CRITICAL SURVEY
OF
DRAMA

CRITICAL SURVEY
OF
DRAMA

REVISED EDITION

A-Chi

1

Edited by
FRANK N. MAGILL

SALEM PRESS

Pasadena, California   Englewood Cliffs, New Jersey

∞ The paper used in these volumes conforms to the
American National Standard for Permanence of Paper
for Printed Library Materials, Z39.48-1984.

Library of Congress Cataloging-in-Publication Data
   Critical survey of drama. English language series/
edited by Frank N. Magill.—Rev. ed.
       p. cm.
   Includes bibliographical references and index.
   1. English drama—Dictionaries. 2. American drama—
Dictionaries. 3. English drama—Bio-bibliography. 4.
American drama—Bio-bibliography. 5. Commonwealth
drama (English)—Dictionaries. 6. Dramatists, English—
Biography—Dictionaries. 7. Dramatists, American—
Biography—Dictionaries. 8. Commonwealth drama (En-
glish)—Bio-bibliography.
I. Magill, Frank Northen, 1907-
PR623.C75   1994
822.009′03—dc20   93-41618
ISBN 0-89356-851-1 (set)   CIP
ISBN 0-89356-852-X (volume 1)

Second Printing

PRINTED IN THE UNITED STATES OF AMERICA

PUBLISHER'S NOTE

Magill's *Critical Survey of Drama, Revised Edition, English Language Series* updates and expands, in seven volumes, the original edition of 1985. This revision of the original set contains a total of 263 articles: 240 on individual dramatists, plus 23 comprehensive "overview" essays, including an annotated bibliography of drama history and criticism and a glossary entitled "Dramatic Terms and Movements." A one-volume *Supplement* to the *Critical Survey of Drama* (which served to update to both the *English Language Series* and the 1986 *Foreign Language Series*) was published in 1987 and contained 49 articles on American and foreign dramatists who were not included in the earlier volumes. The 29 *Supplement* articles on dramatists whose work is written mainly in English were incorporated into the *Revised Edition* and were updated as well.

Of the current edition's 240 articles on individual dramatists, 22 are completely new entries on playwrights who have come to be regarded as established figures in the theater. Included in this group are dramatists who were not included in the original edition, such as Jon Robin Baitz, Caryl Churchill, Richard Foreman, Susan Glaspell, David Henry Hwang, Eduardo Machado, Wendy Wasserstein, and August Wilson. Other dramatists in this group are those who were included in the original edition but whose professional achievements now extend far beyond their work as of 1985; therefore, the original articles were replaced with completely new entries of 5,000 words each. Among these playwrights are Alan Ayckbourn, David Mamet, Sam Shepard, Neil Simon, and Tom Stoppard.

Fully one-third of the essays on individual dramatists—77 articles—have been revised to reflect the current status of the playwright's development and opus, in terms of both life events and literary career. In most of these cases, especially where still-living playwrights are concerned, new productions and publications, new honors and awards, and new biographical events necessitated careful scrutiny of these articles. Some of these articles also contain one or more pages of additional "Analysis," updating the critical interpretation of the dramatists' works in the light of their recent productions. Another group among the revised articles constitutes dramatists who have died in the past decade. These articles underwent similar revision; in cases where little has changed in the playwright's career, the essential facts of death were added and alterations were made in the text.

All articles—whether substantially revised, new, or re-edited—were updated in one substantial respect: In place of the original secondary bibliographies that appeared at the ends of these articles, new, updated, and annotated bibliographies appear. These bibliographies provide the interested reader with possibilities for further reading about the dramatists and their works. This emendation not only provides readers with useful information but also brings this edition in line with the new format of Magill's *Critical Survey* series.

In the final volume, those interested in obtaining an overview of the development of drama will find 23 extensive essays on various aspects of English-language drama.

These essays begin with an examination of dramatic genres and the early forms of drama, such as medieval, Elizabethan, and Restoration drama, and trace the genre's development through the eighteenth, nineteenth, and twentieth centuries. Other essays are those specializing in African drama, African-American drama, Australian drama, Canadian drama, Irish drama, and others, and those treating particular dramatic genres, such as musical, experimental, radio, and television drama. An annotated bibliography of drama criticism and a glossary of terms and movements will prove useful for the beginning student of drama. Finally, the comprehensive subject index, listing names of literary personages, titles of works receiving substantial discussion, and literary terms and concepts, has been revised to cite new material.

Whenever original articles were updated by someone other than the initial contributor, the names of those contributors, and of those who supplied annotated secondary bibliographies, were added at the end of each revised article. Whenever an article was written and updated by the same contributor, or whenever an article was a completely new acquisition, the name of the article's author was simply listed at the end of the article, below the secondary bibliography. The expertise and efforts of all these individuals are gratefully acknowledged.

CONTRIBUTORS

Howard C. Adams
Jacob H. Adler
Thomas P. Adler
Kwaku Amoabeng
Andrew J. Angyal
Stanley Archer
Gerald S. Argetsinger
Edwin T. Arnold
William M. Baillie
Margaret Ann Baker
William Baker
Thomas Banks
Theodore J. Baroody
Kirk H. Beetz
Rebecca Bell-Metereau
Robert Bensen
Anthony Bernardo
Harold Branam
Gerhard Brand
Timothy Brennan
Ward W. Briggs
Hallman B. Bryant
Elizabeth Buckmaster
Donald Burness
Douglas R. Butler
Ralph S. Carlson
Susan Carlson
John Carpenter
C. L. Chua
Lorna Clarke
John W. Crawford
Carol Croxton
J. D. Daubs
William A. Davis
Joan F. Dean
Elliott A. Denniston
Jill Dolan

Henry J. Donaghy
Reade W. Dornan
Susan Duffy
Ayne C. Durham
Ted R. Ellis III
Jane Falco
Patricia A. Farrant
James Feast
John W. Fiero
Edward Fiorelli
Benjamin Fisher
Howard L. Ford
Robert J. Forman
William Frankfather
Lawrence S. Friedman
Steven H. Gale
Edward V. Geist
Donna Gerstenberger
Scott Giantvalley
Richard B. Gidez
E. Bryan Gillespie
Eleanor R. Goldhar
Peter Goslett
Peter W. Graham
Christopher Griffin
Ira Grushow
Angela Hague
Jay Halio
Gertrude K. Hamilton
Robert D. Hamner
Maryhelen C. Harmon
Zia Hasan
William J. Helm
Gordon Henderson
Michael Hennessy
Janet S. Hertzbach
Holly Hill

John R. Holmes
Glenn Hopp
Eril Barnett Hughes
William Hutchings
Philip K. Jason
Vera Jiji
Millard T. Jones
B. A. Kachur
Albert E. Kalson
Irma M. Kashuba
Nancy Kearns
Arthur Kincaid
Anne Mills King
B. G. Knepper
Mildred Kuner
Gregory W. Lanier
Carrol Lasker
Kathleen Latimer
Norman Lavers
Janet Lorenz
Michael Loudon
John R. Lucas
Michael McCully
John F. McDiarmid
James C. MacDonald
Richard D. McGhee
Alan L. McLeod
Christina Hunt Mahony
James E. Maloney
Stella Maloney
Barry Mann
Jonathan Marks
Patricia Marks
Joseph Marohl
Walter J. Meserve
Raymond Miller, Jr.
Leslie B. Mittleman
Christian H. Moe
Michael D. Moore

Michael G. Moran
Laurie P. Morrow
Robert E. Morsberger
Gerald W. Morton
Mary C. Murphy
Helen H. Naugle
Anne Newgarden
Evelyn S. Newlyn
Sally Osborne Norton
George O'Brien
Robert H. O'Connor
Leslie O'Dell
Elizabeth Spalding Otten
Robert M. Otten
Cóilín D. Owens
Philip Oxley
Anthony F. R. Palmieri
Sidney F. Parham
Lisë Pedersen
John Povey
Diane Quinn
Michael L. Quinn
Richard N. Ramsey
Steven Reese
Carl Rollyson
Joseph Rosenblum
Robert Ross
Matthew C. Roudané
Valerie C. Rudolph
Victor Anthony Rudowski
Loren Ruff
Susan Rusinko
Arthur M. Saltzman
Laurence Senelick
Walter Shear
Richard J. Sherry
John C. Shields
Hugh Short
R. Baird Shuman

Charles L. P. Silet
Dale Silviria
Philip E. Smith II
P. Jane Splawn
August W. Staub
Anthony Stephenson
Joseph H. Stodder
Gerald H. Strauss
Edmund M. Taft
Daniel Taylor
Thomas J. Taylor
Christopher J. Thaiss
Ian C. Todd

E. F. J. Tucker
A. Gordon Van Ness III
Doris Walters
James M. Welsh
Craig Werner
Barbara Wiedeman
Edwin W. Williams
David Willinger
Robert F. Willson, Jr.
Ann Wilson
Eugene P. Wright
Michael Zeitlin

New Editorial Provided by

Frank Ardolino
Gerald S. Argetsinger
David Barratt
Rebecca Bell-Metereau
Pamela Canal
Ayne Cantrell
Frank Day
Jon Erickson
James Feast
Howard L. Ford
Irene Gnarra
Sharon L. Gravett
Elsie Galbreath Haley
Peter C. Holloran
John R. Holmes
Glenn Hopp
William L. Howard

William Hutchings
Mildred C. Kuner
Gregory W. Lanier
Katherine Lederer
Robert McClenaghan
Richard D. McGhee
Christian H. Moe
George O'Brien
Robert M. Otten
Michael L. Quinn
James W. Robinson, Jr.
Susan Rusinko
Richard J. Sherry
Genevieve Slomski
Jenny S. Spencer
Thomas J. Taylor
Barry B. Witham

LIST OF AUTHORS IN VOLUME 1

CRITICAL SURVEY
OF
DRAMA

JOSEPH ADDISON

Born: Milston, England; May 1, 1672
Died: London, England; June 17, 1719

Principal drama

Rosamond, pr., pb. 1707 (libretto; music by Thomas Clayton); *Cato*, pr., pb. 1713; *The Drummer: Or, The Haunted House*, pr., pb. 1716.

Other literary forms

Joseph Addison wrote in almost every genre flourishing in British literature during the reigns of William III and Queen Anne. In addition to his three plays, Addison wrote verse in Latin and in English, a travel book, a scholarly account of ancient Roman coins, political pamphlets, and hundreds of essays for *The Tatler*, *The Spectator*, and other periodicals. This variety reflects the active literary culture of the time, Addison's own wide learning, and his search for his proper niche.

Because of Addison's varied canon, there has yet to be a satisfactory complete edition. The first attempt, by Thomas Tickell in 1721, omitted some embarrassing early works and many of the periodical essays. Another collected edition a century later restored some early works and offered a fuller selection of essays. Two good modern critical editions cover most of Addison's corpus: A. C. Guthkelch's *The Miscellaneous Works* (1914) includes the plays as well as the poetry and nonperiodical prose works, and Donald Bond's *The Spectator* (1965) covers Addison's essays for the most famous periodical to which he contributed. Essays written for other journals await modern editions. Addison's *Letters*, an unrevealing collection, was published in 1941.

Achievements

Addison's literary reputation has risen and fallen cyclically for reasons that have little to do with his artistic achievement. His contemporaries and the next generation praised Addison highly for expressing not only Whig political principles but also classical qualities which gave English literature a dignity that it previously lacked. Readers and writers in the Romantic age, however, found Addison unoriginal and conventional. The Victorians restored Addison to the pedestal because he spoke well of virtue and painted the portrait of the Christian gentleman. Twentieth century critics often treat his work as a reflection of the values of the ascendant bourgeoisie; many personally dislike the man for accommodating himself to the class structure of eighteenth century England.

While such judgments affect how often Addison is reprinted and how much he is read, his place in literary history rests firmly on two achievements: his role in the development of the periodical essay and his prose style. Through his collaboration with Richard Steele on *The Tatler* (1709-1711), *The Spectator* (1711-1712, 1714), and *The Guardian* (1713), Addison helped to establish the periodical essay as a literary form. Seemingly informal and natural yet shaped by conscious art, Addison's prose style became for the next two centuries a model for novice writers: Stylists as diverse as Benjamin Franklin and Thomas Hardy began by imitating Addison. Samuel Johnson defined Addison's style in an immortal assessment: "Whoever wishes to attain an English style, familiar but not coarse, and elegant but not ostentatious, must give his days and nights to the volumes of Addison."

If Addison's primary achievement was in periodical prose, his plays rank second, his scholarly prose third, and his poetry last. His plays do not have all the virtues of successful drama but do show that two qualities of his prose—a light comic touch and a skill at putting the best words in the best order—were partially transferable to another genre. There is a consistency to Addison's drama: All three plays are quite competent and worth reading. Historically, the plays received varied reactions: *Rosamond* was a disaster, *Cato* was a huge success, and *The Drummer* was hardly noticed. The reactions to *Rosamond* and *Cato* had little to do with their literary merit, a fate common to other imaginative works in Augustan London, where politics, authorial popularity, and prejudice were often decisive.

Biography

Joseph Addison might easily have followed in his father's footsteps: attending Oxford University, becoming a minister of the Anglican Church, pursuing a series of increasingly important ecclesiastical posts, and supporting the divine right of Stuart kings. Addison, however, took a different path.

Two revolutionary currents swept up Addison while he was at Oxford. The first was an enthusiasm for the "New Philosophy," the scientific method that was challenging the supremacy of classical philosophy; the second was the Glorious Revolution of 1688, which brought William III to the throne in place of James II and established the principle that Parliament's choice for a king weighed equally with God's anointing of His earthly representative. Addison followed the traditional classical curriculum at Oxford (where he achieved his first literary reputation for Latin poetry), but with the idea of supporting a new English culture and political order. Based on the Roman concept of an educated citizenry, this new order, Addison and like-minded revolutionaries hoped, would be the greatest civilization England had yet known: a literate and cultured populace would sensibly cooperate in their own government in order to develop a thriving commercial economy at home and to achieve leadership among European nations.

While at Oxford, Addison expressed his enthusiasm for this new concept of England in poems that brought him to the attention of leading Whig politicians. In 1699, Lord Somers and Lord Halifax secured for Addison a grant from William III, allowing Addison to travel throughout the Continent in preparation for government service. Addison remained abroad until late 1703, when William's death ended the pension. He did little for the next year until, at the request of two of Queen Anne's ministers, he wrote *The Campaign* to celebrate the military victories of the Duke of Marlborough against the French. This successful poem, which was published in 1705, won for Addison a position as commissioner of appeals.

This post placed Addison in a circle of Whig politicians and writers called the Kit-Kat Club. The powerful politicians supported the writers by patronage; the writers helped the politicians gain or keep power by penning public-relations puffs and persuasive pamphlets. Addison's new acquaintances spurred his literary efforts. A Kit-Kat publisher brought out Addison's travels in 1705 to capitalize on the reputation of the author of *The Campaign*. Richard Steele, a Kit-Kat writer, urged Addison to dabble in the drama and to try his hand at an English opera to counteract London's then current passion for Italian opera. Addison's opera, *Rosamond*, was a failure, however, primarily because of Thomas Clayton's poor musical score.

Nevertheless, *Rosamond* was the only setback for Addison between 1705 and 1711. Political contacts at the Kit-Kat Club provided him with increasingly responsible appointments. He served as secretary to a number of important ministers and was elected to Parliament in 1708. His literary output in these years was limited to several political tracts and to a few contributions to the early numbers of Steele's *The Tatler*.

After the Whig ministry lost power in 1710, Addison became a regular partner with Steele in the later issues of *The Tatler* and shared responsibility for founding its successor, *The Spectator*. The new paper was spectacularly successful and was the talk of London's polite society; Addison provided most of the variety in the paper, writing sketches, fables, short stories, and poems in addition to the expository essays which were its staple.

Political events and Addison's high literary reputation conspired to return him to the theater in 1713. The country was torn by the question of the aging Queen Anne's successor: Would the Protestant Prince George of Hanover succeed to the throne according to Parliament's wish, or would a Catholic Stuart attempt to assert his hereditary right by military force? Addison had begun sometime earlier a play about the Roman patriot Cato, who had resisted the dictatorial ambitions of Julius Caesar; his Whig friends encouraged Addison to finish the play and produce it as a clarion call to resist the return of Stuart absolutism. Addison reluctantly agreed and saw the play received with a passionate response from the party faithful. The Whigs' opponents, the Tories, ironically clapped up the play just as loudly, hailing it as a patriotic summons to resist a foreign prince. The play was produced at both London and Oxford with great success, although few paid attention to its literary qualities.

In 1714, the Protestant prince did ascend the English throne as George I, and Addison served as secretary to the council that oversaw the transition. Addison supported the new government with several poems and a political journal, *The Freeholder*. He tried his hand at the theater once more with *The Drummer* in 1716, but it ran for only three nights. Although not roundly scorned, as *Rosamond* had been, this "delicate" comedy (as Steele called it) did not impress audiences. In 1717, Addison reached the height of his political career by becoming secretary of state.

Political and literary success brought substantial rewards. Addison purchased a pleasant estate, Bilton Hall; married the widowed Countess of Warwick; and fathered a daughter, Charlotte. In 1718, however, illness forced him to resign from the government, and the last months of his life were marred by a pamphlet war with his former partner Steele over the Peerage Bill. On his deathbed, legend holds, Addison summoned his dissolute stepson to witness "how a Christian can die." Addison never lacked confidence in his religious, political, or literary convictions.

Analysis

Joseph Addison's three plays indicate important trends in eighteenth century British theater. *Rosamond* attempts to combine music and drama as a domestic alternative to Italian opera, an ambition not realized until two decades later, with the success of John Gay's *The Beggar's Opera* (1728). *Cato* represents a strain of classical tragedy that produced much declamation and little worth, "immortal in the closet" (as the saying went) but stale on the stage. *The Drummer* is an early sentimental comedy whose primary virtue was in being less maudlin than its successors.

None of Addison's plays is a landmark of drama—except *Cato*, by political accident—but none is bad. In fact, each play has its interesting aspects. All of them suffer from a common flaw, the lack of a central character whose plight engages the audience's sympathy, and each play suffers individual minor difficulties. Yet each play has distinctive virtues. *Rosamond* and *The Drummer* have enough comic characters and dialogue to justify, in conjunction with Addison's humorous papers in *The Spectator*, Samuel Johnson's observation: "If Addison had cultivated the lighter parts of poetry, he would probably have excelled." *Cato*'s blank verse, while no rival to Christopher Marlowe's or William Shakespeare's, is a solid achievement and is the best poetry that Addison ever wrote.

Rosamond's three acts tell of the love affair between Henry II and Rosamond Clifford. The main plot concerns Henry's conflict, his love for

Rosamond against his duty to Queen Elinor; the subplot concerns the man whom Henry has set to watch over Rosamond, Sir Trusty, himself in love with his charge and plagued with a shrewish wife, Grideline. Act 1 displays the characters in their frustrations: the queen jealous, the mistress guilty and lonely, the guardian melancholy. Only Henry, returning from France and eager to see Rosamond, seems pleased with the situation. In act 2, Grideline sends a page to spy on Sir Trusty, but the young man discovers instead Queen Elinor plotting to kill her husband's mistress. Hesitating for a moment because Rosamond's death may lead to Henry's, Elinor finally issues an ultimatum to her rival: be stabbed or drink poison. Rosamond chooses poison, and when Sir Trusty finds the corpse, he likewise drinks the fatal concoction. Act 3 begins with Henry asleep and dreaming of martial conquest. Spirits grant him a vision of England's future glory if he gives up his illicit love. Henry awakens and resolves to put Rosamond aside, but hearing of her death, he vows to die in battle. Elinor counters his rashness by revealing that the poison was only a sleeping potion and that Rosamond lives. She retires to a convent to expiate her sin, and Henry returns to Elinor and reestablishes domestic accord. Sir Trusty, awakening to find king and queen happily reunited, now devotes himself wholeheartedly to Grideline.

Addison's opera had several elements that ought to have made it congenial to audiences of the day. The plot came from English history, a strong appeal to the patriotic instincts of a generation locked in a long war with France. The characters were familiar dramatic types: The royal leads experienced the conflicts of love and honor so common to the protagonists of Restoration heroic tragedy, while Sir Trusty and Grideline knew the jealousies and philanderings fundamental to the Restoration comedy of manners. Finally, the play's third act offered a spectacular effect: In Henry's vision, there was a backdrop featuring Blenheim Castle, which was at that moment under construction. The play's theme—that married love conquers all—likewise accorded well with the sentiments for reform which had been growing increasingly fashionable since the accession of William III.

Contemporaries agreed that an atrocious musical score doomed the play, but it must also be admitted that Addison's arrangement of the parts must have seemed odd to his audience no matter how mellifluous the music. A plot recitation indicates those elements which were supposed to predominate: several romantic conflicts, a patriotic theme, an uplifting moral. A close reading of *Rosamond*, however, reveals that the author's best effects are in the comic elements. If the London stage of 1707 had been familiar with the musical comedy, as Bonamy Dobrée points out, Addison's opera would have been comprehensible. It is a play in which the major ingredients are wholesome and bland while the subplot and supporting characters are what the audience enjoys and remembers. The witty but foolish Sir

Trusty steals the show. His superficial passion and foolish suicide, meant to contrast with Henry's love and Elinor's jealousy, instead made the royal lovers look like caricatures. Surely the effect was unintentional; not until Gilbert and Sullivan's operettas would ridiculing the aristocracy become public dramatic entertainment.

The Drummer does not suffer from the same tension between main plot and subplot; in fact, the two are nicely harmonized, although the best character in the play is still the male protagonist of the subplot. What *The Drummer* lacks, in fact, is any strong tension at all. Although its situations and language produce numerous smiles, the play lacks the sharpness that memorable comedy demands.

Addison, drawing on his classical learning, borrowed the plot of *The Drummer* from the last several books of Homer's *Odyssey* (c. 800 B.C.). Like Homer's epic, Addison's play is about a soldier, supposedly dead in a war, who comes home in disguise to find his wife besieged by suitors and his only ally in a faithful servant.

Act 1 depicts the estate of Lady Trueman, supposedly haunted by the drumbeating ghost of her husband, Sir George, killed fourteen months before in battle. The ghost is actually a disguised suitor for the widow's hand in marriage, the London beau Fantome, who has secured the help of a servant, Abigail, in his plot to drive away another suitor, the foppish Tinsel. Though Lady Trueman acts kindly toward Tinsel, she in fact despises both men. When the real Sir George turns up alive in act 2, he enters the household disguised as a conjurer in order to observe his wife's behavior. Throughout act 3, Vellum, Sir George's faithful steward, attempts to help his master expose Tinsel and subvert Fantome by wooing Abigail. In act 4, Fantome disposes of his rival but unknowingly loses Abigail's assistance. In act 5, Sir George tests his wife to determine if she still loves her husband; convinced by her reaction, the real Sir George routs the pseudo-Sir George by appearing as the drumbeating ghost of himself. Sir George and Lady Trueman are reunited, and Vellum earns Abigail's love as well as her rich bribe from Fantome.

Sir George and Lady Trueman are more convincing lovers than Henry and Elinor. Since they do not begin so very far apart, reconciliation is natural. Though fearful that his widow may have been too quick to forget him, Sir George really knows all along that his spouse has more heart than the typically coquettish wife. Though Lady Trueman is quick to have suitors, she keeps them at a distance.

Vellum, not in love with the same woman as his lord, does not undercut Sir George's character as Trusty undercut Henry's. Vellum, in fact, is a reluctant lover, becoming a wooer of Abigail only to help his master and only after he discovers that she responds to his stewardly approach to love. A steward is a careful man who always itemizes and lists what is valuable and keeps an eye on it. Addison skillfully uses the steward mentality both to depict Vellum as a delightful eccentric and to use him as a weapon against the unstewardly figures Tinsel and Fantome, who know how to value nothing.

In addition to Vellum, who is the highlight of the play, Addison creates some humor with three bumbling servants—a butler, a coachman, and a gardener—of whose credulity Sir George takes advantage in order to pass himself off as a conjurer. These four, however, do not have enough stage lines to offset the blandness of the major characters. Sir George and Lady Trueman are loving but not very witty with each other; the fops Tinsel and Fantome are without any distinguishing or distinctive foolishness; Abigail, who has some tendency to be vixenish, slides without ado from corrupted betrayer to protective intriguer. *The Drummer* on the whole does not disappoint the reader, but it cannot lure one back for a second encounter.

If *Rosamond* and *The Drummer* show Addison's comic touch, *Cato* contains his best poetry. For several decades after its first performance, *Cato* maintained a firm stage reputation as well as a solid critical repute, but largely on the strength of its political appeal, the high esteem in which Addison was generally held, and a weakness for declamation among audiences that should have known better. In more recent times, the glaring discrepancy between the main plot and the subplot has become impossible to ignore and the absence of human feeling in the tragic protagonist too obvious to be obscured by the play's virtues. Only the language, which develops subtle and rich image patterns, saves the play from being a mere museum piece.

The main plot and subplot are so different that the play is better summarized in two parts than act by act. The hero is Cato, often praised as the ideal Roman magistrate, who as consul and senator opposed the dictatorial ambitions of Julius Caesar. Cato has led a senatorial army in defense of the Republic, but it is now reduced to a small force trapped at Utica. Like many other cornered generals, Cato confronts, in addition to the enemy, mutiny among his own troops and desertion by allied contingents. Cato personally faces a severe dilemma. Should he fight a glorious but futile battle, dying in defense of his principles? Should he slink out of Utica alone in hopes of raising new allies and a new army elsewhere so that he can carry on the struggle? Should he surrender his troops in order to avoid senseless bloodshed but commit suicide to prevent falling into his enemy's hands? After successfully combating mutiny in the ranks, Cato chooses suicide in order to remain the master of his own destiny.

The subplot, patterned after the romantic dilemmas of Restoration heroic tragedy, seems today to be made out of soap-opera materials. With Cato at Utica are his two sons Marcus and Portius, both of whom are in love with Lucia, the daughter of a Roman general. Portius knows he is his brother's rival and feels badly; Marcus does not know and spills his heart's love to Portius; Lucia knows that both men love her and refuses to choose one lest she make the other despair. With Cato, too, is his daughter Marcia, herself pursued by two suitors: the Roman senator Sempronius and the Numidian prince Juba. Marcia refuses to consider either until the army's fate is decided. Sempronius, however, refuses to wait and plans to revolt against Cato and carry off Marcia. The mutiny helps bring out all the lovers' true feelings. Marcia resists Sempronius and confesses to loving Juba, whom she mistakenly believes has been killed in the rebellion. Lucia refuses Marcus' proposal—painfully delivered by the torn Portius—and the rejected suitor throws himself bravely but recklessly into battle against Sempronius' rebels. Marcus' heroic death leaves Portius and Lucia free to wed, as are Juba and Marcia.

That Cato should have to see to his children happily married as the Republic collapses about him indicates one of the imbalances in the play. Addison, in apparent deference to the theatrical taste of the time, tried to combine a complicated love plot with a tragedy in the Senecan mold which discusses important political issues through declamation. The two plots never mix onstage: The oil of romance remains atop and befouls the waters of political philosophy.

Cato himself is a paragon of virtue. Addison follows most classical authors in depicting the Roman senator as the epitome of Stoic virtue. Seneca, Cicero, and Plutarch all described Cato as a human rock steadfast amid the storms of Fortune. Cato was an attractive model of secular, civic virtue to eighteenth century Englishmen who had seen the results of religious, sectarian virtue in the religious civil wars of the seventeenth century. Reviewing the text of *Cato* before its production, Lady Mary Wortley Montagu praised Cato's plain and great sentiments.

Yet for all the ideals that Cato represented to a contemporary audience, the dramatic fact is that he does not engage one's sympathy. As Samuel Johnson put it, the play's "hopes and fears communicate no vibrancy to the heart." Although Addison has created in the first three acts enough dilemmas to bring out a character's humanity, Cato shows none of it in the last two acts. His reaction to Marcus' death in act 4, glorying in the corpse's wounds as a sign of virtue, seems exaggerated and monstrous. In act 5, he contemplates the immortality of the soul before he commits suicide, but so superficially that he seems to be carrying out a ritual rather than reflecting on eternity. He advises Portius to retire to his estate—prudential wisdom indeed, but not consistent with his own fate or that of Marcus. Worst of all, as a contemporary reviewer observed, *Cato* lacks the reversal of fortune, the moment of realization by a despairing protagonist such as Oedipus which strikes an audience with terror and pity. Cato suffers throughout the play, but he never contributes to his downfall. He stands against superior armed forces and malevolent fate until he chooses no longer to be overwhelmed.

Although Cato's story is not tragic, it is not unmoving. It is a brave tale, a portrait of human greatness, and a paean to devotion to principle. The audience senses these qualities, however, more through the language of the play than through its action. Addison builds around a central metaphor a pattern of imagery that makes sense of otherwise discordant love complications and cardboard characters.

The central metaphor is that of the man who stands so calmly and resolutely amid the storms of civil war that his virtue shines like a beacon through the darkness, the wind, and the rain. Throughout the play, Addison images the forces of rebellion—Caesar, Sempronius, the mutinous troops—as storms that batter Cato. In contrast stands Cato's soul, whose virtuous flame never flickers amid the external mayhem. Shielded by virtue, Cato's soul is all placidity. In each act, this opposition of internal harmony and external chaos becomes an index by which the other characters in the play can be judged.

In language rich with contrasting images of harmony and discord, calm and storm, peace and battle, Addison measures each character against the standard, and with each character the loftiness of the standard becomes more apparent. Sempronius, though like Cato a senator, proves un-Roman because the outer storm of Caesar's rebellion sets off in him corresponding inner storms of rebellion against Cato and of lustful passion for Marcia. Marcus is inwardly as blown about by passion and resentment as is Sempronius, but at least Marcus directs his untamable energies into his country's cause. Juba, prince of a desert kingdom, accustomed to riding the whirlwind of his own desires, gradually acquires a Cato-like serenity by learning the Stoic philosophy.

The remaining characters—Portius, Marcia, and Lucia—are already Cato-like as the play opens. Despite their personal dilemmas about love, each focuses more on Cato's plight and resolves not to let personal fears or jealousies conquer as long as the great man's fate hangs in the balance. In the course of the play, none is lost to frustrated passion; having withstood the storms of civil war as well, each emerges at the play's end pure and rejuvenated:

> So the pure limpid stream when foul with stains,
> Of rushing torrents, and descending rains,
> Works itself clear, and as it runs, refines;
> 'Till by degrees, the floating mirror shines,
> Reflects each flow'r that on the border grows,
> And a new Heaven in its fair bosom shows.

In keeping with the increasingly intellectual preoccupations of the middle class, Addison tried his hand at both the comic and the serious, the delicate and the moral, and the domestic and the philosophical. Even when light in tone, his works reflect the polite society of the day, while revealing an underlying common sense that informs his essays and drama alike. Drawing on his scholarly background, Addison synthesized popular and learned aspects of Augustan society. As a stylist, he gained the respect of his era, and he has continued to exert a formidable influence on later writers.

Other major works

SHORT FICTION: *The Tatler*, 1709-1711 (with Richard Steele; periodical essays); *The Spectator*, 1711-1712, 1714 (with Richard Steele; periodical essays); *The Guardian* 1713 (with Richard Steele, periodical essays); *The Freeholder: Or, Political Essays*, 1715-1716 (periodical essays); *The Spectator*, 1965 (Donald Bond, editor).

POETRY: "To Mr. Dryden," 1693; *A Poem to His Majesty*, 1695; *Praelum Inter Pygmaeos et Grues Commisum*, 1699; "A Letter from Italy," 1703; *The Campaign*, 1705; "To Her Royal Highness," 1716; "To Sir Godfrey Kneller on His Portrait of the King," 1716.

NONFICTION: *Remarks upon Italy*, 1705; *Dialogues upon the Usefulness of Ancient Medals*, 1721; *The Letters of Joseph Addison*, 1941 (Walter Graham, editor).

TRANSLATION: *Fourth Georgic*, 1694 (of Vergil's *Georgics*).

MISCELLANEOUS: *The Miscellaneous Works*, 1914 (A. C. Guthkelch, editor).

Bibliography

Addison, Joseph. *The Letters of Joseph Addison.* Edited by Walter Graham. Oxford, England: Clarendon Press, 1941. Reprint. St. Clair Shores, Mich.: Scholarly Press, 1976. About seven hundred of Addison's letters are represented here, covering a twenty-year period from 1699 to 1719. Among the addressees are William Congreve, Jonathan Swift, and the philosopher Gottfried Wilhelm Leibniz. Forty letters to Addison are included.

Bloom, Edward A., and Lillian D. Bloom. *Joseph Addison's Sociable Animal.* Providence, R.I.: Brown University Press, 1971. The Blooms strive for a "whole view of Addison" and divide their study into three parts. "In the Market Place" treats Addison as a representative of the middle class, "On the Hustings" depicts him as a solid supporter of Whig causes, and "In the Pulpit" describes Addison's "coolness" toward religious dissent.

Elioseff, Lee Andrew. *The Cultural Milieu of Addison's Literary Criticism.* Austin: University of Texas Press, 1963. Elioseff studies Addison in the context of eighteenth century intellectual history. He scrutinizes the critical milieu, looks closely at the sublime and the pastoral in Addison's time, takes up the philosophical issues in empiricism, sums up the last phase of neoclassicism, and adds an appendix entitled "Opera and the Decline of English Virtue."

Johnson, Samuel. "Addison." In *Lives of the English Poets*, edited by George Birkbeck Hill. Vol. 2. Oxford, England: Clarendon Press, 1905. Reprint. Hildesheim, Germany: Georg Olms, 1968. This fine edition is replete with helpful notes. Johnson's praise is high: "Whoever wishes to attain an English style, familiar but not coarse, and elegant but not ostentatious, must give his days and nights to the volumes of Addison."

Kelsall, M. M. "The Meaning of Addison's *Cato.*" *The Review of English Studies: A Quarterly Journal of English Literature and the English Language* 17 (May, 1966): 149-162. Kelsall identifies *Cato* as "one of a long line of 'Roman' plays" and stresses Cato's importance as a symbol of greatness and self-reliance in Addison's London. The success of the play reveals "a tendency in the age to choose its symbols of heroic virtue rather from Roman history than from the Bible."

Macauley, Thomas Babington. *Macauley's Essays on Addison and Johnson.* Edited by Alphonso G. Newcomer. Chicago: Scott, Foresman, 1903, 1920. A student's edition of Macauley's essay on the occasion of Lucy Aikin's life of Addison in 1843. Macauley notes that Addison's greatness as a satirist comes from "the grace, the nobleness, the moral purity" of his work and that his humanity has no parallel in literary history. His account of the reception of *Cato* is finely dramatic.

Smithers, Peter. *The Life of Joseph Addison.* Oxford, England: Clarendon Press, 1954. This full-length biography describes the performance and reception of *Cato* at length in the chapter "Cato in the Wilderness." Smithers spells out well the political ambiguities of *Cato* and explains that "[i]ts strength lies in the eloquence of its appeal to reason for virtue."

Robert M. Otten
(updated by *Frank Day*)

JOANNE AKALAITIS

Born: Cicero, Illinois; June 29, 1937

Principal drama

Dressed Like an Egg, pr. 1977, pb. 1984; *Southern Exposure*, pr. 1979; *Dead End Kids*, pr. 1980, pb. 1982; *Green Card*, pr. 1986, pb. 1987.

Other literary forms

JoAnne Akalaitis is known primarily as a playwright, director, and actress. Her tribute, "Meeting Beckett," appeared in the Fall, 1990, issue of *The Drama Review.* She directed the film version of *Dead End Kids* in 1986.

Achievements

Akalaitis and Mabou Mines, the theater company which she helped form in 1969, are best known for their contributions to multimedia, collaborative work. Akalaitis has received support from the National Endowment for the Arts, the Rockefeller Foundation, and the New York State Creative Artists Public Service Program. Mabou Mines did not originally consider itself to be performance theater; its conceptual collaborations, such as *Red Horse Animation* (1970) and *The Saint and the Football Player* (1976), evolved slowly, taking place first as visual performance pieces in New York's Solomon R. Guggenheim Museum, the Museum of Modern Art, and the Berkeley and Pasadena art museums. Other multimedia events by Akalaitis include performances with the 1976 American Dance Festival. Composer Philip Glass, who was once married to Akalaitis, provided music for Mabou Mines in such productions as *Dressed Like an Egg* and *Dead End Kids*, which was the only New York avant-garde play included in the Toronto Theatre Festival in 1980. She has won three Obie Awards and in August, 1991, succeeded Joseph Papp as director of the New York Shakespeare Festival at the Public Theater, a position she maintained until early 1993.

Biography

The influence of JoAnne Akalaitis' background appears in various forms in her work. Born in Cicero, Illinois, in 1937, she was reared in a predominantly Lithuanian Catholic neighborhood. She studied philosophy at the University of Chicago and Stanford University, training that emerges in her constant fascination with the nature of being. She worked at the Actor's Workshop in San Francisco in 1962, where she first met Lee Breuer and Ruth Maleczech, with whom she formed the theater collective Mabou

Mines in 1969. Her acting teachers included Herbert Berghof, Bill Hickey, and later Spalding Gray and Joyce Aaron of Open Theatre. She has commented in an interview with Jonathan Kalb that having two children with her former husband, composer Philip Glass, may have kept her from doing more work, but that she would not be who she is without them.

In 1993, only twenty months after being appointed artistic director of the Public Theater by Joseph Papp, Akalaitis was dismissed from that position in a sudden Public Theater Board decision. Although the board's decision may have been partly based on Akalaitis' performance of her administrative duties as artistic director, her political agenda, her working style, and various theater business issues, Akalaitis remains an artist who is on the cutting edge of theater.

Analysis

JoAnne Akalaitis' place in the history of theater is, according to her own assessment, not connected with the American theater tradition of such artists as Tennessee Williams, Arthur Miller, and Edward Albee, who, despite their apparent differences, all have family and relationships at the core of their work. Solidly nested in avant-garde theater, Akalaitis' work with Mabou Mines is more international and multimedia in flavor. Surrealist and expressionist elements appear in nontraditional use of objects and lighting. Like Bertolt Brecht, Mabou Mines creates a reflexive world in which the actors call attention to the existence of the stage and their own acting, through nonconcealment of set changes, onstage narration, shifting of character portrayal among various actors, and partial set designs that reveal the bare bones of the stage.

At once grounded in history and deliberately detached from context, Akalaitis' work is highly conceptual, tempting the audience to decipher or create the play's patterns while deconstructing these patterns, even as they grow. Her views on acting include a firm determination not to manipulate actors or audiences but rather to allow whatever works for the moment to happen. The methods of Akalaitis and Mabou Mines stem from their notions of group consciousness, and they aim to create theater from the dialectic between past and present, traditional theater and nontheatrical media, and group and individual.

Her first widely successful production, *Dressed Like an Egg*, first presented by the New York Shakespeare Festival in May of 1977, is a collage piece with ten segments: "Prologue," "The Dance," "The Cage," "The Bath," "The Seaside," "The Cage (Part II)," "The Pantomime," "Opium," "The Novel," and "Age." Based on the writings of Colette, each of the segments deals in some manner with the issue of gender. The prologue begins with a brief recitation on carrying a child high in the womb. The play moves quickly to "The Dance," which explores relationships between men and women, jux-

taposing such romantic elements as a Chopin polonaise to the obvious movements of a stagehand who offhandedly whistles the tune as he works. Flowers
and lines about the ecstasy of love are delivered by males and females wearing turn-of-the-century undergarments and gazing into hand mirrors as they
speak, thus undercutting the emotion and sentimentality of their words.
"The Cage" and "The Bath" feature trapeze work and a bathing scene, followed by "The Seaside," in which a man claims that he writes out titles the
library should have, a service he claims preserves the honor of the Catalogue.
These comic scenes focus audience attention on the concept of the ideal in
sexuality, romance, and intellect.

The structure of the play is not at first apparent, but on closer inspection,
the second half seems more serious, less playful, despite occasional absur-
dities which may draw audience laughter. "The Cage (Part II)" deals with the
ending of romance, and the last line, "I'm cold," hints at death, a line reiterated as the last phrase of the final scene. In absurd recapitulation of the
theme of physical passion, a stagehand commands a woman to "let loose a
breast!" in "The Pantomime." "Opium" and "The Novel" quote extensively
from Colette on the topics of opium dens and the power play of romantic
involvements. These two segments both depict decadent phases of development, one within an individual or culture and one within a relationship. The
historical connections and recurrence of themes achieve full circle in "Age,"
which combines images of American planes and the cycle of Venus, a planet
that grows into its period of greatest brilliance every eight years. The section
on Venus indirectly comments on the waxing and waning of romantic impulses, at both an individual and a cultural level.

As in most of Akalaitis' works, visual and aural richness play an integral
role in the production. *Dressed Like an Egg* contrasts the soft romantic elements of seashell footlights, pastel pinks, blues, and grays, with the crudity
of modern fabrics, silver lamé, a Celastic dress, a mylar rug, and the startling
image of hairy male arms and hands dancing in women's shoes. Stereo-
typically feminine symbols, such as carnations and irises, act as counterpoint
to a woman snoring loudly. *Dressed Like an Egg* explores sexual ambiguity in
other visually shocking scenes: for example, when a woman dressed as a
mummy passionately kisses another woman who is dressed as a man, an allusion to Colette's intimate friendships with other women.

Akalaitis works well with historical information, weaving facts into the fab-
ric of a purely modern vision, including abstract philosophy and absurdist
elements of theater performance. *Southern Exposure*, performed at The New
Theatre Festival, Baltimore, in 1979, is an exploration of exterior and interior poles. The play offers tribute to early explorers of the Antarctic, at the
same time that it explores interior or mental uncharted territory, areas of the
mind untouched by civilization, perhaps seeking the blank spot of pure
being, nonbeing, or Nirvana. As in *Dressed Like an Egg*, past and present

commingle in delightful ways, with the idea of blankness as the element which draws people to superimpose definitions and "culture" on empty space. In the prologue, a woman dressed in Edwardian style builds a penguin nest as she explains the penguin family system, in which the father warms the eggs. Blackout follows this touching scene, after which a film of a modern couple visiting aquarium penguins appears, accompanied by a female voice-over describing the timeless penguin burial ground, where dead penguins float, layer upon layer, preserved in the ice of Antarctica.

In the "Shackleton Story," a scene in *Southern Exposure*, a couple in bed recount the disastrous mission of Ernest Shackleton's Trans-Antarctic Expedition from 1914 to 1917. The melancholy quality of this historical document diminishes as the woman drops black cubes into the man's lap. In "Mirage," a man draws the word "horizon" on a blank paper, then rips and crinkles it, underscoring the failure of art to capture the immediate quality of the environment, just as the explorer fails to encompass the vastness of physical space. "Bed" and "Food" bring the play to a humorous, mundane level, with the account of the Shackleton party's obsession with fantasies of huge repasts. The next segment, "Quilt," takes the audience to the domestic scene of a man and a woman sewing a pattern on the quilt as they discuss the failure of Robert Falcon Scott and Roald Amundsen, as slides are projected onto the background. The quilt and the final reading from the explorer's journal point to humanity's drive to trace the pattern of life, even if this attempt is utterly futile.

The stark set serves as an additional character in the piece. Whites predominate, with only the gray stones of a penguin nest, a book, a grayish chair, and the gray shadow of a canted bed offering contrast to the stark simplicity of the set. The set, costumes, slides, film, and props all call attention to the connections between art and life, between the exploration of geographical domains and the intellectual and spiritual realms of art. Human beings' attempts to impose a design on this blank space are portrayed simultaneously as the origin of nobility and the destruction of the very openness necessary to creativity.

Dead End Kids, one of the group's most widely publicized works and clearly their most didactic, is worthy of detailed analysis. The play's opening at The Public Theatre in November of 1980 exemplifies the group's attempt to break down boundaries between audience and performers, between theater and life, with the performance beginning even before the audience enters the theater. In the lobby, patrons view a 1950's-style science fair, whose theme is "Atoms for Peace." As people enter the theater, they hear the droning voice of a girl describing effective construction and use of home bomb shelters, a haunting recapitulation of many of the defense department films of the 1950's. The girl's speech ends with an admonition to be prepared and to remember President Franklin D. Roosevelt's famous line, "There is nothing to fear but fear itself," a statement whose irony becomes more apparent as the play continues.

The appearance of such characters as alchemists, Madame Marie Curie, Albert Einstein, a lecturer, a magician, a young female doctoral student, and an announcer underscore humanity's communal responsibility for the development of nuclear energy and weapons. When Mephistopheles and Faust appear, reciting in German as Madame Curie conducts a simultaneous commentary, the link between nuclear power and the desire for metaphysical power becomes apparent. In the next scene, army generals and a sexy stenographer join with Mephistopheles, sitting around a conference table, smoking and guffawing at double entendres laced through descriptions of the first nuclear explosion. This scene portrays military knowledge as a means to establish virility and provide male bonding.

After this relatively comic interlude, the intermission actually returns the audience to more sober aspects of the play's nuclear theme, with the fallout shelter tape continuing throughout. Upon return to their seats, audiences witness a film compilation of 1950's government propaganda films for nuclear power and arms. A man and woman recite back and forth all that they have seen in the universe, and they are then joined by a series of characters, including a boy nerd, a Cub Scout, an older woman, and a teenager, all of whom begin dancing the Jerk, until the music ceases and they end frozen in grotesque, strained poses, as a voice recites statistics about the risk of lung cancer caused by plutonium particles. The lecturer continues with graphic information about the effects of radiation sickness, as various listeners display a disturbing lack of emotion. The play closes much as it began, with voices of two girls reciting definitions of nuclear terms; as the audience exits, the fallout shelter tape resumes. The play accomplishes its purpose quite effectively, showing at once the absurdity and logic behind the development of nuclear power, as a natural outgrowth of human intellectual curiosity and the self-destructive impulse toward ultimate domination over life itself.

In keeping with Akalaitis' interest in social responsibility for individual suffering, *Green Card* addresses the issue of United States immigration policies. Through what Akalaitis calls a "collage" of characters, the play presents information about the lives and viewpoints of aliens, from a Salvadoran refugee to a Jewish immigrant of the late 1900's. As with *Dead End Kids*, the opening occurs as the audience enters, with loudspeaker voices delivering lines relevant to the play's theme. A woman's recitation of Emma Lazarus' poem, "Send these, the homeless, tempest-tost to me," fades under a booming male voice reeling off racial slurs and epithets. A spotlight shines on a master of ceremonies who cheerfully calls out insulting terms for different ethnic and racial groups. As if in answer, the light on him fades and another appears, highlighting a collection of men and women grouped together. To the sound of blasting rock music, they break into dance, and then, just as suddenly, stop, paralyzed and frightened-looking, as before.

Green Card opened in Los Angeles' Mark Taper Forum in 1986, a location appropriate to the play's immediate concern. At one point the Salvadoran refugee comments that El Centro, near Los Angeles, is "really a jail," thus bringing the play's suffering into the backyard of the audience. Personal histories of individual men and women interweave with ethnic tidbits in this sometimes humorous, always biting, commentary on the new "melting pot" on the West Coast. The play repeatedly suggests the United States' complicity in the bloody wars and political repression that has driven people from their homelands in Central America and elsewhere in the world. The issue of citizen and government responsibility is not resolved, nor is the fate of the aliens whose lives have been briefly displayed. *Green Card* closes with a line of men and women waiting at a bus stop, all gazing hopefully down the line into a less than rosy future. Some viewers find the play painful to watch, oppressive in its grim depiction of apparently futile struggles. Others see more optimism and a call for action, but regardless of one's interpretation, Akalaitis' work demands that its audience grapple with disturbing political realities.

If Akalaitis creates a stir by her selection of controversial subject matter, she creates an even greater controversy in her treatment of other playwrights' work in her role as director. The most outstanding case is the much-disputed American Repertory Theater production of Samuel Beckett's 1957 *Endgame*, performed in Cambridge, Massachusetts, in 1984. Beckett's stage directions call for an empty room with two small windows, but director Akalaitis placed the work in a subway station with a derailed train in the background. Beckett threatened to halt production but finally agreed to allow the performance to take place with his disclaimer attached to the playbill. Such conflicts between playwrights and performers appeared frequently in the theater of the 1980's, particularly in the protests of minorities seeking more casting of nontraditional actors in traditional roles. Akalaitis later met Beckett, an encounter that she described in a memoriam to him in *The Drama Review*. Profoundly impressed by the sparsity and intense purposefulness of all of his communication, Akalaitis and the Mabou Mines company informed Beckett that they wished to perform his radio play *Cascando* (1963) in Geneva and Zurich. Beckett's agent had earlier denied them permission, but Beckett told them not to worry and handed Akalaitis a napkin signed with his name and his permission to perform the play in Switzerland.

Throughout the 1980's, Akalaitis gained the respect of the theatrical community, eventually working at the Guthrie Theater in Minneapolis, the Goodman Theatre in Chicago, and the New York Shakespeare Festival, directing more traditional works such as Shakespeare's *Cymbeline* (pr. c. 1609-1610, pb. 1623) and John Ford's *'Tis Pity She's a Whore* (pr. 1629[?]-1633, pb. 1633). As with her earlier work, her direction of *Cymbeline* in 1990 caused a critical furor, with much criticism of Akalaitis' liberal interpretation of Shakespeare's intent. Joseph Papp appointed her his successor when his struggle with cancer caused him to give up his directorship of the New York Shakespeare Festival. In spite of entering this mainstream position, Akalaitis maintained a politically activist stance, as demonstrated by her visit to the Middle East to talk with Palestinian dramatists in September of 1991. Her unorthodox interpretations of conventional theater pieces continued to arouse interest and controversy.

The whole issue of the nature of performance, the extent to which directors and actors may tamper with original casting, set design, and text, is central to the fate of directors and groups such as Akalaitis and Mabou Mines. As is the case with many artists, within the strengths of works by Akalaitis reside her limitations and perhaps her downfall. Dedication to timely topics and a collaborative theater style make her work vibrant and electric, but these virtues may condemn her to the same kind of relative obscurity endured by such innovative and polemical artists as Clifford Odets and Elmer Rice. Indeed, Akalaitis and Mabou Mines hope that *Dead End Kids* will become dated, that the dangerous use of nuclear power which inspired their work may someday be eliminated, erasing any need for protest. At the same time, all of their works deal with concepts and human concerns that are timeless. The survival of their plays, however, may not be assured without a change in the very nature of the theater canon. As long as it is a body of literature created by individuals and preserved through conventional publishing methods, dynamic groups such as Mabou Mines and truly collaborative artists may remain in the realm of theater ephemera—which may be exactly where they wish to reside. As a director, however, Akalaitis has established her reputation as a powerful and lasting influence in American theater.

Bibliography

Akalaitis, JoAnne. "JoAnne Akalaitis." Interview by Jonathan Kalb. *Theatre Magazine* 15 (May, 1984): 6-13. Contains photographs of Akalaitis and productions of *Dressed Like an Egg*, *Dead End Kids*, and *Southern Exposure.* The interview deals with Akalaitis' work on the filming of *Dead End Kids*, and she discusses her collaboration with Ruth Malezech, Women's Interart, and Mabou Mines. Akalaitis describes her work on an opera written with John Gibson, supported by National Endowment and Rockefeller grants.

Cohen, Debra. "The Mabou Mines' *The Lost Ones.*" *The Drama Review* 20 (June, 1976): 83-87. This article provides biographical information about Akalaitis, with some analysis of the form and content of her work. In addition, Cohen includes an interview with Akalaitis that provides some background on the development of the company, the company's production of Samuel Beckett's play, and the philosophy of the troupe, contrasting the family-oriented group with other avant-garde artists, who are often younger and more unconventional in their personal lives. Contains photographs.

Gussow, Mel. "Other Ways at the Shakespeare Festival." *The New York Times*, June 17, 1991, p. B5. Gussow devotes a page with photographs to a relatively sympathetic description of Akalaitis' career, as director, playwright, collaborative performance artist, and Joseph Papp's successor as director of the New York Shakespeare Festival. He briefly reviews the critical reception of her writing and directorial career, mentioning the negative critical reception of Akalaitis' direction of Shakespeare's *Cymbeline.*

Lacayo, Richard. "Directors Fiddle, Authors Burn." *Time*, January, 1985, 75. Lacayo's article describes Samuel Beckett's objections to Akalaitis' setting of *Endgame* in a subway station with a derailed train. While less than a page in length, the article places the event in a larger context of modification of well-established plays. Lacayo discusses the legal and artistic dimensions of directorial discretion, with reference to works by Arthur Miller and Edward Albee.

Mehta, Xerxes. "Notes from the Avant-Garde." *Theatre Journal* 31 (March, 1979): 20-24. With bibliographical references and a rich description of *Dressed Like an Egg*, Mehta's essay offers detailed analysis of the costuming, dialogue, and structure of the play. She goes on to describe the history of Lee Breuer, Ruth Maleczech, the Actor's Workshop, and Mabou Mines, their use of Brechtian distancing devices, the influence of Richard Foreman, and the SoHo art world. This article works well to establish the avant-garde context for a variety of experimental artists.

_____. "Some Versions of Performance Art." *Theatre Journal* 36 (May, 1984): 164-191. Mehta gives a thorough, scene-by-scene description of *Southern Exposure*, which was not a production of Mabou Mines. Photographs and notes assist the general reader to picture the simple, almost harsh, set of the play. Mehta places the work in the context of Surrealist and cubist art movements. The analysis may be rather heavily semiological for a general audience, but it provides excellent visual description of each scene.

Rebecca Bell-Metereau

EDWARD ALBEE

Born: Virginia; March 12, 1928

Principal drama

The Zoo Story, pr., pb. 1959; *The Death of Bessie Smith*, pr., pb. 1960; *The Sandbox*, pr., pb. 1960; *Fam and Yam*, pr. 1960, pb. 1963; *The American Dream*, pr., pb. 1961; *Bartleby*, pr. 1961 (libretto, with James Hinton, Jr.; music by William Flanagan; adaptation of Herman Melville's "Bartleby the Scrivener"); *Who's Afraid of Virginia Woolf?*, pr., pb. 1962; *The Ballad of the Sad Café*, pr., pb. 1963 (adaptation of Carson McCullers' novel *The Ballad of the Sad Café*); *Tiny Alice*, pr. 1964, pb. 1965; *A Delicate Balance*, pr. 1966, pb. 1967; *Malcolm*, pr., pb. 1966 (adaptation of James Purdy's novel *Malcolm*); *Everything in the Garden*, pr. 1967, pb. 1968 (adaptation of Giles Cooper's play *Everything in the Garden*); *Box and Quotations from Chairman Mao Tse-Tung*, pr. 1968, pb. 1969 (2 one-acts); *All Over*, pr., pb. 1971; *Seascape*, pr., pb. 1975; *Counting the Ways*, pr., pb. 1977; *Listening*, pr., pb. 1977; *The Lady from Dubuque*, pr., pb. 1980; *Lolita*, pr. 1981 (adaptation of Vladimir Nabokov's novel *Lolita*); *The Man Who Had Three Arms*, pr., pb. 1982; *Finding the Sun*, pr. 1983; *Marriage Play*, pr. 1987; *Three Tall Women*, pr. 1991.

Other literary forms

Although Edward Albee has written the libretto for an unsuccessful operatic version of Herman Melville's story "Bartleby the Scrivener," as well as some occasional essays and a few adaptations, he is known primarily for his plays.

Achievements

Albee is, with David Mamet and Sam Shepard, one of the only American playwrights to emerge since the 1950's with any claim to being considered a major dramatist ranked among the pantheon of Eugene O'Neill, Thornton Wilder, Arthur Miller, and Tennessee Williams. Since *The Zoo Story* first appeared, Albee has produced a sustained and varied body of work, often of considerably higher quality than his critical and popular reputation would suggest. In the introduction to his most experimental works, the two one-acts published together in *Box and Quotations from Chairman Mao Tse-tung*, Albee sets forth the two "obligations" of a playwright: to illuminate the human condition and to make some statement about the art form itself by altering "the forms within which his precursors have had to work." Like O'Neill before him, Albee has always been an experimentalist, refusing to go back and repeat the earlier formulas simply because they have proved commercially and critically successful. Unlike O'Neill's last works in the mode of symbolic realism, which now are generally regarded as his best, Albee's later dramas have failed to garner the critical acclaim that his earliest ones received. Although acutely disturbed by the downward spiral and paralysis of will that seem to have overtaken modern civilization, and committed to charting these in his work, Albee is not primarily a social playwright, and there is hardly one of his plays that is totally naturalistic or realistic. In form and style, they range, indeed, from surrealism (*The Sandbox*) to allegory (*Tiny Alice*), from the quasi-religious drawing-room play (*A Delicate Balance*) to the fable (*Seascape*), from the picaresque journey (*Malcolm*) to the ritual deathwatch (both *All Over* and *The Lady from Dubuque*), and from scenes linked by cinematic techniques (*The Death of Bessie Smith*) to monodrama for a disembodied voice (*Box*).

Though he is touted sometimes as the chief American practitioner of the Absurd in drama, Albee only rarely combines in a single work both the techniques and the philosophy associated with that movement and is seldom as unremittingly bleak and despairing an author as Samuel Beckett. Yet the influence of Eugène Ionesco's humor and of Jean Genet's rituals can be discerned in isolated works, as can the battle of the sexes and the voracious, emasculating female from August Strindberg, the illusion/reality motif from Luigi Pirandello and O'Neill, and the poetic language of T. S. Eliot, Beckett (particularly of *Endgame*), and Harold Pinter, as well as the recessive action and lack of definite resolution and closure often found in Beckett and Pinter. As the only avant-garde American dramatist of his generation to attain a wide measure of popular success, Albee sometimes demonstrates, especially in the plays from the first decade of his career, the rather strident and accusatory voice of the angry young man. The outlook in his later works, however, is more that of the compassionate moralist, linking him—perhaps unexpectedly—with Anton Chekhov; one of the characters in *All Over*, recognizing the disparity between what human beings could become and what they have settled for, even echoes the Russian master's Madame Ranevsky when she says, "How dull our lives are." Even in his most technically and stylistically avant-garde dramas, however, Albee remains essentially very traditional in the values he espouses, as he underlines the necessity for human contact and communion, for family ties and friendships, which provide individuals with the courage to grow and face the unknown. Always prodding people to become more, yet, at the same time, sympathetically accepting their fear and anxiety over change, Albee has increasingly become a gentle apologist for human beings, who need one crutch after another, who need one illusion after another, so that—in a paraphrase of O'Neill's words—they can make it through life and comfort their fears of death.

Biography

Born on March 12, 1928, in Virginia, Edward Franklin Albee was adopted at the age of two weeks by the socially prominent and wealthy New Yorkers Reed and Frances Albee. His adoptive father was the scion of the family who owned the Keith-Albee chain of vaudeville houses; his adoptive mother was a former Bergdorf high-fashion mannequin. Albee's deep-seated resentment of the natural parents who abandoned him finds reflection in the child motifs that pervade both his original plays and his adaptations: the orphans in *The Zoo Story* and *The Ballad of the Sad Café*, the mutilated twin in *The American Dream*, the intensely hoped-for child who is never conceived and the conceived child who is unwanted in *Who's Afraid of Virginia Woolf?*, the dead son in *A Delicate Balance*, the child in search of his father in *Malcolm*. Living with the Albees was Edward's maternal grandmother, Grandma Cotta, whom he revered and would later memorialize in *The Sandbox* and *The American Dream*. After his primary education at the Rye Country Day School, Albee attended a succession of prep schools (Lawrenceville School for Boys, Valley Forge Military Academy), finally graduating from Choate in 1946 before enrolling at Trinity College in Hartford, Connecticut, where he studied for a year and a half. While in high school, he wrote both poetry and plays.

In 1953, Albee was living in Greenwich Village and working at a variety of odd jobs when, with the encouragement of Thornton Wilder, he committed himself to the theater. *The Zoo Story*, written in only two weeks, premiered in Berlin on September 28, 1959; when it opened Off-Broadway at the Provincetown Playhouse on a double bill with Beckett's *Krapp's Last Tape* in January, 1960, it brought Albee immediate acclaim as the most promising of the new playwrights and won for him an Obie Award as Best Play of the Year. *Who's Afraid of Virginia Woolf?*, his first full-length work—and still his most famous—opened on Broadway in October, 1962, winning for him both the Drama Critics Circle Award and the Tony Award for the Best American Play of that season; the Drama Jury voted it the Pulitzer Prize, but the Advisory Board of Columbia University overturned the nomination because of the play's strong language, and, as a result, John Gassner and John Mason Brown resigned from the jury in protest. Albee went on, however, to win two Pulitzers, for *A Delicate Balance* and *Seascape*. Along with the New York productions of seven original one-act plays and eight original full-length works, Albee has done four adaptations for the stage: of Carson McCullers' 1951 novella *The Ballad of the Sad Café*; of James Purdy's 1959 novel *Malcolm*; of Giles Cooper's 1962 play *Everything in the Garden*; and of Vladimir Nabokov's 1955 novel *Lolita*.

From the time of his own early successes, Albee has actively encouraged the development of other young dramatists and, as part of a production team, has also brought the work of major avant-garde foreign dramatists to New York. Under the auspices of the State Department, he toured behind the Iron Curtain and in South America, and he has become a frequent and popular lecturer on the college circuit, as well as a director of revivals of his own plays.

After a residency at the University of Houston, Albee directed the world premieres of *Marriage Play* and *Three Tall Women*, both at the English Theatre in Vienna; he also directed *Marriage Play* at the Alley Theatre in 1991 and at the McCarter Theatre in 1992. Critic David Richards of *The New York Times* noted that Albee, "increasingly introspective over the years," has countered his disappointment with Broadway (*The Man Who Had Three Arms* saw only sixteen performances in 1983) by becoming "a European playwright."

Analysis

The major recurrent pattern in Edward Albee's plays finds his characters facing a test or a challenge to become more fully human. In *The Zoo Story*, Jerry arrives at a bench in Central Park to jar Peter out of his passivity and Madison Avenue complacence; in *The Death of Bessie Smith*, the black blues singer arrives dying at a Southern hospital only to be turned away because of racial prejudice; in *Tiny Alice*, Brother Julian arrives at Miss Alice's mansion to undergo his dark night of the soul; in *A Delicate Balance*, Harry and Edna arrive at the home of their dearest friends to test the limits of friendship and measure the quality of Agnes and Tobias' life; in *Seascape*, the lizards Leslie and Sarah come up from the sea to challenge Charlie to renewed activity and to try their own readiness for the human adventure; and in *The Lady from Dubuque*, the Lady and her black traveling companion arrive to ease Jo to her death and help her husband learn to let go.

In order to effect the desired change in Peter, Jerry in *The Zoo Story* must first break down the barriers that hinder communication. Accomplishing this might even require deliberate cruelty, since kindness by itself may no longer be enough; oftentimes in Albee, one character needs to hurt another before he can help, the hurt then becoming a creative rather than a destructive force. Along with the focus on lack of communication and on a love and concern that dare to be critical, Albee consistently pursues several additional thematic emphases throughout his works. *The American Dream*, which comments on the decline and fall from grace of Western civilization and on the spiritual aridity of a society that lives solely by a materialistic ethic, also decries the emasculation of Daddy at the hands of Mommy; to a greater or lesser degree, *The Death of Bessie Smith*, *Who's Afraid of Virginia Woolf?*, and *A Delicate Balance* all speak as well to what Albee sees as a disturbing reversal of gender roles (a motif he inherits from Strindberg), though Albee does become increasingly understanding of the female characters in his later works. Several plays, among them *Who's Afraid of Virginia Woolf?* and *A Delicate Balance*, consider the delimiting effect of time on human choice and the way in which man's potential for constructive change decreases as time goes on. Characters in both *A Delicate Balance* and *Tiny Alice* face the existential void, suffering the anxiety that arises over the possibility of there being a meaninglessness at the very core of existence, while characters in several others, including *Box and Quotations from Chairman Mao Tse-tung*, *All Over*, and *The Lady from Dubuque*, confront mortality as they ponder the distinction between dying (which ends) and death (which goes on) and the suffering of the survivor. Elsewhere, particularly in *Counting the Ways*, Albee insists on the difficulty of ever arriving at certainty in matters of the heart, which cannot be known or proved quantitatively. Finally, in such works as *Malcolm* and *Seascape*, he explores the notion that innocence must be lost—or at least risked—before there can be any hope of achieving a paradise regained.

If the mood of many Albee works is autumnal, even wintry, it is because the dramatist continually prods his audiences into questioning whether the answers which the characters put forward in response to the human dilemma—such panaceas as religion (*Tiny Alice*) or formulaic social rituals (*All Over*)—might not in themselves all be simply illusions in which human beings hide from a confrontation with the ultimate nothingness of existence. In this, he comes closer to the Absurdists, though he is more positive in his holding out of salvific acts: the sacrifice to save the other that ends *The Zoo Story*, the gesture of communion that concludes *Who's Afraid of Virginia Woolf?*, the affirmation of shared humanness that ends *Seascape*, the merciful comforting of the survivor that concludes *The Lady from Dubuque*. If Albee's characters often live a death-in-life existence, it is equally evident that human beings, God's only metaphor-making animals, can sometimes achieve a breakthrough by coming to full consciousness of their condition and by recognizing the symbolic, allegorical, and anagogical planes of existence.

Who's Afraid of Virginia Woolf?, which brought Albee immediate fame as the most important American dramatist since Williams and Miller, is probably also the single most important American play of the 1960's, the only one from that decade with any likelihood of becoming a classic work of dramatic literature. In this, his first full-length drama, Albee continues several strands from his one-act plays—including the need to hurt in order to help from *The Zoo Story*, the criticism of Western civilization from *The American Dream*, and the Strindbergian battle of the sexes from that play and *The Death of Bessie Smith*—while weaving in several others that become increasingly prominent in his work: excoriating wit, a concern with illusion/reality, the structuring of action through games and game-playing (here, "Humiliate the Host," "Hump the Hostess," "Get the Guests," and "Bringing Up Baby"), and a mature emphasis on the need to accept change and the potentially creative possibilities it offers.

Tightly unified in time, place, and action, *Who's Afraid of Virginia Woolf?* occurs in the early hours of Sunday morning in the home of George, a professor of history, and his wife, Martha, in the mythical eastern town of New Carthage. After a party given by her father, the college president, Martha invites Nick, a young biology teacher, and his wife, Honey, back home for a nightcap. Through the ensuing confrontations and games that occasionally turn bitter and vicious, both the older and the younger couples experience a radical, regenerative transformation. George, who sees himself as a humanist who lives for the multiplicity and infinite variety that have always characterized history, immediately sets himself up against Nick, the man of science, or, better yet, of scientism, whose narrow, amoral view of inevitability—wherein every creature would be determined down to color of hair and eyes—would sound the death knell for civilization. Like the attractive, muscular young men from *The American Dream* and *The Sandbox*, Nick is appealing on the outside but spiritually vapid within. If his ethical sense is undeveloped, even nonexistent, and his intellect sterile, he is also physically impotent when he and Martha go off to bed, though his temporary impotence should probably be regarded mainly as symbolic of the general sterility of his entire life. George apparently intends, much as Jerry had in *The Zoo Story*, to jar Nick out of his present condition, which involves being overly solicitous of his mousey, infantile wife. Though experiencing a false pregnancy when Nick married her, Honey, slim-hipped and unable to hold her liquor—her repeated exits to the bathroom are adroitly managed to move characters on and off the stage—is frightened of childbirth. As George detects, she has been preventing conception or aborting without Nick's knowledge, and in this way unmanning her husband, preventing him from transmitting his genes. By the play's end, Nick and Honey have seen the intense emptiness that can infect a marriage without children, and Honey three times cries out that she wants a child. George and Martha were unable to have children— neither will cast blame on the other for this—and so, twenty-one years earlier, they created an imaginary son, an illusion so powerful that it has become, for all intents and purposes, a reality for them.

If not intellectually weak, George, who is in fact Albee's spokesman in the play, does share with Nick the condition of being under the emotional and physical control of his wife. Ever since the time when Martha's Daddy insisted that his faculty participate in an exhibition sparring match to demonstrate their readiness to fight in the war and Martha knocked George down in the huckleberry bush, she has taunted George with being a blank and a cipher. It is unlikely that he will ever succeed her father as college president—he will not even become head of the history department. Martha claims that George married her to be humiliated and that she has worn the pants in the family not by choice but because someone must be stronger in any relationship. George realizes that if he does not act decisively to change his life by taking control, the time for any possible action will have passed.

In a formulation of the evolutionary metaphor that Albee recurrently employs, George, who, like civilization, is facing a watershed, remarks that a person can descend only so many rungs on the ladder before there can be no turning back; he must stop contemplating the past and decide to "alter the future." Martha, too, seems to want George to take hold and become more forceful; she, indeed, is openly happy when he exerts himself, as when he frightens them all with a rifle that shoots a parasol proclaiming "Bang," in one of the absurd jokes of which Albee is fond. Martha, despite being loud and brash and vulgar, is also sensual and extremely vulnerable. She does indeed love George, who is the only man she has ever loved, and fears that someday she will go so far in belittling him that she will lose him forever.

The imaginary son has served not only as a uniting force in their marriage but also as a beanbag they can toss against each other. When George decides to kill the son whom they mutually created through an act of imagination, Martha desperately insists that he does not have the right to do this on his own, but to no avail. Even if the child, who was to have reached his twenty-first birthday and legal maturity on the day of the play, had been real, the parents would have had to let go and continue on alone, facing the future with only each other. As George says, "It was time." He kills the illusion, intoning the mass for the dead. It is Sunday morning, and Martha is still frightened of "Virginia Woolf," of living without illusion, but also of facing the unknown. "*Maybe* it will be better," George tells her, for one can never be totally certain of what is to come. Just as there can be no assurance—though all signs point in that direction—that Nick and Honey's marriage will be firmer with a child, there can be no certainty that George and Martha's will be better without their imaginary son, though George is now prepared to offer Martha the strength and support needed to see her through her fear. Finally, Albee seems to be saying, human beings must not only accept change but also actively embrace it for the possibilities it presents for growth. The future is always terrifying, an uncharted territory, yet if one does not walk into it, one has no other choice but death.

Tiny Alice is Albee's richest work from a philosophical point of view; it also represents his most explicit excursion into the realm of the Absurd. In it, Albee addresses the problem of how human beings come to know the reality outside themselves, even questioning whether there is, finally, any reality to know. To do this, Albee builds his play around a series of dichotomies: between faith and reason, between present memory and past occurrence, between symbol and substance. The play opens with a scene that could almost stand on its own as a little one-act play, demonstrating Albee's wit at its virulent best. A Lawyer and a Cardinal, old school chums and, apparently, homosexual lovers in their adolescence, attack each other verbally, revealing the venery of both civil and religious authority. The Lawyer has come as the emissary of Miss Alice, ready to bequeath to the Church one hundred million dollars a year for the next twenty years; the Cardinal's secretary, the lay Brother Julian, will be sent to her castle to complete the transaction. For Julian, this becomes an allegorical dark night of the soul, a period when his religious faith will be tempted and tested. On the literal level, the play seems preposterous at times and even muddled; the suspicion that all this has been planned by some extortion ring, though it is unclear what they hope to gain by involving Julian, or even, perhaps, that all this is a charade devised by Julian to provide himself with an opportunity for sacrifice, is never quite dispelled. On the metaphoric and symbolic levels, however, as a religious drama about contemporary man's need to make the abstract concrete in order to have some object to worship, *Tiny Alice* is clear and consistent and succeeds admirably.

Julian, who earlier suffered a temporary loss of sanity over the disparity between his own conception of God and the false gods that human beings create in their own image, is now undergoing a further crisis. His temptation now is to search out a personification of the Godhead in order to make the Unknowable knowable, by making it concrete through a symbol; he hopes to prove that God exists by making contact with an experiential representation of Him. To represent the Deity in this manner is, however, as the Lawyer insists, to distort and diminish It so that It can be understood in human terms. Up to this point, Julian has always fought against precisely such a reduction of the divine. The symbol that Julian now literally embraces—through a sexual consummation and marriage that is both religious and erotic—is Miss Alice, the surrogate for Tiny Alice. That God in Albee's play is named *"Tiny* Alice" points, in itself, to the strange modern phenomenon of a reduced and delimited rather than an expansive deity. Instead of the real (Miss Alice) being a pale shadowing forth of the ideal form (Tiny Alice), here the symbol (Alice) is *larger* than what it represents, just as the mansion in which the action after scene 1 occurs is larger than its replica, exact down to the last detail, that is onstage in the library. The Lawyer insists that human beings can never worship an abstraction, for to do so always results in worshiping only the symbol and never the substance or the thing symbolized. Furthermore, he causes Julian to question whether that substance has any tangible existence: Is it only the symbol, and not the thing symbolized, that exists? If so, then Julian faces the possibility of nothingness, of there being *nothing there*, of there being only the finite, sense-accessible dimension in which people live and no higher order that provides meaning.

In the face of this dilemma, Brother Julian can either despair of ever knowing his God, or he can make a leap of faith. When the financial arrangements have been completed, the Lawyer, who—like the Butler— has had Miss Alice as his mistress, shoots Julian, who has always dreamed of sacrificing himself for his faith. Martyrdom, the ultimate form of service to one's God, always involves questions of suicidal intent, of doing, as Eliot's hero in *Murder in the Cathedral* knows, "the right deed for the wrong reason." Is one dying for self, or as a totally submissive instrument of God? As Julian dies in the posture of one crucified, he demands, in a paroxysm blending sexual hysteria and religious ecstasy, that the transcendent personify itself; indeed, a shadow moves through the mansion, accompanied by ever-increasing heartbeat and ever-louder breathing, until it totally envelops the room. As Albee himself commented, two possibilities present themselves: Either the transcendent is real, and the God Tiny Alice actually manifests itself to Brother Julian at the moment of his death, or Julian's desire for transcendence is so great that he deceives himself. Thus, the play's ending, while allowing for the person of faith to be confirmed in his or her belief about the spiritual reality behind the physical symbol, is at the same time disquieting in that it insists on the equally possible option that the revelation of transcendence is merely a figment of one's imagination. What Albee may well be suggesting, then, and what brings him to the doorstep of the Absurdists in this provocative work, is that there is, finally, nothing there except what human beings, through their illusions, are able to call up as a shield against the void.

A Delicate Balance, for which Albee deservedly won the Pulitzer Prize denied him by the Advisory Board four seasons earlier for *Who's Afraid of Virginia Woolf?*, is an autumnal play about death-in-life. A metaphysical drawing-room drama in the manner of Eliot and Graham Greene, it focuses on a well-to-do middle-aged couple, Agnes and Tobias, who are forced one October weekend to assess their lives by the unexpected visit of their closest friends, Harry and Edna (characters in Albee traditionally lack surnames). The latter couple arrives on Friday night, frightened by a sudden perception of emptiness. Having faced the existential void, they flee, terrified, to the warmth and succor of Agnes and Tobias' home, trusting that they will discover there some shelter from meaninglessness, some proof that at least the personal values of friendship and love remain. As the stage directions imply, an audience should not measure these visitors-in-the-night against the requirements of realistic character portrayal; they function, instead, as mirror images for their hosts, who, by looking at them, are forced to confront the emotional and spiritual malaise of their own lives. Agnes' live-in sister, the self-proclaimed alcoholic Claire—whose name suggests the clear-sightedness of this woman who stands on the side-lines and sees things as they are—understands the threat that Harry and Edna bring with them. Agnes fears that their guests come bearing the "plague," and Claire understands that this weekend will be spent waiting for the biopsy, for confirmation of whether some dread, terminal disease afflicts this family.

Agnes not only has no desire for self-knowledge but also deliberately guards against any diagnosis of the family's ills. As the fulcrum, she is able to maintain the family's status quo only by keeping herself and Tobias in a condition of stasis, insulated from the currents that threaten to upset the "delicate balance" that allows them to go on without ever questioning their assumptions. A somewhat haughty though gracious woman, whose highly artificial and carefully measured language reflects the controlled pattern of her existence and her inability to tolerate or handle the unexpected, Agnes muses frequently on sex roles. A dramatic descendant of Strindberg's male characters rather than of his female characters, she decries all of those things that have made the sexes too similar and have thus threatened the stability of the traditional family unit.

From her perspective, it is the wife's function to maintain the family *after* the husband has made the decisions: She only holds the reins; Tobias decides the route. It is Tobias' house which is not in order, and only he, she says, can decide what should be done. Tobias himself would claim that Agnes rules, but Agnes would counter that this is only his illusion. Clearly, Tobias seems to have relinquished his position of authority after the death of their son, Teddy; at that point, according to their oft-divorced daughter, Julia, now inopportunely home again after a fourth failed marriage, Tobias became a pleasant, ineffectual, gray *non*eminence. Undoubtedly, his insufficiencies as a father have had an adverse effect upon his daughter's relationships with men, and although Tobias rationalizes that he did not want another son because of the potential suffering it might have caused for Agnes, he might equally have feared his own inadequacy as a role model.

That Tobias lacks essential self-criticism and decisiveness is suggested by the motto he has cheerfully adopted: "We do what we can." In other words, he takes the path of least resistance, no longer exerting himself to do more than the minimum in his personal relationships. At one point in the play, Tobias tells a story about his cat and him—a parable similar to Jerry's tale of the dog in *The Zoo Story*—which illustrates Tobias' attitude toward having demands placed upon him and being judged. Believing that the cat was accusing him of being neglectful, and resenting this assessment, he turned to hating the cat, which he finally had put to sleep in an act Claire terms the "least ugly" choice. Now, with Harry and Edna's visit, Tobias is again having his motives and the depth of his concern measured.

He realizes that if he does not respond positively to their needs, he will be tacitly admitting that his whole life, even his marriage to Agnes, has been empty. In one of the verbal arias for which Albee is justly famous, Tobias begs, even demands, that they remain, though he does not want this burden and disruption. When, despite his desperate entreaties, they insist on leaving, Agnes can calmly remark, "Come now; we can begin the day," satisfied that the dark night of terror is safely passed. Her closing line must, however, be understood as ironic. Although it is Sunday morning, there has been no resurrection or renewal; the opportunity for salvation has been missed, and Tobias must now live on with the knowledge that he has failed, that much of his life has been a sham.

As is true of the characters at the end of O'Neill's *Long Day's Journey into Night*, Tobias' tragedy is that he has come to self-knowledge too late to act upon the new recognition. This is perhaps Albee's central perception in *A Delicate Balance*: that time diminishes the possibilities for human choice and change. Try as he might, it is now too late for Tobias to break out of the pattern, and so he is condemned to living out his days with an awareness of how little he has become, since he lacks the comforting illusions of propriety and magnanimity that Agnes can call upon for solace. He has seen his soul, and he has found it wanting, and things can never be the same again. For Tobias, in what is Albee's most beautiful play, the "delicate balance" that everyone erects as a shelter has tipped, but not in his favor. As Agnes muses, "Time happens," and all that remains is rust, bones, and wind. These are Albee's hollow people for whom the dark never ends.

If *Tiny Alice* and *A Delicate Balance* are dark plays, *Seascape* is a play of light, Albee's most luminous work to date. An optimistic tone poem which won for Albee his second Pulitzer, *Seascape* might, indeed, profitably be seen as a reverse image of *A Delicate Balance*, which won for him his first. In the later play, Albee again focuses on a couple in their middle age who ask: Where do we go from here? Are change and growth still possible, or is all that remains a gradual process of physical and spiritual atrophy until death? Nearly the entire first act of *Seascape*—which is primarily a play of scintillating discussion rather than action—is a two-character drama, with the diametrically opposed viewpoints of Nancy and Charlie temporarily poised in a tenuous equilibrium. Nancy's inclination is to follow the urge to ever fuller life, while Charlie is seduced by the prospect of a painless withdrawal from all purposive activity. The "seascape" of the play's title is the literal setting, but it is also an "escape," for the sea lying beyond the dunes is the archetype of both life and death; if it once symbolized Charlie's will-to-life, it now communicates his willed desire for the inertia of death or, at least, for a kind of premoral existence in which life simply passes. The shadow of Albee's dark plays still falls over *Seascape* in Charlie's initial stance as a man experiencing existential angst, terrified by the premonition of loneliness if Nancy should no longer be with him, fearful that even life itself may be only an illusion. In the face of these terrors—symbolized by the recurrent sound of the jet planes passing overhead—death beckons as a welcome release for Charlie, since he has lived well. As his watchword, he chooses "we'll see," just another way of saying that things will be put off until they are blessedly forgotten. Nancy, on the other hand, refuses to vegetate by retreating from life and living out her remaining days in a condition equivalent to "purgatory *before* purgatory," insisting instead that they "*do something*." She understands that if nothing is ever ventured, nothing can be gained. If Charlie, like Agnes in *A Delicate Balance*, desires stasis, a condition comfortable precisely because it is known and therefore can be controlled, Nancy will make the leap of faith into the unknown, accepting change and flux as a necessary precondition for progress and growth. Nancy accuses Charlie of a lack of "interest in imagery"; if, as Albee has frequently said, it is man's metaphor-making ability that renders him truly human, then Charlie's deficiency in this regard signals his diminished condition.

No sooner has Nancy finished her admonition to Charlie that they "*try something new*" than the opportunity presents itself in the appearance of Leslie and Sarah, two great green talking lizards come up from the sea. Their arrival, a startling yet delightful *coup de théâtre*, raises the work to the level of parable and allegory: Leslie and Sarah, existing at some prehuman stage on the evolutionary scale, serve as recollections of what the older couple's heritage was eons ago—as well as of what Charlie desires to become once again. Leslie and Sarah, like Harry and Edna in *A Delicate Balance*, are afraid not of the prospect of dying and finding nothingness or the void but of the challenge of becoming more highly developed, which is to say more human and morally responsible creatures. Life in the sea, unterrifying because a known quantity, was also more restricted and limiting. What inspires them to seek something more are the inklings of a sense of wonder, of awe, and of a childlike enthusiasm—qualities Nancy possesses in abundance. Their choice, then, exactly parallels Charlie's: They can make do by settling for less than a full life, or they can expand their lives qualitatively by becoming conscious of themselves as thinking and feeling beings, though that, of course, requires a willingness to experience consciously suffering as well as joy.

Significantly, it is Charlie, himself afraid, who convinces Leslie and Sarah to remain up on earth rather than descend back into the deep. In the moment of convincing them, he himself undergoes a regenerative epiphany that saves him, too. At the climactic point in *Seascape*, Charlie, like Jerry in *The Zoo Story* and George in *Who's Afraid of Virginia Woolf?* before him, gives Leslie and Sarah a "survival kit." To accomplish this requires that he hurt them, especially Sarah. Since what separates human beings from the lower animals is precisely their consciousness of being alive, of being vulnerable, and of finally being mortal, Charlie realizes that he can help Leslie and Sarah complete their transformation from beast to human only by making them feel truly human emotions. Playing on Sarah's fear that Leslie might someday leave her and never return, he deliberately, in an action that recalls the necessary violence of Jerry toward Peter, makes Sarah cry; that, in turn, makes Leslie so defensive and angry that he hits and chokes Charlie. Having tasted these human emotions of sorrow and wrath, Sarah and Leslie at first desire more than ever to return to the ooze, to the prehuman security of the sea. What quenches their fears is Nancy and Charlie pleading with them not to retreat, extending their hands to the younger couple in a gesture of compassion and human solidarity. In aiding Leslie and Sarah on the mythic journey from the womb into the world that, no matter how traumatic, must in time be taken, Charlie simultaneously leaves behind his desire to escape from life and asserts once more his will to live. If Charlie is a representative Everyman, fallen prey to ennui and despair, then Leslie's "Begin," on which the curtain falls, is a declaration of faith, trust, and determination, uttered not only for himself and Sarah but also for all humankind, who must periodically be roused and inspired to continue their journey.

In *The Man Who Had Three Arms*, Albee abolished the "fourth wall" of the theater in a manner that reminded many critics of the works of Luigi Pirandello; the play's protagonist spends much of the drama lecturing to the audience. Critical reaction was strongly negative, but Albee defended his methods as "a way of involving the audience; of embarrassing, if need be, the audience into participation." Many reviewers, in fact, decried *The Man Who Had Three Arms* as a virtual attack on its audience. Albee concurred, noting that he agreed with Antonin Artaud that at times a dramatist must "literally draw blood." He admitted that the drama was "an act of aggression" and "probably the most violent play I've written."

Marriage Play confines its violence to the stage, where the protagonists, a married couple named Jack and Gillian, alternate between bouts of physical abuse and scenes of tenderness and physical attraction. Jack and Gillian are in some ways reminiscent of the battling couples of *Who's Afraid of Virginia Woolf?*, but the newer play also incorporates the sort of metaphysical speculation that had marked much of Albee's later work. *Marriage Play* thus served to encapsulate many of the principal themes of Albee's dramatic career.

Despite a lengthy career that has, especially in its second half, been marked by more critical downs than ups, Albee has not been satisfied to rest on his successes, such as *Who's Afraid of Virginia Woolf?*, nor has he been content simply to repeat the formulas that have worked for him in the past. Instead, he has continued to experiment with dramatic form, to venture into new structures and styles. In so doing, he has grown into a major voice in dramatic literature, the progress of whose career in itself reflects his overriding theme: No emotional or artistic or spiritual growth is possible without embracing the terror—and perhaps the glory—of tomorrow's unknown, for the unknown is contemporary humanity's only certainty.

Bibliography

Amacher, Richard E. *Edward Albee.* Rev. ed. Boston: Twayne, 1982. Taking Albee's career through *The Man Who Had Three Arms*, this study is part biography, part script analysis, and part career assessment. Amacher is best at discussing Albee's "place in the theatre" and his marriage of the well-made play form with the formless Theater of the Absurd. Good second opinion after C. W. E. Bigsby's edition of essays in 1975. Chronology, notes, bibliography.

Bigsby, C. W. E., ed. *Edward Albee: A Collection of Critical Essays.* Englewood Cliffs, N.J.: Prentice-Hall, 1975. Part of the Twentieth Century Views series, this collection includes notable names in theater and scholarship, such as Gerald Weales, Martin Esslin, Richard Schechner, Alan Schneider, Harold Clurman, Philip Roth, and Robert Brustein. They contribute several interpretations of the symbolic aspect of Albee's plays, usually, but not always, in single-play discussions. Chronology and select bibliography.

Cohn, Ruby. *Edward Albee.* Minneapolis: University of Minnesota Press, 1969. Reprint. Ann Arbor, Mich.: University Microfilms International, 1979. With her usual foresight and insight, Cohn delivers this pamphlet-like first response to early Albee, from *The Zoo Story* to *Box and Quotations from Chairman Mao Tse-tung.* Sees Albee's early predilection for biblical associations and the hidden, often religious, significance of character names. Strong bibliography of early studies.

Hayman, Ronald. *Edward Albee.* London: Heinemann, 1971. Albee is only the second (after Arthur Miller) American playwright to be treated in this Contemporary Playwrights series from England. He is seen here as an "important" newcomer, whose plays are "powerful and moving" despite the failure of *All Over* and three adaptations. "There is still hope that [Albee's talent] will recover," Hayman notes. Biographical outline and list of performances to 1970.

Kolin, Philip C., and J. Madison Davis. *Critical Essays on Edward Albee.* Boston: G. K. Hall, 1986. Part of a series of critical essays on American literature, this collection of original reviews (from *The Zoo Story* to *Counting the Ways*), general criticism, and an overview of Albee's importance to world theater is comprehensive and thorough, with some thirty-seven articles, as well as an annotated bibliography of Albee interviews (with its own index).

McCarthy, Gerry. *Edward Albee*. New York: St. Martin's Press, 1987. Stronger than other studies on Albee's theater sense, as opposed to his plays as dramatic literature, this brief but informative overview puts the work in a dynamic, action-and-reaction-oriented structural perspective. Some production stills, index, and brief bibliography.

Roudané, Matthew. *Understanding Edward Albee*. Columbia: University of South Carolina Press, 1987. Organized chronologically, and pairing the plays in each chapter (*Who's Afraid of Virginia Woolf?* gets its own), this study focuses on Albee's plays in a "culture seeking to locate its identity through the ritualized action implicit in the art of theater." Bibliography and index.

Wasserman, Julian, ed. *Edward Albee: An Interview and Essays*. Houston, Tex.: University of St. Thomas, 1983. This 1981 interview, on translations, audiences, and similar earthly subjects, has a show-biz tone to it, without much of the transcendental abstractions of later interviews. A good place to start a study of Albee, since he articulates his intentions here with some clarity and grace. Wasserman contributes an essay on language; seven other authors offer single-play discussions, not including *Who's Afraid of Virginia Woolf?* but including *The Lady from Dubuque*, *Seascape*, and *Counting the Ways*.

Thomas P. Adler
(Updated by *Thomas J. Taylor*
and *Robert McClenaghan*)

MAXWELL ANDERSON

Born: Atlantic, Pennsylvania; December 15, 1888
Died: Stamford, Connecticut; February 28, 1959

Principal drama

White Desert, pr. 1923; *What Price Glory?*, pr. 1924, pb. 1926 (with Laurence Stallings); *Outside Looking In*, pr. 1925, pb. 1929; *First Flight*, pr. 1925, pb. 1926 (with Stallings); *Three American Plays*, pb. 1926; *Saturday's Children*, pr., pb. 1927; *Gypsy*, pr. 1929; *Elizabeth the Queen*, pr., pb. 1930 (adaptation of Lytton Strachey's history *Elizabeth and Essex*); *Night over Taos*, pr., pb. 1932; *Both Your Houses*, pr., pb. 1933; *Mary of Scotland*, pr., pb. 1933; *Valley Forge*, pr., pb. 1934; *Winterset*, pr., pb. 1935; *The Masque of Kings*, pb. 1936, pr. 1937; *High Tor*, pr., pb. 1937; *Knickerbocker Holiday*, pr., pb. 1938 (lyrics; music by Kurt Weill); *Key Largo*, pr., pb. 1939; *Eleven Verse Plays, 1929-1939*, pb. 1940; *Joan of Lorraine*, pr., pb. 1946; *Anne of the Thousand Days*, pr., pb. 1948; *Lost in the Stars*, pr., pb. 1949 (lyrics; music by Weill; adaptation of Alan Paton's novel *Cry, the Beloved Country*); *Barefoot in Athens*, pr., pb. 1951; *Bad Seed*, pr. 1954, pb. 1955 (adaptation of William March's novel); *The Day the Money Stopped*, pr., pb. 1958 (adaptation of Brendan Gill's novel); *The Golden Six*, pr. 1958, pb. 1961; *Four Verse Plays*, pb. 1959.

Other literary forms

Maxwell Anderson's reputation rests exclusively on his dramatic works. In addition to his works in various forms of drama, he wrote a number of essays on the theater, some of which are collected in *The Essence of Tragedy and Other Footnotes and Papers* (1939) and *Off Broadway: Essays About the Theatre* (1947). Anderson also published two collections of poetry: *You Who Have Dreams* (1925) and *Notes on a Dream* (1971). Finally, he wrote a number of screenplays, including the screenplay for the film adaptation of the play *Joan of Lorraine*, entitled *Joan of Arc* (1948).

Achievements

Anderson was a prolific and versatile playwright, the author of poetic drama and historical drama, realistic plays and thesis plays, radio drama, screenplays, and musical drama (including two collaborations with composer Kurt Weill). At the peak of his success, during one season in the 1930's, he had three plays running on Broadway at the same time. During that same decade, he twice received the New York Drama Critics Circle Award and was also awarded a Pulitzer Prize.

Of the twelve Anderson plays produced on Broadway in his lifetime, nine are verse dramas—a remarkable feat in itself in the twentieth century, with verse drama long an endangered species. Indeed, it is as a rare modern practitioner of that form that Anderson is likely to be remembered.

Even Anderson's lesser achievements attest the enormous vitality of the American theater in his time: The sheer range of his work, including both failed experiments and commercial successes, the stretch of his ambition (even when one concedes that his theory of tragedy, for example, is an intellectual embarrassment)—all of this makes him one of the representative figures of a key period in the history of American drama.

Biography

James Maxwell Anderson was born the son of a Baptist minister in Atlantic, Pennsylvania, on December 15, 1888. The family moved frequently, but in time Maxwell enrolled at the University of North Dakota, where he wrote poetry and drama. Following graduation, in 1911, he married Margaret Haskett. After two years of teaching high school, he enrolled in a master's program at Stanford University and earned his M.A. degree in 1914. After having taught for five years, Anderson went into journalism, working for the *Chronicle* and the *Bulletin* in San Francisco. In 1918, he moved to New York, where he worked on the editorial staffs of *The New Republic*, *New York Evening Globe*, and *New York World*.

Anderson's playwriting did not begin until 1923, when, at the age of thirty-five, he wrote the verse tragedy *White Desert*. The play was a theatrical failure, but it interested another playwright, Laurence Stallings, at that time a successful book reviewer for *New York World*. In 1924, the two collaborated on an antiwar play, *What Price Glory?*, a realistic piece that was extremely well received.

Following this success, Anderson began to broaden his techniques, writing in both verse and prose. When subsequent collaborations with Stallings did not prove successful, Anderson parted company with him. He was to write six more plays before he achieved another success, with *Elizabeth the Queen* in 1930. In this play, Anderson's unusual combination of poetic, dramatic, and philosophical gifts finds brilliant expression in a dramatization of the love affair of Queen Elizabeth I of England and the ambitious Lord Essex.

Anderson's technique of illuminating contemporary issues with historical settings was so successful in *Elizabeth the Queen* that he wrote eight more plays using history for this purpose. *Night over Taos*, *Mary of Scotland*, *Valley Forge*, and *The Masque of Kings* are, like *Elizabeth the Queen*, verse plays, though none of these was as successful as the latter. One of Anderson's musicals, *Knickerbocker Holiday*, which takes as its point of departure Washington Irving's *A History of New York* (1809), also has a historical setting, used to shed a comic and satiric light on the political scene of the 1930's. *Barefoot in Athens* and the perennially popular *Anne of the Thousand Days* combine the historical drama with the drama of ideas, following the pattern of George Bernard Shaw but without Shaw's ability to dramatize intellectual issues. Finally, *Joan of Lorraine* is an examination of Joan's character through a rehearsal for a play during which the actress portraying the saint and the director disagree on the interpretation of her role.

In the 1940's and 1950's, Anderson devoted more of his time to matters outside the theater and produced fewer plays than he had during the 1930's. In 1940, he participated in Wendell Willkie's unsuccessful campaign for the presidency against Franklin Delano Roosevelt. In 1942, Anderson helped to raise money to buy High Tor, and in 1943, it was given to the state of New York for a park, thus saving the real mountain from the fate it suffered in the play of the same title. He spent part of 1943 touring army bases in North Carolina and Virginia, then in England and North Africa. In 1944, he devoted the summer and fall to campaigning against the United States congressman from his home district in New York State and was successful in that venture. In 1947, he toured Greece and wrote a series of essays about the political situation there.

Anderson's first wife died in 1931, and in 1933 he married the actress Gertrude Maynard. They had been estranged for some time when, in March, 1953, she committed suicide. In 1954, Anderson married Gilda Oakleaf. They established a new home in Stamford, Connecticut, where Anderson was to live until his death.

Burdened with tax problems, Anderson in the late 1950's wrote three plays primarily to bring in more money: *Bad Seed* in 1954, *The Day the Money Stopped* in 1958, and *The Golden Six* in the same year. Only *Bad Seed*, however, proved to be a commercial success.

Anderson died on February 28, 1959, following a stroke at his home in Stamford, Connecticut. On March 3, a memorial service was held for him at St. Paul's Chapel, Columbia University.

Analysis

Maxwell Anderson was one among several playwrights, including Eugene O'Neill, Elmer Rice, Sidney Howard, Robert E. Sherwood, George S. Kaufman, and Paul Green, who changed the world's perception of American drama. Before World War I, American drama was purely of local interest, and no great playwrights had appeared in the United States. By the end of the 1920's, however, New York City had become one of the most vital theater centers in the world, and American dramatists were enjoying a period of extraordinary creative flowering.

Although the American playwrights of this period were diverse in their points of view, many of them reflected the disillusionment that followed World War I. Anderson was among these; the basic philosophy of life that informs his drama is typical of the 1920's. In this view, modern man is deprived of religious faith or the opportunity for meaningful social action. Love, although fleeting, is the only thing that gives life meaning. Anderson's first successful play, *What Price Glory?*, on which he collaborated with Laurence Stallings, has affinities with many works of the 1920's; its critical look at the myths surrounding war brings to mind Ernest Hemingway's novel *A Farewell to Arms* (1929). The play centers on a squad of marines in the midst of some of the heaviest fighting in World War I.

The play's disillusioned attitude and profane dialogue may seem mild to today's readers, who are accustomed to stronger stuff, but to the audience of the 1920's, the play was shocking. Stallings and Anderson's soldiers talk like soldiers, and their profanity (toned down after objections from various groups, including the Marine Corps) epitomizes a thoroughgoing irreverence among the characters toward matters that traditionally had been treated with greater respect.

The play uses the war as a symbol for a world that is purposeless and chaotic. Act 1 shows the American marine unit awaiting a battle with the Germans in a French town; act 2 centers on the battle, emphasizing the suffering of Americans and Germans alike; and act 3 reveals the futility of the conflict. In act 1, Sergeant Quirk arrives to take over the duties of a longtime enemy, Captain Flagg, while Flagg goes on a brief leave. Quirk later becomes involved with a prostitute named Charmaine, unaware that Flagg also likes her. The inevitable happens: The girl's father eventually demands that his daughter's honor be saved by marriage. Quirk is threatened by Flagg with court-martial if he does not marry the girl, but the company is ordered to the front before the matter can be resolved. The girl is abandoned so that the men can continue to kill others, rather than themselves.

When *Elizabeth the Queen* was produced on November 3, 1930, Anderson launched the most productive decade of his career and for the first time showed the public the nature of his concern with poetic tragedy. The play was both a popular and a critical success—surprising, perhaps, considering that it was written in verse. The controlled expression of emotion through rhythm and image is well handled in the play, perhaps contributing to the acceptance of the poetic form by the audience. The idea of the play came from Lytton Strachey's history *Elizabeth and Essex*, published in 1928. Anderson, however, shifted the focus from historic transition to individual character. Evident here is a recurring theme in Anderson's Tudor plays: the lust for power in conflict with sexual passion.

The aging Queen Elizabeth suspects that her youthful lover Essex is as enamored of her throne as he is of her person. Two rival courtiers, Sir Robert Cecil and Sir Walter Raleigh, intrigue against Essex by intercepting Essex's and the queen's letters while he is in Ireland on a military expedition, thus sowing further distrust between the lovers. Their plot is successful: Essex is provoked into storming the palace, but once within the throne room, he is outwitted by Elizabeth, who then orders his arrest and execution for treason. In the last act, Elizabeth anxiously waits for Essex to return to her a ring as a sign of his repentence. Finally, she sends for him. Her attempt to save him is futile, however, for Essex is too proud to beg for his life and acknowledges that, were he freed, he would continue his pursuit of the throne. Essex leaves, having accepted his fate, and Elizabeth must wait, in anguish, for his now inevitable execution.

Anderson distrusted the system of government and of power politics in the United States and elsewhere. He believed that persons of goodwill are usually destroyed by evil ones—a sentiment expressed here in the line "The rats inherit the earth." He saw, however, in the struggle of humankind against powerful forces a magnificence in which he found inspiration. *Elizabeth the Queen* revolves around very strong characters motivated by great passion, flawed characters who are nevertheless dignified through suffering. Their sense of loneliness and alienation reflects the fragmentation and isolation of modern society; Elizabeth says "The years are long living among strangers." Such recognition of the lonely state of human beings in a society in which evil is a dominant force recurs throughout Anderson's work.

Soon after the success of *Elizabeth the Queen*, Anderson returned to prose drama with the political satire *Both Your Houses*, which won for him a Pulitzer Prize in 1933. Although the setting of the latter is modern Washington, D.C., rather than historical England, *Both Your Houses*, like its predecessor, centers on the isolation of the honest individual in a predominantly evil society. Alan McClean is a freshman congressman who is appalled by the graft and corruption he finds to be commonplace in Washington. As he explores this rampant corruption, he discovers not only that his own election campaign is tainted but also that, if he votes according to his conscience, he risks financially ruining his fiancé's father, a man whom he admires. McClean is unsuccessful in an attempt to beat his colleagues at their own game and is left, in his own eyes, with no choice but to resign.

Among Anderson's many plays of the 1930's, his most productive decade, one of the most interesting is *High Tor*. Perhaps it is so interesting because the theme is an enduring one in American literature: conservation, or, as it is now termed, ecology. High Tor is a real mountain peak overlooking the Hudson River, near which Anderson lived at the time he wrote the play.

Van Van Dorn, the individualistic owner of High Tor, is determined not to sell his mountain despite the threats of two men who represent a mining company that wants to buy High Tor. Van Dorn is aided in his efforts to preserve the mountain by the ghosts of Henry Hudson's crew, who have been wandering the slopes of High Tor for three hundred years, waiting for their ship to return for them. When the company men are stranded on the mountain after dark, they take shelter in a steam shovel, which the ghosts then hoist high into the air. Morning finds the conflicts resolved. The spectral ship has returned for its crew, and Van Dorn finally agrees to sell High Tor, believing that, like the ghosts, the mountain has vanished overnight.

The play blends realism, fantasy, farce, and satire in a delightfully theatrical mix; it won for Anderson the New York Drama Critics Circle Award. Despite the play's entertaining qualities, however, it reminds the audience that the materialistic modern world will not allow the free and natural to survive.

Throughout his dramatic works, Anderson adhered to the Aristotelian principles of unity and the tragic hero as he explored the myths of his times. Producing the most important body of his work during the Depression era, he addressed social issues and injustices, though his primary purpose seems to have been to place them in their historical, literary, and mythological contexts rather than to raise the audience's awareness of such problems. Clearly, Anderson was interested in dramatic theory and history, and his plays exemplify his concerns with form as well as with theme.

Other major works

NOVEL: *Morning Winter and Night*, 1952 (as John Nairne Michaelson).

POETRY: *You Who Have Dreams*, 1925; *Notes on a Dream*, 1971.

NONFICTION: *The Essence of Tragedy and Other Footnotes and Papers*, 1939; *Off Broadway: Essays About the Theatre*, 1947; *Dramatist in America: Letters of Maxwell Anderson, 1912-1958*, 1977.

SCREENPLAYS: *All Quiet on the Western Front*, 1930 (with others; adaptation of Erich Maria Remarque's novel); *Joan of Arc*, 1948 (with Andrew Solt); *The Wrong Man*, 1956 (with Angus MacPhail).

Bibliography

Adam, Julie. *Versions of Heroism in Modern American Drama: Redefinitions by Miller, Williams, O'Neill, and Anderson.* New York: St. Martin's Press, 1991. This excellent study is an exploration of redefinitions. Adam argues that Arthur Miller, Tennessee Williams, Eugene O'Neill, and Anderson not only do not provide a systematic theory of tragedy but also frequently do not engage in an easily classifiable dramatic practice. Often ignoring the formal aspects and philosophical dimension of traditional tragedy, they instead focus on its intensified character portrayal, which they believe typifies the genre. They identify tragedy with dramatization of heroism and redefine tragedy as primarily a dramatic tribute to individualism and human potential. First-rate bibliography.

Anderson, Maxwell. *Dramatist in America: Letters of Maxwell Anderson, 1912-1958.* Edited by Laurence G. Avery. Chapel Hill: University of North

Carolina Press, 1977. Consists of 212 illuminating letters on a wide variety of topics. The letters are arranged in chronological order, and each is presented in three parts: heading, text, and annotation. Extremely few letters, however, are available from the early period of Anderson's life and from the period during which the author suffered a nervous breakdown. Contains a chronology, a list of letters, and appendices.

Bailey, Mabel D. *Maxwell Anderson: The Playwright as Prophet.* New York: Abelard-Schuman, 1957. A brief but well-written book of dramatic criticism aimed at a general audience. Bailey's aim is to test the validity of Anderson's creative principles—particularly his dramatic theory—by undertaking a critical examination of the plays that Anderson produced in accordance with that theory. Central to this theory is the notion that theme is the thing for which the work of art exists. Bailey offers many perceptive comments, particularly on the drama *Barefoot in Athens.*

Clark, Barrett H. *Maxwell Anderson: The Man and His Plays.* New York: Samuel French, 1933. A pioneer study giving an overview on some of the early plays. The biographical section consists of six brief pages—a testimony to the playwright's polite refusal to volunteer information about his personal life. Clark was one of the earliest critics to recognize Anderson's unusual talent.

Shivers, Alfred S. *The Life of Maxwell Anderson.* New York: Stein & Day, 1983. The first full-length biography of Anderson. It is based on correspondence, diaries, business documents, notes, legal documents, oral and unpublished written reminiscences of Anderson's relatives and friends, and a memoir of Anderson and hitherto unpublished photographs. Also includes a family genealogy, a lengthy bibliography, a list of the Playwrights' Company productions, and a list of Anderson's addresses.

_____. *Maxwell Anderson.* Boston: Twayne, 1976. Based not only on a study of the dramatic works themselves and on the published secondary sources but also on new archival materials and correspondence with Anderson's relatives and friends, who volunteered much fresh information about the playwright and his art. As a result, the first chapter offers much more biography than had yet appeared in print. The remaining chapters consist of critical studies of the major plays and some of the minor ones.

John W. Crawford
(Updated by *Genevieve Slomski*)

ROBERT ANDERSON

Born: New York, New York; April 28, 1917

Principal drama

Come Marching Home, pr. 1945; *All Summer Long*, pr. 1953, pb. 1955; *Tea and Sympathy*, pr., pb. 1953; *Silent Night, Lonely Night*, pr. 1955, pb. 1960; *The Days Between*, pr., pb. 1965; *You Know I Can't Hear You When the Water's Running*, pr., pb. 1967 (comprises four one-act plays: *The Footsteps of Doves*, *I'm Herbert*, *The Shock of Recognition*, and *I'll Be Home for Christmas*); *I Never Sang for My Father*, pr., pb. 1968; *Solitaire/Double Solitaire*, pr. 1971, pb. 1972; *Free and Clear*, pr. 1983.

Other literary forms

Robert Anderson has written numerous radio, television, and film scripts, including screen adaptations of Kathryn Hulme's 1956 novel *The Nun's Story* (1959), of Richard McKenna's 1962 novel *The Sand Pebbles* (1966), and of his own *I Never Sang for My Father* (1970). The only one of these that has been published, however, is the screenplay of *I Never Sang for My Father*. Many interviews with Anderson and essays by him on the practice of playwriting and the state of the theater have been published in various newspapers and journals, but these interviews and essays have not been collected. He has also published the novels *After* (1973) and *Getting Up and Going Home* (1978).

Achievements

Considering Robert Anderson's lifelong devotion to the theater, the number of his plays receiving wide notice has been relatively small. Although he wrote *The Days Between* with Broadway in mind, Anderson offered it to the newly formed American Playwrights Theater when that organization was having difficulty getting good new plays to offer its member theaters. As a result, *The Days Between* was produced during 1965-1966 in fifty regional theaters but was never produced on Broadway. *Come Marching Home*, which did have a short New York run, was never published.

Although Anderson's plays are to some extent marred by imitativeness and by a lack of variation in theme and motif, they nevertheless represent a solid, if modest, achievement. Anderson has created several memorable characters—for example, the rigid, domineering, irascible, charming, and pathetic Tom Garrison of *I Never Sang for My Father*, a self-made man who in his old age is unable to admit to himself, much less communicate to his family, his need for them and his loneliness; the comic, anxiously adaptable actor Richard Pawling of *The Shock of Recognition*, also pathetic in his eagerness to be or to do anything at all in order to get a part in a play; and the middle-class, middle-aged, anguished Chuck of *I'll Be Home for Christmas*, suddenly, by a letter from his son, brought face to face with his own fears about the meaninglessness of his existence.

In addition, Anderson has been willing to take chances in his plays, and in so doing has helped enrich both in subject and in technique the possibilities open to the theater. In subject, for example, *Tea and Sympathy* was the first American play to deal explicitly with homosexuality, and *Double Solitaire* carries frankness in the discussion of sexual experiences to what is probably the limit of public acceptability on the stage; in stage technique, *The Shock of Recognition* introduced for the first time the possibility of presenting male frontal nudity in the theater (though not itself actually presenting such nudity); and in format, his *You Know I Can't Hear You When the Water's Running* successfully defied the well-entrenched belief that a group of one-act plays could not achieve commercial success on Broadway. These accomplishments have established Anderson's reputation as a dramatist seriously interested in making stage depictions of life correspond more closely to real life.

Biography

Robert Woodruff Anderson was born in New York City in April, 1917, to James Hewston and Myra Grigg Anderson. His father was a self-made man who twice made his way from poverty to financial success. Perhaps as a consequence, James Anderson had great respect for the so-called "manly" virtues of self-reliance, determination, and physical courage, but shared none of the aesthetic values which his wife instilled in young Robert. The resultant unhappy relationship between a husband and wife unable to appreciate each other's values has been mirrored in several of Anderson's plays, notably *All Summer Long*, *Tea and Sympathy*, and *I Never Sang for My Father*. The strained relationship between a father with a purely materialistic bent and a son whose artistic and literary bent embarrasses and bewilders his father forms a secondary motif in several of Anderson's plays and provides the central conflict in *I Never Sang for My Father*.

Anderson was educated in private elementary schools; at Phillips Exeter Academy, in Exeter, New Hampshire, where he wrote his first plays; and at Harvard, where he wrote plays, theater reviews, and a senior honors thesis entitled "The Necessity for Poetic Drama." He completed his undergraduate work at Harvard in 1939 and his work for the master's degree in 1940, and continued work toward a Ph.D. there until he entered the navy in 1942. While a graduate student at Harvard, he served as a teaching assistant and also taught drama courses in several small local colleges. During his navy service in World War II, Anderson wrote several plays, including *Come Marching Home*, which won the National Theater Conference Prize in 1945 for the best play written by a serviceman overseas and which subsequently had a very brief run Off-Broadway in New York. This prize helped him to obtain a scholarship to study playwriting under John Gassner, who later became one of Anderson's staunchest supporters among drama critics.

In 1940, Anderson married Phyllis Stohl, a woman ten years older than he, who was beloved in theatrical circles and who all of their married life was working for the theater in one capacity or another—as teacher, director, radio scriptwriter, producer, and finally as a literary agent for playwrights. They had no children, and the last five years of their sixteen-year marriage were dominated for both by the emotional turmoil of her long, and eventually unsuccessful, struggle against cancer. The trauma of this experience and his subsequent feelings of grief and guilt haunted Anderson for many years, leaving its impact on several of his plays, until he finally exorcised it in the pages of a very autobiographical novel, *After*. In 1959, Anderson married another theater personality, the stage and screen actress Teresa Wright, who later originated the role of Alice in the stage version of *I Never Sang for My Father*. This marriage produced no children, although Wright had two children from a previous marriage.

In addition to Anderson's own playwriting, he has contributed to American drama in his organization and support of other playwrights: In 1951 he cofounded New Dramatists; for many years he served as president of the Dramatists Guild; and in 1953, as "the sixth playwright," he revitalized the Playwrights' Producing Company with the success of *Tea and Sympathy*. In December, 1990, he hosted a tea reception for New Dramatists, initiating a series of fund-raisers for this still-flourishing organization.

Only three of Anderson's plays have had any great degree of commercial and critical success: *Tea and Sympathy*, *You Know I Can't Hear You When the Water's Running*, and *I Never Sang for My Father*. The others have had short runs and mixed reviews. In addition to writing for the theater, however, he has produced numerous scripts for radio, television, and motion pictures, many of them highly successful in production, and has been a teacher of drama and playwriting in colleges and universities.

Analysis

Robert Anderson is a heavily autobiographical playwright. His focal character is usually male, is usually a writer, often also a teacher, is misunderstood or not properly appreciated by someone close to him—most often his father or his wife—and is sometimes suffering from a tragedy associated with his wife. This character is young in the plays written when Anderson was young—in *All Summer Long*, he is only twelve, and in *Tea and Sympathy*, he is almost eighteen—but in the plays written as Anderson grew older, the focal character also is older: In *Silent Night, Lonely Night*, he is in his early forties; in *The Days Between*, he is split into two characters, both of whom are around forty; in three of the four one-act plays which make up *You Know I Can't Hear You When the Water's Running*, he is middle-aged, though in one of these he is not a writer; in *I Never Sang for My Father*, he is forty; in *Solitaire*, he is around fifty and, though not a writer since writing is obsolete in his society, a recorder of tapes in a library; and in *Double Solitaire*, he is forty-three.

Anderson's themes derive from the circumstances of this character in various incarnations. One of his most common themes is the incompatibility of a husband and wife, particularly a middle-aged couple who were once madly in love with each other. Their incompatibility may or may not be in values or goals, but its major symptom is always an unhappy sex life. In some cases, it even results in a complete cessation of any sex life within the marriage. Closely related to this theme is the theme of the importance of good sexual experiences in and of themselves, even outside marriage. Sex is seen as therapeutic, and it becomes a charitable obligation for kind and selfless people to fulfill the sex needs which they discern in lonely people with whom they have a mental or spiritual rapport. Another common theme of the plays is an unhappy father-son relationship, usually stemming from the inability of a materialistic, forceful, athletically inclined father to understand or appreciate properly the nature or accomplishments of a more sensitive, thoughtful, artistic son. Two other themes are inherent in these unhappy relationships, whether marital or father-son: the theme of guilt and hostility within the failing or failed relationship, and the theme of loneliness—the loneliness of an individual who is unable to achieve with another a sharing of values, goals and aspirations, tenderness and love.

Surprisingly for a writer so personal in theme and character, Anderson has seldom been innovative in plot, style, or technique. Perhaps because of his many years of formal education in drama, his works are much influenced by earlier writers, particularly Anton Chekhov, John Van Druten, and Tennessee Williams. *All Summer Long*, for example, follows Chekhov's *The Cherry Orchard* (pr. 1904) not only in its slow pace and in the lassitude of its ineffectual characters but also in the loss of the family home, which literally slides into a river because the adults in the family have been unable to put aside their petty personal desires and take some positive action to prevent the erosion of the soil under the house. *Tea and Sympathy* has an equally heavy debt to Van Druten's *Young Woodley* (pr. 1925), and *I Never Sang for My Father* owes several of its important elements to Williams' *The Glass Menagerie* (pr. 1944). Anderson has, however, not been wedded to any particular format or technique, but has been willing to experiment with various techniques introduced by others, using for his settings in some plays the highly realistic, conventional scene behind the proscenium arch and in others settings which are to varying degrees illusionistic and nonrepresentational; using an almost bare stage in some of the one-act plays; and using a narrator-chorus figure in *I Never Sang for My Father*. His attempts to make the theater more frank and open in its treatment of sex stem from his desire to see it become more adult and honest in its treatment of human relationships, particularly the marital and extramarital sexual relationships on which his plays so often center.

The autobiographical influences on *Tea and Sympathy* are readily apparent. The setting is a New England preparatory school similar to the one Anderson attended. Young Tom Lee has an artistic and sensitive nature and aesthetic interests which make him seem an "off-horse" to some of the other boys, to his housemaster, and to his father, who has sent Tom to this school in the hope that the housemaster will develop in Tom what the father considers a more manly character. Tom is not a writer, although in his elementary school days when his class needed a poet he was apparently the automatic choice. His real interest is in music, however, and he hopes for a career as a folksinger. Anderson's own first interest had also been music, and only after a sinus condition ruined his voice did he turn to the writing of plays. Tom falls in love with Laura Reynolds, a woman almost ten years older than he. Like Anderson's first wife, Phyllis, Laura is sympathetic to young people and eager to encourage talent in the young. Anderson's dedication of the play to Phyllis, "whose spirit is everywhere in this play," suggests that Laura resembles Phyllis in many other respects.

In addition to this strong autobiographical influence, however, there are also several strong literary influences on the play. One such influence, although a minor one, is Williams' *A Streetcar Named Desire*. In Williams' play, the young, sensitive first husband of Blanche kills himself when she discovers he is homosexual. His suicide scars Blanche for life, leaving her with feelings of guilt and remorse which she attempts to expiate by having sex with teenage boys even later in life when she is much older than they. In *Tea and Sympathy*, the young, sensitive first husband of Laura, because of some incident unknown to Laura which called his courage and manliness into question, in effect kills himself by risking his life unnecessarily in battle to prove to others that he is not a coward. His death scars Laura and may lead to her desire to experience sexual love with the teenage Tom Lee.

Two more important literary influences are Van Druten's *Young Woodley* and George Bernard Shaw's *Candida*. *Tea and Sympathy* is, in fact, so similar to *Young Woodley* that it might almost be considered an adaptation. In both plays, the young protagonist, a student at a boarding school, is disliked by his housemaster and teased by some of the students because he does not conform to their concept of manliness. Both housemasters hope eventually to become housemasters of their schools, and both are apparently projecting their own weaknesses and self-doubts on the protagonists.

In both plays, the protagonist has been deprived of his mother early in life, in *Young Woodley* by her death and in *Tea and Sympathy* by the divorce of the parents. In both, the student is in love with the housemaster's young wife (in both plays named Laura), whose nature and values are far different from those of her husband. In both, Laura encourages the young man in his artistic pursuits. In both, the young man visits the town prostitute, with resultant feelings of self-disgust, though for different reasons. In both, the young man, in a rage of frustration and despair, makes an attack with a butcher knife, Woodley an attack on another student and Tom an attempt at suicide. One important difference between the two plays is that in the last analysis, Woodley's father is far more helpful and sympathetic to his son than is Tom's father, a difference which reflects the lack of sympathetic understanding between Anderson and his own father. Another major difference is in the ending; Anderson gave his play a conclusion which, for that period in American theatrical history, was quite sensational.

This ending stems from the inspiration which Shaw's play *Candida* gave to Anderson's play. When Candida, the older married woman in Shaw's play, speculates on the effect which her rejection of the young, poetic Marchbanks will ultimately have on him, she wonders whether Marchbanks will forgive her for selfishly maintaining her own purity and chastity instead of initiating him into the mysteries of sexual love. She concludes that Marchbanks will forgive her if some other good woman teaches him about such love, but will not forgive her if he has the disillusioning experience of learning about sexual love from a "bad woman." In *Tea and Sympathy*, Tom asks Laura if she thinks Candida was right to send Marchbanks away, and Laura replies that Shaw "made it seem right." Later, when Tom, overcome by emotion, impulsively embraces and kisses Laura, she momentarily rejects his kisses, and he flees to the arms of the local prostitute, where his repulsion for the prostitute makes him unable to perform sexually and fills him with self-disgust. Laura, hearing about Tom's wretched experience, feels responsible for it, saying that she wishes she had let Tom prove his sexual prowess with her rather than sending him off to such a sordid experience. She has, thus, decided that Candida was wrong after all, and the play concludes as she is offering herself to Tom so that he will be able to prove to himself that he can indeed perform sexually as a man.

Here, Anderson is developing one of his favorite themes—the immorality and selfishness of allowing conventional mores to prevent one from offering a loving sexual experience to a kindred spirit who is lonely and in need of such love. The offering of a spirit of love and understanding is not enough in such circumstances; the truly loving person will feel the obligation to offer the full consummation of a sexual experience and will feel guilty for withholding such an offer. This theme provides the major conflict of Anderson's next play, *Silent Night, Lonely Night*, in which two lonely, unhappy people meet by chance on Christmas Eve, and, though both remain committed to their own unhappy marriages, help and strengthen each other by experiencing together a full sexual communion for that night only. Each has regrets for times in the past when he or she should have offered such an experience but withheld it through mindless obedience to an inappropriate system of morality, and both are seen at the conclusion of the play as better persons because they have learned to overcome such rigid principles. In this play, the Christmas Eve setting seems intended to give a religious sanction to Anderson's thesis.

Not only the morality but also the validity of this thesis can be, and indeed have been, questioned. Gerald Weales has branded it as belonging to the "fashionable sex-as-therapy" school of drama, which he finds unrealistic, and even John Gassner pointed out the strong possibility that in reality, the awe in which Tom Lee held Laura would prevent him from performing sexually with her and would thus compound, instead of alleviating, his trauma. Others have noted the lengths to which Anderson went to make the sensational ending seem right: that he divided his characters for the most part along melodramatic lines into the good and the bad, with both Laura and Tom clearly in the category of the good and with the vicious housemaster clearly in the category of the bad; that the housemaster is revealed as a latent homosexual himself; that Laura unequivocally breaks off her marriage to him before she offers herself to Tom; and even that her seduction of Tom takes place on his eighteenth birthday, so that she cannot be accused of contributing to the delinquency of a minor.

Tea and Sympathy thus takes up all the major themes of Anderson's later plays: the unhappy marital relationship, the unhappy father-son relationship, the feelings of guilt and loneliness deriving from the failure of such relationships, and the moral imperative of offering sexual experiences generously under certain circumstances. While derivative in plot and technique, it does break new ground in treating homosexuality explicitly rather than by innuendo and in the sexual frankness of the scene on which the curtain drops.

I Never Sang for My Father, though produced the year after *You Know I Can't Hear You When the Water's Running*, was written earlier and represents an earlier stage in Anderson's development. It is his most thorough and most successful attempt at exploring a difficult father-son relationship. Again, the autobiographical elements of the play are obvious. Tom Garrison, the father in the play, is like Anderson's father in many respects. He is a self-made man; he loves athletics and athletic values; he was once a mayor (Anderson's father once ran for the office of mayor of New Rochelle); and he has never understood or appreciated the artistic and literary interests of either his wife or his son. The son, Gene Garrison, is like Anderson in being both a writer and a college professor, in having had a wife who died slowly of a lingering illness, in being much closer to his mother than to his father, and in trying unsuccessfully to establish a satisfying relationship with his father.

The most important literary influence on the play is Williams' *The Glass Menagerie*. Anderson's play was first written as a movie script, and when Anderson sought a way of giving the play version a fluidity of movement from short scene to short scene, he borrowed the narrator-chorus figure which Williams had used so successfully in *The Glass Menagerie*. In addition, the two plays are similar in that both protagonists are trying to free their lives from the claims which parents are trying to impose on them, that both do eventually reject those claims and escape their parents' domination, and that neither succeeds in throwing off the consequent feelings of guilt and remorse.

In addition to the unsatisfactory father-son relationship, *I Never Sang for My Father* develops at some length the incompatibility of the interests and values of Margaret and Tom Garrison, thus providing yet another example of Anderson's interest in the theme of the unhappy marital relationship. As in his earlier treatments of this theme, the incompatibility of values is reflected in an unsatisfactory sex life, though this aspect of their lives is barely hinted at by Margaret Garrison.

In its exploration of both the father-son and the marital relationship, *I Never Sang for My Father* is probably Anderson's best play. The characters are real, and the anguish that they experience as they try unsuccessfully to reach one another is deep and moving. Gene's reactions ring true as those of a middle-aged son who loves his mother and tries to love his father but is appalled by the inevitable dependence of both on him. Gene and his mother understand each other well, and their shared understanding of Tom intensifies their closeness. Gene and his father, on the other hand, are diametrically opposed in temperament and values, so that all Gene's efforts at reaching some rapport with his father fail miserably. Nevertheless, Gene continues to try, partly because he feels it his duty to do so, partly because his nature craves a father he can love, and partly—as his sister Alice suggests—because he has never gotten over the fact that he does not measure up to his father's idea of manliness. Tom views with contempt all Gene's accomplishments as a writer and teacher, and only once in his life, when Gene was in the Marines, has Tom felt proud of his son.

Tom is the most rigid character in the play, yet Anderson treats him fairly, showing that his character and attitudes stem from a bad relationship with his own father and from the resultant hardship of his life as a child and as a young man. His unreasonableness is believable, and his son's simultaneous desire and inability to break through it are convincing. Alice is also convincingly complex as the daughter who has succeeded in escaping

Tom's domination, partly because his opposition to her marriage gave her an excuse to do so with a clear conscience, but who in one vulnerable moment unexpectedly reveals how deeply she has been affected by the lack of love from her father.

Although there is nothing new in this play—the characters, their circumstances, and their helpless and mostly ineffectual attempts to deal with those circumstances are very familiar—*I Never Sang for My Father* will probably be remembered for its complex and credible characters and for the sincerity of the emotion the play generates.

In *You Know I Can't Hear You When the Water's Running*, Anderson returned to a form which he evidently found very congenial, the one-act play. Of approximately twenty-four plays which he wrote in his Harvard years, some twenty were one-act plays, and the one nonmusical play he wrote at Exeter was a one-act play. Of the four plays which make up *You Know I Can't Hear You When the Water's Running*, two—*The Footsteps of Doves* and *I'm Herbert*—are mere entertainments, little more than skits. The other two—*The Shock of Recognition* and *I'll Be Home for Christmas*— have much greater significance in acuteness of observation and validity and interest of characterization.

The Footsteps of Doves derives its title from a saying of Friedrich Nietzsche to the effect that major changes in one's life are not announced dramatically, with thunderous crescendos, but slip up on one almost imperceptibly, like the footsteps of doves—a saying which Anderson had used earlier, in *Silent Night, Lonely Night*, and would use again in his novel *After*. In this play, the footsteps are heard only by the husband when a middle-aged couple, George and Harriet, are buying a new bed and Harriet insists on twin beds despite all of George's arguments for the double bed. George and Harriet's sex life has deteriorated badly since the time of their youthful happiness together, and George sees the purchase of the twin beds as symbolic of an utter lack of hope that it will improve. When the younger, more vital Jill appears and makes a thinly veiled offer to share a double bed with George, it becomes apparent that he will accept this offer and thus will thenceforth accept her, rather than his wife, as his permanent sex partner.

This play expresses Anderson's oft-reiterated belief in the importance of a happy sex life to a good marriage, but it is new in its isolation of that element from all the other elements which go into making a good marriage. In his earlier plays, an unhappy sex life is seen as the result of other kinds of incompatibility in the marriage—personality clashes, value clashes, clashes in beliefs and goals—but in this play, one knows nothing about the couple except their sex life.

I'm Herbert also focuses on the sex life of a couple as the sole index of the happiness of their marriage. Some critics have found in the play that theme so common among absurdist playwrights, the lack of communication in modern society; this interpretation, however, is negated by the fact that the lack of communication in *I'm Herbert* stems neither from the specific conditions of modern society nor from the perennial human condition but solely from senility, a specific medical problem found only in some elderly people. Thomas P. Adler sees the play as almost a paean to a happy marriage which has "passed beyond physical sexuality"; this interpretation, however, is negated by the fact that the old couple in the play remember nothing at all about their former or present mates but the sexual experiences they shared, and that the sexual experiences they remember are not attached to any particular person in their minds but are remembered simply for themselves. Love is nowhere to be found in this play, which focuses entirely on the theme of the importance of sexual excitement and gratification. In the absence of any greater depth of meaning, then, it seems to be no more than an extended and tasteless joke based on a highly unfair and inaccurate stereotype of the elderly. *I'm Herbert* is, thus, the least satisfying of the plays in the quartet.

The Shock of Recognition is the first of Anderson's plays to center on the discussion of a particular theatrical issue. Jack Barnstable is an autobiographical character in that he is a writer of plays arguing for a position which Anderson supported, the acceptance in the theater of greater honesty and realism in dealing with sex. Herb Miller is a stereotype of the kind of opponent such a position often meets: a man who prides himself on his virility and who thinks of sex as the appropriate subject for dirty jokes told among men and for broad innuendoes used to embarrass naïve young women, but not as something which can be discussed openly and objectively among adult men and women or can be presented in such a fashion onstage. The really interesting character in this play, however, is Richard Pawling, the actor who will sacrifice anything to get a part in a play. Both ludicrous and pathetic in his eagerness and determination to please, he is Anderson's most richly comic character, and the play is memorable more for this character than for any other element, even the then shocking but now passé idea of presenting male frontal nudity onstage.

I'll Be Home for Christmas, though beginning as comedy and presumably intended to maintain the comic tone to complement the tone of the other plays in this group, is at times too moving and real in its pain to be funny. Chuck's hurt and anguish, his real fear that his life has no meaning, are too strong. Like the other plays in this group, *I'll Be Home for Christmas* deals with the importance of sex, but unlike the others, it demonstrates that a healthy marriage needs more than sexual gratification. Chuck, the middle-aged husband, is appalled at the mechanical, even clinical, view which his wife Edith has of sex, which she considers an extremely important part of a wholesome married life. He is revolted as she discusses the sex education which she has been giving and proposes to continue giving to their children. He has a much more romantic view of sex and demands much more meaning, not only in his marriage but in his entire life, than he discerns around him. Unfortunately, the one-act format works against the play on this point. There has not been room to develop any notion of the values which Chuck has stood for in the past. The values of Edith are, however, both apparent and repugnant, so that as Chuck sits brooding over a letter in which his son Donny has rejected Chuck's way of life as meaningless, the audience is likely to wonder why Donny did not address the letter to his mother, rather than to his father.

The success of this quartet of one-act plays led Anderson to try the one-act format once again in two short plays on the theme of family life, *Solitaire/Double Solitaire*. The lack of success of this duet on Broadway may have helped to push Anderson in the direction of writing novels. Another very important element in his turning to novels, however, was certainly the fact that in *Double Solitaire* he had carried frankness in the discussion and portrayal of sex to the limits which it could reach on the stage. As Anderson has acknowledged, the autobiographical, even confessional, nature of the content of *After* required "so much explicit sex" and "so many interior monologues" that he had to give up his attempts to present it in the form of a play and turn to the novel instead.

In discussing the writing of *After*, Anderson said, "I have always been obsessed with the themes of love and sex and death and marriage." The sources of this obsession in the experiences of his own life are readily apparent, and it well may be that the autobiographical nature of his work has made it difficult for him to achieve the aesthetic distance necessary for effective drama. At the same time, however, this autobiographical impulse is probably what has enabled him to create with sympathy and compassion the characters and scenes on which his reputation as a dramatist rests.

Other major works

NOVELS: *After*, 1973; *Getting Up and Going Home*, 1978.

SCREENPLAYS: *The Nun's Story*, 1959 (adaptation of Kathryn Hulme's novel); *The Sand Pebbles*, 1966 (adaptation of Richard McKenna's novel); *I Never Sang for My Father*, 1970 (adaptation of his play).

TELEPLAYS: *Double Solitaire*, 1972 (adaptation of his play); *The Patricia Neal Story*, 1981; *Absolute Strangers*, 1991.

Bibliography

Ayers, David Hugh. *The Apprenticeship of Robert Anderson.* Ann Arbor, Mich.: University Microfilms, 1970. The first book-length study of the author of *Tea and Sympathy*, with a valuable bibliography of reviews and articles that appeared in *The New York Times.* Also contains a definitive account of Anderson's salad days, Navy plays, the period of his wife's cancer, the lawsuit concerning *Tea and Sympathy*, and the formation of the New Dramatists in 1951.

Bentley, Eric. *The Dramatic Event: An American Chronicle.* New York: Horizon Press, 1954. In his review and essay on Anderson's *Tea and Sympathy*, Bentley calls it "a highly superior specimen of the theatre of 'realist' escape" but states that "one doesn't ask the questions one would ask of a really serious play."

Gassner, John. *Theatre at the Crossroads: Plays and Playwrights of the Mid-Century American Stage.* New York: Holt, Rinehart and Winston, 1960. Gassner is a pessimistic critic here, but he sees Anderson's work as an "affirmation." He discusses the work in relation to Chekhovian influence and credits Anderson with "excellent details of characterization and feeling."

Gordon, A. C. *A Critical Study of the History and Development of the Playwrights' Producing Company.* Ann Arbor, Mich: University Microfilms, 1972. A thorough study of this producing organization, where Robert Anderson and Maxwell Anderson (no relation) crossed careers between 1953 and 1959. The work underlines Robert Anderson's lifelong interest in producing and developing new playwrights.

Guernsey, Otis, Jr., ed. *Playwrights, Lyricists, Composers on Theater.* New York: Dodd, Mead, 1974. Anderson supplies several comments throughout, including one in which he states that "the theater is such an impossible place, maybe it's meant only for miracles," excerpted from *The Dramatists Guild Quarterly.* He also applauds the decentralization of theater.

Wharton, John F. "The Sixth Playwright." In *Life Among the Playwrights.* New York: Quadrangle, 1974. Presents the story of the Playwrights' Producing Company, of which Wharton was a founding member. This chapter introduces Anderson's involvement, claiming he could have been the revitalizing force for the group in its waning years.

Lisë Pedersen
(Updated by *Thomas J. Taylor*)

JOHN ARDEN

Born: Barnsley, England; October 26, 1930

Principal drama

All Fall Down, pr. 1955; *The Waters of Babylon*, pr. 1957, pb. 1964; *Live Like Pigs*, pr. 1958, pb. 1964; *When Is a Door Not a Door?*, pr. 1958, pb. 1967; *Serjeant Musgrave's Dance: An Unhistorical Parable*, pr. 1959, pb. 1960; *The Business of Good Government*, pr. 1960, pb. 1963 (with Margaretta D'Arcy); *The Happy Haven*, pr. 1960, pb. 1964; *Ironhand*, pr. 1963, pb. 1965 (adaptation of Johann Wolfgang von Goethe's *Götz von Berlichingen*); *The Workhouse Donkey*, pr. 1963, pb. 1964; *Armstrong's Last Goodnight: An Exercise in Diplomacy*, pr. 1964, pb. 1965; *Ars Longa, Vita Brevis*, pr. 1964, pb. 1965 (with D'Arcy); *Fidelio*, pr. 1965 (adaptation of libretto of Ludwig van Beethoven's opera); *Left-Handed Liberty*, pr., pb. 1965; *Friday's Hiding*, pr. 1966, pb. 1967 (with D'Arcy); *The Royal Pardon*, pr. 1966, pb. 1967 (with D'Arcy); *The Vietnam War-Game*, pr. 1967 (with D'Arcy); *Harold Muggins Is a Martyr*, pr. 1968 (with Cartoon Archetypal Slogan Theater and D'Arcy); *The Hero Rises Up*, pr. 1968, pb. 1969 (with D'Arcy); *The Soldier's Tale*, pr. 1968 (adaptation of libretto by Ramuz; music by Igor Stravinsky); *The True History of Squire Jonathan and His Unfortunate Treasure*, pr. 1968, pb. 1971; *The Ballygombeen Bequest*, pr., pb. 1972 (with D'Arcy); *The Island of the Mighty*, pr. 1972, pb. 1974 (trilogy; with D'Arcy); *Henry Dubb Show*, pr. 1973 (with D'Arcy); *Portrait of a Rebel*, pr. 1973 (with D'Arcy); *The Non-Stop Connolly Show* (6 parts), pr. 1975, pb. 1977-1978 (5 volumes; with D'Arcy); *The Little Gray Home in the West*, pr. 1978, pb. 1982 (with D'Arcy; revision of *The Ballygombeen Bequest*); *Vandaleur's Folly: An Anglo-Irish Melodrama*, pr. 1978, pb. 1981 (with D'Arcy); *Fire Plays*, pb. 1991 (with D'Arcy); *Arden and D'Arcy Plays*, pb. 1991.

Other literary forms

An important work for understanding the dramaturgy and politics of John Arden is *To Present the Pretence* (1977), a collection of his essays which originally appeared in various publications over a number of years. Many of Arden's plays are also accompanied by informative prefaces, especially concerning the genesis and composition of individual plays, their production, and the dramatist's own sometimes stormy relations with the professional theatrical world. Finally, Arden's first novel, *Silence Among the Weapons*, was published in Great Britain in 1982.

Achievements

Along with John Osborne, Arnold Wesker, and Harold Pinter, John Arden is one of the early leading playwrights of the so-called New Wave (or New Renaissance) of British drama. Encouraged primarily by the English Stage Company, directed by George Devine at London's Royal Court Theatre, the playwrights of the New Wave have given Britain some of the most lively drama in the contemporary world. Arden has been an important part of the movement, both through his own work and through his influence on later dramatists.

Throughout his career, Arden has been a controversial figure in his own country. None of his plays has enjoyed commercial success, and some have been violently attacked by critics. His best-known work, *Serjeant Musgrave's Dance*, lost ten thousand pounds at the Royal Court; the critic Harold Hobson called the play "another frightful ordeal" and *Punch* dubbed it a "lump of absurdity." Arden's early critics complained that he sermonized and that his sermons were not clear. Audiences had trouble identifying with his central characters, and his plays were even called amoral. These confused reactions say as much about the ingrown nature of British drama at the time as they do about the plays themselves, though it is true that in his early plays the young playwright was struggling with his own uncertainties. Arden generally wrote in a mode resembling the "epic theater" of Bertolt Brecht, filling his plays with ballads, narration, emblematic actions and sets, and other "alienating" (that is, deliberately theatrical) effects. Arden's mode also draws on an older tradition in Britain: Besides Brecht, Arden has acknowledged the influence of Ben Jonson, William Shakespeare, and medieval drama. Part of Arden's achievement is that he has helped break down audience expectations of naturalistic drama to reintroduce the British to their own traditions.

Despite the initial critical reception of his work, Arden's reputation grew. Harold Hobson changed his opinion about *Serjeant Musgrave's Dance* as the play became popular with university theater groups; eventually, it reached the status of a set text for secondary school examinations in English. Arden attained a peak of official acceptance in 1965 when the Corporation of the City of London commissioned him to write *Left-Handed Liberty* for the seven hundred fiftieth anniversary of the signing of the Magna Carta. Thereafter, whether by choice or otherwise, Arden gradually drifted further away from the London professional theater, writing mostly in collaboration with his wife, Margaretta D'Arcy, and becoming more involved in experimental, community, and political theater. His new activities also aroused controversy.

Meanwhile, Arden's reputation spread abroad (particularly to Germany), and he has become a subject of scholarly study, including several books. This attention is deserved, even though Arden's work is uneven in quality. For example, the ambitious three-part work *The Island of the Mighty* is a disappointment, and some of the less ambitious short pieces are of minor interest. Arden's best plays seem to be several modern comedies, *The Waters of Babylon* and *The Workhouse Donkey*, and the historical parables *Serjeant Musgrave's Dance*, *Armstrong's Last Goodnight*, *The Hero Rises Up*, and *Vandaleur's Folly*. The key to Arden's best work is the same quality that appeals to university audiences: a combination of Dionysian energy with treatment of the big issues in today's world. Since those issues will not go away soon, it is likely that Arden's dramatic reputation will continue to grow.

Biography

John Arden's development as a playwright can be explained in part by his background, which differs significantly from the London working-class background typical of fellow New Wave dramatists. The product of a Yorkshire middle-class family, Arden was educated at Sedbergh, a private boarding school in Yorkshire's remote northwest dales (where he had been sent to escape World War II bombing raids), took a degree in architecture from Cambridge University (1953), and proceeded to further his study of architecture at Edinburgh College of Art, receiving his diploma from that institution in 1955. Between Sedbergh and Cambridge, the future author of *Serjeant Musgrave's Dance* and writer for *Peace News* served in the military, mostly in Edinburgh, where he attained the rank of lance-corporal in the Army Intelligence Corps.

Arden's background in the North Country, home of medieval drama and balladry and the setting of most of his best work, is a major source of strength in his plays, as is evident from the salty language used in them. His background suggests that Arden was not born to his Socialist sentiments but arrived at them through a lengthy process of observation and deliberation. Such a process of development, involving constant challenge and considerable self-examination, would help account for the ambiguities in his earlier works and for Arden's characterizations of himself as having been a wishy-washy liberal, a sort of Hamlet of the New Wave. Possibly the young playwright also had mixed reactions to the new welfare state in Britain and to the prevailing doctrinaire atmosphere, especially in the universities, where left-wing evangelizing, with its assumptions and jargon, was sometimes reminiscent of Bible-belt fundamentalism: The New Jerusalem did not tolerate its sinners easily, and it found its American devils handy. Although polite and mild-mannered, Arden has always been strongly independent in his thinking. He chose, for example, to study architecture rather than English in order to avoid compromising his creativity as a writer.

Arden's architectural study did not go to waste: It has contributed to his sense of dramatic structure and sometimes to the content of his plays. His education also gave him perhaps the strongest intellectual background of any of the New Wave playwrights. He practiced architecture in London for only two years, however, until his playwriting career was launched by the Royal Court's 1957 presentation of *The Waters of Babylon*.

That same year, Arden married Margaretta D'Arcy, an actress of Irish background. Not only have they had four sons, but D'Arcy has also been closely associated with Arden's career, first as a friendly critic/consultant and later as a collaborator. (An important distinction among their collaborative works is marked by the designations "by Arden and D'Arcy" and "by D'Arcy and Arden.") D'Arcy has influenced Arden's involvement in experimental, community, and political drama and his use of Irish material. Their travels together have also been influential, particularly two trips to the United States (Arden held guest lectureships at New York University in 1967 and, with D'Arcy, at the University of California at Davis in 1973), where they led politically controversial drama projects, and a stay in India (for the centennial celebrations of Mahatma Gandhi's birth), where they were shocked by the depth of that country's poverty. Their most controversial and effective collaboration was the six-part *The Non-Stop Connolly Show*, whose premiere in 1975 ran twenty-six hours. Critics such as Michael Cohen have called it the pair's most strident and convincing work, "probably the most ambitious attempt in English to dramatize working-class and socialist history." In 1988, the British Broadcasting Corporation aired *Whose Is the Kingdom?* (1982) in nine parts, a radio play about early Christianity.

Beginning in the 1960's, the Ardens' residence in the west of Ireland (County Galway) seemed to symbolize their distance from the London political and theatrical establishment—a distance which became manifest in their much-publicized dispute with the Royal Shakespeare Company over its 1972 production of *The Island of the Mighty*. The Ardens ended up picketing the production. How much this unfortunate dispute affected Arden's career is hard to say, but it was certainly controversial.

Interviewed in Galway, Ireland, in 1990, Arden credited early radio plays with his success, reexamined the thematic thrust of his best-known works, commented that the "pox" of *Serjeant Musgrave's Dance* can be compared to acquired immune deficiency syndrome (AIDS) in the 1990's, and lamented that the "epidemic" called "the use of murder to support government" is still raging, not only in Ireland but also in incidents in the Falkland Islands, Panama, and Nicaragua: "I'm thinking of the . . . rise in popularity of such politicians as Thatcher, Reagan, and Bush, and I feel sickened."

Analysis

The controversy accompanying John Arden's career has tended to obscure his rather old-fashioned views of the proper role of the playwright.

He draws not only on an older dramatic tradition but also on an older concept of the dramatist: the playwright as burgher. Arden is an immensely civic-minded playwright, a citizen who chooses to dramatize his concern for the commonweal. This concept of the dramatist—almost antithetical to the commercial theater as it now exists—belongs to an older tradition which embraces Shakespeare, the medieval theater, and the Greek dramatists. In Arden and D'Arcy's three-part Arthurian *The Island of the Mighty*, the ancient poets are not merely entertainers but also political advisers. Arden's concept of the dramatist explains his interest in community theater; increasingly, in the global village, his concerns have become international in scope.

Arden's concept of the dramatist means that his drama has been almost exclusively political, but his politics have changed and his involvement developed over time. In his early plays, although he treated parochial issues, he tended not to take a stand; rather, like the architect he had trained to be, he was merely concerned with how people live, as indicated by such titles as *Live Like Pigs* and *The Happy Haven*. If any stand was implied, it was likely to be anti-Socialist—for example, to condemn heavy-handed administration of the welfare state. Soon, however, through his historical parables, Arden expanded his vision: He began to connect local issues to world issues and to historical processes, and he began to deal either directly or indirectly with pacifist and Socialist concerns: militarism, colonialism, economic and social injustice. Finally, the plays written with D'Arcy take a more militant, partisan approach toward these same issues and others (such as sexism), condemning the imperialist/militarist/capitalist/ exploitative mentality and viewing the Irish situation as a prime result of this mentality.

For Arden, the development in his thinking is summed up in the crisis of the liberal: the conflict between revolution and reform, and the fear that reform is only refining and strengthening an exploitative system. His thinking is influenced not only by the world scene but also specifically by Britain's past experience of empire. Also, Arden's thinking is not unique in contemporary Britain but is only one aspect of a political mood evoked by the title of the first New Wave play, John Osborne's *Look Back in Anger* (pr. 1956).

In three early social comedies, *The Waters of Babylon*, *Live Like Pigs*, and *The Happy Haven*, one sees the young dramatist struggling to find his way. All three plays are generally comic in tone, but some terrible things happen in each one. Some of the humor is undergraduate, but when these were written, the playwright had, after all, only recently been a student (and his most appreciative audience was students). Despite flashes of energy, the action drags in both *Live Like Pigs* and *The Happy Haven*, and both plays mix modes awkwardly: *Live Like Pigs* combines naturalism with the Brechtian mode, while *The Happy Haven* mixes naturalism with a Theater-of-the-Absurd parable.

Live Like Pigs and *The Happy Haven* are notable, however, for their implied criticism of the welfare state, new to Britain after World War II and hence somewhat raw. A coercive bureaucracy and pressures to conform are revealed in *Live Like Pigs* when the Sawneys, a raffish family living in an old tramcar down by the tracks, are forced by officials to move into a public housing estate. The Sawneys turn their new house into a pigsty, offend their proper neighbors, and provoke a bloody riot. The insensitive treatment of people as objects is even more obvious in *The Happy Haven*: Here, the nursing-home setting can be seen as a satire on the welfare state, complete with a presiding doctor who performs experiments on the old people—for their own good, of course (he is perfecting an elixir of youth). Such is the bureaucratic best of all possible worlds.

A much better play is *The Waters of Babylon*, which sticks closer to the Brechtian mode and has a wider scope, showing postwar Britain's legacy of colonialism, militarism, and capitalism. While Britain was building a welfare state, it was being flooded by refugees and immigrants, represented in this play by the Poles, Irish, and West Indians. Their world, as the play's title suggests, is a world of dislocation and exile. Moreover, their world is the true postwar world, a world full of Sawneys, and it is impinging on the tidy British, whether they like it or not. Some do not, a group represented by the insular Englishman Henry Ginger. Others do, represented by Alexander Loap, a Member of Parliament who keeps an expensive redheaded Irish mistress, and by Charles Butterthwaite, a former Yorkshire politician who finds a corrupt mate in Krank, the Polish slum landlord.

Above all, it is Krank, one of Arden's most colorful characters, who represents the soul of postwar Great Britain. His full name, Sigismanfred Krankiewicz, sums up the European history with which Britain has tried not to be involved. Krank himself wants to be uninvolved, left alone, but meanwhile he profits from his own little British empire, a run-down apartment house where he takes in immigrants and operates a prostitution ring. The chickens come to roost for Krank as they do for the British Empire: It is discovered that he spent the war in Buchenwald, all right, but as a German soldier rather than a prisoner, and he is shot by the Polish patriot Paul. Before he dies, however, Krank admits his complicity in recent human history—a lesson, Arden suggests, that we could all learn.

If *The Waters of Babylon* shows some aftereffects of the British Empire, *Serjeant Musgrave's Dance* goes to the Empire's heart, showing its workings. The play is Brechtian in mode, but with an elemental, mythic quality. The time is the Victorian era, around 1880. The place is a wintry North Country coal town, snowbound and starving, in the middle of a strike, the coldness of the setting suggesting the coldness of the empire's discipline. This discipline is maintained in the town by a triumvirate of mayor (who, conveniently, also owns the coal mine), parson, and constable, assisted by the distractions of Mrs. Hitchcock's pub (where a man can purchase grog and the ministrations of Annie). Abroad in the colonies, discipline is even less subtle: It is maintained by the Queen's army, which collects trouble-makers at home to turn them loose on troublemakers in the colonies. In an emergency, the troops can also be used against the home folks. Thus, in the name of prosperity, patriotism, and good order, blessed by religion, the ruthless forces of capitalism, colonialism, and militarism operate together in a vast but tightly enclosed system which benefits the few at the expense and suffering of the many. The ballad chorus captures the spirit of the system: "The Empire wars are far away/ For duty's sake we sail away/ Me arms and legs is shot away/ And all for the wink of a shilling and a drink."

A desperate challenge to this brutal system is mounted by four soldiers who appear in the coal town, ostensibly to recruit but in reality to bring home the truth. The truth about the system is symbolized by the skeleton of Billy Hicks, a young soldier from the town. Billy was murdered in a far-off British "protectorate," and the British army retaliated by indiscrimi-nately wounding thirty-four natives and killing five in a bloody night raid. Now the soldiers, led by Serjeant Musgrave, hoist Billy's skeleton on a market cross in the town square, train rifles and a Gatling gun on the town's citizens (actually, on the play's audience), and proceed to lecture them about the evils of the system and their complicity in it. At first the citizens think Musgrave, who does a little dance under the skeleton, is merely balmy, but then the striking colliers heed his call for solidarity. Not unnaturally, however, they draw back when Musgrave announces plans to kill twenty-five townspeople in retaliation for the five dead protectorate na-tives. The final straw comes when the crowd learns that one of the four soldiers is missing, dead at the hands of his comrades. The townspeople are saved by disagreement among the remaining soldiers and by the arrival of the dragoons. The temporarily challenged system starts up again, sym-bolized by a dance in which all join hands and sing a mindless round, led by the grotesque Bargee, who has been Musgrave's shadow throughout the play.

The trouble is that Musgrave himself is twisted by the system. His inten-tions are good, but his methods are terrible. He thinks he is led by God, but he is instead moved by the military logic he opposes, as indicated by the discipline he maintains over the soldiers even after they are all desert-ers. His protest takes the form of a military exercise, complete with mili-tary mathematics. As the soldier Attercliffe notes, Musgrave tries to end war "by its own rules: no bloody good . . . you can't cure the pox by whoring." Yet it is a protest which will be remembered by the townspeople—and by the people who see the play.

Like *Serjeant Musgrave's Dance*, *Armstrong's Last Goodnight* is "an unhistorical parable"—that is, both plays were suggested by current events: *Serjeant Musgrave's Dance* by events in Cyprus in 1958, *Armstrong's Last Goodnight* by the situation in the Congo in 1961. Setting the plays in the past provides distance from current events but at the same time raises ironic parallels. For example, *Armstrong's Last Goodnight* is ironically subtitled *An Exercise in Diplomacy*, suggesting that much diplomacy has been and is still an exercise in treachery. In *Armstrong's Last Goodnight*, it resides in early sixteenth century Scotland, a vicious land of constant feuding, plotting, and shifting alliances (rather like the early sixteenth century English court described in the play's epigraph from the poet John Skelton), a land where the biggest freebooter prevails.

In *Armstrong's Last Goodnight*, the prescribed strategy is to invite your enemy to go hunting, offer him some of the local brew, shake hands with him, swear friendship forever, and then kill him at the first safe opportunity. Johnnie Armstrong of Gilknockie, a colorful border strongman, does this to James Johnstone of Wamphray, and then James V of Scotland does it to Armstrong. To entice Armstrong, King James needs the help of his scheming ambassador, Sir David Lindsay (another poet who was involved in politics), and of Lindsay's mistress, an earthy lady who even gets used to the smell in Armstrong's castle and who describes her sexuality in terms of a hot pot of red-herring broth (boiling over, of course). This play too has its elemental, mythic qualities, qualities enhanced by the Scots dialect in which it is written, but its overriding reminder is that international relations are still conducted on the primitive level of relations among early Scotch lairds.

Authored by D'Arcy and Arden, *Vandaleur's Folly* has a dialectic pattern familiar from *Serjeant Musgrave's Dance*: thesis, antithesis, fiasco. Here the exploitative system is the prototypical plantation colony of 1830's Ireland, a country of whiskey-drinking British gentry and thirsty Irish tenantry, where the absentee landlords gamble in Dublin's Hell Fire Club and visit their estates occasionally to conduct a "fox" hunt using a lively Irish lass. The play draws parallels between the treatment of the Irish, the American slave trade, and the treatment of women. For example, the slave-trader Wilberforce is the business partner of Major Baker-Fortescue, the vicious Orangeman landlord. The two are opposed by Roxana, an American abolitionist who is part black, and by Micheal, an Irishman who leads the Lady Clare Boys, a peasant guerrilla group.

The most important challenge to the plantation system, however, is Ralahine, a Socialist cooperative set up by Vandaleur, an enlightened landowner. Ralahine, where landowner and tenant share equally and have equal rights, is a financial success and brings peace to the countryside, yet it drives the other landowners wild. The Commune's opponents finally destroy it by taking advantage of a fatal flaw in its makeup: Like Musgrave, Vandaleur is still infected by the system; he retains private ownership of the experimental estate and, in a fit of gambling fever, loses it to Baker-Fortescue in a faro game at the Hell Fire Club.

Subtitled *An Anglo-Irish Melodrama*, *Vandaleur's Folly* fits the description. Its one-sided characterizations result in some loss of artistic power, and the language of the play is not spiced with dialect. Yet *Vandaleur's Folly* is entertaining melodrama, and there is no trouble understanding its partisan point: Private property is wrong, and so is any arrangement which treats people as property.

Like the forthright *Vandaleur's Folly*, Arden's work generally is meant to stir people to think about the issues of today's world and perhaps to take action. One of the current writers most attuned to those issues, Arden is very much a practical playwright: He does not merely look back in anger, but looks forward with hope. As this description implies, he is also a playwright for the young. Although his work embodies prophetic warnings, it does not reflect the despairing tone of earlier twentieth century literature, with its recurring visions of the wasteland; rather, Arden looks beyond the crisis of modern civilization toward solutions.

Other major works

NOVEL: *Silence Among the Weapons*, 1982 (also as *Vox Pop: Last Days of the Roman Republic*, 1983); *Books of Bale*, 1988.

NONFICTION: *To Present the Pretence*, 1977; *Awkward Corners*, 1988 (with D'Arcy).

TELEPLAYS: *Soldier, Soldier*, 1960; *Wet Fish*, 1961.

RADIO PLAYS: *The Life of Man*, 1956; *The Dying Cowboy*, 1961; *The Bagman*, 1970; *Keep Those People Moving*, 1972 (with D'Arcy); *Pearl*, 1978; *To Put It Frankly . . .* , 1979; *Don Quixote* (2 parts), 1980; *Garland for a Hoar Head*, 1982; *The Old Man Sleeps Alone*, 1982; *Whose Is the Kingdom?*, 1982 (9 parts; with D'Arcy).

Bibliography

Gray, Frances. *John Arden.* New York: Grove Press, 1983. The introduction points out the inherently noncommercial "manner" and "matter" of Arden's structure, subject matter, and cast of characters, and it uses the theme as an organizational device for discussing Arden's work. Chronology (to 1982), brief bibliography, and index.

Hunt, Albert. *Arden: A Study of His Plays.* London: Eyre Methuen, 1974. Thirteen plays are given a chapter each of critical discussion, bracketed by illustrations, a chronology, an introductory essay, a postscript (on *The Island of the Mighty*), and two appendices. A bibliographical note and index are added. The most comprehensive study to 1974.

Leeming, Glenda. *John Arden.* Essex, England: Longman, 1974. A brief overview of Arden's work to 1974, with some attention paid to the role of women characters. Notes the division of Arden's "closet" dramas and the more theatrical collaborations with Arden's wife and sometimes director, Margaretta D'Arcy. Bibliography and short list of critical studies.

Page, Malcolm, comp. *Arden on File.* London: Methuen, 1985. An information-age compilation of facts on Arden's productions (twenty-one plays described and annotated), themes, growth as a writer, and self-evaluation through the course of his career. Easy to use, full of names and dates, and the pith of reviews. Contains a chronology and a select bibliography.

Trussler, Simon. *John Arden.* New York: Columbia University Press, 1973. A brief essay without organizational divisions, locating critical discussion inside a sparse biographical chronicle. Trussler sees Arden as Arden sees himself: an English Pieter Brueghel, painting "many of the mythic archetypes of urban life, caught from an unexpected angle." Includes a select bibliography of Arden's works to 1971 and a short list of critical articles from theater journals.

Harold Branam
(Updated by *Thomas J. Taylor*)

W. H. AUDEN

Born: York, England; February 21, 1907
Died: Vienna, Austria; September 29, 1973

Principal drama

Paid on Both Sides: A Charade, pb. 1930, pr. 1931; *The Dance of Death*, pb. 1933, pr. 1934; *The Dog Beneath the Skin: Or, Where Is Francis?*, pb. 1935, pr. 1936 (with Christopher Isherwood); *The Ascent of F6*, pb. 1936, pr. 1937 (with Isherwood); *On the Frontier*, pr., pb. 1938 (with Isherwood); *Paul Bunyan*, pr. 1941, pb. 1976 (libretto; music by Benjamin Britten); *The Rake's Progress*, pr., pb. 1951 (libretto, with Chester Kallman; music by Igor Stravinsky); *Delia: Or, A Masque of Night*, pb. 1953 (libretto, with Kallman; not set to music); *For the Time Being*, pr. 1959 (oratorio; musical setting by Martin David Levy); *Elegy for Young Lovers*, pr., pb. 1961 (libretto, with Kallman; music by Hans Werner Henze); *The Bassarids*, pr., pb. 1966 (libretto, with Kallman; music by Henze); *Love's Labour's Lost*, pb. 1972, pr. 1973 (libretto, with Kallman; music by Nicolas Nabokov; adaptation of William Shakespeare's play *Love's Labour's Lost*); *The Entertainment of the Senses*, pr. 1974 (libretto, with Kallman; music by John Gardiner); *Plays and Other Dramatic Writings by W. H. Auden, 1928-1938*, pb. 1988.

Other literary forms

Although well regarded as a playwright and librettist, W. H. Auden is known chiefly as a poet. During his lifetime, he published more than twenty collections of poetry, establishing himself as a major voice in twentieth century literature. His work includes a remarkable variety of lyric poems, notable for their range of thought and technique. Auden also wrote several longer poems, including *For the Time Being* and *The Sea and the Mirror*, both of which appeared in a 1944 collection, and *The Age of Anxiety* (1947). The shorter as well as the longer poems are in *Collected Poems* (1976) and *The English Auden* (1977), both edited by Edward Mendelson.

In addition to plays, librettos, and poetry, Auden produced a substantial amount of nonfiction prose. Many of his best essays, reviews, lectures, and introductions are collected in *The Dyer's Hand and Other Essays* (1962), *Secondary Worlds* (1969), and *Forewords and Afterwords* (1973). Auden also wrote several scripts for film and radio and worked extensively as an editor and translator.

Achievements

Though W. H. Auden is not regarded as a major playwright, he and his collaborators produced a body of work that is recognized today as a significant contribution to modern drama and opera. His plays with Christopher Isherwood have survived as period pieces and are well regarded as experiments in poetic, didactic drama, written at a time when the English theater offered little more than uninspired Naturalism. *The Dog Beneath the Skin*, probably the most lasting of the Auden-Isherwood collaborations, contains some of Auden's finest verse written for the stage and, though often raw and uneven, remains engaging in its mixture of popular, high-spirited comedy and political satire. Michael Sidnell, while suggesting that personal and artistic difficulties kept Auden and Isherwood from fully committing themselves to the theater, argues, nevertheless, that they "were in advance of their time in using poetry, song, dance, and fable for serious dramatic purposes in a way that did not become common on the English stage until the late 1950's, when the strong influence of Brecht was belatedly felt."

Auden's work for the operatic stage is more difficult to assess, partly because of the complex interdependence of the librettos and their musical settings. Auden saw the librettist's role as clearly secondary to the composer's, yet his librettos with Chester Kallman are regarded by some as significant dramatic and poetic texts in their own right. John Blair, for example, treating *The Rake's Progress* as an "operatic poem," suggests that the libretto can be "seen as an epitome of Auden's mature poetic mode." As opera, the Auden-Kallman collaborations have had mixed success; *The Rake's Progress* (with music by Igor Stravinsky) is generally conceded to be their best and, as Humphrey Carpenter points out, is apparently "one of the very few modern operas to become a permanent addition to the repertoire." In the two years following its premiere, it was staged more than two hundred times.

Biography

Wystan Hugh Auden was born into a middle-class English family in 1907, the son of George Auden, a medical doctor, and Constance Bicknell Auden, a nurse. Auden grew up in an atmosphere that fostered intellectual and cultural growth, and his parents, both the children of clergymen, gave him and his two older brothers a strong sense of traditional religious values. His father was the strongest influence on his early intellectual life, teaching Auden about classical and Norse mythology and encouraging his interest in science. Auden maintained this interest throughout his life, often using scientific concepts and images in his poetry.

In 1915, when he was eight, Auden went as a boarder to St. Edmund's School in Surrey, where he met Christopher Isherwood, later his close friend and collaborator. After St. Edmund's, Auden attended Gresham's School, an institution with a strong reputation in the sciences. During his time there, Auden began to question the religion of his childhood and to distance himself from the traditional values of his middle-class, public-school upbringing. At Gresham's, he acknowledged his homosexuality, and, by the time he left, he had abandoned his faith.

Auden's interest in writing, begun at Gresham's, flourished at Oxford, where he went to read science in 1925. He soon changed to English studies and, before finishing his undergraduate career, resolved to make poetry his vocation. While at Oxford and in the remaining years of the 1930's, Auden established a considerable reputation as a poet and experimental dramatist. In 1928, he wrote his first dramatic work, *Paid on Both Sides,* a brief "charade" that draws heavily on his English public-school experience, his fascination with the lead-mining country of his youth, and the Icelandic legends he learned from his father. Four years later, in 1932, he again turned to theater. In the summer of that year, the ballet dancer Rupert Doone and the painter Robert Medley (whom Auden had known at Gresham's) proposed to Auden the idea of forming an experimental theater company that Doone hoped could be "self-sufficient and independent of any purely commercial considerations." The founders of what came to be known as the Group Theatre wanted to bring to the stage a combination of dance, music, and speech; they also saw in the theater a potential for left-wing social commentary, an idea that appealed to Auden, whose political leanings had become increasingly leftist during the 1930's.

At the urging of Doone and Medley, Auden produced for the Group Theatre a ballet-drama on Marxist themes. In the next several years, he collaborated with Christopher Isherwood on three more plays for the Group, the first of them *The Dog Beneath the Skin*, a work that developed out of earlier dramatic experiments by the two writers—their joint effort, "Enemies of a Bishop" (written in 1929), and two works by Auden, "The Fronny" (written in 1930) and "The Chase" (written in 1934). These plays were not published or performed, and only a few scraps of "The Fronny" survive. By the end of the 1930's, Auden and Isherwood had collaborated on a second and third play for the Group Theatre, both of them more theatrically conventional than their first one.

In 1939, Auden's life took a major turn. He and Isherwood left England for the United States, and, within two years of his arrival, Auden rejoined the Anglican communion, a reaffirmation of his childhood faith toward which he had been moving for some time. From this point in his life, his writing was informed by a Christian perspective spelled out most explicitly in the long poems he wrote during the 1940's, particularly his Christmas oratorio, *For the Time Being.* Though clearly not intended for the stage, his long poems of this period make considerable use of dramatic techniques. Auden's only theatrical work of the time was a brief libretto that he wrote for the British composer Benjamin Britten; *Paul Bunyan* was performed once in 1941 but remained unpublished until after Auden's death.

Auden's dramatic career entered its second phase near the end of the 1940's, when he began the first of his several collaborations with his friend and lifelong companion Chester Kallman, whom he had met shortly after his arrival in America. Together, they wrote for Stravinsky a libretto for *The Rake's Progress* and, later, a briefer one called *Delia*, for which Stravinsky never provided a score. In the last twenty years of his life, Auden continued to write extensively both poetry and prose, living part of each year in New York City and part in Europe. He and Kallman continued their productive collaboration, translating a number of librettos and writing several of their own, two for the German composer Hans Werner Henze and one for the Russian-born composer Nicolas Nabokov. Their final work for the stage, written in the last month of Auden's life, was *The Entertainment of the Senses,* a brief "antimasque" commissioned for the composer John Gardiner. Shortly after completing this piece, Auden left his summer home in Kirchstetten, Austria, to return to Oxford, where he had taken up winter residence the year before. On the way to England, he and Kallman stopped in Vienna for a poetry reading that Auden was scheduled to give there. He died there, suddenly; he is buried, as he wished, in Kirchstetten.

Analysis

W. H. Auden's writing for the stage falls into two distinct categories: the plays of the 1930's, written mostly in collaboration with Christopher Isherwood, and the opera librettos, all but one written with Chester Kallman after Auden's move to America in 1939.

The plays of the 1930's are essentially political and didactic; Auden saw them as a means of reaching a wider audience than he could with his poetry, a way to reunite, as Mendelson puts it, "the private world of the poet with the public world of the theatre." Hence, the plays set forth various psychological and political positions he adopted during the 1930's, offering audiences lessons in the history of their time and awakening them to the possibility of personal and social renewal. Written in a mixture of poetry and prose, Auden's plays borrow theatrical devices from a variety of unlikely sources: ballet, conventional melodrama, music-hall comedy, the variety show, and the cabaret sketch. He combines these devices with serious poetry (often spoken by a chorus), using a blend of popular and literary writing as a vehicle for antiestablishment political commentary. At times, the didacticism outweighs theatrical effectiveness, as it does in *On the Frontier*, a topical and technically conventional play that lacks the energy of Auden's other collaborations with Isherwood. At their best, however, the plays manage to handle political and social themes with a considerable amount of dramatic vitality.

This vitality is best represented in *The Dog Beneath the Skin,* generally recognized as the most successful of the three Auden-Isherwood plays. An odd blend of fable and farce, the plot centers on the quest of Alan Norman to find Sir Francis Crewe, missing heir to the late squire of the English village of Pressan Ambo. Each year, the villagers gather to select by lot a young man to search for Sir Francis (whom they perceive as a sort of idealized lost leader); the ten youths who precede Alan fail in their quest, and two of them never return to the village (though both appear briefly during Alan's quest).

The first part of the play evokes the complacency of the staid and deceptively idyllic English village, whose leading citizens are the town vicar, the pompous General Hothan—a retired military man—and Iris Crewe, Sir Francis' sister, who lives at Honeypot Hall, the family estate. This trio is the object of the play's satire against the established social order. Representing religious, military, and class authority, they begin as conventional reactionaries, but, by the end of the play (and in Alan's absence), they turn to Fascism, establishing a militaristic youth brigade in the village. After a quest that takes up most of the play's action, Alan returns with Sir Francis to discover the altered state of affairs in Pressan Ambo. The lost heir, who had in fact been living in disguise among the villagers for the past ten years, denounces them as "obscene, cruel, hypocritical, mean, vulgar creatures." Taking Alan and a small band of villagers with him, Sir Francis leaves Pressan Ambo to "be a unit in the army of the other side," presumably a political and social order opposite the Fascism now established in the village. Though some argue that Sir Francis does not speak for a specific political doctrine, others such as John Fuller, see his joining of the "other side" as an explicit reference to the Communist Party. His and Alan's conversion represents, in any case, a move away from personal and political stagnation toward an active commitment to regeneration and change, an idea that Auden was working with in his poetry at the time.

Along with its explicit critique of Fascist politics, the play makes a broader political statement on the entire capitalist system. The extent to which Auden embraced Marxism is not entirely clear, but he did for a time sympathize with many of its key tenets. His first play for the Group Theatre, *The Dance of Death*, is an avowedly political one, illustrating the decline and eventual death of the bourgeoisie. In *The Dog Beneath the Skin*, his intent is somewhat less overt, but the bulk of the play (and most of its vitality) comes in the quest scenes, which burlesque the moral and economic decay of European capitalism.

At the beginning of his quest, Alan is joined by a large dog that gives the play its title, provides much of its farcical humor, and, in the end, carries much of the play's thematic weight. The dog, it turns out, is Sir Francis Crewe, the object of Alan's quest. The missing heir of Pressan Ambo has been living in disguise for ten years among the villagers and is now

Alan's companion. In the middle section of the play, the two of them travel together, observing the corruption of the established social order, a corruption that had previously seduced and destroyed two young men from the village; though Alan is temporarily lured toward decadence, he manages—with the help of his dog—to escape, having learned along the way the lessons that lead to his personal salvation.

The scenes that satirize capitalist decay borrow an array of theatrical devices from the popular stage. Using slapstick, farce, burlesque, cabaret songs, doggerel, and a host of other devices, Auden and Isherwood provide a kind of comic revue of modern political corruption and personal decadence. The loosely connected comic scenes are separated by a number of choral poems that develop in a more serious fashion the implications of the play's high-spirited satire. The bulk of the satiric pieces are set in Ostnia, a decadent monarchy in Eastern Europe, and Westland, a Fascist state with clear parallels to Nazi Germany. (Both of these nations reappear in the other Auden-Isherwood collaborations.) In Ostnia, Alan and the dog—accompanied by two journalists—witness a grotesquely comic execution of four workers accused of inciting revolution. The satiric point is unmistakable, as it is later in Westland, where the political system becomes an asylum that "the leader" rules by speaking to the inmates through a megaphone attached to his picture.

One of the most memorable sequences in the play occurs at the Ninevah Hotel, where Alan watches a cabaret act in the hotel restaurant, an act which, as John Fuller points out, "burlesques the sexual tyranny and . . . militant philistinism of the rich." At the end of the first sketch, which includes a crude song performed by the Ninevah Girls, one of the wealthy hotel patrons selects a willing chorus girl and orders her cooked and prepared for his dinner. This satire of wealth and sexual domination is followed by another sketch, in which Destructive Desmond uses a penknife to destroy an original Rembrandt while "a piece of third-rate Victorian landscape painting" stands unharmed beside it. The wealthy patrons applaud ecstatically at this grand entertainment, asserting their aggressive distaste for high culture.

With their "brutal, noisy vulgarity and tasteless extravagance" (as the stage directions put it), the Ninevah Hotel scenes have a comic vitality that prevents the play's didacticism from becoming ponderous. Finally, such scenes, with the chorus's commentary, allow Auden and Isherwood to illustrate pointedly the essential decadence and egotism of modern man, his inability to love and sympathize with his fellowman. This theme, which is implicit throughout the play, becomes overt in a scene at Paradise Park, where Alan meets a poet who insists that he is "the only real person in the world," a notion echoed later in the chorus's warning to the audience: "Beware of yourself:/ Have you not heard your own heart whisper: 'I am the nicest person in this room'?"

If the play finally has a significance beyond social satire, it lies in Auden's suggestion that political solutions are useless without personal regeneration. At the end of the play, back in Pressan Ambo and revealed as the missing heir, Sir Francis tells the gathered villagers that for ten years he had a "dog's eye view" of them, "seeing people from underneath," observing their essential hypocrisy, their lack of common human sympathy. After he, Alan, and a few converted villagers leave for the ill-defined "other side," the chorus offers the audience a choice, suggesting that personal change must precede political action: "Choose therefore that you may recover: both your charity and your place/ Determining/ ... Where grace may grow outward and be given praise." As in much of Auden's work of the 1930's, the exact nature of the proposed solution to personal and political ills is clouded; at the time, Auden was a diagnostician, not a healer. The ending of *The Dog Beneath the Skin* gestures toward an ill-defined "love" that is "loath to enter." Only in his later work, and after his return to Christianity, did Auden arrive at a less clouded notion of love as a means of personal and social redemption.

That notion of love is defined most clearly in the long poems that Auden wrote during the 1940's, a time when his interest in stage drama subsided. Aside from *Paul Bunyan*, the brief libretto written for Britten in 1939, Auden did no writing for the stage until Stravinsky approached him in 1947 about the possibility of doing an opera based on William Hogarth's series of engravings *A Rake's Progress*. Auden agreed to the project and wrote with Chester Kallman the first of their several librettos. Auden saw in opera a logical fulfillment of his earlier interest in poetic drama. In a 1966 interview for the British Broadcasting Corporation, he suggested that "opera is the proper place for lyric theatre, rather than the spoken drama." The "job of the librettist," he wrote in *Secondary Worlds*, "is to furnish the composer with a plot, characters and words." Clearly in a supporting role, the verbal text "is to be judged ... by its success or failure in exciting the musical imagination of the composer."

Though Auden tended to minimize the role of the librettist, his operatic works with Kallman have considerable merit apart from their musical settings. *The Rake's Progress* is particularly well regarded both as a stage opera and as an independent poetic text. The libretto illustrates many of the central themes of Auden's mature work and suggests that several of the techniques he and Isherwood used in the 1930's plays were naturally suited for the operatic stage: the reliance on fable and myth, the use of overstatement and grand gesture, and the emphasis on idea and spectacle rather than character.

The libretto is essentially a moral fable, illustrating in religious terms the Fall and Redemption of man. Auden suggests that through an act of free will, man can choose selfless love (*agape*) and, in doing so, find grace and redemption. This theme is worked out in the fate of the opera's hero, Tom Rakewell, described by Edward Callan as "an aesthetic personality who relies on fortune and believes in his own superior destiny." Auden illustrates the folly of Tom's egotism by giving him three wishes (after the pattern of the archetypal quest hero), each of which leads him further from Anne Truelove, the libretto's symbolic embodiment of selfless love. Rakewell's first wish (for money) is, like his other wishes, fulfilled by Nick Shadow, a satanic servant who secretly aims to damn Rakewell's soul. Removed by his first wish from the redemptive powers of Anne's love, Tom makes a second wish (for happiness), which leads him to an *acte gratuit*, an existential choice to marry Baba, a bearded lady from a fair; Shadow has convinced him that such an act could bring true happiness by freeing him from the demands of necessity. According to Fuller, Auden uses Rakewell's absurd act as a critique of the Existentialist view of free will; his marriage is "a grotesque parody of the true Christian choice" he will make later.

Tom's final wish (to have a magical bread-making machine he has dreamed of) brings about his final ruin. Left at the mercy of Shadow, he is offered—in a Faustian scene—a last, yet apparently hopeless, chance for salvation; recalling Anne's love, he makes an irrational choice when Shadow asks him to name three cards: "I wish for nothing else./ Love, first and last, assume eternal reign;/ Renew my life, O Queen of Hearts, again." The choice is, in effect, a leap of faith, a genuine acceptance of love. The memory of Anne thus saves Rakewell from damnation. Denied Rakewell's soul, Shadow condemns him to madness, but in the concluding scene, Tom (imagining himself as Adonis) is symbolically redeemed from his suffering by Anne (as Venus) and dies reconciled to her.

In a sense, *The Rake's Progress* is a thematic extension of the ideas raised by the Auden-Isherwood plays of the 1930's. Auden's Christianity, his embracing of *agape*, provides a new perspective on the personal and social ills diagnosed in *The Dog Beneath the Skin*. In the later work, Auden sees human failings in personal and religious terms; social and political malaise originates, he seems to suggest, by human imperfection, in man's fallen nature. Only by appealing to powers outside himself can man find redemption.

Auden's dramatic works—both the political plays and the librettos—are concerned at base with the exposition of ideas. In his plays, as in his poetry, he pursues a range of philosophical positions with relish and zest, and his writing for the stage is remarkable, finally, for its managing to bring dramatic vitality to political and theological concepts. His inventiveness, his willingness to experiment, and his masterful use of conventional forms (popular theater as well as opera) guarantee Auden and his collaborators a significant place in the history of modern drama.

Other major works

POETRY: *Poems*, 1930; *The Orators*, 1932; *Look, Stranger!*, 1936 (also as *On This Island*, 1937); *Letters from Iceland*, 1937 (poetry and prose, with Louis MacNeice); *Spain*, 1937; *Journey to a War*, 1939 (poetry and prose, with Christopher Isherwood); *Another Time*, 1940; *The Double Man*, 1941 (also as *New Year Letter*, 1941); *For the Time Being*, 1944 (collection); *The Collected Poetry*, 1945; *The Age of Anxiety*, 1947; *Collected Shorter Poems, 1930-1944*, 1950; *Nones*, 1951; *The Shield of Achilles*, 1955; *Homage to Clio*, 1960; *About the House*, 1965; *Collected Shorter Poems, 1927-1957*, 1966; *Collected Longer Poems*, 1968; *City Without Walls and Other Poems*, 1969; *Epistle to a Godson and Other Poems*, 1972; *Thank You, Fog*, 1974; *Collected Poems*, 1976 (Edward Mendelson, editor); *Selected Poems*, 1979 (Edward Mendelson, editor).

NONFICTION: *Letters from Iceland*, 1937 (poetry and prose, with Louis MacNeice); *Journey to a War*, 1939 (poetry and prose, with Christopher Isherwood); *The Enchafèd Flood*, 1950; *The Dyer's Hand and Other Essays*, 1962; *Selected Essays*, 1964; *Secondary Worlds*, 1969; *A Certain World*, 1970; *Forewords and Afterwords*, 1973.

ANTHOLOGIES: *The Oxford Book of Light Verse*, 1938; *The Portable Greek Reader*, 1948; *Poets of the English Language*, 1950 (5 volumes, with Norman Holmes Pearson); *The Faber Book of Modern American Verse*, 1956; *Selected Poems of Louis MacNeice*, 1964; *Nineteenth Century British Minor Poets*, 1966; *A Choice of Dryden's Verse*, 1973.

MISCELLANEOUS: *The English Auden: Poems, Essays, and Dramatic Writings, 1927-1939*, 1977 (Edward Mendelson, editor).

Bibliography

Bahlke, George W. *The Later Auden: From "New Year Letter" to "About the House."* New Brunswick, N.J.: Rutgers University Press, 1970. A forceful examination of Auden's later writings to show a serious and significant vision. The focus is on the long dramatic poems, including *The Sea and the Mirror*, *For the Time Being*, and *The Age of Anxiety*, as expressions of the interrelationships of art and God in human experience. Includes notes and an index.

Buell, Frederick. *W. H. Auden as a Social Poet.* Ithaca, N.Y.: Cornell University Press, 1973. Arguing that Auden's poetry is an ironic vision of social and moral responsibility, Buell focuses on the 1930's, when Auden was forming his social views. Contains an interesting analysis of the influence of Bertolt Brecht's ideas about theater on Auden, when he lived in Berlin. Footnotes and an index.

Callan, Edward. *Auden: A Carnival of Intellect.* New York: Oxford University Press, 1983. Carefully analyzes Auden's career from 1923 to 1973, focusing on his comic approach to human guilt and his scientific interests. Priority is given to the longer poems and sequences, although selected short lyrics are analyzed as representative of the collections. Contains notes, an index, and two appendices of lists of books made by Auden.

Greenberg, Herbert. *Quest for the Necessary: W. H. Auden and the Dilemma of Divided Consciousness.* Cambridge, Mass.: Harvard University Press, 1968. Examines Auden's canon as questing for what is necessary to heal the sickness of self-division. In *The Sea and the Mirror*, *For the Time Being*, and *The Age of Anxiety*, Auden was attracted to the writings of Søren Kierkegaard as guides for accepting Christianity as the means for that healing. Footnotes, index.

Mendelson, Edward. *Early Auden.* New York: Viking Press, 1981. A brilliant synthesis of Auden's intellectual development and emotional history to 1939. Traces themes back to childhood fantasies, which are the substance of Auden's poetic self-analysis as symbols for public conditions in his time. The main movement of his art was from a private to a public language. Includes notes and index.

Nelson, Gerald. *Changes of Heart: A Study of the Poetry of W. H. Auden.* Berkeley: University of California Press, 1969. Tracing the change in direction that Auden's later works took, Nelson analyzes characters in *The Sea and the Mirror*, *For the Time Being*, and *The Age of Anxiety*. For shorter poems, Auden's "persona" is examined less effectively as a mask for the poet. Complemented by a select bibliography.

Replogle, Justin. *Auden's Poetry.* Seattle: University of Washington Press, 1969. Mechanically analyzes the style of the poems, the conflicting personalities of their speakers as poet-versus-antipoet, and the ideas that they communicate. Unsuccessfully tries, using Søren Kierkegaard and Karl Marx, to demonstrate that Auden was destined to produce comedy through chance and accident. Index.

Michael Hennessy
(Updated by *Richard D. McGhee*)

ALAN AYCKBOURN

Born: Hampstead, London, England; April 12, 1939

Principal drama

The Square Cat, pr. 1959 (as Roland Allen); *Love After All*, pr. 1959 (as Roland Allen); *Mr. Whatnot*, pr. 1963 (revised version pr. 1964); *Relatively Speaking*, pr. 1967, pb. 1968 (originally as *Meet My Father*, pr. 1965); *Ernie's Incredible Illucinations*, pb. 1969, pr. 1971 (for children); *How the Other Half Loves*, pr. 1969, pb. 1972; *Time and Time Again*, pr. 1971, pb. 1973; *Absurd Person Singular*, pr. 1972, pb. 1974; *The Norman Conquests*, pr. 1973, pb. 1975 (includes *Table Manners*, *Living Together*, and *Round and Round the Garden*); *Absent Friends*, pr. 1974, pb. 1975; *Confusions*, pr. 1974, pb. 1977 (five one-acts); *Bedroom Farce*, pr. 1975, pb. 1977; *Just Between Ourselves*, pr. 1976, pb. 1978; *Ten Times Table*, pr. 1977, pb. 1978; *Joking Apart*, pr. 1978, pb. 1979; *Men on Women on Men*, pr. 1978 (lyrics; music by Paul Todd); *Sisterly Feelings*, pr. 1979, pb. 1981; *Taking Steps*, pr. 1979, pb. 1981; *Suburban Strains*, pr. 1980, pb. 1982 (music by Todd); *Season's Greetings*, pr. 1980, pb. 1982; *Way Upstream*, pr. 1981, pb. 1983; *Me, Myself, and I*, pr. 1981, pb. 1989 (music by Todd); *Intimate Exchanges*, pr. 1982, pb. 1985; *A Chorus of Disapproval*, pr. 1984, pb. 1985; *Woman in Mind*, pr. 1985, pb. 1986; *A Small Family Business*, pr., pb. 1987; *Henceforward*, pr. 1987, pb. 1988; *Mr. A's Amazing Maze Plays*, pr. 1988, pb. 1989 (for children); *Man of the Moment*, pr., pb. 1990; *Invisible Friends*, pr., pb. 1991; *The Revengers' Comedies*, pr., pb. 1991; *Body Language*, pr. 1992.

Other literary forms

Alan Ayckbourn is primarily known for his plays.

Achievements

Farceur of contemporary suburbia, Ayckbourn enjoys distinction not only as a prolific writer of entertaining, well-made plays during a stage revolution when the *pièce bien faite* was out of fashion but also as a dramatist who, beginning in 1959, has averaged one play a year, claiming to have surpassed even William Shakespeare in the sheer quantity of plays written by the early 1990's. His early reputation as a commercial dramatist, however, changed with the times and the development of his own style and themes, so that he has enjoyed productions of his plays even at the prestigious National Theatre in London. A critic of contemporary society's greed, he has increasingly honed his farce into black comedy, earning for it the label of "theater of embarrassment." In 1987, Ayckbourn was awarded a royal honor as Commander of the British Empire.

Biography

Alan Ayckbourn was born in Hampstead, London, on April 12, 1939, to Horace and Irene Worley Ayckbourn, his father the first violinist with the London Symphony Orchestra and his mother a novelist and short-story writer for popular women's magazines. In 1943, when he was five, his parents were divorced and his mother married Cecil Pye, a manager for Barclays Bank. Winning a Barclays Bank scholarship, Ayckbourn attended Haileybury School in Hertfordshire, where, during the next five years, he became interested in drama, touring in Holland as Peter in *Romeo and Juliet* and in the United States and Canada as Macduff in *Macbeth.*

Thus began Ayckbourn's lifelong affair with the theater. He left school with "A" levels in English and history and, at seventeen, joined Sir Donald Wolfit's company at the Edinburgh Festival as acting assistant stage manager. He also worked in summer theater at Leatherhead and then at Scarborough's Studio Theatre (under Stephen Joseph, son of actress Hermione Ferdinanda Gingold), writing plays even as he was initiated into the production rites of professional theater.

In 1959, Ayckbourn married actress Christine Roland, had a son (Steven Paul), and saw two of his plays (*The Square Cat* and *Love After All*) produced in Scarborough under the pseudonym of Roland Allen. In 1962, his second son, Nicholas Phillip, was born, and in 1964, Ayckbourn's *Mr. Whatnot* opened at the Arts Theatre in London. Thereafter, he has averaged writing at least one play per year, and he is wont to talk fondly of providing amusement for bored surburbanite vacationers on rainy Scarborough days.

Ayckbourn's early days in the theater included acting in roles such as Vladimir in Samuel Beckett's *En attendant Godot* (pb. 1952, pr. 1953; *Waiting for Godot*, pb. 1954, pr. 1955) and Stanley in Harold Pinter's *The Birthday Party* (pr. 1958, pb. 1960). He was founder-member and associate director of Victoria Theatre in Stoke on Trent, produced dramas on the British Broadcasting Corporation's radio, in Leeds, and, after Stephen Joseph's death in 1967, returned to Scarborough in 1970. After several name changes, the Victoria Theatre became the Stephen Joseph Theatre-in-the-Round, in tribute to Ayckbourn's mentor. It became also Ayckbourn's tryout home prior to openings in theaters in and around London and all over the world.

In the United States, the Alley Theatre in Houston, the Arena Stage in Washington, and the Manhattan Theater Club in New York, among others, became homes for Ayckbourn's plays. Having succeeded in small English theaters such as The Arts, The Roundhouse, and The Richmond Orange Tree, and later in commercial houses in the West End, Ayckbourn's *Bedroom Farce* reached the Royal National Theatre, where both his plays and his directorship (1986) have long enjoyed a liaison. In the best of all possible theater worlds—the provincial, fringe, West End commercial, Royal National, and international theaters producing his plays—Ayckbourn not only has survived the early critical attacks for writing the commercially profitable well-made play but also has continued writing in a long career that has no contemporary equal in quantity and consistency of experimentation. With more than fifty plays, Ayckbourn has continued to be more prolific than any of the new playwrights since the stage revolution began in 1956 with John Osborne's *Look Back in Anger* (pr. 1956, pb. 1957).

Analysis

With labels flourishing during the new era in drama (Osborne's angry theater, Beckett's Theater of the Absurd, Pinter's comedy of menace, Arnold Wesker's kitchen-sink drama), Alan Ayckbourn, too, has been honored with his own, the comedy of embarrassment, based on the increasingly black comedy in his later farces. The term derives from the unease of audiences as their laughter is deflected by the intrusion of realities underlying that hilarity. For example, the accidental murders in *A Small Family Business* and *Man of the Moment* obtrude through the farce, giving it a hollow ring. This jarring union of farce and tragedy, alien to standard farce expectations, in fact, is subtly present even in early comedies such as *How the Other Half Loves*, markedly so in *A Chorus of Disapproval*, and shatteringly so in *A Small Family Business* and *Man of the Moment.* Ayckbourn has become the hilarious tragedian of contemporary life, not unlike Ben Jonson, whose seventeenth century farces about greed seem ancestors to Ayckbourn's. Ayckbourn met the charges of early critics who faulted him for his commercially viable formula plays, commenting that one "cannot begin to shatter theatrical conventions or break golden rules until he is reasonably sure in himself what they are and how they were arrived at." The rules to which Ayckbourn is referring are the time-honored ones practiced by Greeks and Romans, Shakespeare, Jonson, Molière, George Bernard Shaw, and Oscar Wilde.

With the acknowledged influence of William Congreve, Wilde, Georges Feydeau, Anton Chekhov, Noël Coward, Terence Rattigan, J. B. Priestley, and Pinter, Ayckbourn has forged a style of old and new that has given his plays their unique quality. Using the farce conventions of his predecessors, he has experimented with the mechanics of traditional plotting by challenging its limits and extending its boundaries. One of his most noticeable changes in farce techniques is his avoidance of the linear movement of the plot and his replacing it with a sense of indefiniteness. The outcome is a circular movement, resulting in a play structure that is more akin to the static quality of Chekhov's plots than to the active one of Wilde's and Shaw's plays. His disarrangement of linear plot lines creates the illusion of a standard farce, deceiving the audience in its usual comic expectations.

His technique is partly explained by the tripling, sometimes quadrupling, of the number of potentially comic couples or comic situations in the conventional farce. The standard use of the double takes what seems a quantum leap in Ayckbourn's farces.

The tripling extends to the overall architecture of plays, a number of them taking the form of trilogies. In *The Norman Conquests*, each of the three plays treats the same character and situations, one being the offstage action of what happens onstage in another. The order of performance of the three plays, thus, is of little consequence, for each is essentially repetitious of the other two. The chief difference among them is their locale: One occurs in the dining room, the second in the living room, and the third in the garden. The difference is diversionary, suggesting a traditional plot movement where there really is none. Ayckbourn's trilogy *Sisterly Feelings* goes even further in its structural inventiveness, with each play's conclusion in a given performance being determined arbitrarily by a member of the cast. Still another sometimes confusing plot invention is Ayckbourn's use of the same stage space at the same time by two or more different sets of characters (frequently couples), most prominently illustrated in *How the Other Half Loves*, *Bedroom Farce*, and *Taking Steps*. The single most famous of these scenes, in *How the Other Half Loves*, involves two different dinner parties by two different middle-class couples (one having achieved social status and the other desperately trying to do so) seated at the same table, their only common element a third couple who are the guests at both dinners.

Ayckbourn's ingenious plotting strategies provide him ample room to comment on his favorite theme: a satire on the foibles of individuals, his chosen slice of middle-class society in which those individuals function being suburbia. His satire has its brief, unrelieved grim moments as in *A Small Family Business* and *Henceforeward*, plays in which the families' children become victims of the pervasive greed of individuals and their society and are helpless to extricate themselves. The artificially happy ending of a farce is replaced by a realistically sober ending in which the comic surfaces of the plot are maintained, even as they cannot disguise the underlying tragic realities. Thus the play stylistically satisfies the farce's requirement for a happy ending while substantively changing the genre to an ironic farce at its best and a black comedy at its most pessimistic. It is appropriate that the title of one of Ayckbourn's late plays, *The Revengers' Comedies*, derives from Cyril Tourneur's seventeenth century title *The Revenger's Tragedy* (pr. 1606-1607, pb. 1607), with the obvious parallel of the earlier era with Thatcherite England of the 1980's.

Ayckbourn's first London success, *Relatively Speaking*, illustrates his roots in the traditional mechanics of the well-made farce, such as abundant coincidences, well-timed exits and entrances, complicated romantic intrigues, central misunderstandings, quid pro quos, secrets known to the audience but not to the characters, and the crucial use of an object to progress the plot. At the same time, Ayckbourn rejects the suspense-creating, teeter-totter action, the big revelatory scene, and the ending that neatly ties together the loose ends of the plot. Instead, as a keen observer and creator of character, he treats familial and marital situations whose problems are revealed rather than resolved. The results are Chekhov-like revelations of states of being, contained within the guise of farce and an increasingly bitter satire on the moral bankruptcy of contemporary society. Deceptively embodied in the local, his farce is ultimately universal in its depiction of human foibles that know no bounds of time or place.

With echoes of the exploits of Oscar Wilde's Jack and Ernest in *The Importance of Being Earnest* (pr. 1895, pb. 1899), *Relatively Speaking*, a four-character play, involves a young unmarried couple who set off for the country, each for secret reasons withheld from the other. Ginny wishes to retrieve letters from her former lover (and employer) in order to put a definite end to that affair. Unbeknown to her, Greg, her current lover, suspicious because of the flowers and chocolates cluttering Ginny's flat and the address he notices on her cigarette pack (like the cigarette case in Wilde's play), follows her on a different train. Ginny's lie about a visit to her "parents" begins a series of deceptions multiplied at breakneck speed, deceptions that stretch out to include an older couple, Philip and his wife, Sheila. A sine qua non of any farce, the seemingly unstoppable piling up of deceptions, misunderstandings, and coincidences is absurd, one of the most comical being Greg's misinterpretation of Sheila's truthful insistence that she is not Ginny's mother. To Greg, Sheila is merely eluding potential embarrassment at having to reveal the illegitimacy of Ginny's birth.

Like all farceurs, Ayckbourn bases his suspense on secrets known only to some of the characters and on not having all characters on the stage at the same time until the play's end. Consequently, all characters act on the basis of only a partial knowledge of things. While observing this convention, Ayckbourn ignores the artificial disclosure scene (also known as the big scene, obligatory scene, or *scène à faire*) in which all secrets are revealed, all misunderstandings cleared up, and a happy ending contrived. For even as Ginny and Philip depart happily, neither Greg nor Philip is fully apprised of what has happened, the former of Philip's deceptive vacation plans having included Ginny and the latter of Sheila's untruthful claims to having a lover. Thus the turning point in the conventional farce (two of the most famous occurring in Richard Brinsley Sheridan's *The School for Scandal*, pr. 1777, pb. 1780, and Wilde's *The Importance of Being Earnest*) gives way even in Ayckbourn's early farces to a Chekhovian technique of the undramatic.

In *How the Other Half Loves*, Ayckbourn takes his technique one step further, this time in the use of stage space in a simultaneous depiction of two separate dinner parties. He superimposes the dinner party of one upwardly mobile couple (the Fosters) on that of a more affluent couple (the Phillipses), both couples hosts to the same dinner guests (the Featherstones). In an eye-defying sequence of movements, the audience witnesses the two couples preparing for their guests in the same stage space, the distinctions between the relative affluence of the aspiring sets of hosts made clear only by a change in a few minor furnishings, such as pillows. The hilarious scene in which two separate dinner parties at two separate times are staged at one table is Ayckbourn's most inventive climactic scene. Their common guest, Mr. Featherstone, is the victim simultaneously of Teresa Phillips' thrown soup (intended for her husband) and the leaking upstairs toilet at the Fosters' home. Unwitting victim of the accidental physical high jinks of his hosts, Mr. Featherstone is victim in another sense, for although the fortunes of the Phillipses and the Fosters seem to be put to rights at the end of the play, the Featherstones, clearly the couple to be impressed, reveal their own marital problems foreboding, ironically, similar problems for their younger, aspiring hosts.

Up to *Time and Time Again*, Ayckbourn's inventions have focused on plots and staging areas. About this play, however, Ayckbourn speaks of "upsetting the balance," an upsetting involving the nature of his main character. Normally the driving force in the plot, the protagonist, Leonard, is upsettingly passive. According to Ayckbourn, he "attracts people who have an irresistible impulse to push him in one direction, but he slides out of the push." Some audiences, Ayckbourn continues, are "angered by this type," while "others get concerned." Hence, Ayckbourn himself supplies yet another basis for the label applied to him as a writer of the theater of embarrassment.

Leonard's "sliding" in the play is his refusal to be drawn into the banalities of middle-class social lunches and teas. He has developed his own system of quiet resistance. At one point, he relates a tale of a telling of a tale from his former marriage. A schoolteacher at the time, Leonard arrives home one day to find his wife sampling homemade wine with a male friend. Unable or unwilling to react, Leonard spends the evening in the local jail, regaling the officers with his story and retelling it to every fresh batch of police officers as they arrive for duty. Leonard is the first of a series of Ayckbourn's passive heroes, the most humorous being Norman of *The Norman Conquests*; the most sympathetically satiric, Guy Jones in *A Chorus of Disapproval*; and the most devastating, Douglas Beechey in *Man of the Moment*.

There is an aggressive element in Leonard's passivity as he forces others to respond to his lack of involvement. From his school days, he tells yet another story of having developed a system of quoting a line or two of poetry, an "infallible system to fool all headmasters and school inspectors." He continues this pattern of behavior even as an adult. Bored by the others and interested by Leonard's erratic behavior, Joan, his current interest, joins Leonard in his game. Meantime, Leonard's antagonist for Joan's attention, Graham, a husband also attracted to Joan, pushes Peter, another admirer of Joan mistaken by Graham as her lover, into a physical fight. Leonard, as a result of the mistake, goes scot-free. The play ends with Leonard eventually leaving Joan (as he earlier had left his wife and her lover to entertain the local police officers) and walking off compatibly with Peter to the playing field, Graham and Peter still laboring under their misunderstanding.

Another Ayckbourn technique becomes more apparent with every play: his inventive use of the room. As character becomes more important than plot, Ayckbourn utilizes the room (frequently the kitchen) as a microscope under which he examines contemporary middle-class behavior in all of its acquisitiveness and sexual rituals. The kitchen, its appliances emblems of materialistic greed, is an appropriate setting for his examination.

In his *Absurd Person Singular*, structured loosely as three one-act plays, three couples celebrate Christmas Eve in three successive years in three different homes, the kitchen winding up as the room in which most of the action takes place. In the first act, the first host-couple, lowest on the social rung, aspire to the social status of their guests. In the second act, the hosts have to some extent realized their social aims. In act 3, the hosts, having played the social-status game longer than their guests, have long since been in a state of total noncommunication, a direction toward which the other two couples seem to be heading. The final scene of act 3 finds all three couples crowding the kitchen, each person in a wild frenzy of attending to chores such as replacing a light bulb, completely ignoring the suicide attempt of their hostess, with her head in the gas oven. The three couples are a variation on those in *How the Other Half Loves*.

Rooms continue to be the means of Ayckbourn's microscopic examination of suburban rituals in *The Norman Conquests*. Here, Ayckbourn locates the similar actions in three different places: the dining room in *Table Manners*, the living room in *Living Together*, and the garden in *Round and Round the Garden*. The family consists of Annie, who is single and the caretaker of their sick mother, her married sister Ruth, and her married brother Reg (and the spouses of the latter two). All convene in the family's country home to provide some relief for Annie. Norman, Ruth's husband, enjoys hilariously romantic encounters with the women in each location of the three plays.

Like Leonard of *Time and Time Again*, Norman attracts female attention and finds himself in situations not of his making. A Chekhovian immobility asserts itself in Annie's abortive plans for a "dirty weekend" with

Norman in East Grinstead. There is a sixth character, an outsider in the person of a slow-witted local veterinarian, played in the original stage production with exquisitely hilarious dullness by Michael Gambon, who would later become a regular actor in Ayckbourn's plays. He is a foil to Norman, whose sexual attractiveness and agility drive the women to respond to him. Each of the three plays is complete in itself, and the order in which they are performed (or seen) is more or less immaterial to the audience's understanding of each play, since the action in each does not essentially depend on that in the other two and since the actions in all three are essentially the same, their different "rooms" creating different perspectives on the same situation.

Two plays, *Taking Steps* and *Bedroom Farce*, revert to Ayckbourn's reliance on hectic physical stage business as in *How the Other Half Loves.* The action of *Taking Steps* occurs on three different floors of an old Victorian house, but one stage space is used to represent all three floors of the house. Hence the actors must take a variety of steps in imitation of stair climbing. Similarly, in *Bedroom Farce*, one stage area is occupied by three large beds to represent three different bedrooms. The potential audience confusions as to who is doing what in whose bed and the risk of actors in making false steps as they maneuver their way through time and space create suspense and keep the play's pace lively. At times, Ayckbourn's risk taking with physical matters seems its own excuse for being, an entertaining ploy to avoid the greater risk of banality potentially inherent in his repetitive marital and extramarital situations.

In the plays of the 1960's and 1970's, Ayckbourn's ingenious strategies of plot, space, and character dominate, and laughter governs the plays' moods. In the 1980's, however, the hilarity, although remaining intact to the end of the play, is mixed with increasing audience uncertainty—to laugh or not to laugh.

In *Season's Greetings*, a stranger (a writer with only one book to his credit) becomes the romantic object of attention of the females. A guest of the single sister at a Christmas family gathering, he is a later version of the outsider, Leonard, in *Time and Time Again.* When the women of the household (including his hostess, the unmarried sister) are attracted to him, an angry husband shoots and almost kills him. The intrusion on farce of a potential disaster changes the nature of the laughter into the kind produced by Chekhov's Uncle Vanya, whose shot at his rival misfires.

Chekhov-like also in his use of a family gathering as the central event of a play, Ayckbourn has commented on that event as unimportant. It is, rather, "the response to the dinner party, not the dinner party itself." He spoke to author Bernard Dukore of the inevitable line in that response: "Wasn't that a boring dinner party?" In that line and as a consequence of it, revelations occur, not only of the problems of those couples who have succeeded but also of the pending fate of those who have not yet arrived but are on the same path. An attractive outsider acts as a catalyst to reveal the Chekhovian inner states of being that lie beneath the politely banal surfaces.

The outsider in *A Chorus of Disapproval* is Guy Jones, a lonely bachelor drawn into a provincial production of John Gay's *The Beggar's Opera* (pr., pb. 1728), when the leading role is suddenly vacated. A fuller version of dull Tom in *The Norman Conquests*, he rises to the occasion, though untalented and inexperienced, and becomes the hero not only of the production but also of the women who thrust themselves on him as a result of dissatisfactions in their own marriages. He is the means by which they respond to the emptiness of their suburban lives.

In three later plays—*A Small Family Business*, *Henceforward*, and *Man of the Moment*—the farce is increasingly ironic in Ayckbourn's progressive shift to emphasize the emotional and moral bankruptcy of middle-class family life in Thatcherite England of the 1980's. In all three, outside forces exert pressures on family situations, pressures that the family finds difficult or impossible to control. In *A Small Family Business*, the pressure is money, involving a family furniture business in which greed corrupts completely, simultaneously involving a hilariously stereotyped, mafia-like quintet of Italian brothers. In *Henceforward*, a gang-infested neighborhood is a refuge for a divorced composer of electronic music, who contests his wife for custody of their daughter. In a stunning move, Ayckbourn deploys a female robot, the composer's means of assuring the social worker of the presence of a maternal influence in his daughter's life. Ayckbourn compounds this bit of theatricality with the appearance of the teen daughter in full regalia as a member of one of the neighborhood gangs. In *Man of the Moment*, the theatricality takes the form of an overweight woman who accidentally kills a most repulsive character when she steps on him rather than saving him, as was her intention. Individual greed and corruption, although present, are given societal approval in the impunity and impersonality with which a television crew exploits personal tragedy in the name of a good news story. Both business and television interests conspire in a cover-up of the real story.

In these three plays, the laughter caused by coincidences and central misunderstandings is still there, but now the plays are darkened by their context of a pervasive societal hypocrisy. The problems are no longer those of innocently human complications but of socially accepted amorality. In *A Small Family Business*, the last person with any scruples, Jack, the new head of the business, cannot extricate himself from its corruption. The gang-infested neighborhood of *Henceforward* and the moral vacuum of the mass media in *Man of the Moment* remain. Ayckbourn provides no artificial resolutions to the problems, only a microscopic examination of them.

Amid the farcical humor that is sustained to the end in two of the plays, two teenagers, as a result of their being ignored because of other family problems, become innocent victims, one a drug addict and the other a gang member. In the third play, an adult innocent, dull and passive Douglas Beechey, is a subject for both hilarity and tragedy, as he is made into a mass-media hero through no attempt on his part. He belongs to a long gallery of Ayckbourn characters who have their roots in the early outsider characters such as Tom in *The Norman Conquests.*

The traditional purpose of comedy has been to reveal and thereby correct the vices of the society that it portrays by exposing them (usually with a *deus ex machina* ending), thereby bringing about correction of behavior in that society. The exposure involves stereotypical characters whose mechanical behavior engenders laughter. Mere exposure is the punishment for the perpetrator of the vice, either reform or prison frequently being the result of that exposure. The vices of the age have no such corrective results in Ayckbourn's farces.

In his exposure of rampant acquisitiveness, however, Ayckbourn does realize half of the farceur's aim. At the same time, he admits to an unease about the corrective results of prevailing farces. Of the Thatcherite regime he says, "It's no coincidence that you hardly ever see members of the present Government in the theatre. . . . The arts and gentle, civilized living are rapidly being downgraded for the fast buck. It has a narrowing effect. It creates an uncaringness."

The traditional purpose of tragedy has been to cleanse the body politic of its moral stain and to affirm life through increased self-knowledge on the part of the hero, a process in which guilty and innocent alike suffer. As realistic rather than stereotypical characters who embody the values of their respective societies, characters evoke, according to Aristotelian precepts, pity and fear in the polis even as they endure individual punishments and rewards. There is no such individual or collective affirmation in Ayckbourn's plays. Again, the darker elements only continue in their non-resolution, in character-generated farces, such as Jack McCracken of *A Small Family Business* and Douglas Beechey of *Man of the Moment.* Societally, business and mass-media corruptors conspire in their lack of awareness of the morality or immorality of their actions. Individually and collectively, characters continue in a context in which punishment and rewards in a moral sense do not exist.

Ayckbourn regards *Absurd Person Singular* with its three Christmas Eve celebrations as his first "offstage action" play, one in which two socially aspiring couples land in the thick of adversities of the most successful couple. The offstage importance increases with every play, with further inability on the part of the characters to extricate themselves from their adversities. For example, the celebratory tableaulike ending to *A Small Family*

Business coexists with a tableau of the young daughter in her drug-induced pain in the bathroom. John Peter describes an Ayckbourn play as "a requiem scored for screams and laughter."

As a dark farceur par excellence of contemporary suburbia, as an ongoing reinventor of farce technique, and as the most prolific of a huge number of new dramatists in the second half of the twentieth century— Ayckbourn continues to be a force on the world stage.

Other major works

TELEPLAY: *Service Not Included*, 1974.
SCREENPLAY: *A Chorus of Disapproval*, 1989.

Bibliography

Billington, Michael. *Alan Ayckbourn*. New York: St. Martin's Press, 1990. A chronological analysis by a leading critic and scholar of Ayckbourn's plays, from his earliest unpublished works to *The Revengers' Comedies*.

Dukore, Bernard. *Alan Ayckbourn: A Casebook*. New York: Garland, 1992. A compilation of lively, analytical articles on Ayckbourn's plays in terms of their stylistic and thematic characteristics, as well as their effectiveness on stage. Includes an interview with Ayckbourn, a complete chronology, and an extensive bibliography.

Kalson, Albert E. "Alan Ayckbourn." In *Dictionary of Literary Biography*, edited by Stanley Weintraub. Vol. 13, pt. 1, *British Dramatists Since World War II*. Detroit: Gail Research, 1982. Although not up to date, this highly readable essay remains the best short introduction to Ayckbourn's plays. Chronology, bibliography.

Page, Malcolm. *File on Ayckbourn*. London: Methuen Drama, 1989. A compilation of biographical information, production and publication data, synopses and comments on each play, interview excerpts, and a bibliography.

Watson, Ian. *Conversations with Ayckbourn*. Rev. ed. London: Faber & Faber, 1988. Unified into what seems to be an autobiography, Ayckbourn's comments range over the achievements of his entire career. Includes useful play synopses and chronology.

White, Sidney Howard. *Alan Ayckbourn*. Boston: Twayne, 1984. A chronological discussion of Ayckbourn's plays, tracing the dramatist's progress from farce to plays of character up to 1972. Includes a chronology, a bibliography, and an index.

Susan Rusinko

JON ROBIN BAITZ

Born: Los Angeles, California; November 4, 1961

Principal drama

Mizlansky/Silinsky, pr. 1985; *The Film Society*, pb. 1987 (as a play in process), pr. 1988, pb. 1989; *Dutch Landscape*, pr. 1989; *The Substance of Fire*, pr., pb. 1991; *Three Hotels*, pr. 1991 (teleplay), pr. 1993 (staged); *The End of the Day*, pr., pb. 1992.

Other literary forms

Jon Robin Baitz is known only for his plays.

Achievements

Baitz is a dramatist who, at the age of thirty, captured national attention with only two successfully produced plays in New York. Two earlier plays, one a failure and the other a moderate success, along with a play for public television, constitute the work for which fellow playwrights such as John Guare and critics such as Robert Brustein have lauded him, the latter placing Baitz in the company of Sam Shepard and David Mamet. Baitz's not-so-fictional universe is that of unprincipled corporate wealth and private greed, monsters whose tentacles have reached out and strangled any moral sensibility in the last decades of the twentieth century. If Mamet and Shepard are artists of the inarticulate, Baitz cultivates the articulate, easily moving in a given play among a range of styles—realism, expressionism, surrealism, naturalism. His creation of a modern Dantean myth includes references to contemporary figures such as Richard M. Nixon, Henry A. Kissinger, Margaret Thatcher, even George Herbert Walker Bush. International mergers, corporate and private greed, Swiss bank accounts, acquired immune deficiency syndrome (AIDS), poverty, and racial bigotry are among the moral diseases that poison Baitz's stage universe. What little redemption Baitz finds in the world is, as with E. M. Forster, that of personal connection. He finds ideology becoming increasingly laughable and irrelevant. In style or theme, his plays have been likened to those of Caryl Churchill, Joe Orton, Simon Gray, and Tom Stoppard.

Biography

The international flavor of Jon Robin Baitz's plays, which span locales such as Southern California, South Africa, London, New York, Morocco, the Virgin Islands, and Mexico, grows out of Baitz's family life. Born in Los Angeles to a father who was an executive with the international division of Carnation Milk Company and a mother who was "a larger-than-life-Auntie Mame type," Baitz, from the age of seven to seventeen, lived in

Brazil, England, and South Africa. When he returned to Los Angeles, he finished high school but decided against college because being a student seemed unreal and attending college, evasive. When his parents moved to Holland, he continued his travels, using their home as a base, and worked at various odd jobs: as a short-order cook, a tractor driver on a kibbutz, and a painter of an art gallery at The Hague.

He found himself a professional eavesdropper and, as a result of his intense preoccupation with listening to other people, developed into an "elevated yenta." While deciding to be "out of the loop" and thinking of starting a small publishing company or buying a vineyard, he worked temporarily for a film producer as a "sort of" phone answerer. Out of this experience, he wrote a theater piece, *Mizlansky/Silinsky*, and suddenly found himself to be a playwright.

Leaving the United States and then coming back to his country was a trigger to his playwriting, as though the physical distance gave "some kind of clarity to the rage I was feeling at a benumbed, becalmed, morally bankrupt country." Transferred to individuals, this moral bankruptcy or corruption is one against which Baitz's characters struggle, mostly with few or no positive results. These characters are dramatized in the South African teachers of *The Film Society*, the father and children in *The Substance of Fire*, and the psychiatrist-turned-oncologist in *The End of the Day*.

Baitz enjoys membership in the Naked Angels, which he regards as a family of gifted actors and writers. After the devastating experience of the failure of *Dutch Landscape* (a play about Americans living abroad) at the Mark Taper Forum in Los Angeles, he credited the Naked Angels with saving his life. In fact, he wrote the first part of *The Substance of Fire* shortly after his disappointment with *Dutch Landscape*.

Baitz became a playwright-in-residence with the New York Stage and Film Company and settled in a TriBeCa loft in the SoHo district of New York. He has received a Revson Fellowship from Playwrights Horizons, a 1987 Playwright U.S.A. Award, the New York Newsday Oppenheimer Award, a National Endowment for the Arts award, a Humanitas Prize for his television play *Three Hotels*, a Rockefeller Fellowship, and a grant from the Fund for New American Playwrights for the production of *Dutch Landscape* at the Mark Taper Forum.

Analysis

Very emphatically a social critic, Jon Robin Baitz, however, stops short of the extremity to which Mamet carries his concern with moral corruption. In Mamet's world, corruption is a given, and his characters— producers in *Speed-the-Plow* (pr., pb. 1988) and salesmen in *Glengarry Glen Ross* (pr. 1983, pb. 1984)—accept that milieu as one in which they must live. Mamet, a stylistic minimalist and the American counterpart of the English Harold Pinter, is existentially absurdist in his view of life. Baitz, on the other hand, is highly articulate, melodramatic, sometimes flamboyant in his style, and belongs to the tradition of social criticism of dramatists such as Henrik Ibsen and Arthur Miller. His characters attempt to change the total corruption of their situations but, overpowered, only sink more deeply into the system or are defeated by it. That system may be the South African English school in *The Film Society*, the publishing business in *The Substance of Fire*, and the international megacorporate world of *The End of the Day*. Social and private moralities clash, as expressed during the reunion in *The End of the Day* of two medical-school friends (now expatriate Britons living in Southern California) in their erratic recital of Matthew Arnold's poem "Dover Beach," ending with the lines:

> And here we are as on a dark'ning plain
> Swept with confused armies of struggle and flight
> Where ignorant armies clash by night.

One of the Britons, recently returned to California from London, describes London as genuinely sad, "so gussied up. Dolled up. Tarted up. Painted faces. But underneath," London, he continues, is like a certain type in Beverly Hills, old, rich, with stretched skin and impossibly blond hair.

Baitz's plays are searing portraits of contemporary civilization in decay. Three professions—education, publishing, and medicine—provide the context for Baitz's major plays: *The Film Society*, *The Substance of Fire*, and *The End of the Day*, respectively.

With the production of *The Film Society* at the Second Stage on Manhattan's upper West Side, Baitz was declared with near-critical unanimity as the new talent to watch. In the play, two teachers, Jonathan and Terry, find themselves beset on all sides by the run-down conditions in a South African English school named Blenheim, very much like the one that Baitz had attended. The decaying school, with its faded Edwardian old-boy traditions of fingernail inspections, cricket, and the discipline of caning, is obviously still a training ground for the children of those dedicated to preserving the power structure of the Afrikaners of South Africa. Jonathan dreams of changes in the financially strapped school, but in the end he opts for the comforts of the status quo. Terry, on the other hand, refusing to compromise either with his affluent family or with the school administration, is fired. His wife, Nan, also a dedicated teacher in the school, after her husband's departure gives "some sort of madwoman speech in social bloody history class," and as a result, she, too, is fired. Her firing seems doubly monstrous because it is the decision of Jonathan, who, as a result of his mother's generous gift to the school, has been appointed assistant headmaster.

All three teachers are from affluent colonial families whose political ide-
ologies are as decayed as the school's buildings. All three are sensitive,
idealistic, and intelligent, in strong contrast to the older members of the
staff. Jonathan, Terry, and Nan represent different degrees of change. Terry,
although doubting even his radicalism, is still the radical; Nan can work
within the system but on her own terms; and Jonathan eventually capitu-
lates to the terms of the system. Although the story is fairly simple, the
relationships among the three teachers are drawn in painfully complex
terms as the play works its way to the departures of Terry and Nan and to
Jonathan's acceptance of his mother's verdict on his life as passivity, comfort, and loneliness. One sees him destined for the kind of human isolation
found in the many schoolteachers in Simon Gray's plays.

The motif of darkness in *The Film Society* is introduced early in the
allusion to the showing, at the weekly meeting of the school's Film Society, of Orson Welles's film *Touch of Evil* (1958), which was sent to the
school as a result of confusion with the film that had been ordered, *That
Touch of Mink*. Shortly thereafter, Terry, already regarded as a lefty, angers
the hierarchy with his bringing an African speaker to the school, resulting
in the speaker's arrest and Terry's freeing him from prison. His wife, who
at first tried to moderate Terry's radicalism, reaches her own breaking point
when she lectures to her social history class on the necessity of retaining
one's humanness.

The moral darkness, hotly debated in the play, is as visual as it is intellectual, as image after image of decay is evoked. According to Jonathan,
herds of bats living in the mango trees attack the schoolboys; termites the
size of Land Rovers scurry about the school; the swimming pool looks like
a science experiment; the floor of the junior toilets is flooded, with bits of
offal floating toward the showers—like the seventh circle of hell. The
burning of local sugar-cane fields by natives is counterpointed by the race
hatred in statements about the Pakistanis and Arabs taking over London or
stories of African Americans from Harlem coming en masse to South Africa. The burning of the dead by the Hindus, the funeral of an administra-
tor, and talk of past funerals add to the dark ambience of the play.

In its straightforward movement, the action of *The Film Society* progresses rapidly in short scenes, and the characters speak with a literacy
and articulateness rarely found on the contemporary American stage. Its
weakness is the lack of progression necessary to make the characters convincing. They give away their positions too early and too strongly, leaving
little to be proved. The two women, Jonathan's mother and Terry's wife,
who are the supports, respectively, to son and husband, are a bit too obviously only that—supports—as they spell out for the audience the positions of the two men.

Baitz's second play produced in New York, *The Substance of Fire*, continues his attacks on contemporary life, this time pitting a financially troubled publisher, Isaac Geldhart, against two sons and a daughter, who are summoned by him to discuss the fate of the family publishing firm. The daughter, Sarah, is an actress in children's television; the older son, Martin, a teacher of landscape architecture at Vassar College; and the younger son, Aaron, a partner in the family publishing business. At stake is a decision regarding the publishing of a money-losing six-volume work on Nazi medical experiments (Isaac's choice) as opposed to a money-making novel (Aaron's choice). Isaac's children own shares in the firm, Martin and eventually Sarah giving their votes to Aaron. In the second of the play's two acts, Isaac is alone, clinically depressed, in his now shabby and increasingly bare, cold apartment, where he is visited by a social worker and Martin.

As in *The Film Society*, the story and the issues of *The Substance of Fire* are clearly defined. The father is vigorously independent, intellectual, feisty, and stubborn in holding on to his past (his survival of the Holocaust). His children, with whom he enjoys little or no intimacy, stand up to his searingly caustic humor and anger. All are sympathetically portrayed and equally effective in articulating their positions, leaving in question the matter of who is right or wrong, moral or immoral. A traditionally conditioned audience tends to side with the main character, whose role in the play is of heroic dimensions. He is the kind of autocratic publishing lion for which New York is famous. His values, though financially ruinous in an age in which Japanese purchases threaten everything for which he stands, evoke the nostalgia of an irretrievable past.

The second act of *The Substance of Fire* takes place three and a half years later and brings into play a new character. A social worker, Marge Hackett, gives a new dimension to Isaac's future and at the same time expands Baitz's social criticism in the play. As she verbally spars with Isaac in much the same manner of the family gathering in act 1, her self-revelations of the past include a husband whose successful political career came crashing down as the result of a financial scandal. Her self-reinvention, after her husband's downfall, includes a college education to prepare for her current career. She is like Isaac, who, having lost one family to the Nazis and another to new-age values, embarks on a new life, as the play ends with the possibility of future dinners with Marge and with Isaac's conciliatory walk with Martin in snowy Gramercy Park.

The closeness between Baitz's subject matter and his own experience is made clear in this play. He admits that Isaac is drawn from friends, whom he loves and thus refuses to name. He also wrote the part of Isaac for Ron Rifkin, whom he met at Williamstown, where he was impressed by the actor's performance in Arthur Miller's *The American Clock* (pr. 1980, pb. 1982).

As in his earlier play, objects take on symbolic significance beyond their realistic function. Especially striking among Isaac's collection of books and other ephemera is an old postcard with a watercolor scene painted by the youthful Adolf Hitler when he had considered becoming an artist. Isaac's emotional tie to the card is strong, yet rather than selling it, as he had done with other valuable memorabilia, he burns it, an action suggesting his stubborn refusal to capitulate and, as well, the possibility of yet another reinvention of his life.

Baitz's next play, *The End of the Day*, takes gigantic stylistic leaps from the previous two plays. Retaining the brisk movement of scenes that characterizes his earlier work, Baitz indulges in an orgy of stylistic shifts, sliding easily in and out of scenes that are at one moment realistic, then, in turn, expressionistic, naturalistic, and surrealistic. Rapidly changing locales accompany the style changes—from well-heeled Malibu Canyon to a run-down health clinic, to a vulgarly opulent London flat, and back to a Southern California art museum into which megacorporations have poured their money.

Played with larger-than-life zest by the Welsh actor Roger Rees, the leading character, Graydon Massey, gives explicit form to Baitz's idea of reinvention in both word and deed. Now an American citizen with an American wife and a corruptly wealthy American father-in-law intent on political office, Massey opens the play with an erratic rehearsal of the Pledge of Allegiance. He feverishly interrupts his rehearsal with a long stream-of-consciousness flow of fragmented thoughts about the American Dream. The margarita-induced monologue concludes with his reason for emigrating: "The point is, in America, you can reinvent yourself. . . . In America— you can go back for seconds." In one dazzlingly fast scene, Baitz establishes the dream that has motivated emigration to the United States for centuries. From this point on, it is all morally downhill for Massey.

In a dreamlike, expressionistic scene change, reminiscent of August Strindberg's technique in *Ett drömspel* (pb. 1902, pr. 1907; *A Dream Play*, 1907) the same set (Malibu) becomes the San Cristobal Clinic in San Pedro, described by Baitz as a "sort of vast Dantesque hell of patients just outside moaning." At this point, naturalism takes over, as Massey, a psychiatrist retrained as an oncologist, confronts an intractably impoverished clinical system and his first AIDS patient.

Complications with his Mafia-like father-in-law, the result of Massey's intention to divorce his wife, cause Massey to return to his mother, Jocelyn Massey, who lives with her brother-in-law in her vulgarly fashionable London home. To satisfy the demands of his wife and father-in-law for having funded him in his costly reeducation, Massey must wring from his mother a huge sum of money and a grotesque George Stubbs painting of a cat skeleton. This he accomplishes, but at the expense of being drawn into a huge, international, megacorporation, at the head of which is his mother. Massey's corrupted "end of the day" involves a series of oncology centers and an art museum replete with Stubbs paintings—all because of his mother's corporate generosity. Thrown into this maze of actions is an old medical-school friend, Marton, involved in a film business that has become a part of Jocelyn's empire. This second act surrealistically intensifies Massey's American Dream into the nightmare that it has become.

At one point, as Massey and Marton exchange views about politics and Massey speaks of having to vote for American "bastards," Marton reminds him of what he left behind, which was not much better, Margaret Thatcher, "a Stalin in a wig, a cunt. A Medusa; anyone looked at her—straight to stone." The following prime minister, John Major, Marton refers to as "a concierge, a head-waiter at a provincial grill." The Iran-Contra corruption, Britons in Hollywood, the Docklands projects in London, a Kennedy-like "Ich bin un Malibuan," and, searingly, Richard M. Nixon's giving the lie to F. Scott Fitzgerald's assertion that there are no second acts in American life—all these views and many more are references to a modern Dantean world with its vividly depicted circles of sinners. William Shakespeare blends parodically with Dante in a number of references to Hamlet— particularly in a dream in which Massey's dead father appears to him and in Jocelyn's cohabitation with Massey's uncle. Baitz has said that this is "very much a play about a bad man trying to be good and ultimately becoming himself—a bad man."

In *Three Hotels*, which appeared two years before in an earlier version on public television, Baitz carries forward the same themes and style of *The Film Society*. *Three Hotels* is about Kenneth Hoyle, an international business executive with a company that sells unhealthy baby formula to Third World countries. Kenneth, ironically, feels responsible for the death of African children, and his rise to corporate power has alienated him from his wife, Barbara, creating problems in their marriage. What is worse is that the couple's teenage son was killed in Brazil for a beautiful watch he was wearing, which was offered to him by his parents.

Consisting entirely of monologues (two by Kenneth, one by Barbara) and prohibiting any dialogue between the two characters, *Three Hotels*, of all Baitz's work, is closest to his family experience. From seven to seventeen, he observed the kind of life led by his fictional couple. International in the reaches of its corporate corruption, the play moves from Tangier, Morocco, to St. Thomas in the Virgin Islands, and then to Oaxaca, Mexico. The "end-of-the-day" fortunes of the couple parallel those of Terry and Nan in *The Film Society*.

In his mockery of an age of money, Baitz acknowledges his idols, the nineteenth century Anthony Trollope and William Makepeace Thackeray, and his twentieth century contemporaries, Martin Amis and Julian Barnes.

He wants to bring their richness to his depiction of contemporary society. In his mind, he has mapped out three plays that he intends to be the American equivalent of David Hare's trilogy of dramas about English institutions: *Secret Rapture* (government), *Racing Demon* (religion), and *Murmuring Judges* (justice system).

Bibliography

Baitz, Jon Robin. "The Substance of Robin Baitz." Interview by Porter Anderson. *Theater Week*, April 27-May 3, 1992, 20-24. This interview with Baitz is an important source of biographical information, and it shows Baitz's attitudes (resulting from his personal experiences) toward society.

Grimes, William. "The Playwright as Modern Day Moralist." *The New York Times*, May 7, 1992, p. C1, 6. In this overview of three Baitz plays, Grimes links them with biographical information, including the author's homosexuality, not yet dealt with in a major way in his plays.

Rich, Frank. "Baitz's Mockery of an Age of Money." Review of *The End of the Day. The New York Times*, April 8, 1992, p. C17, 21. Calling attention to Baitz's possible youthful excess, Rich reviews *The End of the Day*, paying special attention to the author's flamboyant style and the unprecedented integrity with which Roger Rees plays a man with a complete lack of integrity.

_____. "Resisting the Vortex by Living a Life of Books and Anger." Review of *The Substance of Fire. The New York Times*, March 18, 1991, p. C11. Rich analyzes the major themes of *The Substance of Fire* and sees Isaac as a harbinger of a major playwriting career.

_____. "School as a Symbol of a Society in Decline." Review of *The Film Society. The New York Times*, July 22, 1988, p. C3. Rich's review of *The Film Society* deals with the ambiguities of Baitz's style and themes, focusing on his wit and some weaknesses as well.

Rothstein, Mervyn. "Out of South Africa." *The New York Times*, August 2, 1988, p. C15. Rothstein connects Baitz's South African experience with his dramatization of that experience in *The Film Society*.

_____. "A Play Born from the Friendship Between an Author and an Actor." *The New York Times*, March 28, 1991, p. C11. Rothstein interviews both Baitz and Ron Rifkin, with emphasis on the career of Rifkin, for whom Baitz wrote the role of Isaac in *The Substance of Fire*.

Susan Rusinko

JAMES BALDWIN

Born: New York, New York; August 2, 1924
Died: St. Paul de Vence, France; November 30, 1987

Principal drama
The Amen Corner, pr. 1954, pb. 1968; *Blues for Mister Charlie*, pr., pb. 1964; *A Deed from the King of Spain*, pr. 1974.

Other literary forms
Best known for his novels and essays, James Baldwin contributed to every contemporary genre except poetry. Baldwin established his literary reputation with *Go Tell It on the Mountain* (1953), a novel which anticipates the thematic concerns of *The Amen Corner*. Subsequent novels, including *Another Country* (1962), *If Beale Street Could Talk* (1974), and *Just Above My Head* (1979), along with the brilliant story "Sonny's Blues" (1957) confirmed Baldwin's stature as a leading figure in postwar American fiction. Several of Baldwin's early essays, collected in *Notes of a Native Son* (1955) and *Nobody Knows My Name: More Notes of a Native Son* (1961), are today recognized as classics; his essays on Richard Wright, "Everybody's Protest Novel" (1949) and "Many Thousands Gone" (1951), occupy a central position in the development, during the 1950's, of "universalist" African-American thought. *The Fire Next Time* (1963), perhaps Baldwin's most important work of nonfiction, is an extended meditation on the relationship of race, religion, and the individual experience. *No Name in the Street* (1971), emphasizing the failure of the United States to heed the warning of *The Fire Next Time*, asserts the more militant political stance articulated in *Blues for Mister Charlie*. Less formal and intricate, though in some cases more explicit, statements of Baldwin's positions can be found in *A Rap on Race* (1971), an extended discussion with Margaret Mead, and *A Dialogue: James Baldwin and Nikki Giovanni* (1975). Of special interest in relation to Baldwin's drama are the unfilmed scenario *One Day, When I Was Lost: A Scenario Based on "The Autobiography of Malcolm X"* (1972) and *The Devil Finds Work: An Essay* (1976), which focuses on Baldwin's personal and aesthetic frustrations with the American film industry.

Achievements
Baldwin's image as an African-American racial spokesman during the 1950's and 1960's guarantees his place in American cultural history. His fiction and essays, both aesthetically and as charts of the movement from universalism to militancy in African-American thought, have earned for him serious and lasting attention. Nevertheless, Baldwin's significance as a dramatist remains problematic. In large part because of Baldwin's high public visibility, *Blues for Mister Charlie* was greeted as a major cultural

event when it opened on Broadway at the ANTA Theater on April 23, 1964. Baldwin's most direct expression of political anger to that time, the play echoed the warning to white America sounded in *The Fire Next Time*, the essay that had catapulted Baldwin to prominence in the mass media. Despite its immediate impact, however, *Blues for Mister Charlie* failed to win lasting support. Numerous African-American critics, particularly those associated with the community theater movement of the late 1960's, dismissed the play as an attempt to attract a mainstream white audience. Mainstream critics, drawing attention to the contradiction between Baldwin's political theme and his attack on protest writing in "Everybody's Protest Novel," dismissed the play as strident propaganda. Critics of diverse perspectives united in dismissing the play as theatrically static. The play's closing, following a four-month run, underscored its failure to realize the early hopes for a new era in African-American theater on Broadway. Ironically, Baldwin's reputation as a dramatist now rests primarily on *The Amen Corner*, a relatively obscure play written in the early 1950's, produced under the direction of Owen Dodson at Howard University in 1954, and brought to Broadway for a twelve-week run only in April, 1965, as an attempt to capitalize on the interest generated by *Blues for Mister Charlie*. Examining the tension between religious and secular experience, *The Amen Corner* maintains some interest as an anticipation of the thematic and structural use of music in African-American plays during the Black Arts Movement. Although Baldwin's drama fails to live up to the standards set by his prose, the heated public discussion surrounding *Blues for Mister Charlie* attests its historical importance as one element in the political and aesthetic transition from the nonviolent universalism of African-American thought in the 1950's to the militant nationalism of the 1960's.

Biography

James Baldwin once dismissed his childhood as "the usual bleak fantasy." Nevertheless, the major concerns of his writing consistently reflect the social context of his family life in Harlem during the Depression. The dominant figure of Baldwin's childhood was his stepfather, David Baldwin, who worked as a manual laborer and preached in a storefront church. Clearly the model for Gabriel Grimes in *Go Tell It on the Mountain*, David Baldwin had moved from New Orleans to New York City, where he married James's mother, Emma Berdis. The oldest of what was to become a group of nine children in the household, James assumed much of the responsibility for the care of his half brothers and sisters. Insulated somewhat from the brutality of Harlem street life by his domestic duties, Baldwin sought refuge in the Church. Following a conversion experience in 1938, Baldwin preached as a youth minister for several years. At the same time, he began to read, immersing himself in works such as Harriet Beecher Stowe's *Uncle Tom's Cabin* (1852) and the novels of Charles Dickens. Both at his Harlem junior high school, where the African-American poet Countée Cullen was one of his teachers, and at his predominantly white Bronx high school, Baldwin contributed to student literary publications. The combination of family tension, economic hardship, and religious vocation provides the focus of much of Baldwin's greatest writing, most notably *Go Tell It on the Mountain*, *The Fire Next Time*, and *Just Above My Head*.

If Baldwin's experience during the 1930's provided his material, his life from 1942 to 1948 shaped his characteristic approach to that material. After he was graduated from high school in 1942, Baldwin worked for a year as a manual laborer in New Jersey, an experience which increased both his understanding of his stepfather and his insight into America's economic and racial systems. Moving to Greenwich Village in 1944, Baldwin worked during the day and wrote at night for the next five years; his first national reviews and essays appeared in 1946. The major event of the Village years, however, was Baldwin's meeting with Richard Wright in the winter of 1944-1945. Wright's interest helped Baldwin acquire a Eugene F. Saxton Memorial Trust Fellowship and then a Rosenwald Fellowship, enabling him to move to Paris in 1948.

After his arrival in France, Baldwin experienced more of the poverty which had shaped his childhood. Simultaneously, he developed a larger perspective on the psychocultural context conditioning his experience, feeling at once a greater sense of freedom and a larger sense of the global structure of racism, particularly as reflected in the French treatment of North Africans. In addition, he formed many of the personal and literary friendships which contributed to his later public prominence. Baldwin's well-publicized literary feud with Wright, who viewed the younger writer's criticism of *Native Son* (1940) as a form of personal betrayal, helped establish Baldwin as a major presence in African-American letters. Although Baldwin's first novel, *Go Tell It on the Mountain*, was well received critically, it was not so financially successful that he could devote his full time to creative writing. Returning to the United States briefly in 1954-1955, he saw Dodson's production of *The Amen Corner* at Howard University. For several years, he continued to travel widely, frequently on journalistic assignments, while writing the novel *Giovanni's Room* (1956), which is set in France and involves no black characters.

Returning to the United States as a journalist covering the civil rights movement, Baldwin made his first trip to the American South in 1957. The essays and reports describing that physical and psychological journey propelled Baldwin to the position of public prominence that he maintained for more than a decade. During the height of the movement, Baldwin lectured widely and was present at major events such as the march on Washington and the voter registration drive in Selma, Alabama. In addition, he met with most of the major African-American activists of the period, including Martin Luther King, Jr., Elijah Muhammad, James Meredith, and Medgar Evers. Attorney General Robert Kennedy requested that Baldwin bring together the most influential voices in the black community; even though the resulting meeting accomplished little, the request testifies to Baldwin's image as a focal point of African-American opinion. In addition to this political activity, Baldwin formed personal and literary relationships—frequently tempestuous ones—with numerous white writers, including William Styron and Norman Mailer. A surge in literary popularity, reflected in the presence of *Another Country* and *The Fire Next Time* on the best-seller lists throughout most of 1962 and 1963, accompanied Baldwin's political success and freed him from financial insecurity for the first time. His experiences with the civil rights movement shaped both the narrative material and the political perspective of *Blues for Mister Charlie.*

Partly because of Baldwin's involvement with prominent whites and partly because of the sympathy for homosexuals evinced in his writing, several black militants, most notably Eldridge Cleaver, attacked Baldwin's position as "black spokesman" beginning in the late 1960's. As a result, nationalist spokesmen such as Amiri Baraka and Bobby Seale gradually eclipsed Baldwin in the literary and political spotlight. Nevertheless, Baldwin, himself sympathetic to many of the militant positions, would continue his involvement with public issues, such as the fate of the Wilmington, North Carolina prisoners—an issue which he addressed in an open letter to Jimmy Carter shortly after Carter's election to the presidency. In the early 1980's, Baldwin returned to the South to assess the changes of the last three decades and to examine the meaning of events such as the Atlanta child murders.

Shuttling back and forth between France, where he felt accepted, and the United States, where he felt needed, Baldwin spent the last years of his life between two worlds. The French government made him a Commander of the Legion of Honor in 1986. At the same time, however, the Federal Bureau of Investigation (FBI) generated a 609-page investigative file on his political activities.

Although Baldwin was largely eclipsed in his role as racial spokesman in the 1970's and 1980's, the publication of his collected essays in 1985 and his death in 1987 brought him back into the headlines and led to a reassessment of his life and work. Some critics demurred that Baldwin's celebrity derived principally from his status as a vocal African-American writer rather than from great literary talent, but most observers, stressing Baldwin's passion and honesty, were more generous in their judgments. At Baldwin's funeral, Amiri Baraka delivered a eulogy that praised the late writer for making African Americans feel "that we could defend ourselves or define ourselves, that we were in the world not merely as animate slaves, but as terrifyingly sensitive measurers of what is good or evil, beautiful or ugly. This is the power of his spirit."

Analysis

James Baldwin's plays, like his best prose, examine the self-defeating attempts of characters to protect themselves against suffering by categorizing experience in terms of simplistic dichotomies. Like *Go Tell It on the Mountain*, *The Amen Corner* concentrates on the failure of the dichotomy between "Temple" and "Street" to articulate the experience of the congregation of a Harlem storefront church. Like *The Fire Next Time* and *Another Country*, *Blues for Mister Charlie* emphasizes the black-white dichotomy shaping the murderous racial conflict that devastates both blacks and whites psychologically. Where Baldwin's fiction ultimately suggests some means of transcending these tensions, however, his plays frequently remain enmeshed in dramatic structures which inadvertently perpetuate the dichotomies they ostensibly challenge. Paradoxically, Baldwin's problems as a playwright derive from his strengths as a novelist. His use of the tradition of African-American folk preaching as the base for a narrative voice capable of taking on a powerful presence of its own frequently results in static didacticism when linked to a character on stage. Similarly, the emphasis on the importance of silence in his novels highlights the tendency of his plays to make explicit aspects of awareness which his characters would be highly unlikely to articulate even to themselves. As a result, conceptually powerful passages in which characters confront the tension between their ideals and experiences tend to freeze the rhythm onstage. As African-American playwright Carlton Molette observed in a comment that applies equally well to *Blues for Mister Charlie*, "*The Amen Corner* is at its worst as a play precisely when it is at its best as literature."

Nowhere are these difficulties seen more clearly than in Baldwin's treatment of the tension between institutionalized religion and moral integrity in *The Amen Corner*. Like *Go Tell It on the Mountain*, *The Amen Corner* challenges the dichotomy between the holy Temple and the sinful Street, a tension which shapes the play's entire dramatic structure. Accepted unquestioningly by most members of Sister Margaret Alexander's congregation, the dichotomy reflects a basic survival strategy of blacks making the transition from their rural Southern roots to the urban North during the Great Migration. By dividing the world into zones of safety and danger, church members attempt to distance themselves and, perhaps more important, their loved ones from the brutalities of the city. As Baldwin comments in his introduction to the play, Sister Margaret faces the dilemma of "how to treat her husband and her son as men and at the same time to protect them from the bloody consequences of trying to be a man in this society."

In act 1, Margaret attempts to resolve the dilemma by forcing her son David, a musician in his late teens, into the role of servant of the Lord while consigning her estranged husband Luke, a jazz musician, to the role of worldly tempter. Having witnessed the brutal impact of Harlem on Luke, she strives to protect her son by creating a world entirely separate from his father's. Ultimately, however, the attempt fails as David's emerging sense of self drives him to confront a wider range of experience; meanwhile, Luke's physical collapse, which takes place in the "safe zone," forces Margaret to acknowledge her own evasions. The most important of these, which reveals Margaret's claim to moral purity as self-constructed illusion, involves her claim that Luke abandoned his family; in fact, she fled from him to avoid the pain caused by the death of a newborn daughter, a pain associated with sexuality and the Street.

As he did in *Go Tell It on the Mountain*, Baldwin treats the collapse of the dichotomies as a potential source of artistic and spiritual liberation. David recognizes that his development as a musician demands immersion in both the sacred and the secular traditions of African-American music; Margaret attempts to redefine herself in terms not of holiness but of an accepting love imaged in her clutching Luke's trombone mouthpiece after his death. Both resolutions intimate a synthesis of Temple and Street, suggesting the common impulse behind the gospel music and jazz which sound throughout the play. The emotional implications of the collapse of the dichotomies in *The Amen Corner* are directly articulated when, following her acknowledgment that the vision on which she bases her authority as preacher was her own creation, Margaret says: "It's a awful thing to think about, the way love never dies!" This second "vision" marks a victory much more profound than that of the church faction which casts Margaret out at the end of the play. Ironically, the new preacher, Sister Moore, seems destined to perpetuate Margaret's moral failings. Although Sister Moore's rise to power is grounded primarily in the congregation's dissatisfaction with Margaret's inability to connect her spiritual life with the realities of the Street (Margaret refuses to sympathize with a woman's marital difficulties or to allow a man to take a job driving a liquor truck), she fails to perceive the larger implications of the dissatisfaction. Sister Moore's inability to see the depth of Margaret's transformed sense of love suggests that the simplifying dichotomies will continue to shape the congregation's experience.

Thematically and psychologically, then, *The Amen Corner* possesses a great deal of potential power. Theatrically, however, it fails to exploit this potential. Despite Baldwin's awareness that "the ritual of the church, historically speaking, comes out of the theater, the *communion* which is the theater," the structure of *The Amen Corner* emphasizes individual alienation rather than ritual reconciliation. In part because the play's power in performance largely derives from the energy of the music played in the church, the street side of Baldwin's vision remains relatively abstract. Where the brilliant prose of *Go Tell It on the Mountain* suggests nuances of perception which remain only half-conscious to John Grimes during his transforming vision, David's conversations with Luke and Margaret focus almost exclusively on his rebellion against the Temple while leaving the terms of the dichotomy unchallenged. In act 3, similarly, Margaret's catharsis seems static. The fact that Margaret articulates her altered awareness in her preacher's voice suggests a lingering commitment to the Temple at odds with Baldwin's thematic design. Although the sacred music emanating from the church is theoretically balanced by the jazz trombone associated with Luke, most of the performance power adheres to the gospel songs that provide an embodied experience of call and response; taken out of its performance context, the jazz seems a relatively powerless expression. As a result, *The Amen Corner* never escapes from the sense of separation it conceptually attacks.

Blues for Mister Charlie reconsiders the impact of simplistic dichotomies in explicitly political terms. Dedicated to the murdered civil rights leader Medgar Evers and the four black children killed in a 1963 Birmingham terrorist bombing, the play reflects both Baldwin's increasing anger and his continuing search for a unified moral being. Loosely basing his plot on the case of Emmett Till, a black youth murdered for allegedly insulting a white woman in Mississippi, Baldwin focuses his attention on the unpunished white murderer of Richard Henry, who is killed after returning to his minister father's Southern home to recover from a drug addiction. Baldwin establishes a black-white division onstage as an extension of the sacred-secular dichotomy; the two primary sets are a black church and a white courthouse, both of which are divided into two areas, Whitetown and Blacktown. Underscoring the actual interdependence of the constituting terms, Baldwin insists in his stage directions that the audience be aware of the courthouse flag throughout scenes set in the church and of the Cross during scenes set in the courthouse. Periodically, the dialogue brings the connections between seemingly disparate realities into the foreground. Richard's father, Meridian, responds to the liberal white newspaperman Parnell's surprise over the intensity of rage and hatred in the black community following Richard's death: "You've heard it before. You just never recognized it before. You've heard it in all those blues and spirituals and gospel songs you claim to love so much." The tentative rapprochement of Parnell, Meridian, and Richard's lover Juanita at the end of the play provides an image of a potential community capable of acknowledging the complexity of transforming both the rage and the past failures of perception into a political and moral action. When Parnell, employing a term with particularly charged meaning in the context of the Southern civil rights movement, asks if he can "join you on the march," Juanita's tempered acceptance—"we can walk in the same direction"—represents a profound attempt not to invert the black-white dichotomy following the acquittal of Richard's murderer, Lyle Britten, an acquittal in which Parnell is implicated by his inability to challenge the underlying structure of the white legal system.

As background for this resolution, Baldwin develops three central themes: the growing anger of young blacks, the impact of this anger on the older members of the black community, and the white psychology which enables apparently normal individuals to perpetrate atrocities without remorse. The theme of anger focuses on Richard, whose experiences both in New York and Mississippi generate an intense bitterness against all whites. Articulating a militant credo which Baldwin finds emotionally comprehensible but morally inadequate, Richard tells his grandmother, "I'm going to treat every one of them as though they were responsible for all the crimes that ever happened in the history of the world—oh, yes! They're responsible for all the misery I've ever seen . . . the only way the black man's going to get any power is to drive all the white men into the sea." Backed up by his vow to carry a gun with him at all times, Richard's militancy comes into direct conflict with his grandmother's and his father's traditional values of endurance, hope, and Christian compassion. Ironically, Richard's compassion for his grandmother leads him to give his gun to his father, an act which leaves him defenseless when attacked by Lyle. Baldwin suggests that some adjustment between unbridled violence and naïve faith will be necessary if blacks are to put an end to their victimization without emulating the moral failures of their white persecutors.

Baldwin's comments on *Blues for Mister Charlie* emphasize the importance of the portrait of the white persecutor to his overall design. Attributing his reluctance to write drama to a "deeper fear," Baldwin stresses his desire to overcome his own dichotomizing impulses and "to draw a valid portrait of the murderer." Unfortunately, the dramatic presentation of Lyle Britten in many ways fails to fulfill this desire. Obsessed with racial honor, especially as it involves white women, Lyle seems more sociological exemplar than rounded individual. Despite the fact that he has had at least one sexual relationship with a black woman, Lyle's obsession with interracial sex, grounded in a deep insecurity which leads him to respond violently to any perceived threat to his sense of masculine superiority, dominates every aspect of his character. While sociological works such as Joel Kovel's *White Racism: A Psychohistory* (1970) and Calvin Hernton's *Sex and Racism in America* (1965) support the general accuracy of the diagnosis, Baldwin nevertheless fails to demonstrate its relation to aspects of Lyle's experience not directly involved with the obsession. Lyle's monologues on his poor white heritage and his sexual experience sound stilted and contrived, especially when juxtaposed to a generally unconvincing presentation of whites in the play. Parnell's monologue on "the holy, the liberating orgasm," for example, seems more a didactic parody of Norman Mailer's *The White Negro* (1957) than an aspect of his character.

Although in his fiction Baldwin demonstrates a profound understanding of the psychological reality and aesthetic power of silence, *Blues for Mister Charlie* veers sharply toward an overelaboration which undercuts the validity of his portrait of the white persecutors. This in turn weighs the play more heavily than Baldwin intended toward the black perspective, reinforcing rather than challenging the underlying dichotomy. The conversations among Parnell, Lyle, and Lyle's wife, Jo, concerning their attitudes toward race and sex seem wooden and static largely because they articulate attitudes that if consciously acknowledged would dictate changes in behavior in any realistic, as opposed to demoniac, characters. Although it would be possible to interpret the monologues as Eugene O'Neill-style "stream-of-unconsciousness" passages, the dialogue subverts the effectiveness of the technique, suggesting that Baldwin has simply failed to come to terms with the silence of his characters' personalities. Although *Blues for Mister Charlie* advances Baldwin's belief that imposing dichotomies on experience leads inexorably to emotional and physical violence, it nevertheless perpetuates a dichotomy between abstract statement and concrete experience. Baldwin's decision not to return to drama after *Blues for Mister Charlie* seems an acknowledgment that he is much more comfortable with forms in which his voice can assume a concrete reality of its own, transforming tensions that in his drama remain unresolved.

Other major works

NOVELS: *Go Tell It on the Mountain*, 1953; *Giovanni's Room*, 1956; *Another Country*, 1962; *Tell Me How Long the Train's Been Gone*, 1968; *If Beale Street Could Talk*, 1974; *Just Above My Head*, 1979.

SHORT FICTION: *Going to Meet the Man*, 1965.

NONFICTION: *Notes of a Native Son*, 1955; *Nobody Knows My Name: More Notes of a Native Son*, 1961; *The Fire Next Time*, 1963; *Nothing Personal*, 1964 (with Richard Avedon); *No Name in the Street*, 1971; *A Rap on Race*, 1971 (with Margaret Mead); *A Dialogue: James Baldwin and Nikki Giovanni*, 1975; *The Devil Finds Work: An Essay*, 1976; *The Evidence of Things Not Seen*, 1985; *The Price of the Ticket: Collected Nonfiction, 1948-1985*, 1985; *Conversations with James Baldwin*, 1989.

SCREENPLAYS: *One Day, When I Was Lost: A Scenario Based on "The Autobiography of Malcolm X,"* 1972 (unfilmed); *The Inheritance*, 1973.

CHILDREN'S LITERATURE: *Little Man, Little Man*, 1975.

Bibliography

Fabré, Michel. *From Harlem to Paris: Black American Writers in France, 1840-*

1980. Chicago: University of Illinois Press, 1991. A chapter on Baldwin's Paris experiences, "James Baldwin in Paris: Love and Self-Discovery," brings biographical details to the European experiences of the bicontinental playwright, who owed France "his own spiritual growth, through the existential discovery of love as a key to life." The notes offer interview sources of quotations for further study.

O'Daniel, Therman B. *James Baldwin: A Critical Evaluation.* Washington, D.C.: Howard University Press, 1977. A full study of Baldwin's accomplishments in all genres, with some twenty-three articles. Particularly informative are Carlton W. Molette's examination of Baldwin as playwright, Darwin T. Turner's study of Baldwin as a distinctly African-American dramatist, and Waters E. Turpin's brief "Note on *Blues for Mister Charlie.*" Supplemented by a classified bibliography and an index.

Porter, Horace A. *Stealing the Fire: The Art and Protest of James Baldwin.* Middletown, Conn.: Wesleyan University Press, 1989. Concentrates on Baldwin's literary output rather than his political biography and assesses his talents in the face of the necessity of social themes. Strong discussion of Harriet Beecher Stowe and Richard Wright as influences.

Standley, Fred L., and Nancy V. Standley. *James Baldwin: A Reference Guide.* Boston: G. K. Hall, 1980. A comprehensive bibliography with more than three thousand entries, meticulously annotated, sometimes with almost essay-long commentary. A complicated index aids searches, once mastered. The book is divided into works by Baldwin, generically listed alphabetically, and works about Baldwin, listed chronologically and alphabetically.

Troupe, Quincy, ed. *James Baldwin: The Legacy.* New York: Simon & Schuster, 1989. A collection of essays by and about Baldwin, with a foreword by Wole Soyinka. Contains eighteen essays, five of which were written for this collection, and homage and celebration from many who were profoundly influenced by Baldwin, including Pat Mikell's account of Baldwin's last days in St. Paul de Vence. Brief bibliography.

Weatherby, W. J. *James Baldwin: Artist on Fire.* New York: Donald I. Fine, 1989. A portrait by a personal friend of some twenty-eight years, this study is both insightful and scholarly. The "Baldwin on Broadway" chapter covers the production of *Blues for Mister Charlie* and *The Amen Corner*, and Baldwin's often stormy relationship with the Actors Studio and Lincoln Center; "Down South" discusses a thwarted dramatization of *Giovanni's Room* and Baldwin's special affection for Elia Kazan. Photos and index.

Craig Werner
(Updated by *Thomas J. Taylor*
and *Robert McClenaghan*)

JOHN BALE

Born: Cove, England; November 21, 1495
Died: Canterbury, England; November, 1563

Principal drama

King Johan, wr. 1531(?), pb. 1538, pr. 1539(?); *Three Laws*, wr. 1531(?), pb. 1547; *God's Promises*, wr. 1538, pb. 1547; *John Baptist*, wr. 1538, pb. 1547; *The Temptation*, wr. 1538, pb. 1547; *The Dramatic Writings of John Bale*, pb. 1907 (John S. Farmer, editor).

Other literary forms

A Carmelite friar and scholar turned Protestant propagandist, John Bale wrote literary history, chronicle history, and religious polemics as well as verse drama. While a Carmelite, he edited some devotional works and compiled several Latin-language catalogs of the Order's practices and history in England. His *Illustrium Maioris Britanniae Scriptorum* (famous writers of Great Britain), first issued in 1548, subsequently revised and retitled in 1557, gave biographical information about the important writers of England, Scotland, and Wales and listed the titles and dates of their works.

Bale wrote chronicles of persons he deemed noteworthy Protestant martyrs: *A Brief Chronicle of Sir John Oldcastle, the Lord Cobham* (1544), *The First Examination of Anne Askew* (1546), and *The Latter Examination of Anne Askew* (1547).

A bitter opponent of the traditional Catholicism, from which he converted in mid-life, Bale wrote polemics combining dialogue with diatribe. He interpreted the pope as the Antichrist in *The Image of Both Churches* (part 1, 1541; part 2, 1545; part 3, 1547). In *The Acts of English Votaries* (1546), Bale attacked the behavior of those in religious orders. He disputed the positions of various Catholic apologists in the verse tract *An Answer to a Papistical Exhortation* (1548), and in prose in *An Expostulation Against the Blasphemies of a Frantic Papist* (1552) and *The Apology of John Bale Against a Rank Papist* (c. 1555). Bale attacked the papacy in *Acta Romanorum Pontificum* (1558; acts of the Roman pontiffs), and he criticized opponents nearer to home in his book *A Declaration Concerning the Clergy of London* (1561).

Bale edited a work on the sacrament of Holy Communion by John Lambert, *A Treatise to Henry VIII* (c. 1548). In 1538, he translated from the German Thomas Kirchmayer's Protestant play *Pammachius*, though his translation is not extant. Bale's *The True History of the Christian Departing of Martin Luther* (1546) is a translation of German accounts originally collected by Justus Jonas, Michael Cellius, and Joannes Aurifaber.

Achievements

A controversialist living in chaotic times, Bale is known less for originality in his own work than for setting precedents which other talents brought
to flower.

Bale's own literary catalogs include a sprinkling of medieval trivia, such
as attribution of certain literary works to the biblical Adam, yet his work
provided a model for persistence in research, acknowledgment of sources,
and comparative thoroughness in the entries on the writers of his own era.
Modern literary biographers are still drawing on Bale's *Illustrium Maioris
Britanniae Scriptorum* and its expanded editions for information on sixteenth century writers.

In his time, Bale was known for his Protestant propaganda, which
attacked various doctrines and practices of Roman Catholic tradition as
well as the views of other Protestants whom Bale believed to be extreme or
misguided. Hence, in all genres, dogmatic Protestant zeal motivated his
writing.

Bale's chronicle on Sir John Oldcastle was intended to rehabilitate the
fourteenth century nobleman's reputation. As a follower of early reformer
and Bible translator John Wycliffe, Oldcastle was depicted unfavorably in
traditional records. Bale's wish that Protestant martyrs be viewed sympathetically was not unique, but according to his friend John Foxe, Bale's
chronicle influenced in perspective and substance the histories written by
Edward Hall and Raphael Holinshed, as well as Foxe's *The Book of Martyrs* (1559). All three writers reflected to some degree a break from traditional Catholic perspectives, and the chronicles of Hall and of Holinshed
were to become sources for William Shakespeare's history plays.

Although Bale recorded titles of twenty-one plays that he wrote, only
five are extant. The titles of the lost works, such as *Against Adulterators of
God's Word, Christ's Passion*, and *Simon the Leper*, imply that the lost
plays share the dogmatic purpose and medieval conventions of the plays
that survive.

The extant play *King Johan*, however, includes a basic innovation which
later writers worked to full advantage. Among the familiar walking, talking
abstractions of the morality play's virtue and vice characters, Bale placed
the thirteenth century monarch King Johan (King John) and a few of his
historical enemies. King Johan's ill repute easily outlasted Bale's attempt to
make him a Protestant saint and hero of English sovereignty and therefore
a villain to Roman Catholic historians. Still, *King Johan* is a prototype
drama including historical persons and events in English theater. The history plays of Shakespeare and Christopher Marlowe display far greater
sophistication in plot, characterization, and theatricality, but Bale set the
precedent for the history play as a type. He also, in perspective and substance, influenced the chronicle histories of Hall and Holinshed that Shake-

speare used extensively in writing his history plays and stirred the debate over Sir John Oldcastle's true character that gave Shakespeare material for his rascal Falstaff.

Biography

John Bale included autobiographical notes in his literary catalogs. Beginning with those entries, then studying correspondence between Bale and his contemporaries and reviewing official records of the era, Jesse W. Harris has provided considerable background data in his book *John Bale: A Study in the Minor Literature of the Reformation* (1940), to which the following summary is indebted.

Bale was born to Henry and Margaret Bale at Cove, County Suffolk, near Dunwich, England. At age twelve, he began study with the Carmelite friars at Norwich, whose monastery had a good library. Bale learned Latin, the rites and customs of the Order, and the principles of careful study and research.

In 1514, Bale entered Jesus College in Cambridge University. College policy apparently required that he reside at Jesus College rather than with fellow Carmelites in lodgings that the order maintained at the university. When Bale arrived at Cambridge, interest in the New Learning was high and Continental Reformation influences were strong; Erasmus, the Dutch theologian and New Testament scholar, was in residence there. A number of Bale's fellow students, including Hugh Latimer, Thomas Cranmer, Stephen Gardiner, and Matthew Parker, were to become important figures in the religious and political struggles that erupted when Henry VIII assumed control of the English Church and that did not significantly subside until after the accession of Elizabeth I.

Bale took his bachelor of divinity in 1529 and his doctor of divinity not long afterward. He served briefly as prior of the Carmelite monastery in Maldon in 1530, then moved to the priory at Doncaster. In 1533, he became prior at Ipswich, not far from his hometown of Cove; by then, he had a reputation for unorthodox teaching. One William Broman, when questioned about his religious views in 1535, testified that Bale had taught him in Doncaster in 1531 that Christ was not physically present in the Eucharist.

At Ipswich, Bale grew close to Thomas Wentworth, an active Protestant who led the unorthodox friar to act more decisively on his reform convictions. Bale converted to Protestantism, left the priesthood, and married a young woman named Dorothy. On the strength of some fourteen Protestant plays already written for patron John de Vere, Wentworth recommended Bale to Thomas Cromwell, a major power in the Protestant movement. Cromwell encouraged Bale to continue writing plays and other materials to further the Protestant cause. On at least two occasions, Bale's outspoken views brought sanctions from authorities. He even spent time in Greenwich jail, but Cromwell was able to bring pressure to bear on the authorities involved, and Bale was released.

For several years, the nature of the Church in England was fiercely debated. Henry VIII's assumption of headship did not eradicate in one stroke all the centuries of Roman Catholic tradition in England, and among those who called for reform, there was no consensus on how much reform was enough. The relative influence of various factions waxed and waned. For a time, Cromwell's influence was substantial. Anne Boleyn's execution in 1536, however, set off a wave of pro-Catholic activity. By 1540, Henry VIII was less worried about the definition of the national Church than he was about the deep divisions within the body politic. He moved to solve his political problems as he had his personal problems—by execution. To be fair, he beheaded or burned three Catholic and three Protestant leaders, including Cromwell.

His patron gone, Bale fled with his wife and children to the Continent in 1540. He presumably spent time in Holland, Switzerland, and northern Germany. The publication notices in books he issued while in Europe cite places of publication such as Basle, Switzerland; Antwerp, Belgium; and Wesel, Germany. Collateral evidence indicates that he sometimes published in cities where he lived at the time. On occasion, too, whether because of a publishing opportunity or because of concern for personal safety, his works were published in cities where he did not reside. A few items were issued under pseudonyms.

In Europe, Bale developed further contacts with various reform leaders and continued his relationship with a number of exiled English Protestants as well. Meanwhile, his writings continued to stir controversy at home in England. In 1546, his books were banned along with the writings of several other authors, including the Bible translators John Wycliffe and Miles Coverdale. Bale's work on Anne Askew was particularly disturbing to the authorities.

In 1547, Henry VIII was succeeded by his nine-year-old son, Edward VI. The council of regents advising the boy-king was predominantly Protestant. Bishop Stephen Gardiner, who had strongly opposed Bale's writings, was imprisoned in the Tower of London. Bale then returned to England.

Through 1551, Bale continued research for his literary histories and continued writing in support of the Reformation. He was appointed rector of Bishopstoke, Hampshire, in June of 1551, and later of Swaffham, Norfolk. In August of 1552, Edward VI appointed Bale Bishop of Ossory in Ireland. Given the staunch Catholic convictions among most of the Irish clergy and laity in his bishopric, Bale provoked continually bitter conflict by attempting to limit or abolish various traditional customs and forms of worship.

Edward VI died in July of 1553 to be succeeded by Mary I, also known as Bloody Mary because of the number of executions carried out during her reign. The Catholic queen brought a return of Catholic influence to the court and to the English Church. Mary released Bishop Stephen Gardiner from the Tower to be her Lord Chancellor. Thereafter, an English translation of Gardiner's *De Vera Obedientia* (1553; of true obedience) began to circulate in England. Written in earlier days to support King Henry VIII's break with Rome, the book was a certain irritant to the older and more conservative Gardiner, in service to a Catholic queen. Bale is suspected of having done the English translation.

During 1554 and 1555, Bale lived in Frankfurt, Germany. When the English exile Church in Frankfurt split over issues of forms of worship, Bale and his friend John Foxe moved to Switzerland and stayed with a printer, Johannes Oporinus, who issued Bale's literary histories in 1557 and 1559.

Elizabeth I succeeded Mary in 1558. In 1559, Bale returned to England. Other Protestant churchmen were appointed to bishoprics. Bale was named to a prebendary, a modest position at Canterbury. He continued research and writing, though ill, and made many appeals to friends and officials for help in recovering books and manuscripts he had left in Ireland in 1553. Unfortunately, not even a letter from Queen Elizabeth could produce results. Bale died at Canterbury in November of 1563.

Analysis

Discussion of John Bale's drama requires some background on the theatrical conventions of the times. At festivals, common folk enjoyed song, dance, games, and ritual skits satirizing the nobility and the clergy. Some plays were enacted, drawing from English folklore. Also in medieval England there had developed a tradition of religious instruction through drama. Certain towns presented annual cycles of plays, productions lasting three days and made up of individual plays dramatizing selected Bible stories. Such series were designed to present a Christian worldview from the creation of Adam through the life of Christ and on to the Last Judgment. The religious purpose, however, did not preclude use of humorous, even bawdy, stage business and dialogue. Depictions of saints' lives and of moral fables were also common.

Medieval religious drama, which provided a rich heritage for English Renaissance drama, included three major categories: the mystery play, the miracle play, and the morality play. The mystery play drew on liturgy and on episodes of the life of Christ, dramatizing the "mysteries" of divine intervention in the temporal world. The miracle play presented events from lives of saints or martyrs for the purpose of asserting the virtue of faith in divine power and intervention. The morality play personified abstractions such as hope and charity in conflict with vices such as pride or greed in simple stories designed to teach moral, ethical, or theological premises.

Bale's verse drama *God's Promises* fits expectations of the mystery play. While it does not focus on the life of Christ directly, it presents a pattern of biblical characters—Old Testament personalities and John the Baptist from the New Testament—as the essential preface to Christ's coming. It is understood to be a play that Bale would use as the first in a trilogy. Second and third plays would cover Christ's life, death, and resurrection and possibly the Second Coming and Last Judgment.

God's Promises consistently embodies a Christian vision of pre-Christian scriptures as the record of preparation for and prophecy of Christ's appearance on earth. Ancient and medieval theology included searches for proofs of divine order both in the natural world and in Scripture. Numerological formulas were invoked to prove the divine source of Scripture. The number one, for example, was the number of God; three represented the trinity of Father, Son, and Holy Spirit. Six was the number of mortals, while seven, combining the mortal and the divine, was the perfect number.

Bale includes himself as a commentator in *God's Promises*, but the scriptural characters of this seven-act verse drama are seven in number—one divine, *Pater Coelestis* (Heavenly Father), and six mortal: *Adam Primus Homo* (Adam, the First Man), *Justus Noah* (Noah the Righteous), *Abraham Fidelis* (Abraham the Faithful), *Moseh Sanctus* (Moses the Holy), *David Rex Pius* (David the Pious King), *Esaias Prophetas* (Isaiah the Prophet), and *Joannes Baptista* (John the Baptist). Hence, the very structure of the play projects a conventional Christian view of pre-Christian history consisting of six eras leading to a seventh in which Christ appears.

Although one might expect a play featuring Old Testament figures to begin with material from Genesis, Heavenly Father's opening is a Trinitarian self-description that seems a creedal expansion of the first chapter of the Gospel of John. Following Heavenly Father's introduction, which includes references to Adam's fall and God's judgment on both man and woman, Adam enters to plead for mercy. The second act summarizes the era of Noah. Heavenly Father recites the evils which provoked his judgment on mortals, and Noah, like Adam, pleads for mercy. Heavenly Father, in the third act, expresses displeasure over the depravity of Noah's descendants, particularly their falling to idolatry and sodomy. Abraham, on behalf of his nephew Lot, who lives in the vicinity of Sodom and Gomorrah, appeals for mercy. He bargains with Heavenly Father until he secures a promise that God will spare the cities if ten righteous citizens can be found in them. Despite the flood of Noah's era, and despite the witness of faith in Abraham, mortals continue to sin. In the fourth act, Heavenly Father gives the Law to Moses for the people of Israel and for all nations. Dialogue in the fourth act reviews major events of Moses' life—the plagues of Egypt, the Exodus and provision of manna in the desert, Israel's apostasy with the golden calf, and so on. For Israel's idolatry, Heavenly Father again pronounces judgment but tempers his decree with the promise of a prophet to come.

The fifth act sets Heavenly Father in dialogue with David the Pious King. Their exchanges survey the leadership of priests and prophets between the time of Moses and the accession of Saul, David's predecessor. Heavenly Father condemns David for taking the wife of Uriah the Hittite and for taking a national census (a sign of faith in mortal strength rather than in divine protection). David must choose a punishment, but again the judgment is linked with a promise. In David's case, the promise is for the greatness of his son Solomon. Heavenly Father, in the sixth act, discourses with the prophet Isaiah, recounting the infidelity of Israel after Solomon, the split into the kingdoms of Israel and Judah, the Babylonian conquest, and the Babylonian captivity of Israel as punishment for recurrent idolatry. Isaiah, continuing the pattern that Bale has set for his mortal characters in dialogue with Heavenly Father, appeals for mercy. In response, Heavenly Father cites messianic verses from the Old Testament book of Isaiah which Christian tradition has long held to be predictions of Christ's birth.

With John the Baptist, in the seventh act, Heavenly Father surveys events from the time of the Babylonian Captivity through the age of latter prophets, giving special note to the restoration of the temple in Jerusalem and to the religious renewal under King Josiah. In closing, Heavenly Father names John the Baptist the messenger to announce the coming of Christ. In a very clear paraphrase of reactions to divine call in the biblical stories of Moses, Isaiah, and others, John objects, contending that he lacks the learning and eloquence necessary for such awesome duties, but Heavenly Father prevails.

The text of *God's Promises*, then, employs close paraphrase of Scripture and creedal statements throughout. For each era in the schema, Heavenly Father is a rigorous judge, punishing idolatry yet promising some form of relief to come. The emphases in dramatizing these particular characters in dialogue with, and in service to, Heavenly Father are not only traditionally messianic but also decidedly Protestant in their management.

As a friar who left holy orders to marry, Bale offers an interesting view of the Fall of Adam and Eve. Medieval tradition includes much misogynistic coloring of the Fall. Some interpreters made much of Eve's yielding to desire and then inducing Adam to yield to desire as well. Bale, however, poses Heavenly Father attributing Adam's Fall to a failure to use reason. Such a stance might be expected from a reformer quite given to scholarship and seeing in literacy and clear thinking a means to escape what he considered decadent superstition in religion. Furthermore, keeping the responsibility with Adam rather than with Eve, Bale sidesteps a conventional argument for clerical celibacy—namely, that a married cleric would be more concerned with a wife than with his religious duties.

Bale's focus on the Sodom and Gomorrah episode from Abraham's era is a means for him to stress divine judgment upon sodomy. Bale insisted that the rule of celibacy for those in holy orders simply led many to engage in homosexual or illicit heterosexual activity—observing the letter of the vow but not the spirit. Also, every act of *God's Promises* includes condemnation of idolatry. As a Protestant strongly opposed to veneration of saints and sacred relics, Bale keeps the anti-idolatry theme dominant.

In aspects of form other than the structural symbolism mentioned above, *God's Promises* is typical of Bale's style. The lines of verse are roughly pentametric, sometimes straggling into six- or seven-beat lines. End rhymes appear in various groupings, often approximating stanzas of five, seven, or nine lines by interlocking couplets, tercets, and quatrains of sometimes exact, sometimes slant rhyme. The verse functions mainly to keep the great patches of biblical and creedal paraphrase memorable for actors faced with long, set speeches and dialogues only occasionally relieved by some stage business. Religious songs between acts provide some variety, though the texts of certain songs do not seem wholly pertinent to the issues in the bracketing acts. The music itself may be a counter to the radical reform views which minimized or eliminated the role of music in worship.

For *Three Laws*, Bale used the morality play format. The opening is given by *Baleus Prolocutor* (Bale the Commentator). The first act stages the lead character *Deus Pater* (God the Father) calling out the three laws: *Lex Naturae* (the Natural Law), *Moseh Lex* (the Law of Moses, sometimes termed the Law of Bondage), and *Christi Lex* (the Law of Christ, sometimes termed the Law of Grace). At first, as in *God's Promises*, the divinity, God the Father, defines his Triune nature. He then defines each law. The Natural Law has sway in human hearts for three ages: from Adam to Noah, from Noah to Abraham, and from Abraham to Moses. The Law of Moses obtains in another three ages: from Moses to David, from David to the Babylonian Exile, and from the Exile to the appearance of Christ. The Law of Christ dominates the last age. Hence, though the characters staged are abstractions rather than biblical characters, *Three Laws* shares with *God's Promises* Bale's structural reinforcement of numerological symbols. The two sets of three eras equal the mortal number six, and the age of Christ brings the sum to the perfect seven, adding the divine number, one, to the mortal number.

The second act sets Natural Law in dialogue with *Infidelitas* (Infidelity). Natural Law declares, "A knowledge I am whom God in man does hide/ In his whole working to be to him a guide." Infidelity debates the very existence of Natural Law. If, indeed, God has created such an orderly world, why are there severe storms or wild animals that attack people or other extreme disruptions of order? Natural Law answers that such events are divine punishment for disregard of God. Having failed to best Natural Law in debate, Infidelity conjures the demons *Sodomismus* (Sodomy) and *Idolatrias* (Idolatry), who help him overcome Natural Law.

The third act brings the Law of Moses as a successor to Natural Law. To counter the force of the Law of Moses, Infidelity brings in *Avaritia* (Covetousness) and *Ambitio* (Ambition), who render the Law of Moses lame and blind. *Evangelium* (Christ's Gospel) enters in the fourth act to oppose Infidelity. The vice again produces assistants, *Pseudodoctrina* (False Doctrine) and *Hypocrisis* (Hypocrisy), and these three vice characters burn Christ's Gospel at the stake.

Vindicta Dei (God's Wrath) takes the lead in the fifth act. Infidelity offers God's Wrath a bribe to avoid conflict but is confronted and overcome. God the Father recalls the three laws for renewal and cleansing, after which the three sing praise. God the Father then announces restoration of "true faith and religion" and calls in *Fides Christiano* (Christian Faith) for closing doctrinal explanations.

Three Laws includes some passing references to historical figures, such as a comparison of King Henry VIII to the Hebrew reformer-king Josiah, but does not include those historical figures as active characters in the play.

While Bale's anti-Catholicism is occasionally stated outright in *God's Promises*, it runs rampant in *Three Laws*. Costuming notes at the play's end call for visual parodies. Sodomy is to be dressed as a monk, False Doctrine as a "popish doctor," and Hypocrisy as a Gray Friar. Infidelity frequently uses oaths such as "by the mass," and "by St. Stephen"; he also makes a number of coarse, offensive remarks to which the virtuous characters take exception.

Infidelity's introduction of Idolatry continues the anti-Catholic matter. Idolatry is credited with curing toothache, ague, and pox and with conjuring the Devil by saying the Hail Mary. The entrance and introduction of Sodomy carries similar attacks. Sodomy claims that clergy in Rome and elsewhere turn to him because they lack wives and do not fear divine retribution.

Bale builds a long list of Protestant propaganda charges into *Three Laws*: Veneration of saints equals idol worship; the doctrine of purgatory is a device to rob the poor; Latin rites, Scriptures, and prayers censor the true message of the Scriptures, while English is used for those customs and practices which bring cash to church coffers. Bale gives Covetousness a parodic creed that avers faith in the pope rather than faith in God, then continues listing various usages which Bale believed served a corrupt religious establishment while faithful parishioners were misled. Other writers and thinkers in the troubled times of the Reformation and the Counter-Reformation may have been opinionated, even bigoted. Among English writers of his day, Bale was so aggressive that he became known to succeeding generations as "Bilious Bale."

Bale's more noted play, *King Johan*, was probably written several years before 1538, its year of publication. The extant manuscript is likely two or three removes from the original, as its closing lines refer to Queen Elizabeth. The play consists of two long acts, the first with a shift of scene from England to Rome. The entrances and exits of characters, a bit of song, and various opportunities for stage business allow some relief from the steady onslaught of didactic dialogue. Formally, the play lacks the structural concern for symbolism found in *God's Promises* or for the classical convention of five acts as found in *Three Laws*. The political purpose of the drama seems its major shaping force.

The play opens with King Johan declaring that citizens should be loyal to their king, thus following the example of Christ's obedience to civil authorities. England, a widow, enters, complaining that the clergy has abused her rights and estranged her from God, her spouse, by refusing to honor God's word. Sedition derides England, then boasts to King Johan that he, Sedition, has papal authority to overcome secular rulers. King Johan confronts Nobility, Clergy, and Civil Order with the problem. Nobility says that his oath of knighthood requires that he defend the Church. Echoing Peter's denial of Christ, Nobility three times denies knowing Sedition. Civil Order declares loyalty to the king. In debate over the legitimacy of the many religious orders in a single church, Civil Order supports King Johan while Nobility sides with Clergy. The king contends that prayers and masses for the dead counter the premise that Christ's death was efficacious once for all. Nobility, Civil Order, and Clergy all submit to the king and vow to defend the realm. King Johan and Civil Order leave, and Clergy then persuades Nobility to reverse himself and believe what the Church teaches rather than reason for himself.

The scene shifts to Rome. Sedition meets Dissimulation, who, singing a litany, prays to be freed of King Johan. The two vices identify themselves as cousins, sons of Falsehood and Privy Treason, respectively, and as grandsons of Infidelity. Together they boast of various forms that the Church establishment can use for deceit. To help preserve the system, Dissimulation calls in Private Wealth. With Sedition's help, the latter two vices bring in Usurped Power, who reveals that he is Pope Innocent III in unofficial garb. Dissimulation asks the pope's blessing, then reports Clergy's complaints against King Johan of England. He has taxed the clergy, has held them accountable to civil justice rather than leaving offending clergy to ecclesiastical justice, and has forbidden bishops to appeal to Rome. Four English bishops have already pronounced the king excommunicated. He has seized church properties and has collected the revenues from salaries owed to exiled clergy. While the other characters move offstage for costume change, Dissimulation expounds on the measures which the pope will take to counter King Johan.

Returning to stage, the other vices have changed both appearances and identities. Usurped Power has become Pope Innocent III both in costume and in name. Sedition has become Steven Langton, Archbishop of Canterbury. The pope performs a ritual cursing King Johan with bell, book, and candle and declares him excommunicated. To close the first act, an Interpreter appears and summarizes the consequences in England of the king's excommunication and the interdiction of the realm (the banning of the Sacraments in the nation's churches).

In the second act, Nobility bemoans the conflict between king and clergy. Sedition, calling himself Good Perfection, offers Nobility pardon for sin in exchange for support of the Church. Nobility makes confession in rather general terms, but Sedition withholds absolution until Nobility again pledges to oppose King Johan. Met by Clergy and Civil Order, Sedition identifies himself as Archbishop Steven Langton. Clergy kneels for absolution and is presented with parodic relics including a louse and a "turd" from certain saints.

Absolution complete, Langton orders Clergy to provoke insurrection in England. Civil Order, formerly loyal to the king, now sides with the opposition. If the fortunes of the Church decline, so will the fortunes of lawyers.

Private Wealth, dressed as a cardinal, demands that King Johan restore all church property he has seized, accept Langton as Archbishop of Canterbury, and allow the return of all exiled clergy. The king insists that, in taxing the clergy, he is simply following biblical precedent. He offers to accept exiled clergy but balks at the appointment of Langton. At this, Private Wealth officially invokes the papal curse and excommunication of the king as well as the interdiction of the nation.

Nobility, Clergy, and Civil Order report the consequences of the excommunication. King Johan insists that the authority of Scripture is superior to the authority of the pope. He cites instances of Old Testament kings appointing priests. Still, he gains no support from his hearers, who reiterate their ties to the Church.

England again appeals to the king. She brings Commonality, who represents the populace and who is afflicted with poverty and blindness. As cardinal, Private Wealth orders Commonality to leave and advises King Johan to capitulate. Papal influence has raised threats of invasion from Scotland, France, and other lands. The danger is too great for King Johan. He regretfully surrenders his crown to the cardinal, submitting to papal authority and consenting to pay heavy fines.

Treason enters in chains. He recites a catalog of Catholic beliefs and practices in parody as his "crimes," then ends the list with civil felonies including "coin clipping" and counterfeiting. King Johan invokes civil justice and orders him hanged. Treason, however, is a priest. The cardinal releases him and demands that King Johan sign over a third of his realm to a sister-in-law. Widow England, in rebuttal, reports that the woman is dead. Johan confirms his submission to the pope. Sedition leaves to stir up trouble in France. Under the name Simon of Swinsett, Dissimulation concocts poison and drinks half the cup himself in order to ensure that King Johan drinks the rest. Each dies justifying himself. Dissimulation, too, relies on anticipatory pardon for his deed and on prayers and masses being said for his soul.

Verity appears to explain that in chronicles written by traditional churchmen, King Johan cannot but have a bad reputation. Nobility, Clergy, and Civil Order debate the quality of the dead king's life, then repent of their failure to support him. Next appears Imperial Majesty, who presses the trio to support their monarch, not to please the ruler personally, but on biblical authority. Sedition, threatened with hanging, also repents but, once pardoned, insists that papal supporters will continue to seek control of England. Imperial Majesty then reinstates the sentence, and Sedition is taken to be hanged. Nobility, Civil Order, and Clergy repent once more and accept the primacy of Imperial Majesty. They label the pope the Antichrist.

By parody in plot and characterization, Bale offers *King Johan* as another play to declare his usual Protestant arguments and to vilify his Roman Catholic opposition. Thematically, it varies somewhat from *Three Laws* and *God's Promises*, as it raises the issue of English sovereignty to the fore. Nevertheless, by structure and dialogue, it emphasizes the familiar anti-Catholic rant apparent in Bale's other plays. In versification and style, it is no more refined. The stiff convention of keeping two characters in extended dialogue, with only occasional exchanges among three or more, is employed in *King Johan* as in Bale's other works. His reliance on paraphrase of Scripture, creeds, and traditional ceremonies is equally evident.

While Bale seems not to have carried dramatic innovation any further in his extant plays, he did set a significant premise by setting the thirteenth century English king and his opponents onstage to enact historical events. His interpretation is warped by his propagandistic intent, and his flair for theatricality and creative characterization, evident in certain parodic scenes, is always subordinate to his doctrinal persuasion. It therefore remained for playwrights more concerned with drama as an art form, more willing to let their characters enact or show, rather than tell, their discoveries in life, and able to present life in its complexities onstage, rather than to reduce it to a set of foregone conclusions, to move further. Indeed, playwrights such as Shakespeare and Marlowe moved well beyond Bale's first mixture of a historical king and his enemies with the stock virtue and vice characters of the medieval morality play. They carried the history play to full development on the Renaissance stage.

Other major works

NONFICTION: *The Image of Both Churches*, 1541 (part 1), 1545 (part 2), 1547 (part 3); *A Brief Chronicle of Sir John Oldcastle, the Lord Cobham*, 1544; *The Acts of English Votaries*, 1546; *The First Examination of Anne Askew*, 1546; *The Latter Examination of Anne Askew*, 1547; *An Answer to a Papistical Exhortation*, 1548; *Illustrium Maioris Britanniae Scriptorum*, 1548; *An Expostulation Against the Blasphemies of a Frantic Papist*, 1552; *The Apology of John Bale Against a Rank Papist*, c. 1555; *Illustrium Maioris Britanniae Catalogus*, 1557, 1559 (revision of *Illustrium Maioris Britanniae Scriptorum*); *Acta Romanorum Pontificum*, 1558 (in Latin), 1561 (in French), 1571 (in German), 1574 (in English as *The Pageant of the Popes*); *A Declaration Concerning the Clergy of London*, 1561.

TRANSLATIONS: *Pammachius*, 1538 (of Thomas Kirchmayer's German play; no longer extant); *The True History of the Christian Departing of Martin Luther*, 1546 (from German accounts collected by Justus Jonas, Michael Cellius, and Johann Aurifaber).

EDITED TEXT: *A Treatise to Henry VIII*, c. 1548 (of John Lambert's work).

Bibliography

Bale, John. *King Johan.* Edited by Barry B. Adams. San Marino, Calif.: Huntington Library, 1969. Primarily prepared for the specialist, this volume is a definitive analysis of the sole surviving manuscript of *King Johan*, with discussion of the play's date, sources, costuming, and staging. Contains an analysis of the verse, with commentary on the play's association with other plays of its time. Several appendices, one on the eccentricities of Bale's orthography.

Bevington, David. *Tudor Drama and Politics: A Critical Approach to Topical Meaning.* Cambridge, Mass.: Harvard University Press, 1968. Bale's *Three Laws* (of nature, Moses, and Christ) is seen as an attack of precisely those elements of Roman Catholicism hated by the clergy among the Tudor ruling elite. Bevington finds *King Johan* to be an expression of England's fears of a Catholic Europe uniting against her.

Bryant, James C. *Tudor Drama and Religious Controversy.* Macon, Ga.: Mercer University Press, 1984. Bryant considers Bale's play *King Johan* as a polemic supporting Henry VIII's First and Second Royal Injunctions of 1536 and 1538, respectively. He also finds him to be a satirist of many elements of the Roman faith, including the allegorization of scripture.

Fairfield, Leslie P. *John Bale: Mythmaker for the English Reformation.* West Lafayette, Ind.: Purdue University Press, 1976. Argues that Bale's conversion from Catholicism led to his reinterpretation of England's past (including concepts of sainthood), that Bale's search for victims and opponents of Roman Catholicism led to his focus on Sir John Oldcastle and King Johan (King John), and that Bale wrote to correct Polydore Vergil's slander of Oldcastle.

Harris, Jesse W. *John Bale: A Study in the Minor Literature of the Reformation.* Urbana: University of Illinois Press, 1940. Excellent coverage of the major events of Bale's life, including two periods of exile in Germany. Contains a discussion of Bale's dramas, with attention to their actual performances and their relationship to the drama of the time. Also includes a discussion of Bale's historical writings.

Mattsson, May. *Five Plays About King John.* Stockholm, Sweden: Almqvist & Wiksell, 1977. Bale's play is discussed in every chapter and is studied in connection with the anonymous *The Troublesome Reign of King John*, William Shakespeare's *King John* (c. 1596-1597), and two later plays about that monarch. Bale's play is considered in connection with the exercise of royal power, the throne's relationship to the church and the temporal lords, and the issues of public and private morality.

Walker, Greg. *Plays of Persuasion: Drama and Politics in the Court of Henry VIII.* New York: Cambridge University Press, 1991. Deals with Bale's connections with Thomas Cranmer, Thomas Cromwell, and John de Vere. Sees *King Johan* as a reflection of the dangers facing the Henrician court in 1538-1539, when Bale's play was performed at Cranmer's residence, the timing suggestive of Bale's fears of the French-Spanish truce and the schemings of an English cardinal, Reginald Pole.

Ralph S. Carlson
(Updated by *Howard L. Ford*)

AMIRI BARAKA
LeRoi Jones

Born: Newark, New Jersey; October 7, 1934

Principal drama

The Baptism, pr. 1964, pb. 1966; *Dutchman*, pr., pb. 1964; *The Slave*, pr., pb. 1964; *The Toilet*, pr., pb. 1964; *Experimental Death Unit #1*, pr. 1965, pb. 1969; *Jello*, pr. 1965, pb. 1970; *A Black Mass*, pr. 1966, pb. 1969; *Arm Yourself, or Harm Yourself*, pr., pb. 1967; *Great Goodness of Life (A Coon Show)*, pr. 1967, pb. 1969; *Madheart*, pr. 1967, pb. 1969; *Slave Ship: A Historical Pageant*, pr., pb. 1967; *The Death of Malcolm X*, pb. 1969; *Bloodrites*, pr. 1970, pb. 1971; *Junkies Are Full of (SHHH . . .)*, pr. 1970, pb. 1971; *A Recent Killing*, pr. 1973; *S-1*, pr. 1976, pb. 1978; *The Motion of History*, pr. 1977, pb. 1978; *The Sidney Poet Heroical*, pb. 1979 (originally as *Sidnee Poet Heroical*, pr. 1975); *What Was the Relationship of the Lone Ranger to the Means of Production?*, pr., pb. 1979; *At the Dim'cracker Convention*, pr. 1980; *Weimar*, pr. 1981; *Money: A Jazz Opera*, pr. 1982; *Primitive World*, pr. 1984; *The Life and Life of Bumpy Johnson*, pr. 1991; *Meeting Lillie*, pr. 1993.

Other literary forms

Amiri Baraka is a protean literary figure, equally well-known for his poetry, drama, and essays. In addition, he has written short stories, collected in *Tales* (1967), and an experimental novel, *The System of Dante's Hell* (1965), which includes numerous poetic and dramatic passages. Baraka's early volumes of poetry *Preface to a Twenty Volume Suicide Note* (1961) and *The Dead Lecturer* (1964) derive from his period of involvement with the New York City avant-garde. Other volumes, such as *Black Magic* (1969) and *It's Nation Time* (1970), reflect his intense involvement with black nationalist politics. Later volumes, such as *Hard Facts* (1975) and *Reggae or Not!* (1981), reflect his developing movement to a leftist political position and have generally failed to appeal to either his avant-garde or his black nationalist audience. Baraka's critical and political prose has been collected in *Home: Social Essays* (1966), *Raise Race Rays Raze: Essays Since 1965* (1971), *Selected Plays and Prose* (1979), and *Daggers and Javelins: Essays* (1984). *The Autobiography of LeRoi Jones/Amiri Baraka* was published in 1984.

Achievements

One of the most politically controversial playwrights of the 1960's, Amiri Baraka is best known for his brilliant early play *Dutchman* and for his contribution to the development of a community-based black nationalist theater. Throughout his career, he has sought dramatic forms for expressing the consciousness of those alienated from the psychological, economic, and racial mainstream of American society. Even though no consensus exists concerning the success of his experiments, particularly those with ritualistic forms for political drama, his challenge to the aesthetic preconceptions of the American mainstream and the inspiration he has provided younger black playwrights such as Ed Bullins and Ron Milner guarantee his place in the history of American drama.

Already well known as an avant-garde poet, Baraka, then LeRoi Jones, first rose to prominence in the theatrical world with the 1964 productions of *The Baptism*, *Dutchman*, *The Slave*, and *The Toilet*, which established him as a major Off-Broadway presence. Shortly after winning the Obie Award for *Dutchman*, however, Baraka broke his ties with the white avant-garde to concentrate on the creation of a militant African-American theater. Turning away from the psychological complexity of his early plays, most of which treat race simply as one aspect of a disorienting reality, Baraka openly denounced the racism of American culture, endorsing a militant and, if necessary, violent black response. Although mainstream critics harshly denounced his new work, Baraka continued to experiment with radical theatrical forms. Political plays such as *Madheart* and *Slave Ship* are in some ways more technically innovative than his earlier works. As Baraka's mainstream reputation declined, he gained recognition as a leading voice of the Black Arts Movement, ultimately assuming a position of public political visibility matched by only a handful of American literary figures.

Biography

Everett LeRoi Jones, who took the name Amiri Baraka in 1967, was born into a black middle-class family in Newark, New Jersey. An excellent student whose parents encouraged his intellectual interests, Jones was graduated from Howard University of Washington, D.C., in 1954, at the age of nineteen. After spending two years in the United States Air Force, primarily in Puerto Rico, he moved to Greenwich Village, where he embarked on his literary career in 1957. During the early stage of his career, Jones associated closely with numerous white avant-garde poets, including Robert Creeley, Allen Ginsberg, Robert Duncan, and Dianne DiPrima, and, with DiPrima, he founded the American Theatre for Poets in 1961. He married Hettie Cohen, a white woman with whom he edited the magazine *Yugen* from 1958 to 1963, and he established himself as an important young poet, critic, and editor. Among the many magazines to which he contributed was the jazz journal *Downbeat*, where he first developed the interest in African-American musical culture which helped shape his theatrical "rituals." The political interests that were to dominate Jones's later work were unmistakably present as early as 1960, when he toured Cuba with a group of black intellectuals. This experience sparked his perception of the United States as a corrupt bourgeois society and seems particularly significant in relation to his subsequent Socialist stance. Jones's growing political interest influenced his first produced plays, including the Obie Award-winning *Dutchman*, which anticipated the first major transformation of Jones's life.

Separating from Hettie Cohen and severing ties with his white associates, Jones moved from Greenwich Village to Harlem in 1965. Turning his attention to direct action within the black community, he founded the Black Arts Theatre and School in Harlem and, following his return to his native city in 1966, the Spirit House in Newark. After marrying a black woman, Sylvia Robinson (Amina Baraka), in 1966, Jones adopted a new name, Amiri (which means "prince") Baraka ("the blessed one"), to which he added the honorary title "Imamu." Over the next half-dozen years, Baraka helped found and develop organizations such as the Black Community Development and Defense Organization, the Congress of African Peoples (convened in Atlanta in 1970), and the National Black Political Convention (convened in Gary, Indiana, in 1972). As a leading spokesman of the Black Arts Movement, Baraka provided personal and artistic support for young black poets and playwrights, including Larry Neal, Ed Bullins, Marvin X, and Ron Milner. During the Newark riots of 1967, Baraka was arrested for unlawful possession of firearms. Although convicted and given the maximum sentence after the judge read the jury his poem "Black People!" as an example of incitement to riot, Baraka was later cleared on appeal.

Baraka supported Ken Gibson's campaign to become the first black mayor of Newark in 1970, but later broke with him over what he perceived as the Gibson administration's bourgeois values. This disillusionment with black politics within the American system and Baraka's attendance at the Sixth Pan-African Conference at Dar es Salaam in 1974 precipitated the next stage of his political evolution. While not abandoning his commitment to confronting the special problems of African Americans in the United States, Baraka began interpreting these problems within the framework of an overarching "Marxist-Leninist-Mao Tse-tung" philosophy. In conjunction with this second transformation, Baraka dropped the title Imamu and changed the name of his Newark publishing firm from Jihad to People's War. He undertook visiting professorships at Yale and George Washington universities before accepting a more permanent position at the State University of New York at Stony Brook. In 1979, Baraka was arrested during a dispute with his wife; he wrote *The Autobiography of LeRoi Jones* while serving the resulting sentence at a halfway house in Harlem. In 1990, he was involved in a widely publicized dispute with Rutgers University officials who had denied him tenure; he compared the school's faculty to the Ku Klux Klan and the Nazi Party. Though such controversies perhaps exacerbated the difficulty Baraka experienced in finding publishers for his socialist writings, he remained an important voice in the literary world and the African-American community.

Analysis

Working with forms ranging from the morality play to avant-garde expressionism, Amiri Baraka throughout his career has sought to create dramatic rituals expressing the intensity of the physical and psychological violence which dominates his vision of American culture. From his early plays on "universal" alienation through his black nationalist celebrations to his multimedia proletarian pageants, Baraka has focused on a variety of sacrificial victims as his central dramatic presences. Some of these victims remain passive scapegoats who allow a corrupt and vicious system to dictate their fate. Others assume the role of heroic martyr in the cause of community consciousness. Yet a third type of victim is the doomed oppressor whose death marks the transformation of the martyr's consciousness into a ritual action designed to free the community from continuing passive victimization.

The dominant type in Baraka's early plays, the passive scapegoats unaware of their participation in ritual actions, condemn themselves and their communities to blind repetition of destructive patterns. Their apparent mastery of the forms of Euro-American cultural literacy simply obscures the fact of their ignorance of the underlying reality of oppression. Responding to this ironic situation, Baraka's black nationalist plays emphasize the new forms of consciousness, their roots in Africa rather than Europe, needed to free the African-American community from the historical and psychological forces which enforce such blind repetition. Inverting the traditional moral symbolism of Euro-American culture, Baraka creates rituals which substitute symbolically white scapegoats for the symbolically black victims of his earlier works. These rituals frequently reject the image of salvation through self-sacrifice (seen as a technique for the pacification of the black masses), insisting instead that only an active struggle can break the cycle of oppression.

Because the rituals of Baraka's black nationalist plays frequently culminate in violence directed against whites, or symbolically white members of the black bourgeois, or aspects of the individual black psyche, numerous critics have attacked him for perpetuating the violence and racism he ostensibly criticizes. These critics frequently condemn him for oversimplifying reality, citing his movement from psychologically complex ironic forms to much more explicit allegorical modes in his later drama; the most insistent simply dismiss his post-*Dutchman* plays as strident propaganda, lacking all aesthetic and moral merit. Basing their critiques firmly on Euro-American aesthetic assumptions, such critics in fact overlook the central importance of Baraka's changing sense of his audience. Repudiating the largely white avant-garde audience which applauded his early work, Baraka turned almost exclusively to an African-American audience more aware of the storefront preacher and popular music groups such as the Temptations than of August Strindberg and Edward Albee. In adopting a style of performance in accord with this cultural perception, Baraka assumed a didactic voice intended to focus attention on immediate issues of survival and community or class defense.

First produced in leading New York theaters such as St. Mark's Playhouse (*The Slave* and *The Toilet*), the Cherry Lane Theatre (*Dutchman*), and the Writers' Stage Theatre (*The Baptism*), Baraka's early plays clearly reflect both his developing concern with issues of survival and his fascination with Euro-American avant-garde traditions. *The Baptism*, in particular, draws on the conventions of expressionist theater to comment on the absurdity of contemporary American ideas of salvation, which in fact simply mask a larger scheme of victimization. Identified only as symbolic types, Baraka's characters speak a surreal mixture of street language and theological argot. While the slang references link them to the social reality familiar to the audience, their actions are dictated by the sudden shifts and thematic ambiguities characteristic of works such as Strindberg's *A Dream Play* and the "Circe" chapter of James Joyce's *Ulysses.*

The play's central character, named simply the Boy, resembles a traditional Christ figure struggling to come to terms with his vocation. Baraka treats his protagonist with a mixture of irony and empathy, focusing on the ambiguous roles of the spirit and the flesh in relation to salvation. Pressured by the Minister to deny his body and by the cynical Homosexual to immerse himself in the profane as a path to the truly sacred, the Boy vacillates. At times he claims divine status; at times he insists, "I am only flesh." The chorus of women, at once holy virgins and temple prostitutes, reinforces his confusion. Shortly after identifying him as "the Son of God," they refer to him as the "Chief Religious jelly roll of the universe." Given these irreconcilable roles, which he is expected to fulfill, the Boy's destiny as scapegoat and martyr seems inevitable; the dramatic tension revolves around the question of who will victimize him and why. Baraka uses a sequence of conflicting views of the Boy's role, each of which momentarily dominates his self-image, to heighten this tension.

Responding to the Homosexual's insistence that "the devil is a part of creation like an ash tray or senator," the Boy first confesses his past sins and demands baptism. When the Women respond by elevating him to the status of "Son of God/ Son of Man," he explicitly rejects all claim to spiritual purity. The ambiguous masquerade culminates in an attack on the Boy, who is accused of using his spiritual status to seduce women who "wanted to be virgins of the Lord." Supported only by the Homosexual, the Boy defends himself against the Women and the Minister, who clamor for his sacrifice, ostensibly as punishment for his sins. Insisting that "there will be no second crucifixion," the Boy slays his antagonists with a phallic sword, which he interprets as the embodiment of spiritual glory. For a brief moment, the figures of Christ as scapegoat and Christ as avenger seem reconciled in a baptism of fire.

Baraka undercuts this moment of equilibrium almost immediately. Having escaped martyrdom at the hands of the mob (ironically, itself victimized), the Boy confronts the Messenger, who wears a motorcycle jacket embellished with a gold crown and the words "The Man." In Baraka's dream allegory, the Man can represent the Roman/American legal system or be a symbol for God the Father, both powers that severely limit the Boy's control over events. The Boy's first reaction to the Messenger is to reclaim his superior spiritual status, insisting that he has "brought love to many people" and calling on his "Father" for compassion. Rejecting these pleas, the Messenger indicates that "the Man's destroying the whole works tonight." The Boy responds defiantly: "Neither God nor man shall force me to leave. I was sent here to save man and I'll not leave until I do." The allegory suggests several different levels of interpretation: social, psychological, and symbolic. The Boy rejects his responsibility to concrete individuals (the mob he kills, the Man) in order to save an abstract entity (the mob as an ideal, man). Ultimately, he claims his right to the martyr's death which he killed the mob in order to avoid, by repudiating the martyr's submission to a higher power. Losing patience with the Boy's rhetoric, the Messenger responds not by killing him but by knocking him out and dragging him offstage. His attitude of boredom effectively deflates the allegorical seriousness of the Boy's defiance, a deflation reinforced by the Homosexual's concluding comment that the scene resembles "some really uninteresting kind of orgy."

The Baptism's treatment of the interlocking themes of sacrifice, ritual, and victimization emphasizes their inherent ambiguity and suggests the impossibility of moral action in a culture that confuses God with the leader of a motorcycle gang. The encompassing irony of the Christ figure sacrificing his congregation to assure universal destruction recalls T. S. Eliot's treatment of myth in *The Waste Land* and his essay "Ulysses: Myth and Order." Eliot's use of classical allusions and mythic analogies to underscore the triviality of modern life clearly anticipates Baraka's ironic vision of Christian ritual. Baraka's baptism initiates the Boy into absurdity rather than responsibility. If any sins have been washed away, they are resurrected immediately in pointless ritual violence and immature rhetoric. Although he does not develop the theme explicitly in *The Baptism*, Baraka suggests that there is an underlying philosophical corruption in Euro-American culture, in this case derived from Christianity's tendency to divorce flesh from spirit. Increasingly, this philosophical corruption takes the center of Baraka's dramatic presentation of Western civilization.

Widely recognized as Baraka's greatest work in any genre, *Dutchman* combines the irony of his avant-garde period with the emotional power and social insight of his later work. Clay, a young black man with a highly developed sense of self, occupies a central position in the play analogous to that of the Boy in *The Baptism*. The central dramatic action of the play involves Clay's confrontation with a young white woman, Lula, who may in fact be seen as an aspect of Clay's own self-awareness. In both thematic emphasis and dramatic structure, *Dutchman* parallels Edward Albee's *The Zoo Story* (pr. 1959). Both plays focus on a clash between characters from divergent social and philosophical backgrounds; both comment on the internal divisions of individuals in American society; both culminate in acts of violence which are at once realistic and symbolic. What sets *Dutchman* apart, however, is its intricate exploration of the psychology that leads Clay to a symbolic rebellion which ironically guarantees his real victimization. Clay *thinks* he exists as an autonomous individual struggling for existential awareness. Baraka implies, however, that this Euro-American conception of self simply enforces Clay's preordained role as ritual scapegoat. As the Everyman figure his name suggests, Clay represents all individuals trapped by self-deception and social pressure. As a black man in a racist culture, he shares the more specific problem of those whose self-consciousness has been determined by white definitions.

The stage directions for *Dutchman* emphasize the link between Clay's situation and the decline of Euro-American culture, describing the subway car where the action transpires as "the flying underbelly of the city . . . heaped in modern myth." Lula enters eating an apple, evoking the myth of the Fall. Together, these allusions contribute a literary dimension to the foreboding atmosphere surrounding the extended conversation which leads to Clay's sacrifice at the hands of Lula and the subway riders, mostly white but some black. Throughout, Lula maintains clear awareness of her symbolic and political intentions, while Clay remains effectively blind. Lula's role demands simply that she maintain the interest of the black man until it is convenient to kill him. Meanwhile, Clay believes he can somehow occupy a position of detachment or spiritual superiority. Changing approach frequently, Lula plays the roles of temptress, intellectual, psychologist, racist. Clay responds variously to these gambits, sometimes with amusement, ultimately with anger and contempt. Consistently, however, he fails to recognize the genocidal reality underlying Lula's masquerade, unwittingly assuming his preordained role in the controlling ritual of black destruction. Much like the legendary ghost ship for which it was named, the "Dutchman," Baraka implies, will continue to sail so long as blacks allow the white world to control the premises of the racial debate.

This rigged debate reflects Baraka's reassessment of his universalist beliefs and his movement toward black nationalism. Clay resembles the early
LeRoi Jones in many ways: Both are articulate natives of New Jersey with
aspirations to avant-garde artistic success. *Dutchman* implies that both are
subject to fantasies about the amount of meaningful success possible for
them in the realm of Euro-American culture. Lula alternately reduces Clay
to a "well-known type" and condemns him for rejecting his roots and embracing "a tradition you ought to feel oppressed by." During the first act,
Clay stays "cool" until Lula sarcastically declares him the "Black
Baudelaire" and follows with the repeated phrase "My Christ. My Christ."
Suddenly shifting emphasis, she immediately denies his Christ-like stature
and insists, "You're a murderer," compressing the two major attributes of
the Boy in *The Baptism*, this time with a specifically social resonance. The
sudden shift disrupts Clay's balance. Ironically restating and simplifying
the thesis of Ralph Ellison's universalist novel *Invisible Man*, Lula concludes the opening act with an ironic resolution to "pretend the people
cannot see you . . . that you are free of your own history. And I am free
of my history." The rapid movement from Clay as Christ and murderer—
standard black roles in the fantasy life of white America—to the *pretense*
of his freedom underscores the inevitability of his victimization, an inevitability clearly dictated by the historical forces controlling Lula, forces
which Clay steadfastly refuses to recognize.

Clay's lack of awareness blinds him to the fact that the subway car,
occupied only by himself and Lula during act 1, fills up with people during
act 2. Continuing to manipulate Clay through rapid shifts of focus, Lula
diverts his attention from the context, first by fantasizing a sexual affair
with him and then by ridiculing him as an "escaped nigger" with absurd
pretensions to cultural whiteness. Abandoning his cool perspective for the
first time, Clay angrily takes "control" of the conversation. His powerful
soliloquy establishes his superior understanding of his interaction with
Lula, but only in the theoretical terms of Euro-American academic dis-
course. Admitting his hatred for whites, Clay claims a deep affinity with
the explosive anger lying beneath the humorous surface of the work of the
great black musicians Bessie Smith and Charlie Parker. Ridiculing Lula's
interpretation of his psychological makeup, Clay warns her that whites
should beware of preaching "rationalism" to blacks, since the best cure for
the black neurosis would be the random murder of whites. After this dem-
onstration of his superior, and highly rational, awareness, Clay turns to go.
He dismisses Lula with contempt, saying, "we won't be acting out that
little pageant you outlined before." Immediately thereafter, Lula kills him.
The murder is in fact the final act of the real pageant, the ritual of black
sacrifice. Seen from Lula's perspective, the entire conversation amounts to
an extended assault on Clay's awareness of the basic necessities of survival.

Seen from Baraka's viewpoint, the heightened racial awareness of Clay's final speech is simply an illusion, worthless if divorced from action. Clay's unwilling participation in the pageant of white mythology reveals the futility of all attempts to respond to white culture on its own terms. Regarded in this light, Baraka's subsequent movement away from the theoretical avant-garde and from Euro-American modes of psychological analysis seems inevitable.

Baraka's black nationalist plays, many of them written for community theater groups such as Spirit House Movers and the San Francisco State College Black Arts Alliance, occasionally employ specific avant-garde techniques. His earlier works take the techniques "seriously," but even his most experimental nationalist plays, such as *Experimental Death Unit #1*, clearly attempt to subvert the values implied by the Euro-American aesthetic. Determined to communicate with his community through its own idiom, Baraka sought new forms in the African-American aesthetic embodied in dance and music, African chants, experimental jazz, rhythm and blues, and reggae. Particularly when performed in predominantly black contexts, his work in this idiom creates an emotional intensity difficult to describe in standard academic terms, an atmosphere often extremely uncomfortable for white viewers. Even while embracing and exploiting the aesthetic potential of the idiom, however, Baraka attempts to purify and transform it. Repudiating his earlier vision of universal alienation and victimization, Baraka no longer sympathizes with, or even tolerates, passive scapegoats such as Clay and the Boy. He does not, however, remove the victim from the center of his drama. Rather, he emphasizes two new types of victims in his nationalist rituals: the clearly heroic African-American martyr in *Great Goodness of Life (A Coon Show)* and *The Death of Malcolm X*, and the whitewashed black and overthrown white oppressor in *Madheart* and *Slave Ship*, portrayed as deserving their death.

Madheart and *Great Goodness of Life (A Coon Show)* employ different constellations of these figures to criticize the failure of the black community to purge its consciousness of Euro-American values. Like *A Black Mass*, *Madheart* borrows the image of the "white devil" from the theology of the Nation of Islam (sometimes referred to inaccurately as the Black Muslims) to account for the fallen condition of black awareness. Beginning with a confrontation between allegorical characters identified as Black Man and Devil Lady, *Madheart* focuses on the Devil Lady's influence over the Black Man's Mother and Sister, whose red and blonde wigs indicate the extent of their corruption. Aided by the supportive Black Woman, Black Man rejects and sacrifices the Devil Lady, symbolically repudiating white culture. Mother and Sister, however, refuse to participate in the ritual of purification. Sister loses consciousness, believing that the death of the Devil Lady is also her own death. Lamenting over her daughter, Mother calls on white "saints" such as Tony Bennett, Beethoven, and Batman for deliverance. Clinging to their belief in whiteness, Mother and a revived Sister descend to the level of slobbering animals. Motivated by love rather than hatred, Black Man turns a firehose on them as the play ends. His concluding speech echoes Baraka's basic attitude toward his suffering community: "This stuff can't go on. They'll die or help us, be black or white and dead. I'll save them or kill them." To avoid being sacrificed like Clay, Baraka implies, the African-American community must repudiate its internal whiteness. The elimination of the white "devil," far from being an end in itself, is simply a preliminary step toward the purification of the black self-image.

Extending this critique of the internalization of white corruption, *Great Goodness of Life (A Coon Show)*, with its title ironic at several levels, focuses on the trial of Court Royal, a middle-aged black man accused of unspecified crimes. An offstage voice, supported by a sequence of increasingly respectable-looking Ku Klux Klan figures, echoes Lula in *Dutchman*, claiming that Court Royal has been harboring a murderer. Although Court Royal interprets the claim in concrete terms, the voice seeks primarily to bring about his repudiation of his black identity. Manipulating his fear of personal loss, the voice forces Court to preside over the ritual murder of a black martyr whose body is carried onstage to the accompaniment of projected slides showing martyrs such as Malcolm X and Patrice Lumumba. Ordering the disposal of the corpse, the voice says: "Conceal the body in a stone. And sink the stone deep under the ocean. Call the newspapers and give the official history. Make sure his voice is in that stone too." In fact, the primary aim of the voice is to silence the African-American cultural tradition by encouraging individuals to see their own situations as divorced from that of their community. Despite Court Royal's dim awareness that the "body" is that of a collective figure, the voice forces him to deny his sense that "there are many faces." After Court Royal acquiesces to this Euro-American vision of individualism, the voice declares him "free," stipulating only that he "perform the rite." The rite is the execution of the "body."

Assuring Court Royal that the murderer is already dead, the voice nevertheless demands that he actively contribute to the destruction of the African-American tradition by sacrificing the "murderer" within. To distract Court Royal from the genocidal reality of his act, the voice delivers an intricate statement on the nature of ritual action. Court, caught in the trap of Euro-American rhetoric, ironically assumes the role of the white God and executes his symbolic son; the young black man cries out "Papa" as he dies. His soul "washed white as snow," Court merely returns to his night-out bowling. His voice sunk beneath the sea, he can only echo the white voice which commands his passive acceptance of Euro-American rituals. Where Clay was killed by white society directly, the martyr in *Great*

Goodness of Life (A Coon Show) is killed by white society acting indirectly through the timorous and self-deluded black bourgeois. Ritual murder metamorphoses into ritual suicide. Baraka clearly intimates the need for new rituals that will be capable of presenting new alternatives not under the control of the white voice.

Slave Ship, Baraka's most convincing and theatrically effective black nationalist play, develops both the form and the content of these rituals. Thematically, the play places the perceptions of *Madheart* and *Great Goodness of Life (A Coon Show)* in a broader historical perspective. Beginning in West Africa and progressing through the American Civil War, Baraka traces the evolution of African-American culture, stressing the recurring scenes of betrayal in which traitors, frequently preachers, curry favor with their white masters by selling out their people. Such repeated betrayals, coupled with scenes of white violence against blacks, create a tension which is released only with the sudden ritual killing of the white voice and the black traitor. This sacrifice emphasizes Baraka's demand for an uncompromising response to the forces, inside and outside the community, responsible for centuries of black misery.

The real power of *Slave Ship*, however, stems from its performance style, which combines lighting, music, at times even smell, to create an encompassing atmosphere of oppression which gives way to an even more overwhelming celebration. The sound of white laughter and black singing and moaning surrounds the recurring visual images which link the historical vignettes. A drumbeat reasserts itself at moments of tension and seeming despair, suggesting the saving presence of the African heritage. The drum, joined by a jazz saxophone as the black community rises to break its chains, initiates the celebratory chant: "When we gonna rise up, brother/ When we gonna rise above the sun/ When we gonna take our own place, brother/ Like the world had just begun?" Superimposed on the continuing background moaning, the chant inspires a communal dance which combines African and African-American styles. Invoking the choreography of the "Miracles/Temptations dancing line," Baraka calls the dance the Boogalooyoruba, compressing historical past and present in a ritual designed to create a brighter future. Following the climactic sacrifice, the severed heads of black traitor and white oppressor are cast down on the stage. Given ideal context and performance, the dancing of the Boogalooyoruba will then spread through the audience. *Slave Ship* thus exemplifies African-American ritual drama of the 1960's; merging aesthetic performance and political statement, it marks the culmination of Baraka's black nationalist work.

Baraka's later plays express the Marxist-Leninist-Mao Tse-tung philosophy he embraced in the mid-1970's. Gauging the success of monumental dramas such as *The Motion of History* and *The Sidney Poet Heroical* is difficult, in part because they are rarely performed, in larger part because of a generally hostile political climate. The texts of the plays reflect Baraka's continuing interest in multimedia performance styles, incorporating a great deal of musical and cinematic material. Both plays comprise numerous brief scenes revealing the action of historical forces, primarily economic in *The Motion of History* and primarily racial in *The Sidney Poet Heroical*. Both present images of martyr-heroes and oppressor-scapegoats. On the page, however, both appear programmatic and somewhat naïvely ideological. The climaxes, for example, feature mass meetings intended to inspire the audience to political commitment, a technique anticipated in proletarian dramas of the 1930's such as Clifford Odets' *Waiting for Lefty* (pr. 1935). The cries "Long live socialist revolution" and "Victory to Black People! Victory to all oppressed people!" which conclude *The Motion of History* and *The Sidney Poet Heroical* obviously require both a sensitive production and a politically sympathetic audience to work their desired effect. In the political climate of the late 1970's and 1980's, neither element was common, and Baraka's plays of this period could be considered closet dramas. His early 1990's plays *The Life and Life of Bumpy Johnson* and *Meeting Lillie* were somewhat less strident and, perhaps as a result, somewhat better received by mainstream critics.

Other major works

NOVEL: *The System of Dante's Hell*, 1965.

SHORT FICTION: *Tales*, 1967.

POETRY: *Spring and Soforth*, 1960; *Preface to a Twenty Volume Suicide Note*, 1961; *The Dead Lecturer*, 1964; *Black Art*, 1966; *A Poem for Black Hearts*, 1967; *Black Magic: Sabotage—Target Study—Black Art: Collected Poetry, 1961-1967*, 1969; *It's Nation Time*, 1970; *In Our Terribleness: Some Elements and Meaning in Black Style*, 1970 (with Fundi [Billy Abernathy]); *Spirit Reach*, 1972; *Afrikan Revolution*, 1973; *Hard Facts*, 1975; *Selected Poetry of Amiri Baraka/LeRoi Jones*, 1979; *Reggae or Not!*, 1981.

NONFICTION: *Blues People: Negro Music in White America*, 1963; *Home: Social Essays*, 1966; *Raise Race Rays Raze: Essays Since 1965*, 1971; *The New Nationalism*, 1972; *The Autobiography of LeRoi Jones/Amiri Baraka*, 1984; *Daggers and Javelins: Essays*, 1984; *The Music: Reflections on Jazz and Blues*, 1987 (with Amina Baraka).

ANTHOLOGIES: *The Moderns: New Fiction in America*, 1963; *Black Fire: An Anthology of Afro-American Writing*, 1968 (with Larry Neal).

MISCELLANEOUS: *African Congress: A Documentary of the First Modern Pan-African Congress*, 1972 (editor); *Selected Plays and Prose*, 1979.

Bibliography

Benston, Kimberly W., ed. *Imamu Amiri Baraka (LeRoi Jones): A Collec-*

tion of Critical Essays. Englewood Cliffs, N.J.: Prentice-Hall, 1978. A whole section, entitled "Black Labs of the Heart," examines Baraka's drama in six essays on *Dutchman*, *The Slave*, *The Toilet*, *Great Goodness of Life (A Coon Show)*, *Madheart*, and *Slave Ship.* "Baraka's theatre is one of deliverance, inexorably oriented toward liberation through confrontation," says Benston in her introduction. Contains a bibliography.

Brown, Lloyd W. *Amiri Baraka.* Boston: Twayne, 1980. Separating Baraka's literary output by major genre, Brown covers drama last, beginning with Mao Tse-tung's influence on the socialist perspective of such plays as *The Motion of History* and *S-1.* Even in Baraka's four early plays—*The Baptism*, *The Toilet*, *Dutchman*, and *The Slave*—Brown sees not an advocacy of revolution but "a highly effective analysis of American society" before his political views find an ideology. *Slave Ship* is a successful "ritual drama," Brown notes. Chronology, bibliography, index.

Hudson, Theodore R. *From LeRoi Jones to Amiri Baraka: The Literary Works.* Durham, N.C.: Duke University Press, 1973. The last chapter, "Not the Weak Hamlets," deals with Baraka's almost single-handed invention of black theater and his theory of the drama as "a device for [political] edification and motivation." Hudson states that six plays produced in 1964 and an Obie Award established Baraka as "the subject of serious critical consideration by the American theatre establishment." Index and bibliography.

Lacey, Henry C. *To Raise, Destroy, and Create: The Poetry, Drama, and Fiction of Imamu Amiri Baraka (LeRoi Jones).* Troy, N.Y.: Whitston, 1981. Unlike other studies, which separate the works by genres, this volume divides Baraka's life into a Beat period, a transition, and a rebirth symbolized by taking on a new name. Also discusses Baraka's dramatic work in context with his writing in other genres. Supplemented by an index and a list of Baraka's works.

Sollors, Werner. *Amiri Baraka/LeRoi Jones: The Quest for a "Populist Modernism."* New York: Columbia University Press, 1978. Three chapters of this study deal with Baraka's drama. "From Off-Bowery to Off Broadway" provides a close study of *The Baptism* and *The Toilet*; *Dutchman* gets a whole chapter to itself. Good photograph section of production stills. Bibliography and index.

Craig Werner
(Updated by *Thomas J. Taylor*
and *Robert McClenaghan*)

JAMES NELSON BARKER

Born: Philadelphia, Pennsylvania; June 17, 1784
Died: Washington, D.C.; March 9, 1858

Principal drama

Tears and Smiles, pr. 1807, pb. 1808; *The Embargo: Or, What News*, pr. 1808 (no longer extant); *The Indian Princess: Or, La Belle Sauvage*, pr., pb. 1808 (libretto; music by John Bray); *Travellers: Or, Music's Fascination*, pr. 1808 (adaptation of Andrew Cherry's play; no longer extant); *Marmion: Or, The Battle of Flodden Field*, pr. 1812, pb. 1816 (based on Sir Walter Scott's poem); *The Armourer's Escape: Or, Three Years at Nootka Sound*, pr. 1817 (no longer extant); *How to Try a Lover*, pb. 1817, pr. 1836 (as *The Court of Love*; based on Pigault-Lebrun's novel *La Folie espagnole*); *Superstition: Or, The Fanatic Father*, pr. 1824, pb. 1826.

Other literary forms

Although known chiefly as a dramatist, James Nelson Barker wrote some occasional verse, political poems and orations, and several newspaper essays on contemporary drama. His six biographical essays on notable Americans, including DeWitt Clinton, Robert Fulton, and John Jay, appeared in *Delaplaine's Repository of the Lives and Portraits of Distinguished Americans* (1817).

Achievements

In the first half of the nineteenth century, when many American writers were struggling against a literary inferiority complex, Barker was among the earliest of American dramatists to break new ground. His *The Indian Princess*, which took the story of Pocahontas as its central theme, was the first American "Indian" play ever to be performed. It began a dramatic tradition, providing a motif for American playwrights for the next fifty years. Not until the eve of the Civil War, when drama turned more toward realism, had the Pocahontas material run its course. Barker's use of the Indian as a literary motif predates by more than ten years the depiction of the Indian in the novels of James Fenimore Cooper and in the works of his contemporaries.

Barker was thus among the first American writers to use native material as a corrective to what was perceived as the American writer's servile dependence on European, particularly British, literary influence. His most creative period, from 1808 to 1824, coincided with America's growing sense of literary nationalism, that sentiment by which American authors sought to produce a native literature that reflected the nation's character, customs, manners, and ideals. The forceful preface to his *Tears and Smiles*, for example, condemns the reverent attitude of American critics toward European standards. Denouncing these reviewers as "mental colonists," intellectually submissive to British opinion, Barker calls for a sort of declaration of literary independence, a repudiation of foreign models and an embracing of national cultural material.

Tears and Smiles, Barker's first play, contributed to the development of the stage Yankee, that bumbling yet shrewd New Englander whose individualism was distinctively American. Only twenty years after Royall Tyler introduced the stage Yankee in *The Contrast* (pr. 1787), Barker created the character of "Nathan Yank," a major link in the chain of Yankee plays that were to remain popular throughout the first half of the nineteenth century.

Barker's crowning achievement was the last of his five extant plays. First performed in 1824, *Superstition* is one of the earliest dramas to use colonial history as its source. Dealing primarily with the bigotry and fears of a New England village in the late seventeenth century, the play is a tragedy that anticipates some of the ideas and characters later to be found in the works of Nathaniel Hawthorne. It is the most controlled of Barker's dramas, and in its fusion of historical material with convincing character motivation, it remains the best American play of its time.

In his use of native material, then, together with his lifelong advocacy of a native American theater, Barker must be considered a significant influence in the history of American drama.

Biography

The fourth son of John Barker, one of Philadelphia's foremost citizens, James Nelson Barker was educated in public schools and became, in his early teens, a wide reader. Though he did not go to college, he was familiar enough with some of the world's great authors to begin, at the age of twenty, his first play, based on a story by Miguel de Cervantes. This play, "The Spanish Rover," was left unfinished and has not survived. By 1805, Barker had completed two acts of a proposed tragedy entitled "Attila," suggested by his reading of Edward Gibbon's five-volume work, *The History of the Decline and Fall of the Roman Empire* (1776, 1781, 1788); this play has also been lost. The only knowledge of these early efforts comes from Barker's autobiographical account of his dramatic career, written for William Dunlap's *History of the American Theatre* (1832).

Though these fledgling works attest Barker's early interest in the drama and indicate the scope of his reading, they also make a point about his creative imagination. The subject matter, the setting, even the characters of both works were foreign. Attila's Rome and Cervantes' seventeenth century Spain were far removed from the bumptious America of the early Republic; the results were therefore simple false starts. In contrast, when the occasion arose for the writing of a play with an American milieu as its setting, Barker's imagination took fire.

That occasion was a hunting trip in 1806. One of Barker's companions, a theater manager, knowing of the young man's dramatic interests, asked Barker to write an American play, and a prominent actor of the day, Joseph Jefferson, who specialized in Yankee characterizations, asked that Barker include a Yankee type. Barker set to work, and in forty-three days he completed his first play, *Tears and Smiles*, produced the following year. In his preface to the published work, Barker derides the popular opinion among critics that a successful drama had to be European in plot, setting, and character. As if poking fun at himself and his two earlier, abortive efforts, he quotes a fictitious friend who suggests that he, Barker, abandon his scheme of delineating American manners and instead "write a melodrama [*sic*] and lay [your] scene in the moon."

With one successful play behind him, Barker, now only in his early twenties, turned his youthful exuberance into more worldly pursuits. At this time, the city of Philadelphia had fallen under the spell of a sort of soldier of fortune, General Don Francisco de Miranda. Miranda wanted to liberate Venezuela and in time secure independence for all South America. In pursuit of this goal, he was seeking enlistments, promising wealth and glory to all who volunteered for the cause of freedom. Whether Barker was moved by the democratic fervor of the times or had merely surrendered to the swashbuckling Byronism of the scheme, he nevertheless left for the port of New York in August, 1806, with the idea of joining the expedition in Trinidad, West Indies. News of Miranda's defeat, however, and a series of letters from his father urging him to come home resulted in Barker's return to Philadelphia early in 1807.

This frustrated adventure can be seen as a catalyst in Barker's creative process, for his next play, first acted in March, 1808, was a political satire, *The Embargo*. Borrowing extensively from a British play by Arthur Murphy, *The Upholsterer* (1757), Barker's comedy was to be the most topical of his works. Never printed and since lost, the play was probably heavily allusive to President Thomas Jefferson's embargo of British shipping, in commercial retaliation for British seizures of American vessels during this period when Britain was engaged in a war with France, led by the Emperor Napoleon Bonaparte. Little else is known about what was probably Barker's least important work.

In April, 1808, Barker's third completed play was produced. *The Indian Princess* was a historically significant production, the first dramatization of the Pocahontas story. The play was enormously influential—so popular, in fact, that, by Barker's own account to Dunlap, it was eventually acted in every theater in the country. It was also the first original American play to be performed in England after its premiere in the United States.

Barker's next dramatic work was a trivial affair, an adaptation of *Travel-*

lers: Or, Music's Fascination (pr. 1806), by British author Andrew Cherry. A kind of musical panorama, the play was never printed, and though it was a modest success when performed during the Christmas season of 1808, it was, by Barker's admission, only "a little less absurd" than its original. It has been deservedly forgotten.

After this flurry of dramatic activity, Barker began to sow the seeds of his own political future, probably at the urging and with the help of his father, who was by 1809 the mayor of Philadelphia. Becoming active in the Democratic party of the city, Barker was sent to Washington with letters of introduction from his father to President James Madison. There he served as his father's lobbyist and listening post; his letters to the mayor, from his arrival in the capital in December, 1809, to his departure in March, 1810, are filled with political gossip, reports of evening balls and social entertainments, and frequent pleas for more money, always postscripted by appropriately filial apologies.

Returning to Philadelphia, Barker met and married Mary Rogers in 1811, took up portrait painting as a hobby, and wrote *Marmion*. The product of his reading of Sir Walter Scott, the play was not only a dramatization of Scott's poem of the same title but also a skillful conflation of other sources relating to the subject. In particular, Barker used material from the chronicles of Raphael Holinshed; the result was a play that was fast-paced and tightly structured. *Marmion* turned out to be Barker's longest-running stage work; it is interesting that it was his first successful drama on a non-native subject, and this on the eve of the War of 1812, when national pride and patriotism were rising.

As it did for many, the war enabled Barker to develop his political career. Appointed a regimental captain of artillery, Barker soon saw active service at Fort Erie and at Buffalo, New York. Returning to Philadelphia, he became a principal recruiting officer in the region, mustering several hundred men; served as captain in the Artillery Corps; and was appointed brevet major by 1814.

At the war's end, Barker ran for the Pennsylvania Assembly on the Democratic ticket. Though defeated, he made many political friends, who helped him a short time later to be appointed a city alderman. It was a crucial political position, for only two years later, in 1819—and like his father—Barker himself became the mayor of Philadelphia. His one-year term, from October, 1819, to October, 1820, was marked by honesty, efficiency, and courage. He trimmed the city budget, cutting his own salary first; raised money for national relief programs; and reorganized the city's police and militia during a time of civil unrest.

Defeated for reelection, Barker also suffered a deep personal loss: Over the next two years, three of his children died. Barker's loyalty to the Democratic party was remembered, however, when Andrew Jackson became president and named Barker to the post of collector of the port of Philadelphia, a political plum, one of the choicest fruits of Jackson's spoils system. Barker held this post from 1829 to 1838.

Meanwhile, Barker's literary career continued to flourish. In the midst of his political activities leading to his post as alderman, Barker returned to a native subject for a play. *The Armourer's Escape* was a dramatization of John Jewitt's narrative of his captivity among the Nootkian Indians. Captivity narratives, real or fictional, were popular in England and in the United States during the late seventeenth and eighteenth centuries; Jewitt was counting on such literary precedent to promote the sales of his own adventures. His book was a failure, however, and he turned to the dramatist for help. The play was never printed and is now lost.

How to Try a Lover, though written shortly after the Jewitt dramatization, was not produced until almost twenty years later, though Barker remarked to Dunlap that it was the play with which he was most satisfied. Set in thirteenth century Spain, this comedy of love forsworn and finally consummated was based on Pigault-Lebrun's novel *La Folie espagnole* (1801). It is a charming, extremely actable play but not representative of that aspect of Barker's work which is most notable—namely, his use of native material.

Barker's use of such native sources resulted in his finest work, *Superstition*. In this work, the use of history meshes with sound dramatic instinct; the drama is regarded as one of the best American plays of the period. Serious, dark, and intense, the play shows a control of plot, character, and language that few dramatists had yet attained and which gains in effectiveness when one remembers that Barker wrote the play in the years immediately following the deaths of his children and his defeat for reelection to the mayoralty.

Although *Superstition* was Barker's last play, he continued, throughout the next decade, to supply newspapers and magazines with pedestrian occasional verse, patriotic centennial odes on such themes as the birthday of George Washington and on the founding of the state of Pennsylvania.

The last twenty years of Barker's life were spent in various positions in the United States Treasury Department in Washington, D.C. The demands of such service effectively curtailed his literary career. He remained a respected figure in Washington until his death on March 9, 1858.

Analysis

James Nelson Barker's earliest play, *Tears and Smiles*, succeeds on two counts. It is, first, a quickly moving, sprightly work, filled with the youthful exuberance of an author in his early twenties. Exuberance, indeed, is a crucial ingredient, for the recipe of plot and character is otherwise spoiled by convention and claptrap. Second, the piece has some genuine historical value as an early example of the portrayal of the stage Yankee, here named Nathan Yank.

Influenced by Tyler's *The Contrast*, *Tears and Smiles* relies on traditional elements of melodrama. Louisa Campdon, the heroine, has been promised by her father to the delicate dandy, Mr. Fluttermore, whose very name is suggestive of characters from Restoration drama. Louisa, however, is in love with Sydney, a young man of recognized valor but uncertain parentage who has returned from Tripoli and the wars against the Turkish pirates to reclaim her love. The Turkish allusions show how alert Barker was to literary and theatrical trends. Tyler had used the motif in his novel *The Algerine Captive* (1797), and the Turkish or Oriental motif had been popular in the early Gothic romances; in addition, operatic composers such as Christoph Gluck, Wolfgang Amadeus Mozart, and Gioacchino Rossini (Barker's contemporary) had staged Turkish operas.

By the end of the comedy, thanks to the intercession of characters such as General Campdon (Louisa's uncle) and the Widow Freegrace, the lovers are united and the fop appropriately chastened. Sydney is also reunited with his long-lost parents, who have been separated for years and suffered from pirates, slavery, and family disapproval. Such characters and situations were typical of the drama of the period, and *Tears and Smiles* is grievously weakened as art by its heavy reliance on them.

Still, the play is worthy of attention for its lively humor and satire as Barker pokes fun at Americans' seduction by European modes and manners. The opening scene quickly clears the ground for satire when Louisa's uncle protests her proposed marriage to Fluttermore, who, when he left America, was a clever, honest fellow but who has returned from his travels abroad "a puppy . . . with a pale face and a hearty contempt for everything this side of the water." Meanwhile, Barker skillfully delays Fluttermore's entrance until near the end of act 1, when Fluttermore saunters onstage with Monsieur Galliard, a combination companion and valet. The scene is deliciously funny, with bluff Jack Rangely, the second lead, shaking hands so cordially that he knocks the powder from Fluttermore's wig. By giving Fluttermore "Frenchified" rather than Anglicized affectations, Barker provides a variation on the standard portrayal of the British fop and makes a topical point about French influence on American fashion and theater at the time. "I can't conceive what you possibly do in this corner of the globe," says Fluttermore, disparaging American manners. "No opera; no masquerade, nor *fête*, nor *conversazione*." Later, writers from Hawthorne to Henry James would seriously lament America's lack of European refinement, that sense of history and rich cultural precedent, a lack which they saw as a limiting force on the American imagination. Yet here, at the dawn of American literary nationalism, foppish Fluttermore's denigration of American culture is distinctly comic.

Of special comic interest in *Tears and Smiles* is Nathan Yank, the first stage Yankee of the nineteenth century. Introduced in Tyler's *The Contrast*, this comic figure was to be one of the most popular and enduring types on the American stage. He was generally depicted as an honest, homespun bumpkin who very often was the butt as well as the perpetrator of jokes and whose comic antics were often dramatic set pieces, independent of the main action. Actors such as Joseph Jefferson, George Handel Hill, and Joshua Silsbee made their living playing Yankee characters. "Yankee" Hill was particularly notable for delivering Yankee monologues or yarns, a device that surely must have provided comic precedent for Mark Twain.

Barker's Nathan Yank added little to the characterization already drawn by Tyler some twenty years before. Nathan retains his predecessor's bumptiousness, for example, and holds the same status, that of servant, but whereas Tyler's Jonathan is boorish, he is also his own man. Jonathan shows a Puritan reliance on biblical precept as well as a practical sense of getting on in the world. His love scenes with Jenny, his social equal, prove him to be a man as well as a clown, a man of independent temperament, despite his status as servant.

In contrast, Nathan Yank never goes beyond the range of low comedian. He misdirects his master, Rangely, for example, by mistaking one house for another, and he indulges in a series of puns at the expense of Rangely's lover. To Rangely, who does not know her name, she is his "incognita," but Nathan henceforth refers to her as "Cognita." Inexplicably, Barker drops Nathan from the action by act 4, and Nathan is noticeably absent at the finale in act 5.

Although Nathan's shallow, one-dimensional buffoonery and his rather peripheral position in the action seem to represent a retrogression or at least a pause in the development of the stage Yankee, there is, on a closer reading of the play, an important advance in his use of dialect. While Tyler's Jonathan used dialect inconsistently, shifting arbitrarily from formal English to homely solecism, Nathan Yank is almost always dialectical, more consistently ungrammatical. From his first "I reckon" in act 1 to his "tarnal long" in his last appearance, Yank speaks strictly homespun American. This move toward a more consistent use of dialect was an important step in the transmission of the Yankee type.

If *Tears and Smiles* is notable for its exuberance, *The Indian Princess* is marked by a self-consciousness and a nationalistic sense of purpose. The very preface to the printed edition begins with a plea to both critics and theatergoers to take American drama seriously. Barker laments the poor reception American plays have received from critics and publishers, decrying the fact that acknowledged American productions simply die, like orphans, from "total neglect." As for *The Indian Princess* in particular, he urges the public not to denigrate the play simply because it "cannot lisp the language of Shakespeare." Like all living things, he says, American drama must first creep before it can walk. Finally, in a tone which adumbrates the pronouncements of Ralph Waldo Emerson and Walt Whitman, Barker predicts that America will bring forth "a dramatic genius" once the "stagnant atmosphere of entire apathy" is dispelled.

Though Barker's remarks may be seen as a self-serving acknowledgment of his pioneering role in the development of native drama, *The Indian Princess* is far from the work of genius predicted so confidently by its author. Despite its numerous failures, however, the play has genuine merit.

The first play in the literature to use the story of Pocahontas as its central idea, *The Indian Princess* was also the first of Barker's plays based on an authentic historical text. The advertisement to the 1808 edition credits Captain John Smith's *The Generall Historie of Virginia, New England, and the Summer Isles* (1624) as being the principal source, adding that the author has preserved "as close an adherence to historic truth" as the demands of the drama allowed.

An examination of Smith's account reveals just how cannily Barker used his source material. The Pocahontas episode in Smith (which in the opinion of some historians is of questionable truth) is narrated in the third person and is quickly told in a brief paragraph. The central scene in which Pocahontas puts her own head on the block to save Smith takes only a sentence. Barker casts this somewhat fleeting, almost offhand reference into the central episode of the play. It comes in the opening of act 2, not quite halfway through the three-act drama. Some critics, among them Arthur Hobson Quinn, have suggested that this crucial scene comes too early in the play, with the result that the third act tends to be rather anticlimactic.

If the statement in the advertisement about adhering to historical truth is taken as significant of Barker's intention, then the scene is rightly placed, for it serves as the central link in the chain of historical events that follow—namely, John Rolfe's love of the Indian Princess and their subsequent marriage, which cemented the bond between the English colonists and an important Indian tribe in the region, headed by Pocahontas' father, Chief Powhatan. Historically, Powhatan did seek English allies for his fight against the Susquehannocks, and in the closing scenes of Barker's play such an alliance takes place, both historically and symbolically, when all the lovers are united: Rolfe with Pocahontas; Robin (one of Smith's men) with Nima, Pocahontas' lady in waiting; and no less than three other pairs of lovers, Indian and white.

At the end of the play, Smith praises America as the new Eden, a new world "disjoined from old licentious Europe." This idea of America as a fresh start, an innocent, uncorrupted land untainted by history and therefore rich in human possibility, was a common thread in the skein of American literature during the nineteenth century. Barker's use of the idea so early in the century points out once again his pioneering sense of literary nationalism.

For all of its dramatic interest, however, the play is not without serious flaws. As in *Tears and Smiles*, Barker relies on conventional characters and situations, particularly in the scenes involving the minor pairs of lovers, such as Larry, the stage Irishman who loves Kate and who carries a potato in his pocket and commits execrable puns.

The play was originally intended as a straight drama, but Barker was persuaded to turn it into an opera—"an operatic melodrame," as the title page announces. As a result, some of the scenes are mere interludes, set pieces of vapid verse, set to music by a composer named Bray, which do little to advance the action or to discover character.

The most damaging weakness of *The Indian Princess* is Barker's inability to render effective, believable dialogue. The Indians speak, like their white counterparts, in blank verse or in orotund periods. Only on rare occasions does Barker even attempt to distinguish the speech of Indians from that of whites. These attempts often result in such rhetorical infelicities as Powhatan's exclamation at seeing Captain Smith for the first time: "Behold the white being." The love scene between Pocahontas and Rolfe is tender, evocative, and romantic, but echoes of William Shakespeare's *Romeo and Juliet* make Pocahontas' blank verse difficult to credit:

> Thou art my life!
> I lived not till I saw thee, love; and now
> I live not long in thine absence . . . .

Barker's failure to treat the Indian in other than romantic terms (even the evil medicine man, Grimosco, and the rival, Miami, are but red-skinned Gothic villains) typifies the problem faced by the early American writer who recognized the Indian as a legitimate literary property but who could not properly assimilate him into a creditable literary context because of subversive cultural differences.

For his finest work, *Superstition*, Barker once again turned to authentic colonial records. Drawing its main outlines from Thomas Hutchinson's *The History of Massachusetts* (1795), *Superstition* is set in a New England village in 1675. Ravensworth, the minister, is a zealous but cold man who is obsessed with what he sees as "the dark sorcery" practiced by Isabella, a late arrival to the village, who "scorns the church's discipline" and holds herself aloof from the neighbors. Isabella's son Charles is in love with Ravensworth's daughter Mary, an added motive feeding Ravensworth's obsession.

To this basic plot situation Barker successfully fuses a second motif, based also on a historical incident. A small group of Puritans who had presided over the execution of Charles I in January, 1649, were forced to flee

England at the restoration of Charles II in 1660. Though the majority were later granted amnesty, some were excepted and lived under assumed identities in the New World. Barker drew on this theme of the so-called regicides for the creation of the character of the Unknown, a mysterious figure living in exile in a cave deep in the wilderness. As the play unfolds, the Unknown saves the village from Indian attack by instilling courage and leading the colonists in a counter-offensive. In the end, he turns out to be a regicide and Isabella's long-lost father, in search of whom she has come to the New World.

The melodramatic elements inherent in this character and in his discovered relationship with Isabella seriously mar the aesthetic integrity of the play. Similarly, Ravensworth, whose obsession ultimately causes the deaths of Charles, Isabella, and his own daughter, has much of the melodramatic one-sidedness of a Gothic villain.

Yet the power of *Superstition* is undeniable. Its effectiveness lies in Barker's complete mastery in fusing historical event with psychological motivation. The characters' behavior and their various fates are dramatically represented as largely the results of the historical forces at work; there is an inevitability to the action. Action and character, in fact, are inseparable, as in all effective tragedy. Ravensworth's single-minded determination to root out "with an unsparing hand/ The weeds that choke the soil," his conviction that "the powers of darkness are at work among us," is made clear in the opening scene, and this obsession hangs over the characters and the action as a central, remarkably sustained idea.

Finally, there is strong temptation to speculate on the influence of *Superstition* on Hawthorne, who was an undergraduate at Bowdoin College when the play was first produced. Hawthorne, indeed, would later use the theme of the regicides in his short story "The Gray Champion," and Ravensworth's obsession is anticipatory of the diabolic singleness of purpose of Roger Chillingworth in Hawthorne's *The Scarlet Letter* (1850); even the similarity of surnames is notable. It could be argued, as well, that Isabella's independent piety and relative isolation are strongly suggestive of the character of Hester Prynne.

Regardless of whether *Superstition* was a direct early influence on Hawthorne, it stands on its own as a convincing treatment of a dark episode in American colonial history and as solid evidence of James Nelson Barker's legacy to the American theater.

Other major works

NONFICTION: "Peyton Randolph," "Thomas Jefferson," "John Jay," "Rufus King," "DeWitt Clinton," "Robert Fulton," in *Delaplaine's Repository of the Lives and Portraits of Distinguished Americans*, 1817.

Bibliography

Hodge, Francis. *Yankee Theater: The Image of America on the Stage, 1825-1850.* Austin: University of Texas Press, 1964. Deals with portrayals of the stage Yankee, a popular comic figure in American drama of the period. Sees Barker's *Tears and Smiles* as only a curiosity among Yankee plays, since Barker himself had never seen a Yankee and since the leading character was played by a British actor.

Moody, Richard. *America Takes the Stage.* Bloomington: University of Indiana Press, 1955. The author particularly notes Barker's use of native themes and characters. Though his *The Indian Princess* was the first play in which Pocahontas appeared as a principal figure, Barker relied too closely on the undramatic nature of his source, John Smith's *The Generall Historie of Virginia, New England, and the Summer Isles* (1642), and presented the famous scene too early. Much of the rest of the play is thus anticlimactic.

Musser, Paul. *James Nelson Barker, 1784-1858.* New York: AMS Press, 1969. This definitive study, though brief, traces Barker's life and career from his early education in Philadelphia to his political career as collector of the port during the administration of President James K. Polk. Musser includes the complete text of *Tears and Smiles* and sees Barker as a writer who, by temperament and training, was a leading advocate of native material in American drama.

Quinn, Arthur Hobson. *A History of the American Drama from the Beginning to the Civil War.* 2d ed. New York: F. S. Crofts, 1951. Though now a venerable source, Quinn's study is still valuable, drawing as it does on personal material then extant. Scholarly, precise, and clear, Quinn's work is probably the most accessible. Part of one chapter presents an overview of Barker's plays, noting the later revivals and the actors who were then popular.

Vaughan, Jack A. *Early American Dramatists from the Beginnings to 1900.* New York: Frederick Ungar, 1981. One chapter presents a short study of Barker's five extant plays. Though noting Barker's use of melodrama and sentimentality, Vaughan also says that Barker knew how to write effective drama and could be "genuinely moving," especially in *Superstition*, probably his best play.

Edward Fiorelli

PETER BARNES

Born: London, England; January 10, 1931

Principal drama

Sclerosis, pr. 1965; *The Ruling Class: A Baroque Comedy*, pr. 1968, pb. 1969; *Leonardo's Last Supper*, pr. 1969, pb. 1970; *Noonday Demons*, pr. 1969, pb. 1970; *Lulu*, pr. 1970, pb. 1971 (conflation of Frank Wedekind's *Der Erdgeist* and *Die Büchse der Pandora*); *The Bewitched*, pr., pb. 1974; *The Frontiers of Farce*, pr. 1976, pb. 1977 (adaptations of Georges Feydeau's *On purge Bébé!* and Wedekind's *Der Kammersänger*); *Antonio*, pr. 1977 (radio play), pr. 1979 (staged; adaptation of John Marston's plays *Antonio and Mellida* and *Antonio's Revenge*); *Laughter!*, pr., pb. 1978; *Collected Plays*, pb. 1981; *Red Noses*, pr., pb. 1985; *Plays I*, pb. 1989; *Revolutionary Witness, and Nobody Here but Us Chickens*, pb. 1989; *The Spirit of Man and More Barnes' People: Seven Monologues*, pb. 1990; *Sunsets and Glories*, pr., pb. 1990.

Other literary forms

Peter Barnes is known primarily for a wide range of theater-related activities. He is an editor, adapter, and director of stage and radio plays and cabaret. He has also written many screenplays as well as worked as a story editor for Warwick Films. Barnes draws an important distinction between his film work, in which he is simply practicing a craft, and his stage plays, which are the product of an inner compulsion.

Achievements

Barnes is a controversial English playwright with an international reputation. His plays are all complex, seriocomic or satirical studies in opposites and extremes. For the most part, he writes highly theatrical, nonrealistic, antiestablishment plays, which employ elements of farce; alienation or dislocation effects such as the rapid succession of short, contrasting scenes or the unexpected introduction of songs and dance; and surrealistic devices. His work contains echoes of English Renaissance dramas, English music hall, American vaudeville, musical comedy, and motion pictures. His theatrical language is richly textured, full of neologisms, literary, biblical, and historical allusions, and British and American slang. In his historical plays, he creates special, eccentric languages with their own period flavor. Most of his own radio plays are more realistic, but his characters and situations are always extraordinary or disturbing. Barnes constantly attacks the corruption of the powerful, the greedy, and the obsessed, and defends the victims of society: the lonely, the old, the dispossessed, the disadvantaged.

Although Barnes' view of the world is pessimistic, there is, particularly in the plays after 1978, a glimmer of hope that the world can be improved. Laughter can be used by the powerful to divert attention from their oppression of the less fortunate, but it can also be a major source of good, and Barnes' plays reverberate with irreverent laughter at social or religious pretensions and an absurd universe. Barnes' work is distinguished by its disturbing subject matter, its rough, often vulgar energy, and its spectacular stage effects. His universe is in turmoil, with no clear direction or purpose. Barnes mirrors ontological anxiety by playing on the paradoxes and ambiguities of life and by juxtaposing contrasting moods, which ultimately prevent any true comic or tragic resolution.

Barnes has also made considerable contributions to the theater and to radio drama as reviver, editor, adaptor, and director of plays, both English and European, hitherto neglected in England. His own collections of radio plays for the British Broadcasting Corporation (BBC) earned for him the Giles Cooper Award for Radio Drama in 1981 and 1984. For his stage plays he won the John Whiting Award in 1968 and the *Evening Standard* Award in 1969 for *The Ruling Class*, and the Olivier Award for Best Play of the Year, 1985, for *Red Noses*. In 1989, *Nobody Here but Us Chickens* won the Royal Television Society Award as the year's best television drama.

Biography

Peter Barnes was born in the East End of London on January 10, 1931. His parents, assimilated Jews, later moved the family to the holiday resort of Clacton-on-Sea, Essex, where they ran an amusement arcade on the pier. He has one younger sister. During World War II, Barnes was evacuated to the county of Gloucestershire. After the war, he returned to Clacton and completed his formal education at a local grammar school, followed by a year's compulsory military service. He continued his education at night school in London while working as a civil servant for the Greater London Council and as a free-lance film critic. In 1954 he was film critic for *Films and Filming*, and the following year he became a story editor for Warwick Films. From about 1958 to 1967, he worked free-lance on a number of screenplays, including *Violent Moment* (1958), *The Professionals* (1960), *Off Beat* (1961), and *Ring of Spies* (1964). In 1961, he married Charlotte Beck, a secretary at the British Film Institute.

His own first play, *The Man with a Feather in His Hat*, was produced for television in 1960. His first stage play, *The Time of the Barracudas*, was produced in San Francisco and Los Angeles in 1963, but it failed, and Barnes refused permission for any subsequent productions. In 1965, his one-act play *Sclerosis* was produced at the Edinburgh Festival and later at the Aldwych Theatre, London, directed by Charles Marowitz. In 1968, Barnes achieved considerable public success with his award-winning play, *The Ruling Class*, at the Nottingham Playhouse, later performed at the Piccadilly Theatre, London, directed by Stuart Burge. This play, more than any other of Barnes' works, has been staged all over the world, and a film version, starring Peter O'Toole, with screenplay by Barnes, released in 1972, established his international reputation.

Also in 1969, Barnes' two one-act plays *Leonardo's Last Supper* and *Noonday Demons* were played at the Open Space Theatre, London, directed by Charles Marowitz. His next full-length play, *The Bewitched*, was produced in 1974 by the Royal Shakespeare Company at the Aldwych, directed by Terry Hands, and received mixed reviews. *Laughter!* was produced by the Royal Court Theatre in 1978, directed by Charles Marowitz, Barnes having correctly anticipated that this work would displease most critics. That same year he completed *Red Noses, Black Death*, which, thanks at least in part to the unfavorable reception of *Laughter!*, was not to be seen until 1985 in a production by the Royal Shakespeare Company at the Barbican, London, directed by Terry Hands, the title shortened to *Red Noses*.

Barnes occupied himself between stage productions by editing, conflating, or adapting, and occasionally directing, plays by Ben Jonson: *The Alchemist* (1610) and *The Devil Is an Ass* (1616) at the Nottingham Playhouse, co-directed by Stuart Burge; *Bartholomew Fair* (1614) at the Roundhouse, London, under his own direction; and also plays by Thomas Middleton, George Chapman, Thomas Otway, Georges Feydeau, and Frank Wedekind, both for the stage and for radio. One notes particularly the success of *Lulu*, produced in Nottingham and London in 1970; *Antonio*, an adaptation/conflation of John Marston's *Antonio and Mellida* (1599) and *Antonio's Revenge* (1599), first heard on BBC radio in 1977 and later staged at the Nottingham Playhouse in 1979; and *The Frontiers of Farce*, produced at the Old Vic in 1976.

In a conscious effort to refine his skills and experiment with plays employing smaller casts, Barnes worked on three sets of short radio dramas—monologues, duologues, and three-character plays—produced by the BBC in 1981, 1984, and 1986 respectively, under the headings of *Barnes' People I*, *Barnes' People II*, and *Barnes' People III*. These plays, acted by such great performers as Sir John Gielgud, Dame Edith Evans, Paul Scofield, Alec McCowen, Peter Ustinov, and Ian McKellen, were very well received in Great Britain and won two drama awards. He also remained active in live theater, directing a 1987 London production of *Bartholomew Fair* and writing *Sunsets and Glories*, which was produced in 1990.

Analysis

Peter Barnes' plays are a heady mixture of many theatrical forms in which the visual elements are important; the written text falls far short of offering the true effect of a good production. Barnes claims that "the aim is to create, by means of soliloquy, rhetoric, formalized ritual, slapstick, songs and dances, a comic theatre of contrasting moods and opposites, where everything is simultaneously tragic and ridiculous." Most reviewers and critics agree about the theatrical brilliance and ingenuity of his plays, but opinion is divided about the significance or depth of his views of the human condition. Barnes is concerned with the pressures of society (authority) which suppress openness of feeling and deny happiness (freedom). His plays attack class, privilege, and whatever prevents the realization of individual or group fulfillment; revolution, even anarchy, may be better than meek submission. Above all, Barnes reveals the fierce tenacity with which groups or individuals hold on to or grasp at power and make society less human. Even devotion to God conceals selfishness, encourages persecution, or is a form of madness or obsession. Barnes is constantly preoccupied with man's inhumanity to man and with God's seeming indifference to human suffering. While most of his plays suggest that the world is beyond redemption, there are small but significant gleams of hope in the darkness, especially in the plays after 1978, and the comic vitality in all of his works mitigates Barnes' anger and pessimism.

Barnes' first published play, *The Ruling Class*, ridicules the English upper classes, the House of Lords, the Anglican Church, public schools (expensive private upper-class institutions), the police, English xenophobia, psychiatrists, snobbery, and complacency. The play begins with the death of the thirteenth Earl of Gurney. Dressed in a tutu and military dress hat and jacket, and brandishing a sword, the Earl indulges in a recreational mock-hanging in order to induce intoxicating visions; he accidentally kills himself. His son, Jack, the fourteenth Earl, becomes the focus of the family's efforts to marry him off to Grace Shelley, have him produce an heir, and then certify him insane. He is a threat because of his egalitarian views; he believes himself to be the God of Love reincarnated.

The loving Earl is a paranoid schizophrenic with enormous energy and an eccentric verbal exuberance, but his delusions make him an easy victim. When asked why he thinks he is God, he replies, "Simple. When I pray to Him I find I'm talking to myself." His uncle, Sir Charles, persuades Grace, his mistress, a former actress and stripper, to impersonate Marguerite Gautier, the Lady of the Camelias, to whom the Earl thinks he is already married. She arrives at a crucial moment dressed as the heroine of Giuseppe Verdi's *La Traviata* (1853), complete with wax camelias, singing the famous "Godiam" aria. In this splendid scene, the Earl sings and dances with her.

The main focus of the play is on Jack as the New Testament God of Love and what he becomes after Dr. Herder's "cure": the Old Testament God of Wrath and Justice, and Jack the Ripper. No longer open, spontaneous, and joyful, Jack becomes repressed, Victorian, and as such acceptable to the ruling class. The pivotal scene is the confrontation arranged by Dr. Herder between the madman McKyle, the High-Voltage Messiah, and Jack, the God of Love. This scene presents the symbolic death of Jack as Jesus, and his rebirth, coinciding with the birth of Jack's son and heir, as God the Father.

Jack's "change" is demonstrated by his being attacked by a surreal, apelike monster dressed in Victorian garb, a Victorian Beast which possesses him, although it is unseen by the others onstage, and Jack's pummeling seems to be an epileptic seizure. Act 2 shows Jack's successful efforts to establish his normality, dominate his family, and become a bulwark of respectability, while as Jack the Ripper he carries on a private war against sexuality by murdering his amorous Aunt Claire and, ultimately, his wife. His maiden speech in the House of Lords on the need of the strong to crush the weak receives rapturous applause: He is one of them at last.

Noonday Demons also deals with religion, this time the folly of the "saintly" anchorite's wish to purge himself of the sins of the flesh. Saint Eusebius is shown in his cave in the Theban desert, ragged and in chains, attempting to rid himself of "old style man": "In destroying my body I destroyed Space and Time," he claims. He can see into the future, and communes with angelic voices. Challenged and tempted by an inner demon, he successfully resists wealth, lust, and power. When another anchorite, Saint Pior, arrives and lays claim to Saint Eusebius' cave, conflict between the two holy men quickly develops, each saint being convinced that he alone interprets God's will and that the other must be a demon. Saint Eusebius kills Saint Pior, and he is again able to commune with the angels, but the play's ending undercuts his triumph as, transported to the present, he can see how the theater audience watching *Noonday Demons* regards his life as meaningless and bizarre.

Leonardo's Last Supper, set in the grisly Ambois charnel house to which Leonardo da Vinci's corpse has been taken, introduces the audience to the squabbling Lasca family, forerunners of modern morticians, fallen on hard times. They toast their good luck in having been sent a "golden carcass" which will restore their wealth and reputation. Yet Leonardo is not dead, although when he awakes in such a place he finds it hard to believe that he is alive. The Lascas are not interested in the gratitude of future generations for preserving "the universal man." They are the new men: "Men o' trade, o' money, we'll build a new heaven and a new earth by helping ourselves." To them, Leonardo is a luxury, as are the things he represents: beauty, truth, knowledge, humanity. Seeing their trade being taken away from them, they seize, kill, and prepare Leonardo for burial, a family happily reunited in their business pursuits.

The Bewitched is long and complex, but one can recognize in it many of the themes explored in Barnes' earlier plays, with a heightened savagery and ironic intensity to them: cruelty and violence performed in the name of a God of Love; demoniac possession and angry confrontations between "holy" men; the professional pride and dedication of destroyers of men, from doctors and astrologers to torturers for the Inquisition; the absurd tenacity with which the Spanish grandees cling to their often ludicrous privileges; and the unscrupulous ways in which men behave when driven to pettiness, greed, folly, jealousy, murder. *The Bewitched* is a concentrated attack on the madness of man's blind respect for hierarchical order.

The play deals in particular with the reign of Carlos II, the last of the Spanish Habsburgs. The end product of prolonged inbreeding, Carlos is sickly, impotent, epileptic, and the pawn of unscrupulous politicians, leaders of church and court. The play records some of the intrigues and incredible devices used to keep Carlos alive and to induce him to produce an heir to the Spanish throne and thus preserve the privileged caste. Carlos dies childless, his throne passes to the Bourbons, and the terrible War of the Spanish Succession follows: "One million dead. Two million wounded. Western Europe is in ruins." The reign of Carlos is "a glorious monument to futility." In one of his few lucid moments in the play, Carlos presents Barnes' most open attack on the system when he says,

> Now I see Authority's a poor provider.
> No blessings come from 't
> No man born shouldst ha' t', wield 't . . .
> 'Twill make a desert o' this world
> Whilst there's still one man left t' gi' commands
> And another who'll obey 'em.

Laughter! is the most extreme and most controversial of Barnes' plays. Its thesis is voiced by the character of the Author, who introduces the play: "Comedy is the enemy," the ally of tyrants. "It softens our hatred. An excuse to change nothing, for nothing needs changing when it's all a joke." He asks the audience to root out laughter, "strangle mirth, let the heart pump sulphuric acid, not blood." This plea is accompanied by some diverting, zany stage business, including a whirling bow tie and trousers falling to reveal spangled underpants.

Part 1 deals with the reign of Ivan the Terrible; part 2 with Auschwitz. Ivan is reluctant either to wield power or to surrender it; nevertheless, in the name of authority he slaughters thousands and kills his own son to protect him from the pain of exercising power. Finally, an Angel of Death, dressed like a seedy office clerk, confronts Ivan. After wrestling with this relentless antagonist, Ivan is petrified into a statue, befouled by bird droppings.

In part 2, the setting is Berlin, where petty bureaucrats Else Jost, Victor Cranach, and Heinz Stroop live out their working lives. It is Christmas Eve, 1942. They are visited by the snooping, fanatical Nazi, Gottleb. In spite of wartime shortages and constant fear of the authorities should they deviate from the expected norm, they manage a kind of drunken festivity, and induce an ambiguous vision of the truth behind their façade of loyalty. They rail against their superiors and intellectuals, and finally fire off a round of subversive anti-Hitler jokes. Gottleb then summons a vision of what their paperwork is really masking: the production of flues for the crematoriums at Auschwitz. Onstage, a graphic, horrible representation of the death agonies of those gassed by hydro-cyanide is shown with dummies in place of human beings. Horrified, the bureaucrats cannot translate coded office numbers into the brutal facts. They throw out Gottleb and find solace in being "ordinary people, people who like people, people like them, you, me, us." The epilogue introduces the farewell Christmas concert appearance of the Boffo Boys of Birkenau, Abe Bimko and Hymie Bieberstein, whose awful dance and patter routine comes to an end as the gas does its work.

Red Noses, a most complex play, elaborates many of the themes found in *The Bewitched*, and modifies some of the ideas expounded in *Laughter!* Faced with the horror of the Black Death, which has removed more than a third of the population of Europe, what can a small, bizarre group of entertainers do to improve the world? Given the facts that the Church, prayers, medicine, and wealth are helpless against the plague, Father Flote and his group of "Christ's Clowns," wearing red noses, can at least give the dying some consolation. They are sanctioned by Pope Clement VI and become agents of Church power, a distraction from the real world.

Yet Barnes also suggests that laughter can be associated with revolution and redemption. Opposed to the Floties are the Black Ravens, who see the plague as a chance to create an egalitarian society. Another opposing group, the Flagellants, seek no social change but defy the Church establishment and wish to atone for sin by self-inflicted punishment and direct appeal to God. Inevitably the Church cannot tolerate such deviations and eventually destroys both the Black Ravens and the Flagellants. The Church tolerates the Floties, however, even after the end of the plague, until Father Flote, realizing that there are valuable qualities in the beliefs of the two outlawed groups—that laughter is in fact revolutionary as well as a corrective to sin—defies papal authority and advocates SLOP, "Slow, Lawful, Orthodox Progress." Laughter will no longer be only for losers but can be a force for social and personal improvement. The Church regards Father Flote's defiance as a threat, and the Red Noses are executed. The importance of the individual, the need for social reform, and the positive power of "the laughter of compassion and joy" are at last united in a new and more positive way in a play that is highly complex and richly textured.

The three collections of radio plays, too numerous to discuss here, are particularly interesting as illustrations of the transition Barnes makes from deep pessimism to a more positive view of the world. The outstanding play in *Barnes' People I* is "Rosa," about an aging, disillusioned, but still dedicated social worker. She has a brief, devastating vision of an army of geriatrics on the rampage, raging against the waste of their lives; her vision ends, however, and she knows that she must go on, working with the system, however imperfect it may be: "Slow, Lawful, Orthodox Progress." "The Three Visions," the last play of *Barnes' People III*, is a discussion between Barnes at ages thirty-one, Barnes at age fifty-five, and Barnes at age seventy-four. It is clear that however little he believes he has contributed to his profession, he goes on with the struggle, and never compromises.

Other major works

TELEPLAY: *The Man with a Feather in His Hat*, 1960.

RADIO PLAYS: *Barnes' People I: Seven Monologues*, 1981; *Barnes' People II: Seven Duologues*, 1984; *The Real Long John Silver and Other Plays: Barnes' People III*, 1986.

TRANSLATION: *Tango at the End of Winter*, 1991.

Bibliography

Barnes, Peter. "Theater of the Extreme: An Interview with Peter Barnes." Interview by Mark Bly and Doug Wager. *Theater* 12 (Spring, 1981): 43. The interviewers get Barnes talking on his relationship to Brechtian imagination and rules for the theater, as a catalyst for social change. Barnes calls for the revival of English dramatic classics (a Barnes specialty) not the stagings of Charles Dickens' novel *Nicholas Nickleby* (1838-1839). "Comedy transcending tragedy" is a characteristic of modern times, he states.

Hiley, Jim. "Liberating Laughter: Peter Barnes and Peter Nichols in Interviews with Jim Hiley." *Plays and Players* 25, no. 6 (March, 1978): 14-17. Barnes discusses *Laughter!*, his 1978 play at the Royal Court, dealing with "man's inhumanity to man" in the form of Ivan the Terrible and Auschwitz. "Cruelty . . . has progressed into something more systematic" than the personal affair of the feudal times, he says. Discusses his adaptation of Ben Jonson's plays and his controversy with critics over his style and content.

Hinchliffe, Arnold P. *British Theatre, 1950-1970.* Totowa, N.J.: Rowman & Littlefield, 1974. A journalistic style introduces the "rocket that came from Nottingham," with his play *Sclerosis*, produced at the Traverse Theatre. The author notes that Barnes "had been a playwright for ten years and screenwriter for fourteen" before his success with *The Ruling Class.* Also discusses *Lulu* and two one-act plays. Good midcareer assessment.

Taylor, John Russell. *The Second Wave: British Drama for the Seventies.* New York: Hill & Wang, 1971. Barnes is among the "Dark Fantastic," with David Hare, Howard Brenton, and others, who "have distinguished themselves in a kind of baroque black comedy, related in its turn to the plays of Joe Orton. . . ." *The Ruling Class* and *Leonardo's Last Supper* ("a briskly ironic fantasy") are dealt with, and *Noonday Demons* is mentioned.

Worth, Katharine J. *Revolutions in Modern English Drama.* London:

G. Bell & Sons, 1972. The chapter entitled "Forms of Freedom and Mystery: Beneath the Subtext" places Barnes in the company of Samuel Beckett, Joe Orton, and Heathcote Williams. Worth describes Barnes as taking the "farce in curious new directions, mixing it with melodrama in a most unlikely and distinctive style." Contains a long discussion of *The Ruling Class.*

Worthen, W. B. *Modern Drama and the Rhetoric of Theater.* Berkeley: University of California Press, 1992. Deals with *Laughter!* at length: "To read *Laughter!* as about Auschwitz alone is crucially to misread the play's theatrical design," says Worthen, adding that the play "stages the spectator's performance as part of its critique of history." Good index.

Ian C. Todd
(Updated by *Thomas J. Taylor*)

SIR JAMES BARRIE

Born: Kirriemuir, Scotland; May 9, 1860
Died: London, England; June 19, 1937

Principal drama

Ibsen's Ghost: Or, Toole Up to Date, pr. 1891, pb. 1939; *Richard Savage*, pr., pb. 1891 (with H. B. M. Watson); *Walker, London*, pr. 1892, pb. 1907; *The Professor's Love Story*, pr. 1892, pb. 1942; *The Little Minister*, pr. 1897, pb. 1942 (adaptation of Barrie's novel); *The Wedding Guest*, pr., pb. 1900; *Quality Street*, pr. 1902, pb. 1913; *The Admirable Crichton*, pr. 1902, pb. 1914; *Little Mary*, pr. 1903, pb. 1942; *Peter Pan: Or, The Boy Who Wouldn't Grow Up*, pr. 1904, pb. 1928; *Alice-Sit-by-the-Fire*, pr. 1905, pb. 1919; *Josephine*, pr. 1906; *Punch*, pr. 1906; *What Every Woman Knows*, pr. 1908, pb. 1918; *The Twelve-Pound Look*, pr. 1910, pb. 1914; *The Will*, pr. 1913, pb. 1914; *Der Tag: Or, The Tragic Man*, pr., pb. 1914; *The New Word*, pr. 1915, pb. 1918; *A Kiss for Cinderella*, pr. 1916, pb. 1920; *Dear Brutus*, pr. 1917, pb. 1923; *The Old Lady Shows Her Medals*, pr. 1917, pb. 1918; *Barbara's Wedding*, pb. 1918, pr. 1927; *A Well-Remembered Voice*, pr., pb. 1918; *Mary Rose*, pr. 1920, pb. 1924; *Shall We Join the Ladies?*, pr. 1921, pb. 1927; *The Boy David*, pr. 1936, pb. 1938; *Representative Plays*, pb. 1954.

Other literary forms

The sheer volume of Sir James Barrie's literary output, together with the fact that his most successful and enduring works were written for the stage, tends to obscure recognition of his talent in other genres. His success as a playwright came when he was already launched as a writer. The vignettes and anecdotes of his literary apprenticeship had formed the basis for the successful *Auld Licht Idylls* (1888), and Barrie might have been content to continue drawing on his Scottish experiences in the form of articles and essays in the then popular "Kailyard" (cabbage-patch) style but for his determination to write a novel. Success in this genre came eventually with *The Little Minister* (1891), written in the same vein as the *Auld Licht Idylls*.

Barrie returned to the Scottish setting in *Margaret Ogilvy* (1896), a biography based on sentimental recollections of his mother. Questions were raised as to the genre of the work, and reviewers in Scotland were shocked by the detailed ruthlessness of his observation. No less revealing is the largely autobiographical novel *Sentimental Tommy* (1896), which, together with its sequel, *Tommy and Grizel* (1900), throws considerable light on Barrie's complex personality.

The novel *The Little White Bird* (1902) contained a blueprint for the development of the Peter Pan theme, but it was the successful dramatization of *The Little Minister* which finally channeled Barrie's literary efforts away from the novel toward the stage. The foundation of Barrie's career as a playwright was his determination to master the novel and to capitalize on his potentially limiting Scottish background and childhood experiences.

Achievements

Barrie was a prolific and versatile writer who enjoyed great popularity in his day, but he tends to be remembered only as the creator of *Peter Pan*. This enduringly popular work was the most successful play of Barrie's entire career, but it is uncharacteristic of his writing in that it was aimed at a children's audience. The secret of its undiminished popularity lies in Barrie's ability to appeal on different levels to both adults and children.

The bulk of Barrie's writing has now sunk into relative obscurity. It may be that his other works, and particularly his plays, are too closely tied to the spirit of the age in which they were conceived, or that their psychology is too naïve and their characters too transparent for modern taste. Nevertheless, Barrie's achievements as a playwright should not be assessed on the merits of *Peter Pan* alone.

Taken in the context of his dramatic works as a whole, *Peter Pan* can be seen to be a natural development of an escapist tendency which frequently motivates Barrie's plays. Often his plots center on a juxtaposition of a fantasy world with the "real" world as it is represented on the stage—real for the characters themselves and accepted as such by the audience. Barrie's preoccupation with psychological escapism can be attributed to his own tendency to fantasize in his closest personal relationships. Additionally, by involving his characters in the mechanics of a fantasy world as distinct from a theatrical representation of the real world, Barrie gives himself much greater scope for social criticism: Fantasy worlds are used to highlight the shortcomings of the real world.

Biography

James Matthew Barrie was of humble origins, the seventh of the eight surviving children of David Barrie, a Scottish weaver. Barrie's mother, Margaret Ogilvy, was a strict Puritan, reared in the fundamentalist beliefs of the Auld Lichts (Old Lights), a sect of the Presbyterian Church of Scotland. The unusual strength of the influence she exerted over Barrie throughout his life was detrimental to him in many ways. When he was six, his older brother David, aged nearly fourteen and his mother's favorite, died after a skating accident. Margaret Ogilvy was desolate in her loss, and the young James made a conscious effort to become a substitute for David, to help her overcome her grief. This was the beginning of the sharp division for Barrie between home, where he was acting out a fantasy in his most intimate relationship, and the outside, real world.

Barrie entered Dumfries Academy in 1873, and while there he began to be interested in all aspects of the theater. He was a founding member of a school dramatic society, and left school intent on becoming a writer. Family opposition was strong, however, and reluctantly he entered Edinburgh University, graduating in 1882. During his years as an undergraduate, he wrote as a free-lance drama critic for the Edinburgh *Courant*. After an unsuccessful year spent in Edinburgh researching a book on the early satirical poetry of Great Britain, he answered an advertisement for a job as leader-writer for the *Nottingham Journal*. Editorial supervision was virtually nonexistent, and Barrie wrote extensively for the paper under a variety of names. He began sending articles to London, undaunted by frequent rejections.

In 1884, Barrie returned to Scotland, where he wrote up his mother's childhood memories. "An Auld Licht Community" was published in the *St. James's Gazette*, and the editor requested more in the same vein, which Barrie found easy to provide. The following year, he decided that to make a career of writing he would have to be in London, so he moved south. He managed to sell articles steadily and before long was making a respectable living. His first successful book, a collection of Scottish articles, *Auld Licht Idylls*, appeared in 1888; together with *A Window in Thrums* (1889), it raised a storm of protest in Scotland, but Barrie was undeterred.

Barrie was now writing furiously, working simultaneously on a novel, *The Little Minister*, and a play. The part of the second leading lady in *Walker, London* went to Mary Ansell, whom Barrie ultimately married in 1894. The marriage, apparently unconsummated, ended in divorce in 1909, their companionship having been disrupted by the extraordinary way that Barrie was attracted to the Llewelyn Davies family, initially to the children, George (born 1893), Jack (born 1894), and Peter (born 1897), but later to Sylvia Jocelyn Llewelyn Davies, their mother. Barrie met her at a dinner party in 1897 and subsequently met the children in Kensington Gardens. They were enchanted by his stories, and he would frequently accompany them home. It was not long before he was behaving like a member of the family, despite the reluctance of their father, Arthur Llewelyn Davies, to accept this situation.

The year 1900 saw the birth of the Llewelyn Davies' fourth son, Michael, and Mary Barrie's purchase of Black Lake Cottage on the outskirts of Farnham, Surrey. Here Barrie and the three older Davies boys spent the summer of 1901 enacting adventures and fantasies in the overgrown gardens, setting the scene for *Peter Pan*; it was not until 1903, however, after the success of *Quality Street*, *The Admirable Crichton*, and *Little Mary*, that Barrie began the play which was to make him a household name.

In 1906, two years after the birth of his fifth son, Nicholas, Arthur Llewelyn Davies was diagnosed as having cancer. Unable to earn at the

Bar, he had no alternative but gratefully to accept Barrie's offer of financial support for his family. Barrie was by now spending almost all of his free time with the Davies family, leaving his own wife, Mary, very much alone. In the three-year period between Arthur's death and her own in 1910, Sylvia Davies received continuous support and attention from Barrie, and when she died Barrie took upon himself the guardianship of her sons— "My Boys," as he called them. Of the five, he seems to have been closest to George, killed in France in 1915, and Michael, drowned at Oxford in 1921. Michael's death prostrated Barrie, but he was helped over it by Lady Cynthia Asquith, who had been acting as his personal assistant since 1917. Barrie's relationship with her developed along similar lines to his relationship with Sylvia Llewelyn Davies. He frequently assisted the Asquiths out of financial difficulties with generous presents to Cynthia, and became imperceptibly an extension of their family, in the face of the opposition and dislike of Herbert (Beb) Asquith, an aspiring writer.

For a shy man, Barrie was by this time a very prominent figure. Having declined a knighthood in 1909, he had accepted a baronetcy in 1913 and was awarded the Order of Merit in 1922. He was unfailingly generous with his money, and during World War I he funded and organized the establishment of a home for refugee mothers and children in France. He continued a voluminous correspondence even after being forced by pain in his right hand to train himself to write with his left.

Barrie's last play, *The Boy David*, written for the Austrian actress Elisabeth Bergner, received highly critical notices. Cynthia Asquith arranged a command performance which should have been a triumph for Barrie but ended up as an unremarkable matinee, and the playwright died shortly afterward, a disappointed man.

Analysis

Walker, London was Sir James Barrie's third attempt at writing for the stage, but the first to meet with any real success. The idea for the setting came from a summer Barrie had spent on a houseboat on the Thames, and the play captures the lazy indolence of life moored to the riverbank. It is not by any means an outstanding work but is of interest as an early approach to the question of the relationship between fantasy and the real world, which was to become a constant preoccupation in Barrie's subsequent works.

The pleasant lethargy of the party on the houseboat is disturbed but not spoiled by an uninvited guest, an undistinguished London barber by the name of Jason Phipps. Phipps has run away from the reality of his everyday life, and for the duration of his holiday, which should have been his honeymoon, has decided to assume the identity of one of his customers, the celebrated African explorer Colonel Neil. Mrs. Golightly and the other members of the houseboat party are indebted to the newcomer for his ostensibly heroic action in saving Bell Golightly from drowning in a punting accident, and they are delighted to be able to offer hospitality to one so famous. The audience, however, is well aware that Neil is an impostor. He has bribed the only witness of the accident to support the heroic version of the episode, and he is being diligently searched for by his jilted fiancée. During the week that Phipps spends on board the houseboat, he regales the company with vivid descriptions of the adventures he has had on his explorations, drawing his listeners unwittingly into the fantasy he is building. As Neil, Phipps makes proposals to both Bell Golightly and her cousin Nanny O'Brien—proposals which they find difficult to reject, because they are caught up in the fantasy, too; as himself, however, Phipps realizes that the girl for him is the faithful Sarah, who catches up with him in the end. The last act is virtually pure farce and ends with Phipps making a quick exit into his everyday life before he can be unmasked.

Barrie had originally intended the play to be entitled "The Houseboat," but there was another work in existence by that title and thus a new one had to be found. As Phipps leaves the stage for the last time he is asked for his address. He gives it as Walker, London, the new title of the play: "Walker" was a slang word meaning a hoaxer.

The theme of assumed identity recurs in *Quality Street*, which was first produced in October, 1902, only one month before the equally successful *The Admirable Crichton*, enjoying a run of fourteen months. As with *Walker, London*, the definitive title of the play was a later alteration. The working title was "Phoebe's Garden," but Quality Street, the name of an actual town between Leith and North Berwick, appealed to Barrie; the final title subtly reinforces the notions of hidebound respectability with which the play deals.

The action takes place in Quality Street during the Napoleonic Wars. The heroine, Miss Phoebe Throssel, has fallen in love with a local doctor, Valentine Brown. Both Phoebe and her sister Susan, an old maid, expect that "V. B.," as they refer to him, is calling to make his declaration and ask for Phoebe's hand. Unfortunately, it becomes apparent that he has other news: He has enlisted in the army and will be leaving forthwith to join the campaign against the French. The Misses Throssel cover their disappointment admirably and, as convention demands, say nothing of love.

The second act takes place ten years later. The blue and white frilliness of the Throssel parlor has been subordinated to the requirements of a classroom. It transpires that Phoebe and Susan, having invested their money according to Brown's advice, have suffered a substantial loss and have been forced to earn their living by opening a school. Phoebe appears to have aged much more than ten years, assuming prematurely the garb and attitudes of the old maid she seems destined to become. The sisters' new way of life is highly distasteful to them, but for respectable women in their position, society offers no other choice. Their drab existence is suddenly brightened by the return of Valentine Brown and the rest of the troops. The doctor is visibly struck by the change in Phoebe when he calls on the Throssels unexpectedly, for she is at her most severe in her schoolmistress attire. Phoebe suddenly realizes that she no longer has to act older than her years. They have caught up with her, and she has come a long way from being the pretty girl that she was when the troops left for the war.

When Phoebe next appears on the stage, she has discarded her cap and drab clothes and has pulled out all her ringlets, so that she is virtually her former self, except for what she has experienced during the ten years. It is in this guise that Brown sees her next. She is inspired to pass herself off as her own niece, Miss Livvy, a ploy which her sister is pushed into supporting. The mechanics of the deception give rise to some comic scenes, particularly when the sisters find themselves having to deceive their gossipy and envious friends, the Misses Willoughby. By wearing the same fashionable veil as her friend, which can be opened or closed at will by the wearer, Phoebe is accepted as Miss Livvy, but the ladies sense a mystery and are desperate to find out what is happening.

Phoebe daringly sets out on a round of balls given to celebrate the victory, and act 3 shows her in full swing, acting in her assumed identity in an outrageously flirtatious way and turning the heads of all the men present. She is determined to take revenge on Valentine Brown for having forgotten that he kissed her once, ten years before. For all of those years she treasured both the memory of the kiss and her guilt at the impropriety of having allowed him to kiss her, only to find upon his return that he does not even remember the event. The climax comes when it looks as though Brown is going to propose to Livvy, and she is preparing to reject him out of hand. Much to her surprise, however, he confesses that it is her aunt Phoebe whom he really loves; in courting her, so much like her aunt in appearance but so different in behavior, he has come to realize where his affections really lie, and where they have always lain.

The sisters now have to find a way of getting rid of the unwanted Livvy. She takes to her bed and Phoebe reappears, but the Misses Willoughby are extremely solicitous. As it seems inevitable that the deception will be discovered, the tension rises until Valentine Brown, in his capacity as a doctor, goes into Livvy's bedroom and reappears to report on the progress of the patient who does not exist. He then joins forces with the sisters to dispose of Livvy. He wraps the phantom up and takes her out to his carriage, which is sent off with the maidservant in attendance to convey the sick Livvy home. The suspicions of the watching neighbors are lulled and the way is clear for Valentine Brown to make his proposal and for it to be accepted by his beloved Phoebe.

In *Quality Street*, the assumption of a new identity is not a *fait accompli* as in *Walker, London*. It is a deliberate ploy, but it is seen to happen on-stage in direct response to a development in external circumstances affecting the character. Whereas the character assumed by Jason Phipps was based on an idealization of the attributes of a person unknown to the audience, Phoebe finds her model in her own past, so her escape from her own personality is more pragmatic and less fanciful; the essence of her assumed nature has lain dormant within her. It is only in her uncharacteristic co-quetry that Livvy is different from Phoebe, and in this there is a large measure of making up for lost opportunity, a foreshadowing of the development of this theme in *Dear Brutus*.

The approach to fantasy in *The Admirable Crichton* is quite different. In this play, Barrie draws a definite line between the "real" world, where the characters originate, and the fantasy one, where they end up after the shipwreck. The desert island, however, is only fantasy to the audience; for the characters, it becomes reality, and they journey from the reality of the "real" world to the reality of the fantasy and back again in the course of the play.

The Admirable Crichton, one of Barrie's most successful plays, is a comedy with a social message. The dominant theme is the equality of all individuals. As a philosophical ideal, the concept that all human beings are naturally equal is espoused by the Earl of Loam and is fashionably exploited in the peer's unprecedented declaration that one day a month all of his servants will meet the other members of his household on equal terms. Thus, the first act of the play opens on one such day, when the house is in a turmoil. It is immediately apparent to the audience that both masters and servants alike find the imposition of equality frustrating and unnatural. For the daughters of the house, it is a tiresome bore to receive their servants in the drawing room and address them as social equals using a respectful form of address. When "Miss" Fisher, Lady Mary's maid, is piqued by not taking precedence over the lower-ranking Tweeny, the audience may laugh at such trivial preoccupation with position in circumstances of temporary, but nevertheless total, equality, but Barrie is reminding them how deeply ingrained in society are the distinctions of rank and privilege.

The second act takes place a short time after the first, but the setting is a remote desert island. The main characters have been shipwrecked, and they appear on the stage immediately after the catastrophe; a particular feature of the set is that unidentified objects drop at intervals from the trees to the ground, adding to the strangeness and hostility of the environment in which the castaways now find themselves. It is not long before both the audience and the characters become aware that the man best equipped to lead the castaways in their survival effort is not the earl, the socially superior and conventionally obvious candidate, but Crichton the butler. Crichton is a man who knows his place both with respect to his employers, to whom he knows he is inferior, and with respect to his fellow servants, to whom he is undoubtedly superior. His progressive assumption of authority on the island is a natural extension of his regular duties, and he is accustomed to having other people under his authority. What is unforeseen, but very humorous, is the total inability of the upper-class members of the shipwrecked party to make any practical contribution to attending to their immediate survival needs. Even with three minutes' warning of the impending disaster, they were unable to dress themselves suitably and have only one pair of boots between them. The most useful contribution the Honorable Ernest can make is to compose exasperating epigrams, and the three young ladies seem unaware of the seriousness of their predicament as they bemoan the loss of their hairpins. Such concern for trivia in the face of a desperate situation does not inspire confidence in their ability to survive.

That the relationship between master and servant is already becoming strained is apparent from the way Crichton follows the example of the peer's daughters and criticizes him for having left behind the hairpin he found on the beach. While the girls cannot see beyond the normal function of the hairpin, Crichton can visualize its use in a number of ways. The Earl of Loam is quick to realize that Crichton may be stepping out of line, and a discussion of leadership develops, with the peer and the butler arguing from exactly opposite viewpoints from the ones they took in the first act. Indignantly, the upper-class members of the party decide to go it on their own, despite having saved nothing at all from the wreck. That anything was salvaged was only because of the foresight and industry of Crichton, and in due course the smell of his stew wafting along the beach brings the others crawling back to the campfire.

The events of the third act take place after a lapse of three years or so. The physical conditions of the party have taken a turn for the better, and they are comfortably housed and well fed. A number of ingenious contraptions have been devised to improve the quality of their lives, and it transpires that this is all because of the drive and ability of "the Guv." The audience may suspect that Crichton is "the Guv" but does not know for certain until he appears on the stage, a distinctly regal figure. There has been much discussion among the women prior to his appearance about who will have the honor of serving him, and the honor falls to Lady Mary, now known as Polly, who begs Tweeny to let her wear "It" for the occasion. "It" is the skirt Tweeny was prudent enough to put on the night they escaped from the wreck, the only such garment on the island.

While the audience may have admired Crichton's quiet efficiency and obvious leadership potential in act 2, the figure he cuts in act 3 is disquieting.

Despite the order and efficiency he has imposed on life on the island, despite the benefits he has brought to the others who clearly would not have survived long without him, he is, nevertheless, a dictator, and it is galling to see the women courting his attentions. At a time when the Labour movement was gathering strength and the Fabians were active, Barrie may well have intended a warning to the upper echelons of society of impending social change. After all, he, himself, was nearing the top of the social ladder, having started off on its lowest rungs. It is reassuring to see the old order restored in the last act, with a return to the status quo.

Having seen a more worthy side of the upper-class characters in their newly found identities on the island, the audience might expect to see them retain some of their improved qualities, but this is not to be. When they regain their former position of social superiority, they also become subject once again to the shallow conventions and superficial moral preoccupations of society, as exemplified by the attitudes of the dowager. The distorted account that emerges of their life on the island is not a willful fabrication by the characters. It is a fantasizing of the reality of the fantasy. It is what would be expected of them by society, and in this deception it is society that should be condemned. Through the medium of humor, Barrie thus succeeds in criticizing both the philosophy that all human beings are equal and the idea that any kind of social revolution would be an improvement on the existing social order. That the existing social order is not without its defects is freely admitted, but any social critique is subordinate to the primary purpose of the play, which is to entertain and amuse.

Reality and fantasy coexist in *Peter Pan,* also, but in contrast to *The Admirable Crichton,* the boundaries between the two states are fluid and indistinct. Barrie is concerned above all with the progression from the one to the other, and in most cases this is the progression from the imaginative existence of the child into the prosaic life of the adult. At first, adult reality and childhood fantasy seem diametrically opposed and mutually exclusive, but it soon becomes apparent that the degree to which the characters in *Peter Pan* are able to enter into and become part of the fantasy is directly dependent on their distance from childhood. Wendy, like her mother, will always retain a childlike streak in her nature which will ensure that her memory of Never Land will never fade completely, no matter how old she becomes, but Peter Pan will never leave Never Land because of his refusal to progress to adulthood.

The archetypal boy who never grew up, Peter Pan evolved in the stories of Kensington Gardens with which Barrie enchanted the Davies boys. The earliest literary version of these stories was a novel, *The Little White Bird,* which, contrary to Barrie's original plan, came to be dominated by Peter Pan. Barrie was increasingly attracted by this new character as his ties with the Davies family became even closer, and in 1903 he grew absorbed in writing a new play which would have Peter Pan as the central character. The scene for the play had already been set two years earlier in the gardens of Black Lake Cottage. At that time, Barrie had made a photographic record of the boys' adventures, with a preface ostensibly written by Peter Llewelyn Davies, whose name the hero of the new play assumed. Using the working title of "Peter and Wendy," Barrie offered his play to Herbert Beerbohm Tree, knowing it would entail an elaborate and expensive production, but he was not interested. It was Barrie's American associate, the impresario Charles Frohman, who grasped the play's potential and spared no effort to make it a success. He engaged the talented Dion Boucicault as producer, a recent innovation in the theatrical world, where production had traditionally been the concern of the actor-managers, and the play opened at the Duke of York's Theatre on December 27, 1904.

The plot of *Peter Pan* is calculated to appeal to the imaginations of the young. The Darling children, Wendy, John, and Michael, are induced by the intriguing, magical boy Peter Pan and his fairy acolyte Tinker Bell to abandon their comfortable nursery and savor the delights and perils of Never Land. The climax of the first act comes as they fly out the nursery window.

In the second act, the children become acquainted with the other inhabitants of Never Land. The Lost Boys, children without mothers who as babies fell out of their baby carriages, recognize Peter as their natural leader. They are permanently in danger from the Pirates, a motley crew led by the dastardly Captain Hook. The Redskins are enemies of both the Lost Boys and the Pirates until Peter and the Lost Boys rescue the belle of the tribe from death by marooning at Hook's hands. The appeal of the island is enhanced by the antics of the mermaids, the threat of the wolves and the Never Bird, not to mention the ticking crocodile which follows Hook inexorably around and around the island, waiting for the moment when it can finish making a meal of him.

In the fourth act, a great battle between the Redskins and the Pirates ends in victory for Hook, and it is then very easy for him to abduct Wendy and the Lost Boys as they prepare to leave Never Land. Only Peter can rescue them from the pirate ship before they are made to walk the plank, and this he does with great enthusiasm. Hook meets his nemesis, the crocodile, and the Darling children return to the security of their nursery.

Peter is unique among the characters in his insistence that he does not want to grow up. The Lost Boys have no fixed opinion on the subject and are easily talked into going back with Wendy and her brothers to be adopted, and Wendy herself realizes that growing up is inevitable. It is easy to see the parallel between Peter's refusal to countenance even the thought of growing up with the singular circumstances of Barrie's own childhood. Physically, he remained a child longer than most of his contemporaries and was marked throughout his adulthood by his short stature (he was just over five feet tall); on the other hand, carefree childhood ended abruptly for him at the age of six when he embarked on the fantasy relationship with his mother, trying to live up to her expectations for his older brother.

Barrie's emphasis on the reluctance of Peter Pan to grow up is often interpreted as a disenchantment with adult life and an idealization of childhood, but Never Land offers only a temporary refuge from, and not a permanent solution to, the problems of growing up; childhood as epitomized by Peter, and to a lesser extent, the Lost Boys, is not ideal. Peter is callous and self-centered. He is illogical, inconsiderate, irresponsible, and irrepressible, but nevertheless endearing. His insouciance sets him apart from Wendy, who is already burdened with responsibilities and is happy to assume more.

If Peter Pan is a combination of Barrie himself and the characteristics that most appealed to him in the children of whom he was so fond, then Wendy must surely be a distillation of elements from the women in Barrie's life. The strongest parallel is with his mother, particularly as she emerged for him in her stories of her early childhood. Domestic responsibility came early to her, and she was already mothering her younger brother at the age of eight. The theme of motherhood is very strong in Peter Pan, and the maternal qualities of Sylvia Llewelyn Davies with her five sons must have served as a model for the scenes of Wendy and the Lost Boys. At the same time, Wendy's commonsense organization of the unpredictabilities of life in Never Land does not exclude her from participating in the great adventure. She is still a child and eligible to enjoy the delights of this children's preserve. She is already marked by feminine intuition, however, and if she is mother to the Lost Boys, then she expects Peter to be the father, a role of which he is particularly wary. The whole of the scene in the house underground in act 4 is built around Wendy's enactment of an adult role into which she will inevitably grow and Peter's avoidance of the parallel one which he will never accept.

Dreams are the substance of *Peter Pan*, and Barrie leaves the skeptical with the option of interpreting the fantasy on this level. On the other hand, even Mrs. Darling knows that Peter's shadow has substance: She has rolled it up and put it away in a drawer, and Tinker Bell's remarkable recovery after drinking the poison intended for Peter convinces every child in the audience, at least for the duration of the play, that fairies do exist.

If Peter Pan epitomizes childhood, then Lob in *Dear Brutus* is the essence of worldly experience. He is likened, by the other characters in the play at the beginning of the first act, to Puck, or what Puck would have looked like if he had forgotten to die. He is thus at the opposite end of the age spectrum to Peter but like Peter is instrumental in strangely altering the lives of the other characters. The first act opens in a darkened room in his house, looking out onto a moonlit garden, a pertinent reversal of the usual situation. When the main characters enter the dark room the lights go up and the ladies of the house party attempt to discover why they, particularly, have been invited. The butler, Matey, is blackmailed into giving them as much information as he knows, which is little. All he can say is to beware of the wood, and not to venture out beyond the garden. His advice sounds ridiculous, because as the characters all know there is no wood for miles around, but it is Midsummer's Eve, and strange tales are told about a magic wood and its properties. When the men of the party join the ladies, they are full of enthusiasm for a project clearly suggested by Lob—namely, to go out to find the fabled wood.

During the remainder of this act, it becomes apparent that the lives of all the guests are marred in some way. Purdie, for example, cannot help being attracted to women other than his wife, and the current object of his attentions is Joanna Trout; Will Dearth is a failure and an alcoholic who is despised by his wife; Coade has achieved nothing at all in his life and even confuses his second wife with the memory of his first. Will Dearth observes that there are three things generally viewed as never returning to people: the spoken word, past life, and neglected opportunity. They would all welcome a second chance at life, and this the wood could provide. The climax to the first act is the discovery that the mysterious wood now entirely surrounds Lob's house, and one by one the characters venture out into it.

Act 2 shows how the characters react to the boon of a second chance to live their lives. It is entirely predictable that they will repeat the mistakes of their lives in the real world, and this they proceed to do. Purdie, married to Joanna, chases after Mabel, in reality Mrs. Purdie; Alice Dearth has married her other suitor, and although she is the Honorable Mrs. Finch-Fallowe in name she is now only a vagrant. Of all of them, only Will Dearth has benefited, possibly because the value of his life only declined once his wife saw him as a failure. He now delights in the daughter he wanted, but never had in reality.

The third act takes place back in Lob's house. The characters drift in from the wood, leaving their fantasy existence, and in Dearth's case, his darling Margaret, behind. Their return to reality is gradual, however, and they are able to compare their two states, to arrive at some profound but depressing conclusions about the flaws in their characters which have made their lives what they are. It is Purdie, the now self-confessed philanderer, who quotes the lines from Julius Caesar that furnish the elliptical title of the play: "The fault, dear Brutus, is not in our stars, but in ourselves. . . ."

Only once (in *Der Tag*) did Barrie abandon comedy as his medium of expression. His plays are known for their lighthearted whimsicality, and are enjoyed for the elements of farce that even the more serious ones, such as *Dear Brutus*, contain. The majority of his characters are little more than caricatures, but Barrie nevertheless succeeds in capturing the essence of each, not least because of the careful notes about them which usually form part of the text of a given play. Comedy of character is augmented by verbal humor and a deft handling of the comic situation to put the theme of the play across to the audience with a minimum of effort. The result is that a Barrie play seems light, almost flippant, with the underlying social message only fleetingly apparent. Although the tenor and atmosphere of his plays faithfully reflect the society that filled the theaters when they were first produced, Barrie's themes and preoccupations are no less relevant today.

Other major works

NOVELS: *Better Dead,* 1887; *When a Man's Single,* 1888; *The Little Minister,* 1891; *Sentimental Tommy,* 1896; *Tommy and Grizel,* 1900; *The Little White Bird,* 1902.

SHORT FICTION: *Auld Licht Idylls,* 1888; *A Window in Thrums,* 1889.

NONFICTION: *Margaret Ogilvy,* 1896.

Bibliography

Asquith, Cynthia, Lady. *Portrait of Barrie.* New York: E. P. Dutton, 1955. Written by Barrie's friend and secretary, this biography is a sympathetic portrait of an enigmatic man, his early life, his relationship with his mother, his friendships (notably with H. G. Wells and George Bernard Shaw), his unhappy personal life and its attendant depressions, his shyness, his genuine modesty, and his extraordinary generosity. What the author most admired in Barrie was his talent for giving people hope and courage when their spirits were low despite his own sorrows. Illustrations.

Dunbar, Janet. *J. M. Barrie: The Man Behind the Image.* Boston: Houghton Mifflin, 1970. Barrie was a figure of legend even in his lifetime. Because the biographer had access to private papers, she was able to reveal more of Barrie's life than had commonly been known. The book deals with the influence of various women in his life, including his mother, his wife, his secretary, and the mother of the five boys he adopted, one of whom became the model for *Peter Pan.* The relevant facts are used to show how they supplied Barrie with the material for his plays. Illustrations.

Eaton, Walter Prichard. *The Drama in English.* New York: Charles Scribner's Sons, 1930. A chapter on the playwright, written by a distinguished critic of the day, attempts to define Barrie's contribution to theater. In his own day as well as in modern times, Barrie has been accused of excessive sentimentality and escapism, but Eaton saw him as a satirist who used bitter humor to achieve reality without realism. Thus,

The Admirable Crichton, which appears to be a comedy of manners, is a subtle attack on the class system; *Dear Brutus*, which is a fantasy allowing people to have a second chance at life, shows that they would make precisely the same mistakes; and *Peter Pan*, which is about a boy who can fly, proves that the world of grown-ups is so ugly that it is better to remain forever a child.

Gassner, John. *Masters of the Drama*. 3d rev. ed. New York: Dover, 1954. In contrast to Walter Prichard Eaton (above), Gassner characterizes Barrie's dramas as "pulverized sugar," arguing that he always left his audiences feeling comfortable about the resolution of his plays. Gassner considered Barrie to be in the tradition of Arthur Wing Pinero, a compromiser who raised questions but never honestly answered them.

Geduld, Harry M. *Sir James Barrie*. New York: Twayne, 1971. An excellent study of Barrie's plays and novels, which are reappraised following the decline in his reputation. The author, while admitting that Barrie may have been overpraised in his lifetime (only *Peter Pan* is frequently produced, in addition to receiving a new life both as a musical and as a film), nevertheless argues that modern critics have failed to appreciate the satirical elements in Barrie's writings and have too often dismissed him as a sentimentalist. Bibliography.

Hammerton, J. A. *Barrie: The Story of a Genius*. London: Sampson Low, Marston, 1929. Written eight years before Barrie's death, this biography is a trifle too adulatory, but it offers a fair view of contemporary estimates of Barrie's life and contributions. It is particularly valuable because of the illustrations, not found in other biographies.

Mackail, Denis. *The Story of J. M. B.* London: Peter Davies, 1941. One of the best biographies of Barrie, with emphasis on the way Barrie's life and art blended. The author discusses Barrie's affinity for children whom he understood as few adults do, and it was this childlike quality that was the hallmark of his writing. Includes a frontispiece and a portrait of Barrie.

Zia Hasan
(Updated by Mildred C. Kuner)

PHILIP BARRY

Born: Rochester, New York; June 18, 1896
Died: New York, New York; December 3, 1949

Principal drama

Autonomy, pr. 1919 (one act); *A Punch for Judy*, pr. 1921, pb. 1925; *You and I*, pr., pb. 1923 (originally as *The Jilts*, pr. 1922); *The Youngest*, pr. 1924, pb. 1925; *In a Garden*, pr. 1925, pb. 1926; *White Wings*, pr. 1926, pb. 1927; *John*, pr. 1927, pb. 1929; *Paris Bound*, pr. 1927 (as *The Wedding*), pb. 1929; *Cock Robin*, pr. 1928, pb. 1929 (with Elmer Rice); *Holiday*, pr. 1928, pb. 1929; *Hotel Universe*, pr., pb. 1930; *Tomorrow and Tomorrow*, pr., pb. 1931; *The Animal Kingdom*, pr., pb. 1932; *The Joyous Season*, pr., pb. 1934; *Bright Star*, pr. 1935; *Spring Dance*, pr., pb. 1936 (adaptation of Eleanor Golden and Eloise Barrington's play); *Here Come the Clowns*, pr. 1938, pb. 1939 (adaptation of his novel, *War in Heaven*); *The Philadelphia Story*, pr., pb. 1939; *Liberty Jones*, pr., pb. 1941; *Without Love*, pr. 1942, pb. 1943; *Foolish Notion*, pr. 1945; *My Name Is Aquilon*, pr. 1949 (adaptation of Jean Pierre Aumont's play *L'Empereur de Chine*); *Second Threshold*, pr., pb. 1951 (completed by Robert E. Sherwood); *States of Grace: Eight Plays*, pb. 1975.

Other literary forms

Philip Barry published one novel, *War in Heaven* (1938), which was dramatized as *Here Come the Clowns*, and a short story in *Scribner's Magazine* in 1922 that, along with his juvenilia and some nonfiction works, constitute his only literary output other than his plays.

Achievements

Barry will always be regarded primarily as a writer of superb drawing-room comedies, full of wit and sophistication and charm; indeed, Barry did write such skillful comedies of manners. Even during his own lifetime, however, critics perceived a duality in his dramatic output and were somewhat perplexed by the variety of Barry's experimentation on the stage. As easy as it would have been for him to stick to a comedic formula, grinding out comedies year after year, Barry proved an adventuresome dramatist and thereby cast confusion among the critical community. In spite of repeated failure at the box office, Barry continued with engaging persistence to write and produce serious drama in a variety of forms—serious drama, tragedy in some cases, which in retrospect is of considerable interest even if it is far less pleasurable to study than are the mannered comedies.

Barry was neither as funny as George S. Kaufman nor as deeply brooding (or tedious) as Eugene O'Neill. His comedies, especially *You and I*, *Paris Bound*, *Holiday*, and *The Philadelphia Story*, attracted widespread attention when they were first produced and are still regularly revived by amateur theatrical groups. His serious dramas for the most part met with scant critical recognition and usually even less financial success, but such plays as *In a Garden*, *Hotel Universe*, *Tomorrow and Tomorrow*, *Here Come the Clowns*, and *Foolish Notion* are well within the traditions more fully exploited by such contemporaries as O'Neill, Robert E. Sherwood, Lillian Hellman, and Elmer Rice. What is often overlooked when discussing Barry's career is that he, too, was in on the beginnings of the new American drama, interested in many of the same innovations that were more highly publicized in the works of others. Partly because of his reticence, partly because his working methods eschewed the obvious, the self-consciously "serious" elements that were highlighted in the work of his contemporaries, Barry's message was often concealed by the charm of his characters and the smoothness of his dialogue.

Barry was among the earliest of American playwrights to incorporate the new Freudian psychology into his drama. Barry also did much to adapt Maeterlinckian fantasy for the Broadway stage, as in *In a Garden*. Symbolism, tragedy, realism, and poetic drama were used by Barry in his various dramatic experiments. Even social criticism forms a central part of his plays, and although he was criticized for not joining in the political movements of the 1930's, his work presents one of the most sustained and devastating critiques of the narrowness and aridity of American capitalism in the history of modern theater. All of this Barry accomplished without the intellectual posing or the critical backstabbing so often associated with the theater. In spite of these credentials, however, Barry's drama has all but disappeared from American literature—a fate that raises some awkward questions for anyone interested in assessing his work. In part it can be attributed to the lack of homogeneity among his plays. He skipped from one form to another and, except for high comedy, never seemed completely successful at any. He lacked the consistent vision of O'Neill, the virtuosity of Kaufman, the social commitment of Hellman and Clifford Odets. Finally, the diffidence which allowed him social mobility denied him the passionate engagement that might have made him a great rather than merely a fascinating playwright.

Biography

Outwardly, Philip Barry led a charmed life: He married the right woman, made lots of money, and ran with the rich and famous. Inwardly, however, his life was not as fortunate. By the time Barry died in 1949, at the comparatively young age of fifty-three, he had experienced more failures on Broadway than successes, and he was plagued by depression and religious doubts severe enough to disrupt his otherwise disciplined and orderly work habits. In addition, all of his life Barry remained on the periphery of the upper-class world he depicted in so many of his plays and emulated in his life. As Brendan Gill has perceptively noted, Barry, like such other Irish-Catholic writers of his generation as Eugene O'Neill, F. Scott Fitzgerald, and John O'Hara, spent his creative career striving for the perquisites and assurance of his Protestant betters.

Philip James Quinn Barry was born on June 18, 1896, in Rochester, New York, to James Corbett Barry and Mary Agnes Quinn. He was the youngest of four children. His father, who emigrated from Ireland as a boy, became wealthy in a marble and granite business, and when he married Mary Agnes, they brought together two well-to-do Irish families who were obviously going to make their mark in the prospering Upstate city. Unfortunately, James Barry died the year after Philip's birth, leaving his youngest son to be brought up by his sister and mother and under increasingly reduced circumstances, for despite the best efforts of the two older Barry sons, the granite business gradually declined. Barry attended Nazareth Hall Academy, a Roman Catholic secondary school, and East High School in Rochester. He attempted his first three-act play, "No Thoroughfare," in 1909, but other than a story, "Tab the Cat," which he wrote for publication in the *Rochester Post Express*, the young Philip did not show any precocious literary talent. In the autumn of 1913 he entered Yale.

The combination of East High and Yale did much to broaden Barry's world beyond the rather narrow Catholicism of his family. Especially at Yale, where he was thrown in among the Protestant elite, Barry decided to work his way into the larger, more sophisticated world of money. Because of defective eyesight, he had not been an athlete in school, so Barry turned to writing, and over the next three years he contributed poetry, short stories, and editorials to the *Yale Literary Magazine*. World War I disrupted Barry's education, and he went to work for the American Embassy in London as a code clerk after he was rejected for military service. He used the time to advantage, however, completing a three-act play, which he unsuccessfully tried to get produced. In March of 1919, he was back at Yale, his work done in London, and in June the Dramatic Club produced his only known one-act play, *Autonomy*. That September, after receiving his degree, Barry enrolled in George Pierce Baker's Workshop 47 at Harvard, and during the next year he wrote another three-act play, *A Punch for Judy*. Temporarily out of funds, Barry wrote copy for a year at W. A. Erickson, an advertising agency. During this time, he became engaged to Ellen Semple, daughter of a wealthy international lawyer, Lorenzo Semple, who with his wife lived in New York City and Mt. Kisco, New York. In the summer, Barry received word that *A Punch for Judy* would be produced by Workshop 47, would open in New York, and would go on tour. In the fall, Barry left advertising and returned to Baker's Workshop 47, where during the next few months he wrote the drafts of two plays, *The Jilts*, later retitled *You and I*, and "Poor Richard," which underwent several title changes before being published as *The Youngest*. On July 15, 1922, he married Ellen Semple, and they spent the rest of the summer honeymooning in Europe. On the return voyage, Barry, who had few prospects for employment, learned that *The Jilts* had won the Herndon Prize for the best full-length play written in Workshop 47 and that it would be produced on Broadway early in the new year. Retitled *You and I*, Barry's play became a rousing success and established him as one of the rising stars of the new American theater. Later that same year, his first son was born.

In spite of his impressive beginning, over the next few years Barry's plays were increasingly unsuccessful. *The Youngest* ran for 104 performances, *In a Garden* survived for seventy-four performances, *White Wings* ran for twenty-seven, and *John* lasted only eleven performances. During the summer of 1927, however, while Barry was living at Cannes in Southern France, his luck changed.

On the trip over, Barry and Rice had begun collaboration on a mystery play, *Cock Robin*, which Barry completed along with *Paris Bound* during his stay in France. *Paris Bound* opened in December and *Cock Robin* in January, 1928, both to good audiences. Barry followed these successes in the fall with *Holiday*, his eighth Broadway production, and it ran 230 performances at the Plymouth Theater. Thereafter, although his plays would often have a disappointing box office or receive mediocre reviews, Barry was at least financially secure. He earned increasing sums from the sale of his properties to Hollywood, and amateur performances continued to boost the revenues on each play he wrote. His second son was born in 1926. Although Barry's mother had died in 1927, his marriage, the most fortunate part of his exceptionally fortunate life, continued to provide him with sustenance. As one critic has described it, his marriage was itself "Barryesque," full of charm, intelligence, wit, and concern.

The 1930's treated Barry, professionally at least, much in the same way the 1920's had. He began strong with the successful run of *Tomorrow and Tomorrow*, slumped downward during the middle of the decade, his career reaching what was perhaps its nadir when *Bright Star* closed after seven performances, only to rise spectacularly in 1939 with the overwhelming success of *The Philadelphia Story*. The latter, starring Katharine Hepburn, ran for more than four hundred performances and is credited with restoring to solvency the Theatre Guild, which Barry had joined a decade earlier. Barry also published his only novel, *War in Heaven*, in 1938, and earlier in the decade he spent a brief stint in Hollywood as a screenwriter for Metro-Goldwyn-Mayer.

Barry came under increasing criticism during this period of social and political unrest. He was roundly condemned for writing frivolous plays at a time when many critics felt that all artists should be engaged in the struggle for economic and social justice. In particular, his refusal to write overtly about political causes lost him support among the younger drama critics of the period. In addition, Barry suffered two personal losses in these years: Both his brother, Edmund, and an infant daughter died.

World War II suspended the Barrys' routine of living most of the year in Southern France, but it hardly diminished Barry's output: He produced plays in 1941 (*Liberty Jones*), in 1942 (*Without Love*), and in 1945 (*Foolish Notion*). When the war was over, the Barrys returned to France. For the next three years, Barry had nothing running on Broadway, but in 1949, *My Name Is Aquilon*, his adaptation of Jean Pierre Aumont's *L'Empereur de Chine*, opened as his twentieth Broadway production and, as it would turn out, his last. After submitting the draft of his next play, *Second Threshold*, to the Theatre Guild, Barry died suddenly of a heart attack at his apartment in New York City. On December 5, a requiem mass was said at the Church of St. Vincent Ferrer, and he was buried at East Hampton, Long Island. *Second Threshold* was completed by Robert E. Sherwood in 1951 and, in the same year, it opened at the Morosco Theatre and ran for 126 performances.

Although Barry shared certain accidents of birth and background with other Irish-Catholic writers of his generation, he succeeded, unlike many of the others, in gaining acceptance into the moneyed world of the Protestant upper class. Even so, he always remained apart; the role of an observer was congenial to him. In the end, perhaps, Barry saw the upper classes clearly not only because of his proximity but also because of his restraint; by avoiding the excesses of O'Hara, Fitzgerald, and O'Neill, he was able to cross the social and financial barriers into the world which receded before the others like Gatsby's rolling prairie out into the night.

Analysis

Philip Barry made his mark in American theater as a writer of high comedy and as an experimentalist, and during three decades of playwriting he explored to the full both of these artistic tendencies in his work. In the process, he came to occupy a kind of middle ground between dramatic extremes; in the words of John Gassner, Barry tried to arrive at a point of reasonableness in an unreasonable world. As a theatrical moderate, he faced a much more difficult task than did the more extreme dramatists of the period between the two world wars. Neither a social satirist nor a vacuous entertainer, a partisan politico nor a know-nothing fool, an unthinking realist nor a muddled metaphysician, Barry's art was a healing art and his mission to reduce the dissonance of the modern American theater. Barry's diffidence, however, made him difficult to classify, and literary history has not treated him well. Often misunderstood when he was alive, he now resides in a critical limbo in American theatrical history. As a Catholic, it is a position he would have understood and perhaps relished.

Barry established his reputation with his play *You and I*, which under the working title *The Jilts* had won an award as the best play of Baker's Workshop 47. Under the terms of the award, the play chosen was to be produced on Broadway and then taken on tour. *You and I* was a resounding success, both in New York and on tour, and set the pattern for Barry's other drawing-room comedies, most notably *Paris Bound*, *Holiday*, and *The Philadelphia Story*. With witty dialogue and a modish plot, the play revealed the essentially corrupt spirit of capitalism and concluded with a realistic vision of life's limitations. The action centers on Maitland White, a fortyish businessman who decides to give up his comfortable advertising job in a soap company and return to the ambition of his youth, to become a painter. His wife rather generously agrees to give up her affluent life-style in order to help him realize his dream. His son, who is just embarking on his own life, has fallen in love with a girl and is about to give up his ambition to become an architect and go to work for the firm his father has just quit. The play concludes as the father returns to work, thereby freeing the son both to marry and to realize his dream of studying architecture in Paris. Matey realizes by the play's end that time has robbed him of any chance to become anything but a mediocre artist and that his family obligations must take precedence over his individual desires. Dreams, ambition, and talent can all die with age and obligation; such is the rather sobering resolution to Barry's witty plot.

This pattern of hope, loss, and reconciliation (or resignation) marked all of Barry's most famous and successful comedies. *Paris Bound*, which was produced in 1927 following a series of increasingly unsuccessful dramas, also contains a cautionary ending. Jim and Mary Hutton have been married for six years when Mary learns that her husband has committed casual adultery. Deeply hurt at such a betrayal, she leaves for Paris to sue for divorce. In spite of her "modern" attitude about such things, announced on her wedding day, Mary is now prepared to forsake her liberality in favor of a more conventional morality—until she, too, is faced with temptation by Richard, a bright, attractive, young composer. Although she does not have an affair with Richard, she learns the ease of such venial sins and accepts her husband back without revealing her own involvement. She has learned that the spiritual bond within marriage should be valued above mere physical fidelity. Again, Barry's dialogue was praised by the critics, while audiences were titillated by his unconventional attitude toward extramarital affairs. A smash hit on Broadway, the play was also included in the ten best list for 1927, and screen rights were purchased by Pathé. Once again, Barry's wit and charm obscured a more serious theme, one that would surface again and again in his later plays—namely, the question of marriage and resolutions to marriages in trouble. Like that of Tracy Lord in *The*

Philadelphia Story, Mary Hutton's resolution in *Paris Bound* strikes one as a little too pat for the anguish that has been expended. The problem of divorce and broken relationships was of considerable social interest during the 1920's, but Barry declined to confront it head-on.

Indeed, Barry was always able in his high comedies to skirt popular and often controversial issues by placing them in warm and sunny settings. One of the ways in which he used the upper-middle-class milieu for which he became famous was to couch radical themes in comfortable surroundings and thereby make them more palatable to his audiences. A case in point is his next broadly successful comedy, *Holiday*. Returning to the theme of a young man's dreams, *Holiday* deals with Johnny Case, who wants to risk his small fortune in order to go off and find himself, in spite of the fact that he has just met and fallen in love with the wealthy Julia Seaton. The play's plot hinges on whether Johnny, who has little prospect of earning a living and no money to fall back on, will withstand the financial and sexual pressures of Julia in order to be true to himself. As it turns out, Johnny does break off with Julia but is followed on his travels by the less frivolous and more understanding Linda, Julia's sister. Like *You and I*, the play centers on the various pulls made on the young hero by competing value systems and by competing girls. More upbeat than the earlier play, *Holiday* seems to suggest that it is possible to have it all but that such ventures are not without risks and finally entailments, albeit not necessarily strangling ones. Barry was saying that money should not be an end in itself and that all people should have the opportunity to make life choices for themselves and to assume responsibility for such choices. His point was well taken but came at a particularly inappropriate moment: The year after the play was produced, the stock market crashed, plunging the United States into unparalleled financial decline. The ensuing Depression denied to millions the opportunities afforded Johnny, and the optimism of *Holiday* rang hollow.

Barry was not to write another successful comedy of this type for four years. By 1932, the Depression was well established, with no end in sight. *The Animal Kingdom*, produced in that year, was originally written for a young Hepburn, then just beginning her stage career. For a variety of reasons, Hepburn was dropped from the cast of *The Animal Kingdom* at the last minute, but the play is now seen to be an earlier version of her hit *The Philadelphia Story*. *The Animal Kingdom* also bears a resemblance to *Paris Bound*. Tom Collier, a publisher, who has been living with Daisy Sage, a journalist, for three years, falls in love with and marries Cecelia Henry. Cecelia seduces Tom into publishing trash for a quick profit, to the damnation of his publisher's soul. Realizing the immorality of their marriage, Tom leaves Cecelia, who is more mistress than helpmate, to return to his mistress, Daisy, who is more wife than paramour. Daisy's love for Tom wins out over Cecelia's manipulation of his affection for profit. Again, Barry suggests that a marriage built only on the appetites of the animal kingdom is not a true marriage, and Daisy's pure love finally gives Tom the strength to free himself and discover who he really is. By rejecting the dictates of society, Tom is able, unlike Matey, to regain his individual integrity.

For the rest of the 1930's, Barry seemed unable to write anything that would capture the imagination of his public. In 1939, however, with a second chance to work with Hepburn, Barry wrote the play for which he is probably best remembered, *The Philadelphia Story*. For Hepburn, Barry, and the Theatre Guild, which produced it, the new play was crucial. None of the principals should have worried: *The Philadelphia Story* saved the Guild financially, helped establish Hepburn's career, and rescued Barry's reputation.

As the play begins, Tracy Lord is preparing to marry for the second time, but her plans are complicated by a series of family entanglements: Her boozy ex-husband shows up, a reporter from a national magazine arrives to do an in-depth piece on the family, her father has developed an attachment to a lady of questionable (or perhaps "unquestionable" would be better) morals, her sister's behavior is erratic, and her uncle goes around pinching young girls. Tracy's high moral principles match the priggishness of her husband-to-be until she gets roaring drunk one night and swims nude with the journalist who is covering the family. Like Mary in Barry's *Paris Bound*, Tracy learns tolerance. Rejecting her intolerant would-be second husband, she is reunited with her estranged father and former husband. Human warmth and understanding, Barry implies, are worth more than unthinking moral rectitude, and people with social position and wealth have no hold on individual morality, as the uprightness of the young reporter has proved. *The Philadelphia Story* was to be the last of Barry's high comedies and the last of his successful plays, for although two of Barry's later plays performed creditably at the box office, their success was nothing compared to that of *The Philadelphia Story*. The film version of the play, starring Hepburn as well, became one of the most successful screwball comedies of the late 1930's, while the 1956 musical film version, *High Society*, was a successful vehicle for a girl from Philadelphia, Grace Kelly.

Although Barry will probably always be known primarily for his high comedies, he was proudest, as John Mason Brown has written, of his failures, his experimental dramas. Underneath his surface gaiety and wit, Barry was a serious student of the theater, one who was in touch with the current trends in European as well as American avant-garde drama. His so-called failures represent that audacious, unconventional side of his theatrical nature. It must be understood that in all of his plays, Barry experimented. He played with dialogue, setting, character, and most of all subject matter, but those comedies which established his reputation in the American theater tended to be the least audacious stylistically. Then as now, audiences did not like to be jolted out of their complacency by too radical a form. They liked changes in the language, the plots, the themes, but not in the form of the drama. When Barry wrote a play without an intermission, when he introduced allegory or fantasy, his audiences did not respond as fully as they did to his more conservative comedies.

Barry's first obviously experimental drama, *In a Garden*, not only employed a play within a play (in itself not a radical device) but also incorporated a deliberately poetic plot and dealt in a more overt way with self-consciously "serious" topics, two elements which Barry had kept discreetly in the background of his previous plays. There is an element of Luigi Pirandello in the fey qualities of the characters, especially the girl, Lissa, and several of the critics likened Barry's work to Henrik Ibsen's *A Doll's House* (pr. 1879). The play closed after seventy-four performances.

Barry followed *In a Garden* with another, even more fantastic play. *White Wings* is almost totally symbolic, dealing with a family of street cleaners whose livelihood is passing with the coming of the automobile and the disappearance of the horse. Although the play intrigued the critics, it baffled the public and ran for only twenty-seven performances. Clearly, *White Wings* is concerned with modernity's impact on traditional values, but the play's symbolic manner leaves Barry's precise intentions in doubt. One critic has suggested that Barry's faith had been called into question by his rereading of the Gospels and that the "faith of the fathers" which is portrayed and undercut in *White Wings* is the Catholicism of Barry's youth. Whatever the sources of *White Wings*, Barry continued in this vein in his next play, *John*, based on the life of John the Baptist.

John, the most serious work Barry had yet attempted, reflected the religious turmoil that he was experiencing at the time. Running for only eleven nights, the play was a disaster from the beginning; in particular, its language was too colloquial for its biblical subject matter. Still, in retrospect, the play looks better than its initial reception would indicate. The dialogue is less off-putting to the contemporary sensibility than it was to audiences in the late 1920's; indeed, *John* has affinities with Archibald MacLeish's highly successful *J. B.* (pr. 1958). Nevertheless, Barry was sufficiently discouraged by the failure of *John* to agree to collaborate with Rice on a mystery play, *Cock Robin*, which, along with *Paris Bound* and *Holiday*, managed to reestablish Barry's career at the end of the decade.

Hotel Universe was Barry's first play of the 1930's, a play which captured the critics' fancy but was only mediocre at the box office. A parable that mixes Freudianism and Christianity, *Hotel Universe* is set in a large house that once was a hotel. Ann Field has assembled a number of guests who have in various ways rebelled against society but who have achieved only purposeless personal freedom and who now face the emptiness of their lives with increasing despair. Running without intermissions, the play is an extended psychodrama in which the various characters reenact scenes from the past, experiencing catharsis in the process. Barry's parable, however skillfully presented, did not attract an audience. Its failure with the public followed the pattern set by his earlier experimental dramas, a pattern to which most of his later serious plays were also subject.

It is difficult to sum up Barry's career. He became one of the United States' most financially successful playwrights, earning enough money to allow him to live in the manner of one of his own characters. He was perhaps the most accomplished writer of high or sophisticated comedy between the wars, a period notable for its witty comedies of manners. He was among the most innovative American playwrights working on Broadway during the 1920's and the 1930's. In spite of all of these accomplishments, however, Barry remains largely excluded from serious discussions of American literature. The reasons for this are complex but center on Barry's need to be a maverick, an eccentric in a world dominated by corporate mentalities. Barry's plays, for all their commonality of themes, are just quirky enough to avoid easy synthesis. Both experimental and traditional, comic and serious, religious and skeptical, Barry's work provides enough ambiguity and variety to place him in his own category, which is to say, by himself, alone. It is a position Barry would have welcomed, for like so many of his characters he eschewed easy answers and sought salvation on his own terms.

Other major works

NOVEL: *War in Heaven*, 1938.

SHORT FICTION: "Meadow's End," 1922.

NONFICTION: *The Dramatist and the Amateur Public*, 1927; "Here Come the Clowns," 1938; "Liberty Jones," 1941.

CHILDREN'S LITERATURE: "Tab the Cat," 1905; "The Toy Balloon," 1917.

Bibliography

Broussard, Louis. *American Drama: Contemporary Allegory from Eugene O'Neill to Tennessee Williams.* Norman: University of Oklahoma Press, 1962. In tracing the evolution of the American allegorical play treating contemporary human beings and their problems, Broussard centers a twelve-page chapter on Barry, whom he identifies as a pioneer of a new genre: the comedy of moral purpose. Takes *Hotel Universe* and *Here Come the Clowns* as chief examples of Barry's predilection for forcing characters to exhume and confront a repressed past in a search for self-realization. Bibliography, index.

Gassner, John. "Philip Barry: A Civilized Playwright." In *The Theatre in Our Times.* New York: Crown, 1954. Gassner succinctly examines Barry's life and dramatic works, and he avows that the playwright merits an honored place in American theater both as a cultivated writer of high comedy and as an experimentalist. Includes an index.

Gill, Brendan, ed. "The Dark Advantage." In *States of Grace: Eight Plays.* New York: Harcourt Brace Jovanovich, 1975. Gill precedes a collection of Barry's major plays with an excellently condensed biographical portrait, placing Barry not only in his period but also in his favored milieu (among the rich) and in his relationships to such friends of similar Irish-American background as F. Scott Fitzgerald and John O'Hara. Barry's plays are mentioned but not fully explored. Includes a photograph of Barry.

Gould, Jean. *Modern American Playwrights.* New York: Dodd, Mead, 1966. Gould devotes a twenty-page chapter to Barry, intermixing biographical details with an informal yet substantive analysis of the plays. Emphasizes Barry's yearning to succeed as a serious dramatist despite his recognition as a writer of high comedy. Contains an index and a select bibliography. High school students will find the essay accessible.

Krutch, Joseph Wood. *American Drama Since 1918.* New York: Random House, 1939. Krutch furnishes a lucid sixteen-page appraisal of Barry's plays up to *The Philadelphia Story.* The discussion clearly favors Barry more for his sophisticated social comedies than for his serious dramas. Index.

Roppolo, Joseph Patrick. *Philip Barry.* New York: Twayne, 1965. Roppolo's biographical and critical study provides the most comprehensive treatment of the playwright and his work. It encompasses chapters on Barry's major themes, dramaturgical techniques, and plot structure. Contains a chronology, a detailed index, and an annotated list of secondary sources.

Sievers, Wieder David. *Freud on Broadway.* New York: Heritage House, 1955. In a chapter entitled "The Psychodrama of Philip Barry," Sievers traces and commends Barry's knowledgeable and skillful use of psychology and psychoanalysis in his major plays. Barry is cited as being second only to Eugene O'Neill in his contribution to modern psychological drama.

Charles L. P. Silet
(Updated by *Christian H. Moe*)

FRANCIS BEAUMONT

Born: Grace-Dieu, England; c. 1584
Died: London, England; March 6, 1616

Principal drama

The Woman Hater, pr. c. 1606, pb. 1607 (with John Fletcher); *The Knight of the Burning Pestle*, pr. 1607, pb. 1613; *The Coxcomb*, pr. c. 1608-1610, pb. 1647 (with Fletcher); *Philaster: Or, Love Lies A-Bleeding*, pr. c. 1609, pb. 1620 (with Fletcher); *The Captain*, pr. c. 1609-1612, pb. 1647 (with Fletcher); *The Maid's Tragedy*, pr. c. 1611, pb. 1619 (with Fletcher); *A King and No King*, pr. 1611, pb. 1619 (with Fletcher); *Cupid's Revenge*, pr. 1612, pb. 1615 (with Fletcher); *Four Plays, or Moral Representations, in One*, pr. c. 1612, pb. 1617 (with Fletcher; commonly known as *Four Plays in One*); *The Masque of the Inner Temple and Grayes Inn*, pr., pb. 1613 (with Fletcher); *The Scornful Lady*, pr. c. 1615-1616, pb. 1616 (with Fletcher); *The Tragedy of Thierry, King of France, and His Brother Theodoret*, pr. 1617(?), pb. 1621 (with Fletcher; commonly known as *Thierry and Theodoret*); *The Dramatic Works in the Beaumont and Fletcher Canon*, pb. 1966-1985 (6 volumes).

Other literary forms

Known almost exclusively as a dramatist, Francis Beaumont did publish one verse satire, *Salmacis and Hermaphroditus* (1602), and several lyrics. A collection of his verse, entitled *Poems*, was published in 1640.

Achievements

Francis Beaumont's imprint on seventeenth century drama cannot be distinguished from that of John Fletcher, since their jointly written plays secured the reputations of both men. Indeed, the success of their collaboration from about 1606 until 1613 was such that later editors assumed their few solo plays to have been joint productions; moreover, Fletcher's many collaborations with other writers, most notably Philip Massinger, were widely regarded throughout the seventeenth century as the works of Fletcher and Beaumont.

Though rarely produced after the Restoration and without critical stature since that time, the Beaumont-Fletcher collaborations, including, among others, *Philaster*, *The Maid's Tragedy*, and *A King and No King*, captured large, fashionable audiences with their blend of satire, sophisticated dialogue, and sexual titillation. These plays perfectly suited the tastes of the more affluent theatergoers who patronized the indoor Blackfriars playhouse, while the outdoor theaters catered to the middle-class taste for farce, romance, and patriotic heroism. Beaumont and Fletcher's comedies and tragicomedies expose middle-class optimism as mere naïveté or ignorant ambition. Though never creating worlds as darkly depraved as those of John Webster or George Chapman, Beaumont and Fletcher nevertheless pictured society as corrupt, its rulers as venal, its populace as stupid and conniving. Their main characters, neither heroes nor villains, typically represent the educated gentry; worldly, well-spoken, vain, they assume aristocratic privilege almost as a virtue and thus are frequently boors, though never unwitty ones. Good and evil have little relevance in the Beaumont-Fletcher world; favor is granted those who can seduce or acquire wealth with the greatest aplomb, the most studied indifference. Overt ambition, lack of humor, bad manners, and slow wits mark the losers.

Though the Beaumont-Fletcher partnership ended in 1613 and both playwrights were dead by 1625, their collaborations stayed popular for the rest of the century, Restoration critics regarding them as contemporary masterpieces while reducing the works of William Shakespeare and Ben Jonson to the status of mere classics. William Wycherley, Sir George Etheredge, William Congreve, and, to some extent, John Dryden all wrote as followers of the Beaumont-Fletcher tradition. Those tastes in drama to which the pair had appealed at the Blackfriars were confirmed and intensified in the self-consciously fashionable audiences after 1660.

When fashions changed early in the eighteenth century, the Beaumont-Fletcher collaborations disappeared from the stage and have rarely been revived. Ironically, the least popular play in the canon, Beaumont's *The Knight of the Burning Pestle*, has been increasingly performed, particularly in the twentieth century, and is now critically regarded as one of the greatest Renaissance comedies. Structurally a daringly original play, *The Knight of the Burning Pestle* deliberately blurs the distinctions between players and audience, play and reality. In an era when taste in drama has been molded by Eugène Ionesco, Samuel Beckett, and Thornton Wilder, *The Knight of the Burning Pestle* is perhaps more at home than at any previous time.

Biography

Francis Beaumont's life varied significantly from that of the stereotypical Elizabethan playwright, who emerged from the trade class, worked his way through Oxford or Cambridge, and struggled for an insecure living by writing for the stage, the press, and occasional patrons. As the son of a wealthy Leicestershire judge descended from the Norman nobility, Beaumont seems not to have pursued either his education or his writing out of burning ambition or necessity. Entering Broadgates Hall (later Pembroke College), Oxford, at age twelve, Beaumont left a year later, upon the death of his father, and never returned to the university. He turned instead to the family profession, law, being admitted to the Inner Temple in 1600, but, again, he did not complete his studies.

During this time, Beaumont became one of the habitués of the London literary scene, befriending such luminaries as Michael Drayton and Ben Jonson. Drayton called Beaumont and his brother John, a poet, "My deare companions whom I freely chose/ My bosome friends," while the first quarto of Jonson's *Volpone* (pr. 1606) includes commendatory verses by one "F. B.," probably Beaumont. The playwright's famous association with fellow dramatist John Fletcher began in these years also, with the first of their collaborations occurring about 1606. A bishop's son, Fletcher shared with Beaumont an aristocratic heritage; in addition, he shared Beaumont's Bohemian tastes. According to contemporary chronicler John Aubrey, the friends enjoyed "a wonderful consimility of phansey": "They lived together on the Banke side, not far from the Playhouse, both batchelors; lay together; had one Wench in the house between them, which they did so admire; the same cloathes and cloake, etc. between them."

Though immersed in the life of the city, Beaumont remained a member of the gentry, having inherited the family holdings upon the death of his elder brother Henry in 1605. A verse letter to Jonson indicates his occasional sojourns at Grace-Dieu throughout his London years. Finally, in 1613, the same year that Shakespeare left London for Stratford, Beaumont ended his collaboration with Fletcher in order to marry Ursula Isley, heiress of Sundridge Hall in Kent, and return to country life. The marriage, which produced two daughters, abruptly ended three years later with Beaumont's death, on March 6, 1616.

Analysis

To describe the style of a writer whose greatest body of work was done in collaboration is, to say the least, difficult. Three centuries of commentators have arrived at widely differing judgments of the contributions of John Fletcher and Francis Beaumont to the plays they are known to have written together. Since nothing is known of their characteristic collaborative process, it is presumptuous to look at linguistic cues or at staging patterns as indicators of the dominant hand in certain plays or even in particular scenes. Moreover, since their collaboration produced works remarkably distinct in style from the few solo works by either man, one cannot say which characters or ideas seem typical of Beaumont and which of Fletcher.

What one can do is compare a typical work of the Beaumont-Fletcher collaboration with the single play, *The Knight of the Burning Pestle*, which is believed to be wholly Beaumont's, in order to understand his work; in these different contexts, remarkably different pictures of Beaumont the playwright emerge.

Though the first version of *The Woman Hater* is considered to have been Beaumont's alone, the only extant version of the play is that revised by Fletcher in 1607, the first year of their collaboration; it well represents the typical features of the Beaumont-Fletcher plays. Acted early in 1606 by the

Children of St. Paul's, *The Woman Hater* was among those plays taken over by the King's Men when the children's company disbanded later that year. The play was acted periodically, to some acclaim, throughout the decades before the closing of the theaters in 1642. Its longevity is attested by the publication of two quartos, the first in 1607, the second in 1648-1649.

The 1607 prologue proclaims the play neither comedy nor tragedy: "A Play it is, which was meant to make you laugh, how it will please you, is not written in my part." This vagueness about form is understandable: Though the play holds together, at least somewhat, as a satire of classes and mores, the trivial plot and superficial characters make it incoherent and formless as a complete play. The pleasure it gave its audiences derives primarily from the satire—and, perhaps, from its mildly titillating dialogue between Gondarino, the misogynist, and the coquettish, though technically virginal, Oriana. The satire bites broadly rather than deeply, cutting across the ranks and occupations of society rather than exploring the corruption of a few significant individuals. One reason for the thinness of the play is that both playwrights are satisfied to have all characters function as mere caricatures of familiar court and city types: the officious minister, Lucio, a would-be Machiavel; the feckless nobleman, Count Valore, who whiles away his hours with petty practical jokes; a nameless mercer, representative of the London middle class, a man easily gulled by a pimp into marrying a prostitute. Skulking through the play are also two anonymous intelligencers, courtiers of the most base and vicious sort, who feed the appetite of a decadent court for scandals and plots.

Perhaps the most extreme caricatures are the principals, Gondarino and Oriana, who embody in almost grotesque form the essential pointlessness, in the playwrights' view, of court life. In a Shakespearean comedy, the pair, a professed enemy of womankind and a clever, rich maiden, would gradually fall in love and, in the finale, marry. Beaumont and Fletcher continually tease the audience with this expectation, but the play ends with the two still mutual enemies and love nowhere to be found. At different points in the play, each professes eternal devotion to the other, but these exclamations are nothing more than tricks. There is, however, no real malice in their actions; the overwhelming impression one receives is that these deceptions are motivated merely by boredom.

The only genuine passion in *The Woman Hater* is that of the gluttonous courtier Lazarello, who gives his all in word and deed to win dinner invitations. His particular quest throughout the play is for the head of an umbrana fish, a rare delicacy, which is passed from courtier to courtier in return for favors. Though Lazarello's interest is the basest, he sparks more interest than any other character, because he seems to be the only figure who clearly attaches value to anything.

Although many commentators consider *The Woman Hater* primarily the work of Beaumont, with relatively few scenes exhibiting characteristic Fletcherian diction, the play must be considered essentially a collaboration. Its tone of cynical ennui, besides its structural emphasis on the individual scene rather than on the architectonics of the whole play, makes it very similar to *Philaster, A King and No King*, and other Beaumont-Fletcher tragicomedies. It is also so different in every way from *The Knight of the Burning Pestle* that one has no reason to consider *The Woman Hater* substantially the work of Beaumont alone.

The differences in tone and structure between *The Woman Hater* and *The Knight of the Burning Pestle* are so great that they can hardly be overstated. Where the earlier play exemplifies the typical jadedness of court life in the Beaumont-Fletcher world, the play of one year later offers an optimistic, highly original vision of human harmony. *The Knight of the Burning Pestle* is a boldly imaginative play, unconventional in some startling ways, yet fruitfully adapting conventions of the Elizabethan comic stage to Beaumont's fresh purpose. For example, the play features even more music and song than a typical Shakespearean comedy, with popular tunes and love lyrics helping to create and sustain an atmosphere of romance that would be for Beaumont's audience both idyllic and familiar. From Jonson's early comedies, such as *Every Man in His Humour* (pr. 1598, pb. 1601), Beaumont borrows a satiric perspective within which human foibles and pretensions are seen not as evil but as humbling and ironic. To Robert Greene, Thomas Dekker, and Thomas Heywood, he owes the ebullience of his middle-class characters, who carry his message of joy and harmony, even though his satire frequently makes sport of the outspoken citizen.

The Knight of the Burning Pestle is clearly Beaumont's work alone. The Beaumont-Fletcher plays have been frequently characterized as dominated by the sensational scene rather than moved forward by the plot. In plays such as *Philaster* and *A King and No King*, the plots often seem absurdly manipulated to bring certain volatile characters into confrontation; little thought seems to have been paid to the dramatic working out of a key idea or to the meaning of a conflict beyond the voltage which it can generate. In *A King and No King*, for example, the audience knows that the hero and heroine are brother and sister; the characters do not. The plot is constructed so that the two fall in love, are brought together in a passionate love scene, and then are shocked to discover the truth. There is no exploration of the moral alternatives, no facing up to the conflict between taboo and instinct; there is only the voyeuristic titillation of the audience. Conversely, *The Knight of the Burning Pestle* de-emphasizes the individual scene; all scenes are brief, with dialogues frequently interrupted by the surprising arrival of new characters. Emphasis is on movement toward resolution of the central conflict, which is nothing less than the open clash of two bourgeois ideas: romantic optimism and the virtues of industry.

Through a plot that juggles two or three subplots simultaneously, so that even as one story progresses, the audience is aware of events occurring elsewhere, momentum builds to a romantic resolution that leaves all characters reconciled and the spirit of comedy triumphant.

A description of the play's movement suggests some of the complexity of its structure. The players enter, purporting to present a play entitled *The London Merchant*, presumably a typically anti-middle-class vehicle suited to Blackfriars taste. From the audience, however, comes a "Citizen," George the grocer, and his wife, Nell, who upbraid the players for their prejudice and demand that their apprentice, Rafe, be allowed to perform heroic scenes to honor the grocers of London. To humor the obstreperous pair, the players let Rafe give his speeches, similar to those that bourgeois audiences would have heard in the chivalric fantasies played at the outdoor theaters. At various points throughout the play, the intended performance is again interrupted by outbursts from the Citizens, so that Rafe can orate, sometimes alone but also in impromptu scenes hastily concocted between Rafe and one or two of the players. Surprisingly, Rafe turns out to be no ignorant blowhard, but a marvelously bright and multifaceted performer. Though the players never admit Rafe's talents, the audience observes as the play proceeds how readily they adapt themselves to meet the histrionic whims of George and Nell.

Meanwhile, the intended play also proceeds. As George had suspected, it does make "girds at Citizens," but, ironically, its hero and heroine are also middle-class; thus, the overall tone is not antibourgeois. Moreover, the satire always remains gentle. The play's most amazing character, old Merrythought, displays an utterly joyful faith in Providence that allows romantic optimism always to dominate the urge to find fault.

Simply told, *The London Merchant* begins by presenting the plan of Venturewell—the London merchant of the title—to marry his daughter, Luce, to a loyal but dull apprentice, Humphrey. Luce, however, loves Jasper Merrythought, another apprentice, who has been discharged by the merchant for his outspokenness—and for his attentions to Luce. Jasper has also been exiled from his home by his mother, who has decided to take the family belongings and leave her husband, whose carefree ways she can no longer tolerate. With no money and in fear of the merchant, Jasper and Luce run off to be married; they, like old Merrythought, believe that things will always turn out for the best, if one does not worry.

Lo and behold, they are right. Through a surprising set of coincidences and a clever stratagem engineered by Jasper, the couple eventually wins the father's blessings, and the Merrythoughts, husband and wife, mother and son, are reconciled. Indeed, the sense of harmony is so pervasive that even the interludes by Rafe contribute to the overall effect. The players' growing acceptance of Rafe as a performer parallels the merchant's acceptance of Jasper and Luce and Mistress Merrythought's return to her husband.

It is easy to see why *The Knight of the Burning Pestle* failed in its time. For one reason, Beaumont seems to have tried the play on the wrong audience. Romantic comedies about grocers (the pestle was the symbol of the grocers' guild) and other members of the middle class were doomed at the Blackfriars, even if they satirized tradesmen and their wives for their bluntness, ignorance, greed, and gullibility. Beaumont and the players perhaps thought, wrongly, that the sparkling good fun of this play would make the audience forget its animosities.

An equally important reason for its contemporary failure was its unconventional structure, and this might have ruined it for an audience at the outdoor theaters as quickly as it did for the viewers at the Blackfriars. Other plays, such as John Marston's *The Malcontent* (pr. 1604), include feigned confrontations between audiences and actors, but there are not any so fully instrumental to the play as those in *The Knight of the Burning Pestle*. No doubt the Blackfriars audience expected George and Nell to be harshly put down by the players when the couple first interrupted the action. When, however, their behavior was condoned and when, even worse, Rafe became a key performer, the audience was certainly confused, its dramatic expectations thoroughly thwarted. Though Elizabethan and Jacobean theatergoers tolerated many structural innovations, one does not find in this period any other play that so deeply questions the relationship between actor and spectator. One wonders indeed if Beaumont realized the originality of his venture before it was produced. Whatever the answer, one can speculate that the failure of this wonderful play led him to distrust his singular talents and to cultivate the partnership with Fletcher that won him popularity, but not lasting fame.

Other major works

POETRY: *Salmacis and Hermaphroditus*, 1602; *Poems*, 1640.

Bibliography

Appleton, William W. *Beaumont and Fletcher: A Critical Study*. London: Allen & Unwin, 1956. This book explores literary questions in Beaumont's plays, though, as the title suggests, the focus is on the literary collaboration of Beaumont with John Fletcher. The index is helpful in separating the works of Beaumont, and the second chapter, on their partnership, is a good starting point for understanding Beaumont's style.

Bliss, Lee. *Francis Beaumont*. Boston: Twayne, 1987. This readable book, medium in length, opens with a biographical sketch and continues with detailed analyses of all Beaumont's major works. This book reproduces a portrait of Beaumont and includes a thorough, well-annotated bibliography. Though it is part of a standard series, it is for advanced readers.

Gayley, Charles Mills. *Beaumont, the Dramatist.* New York: Russell & Russell, 1914. Though somewhat dated, this biography is still the most thorough account of Beaumont's life. Readers looking for answers to literary questions will not find them here, though any line from Beaumont's plays that can be construed as biographical is quoted and explained. Gayley favors Beaumont in all controversies.

Waith, Eugene. *The Pattern of Tragicomedy in the Works of Beaumont and Fletcher.* New Haven, Conn.: Yale University Press, 1952. This book is of interest to the student who desires to focus on the genre of tragicomedy, as Beaumont and Fletcher developed it. Covers other aspects of Beaumont's works only insofar as they touch on such formal matters. Waith explains the stylized nature of Beaumont's drama.

Wallis, Lawrence B. *Fletcher, Beaumont, and Company: Entertainers to the Jacobean Gentry.* New York: King's Crown Press, 1947. Unlike other studies that concentrate on the plays, this one looks to the audience, seeing Beaumont and John Fletcher in the context of the society from which they made their living. Wallis speculates on how many scenes might have been played, explaining many matters that textual analysis alone leaves dark.

Christopher J. Thaiss
(Updated by *John R. Holmes*)

SAMUEL BECKETT

Born: Foxrock, Ireland; April 13, 1906
Died: Paris, France; December 22, 1989

Principal drama
Le Kid, pr. 1931; *En attendant Godot*, pb. 1952, pr. 1953 (*Waiting for Godot*, pb. 1954, pr. 1955); *All That Fall*, pr., pb. 1957 (radio play; revised 1968); *Fin de partie: Suivi de Acte sans paroles*, pr., pb. 1957 (*Endgame: A Play in One Act; Followed by Act Without Words: A Mime for One Player*, pr., pb. 1958); *Krapp's Last Tape*, pr., pb. 1958 (one act), pb. 1992 (revised); *Embers*, pr. 1959 (radio play); *Act Without Words II*, pr., pb. 1960 (one-act mime); *The Old Tune*, pr. 1960 (radio play; from a play by Roger Pinget); *Happy Days*, pr., pb. 1961; *Words and Music*, pr. 1962 (radio play; music by John Beckett); *Cascando*, pr. 1963 (radio play); *Play*, pr. 1963, pb. 1963-1964 (in German), pr., pb. 1964 (in English; one act); *Come and Go: Dramaticule*, pr., pb. 1965 (in German), pr., pb. 1966 (in French), pb. 1967, pr. 1968 (in English; one scene); *Film*, pr. 1965 (screenplay); *Eh Joe*, pr. 1966 (*Dis Joe*, 1967; teleplay); *Breath*, pb. 1969; *Not I*, pr. 1972, pb. 1973; *That Time*, pr., pb. 1976; *Footfalls*, pr., pb. 1976; *Rough for Radio*, pr. 1976 (radio play); *Tryst*, pr. 1976 (teleplay); *Shades*, pr. 1977 (includes *Ghost Trio, Not I, . . . but the Clouds . . .*); *A Piece of Monologue*, pr., pb. 1979; *Quad*, pr. 1981 (teleplay); *Rockaby*, pr., pb. 1981; *Ohio Impromptu*, pr., pb. 1981; *Catastrophe*, pr. 1982, pb. 1983; *Company*, pr. 1983; *Nacht und Träume*, pr. 1983 (teleplay); *What Where*, pr. 1983, pb. 1984; *Collected Shorter Plays*, pb. 1984.

Other literary forms
Samuel Beckett worked in literary forms other than drama. Although his radio plays, film script, and teleplays may be viewed as dramas that differ only in their use of various media, they nevertheless indicate his versatile and experimental approach to literary form. In prose fiction, he wrote both novels and short stories. The trilogy of novels, *Molloy* (1951; English translation, 1955), *Malone meurt* (1951; *Malone Dies*, 1956), and *L'Innommable* (1953; *The Unnamable*, 1958), written in French between 1947 and 1949, constitutes a major accomplishment in the genre. These works, like the earlier novel *Murphy* (1938), developed a monologue style of unique tone, with which Beckett had first begun to experiment in his short stories, collected as *More Pricks than Kicks* (1934). His first published literary work, however, was a poem on time and René Descartes, *Whoroscope* (1930), which won for him a prize; this work was followed by a collection of poems entitled *Echo's Bones and Other Precipitates* (1935). Beckett also turned to translations of Spanish poetry with Octavio Paz's *An Anthology of Mexican Poetry* in 1958. In addition, he distinguished himself with his

several translations of his own work, from English into French (such as *Murphy*) and French into English (such as *Malone meurt*); Beckett continued this practice throughout his career as dramatist, notably with *En attendant Godot*, which he translated into *Waiting for Godot*, and *Fin de partie*, which he translated into *Endgame*.

Achievements

Beckett is famous for his fiction and drama, which he wrote both in French and in English. *En attendant Godot* established the Irish Beckett as a unique writer because he elected the French language as his primary means of composition and English as his secondary one. The success of *Endgame* and *Krapp's Last Tape*, as well as his trilogy of French novels, led to Trinity College's awarding Beckett an honorary doctorate in 1959. Beckett also explored radio, cinema, and television for his art. So conscious was he of style that people disappeared into mere voices, mere echoes, and his plays could be called, as one was, ironically, simply *Play*, performed in 1963 at about the same time as his screenplay, *Film*, was being made. In 1961, Beckett received the International Publisher's Prize with Jorge Luis Borges, and in 1970, he was awarded the Nobel Prize in Literature for artistic achievements that define the ironic stance of modern reactions to an increasingly meaningless existence.

Biography

Samuel Barclay Beckett was born at Foxrock, near Dublin, Ireland, on April 13, 1906, the second son of Mary and William Beckett. In 1920, he was sent to Portora Royal School, Enniskillen, and in 1923, he proceeded to Trinity College, Dublin, to study Italian and French. After receiving his B.A. degree in 1927, he went to Belfast as a French tutor, then to the École Normale Supérieure in Paris as a lecturer for two years, a period during which he became acquainted with James Joyce. Beckett then became lecturer in French at Trinity College and studied for his M.A. After two years, he left for Germany and returned to Paris in 1932. Doing odd jobs and writing when he could, he traveled to London, through France and Germany. This trip led to two publications: *More Pricks than Kicks* in 1934 and *Echo's Bones and other Precipitates* in 1935. Meanwhile, he had inherited an annuity after his father's death in 1933, allowing him to concentrate on his writing.

In 1937, Beckett returned again to Paris, where he began to write in French. At the same time, he was preoccupied with the English text of his first novel, *Murphy*, which was published in 1938, the same year that he was stabbed on a Paris street and nearly died. He recovered, however, and established himself in an apartment where he would live throughout World War II and long after, at 6, rue des Favorites. There, he began, with Alfred

Péron, to translate *Murphy* into French. His friendship with Péron, however, was doomed by the war, which began while Beckett was visiting his mother in Dublin.

Nevertheless, Beckett returned to Paris, where he joined the French Resistance. Most of his colleagues, including Péron, disappeared, and Beckett himself barely escaped capture by the Nazis in 1942, when he fled to Free France with· Suzanne Deschevaux-Dumesnil, whom he married in 1961. While in Free France, he worked on a farm for two years and began his novel *Watt* (1953). After the war, in 1945, Beckett began a remarkable period of five years during which he wrote most of his important fiction and drama. His fame began, though, with productions of *Waiting for Godot* in French in 1953 and in English in 1955, followed by productions of *Endgame* in French in 1957 and in English in 1958.

Meanwhile, other plays were produced, including his radio dramas *All That Fall* and *Embers*, broadcast by the British Broadcasting Corporation in 1957 and 1959, respectively. These productions complemented the mimes that Beckett prepared for the stage at about the same time, beginning with *Act Without Words*, which was produced on a double bill with *Endgame*, and continuing with variations to the end of Beckett's career with *Nacht und Träume* in 1983. He also prepared the script for a motion picture, *Film*, with Buster Keaton in the leading role, filmed in New York in 1964. After *Endgame*, Beckett composed two important stage plays, *Krapp's Last Tape* first produced in 1958, and *Happy Days*, in 1961. Radio and television, however, were his favorite media. From 1959, with *Embers*, and 1966, with *Eh Joe*, to the time of his death in 1989, Beckett devoted much of his talent to numerous radio and television works, testing the limits of audience understanding.

Analysis

The dramatic works of Samuel Beckett reflect the evolution of his interests in various means of artistic expression, as he composed plays for stage, radio, cinema, and television. In his stage plays, he parodies traditional dramatic action and borrows the techniques used in other modes of entertainment. His themes are not constant, but they are grimly developed through a steady mood of ironic laughter if not outright sarcasm. Like the character "O" who runs from the camera's eye ("E") in *Film*, Beckett's art finds its form in a flight from conventional expectations and traditional observations. What seems meaningless and absurd is shown to be the only meaning possible in a universe where the human experience of consciousness (as subject) seems trapped by a nature and body (as object) without consciousness. Laughter is an intellectual triumph over material absurdity, and self-denial is self-affirmation. Beckett's plays are made of such paradoxes.

Beckett is best known as the author of four intriguingly powerful stage plays; *Waiting for Godot*, *Endgame*, *Krapp's Last Tape*, and *Happy Days*. His later work has begun to receive critical attention, particularly those plays which focus on women, such as *Play* and especially *Not I*. With his first stunningly successful stage play, however, there is not a woman to be seen. Only two tramps, two strangely united male travelers, and a boy are on the stage of *Waiting for Godot*.

In this play, Beckett established his major tone of comic despair, with his characters resigned to waiting for something to happen that never happens. He also created his major dramatic style out of vaudevillian and silent-film skits by clownish characters who are determined to endure without understanding why they must. In two acts that mirror each other in language and action, *Waiting for Godot* mocks audience desire for significant form and visionary comprehension of human experience. The two protagonists are tramps by the name of Estragon (called Gogo) and Vladimir (called Didi). They seem doomed to repeat forever the experiences played out in the two acts, as they wait for the arrival of a mysterious person known to them only as Godot. This Godot never does arrive. Instead, a lordly fellow named Pozzo appears in the first act, leading his servant Lucky by a rope; in the second act, these two reappear, though Pozzo is now blind and Lucky is dumb.

The spareness of plot and scarcity of characters are reinforced by the stark setting. Only a tree (leafless in act 1, bearing a few leaves in act 2) and a lonely country road mark the location of this play's action through a day of trivial concerns by the two tramps. The interruption by Pozzo and Lucky of their monotonous life of waiting is dramatic, but it is drained of its significance by the incomprehension of the characters who participate in it. The dialogue of the four characters is, in its variety, a counterpoint to the monotony of the slapstick action: The tramps talk in short, quick bursts of verbal response to each other, Pozzo exclaims himself in bombastic rhetoric, and Lucky overflows once in a stream-of-consciousness monologue called "thinking." When they reappear in act 2, Pozzo's pomposity has been deflated into whining, and Lucky cannot speak at all. Thus does this play illustrate Beckett's intense concern for the nature and function of language itself in a world where there is so little worth communicating.

At the end of each act, Vladimir and Estragon threaten to separate, to leave—but in each act, they do not move as the curtain descends on them. The two tramps play word games to pass the time, and they entertain themselves with strategies for suicide, but they cannot kill themselves. Waiting is a part of their fate. Each act ends with the arrival of a boy to announce that Godot will not arrive this evening, but that he will come another time. The boy's claim that he is not the same boy who appeared in the first act, that he tends sheep and that the other boy is his brother, a goatherd, constitutes allusions hinting at some religious mystery in the identity of Godot, the god who will separate sheep from goats on the day of judgment. If Didi and Gogo are denied their meeting with Godot, they are no less heroic for their waiting.

Endgame is one act of waiting also, not for an arrival but rather for a departure. The servant of this play, called Clov, threatens to leave his master, Hamm, when a boy is sighted through one of the two windows in the room, or "shelter," that makes the setting for this play's action. The curtain drops without a definite commitment by Clov to move outside, and the boy is never seen by anyone except Clov. The title refers to the last phase of a game of chess, and two of the four characters move as if they were pieces in such a game. Hamm is unable to leave his chair, and Clov is unable to sit; Hamm orders Clov about, and Clov moves Hamm around. A blind ruler of his household, Hamm is a modern King Lear, blind and helpless to tend to his bodily needs. He wants his painkiller, and Clov tells him it is depleted. Hamm wants the ultimate painkiller of death but seems elusive as well. Both Hamm and Clov wait for the end of the game of life, as all life outside their room seems at an end, except for the mysterious arrival of the boy.

On the stage are two other characters, Nagg and Nell, Hamm's parents. They have lost their legs in an accident and are as immobile as their son. They are kept by Hamm inside ash bins, pathetically reminiscing about their lives until the mother, Nell, dies and Nagg is sealed in his bin by Clov on orders from Hamm. Family values are far from the traditional ones of conventional domestic plots. Hamm tortures his father, or what remains of him, and Nagg torments his son exactly as he did when Hamm was a child. There is some remnant of affection in this play, though, just as there was in *Waiting for Godot*; the emotional tie between Gogo and Didi is repeated between Hamm and Clov, whose past binds them together even while they express a wish to separate. There is also a tie of romance holding the two parents together, though they cannot now reach each other for a kiss, and one of their most romantic adventures led to their helplessness—they lost their legs in a bicycle accident.

This play hints, through various allusions, at a meaning that transcends its apparent lack of meaning. Hamm is both an acting ham and a Prince Hamlet, calling attention to his role as a mockery of art in a meaningless universe; Hamm is also a piece of meat spiced by Clov in a world where human dignity no longer exists. The words and postures of both Hamm and Clov sometimes suggest that they are parodies of Christ on the Cross (where flesh is hammered with nails, puns on the names of the four characters), but there is no salvation for anyone in this play's world, unless it is to be in the boy waiting, perhaps contemplating his navel, beside a rock outside. Hamm is anxious for all life to end, even including that of a louse, so that the absurdity of human consciousness will cease. That boy outside is a threat, and so Hamm wants his life. Will life go on despite Hamm and evolve again, or will it finally wind down into nothingness? The play does not provide a clear sign of the answer as it concludes: Hamm replaces a bloody handkerchief over his blind eyes, and Clov, dressed as if for traveling, stands immobile watching the last pathetic moves of his master.

Pathos is not the essence, however, of *Endgame*, though it may threaten to become so, as in the relationship of the tramps in *Waiting for Godot*. At the point of revealing a depth of passion that might pass for pathos, Beckett's plays pull back and laugh at the pointlessness of the possibility. Everything falls into nothing, everything dies, everything comes to a stop, though not quite, and that is the wild absurdity of it all. If the drama of entropy cannot quite come to a complete stop, that is not the fault of desire for it. In *Krapp's Last Tape*, where an ingenious use of recording tapes creates a dimension of time always present in its absence, the protagonist (and only character on stage) listens to recordings of his own voice from many years past, especially one when he was thirty-nine years old, some thirty years before. Krapp's wait for death, for an end to entropy, is supported by his ironic dismissal of all that was meaningful at the time that he recorded the most important events of his life. In the present time of the play, Krapp is about to record the fact that the sound of the word "spool" is important, but he is drawn back to listen again and again to his recording of thirty years ago, when he described a lovemaking scene on a boat. His lust has declined, but his hunger for bananas and his thirst for wine have not, as he records his last tape.

Krapp's sense of himself, however, is threatened by the fragmented voices from his past; indeed, there is no continuous identity in this character, whose self-recording is a figure for the author's work itself. There is an irony of similarity here, for Beckett's own work may be reflected by the "plot" of *Krapp's Last Tape*. Voices are separated from the body, memories are mixed by mechanical forms, and the self is a stranger to itself. The drama of this discovery is in the encounter of one self with another, of silence yielding to voice, and voice subsiding into silence. These features increasingly preoccupied Beckett, as he moved his wit more and more into the regions of radio (all sound and voice) and mimes (no sound or voice).

More pathetic than all is the situation of Winnie in *Happy Days*. Entropy is visually represented by the intensifying imprisonment of Winnie, who appears in act 1 buried in a mound up to her waist and then, in act 2, up to her neck; she has become increasingly immobilized, and through it all she maintains her view of life as one of "happy days." She is happily stupid or courageously optimistic as she recounts her life's pleasures against the background of an unresponsive husband, Willie. At the end, dressed fit to kill, Willie calls his wife "Win" and seems prepared to shoot her with a pistol that she cannot seize for herself. She may be happy because she expects now to end it all with her death at last. Winnie's immobility is unchosen, and her waiting is absurdly imposed by the earth itself. As a ridiculous version of the earth-mother, Winnie is the opposite of her lethargic though "free" husband, and so she reflects the social condition of all women as well as the exploitation of that condition by men. *Happy Days*, like *Krapp's Last Tape*, develops through monologue rather than dialogue, though in both plays the possibility for dialogue is kept alive for the sake of its ironic futility.

The futility of dialogue, of communication, even perhaps of drama itself seems to direct the shape of the play called *Play*, which appears to have three characters who talk to one another, but in fact it has three characters who talk without regard for, or awareness of, one another. The ash bins of Nell and Nagg in *Endgame* have become three gray urns in *Play*, and these contain the three characters—rather, they contain the heads of three characters who stare straight ahead, as if at the audience, but in fact only into a fiercely interrogating spotlight. Their predicament, like that of Winnie in *Happy Days*, is more frustrating for communication and self-dignity than that of Winnie or Nell and Nagg, whose memories are functional for some modicum of dialogue with another who shares those memories with them. The nameless characters of *Play* are two women and one man, once involved in a shabby conventional love tryst of a married couple and "another woman."

The drama of *Play* is a hell of isolation, regrets, emotional ignorance, and intellectual darkness. The play proceeds from a chorus of three voices in counterpoint, interrupted reminiscences without self-understanding, and a concluding chorus that repeats the opening, as if about to begin again. The urns are funereal wombs for talking heads. The emptiness of meaning from the lives of these characters is the utmost meaning they can express, and their lack of relationship is a judgment by the play on the failure of relationships in modern life generally. As in other Beckett plays of this period, the women of *Play* have a particularly painful message to deliver: Love and marriage do not exist as real possibilities for meaning for anyone anymore, especially for women who have depended on them far more than men. The refusal to accept this predicament without a protest is dramatized in *Not I*, a play in which an apparently female character is divided between a Mouth of denial and an Auditor of silent protest. Here, Beckett has combined mime with radiolike monologue, and he has done it through a sexual pun on "ad-libbing."

To his achievements in stage plays, Beckett added successful accomplishments in radio and television drama, as well as one interesting script for motion pictures, *Film*. The radio plays of note are *All That Fall* and *Embers*; the teleplay deserving attention is *Eh Joe*. Communication, its failure or its emptiness, is a common theme running through Beckett's writing, and his experiments in various modes of artistic expression illustrate his search for success in communication. Radio was a challenging medium, using voice and other sounds to create imaginative shapes for audiences. *All That Fall* uses the muttering voice of an overweight old woman, Mrs. (Maddy) Rooney, making her way to a train station to meet her blind husband, Mr. (Dan) Rooney; her innermost thoughts and feelings are easily expressed in this medium, as are the concerns of those she meets along her way.

Like Beckett's other women, Mrs. Rooney has little to report that is fulfilling in her marriage; indeed, she mourns the loss of her one child, a daughter who would have been forty had she lived. Mrs. Rooney's real character is in her voice, not in her body; she can feel her self through her peculiar choice of words and sentence arrangements. This attention to vocabulary reveals Beckett's profound interest in the power of language as shaped and shaping sound. Of lesser interest is the terrible deed that lies at the center of this play's plot, the death of a child beneath the wheels of a train. Whether Mr. Rooney killed the child or not is less important than whether the audience can be moved by the mere articulation of sound to feel the horror of such a life-denying deed. *All That Fall* takes its title from a biblical verse that praises the power of a deity who protects "all that fall." The Rooneys hoot at this notion, though the child that fell beneath the train may, for all they can know, be better off than all those who, like the Rooneys, merely endure as they slowly decay with the rest of the universe.

Like them, the narrating speaker of *Embers*, Henry, endures through a failing nature, but he uses language to explain rather than affirm failure and death. Like the waves of the sea beside which he sits while he speaks, Henry returns again and again to the same scenes of his life, trying to make them acceptable, especially his father's death and his wife's love. They are not yet coherent for him because they were experiences of futility rather than fulfillment, and so he goes on telling his story, revising as he composes, and composing as he speaks. Henry's regrets are motives for his narratives, and in *Eh Joe*, Joe's refusal to feel regret is a motive for the teleplay. As the television camera moves, like an interrogator or conscience, for an ultimate close-up of Joe's face, a voice interrupts, or propels, the camera's movement to tell a tale of suicide by a woman condemning Joe.

This technique is similar to that of *Film*, in which a male figure (played by Buster Keaton) unsuccessfully fails to avoid self-perception, self-condemnation. In the movement of the film's narrative, the male figure is an Object ("O") for the subject of the camera's Eye ("E"); the whole action is a movement of avoidance by the object from becoming a subject. The drama of the story ends with the failure of avoidance: Art exists because of the duality narrated by the action of the film, and when the duality approaches unity, as self recognizes itself, the art ends and the object fades into a rocking subject. All that man the object, or the male figure, seems to be an attempt to escape his consciousness of himself, including his destruction of photographs (apparently of himself) from his past. Ironically, however, in that final desperate attempt to remove images of himself, he is most fully brought to recognize himself as a subject.

The destructive deed turns out to be a constructive act, as if Beckett's film were commenting on the nature of his own art as a successful communication about failures of communication, an integration of disintegrating forms, and a discovery of meaning in meaninglessness.

Whether it is in the nameless characters in *Play*, the lone and aging Krapp awaiting imminent death in *Krapp's Last Tape*, the pathetic Winnie sinking in her grave in *Happy Days*, the dying family in the masochistic *Endgame*, the monotonous life of waiting of Estragon and Vladimir in *Waiting for Godot*, or the down-and-outers in other dramatic works, Beckett shows his preference for passive characters who attempt to make sense of an increasingly absurd existence and who struggle to survive in a universe that lacks love and meaningful relationships.

As a critic, a transitional thinker, an innovator, and a postmodernist who probed the human condition and sensed the absurdity of the modern world, Beckett tried to link art and life into unusual theatrical images in order to etch human beings' inner world and the human experience of consciousness.

Even though his vision of life and the human predicament is discouraging, his plays are rich with clownish characters, slapstick humor, word games, irony, and sarcasm, allowing laughter to triumph over material absurdity.

Other major works

NOVELS: *Murphy*, 1938; *Malone meurt,* 1951 (*Malone Dies*, 1956); *Molloy*, 1951 (English translation, 1955); *L'Innommable*, 1953 (*The Unnamable*, 1958); *Watt*, 1953; *Comment c'est*, 1961 (*How It Is*, 1964); *Imagination morte imaginez*, 1965 (*Imagination Dead Imagine*, 1965); *Mercier et Camier*, 1970 (*Mercier et Camier*, 1974); *Le Dépeupleur*, 1971 (*The Lost Ones*, 1972); *Company*, 1980; *Mal vu mal dit*, 1981 (*Ill Seen Ill Said*, 1981); *Worstward Ho*, 1983.

SHORT FICTION: *More Pricks than Kicks*, 1934; *Nouvelles et textes pour rien*, 1955 (*Stories and Texts for Nothing*, 1967); *No's Knife: Collected Shorter Prose, 1947-1966*, 1967; *Sans*, 1969 (*Lessness*, 1970); *First Love and Other Shorts*, 1974; *Pour finir encore et autres foirades*, 1976 (*Fizzles*, 1976; also as *For to End Yet Again*, 1976).

POETRY: *Whoroscope*, 1930; *Echo's Bones and Other Precipitates*, 1935;

Poems in English, 1961; *Collected Poems in English and French*, 1977.
NONFICTION: *Proust*, 1931.

TRANSLATIONS: *An Anthology of Mexican Poetry*, 1958 (of Octavio Paz's anthology); "Zone," 1972 (of Guillaume Apollinaire's poem); *Drunken Boat*, 1976 (of Arthur Rimbaud's work).

MISCELLANEOUS: *I Can't Go On, I'll Go On: A Selection from Samuel Beckett's Work*, 1976 (Richard Seaver, editor); *As the Story Was Told*, 1987.

Bibliography

Ben-Zvi, Linda, ed. *Women in Beckett: Performance and Critical Perspectives.* Urbana: University of Illinois Press, 1990. The authors, having interviewed twelve actresses, present eight essays that study the role of women in Beckett's fiction. An essay on Beckett's late fiction and drama is followed by eleven articles on his stage plays, radio plays, and teleplays, emphasizing the later writings, especially *Not I.* Contains an index.

Cohn, Ruby, ed. *Samuel Beckett: A Collection of Criticism.* New York: McGraw-Hill, 1975. Contains three essays that offer general analyses of Beckett's work, essays on his poetry and fiction, and two discussions of religious themes and storytelling characters in his drama. The final essay concentrates on the influence of visual arts in Beckett's career. Chronology, select bibliography.

_____. *Samuel Beckett: The Comic Gamut.* New Brunswick, N.J.: Rutgers University Press, 1962. This major scholar analyzes in thirteen chapters Beckett's fiction, then his plays through *Happy Days.* Studies Beckett as a French intellectual with a sharp Irish humor and devotion to art. An appendix contains *Whoroscope* and other pieces. Includes notes and a bibliography.

Esslin, Martin. *The Theatre of the Absurd.* Rev. ed. Garden City, N.Y.: Anchor Books, 1969. Contains one chapter on Beckett devoted to his works through *Eh Joe* as searches for self-identity. An important essay for appreciating the influence of Beckett on modern drama throughout Europe and the United States. Complemented by a bibliography and an index.

Kenner, Hugh. *Samuel Beckett: A Critical Study.* Rev. ed. Berkeley: University of California Press, 1968. This difficult, influential study emphasizes Beckett's art of the circus clown—exploring techniques of self-denial and discipline. The focus on the drama is limited to two chapters on *Waiting for Godot* and *Endgame*, with a supplementary chapter surveying the writing through *Eh Joe.* Contains a chronology in the first chapter.

Robinson, Michael. *The Long Sonata of the Dead: A Study of Samuel Beckett.* London: Hart-Davis, 1969. Robinson analyzes Beckett's poetic stance on necessary failure and examines the fiction and drama, with play-by-play discussions through *Play.* Emphasizes the paradox of Beckett's creativity in the context of his skeptical attitude toward the meaning of life. Supplemented by notes, an index, and a bibliography.

States, Bert O. *The Shape of Paradox: An Essay on "Waiting for Godot."* Berkeley: University of California Press, 1978. A debatable analysis of language restraining mythic form in *Waiting for Godot*, this book argues that the play is about the fall of humanity. Six chapters study details of literary allusion, echoes, and similarities. The shape of language shapes the play, which expresses dialectical skepticism. Contains an index.

Richard D. McGhee

BRENDAN BEHAN

Born: Dublin, Ireland; February 9, 1923
Died: Dublin, Ireland; March 20, 1964

Principal drama

Gretna Green, pr. 1947; *The Quare Fellow*, pr. 1954, pb. 1956 (translation and revision of his Gaelic play "Casadh Súgáin Eile," wr. 1946); *The Big House*, pr. 1957 (radio play), pr. 1958 (staged), pb. 1961; *An Giall*, pr. 1958, pb. 1981 (in Gaelic); *The Hostage*, pr., pb. 1958 (translation and revision of *An Giall*); *Richard's Cork Leg*, pr. 1972, pb. 1973 (begun 1960, completed posthumously by Alan Simpson, 1964); *The Complete Plays*, pb. 1978.

Other literary forms

Brendan Behan's literary reputation rests on the merits of three works: *The Quare Fellow* and *The Hostage*, his dramatic masterpieces, and *The Borstal Boy* (1958), his autobiography, published in England by Hutchinson and in the United States by Alfred A. Knopf. The two plays were performed several times prior to their publication, and the performance rights are still retained by the Theatre Workshop in East London. *The Borstal Boy*, set in 1931-1941, is an autobiographical narrative of Behan's adolescent years in prison. Several of the stories included in *The Borstal Boy* appeared initially in literary magazines and journals. *Brendan Behan's Island* (1962) was intended by Behan to be similar in tone and structure to John Millington Synge's *The Aran Islands* (1907), but it does not stand up to this literary comparison. Unable to write for extended periods of time in his later years, Behan began taping his stories and subsequently had them edited by his publishing guardian angel and friend, Rae Jeffs. *Brendan Behan's Island*, *Hold Your Hour and Have Another* (1963), *Brendan Behan's New York* (1964), and *Confessions of an Irish Rebel* (1965) are all edited results of taping sessions. *The Scarperer* (1964) was published in book form the year Behan died but had been published first as a series in *The Irish Times*, in 1953, under the pseudonym "Emmet Street." Several of Behan's works were published posthumously. Among these are *Confessions of an Irish Rebel*, *Moving Out* (1952), *A Garden Party* (1952), and *Richard's Cork Leg*, the latter of which was begun by Behan in 1960 and ultimately completed by Alan Simpson. In addition to his plays and books, Behan contributed scores of short stories and poems on a variety of subjects to journals and newspapers throughout his life. He was as renowned for his balladeering as he was for his writings, and he composed the songs for his plays. A recording entitled *Brendan Behan Sings Irish Folksongs and Ballads*, produced by Spoken Arts Inc., provides insight into Behan's passionate personality.

Achievements

Behan has been called the most important postwar Irish writer by contemporary Irish, English, and American critics. His works represent an extraordinary mixture of Irish romance, history, patriotism, and racism. All of his works reflect, in some measure, the Irish Republican Army's efforts to rid Northern Ireland of the English. Paradoxically, his major literary successes came first in England, and though productions of *The Quare Fellow* and *The Hostage* met with moderate success in America, his most receptive audience was always in London.

Stylistically, Behan has been compared to Jonathan Swift, James Joyce, Synge, and Sean O'Casey. His treatment of the Irish in his plays and stories is simultaneously warm and biting. Clearly a social critic, Behan's writings indict law, religion, Ireland, England, and the absurdity of politics. His literary career spans barely twenty years, though the most productive of these amount to less than a decade. His first story, "I Become a Borstal Boy," was published in June, 1942, after which he regularly contributed nationalistic essays, stories, and poems to various Irish periodicals, including organs of the Irish Republican Army (IRA) such as *Fianna: The Voice of Young Ireland* and the *Wolfe Tone Weekly*.

Behan's most productive years (1953-1959) were marked by the production of both *The Quare Fellow* and *The Hostage* and the publication of *The Borstal Boy*. During these years, Behan's fame began to wane, and his creative talent floundered in a sea of alcohol. Behan wrote principally of a world of men, yet ironically it was his association with two women that accounted for much of his artistic success. Joan Littlewood, director and manager of the Theatre Workshop at the Theatre Royal, Stratford East, London, directed *The Quare Fellow* in 1956 and catapulted Behan into the international limelight. Her production of *The Hostage* in 1958 earned for Behan equally high praise. His friend Jeffs can be credited with virtually all of Behan's productivity during his final years. The publicity manager for Hutchinson's Publishing Company, she was "assigned" the obstreperous Behan in 1957. From 1957 to 1964, Jeffs's formidable task included following Behan from pub to pub, trailing and assisting him on his trips from England to America to Ireland, all the while making sure he was writing or taping his work, to be edited later. Ultimately, she performed her task as a labor of love, serving as friend and confidante to both Behan and his wife, Beatrice. Without Jeffs's tenacity, Behan's literary career would have ended in 1957 in an alcoholic stupor. In his final years, Behan became a drunken caricature of himself. The early works evidence the true spark of genius that carried him through the years of honor to the dark years plagued by alcoholism and self-doubt. It is to these early works that one must turn to capture the real genius embodied in the literature of this twentieth century Irish phenomenon.

Biography

Brendan Behan was born February 9, 1923, in Dublin, Ireland, the first child of Stephen and Kathleen (Kearney) Behan, though his mother had two sons by a previous marriage. Born into a family with radical political leanings, Behan was reared on a double dose of IRA propaganda and Catholicism. The radical Left was part of his genetic makeup. His grandmother and a grandfather were jailed for their roles in the revolution, the former for illegal possession of explosives when she was seventy years old and the latter for his part in the murder of Lord Cavendish. Both of Behan's parents fought in the Irish Revolution and in the Troubles. Ultimately jailed for his participation in the violence, Behan's father saw his son for the first time through prison bars.

Behan was a precocious child whose reverence for writers was spawned by his father's readings of Samuel Pepys, Charles Dickens, Émile Zola, George Bernard Shaw, and various polemical treatises to his children. By Behan's own account, his home was filled with reading, song, and revolution. Juxtaposed to this violent heritage was Behan's conservative religious training. He attended schools run by the Sisters of Charity of St. Vincent de Paul, where he was a favorite, and another operated by the Irish Christian Brothers, where he found himself in constant disfavor. His militant disposition surfaced early, when at the age of nine he joined the Fianna Éireann, the junior wing of the IRA. Most of his early adult years were spent in prison. Arrested in Liverpool at the age of sixteen for participating in IRA bombings in England, Behan spent three years in the Borstal, the English correctional institution for juvenile delinquents. Released in 1941 and deported to Ireland, Behan was again incarcerated the following year for shooting at a policeman. He had served four years of a fourteen-year sentence when he was released in 1946. Additional stays in jail followed throughout his life.

The worldview projected in Behan's works recalls the environment in which he matured, one dominated by a radical family and by his prison experience. Cradled in the romance of revolution, Behan was cultured in a more traditional sense. Kathleen and Stephen Behan reared their children with a love for music and literature. Nurtured with a reverential attitude toward Kathleen's brother Peadar Kearney, a noted composer who wrote the Irish national anthem, the Behan children learned his marches and ballads in a home continuously filled with music. According to Colbert Kearney, Behan's precociousness as a child was largely attributable to the education he received at home. His father instilled in him a deep-seated respect for Irish writers and rhetoricians. He learned to read at an early age and was fond of memorizing speeches by Irish patriots such as Robert Emmet. Not as readily discernible in Behan's work is the influence of his strict upbringing in Catholicism. Behan had a love-hate relationship with the Church, and often his works condemn religion. Yet one of his most bitter disappointments came when he was excommunicated while serving time in prison. Some critics believe that this was a crisis in Behan's life from which he never recovered.

Behan began writing while in prison, and his first story, "I Become a Borstal Boy," was published in *The Bell* in 1942. The plays, poems, and short stories written during his prison terms are all autobiographical. The years from 1946 to 1956 were the most ambitious of his career. For a time he lived in Paris, but he was eventually drawn back to Ireland, where he worked as a housepainter and free-lance journalist. During this hiatus from serious encounters with the law, he married Beatrice Salkeld, daughter of the noted Irish artist Cecil Salkeld. Behan's major break came when Alan Simpson agreed to produce *The Quare Fellow* at the Pike Theatre in Dublin in 1954. The play met with critical acclaim, but, to Behan's disappointment, the more prestigious Irish theaters such as the Abbey refused to stage it. This rejection spurred in Behan an overwhelming desire to be accepted as an artist in his own country. *The Quare Fellow* was noticed by Joan Littlewood, whose 1956 London production made Behan an international sensation. He followed this success with another play, *An Giall*, which he wrote in Gaelic and later translated as *The Hostage*. Littlewood's subsequent production of *The Hostage* proved an even greater success than *The Quare Fellow*.

Critics proclaimed Behan a literary genius, but he was destroyed by his success. His notorious interruptions of his plays with drunken speeches shouted from his seat in the audience and his intoxication during interviews for the British Broadcasting Corporation enhanced the "bad boy" image he so carefully cultivated, but ultimately it killed him. The most tragic repercussion of his alcoholism proved to be his inability to sit and write for an extended period of time. *The Hostage* was Behan's last good work. When his writing sojourns to Ibiza, his favorite retreat, and America and Canada produced little, he resorted to taping sessions to meet his publication contracts. By 1960, after two major breakdowns as well as intermittent stays in hospitals to dry out, Behan was a shell of his former robust personality. Riding on his reputation of acknowledged artistry, he found himself incapable of writing, which led him to drink even more. Behan died March 20, 1964, at the age of forty-one. Several of his edited works published after his death created a brief, cultish interest in the man and his writing, but this adulation soon passed. What remains is the recognition that Behan was one of the finest twentieth century Irish writers. His talent will be recognized long after his colorful reputation has faded.

Analysis

To understand Brendan Behan's work, one must first recognize the underlying Behan legend, which is built on paradox. Frank O'Connor, writing in the *Sunday Independent* (Dublin), said of Behan that "under his turbulent exterior there was quite clearly the soul of an altar boy." Behan was a kind, gentle man who acted violently. He was insecure and feared publicity yet perpetrated outrageous stunts to capture attention; he wrote of reasonableness and absurdity in the world yet persisted in his personal irrationality. Behan was saint and sinner, moralist and profligate, and this dichotomy is carried over into his works. Even his overriding thematic consideration, a politically divided Ireland, is complex. Gordon Wickstrom believes Behan writes of three Irelands: the Ireland of contemporary, illegal Republican fanaticism, dedicated to the destruction of everything English; the Ireland of glorious memory of the Troubles and Easter Week, needing no justification beyond the private experience of valor and sacrifice; and Ireland as it actually exists, complete with police attacks, sirens, bloodbaths, and terror.

The principal themes in Behan's works are culled from his close association with the Irish Republican Army: death, freedom, and the absurdity of humanity's impermanence in a hostile world. Behan's major plays, *The Quare Fellow* and *The Hostage*, examine these themes through the eyes of a prisoner, a character-type that figures prominently in Behan's works. As his life stands as a series of paradoxes, so, too, does his style. Behan fills his works with unsavory gallows humor and swings erratically between comedy and tragedy in a decidedly Brechtian manner. Yet the early works are tightly structured and astonishingly poetic. Songs incorporated into his plays serve as lyric Gaelic laments but can quickly turn into obscene ditties. Behan's use of vernacular and the overwhelming sense of freedom in the lines contribute to the impressive strength of his writing. An unlikely coupling of naturalism and absurdism is characteristic of his best work. His characters are drawn from the lower classes, with Irish nationalism, bordering on racism, binding them together. Ironically, Behan's genteel audiences find it easy to empathize with his murderers, prostitutes, homosexuals, and radicals, perhaps because the sordid individuals in Behan's plays and stories are presented with a depth of compassion and understanding usually reserved for more noble literary characters.

Behan's prison years had a profound influence on him. During these stultifying periods, he became preoccupied with the two themes that dominate his works: death and freedom. In the cells and work yards of the Borstal and Mountjoy prisons, Behan mentally cataloged information about individuals, human nature, and the absurdity of the world and its systems. The examination of conflicts between gentleness and violence, a trademark of Behan's work, stems directly from his own divided nature as much as his early background. Major characters such as Dunlavin and the Warder in *The Quare Fellow*, Monsewer and Williams in *The Hostage*, or the prisoner in *The Borstal Boy* reflect various facets of his personality.

In November, 1954, *The Quare Fellow* was labeled "a powerful piece of propaganda" by A. J. Leventhal, writing in *Dublin Magazine*. This assessment of Behan's first literary and theatrical success holds true for all of his works. Though his plays do not strictly adhere to agitation-propaganda techniques used by earlier European playwrights, Behan's works are obviously propagandistic. *The Quare Fellow*, the most structured of his plays, examines the issue of capital punishment. Set in a prison, *The Quare Fellow* is a series of episodes in which the prison community prepares for the execution of the unseen titular character.

Tension is deftly established on two levels: the friction maintained in the relationship between prisoners and warders and the more insidious anxiety, hidden beneath the prattle and routine of the prison, that eats at the souls of both warders and prisoners as the moment of execution draws near. Every character waits in dread for the final moment when a man will die. Their empathetic response to ritualized, state-supported death reinforces the horror felt by the audience. The prison serves as Behan's microcosm of the world in which primal struggles of life and death as well as social struggles of promotion, acceptance, pretense, and charity are all in evidence.

The Quare Fellow opens with the singing of a man in solitary confinement, trying to keep his sanity. His haunting lament, floating over the prison grounds, becomes almost a dirge as the play progresses. The plot is moved by the institution's preparations for the day of execution. Each character fears the approach of the hour of death and manifests his uneasiness in a different way. The prisoners attempt a forced jauntiness and irreverence but are unable to call the condemned man by his Christian name, preferring instead to force on him anonymity, calling him only "the quare fellow." As the climax approaches and the moment of death is imminent, a prisoner cynically announces the offstage procession to the gallows as though it were the start of a horse race: "We're off, in this order: The Governor, The Chief, two screws Regan and Crimmin, the quare fellow between them. . . ." Yet this comic diversion is incapable of diluting the dramatic effect of the climax when the clock strikes the hour and the prisoners wail, howl, and roar in primal lamentation, as the trap drops and the quare fellow hangs. The hero of the play, the quare fellow, never appears onstage. Dunlavin, a crusty, experienced prisoner, and Regan, a compassionate warder, are the principal characters. This den of thieves and murderers has its own order, a social hierarchy based on criminal offenses and experience. Sex offenders are ostracized by the prison community, and Dunlavin bemoans his misfortune at having one placed in the cell next to his. The sex offender, for his part, is appalled that he must live among murderers and takes to quoting Thomas Carlyle.

Religion is brutally satirized in *The Quare Fellow*. The hypocritical representative from the Department of Justice is dubbed "Holy Healey" by the inmates, who paste religious pictures on their walls to curry favor during his visits. Dunlavin's friend and neighbor in the cellblock comments on the importance of the Bible to prisoners, stating, "Many's the time the Bible was a consolation to a fellow all alone in the old cell," not for its spiritual comfort, but because prisoners rolled mattress bits within its pages and smoked them. Dunlavin, in turn, recounts how in his first twelve months he smoked his way halfway through Genesis. The executioner, referred to imperially as "Himself," cannot face his job in a sober state and must be accompanied by a teetotaling, Bible-quoting, hymn-singing assistant to see him to his appointed rounds. The incongruity of this misallied pair is obvious as Jenkinson, the assistant, sings a hymn while the hangman audibly calculates the weight of the condemned man and the height of the drop needed to kill him.

Behan's vision of the value of life and the awesome power of death is painted in masterful strokes throughout *The Quare Follow*. The dignity of man, the worth of an individual life, and the inhumanity of a system devised for correctional purposes are powerfully juxtaposed in this play. The 1954 Pike Theatre production of *The Quare Fellow* was well received, but it was Joan Littlewood's direction in 1956 that made it a modern classic. Although the play has been criticized as being melodramatic, Behan mixes well-developed characters with stereotypes and caricatures to provide diverse opportunities for commentary on various levels. *The Quare Fellow* is not wholly a tragedy, nor is it merely black comedy. It is an unnatural two-backed beast that violently gives birth to Behan's pessimistic worldview.

The music-hall atmosphere of *The Hostage* differs radically from the sterile environment of *The Quare Fellow*. From the opening jig, danced by two prostitutes and two homosexuals, to the rousing chorus, sung by the corpse, Behan jars his audience with the unexpected. Like Bertolt Brecht's *The Threepenny Opera* (pr. 1928), *The Hostage* is populated by a cast of societal misfits. Brechtian influences can be noticed in the play's structure as well. *The Hostage*, according to Richard A. Duprey in *The Critic*, is an indictment of law, religion, home, country, human decency, art, and even death. What is espoused within its tenuous structure is IRA radicalism, but even this cannot escape Behan's satiric barbs. The IRA officer in the play is outraged by the shoddy accommodations—a brothel—afforded him and his political prisoner, while Pat, manager of the "brockel" and a veteran of the Easter Rebellion and the Troubles, denounces the new IRA soldiers as "white-faced loons with their trench coats, berets and teetotal badges."

Thematically, *The Hostage* compares with Behan's other major works in that the protagonist is a prisoner. Leslie Williams has committed no crime except that he is an English soldier in Ireland. Taken as a hostage by IRA reactionaries, Williams is offered in trade for a jailed Irish youth sentenced to hang. The IRA cause is felt most strongly in this play, and Behan's nationalistic biases are given ample voice in the songs about the Easter Rebellion, Monsewer's senile ravings about the days of glorious conflict, and Pat's diatribes against modern Ireland. Hidden beneath the brash, gaudy, and colorful language of the play, such weighty underpinnings emerge in flashes of seriousness.

A mélange of dramatic styles pushes the plot through a series of vignettes, comedy routines, and song-and-dance numbers. Songs, jokes, and malapropisms abound in this very political play. Individually, the characters lack depth and are only one step removed from the stereotyped clowns of burlesque houses. Collectively, they champion traditional Irish Republicanism while at the same time denouncing the absurdity of its violent contemporary manifestations. This is a play about the Republican cause; it is also a play about the value of life. Leslie Williams is an apolitical character who dies needlessly, an injustice which Behan adroitly condemns. Life and death in Behan's work are never equal forces; life always triumphs. He breaks the serious mood of his final scene, in which Williams' death is disclosed, by having the corpse jump up and sing, "The bells of hell go ting a ling a ling for you but not for me...."

The original Gaelic-language version of the play, *An Giall*, was a much more serious play than the version presented in the internationally acclaimed 1958 London production. The seminal version had but ten characters, whereas *The Hostage* has fifteen. Colbert Kearney notes that *An Giall* is essentially a naturalistic tragedy, while *The Hostage* is a musical extravaganza. Certainly, the latter tolerates a greater degree of bawdiness than the original. Critics charged that Joan Littlewood's company substantially altered *An Giall* while in production for *The Hostage*, yet this was partially Behan's fault. During 1957 and 1958, he was committed to two projects: translating *An Giall* into *The Hostage* for Littlewood and finishing *The Borstal Boy*. He became preoccupied with the publicity and lavish promotion given the latter and neglected his commitments to Littlewood. Consequently, parts of *The Hostage* grew out of the improvisations of the Theatre Workshop and, though sanctioned by Behan, changed the play significantly from the original work. Ulick O'Connor believes several of the non sequitur scenes in *The Hostage* were invented by Littlewood and do not reflect Behan's hand in the revision. Nevertheless, the production was a hit. *The Hostage* was selected to represent Great Britain at the prestigious Théâtre des Nations festival in 1959, and it moved to the fashionable Wyndham Theatre on London's West End. Productions of Behan's plays opened in Dublin, New York, Paris, and Berlin.

The Hostage proved to be Behan's last theatrical success. His reputation sustained him as an artist for the next six years, but his talent abandoned him. He began another play, *Richard's Cork Leg*, but it remained unfinished at his death. *The Hostage* is not as neatly structured as *The Quare Fellow*, though Behan's genius for dialogue and *mise en scène* pervade the work. Behan—patriot, nationalist, and racist—is plainly seen in *The Hostage*, yet his persona, so dominant in his plays, turns to reveal Behan the humanitarian in equally sharp focus. Brendan Behan's works, like the man, are paradoxical. His legend lives on, supported by contemporary interest in Behan the revolutionary and artist.

Other major works

NOVEL: *The Scarperer*, 1964 (serialized 1953, as by Emmet Street).

SHORT FICTION: *After the Wake*, 1981.

NONFICTION: *The Borstal Boy*, 1958; *Brendan Behan's Island: An Irish Sketchbook*, 1962; *Hold Your Hour and Have Another*, 1963; *Brendan Behan's New York*, 1964; *Confessions of an Irish Rebel*, 1965.

RADIO PLAYS: *A Garden Party*, 1952; *Moving Out*, 1952.

MISCELLANEOUS: *Poems and Stories*, 1978; *Poems and a Play in Irish*, 1981 (includes the play *An Giall*).

Bibliography

Boyle, Ted E. *Brendan Behan*. New York: Twayne, 1969. This concise overview of Behan's life and works includes an especially useful chapter entitled "Some Relevant Theories of Comedy." In his analysis of Behan's writings, Boyle focuses on "this peculiar juxtaposition of laughter and death . . . [that] could be said to be his most characteristic theme." Annotated bibliography of secondary sources, notes.

Kearney, Colbert. *The Writings of Brendan Behan*. New York: St. Martin's Press, 1977. In this overview of Behan's life and works, the playwright is seen primarily as an iconoclast who pushed broad-mindedness to its limits, both in the theater and in his personal activities.

McCann, Sean, ed. *The World of Brendan Behan*. New York: Twayne, 1966. Published two years after Behan's death, this collection of twenty-four essays, recollections, and tributes provides a personal overview of Behan's life. Though useful and interesting, it is less comprehensive than the Mikhail volumes cited below, and its approach is affectionately anecdotal rather than critical. A sample listing of Behan's epigrams is also included. Drawings by Liam C. Martin.

Mikhail, E. H., ed. *The Art of Brendan Behan*. Totowa, N.J.: Barnes & Noble Books, 1979. This compilation of forty-nine articles and reviews emphasizes Behan the writer rather than the man. Selected reviews of each of Behan's works are arranged chronologically, following six tributes by contemporary writers.

_____. *Brendan Behan: Interviews and Recollections*. 2 vols.

Totowa, N.J.: Barnes & Noble Books, 1982. A collection of extracts from published memoirs and interviews given by those who knew Behan. Contains fifty-one items in volume 1 and fifty-five in volume 2. Mikhail's introduction insightfully compares Behan and Oscar Wilde.

O'Connor, Ulick. *Brendan.* London: Hamish Hamilton, 1970. This excellent, judicious biographical and critical study effectively captures not only Behan's charm and wit as a raconteur and celebrity but also the self-destructiveness and pain of Behan's later life. Photographs, notes, bibliography.

Witoszek, Walentyna. "The Funeral Comedy of Brendan Behan." *Études irlandaises* 11 (December, 1988): 83-91. Witoszek discusses the puzzling presence of laughter in Behan's writings in which execution is imminent. Though Death is the "central character" in all Behan's plays, there is also an orgiastic atmosphere of carnival madness, which is analyzed in terms of ritual, the Irish image of the laughing death, and Mikhail Bakhtin's theories of the carnivalesque.

Susan Duffy
(Updated by *William Hutchings*)

APHRA BEHN

Born: England; July(?), 1640
Died: London, England; April 16, 1689

Principal drama

The Forced Marriage: Or, The Jealous Bridegroom, pr. 1670, pb. 1671; *The Amorous Prince: Or, The Curious Husband*, pr., pb. 1671; *The Dutch Lover*, pr., pb. 1673; *Abdelazer: Or, The Moor's Revenge*, pr. 1676, pb. 1677; *The Town Fop: Or, Sir Timothy Tawdry*, pr. 1676, pb. 1677; *The Rover: Or, The Banished Cavaliers, Part I*, pr., pb. 1677, *Part II*, pr., pb. 1681; *Sir Patient Fancy*, pr., pb. 1678; *The Feigned Courtesans: Or, A Night's Intrigue*, pr., pb. 1679; *The Young King: Or, The Mistake*, pr. 1679, pb. 1683; *The Roundheads: Or, The Good Old Cause*, pr. 1681, pb. 1682; *The City Heiress: Or, Sir Timothy Treat-All*, pr., pb. 1682; *The Lucky Chance: Or, An Alderman's Bargain*, pr. 1686, pb. 1687; *The Emperor of the Moon*, pr., pb. 1687; *The Widow Ranter: Or, The History of Bacon of Virginia*, pr. 1689, pb. 1690; *The Younger Brother: Or, The Amorous Jilt*, pr., pb. 1696.

Other literary forms

In addition to her plays, Aphra Behn's literary legacy includes many noteworthy works of fiction and poetry. The three-part novel entitled *Love Letters Between a Nobleman and His Sister* (1683-1687) is both her earliest and her longest narrative effort. A fictionalized version of a notorious contemporary scandal, this novel was extremely popular at the time, but it is little read today. Of much more interest to present-day readers are the shorter novels such as *The Fair Jilt: Or, The History of Prince Tarquin and Miranda* (1688) and *Oroonoko: Or, The Royal Slave, a True History* (1688). The latter is undoubtedly Mrs. Behn's most enduring literary creation in any genre. Allegedly based on her own experiences in Surinam during the 1660's, the narrative relates the tragic history of a slave of African origin named Oroonoko and his wife, Imoinda, from the viewpoint of the author herself. As the story unfolds, Mrs. Behn repeatedly exposes the deceitful and greedy nature of the European settlers and underscores the innate virtue of the novel's eponymous hero. He is, therefore, one of the earliest fictional manifestations of the archetypal "noble savage." Because of its implicit condemnation of slavery and colonialism, the novel is highly regarded as a harbinger of the crisis in political and social morality that was to trouble the conscience of Europeans in their dealings with the nonwhite population of the globe over the succeeding centuries.

Mrs. Behn's poetry is widely diverse in character. In keeping with the convention of the time, she made it a practice to provide her plays with prologues and epilogues in verse form. She also interspersed many songs within the prose dialogue of her plays. In both instances, the quality of her poetry is usually of a high order. Two of her most successful poems, in fact, appear in *Abdelazer*. The song which begins with the line "LOVE in fantastick Triumph sat" comes at the opening of act 1, and the one commencing "MAKE haste, Amintas, come away" is to be found near the end of act 2. Both of these songs are frequently anthologized. Likewise commendable are two short narrative poems entitled "The Disappointment" and "The Golden Age." While most of her occasional poetry consists of overly rhetorical panegyrics to illustrious personages, a few of the elegies are moving expressions of private grief. Perhaps the best of these are "To the Memory of George, Duke of Buckingham" and "On the Death of Edmund Waller, Esq."

Being fluent in French, Mrs. Behn began making translations from that language as a source of income late in her career. Among the French works that she translated are the maxims of the Duke François de La Rochefoucauld and two works of fiction by Bernard le Bovier de Fontenelle. More in the nature of an adaptation is her translation of Abbé Paul Tallemant's *Le Voyage de l'isle d'amour* (1663), which she published under the title *A Voyage to the Island of Love* in 1684. Tallemant's piece of fantasy is, for the most part, a prose narrative interspersed with songs, but Mrs. Behn chose to render all the prose passages as rhymed couplets. In *Lycidus: Or, The Lover in Fashion* (1688), including an adaptation of Tallemant's second voyage to the Island of Love, however, she adheres to the prose and poetry distinctions of the original text. One of the songs in *Lycidus*, starting with the line "A thousand Martyrs I have made," has proved itself to be a perennial favorite with the reading public. The fact that Mrs. Behn knew little Latin and less Greek did not prevent her from "translating" works written in those tongues. With the aid of French and English translations, she managed to turn out excellent versions of Aesop's fables for an illustrated edition published in 1687. Working chiefly from a prose paraphrase, she also produced a rhymed translation of book 6 (*Of Trees*) from Abraham Cowley's poetic treatise entitled *Sex libri plantarum* (1668). The preceding five books were translated by others, and the complete text of the *Six Books of Plants* was published shortly before Mrs. Behn's death in 1689.

Achievements

Mrs. Behn came of age during the period in English history known as the Restoration. The epoch began in 1660 with the Stuart monarchy being restored in the person of Charles II. His Royal Highness was passionately fond of the theater, and one of his first acts was to rescind the laws prohibiting the performance of plays that had been enacted in 1642 by the Long Parliament under the domination of Oliver Cromwell. While all forms of drama were thenceforth permitted to flourish, the best plays written in the succeeding era turned out to be comedies. The masterpieces of this genre were created by Sir George Etherege, William Wycherley, and William Congreve, among others. While it would be injudicious to claim that any of Mrs. Behn's comedies should be ranked with the best of Etherege, Wycherley, or Congreve, many of her plays have withstood the test of time and are fully deserving of a contemporary readership. The same is true with respect to her novel *Oroonoko*. The dramatic vitality of *Oroonoko* and many of her other works of narrative fiction is attested by the fact that several of them have been successfully adapted for the theater by other hands. Using the novel *The History of the Nun: Or, The Fair Vow-Breaker* (1689) as the source for his plot, Thomas Southerne scored one of his greatest successes as a playwright with the tragedy entitled *The Fatal Marriage: Or, The Innocent Adultery* (pr. 1694). Two years later, in 1696, he repeated this success with a dramatization of *Oroonoko*. In the same year, moreover, Mrs. Catherine Cockburn offered the theatergoing public the opportunity of seeing a play based on Behn's novel *Agnes de Castro* (1688). These adaptations continued to be popular into the eighteenth century.

Literary historians will always accord an honorable place to Behn for being the first Englishwoman to become a professional author and to support herself solely by means of income derived from her writings. While it must have been a bold decision on her part to defy conventional wisdom regarding the proper mode of existence for a woman of her class, she seems not to have been seriously disadvantaged on account of her gender in pursuing a literary career and may have actually been helped by it. The only apparent adverse effect which she suffered by being a woman stemmed from the generally held belief that women are innately more virtuous than men. As a consequence of this social attitude, there was a propensity on the part of some critics, as well as the public at large, to regard her comedies as being more immoral than those of her male colleagues. This charge has been immortalized in Alexander Pope's satire *The First Epistle to the Second Book of Horace* (1737). Here, in a couplet in which he refers to Mrs. Behn by a pseudonym under which she frequently published her poetry, Pope writes: "The stage how loosely does Astraea tread,/ Who fairly puts all Characters to bed." Pope's imputation is unfair, for Mrs. Behn's plays are no more licentious, and frequently less so, than others written in that era. These charges, moreover, never proved detrimental to public attendance at performances of her plays. That she was one of the most popular playwrights of her age is a matter of historical record.

Biography

Reliable information pertaining to the first half of Aphra Behn's life is virtually nonexistent. The sparse biographical information for this period is, moreover, frequently contradictory. The earliest account of her career is to be found in the introduction to an edition of her fictional works that was published posthumously in 1696, which purports to be memoirs on her life written by a "gentlewoman" of her acquaintance. It is now believed that the "gentlewoman" in question was, in fact, Mrs. Behn's personal friend and editor Charles Gildon (1665-1724). According to his account, she was born into a good family by the name of Johnson, whose ancestral roots lay in the city of Canterbury in Kent. Her father, furthermore, was reported as being related to Lord Francis Willoughby of Parham, a man who used his good offices to secure Johnson an appointment to the administrative post of lieutenant-governor over many islands in the West Indies and the territory of Surinam. When Gildon's memoirs were reprinted a year later in an anthology devoted to the lives of dramatic poets, the text was revised in such a way as to state explicitly that Mrs. Behn was herself born in the city of Canterbury.

Information that runs counter to Gildon's memoirs on two important issues, however, comes from the hand of another contemporary writer, Anne Finch (1661-1720). Finch, who is better known as the Countess of Winchelsea, left a marginal note in a manuscript copy of some unpublished poems of her own in which she mentions that the place of Mrs. Behn's birth was the small market town of Wye, near Canterbury, and that her father had been a barber by trade. Finch's account was first discovered by an English literary scholar in 1884, but it was not until the opening decade of the twentieth century that the pertinent entry in the baptismal registry at Wye received a thorough scrutiny. It was thereupon learned that a child listed as Ayfara, along with a brother named John, was duly baptized there on July 10, 1640, but that her family name was not Johnson at all. The parents of Ayfara and her brother are, in fact, identified as a couple named John and Amy Amis. Then, in the 1950's, another English scholar perused the burial registry at Wye and found that both of these children had died a few days after their baptism: Ayfara on July 12 and John on July 16. In neither the baptismal nor the burial registries, moreover, is there any reference to Mr. Amis' being a barber by trade. In the light of these discrepancies, it is difficult to avoid drawing the conclusion that Finch's marginal note is nothing more than a false lead.

The only other contemporary evidence pertaining to Mrs. Behn's birth comes from some manuscripts now held in the British Library that were composed before 1708 by a member of the gentry named Thomas Culpepper. Culpepper reports that Mrs. Behn was born at Canterbury or Sturry and that her maiden name was Johnson. He further claims that she was also his foster-sister by virtue of the fact that her mother was his nurse at one time. A subsequent check of the marriage registry at St. Paul's in Canterbury corroborated Culpepper's account insofar as a couple named

Bartholomew and Elizabeth Johnson was married there on August 25, 1638. It has also been ascertained that Bartholomew Johnson was a yeoman (that is, a member of the class of small freeholding farmers) and that he originally came from Bishopsbourne, a village situated three and a half miles from Canterbury. The first of the couple's four children was, moreover, named Eaffry (Aphra), but she appears to have been born in neither Canterbury nor Sturry. The baptismal records of St. Michael's in the village of Harbledown, located just outside the walls of Canterbury, list her as being baptized there on December 14, 1640. Since Culpepper himself was born on Christmas Day in 1637, there would appear to be some question whether Mrs. Johnson could have served him in the capacity of a wet-nurse.

The question of Mrs. Behn's parentage is further complicated by a passage appearing in James Rodway's *Chronological History of the Discovery and Settlement of Guiana, 1493-1796*, a work first published in 1888. Here it is reported that a relative of Lord Willoughby named Johnson left his homeland toward the end of 1658 bound for Surinam in the company of his wife and children, along with an adopted daughter named Afra or Aphra Johnson. In the absence of any further corroborative evidence, however, the claim regarding Aphra's status as Johnson's foster child is still viewed with a large measure of skepticism by most literary scholars at the current time. Rodway goes on to assert that Johnson never assumed his administrative duties in Surinam, since he fell ill during the voyage and died at sea. The rest of the family, according to this history, duly disembarked at Surinam and spent the next two or three years residing on one of Lord Willoughby's estates in that land.

Rodway's assertion that Johnson died before reaching Surinam is corroborated by some autobiographical remarks that Mrs. Behn makes in her novel *Oroonoko*. Other statements in *Oroonoko*, however, are at variance with several items in Rodway's account of the surviving family's subsequent sojourn in the New World. For one thing, Mrs. Behn herself maintains that their stay in Surinam was a matter of months rather than the two or three years mentioned by Rodway. On the basis of references made to actual events and historical personages in the course of her narrative, it is also most likely that the period of young Aphra's residence in Surinam lasted from November, 1663, to February, 1664.

Shortly after her return to England, she married a London merchant of Dutch ancestry whose surname was Behn. This marriage ended quite abruptly in 1665 or 1666, owing to the death of Mr. Behn, an apparent victim of the plague which raged throughout London during these years. At this point in her life as at several others, Mrs. Behn appears to have been in need of money. Whether for financial or for idealistic reasons, she chose to become a spy for the recently restored British monarchy, which was at that point engaged in a war with the States of Holland—hostilities that were soon extended to France. She was to take up residence in Antwerp (then part of Holland) for the purpose of collecting information pertaining to the activities of dissident English exiles (supporters of Cromwell) as well as the military plans of the Dutch government. Her Dutch surname must surely have been advantageous to her in this mission.

Mrs. Behn is believed to have gone to Antwerp in July, 1666, and for the ensuing six months or so she continued to send cryptographic reports back to her superiors in England, using the code name Astrea to identify herself. It is widely held that she had already adopted this pseudonym while still in Surinam. Although Astrea (or Astraea) is the Greek goddess of justice, the name was quite likely suggested by Honoré d'Urfé's popular three-part novel *Astrea* (1607-1628). The eponymous heroine of this novel had a lover called Celadon, a name which came to be employed as a code name for Aphra's good friend William Scot. This individual was the son of Thomas Scot, a man who was one of the judges at the trial which ended with the execution of Charles I in 1649 and who was himself put to death as a regicide in 1660. Since William Scot was in both Surinam and Antwerp at the same time that "Astrea" was in these places, it is tempting to surmise that a close amorous relationship existed between them. It is, moreover, indisputable that Mrs. Behn diverted much of her energies while in Antwerp to the task of obtaining a royal pardon on behalf of William Scot for political offenses which he had committed against the crown in past years.

Whether Mrs. Behn received adequate financial compensation from the crown for her espionage mission on the Continent is still a debatable issue. There is no doubt, however, that she was in desperate need of money after her return from Antwerp, for she was jailed for a brief period in 1668, as a result of her inability to repay outstanding debts that she had lately contracted. Upon her release from debtors' prison, Mrs. Behn made a bold decision to try her hand at writing for the theater as a means of achieving financial independence. It is likely that her release from confinement was achieved through the intercession of Thomas Killigrew (1612-1683). Killigrew, himself the author of several noteworthy dramas, devoted most of his energies to managing the affairs of the Theatre Royal at Drury Lane. This organization, commonly referred to as the King's Company, was the first of two acting ensembles to be granted a monopoly over theatrical performances within the city of London. The other group, known as the Duke's Company, was managed by Sir William Davenant until his death in 1668. Both of these companies, incidentally, were the first in England to engage actresses to play the roles of women, rather than following the traditional practice of using boys and young men to perform these parts. Despite her close friendship with Killigrew, Mrs. Behn's own plays were staged by the Duke's Company, under the supervision of Davenant's successors, from the time that her first play was produced in 1670 to the year 1682. The plays that she composed during this period, except for an occasional failure, proved to be popular successes, and she soon established herself as one of the public's favorite playwrights.

Mrs. Behn's career as a playwright was nevertheless placed in severe jeopardy when she decided to promote the fortunes of the Stuart monarchy by using the stage to attack powerful Whig opponents of Charles II. Her chief contribution as a propagandist for the Tory cause is to be found in the pair of plays entitled *The Roundheads* and *The City Heiress*. What precipitated a crisis in Mrs. Behn's partisan political activity, however, was her composition of a sardonic prologue and epilogue for the production, in 1682, of *Romulus and Hersilia*, a play by an anonymous author. These supplementary contributions were deemed to be unwarranted aspersions upon the character of the Duke of Monmouth as well as other persons of quality, and a warrant for Mrs. Behn's arrest was issued by the Lord Chamberlain. Subsequent events remain unclear, but she appears to have gotten off lightly in terms of actual confinement. The effect on her literary creativity was far more profound, for she ceased writing plays for a period of nearly four years. During this hiatus from the theater, she found an outlet for her literary talents in composing poetry and narrative fiction. Even though she resumed writing for the theater in the spring of 1686, most of Mrs. Behn's succeeding plays never matched the success of her earlier ones, and she increasingly devoted her time to writing fictional works and to translating plays and novels of foreign authors, perhaps deeming this a superior means of earning a livelihood by the pen.

Since Mrs. Behn was both beautiful and witty, she was highly successful in forming close associations with a great number of prominent persons from literary and social circles in London. The literary figures among her acquaintance included John Dryden, Edmund Waller, and Thomas Otway. The full extent of her friendship with the rakish Earl of Rochester, John Wilmot, is still a matter of conjecture; whether he was among their number, it was common knowledge that Mrs. Behn had a variety of lovers during the 1670's and 1680's. Her most abiding romantic favor appears to have been bestowed upon John Hoyle, a lawyer noted for his witty repartee and ready swordsmanship. Mrs. Behn's relationship with Hoyle was greatly complicated by his unrepressed bisexual proclivities, and they parted ways several years before her death. She died after a long physical illness the exact nature of which is still not fully established. Mrs. Behn was buried in the cloisters of Westminster Abbey. On her tombstone is a wry couplet alleged to have been written by Hoyle himself that runs as follows:

Here lies a proof that wit can never be
Defence enough against mortality.

These lines proved to be even more apposite in regard to Hoyle's personal fate, for his own life came to an abrupt end as the result of a tavern brawl in 1692.

Analysis

Aphra Behn began her literary career with two plays whose technique and style are based on the romantic tragicomedies written in collaboration by Francis Beaumont and John Fletcher. Plays of this type permit a serious subject to be explored while avoiding a tragic resolution of the conflict. The first of her dramas in this vein was entitled *The Forced Marriage*, a work whose theme is the conflict between love and honor. This play was followed by *The Amorous Prince*; Mrs. Behn uses a double plot in which the worldly protagonist first seduces an innocent country lass and then proceeds to fall in love with his best friend's fiancée. The play thus contrasts rural innocence with urban corruption and probes the competing claims of love and friendship. The plot is resolved happily when the repentant prince agrees to marry the country lass and renounces his designs on the friend's fiancée. Neither of these plays has much to interest present-day readers, but they were received enthusiastically by London audiences at the time, and Mrs. Behn's future in the theater appeared to be assured.

The performance of her third play, however, ended in failure. Despite the fact that *The Dutch Lover* is much better than either of its predecessors, the public proved unreceptive. Much of the blame for its failure, however, may justly be attributed to a poor production. Based on a contemporary novel with a Spanish setting, the intricate plot of *The Dutch Lover* involves seven sets of lovers—four of them being of earnest intent and the other three being comic in nature. One of the males who is featured in a comic pair of lovers is a Dutchman, and the play derives its name from his prominence in many of the comedic scenes. The various strands of plot mesh nicely—with the aid of multiple disguises and mistaken identities reminiscent of plays constructed in the manner of Spanish intrigue. Such comedies emphasized action and intricate plotting at the expense of character development and usually incorporated the element of spectacle. Mrs. Behn's fondness for this kind of drama was an abiding one, and she persisted in writing works of this style long after its popularity with English audiences had waned.

Discouraged by the failure of *The Dutch Lover*, Mrs. Behn offered the public no new plays from February, 1673, to the time when *Abdelazer* was produced in July, 1676. This work is a romantic tragedy in the grand manner, with much turgid rhetoric. The plot was derived from an anonymous sixteenth century play, and its action takes place in a Spanish-Moorish milieu. Although it met with public approbation, it is decidedly inferior to plays of this genre written by Dryden and Otway. Sensing that she lacked the temperament needed to create heroic drama, Mrs. Behn did not again attempt to write tragedy. For her next play, she turned to more congenial subject matter and for the first time composed a play whose setting lay within the city of London. Entitled *The Town Fop*, it is a marked improvement over any of her previous works for the theater. Indebted in the main features of its plot to George Wilkins' *The Miseries of Enforced Marriage* (pr. 1605), it deals with a young man whose guardian forces him to marry against his will, despite the fact that he has already promised to wed a girl with whom he is deeply in love. The girl disguises herself as a young man and feigns an attempt to make love to the wife of her former fiancé before he has had a chance to consummate their marriage. Believing that his wife has been morally compromised by this encounter, the young man divorces her and then marries his former sweetheart. The problem of enforced marriage is a major theme in the works of Mrs. Behn and recurs in many of her other plays.

The problem of enforced marriage is, in fact, the chief dramatic conflict in Mrs. Behn's most famous play, *The Rover*. Like many of her plays, it is an adaptation of an earlier work by a different hand. In this case, the source was Thomas Killigrew's closet drama *Thomaso: Or, The Wanderer*. Killigrew's play has seventy-three scenes that are organized into ten acts. He wrote this work in 1654 while in exile, but it was not actually published until ten years later. While there is no direct evidence that Killigrew granted permission to Mrs. Behn to make the adaptation, it is quite unlikely that she would have done so without his express consent. Killigrew's *Thomaso* contains so much material that Mrs. Behn needed two full-length plays to encompass the entire story despite her drastic condensation of certain features of the original plot. The first part of *The Rover* was produced in March, 1677, and the second part almost four years later, in January, 1681. Whereas Killigrew's entire play is set in Madrid, Mrs. Behn shifted the setting for the first part of *The Rover* to Naples during the climax of its carnival season. Since mistakes in identity are rendered more credible when the populace at large is in masquerade, the change of scene has obvious advantages for a comedy of intrigue in which duels are fought based on mistaken identities.

The banished cavaliers referred to in the subtitle of *The Rover* are a group of Englishmen who are compelled to live in exile as a result of Oliver Cromwell's abolition of the Stuart monarchy in 1642. Although not as complex as *The Dutch Lover*, the plot of the first part focuses on the romantic maneuvers of three Englishmen and three Spanish ladies that eventually culminate in the matrimonial union of each pair. The central couple consists of a spirited young Spanish lady named Hellena and a witty Englishman known as Wilmore the Rover. Wilmore is believed to be a composite character based on two of Mrs. Behn's close friends: John Hoyle and John Wilmot, the Earl of Rochester. Wilmore is such an attractive rake that he is said to have made vice alluring to a good part of the audience. Hellena, on the other hand, was originally destined for life in a cloister. It is her sister, Florinda, who is being coerced into an arranged marriage for the sake of prestige and economic advantage. All ends well, and both sisters manage to avoid the respective forms of bondage that threaten their future happiness. There are, it must be acknowledged, many implausibilities in the plot, and some actions appear to be insufficiently motivated. These deficiencies, however, are transcended by the sparkling dialogue that flows from Mrs. Behn's pen, and it is this witty repartee that constitutes the play's chief virtue. Its sequel, generally regarded as inferior to the first part, is most noteworthy for the fact that Mrs. Behn introduced two *commedia dell'arte* figures into its plot: Harlequin and Scaramouche.

Of the plays produced after the first part of *The Rover*, *Sir Patient Fancy* and *The Emperor of the Moon* are probably the most outstanding examples of Mrs. Behn's dramatic craftmanship. Much of the inspiration for *Sir Patient Fancy* is derived from three of Molière's comedies—especially *The Imaginary Invalid* (1673). Her play, however, should be judged on its own merits, for she borrows incidents rather than themes from the French master. While Molière asserted that the purpose of comedy is to correct men by entertaining them, Mrs. Behn herself did not ascribe any pedagogical function to the theater. She wrote her plays solely for the sake of entertaining the public. In *Sir Patient Fancy*, Mrs. Behn succeeds perhaps too well, for the play is undoubtedly her bawdiest. Many women in the audience were offended by the play's overt sexual escapades, and Mrs. Behn had to go to great lengths to defend herself against charges of obscenity. Had the play been written by a man, she argued, the issue of licentiousness would never have arisen.

The Emperor of the Moon, on the other hand, is a model of decorum. This love intrigue successfully integrates a number of distinct styles, including those of grand opera and *commedia dell'arte*. Although the figures of Harlequin and Scaramouche were previously used in the second part of *The Rover*, they are incorporated much more effectively in *The Emperor of the Moon*. The plot centers on a pair of men who masquerade as the King of the Moon and Prince Thunderland as a stratagem of courtship in wooing the daughter and niece of a gullible astrologer. Before their ruse is uncovered, the two masqueraders succeed in marrying the objects of their affection. The astrologer, for his part, duly recognizes the folly of living in a world of fantasy. An immediate success when first performed in 1687, the play continued to be popular with London audiences for most of the eighteenth century.

Although Mrs. Behn lived in an age of great intellectual ferment, her ideas on politics and society are usually commonplace and traditional. In reading her plays, one is tempted to look for connections with current feminist concerns, but except for her deep concern that marriage be entered into on the basis of mutual affection and not contracted for social or monetary reasons, there is little that Mrs. Behn wished to change in the relationship between the sexes. She knew herself too well, furthermore, to attribute greater virtue to women than to men. If she did not appear to be interested in demonstrating the virtue of her sex, she at least used her plays to celebrate its power.

Other major works

NOVELS: *Love Letters Between a Nobleman and His Sister*, 1683-1687 (3 volumes); *The Fair Jilt: Or, The History of Prince Tarquin and Miranda*, 1688; *Oroonoko: Or, The Royal Slave, a True History*, 1688; *Agnes de Castro*, 1688; *The History of the Nun: Or, The Fair Vow-Breaker*, 1689; *The Lucky Mistake*, 1689; *The Nun: Or, The Perjured Beauty*, 1697; *The Adventure of the Black Lady*, 1698; *The Wandering Beauty*, 1698.

POETRY: *Poems upon Several Occasions, with A Voyage to the Island of Love*, 1684 (including adaptation of Abbé Paul Tallemant's *Le Voyage de l'isle d'amour*); *Miscellany: Being a Collection of Poems by Several Hands*, 1685 (includes works by others).

TRANSLATIONS: *Aesop's Fables*, 1687 (with Francis Barlow); *Of Trees*, 1689 (of book 6 of Abraham Cowley's *Sex libri plantarum*).

MISCELLANEOUS: *La Montre: Or, The Lover's Watch*, 1686 (prose and poetry); *The Case for the Watch*, 1686 (prose and poetry); *Lycidus: Or, The Lover in Fashion*, 1688 (prose and poetry; includes works by others); *The Lady's Looking-Glass, to Dress Herself By: Or, The Art of Charming*, 1697 (prose and poetry); *The Works of Aphra Behn*, 1915, 1967 (6 volumes; Montague Summers, editor).

Bibliography

Duffy, Maureen. *The Passionate Shepherdess: Aphra Behn, 1640-89.* London: Jonathan Cape, 1977. Duffy deplores the "fictionalizing process that has taken over to make nonsense or romance of the facts" of Behn's life and attempts to distinguish between fact and conjecture in this important biography. On questions regarding the identities of Behn's parents and husband, Duffy concludes that Behn was the daughter of Bartholomew and Elizabeth Denham Johnson and that two possibilities exist for the "Mr. Behn" she married. Separate chapters treat selected works.

Goreau, Angeline. "Aphra Behn: A Scandal to Modesty, 1640-1689." In *Feminist Theorists: Three Centuries of Key Women Thinkers*, edited by Dale Spender. New York: Pantheon Books, 1983. This biographical essay focuses on Behn's contribution to the debate over the function and nature of theater that pitted the "Ancients" against the "Moderns." Goreau notes that Behn refused to be "intimidated into a sense of inferiority because of her sex's ignorance" of the classics and dismissed "the much-vaunted 'learning' that she had been denied as so much 'academic frippery.'" Works receiving attention are *The Amorous Prince*, *The Dutch Lover*, and *Poems upon Several Occasions.*

_____. *Reconstructing Aphra: A Social Biography of Aphra Behn.* New York: Dial Press, 1980. Goreau sees in Behn a contradictory feminist heroine who "raged against the oppression of women" while defining the poet in herself as "masculine." By relying heavily on contemporary documents, Goreau is successful in placing Behn's life and work in the context of her times. The study includes a brief chronology of Behn's life and works, and a lengthy bibliography reveals Goreau's exhaustive research.

Link, Frederick M. *Aphra Behn.* New York: Twayne, 1968. Link's critical study is a comprehensive survey of Behn's plays, poems, translations, and novels. The plays, examined in chronological order, receive the greatest attention. Link finds that Behn was not a great writer but "an unusually interesting and varied artist whose best comedies have not had the attention they deserve. She was not an innovator but a craftsman strongly responsive to the immediate demands of her audience." Includes a select bibliography.

Sackville-West, Victoria. *Aphra Behn: The Incomparable Astrea.* New York: Russell & Russell, 1927. This short study of Behn's life (less than one hundred pages) relies heavily on biographical passages in Behn's novels. Whereas Sackville-West finds her subject engaging as a woman, she does not wholeheartedly admire Behn's writing. Behn is important because "she was the first woman in England to earn her living by her pen," observes Sackville-West. "The fact she wrote is much more important than the quality of what she wrote." An appendix lists Behn's works and production or publication dates.

Woodcock, George. *The Incomparable Aphra.* London: Boardman, 1948. This early, but important, biography of Behn refutes Ernest Bernbaum's allegation that Behn had never visited Surinam. In the final chapter, Woodcock assesses Behn's work. He writes that "in the perspective of social and literary history, it is her fiction and the almost adventitious fact of her struggle to live as a pioneer woman writer that contain her most influential achievements."

Victor Anthony Rudowski
(Updated by *Ayne Cantrell*)

S. N. BEHRMAN

Born: Worcester, Massachusetts; June 9, 1893(?)
Died: New York, New York; September 9, 1973

Principal drama
Bedside Manners, pr. 1923, pb. 1924 (with J. Kenyon Nicholson); *A Night's Work*, pr. 1924, pb. 1926 (with Nicholson); *The Man Who Forgot*, pr. 1926 (with Owen Davis); *The Second Man*, pr., pb. 1927; *Serena Blandish: Or, The Difficulty of Getting Married*, pr. 1929, pb. 1934; *Meteor*, pr. 1929, pb. 1934; *Brief Moment*, pr., pb. 1931; *Biography*, pr. 1932, pb. 1933; *Rain from Heaven*, pr., pb. 1934; *End of Summer*, pr., pb. 1936; *Amphitryon 38*, pr. 1937, pb. 1938; *Wine of Choice*, pr., pb. 1938; *No Time for Comedy*, pr., pb. 1939; *The Talley Method*, pr., pb. 1941; *The Pirate*, pr. 1942, pb. 1943 (adaptation of Ludwig Fulda's play *Die Seerauber*); *Jacobowsky and the Colonel*, pr., pb. 1944 (based on Franz Werfel's play *Jacobowsky und der Oberst*); *Dunnigan's Daughter*, pr., pb. 1945; *I Know My Love*, pr., pb. 1949 (adaptation of Marcel Achard's play *Auprès de ma blonde*); *Jane*, pr., pb. 1952 (based on a story by W. Somerset Maugham); *Fanny*, pr. 1954, pb. 1955 (with Joshua Logan; music and lyrics by Harold Rome; based on Marcel Pagnol's plays *Marius* and *Fanny* and his screenplay *César*); *The Cold Wind and the Warm*, pr. 1958, pb. 1959; *Lord Pengo*, pr. 1962, pb. 1963; *But for Whom Charlie*, pr., pb. 1964.

Other literary forms
S. N. Behrman wrote two "profile"-type biographies: *Duveen* (1952) and *Portrait of Max: An Intimate Memoir of Sir Max Beerbohm* (1960). *The Suspended Drawing Room* (1965) is a collection of (mostly) familiar essays focusing on such notables as Robert E. Sherwood, Ferenc Molnár, and A. E. Kazan; *The Worcester Account* (1954), the best of Behrman's prose works, is a collection of pieces originally published in *The New Yorker*; *The Burning Glass* (1968) is a semiautobiographical novel; and *People in a Diary* (1972; reissued as *Tribulations and Laughter*, 1972) is a memoir containing brief, often poignant essays and sketches.

Behrman was also the author of numerous screenplays, including several adaptations of his own and others' works.

Achievements
Although Behrman's career as a dramatist spanned several decades, his major impact upon the American theater covered roughly two and a half decades, from 1927, with the great success of *The Second Man* (178 performances in New York City), to 1944, with *Jacobowsky and the Colonel*, which had a run of 415 performances, also in New York City. Excluding his

earlier apprenticeship plays, written during and after studies at Harvard University, Behrman's career as a dramatist ranged from 1923, with *Bedside Manners* (in collaboration with J. Kenyon Nicholson), to 1964, with *But for Whom Charlie*. During this period, the playwright offered to the New York stage—without counting other locales—a total of twenty-two plays in full production, most of them enjoying considerable or at least moderate success. Only three plays were (relatively speaking) unsuccessful—*Wine of Choice*, *Dunnigan's Daughter*, and *But for Whom Charlie*—and even these works attracted some favorable critical notice. Along with *Jacobowsky and the Colonel*, which later became a motion picture, *Fanny* (written as a musical comedy in collaboration with Joshua Logan) and *I Know My Love* enjoyed the longest runs. These works were essentially entertainments, written with a shrewd sense of the audience response yet without the writer's special touches of mannered comedy. Earlier, during the "vintage" years, as Kenneth T. Reed (*S. N. Behrman*, 1975) describes the period between 1927 and 1936, when the writer had seven plays in production on Broadway, a new comedy by Behrman was a special event, one eagerly awaited.

For this audience, a particular quality that marked the author's comedies was "sophistication." This term, still generally applied to Behrman, has only limited usefulness. For one matter, not all of his plays belong to this mode—the most significant exception is *The Cold Wind and the Warm*, a semiautobiographical work, impressionistic and poetic. Moreover, the word "sophistication" has negative connotations, perhaps carrying over from social criticism of the 1930's and 1940's. From this point of view, the word denotes, among other negative attitudes, frivolity, urbane elegance, and elitism. To be sure, most of Behrman's early comedies are set in the drawing rooms of the privileged class, with a clash between intellectuals (either true or sham), together with grasping middle-class parvenues whose special concerns are money, status, and advantageous marriage. Nevertheless, Behrman's judgment of privilege in these comedies is critical and gently satiric, not approving.

By more narrowly construing "sophisticated," the word may be applied with greater confidence to the wide range of Behrman's drama. In the general class of comic ironists such as Oscar Wilde, George Bernard Shaw, W. Somerset Maugham, and Noël Coward (also, arguably, Neil Simon), Behrman writes plays that resemble comedies of manners or polite comedies, but unlike Wilde (although he admired the Irishman's *The Importance of Being Earnest*, pr. 1895), Behrman never treats frivolity or triviality as a prime theme, and unlike Coward (although he also admired Coward's *Blithe Spirit*, pr. 1941), Behrman avoids sentimental fantasy. Curiously, Behrman's work more closely resembles the lighter drama of Shaw and the less farcical comedies of Maugham. Behrman's comedy does not propagandize in favor of socialistic causes, but beneath the surface banter of the American writer is a tough realistic edge, a sharp awareness of the vulgar display of wealth and the brutality of social intolerance. Also, in its satiric wit stopping short of misanthropy, Behrman's work reminds one of certain Maugham plays, such as *Our Betters* (pr. 1917) and *The Circle* (pr. 1921).

Judging the impact of his own work, Behrman was modest. In *People in a Diary*, he wrote: "For a time, Philip Barry, Paul Osborn, and I were the only American writers of high comedy." Of these playwrights, only the first is still remembered. By the late 1930's, Behrman had already established his reputation: In *The American Drama Since 1918: An Informal History* (1939), Joseph Wood Krutch wrote that Behrman had secured for himself "as sure a position in the contemporary American theater as any writer can claim."

Biography

Samuel Nathaniel Behrman was the third child of Joseph and Zelda (Feingold) Behrman and was born in Worcester, Massachusetts. The first two children in the Behrman family, Hiram and Morris, were born in Eastern Europe (in or near Vilna, Lithuania). Because no official record of the writer's birthdate was ever recorded in Worcester, he arbitrarily selected his own "birthday" as June 9, 1893. In *The Worcester Account*, Behrman humorously described the circumstances of his search for his true date of birth and concluded that "common sense tells me that 1893 must be reasonably close."

Readers interested in the details of Behrman's youth and schooling should turn to *The Worcester Account*, a colorful but by no means sentimentalized review of his adventures, the chapters originally written as short narratives for *The New Yorker*. From these pieces one learns that, although poor, Behrman's family enjoyed some distinction among the other Jewish residents of the neighborhood because the father was a Talmudic scholar. From him, Samuel learned "the Old Testament stories as if they had taken place recently—as if they constituted his personal past."

In 1899, Behrman entered Providence Street School, and in 1902, he heard a political speech delivered by Eugene V. Debs, then the Socialist Labor Party candidate for president. That chance occasion, as he later remarked, began in his life "an orientation it would otherwise not have had—a bias in favor of those who had suffered from cruelty or callousness." Another direction in his life was pointed by his friend Daniel Asher (who appears as the character Willie Lavin in *The Cold Wind and the Warm*); with Asher, he witnessed at Lothrops's Opera House in 1904 a melodrama entitled *Devil's Island*, and years later he still recalled the enchantment of that performance.

By 1907, when he entered Classical High School in Worcester, Behrman had begun his lifelong habit of omnivorous reading. Among his early favorites were William Shakespeare and Horatio Alger. He could, for his high school classes, recite from memory passages from *Hamlet* and *Macbeth*, and he acquired an elementary knowledge of Latin and Greek, useful tools in his cultivation of language skills. During these years, also, he deepened his friendship with Asher, who urged Behrman to write and who analyzed all the youth's fledgling manuscripts.

In 1911, Behrman toured on the Poli vaudeville circuit for some months with a skit that he had written himself, entitled "Only a Part." The circuit covered a number of theatrical points, including a New York vaudeville house on Fourteenth Street. Behrman's health, in those years precarious, obliged him to cut short the tour with two others, and he returned to Worcester. In 1912, at the family's urging, he entered Clark College. As a special student at this local school, he continued to write and act, also turning his attention to oratory. His academic work as an English major was successful, but he failed to report to physical education classes and was suspended from Clark. In the summer of 1913, he enrolled at Harvard, then reentered Clark in 1914, but was again suspended for neglecting physical education classes. The next year, he sold his first story, "La Vie Parisienne," which he wrote as a student in Charles Townsend Copeland's class at Harvard. By 1916, he had enrolled in Professor George Pierce Baker's Workshop 47, the only undergraduate admitted to Baker's famous playwriting course. Also in that year, Behrman was graduated from Harvard with a bachelor's degree. After failing to find a job in newspaper offices in several cities, he decided to continue his education at Columbia University, where he studied under Brander Matthews and other notable teachers. In 1918, Behrman earned his master's degree at Columbia. Offered a teaching appointment at the University of Minnesota, Behrman decided instead to hazard his fortune in writing. For the next two years, he worked for *The New York Times*, at first as a typist of classified ads and later as a book reviewer. Before and during this time, he sold stories and essays to several magazines. One of the most influential of them, *The Smart Set*, carried in its November, 1919, issue "The Second Man," a story that he later rewrote into the play of the same title.

For the young journalist with dreams of becoming a playwright, the early years of the 1920's were arduous, mostly frustrating, with only occasional periods of publishing success. This period came to an end in 1926, when Behrman developed a working friendship with a more established dramatist, Owen Davis, with whom he collaborated on a play entitled *The Man Who Forgot*. Later that year, *A Night's Work*, written in collaboration with J. Kenyon Nicholson, was produced on Broadway. Through these efforts and the contacts that he established with producers Ned Harris and Crosbie Gaige, Behrman was able to supplement his income with publicity work for other New York-based plays.

Finally, on April 11, 1927, Behrman's years of apprenticeship came to an end when the Theatre Guild presented *The Second Man*. After that popular and critical success, Behrman's labors were often divided between playwriting and scriptwriting for Hollywood. Also dating from this period was his long-lasting association and friendship with Harold Ross of *The New Yorker*. Over the years, Ross commissioned Behrman to write many essays, including "profiles," for his magazine—the first of which was on George Gershwin and appeared in 1929.

During the late 1920's and the decade of the 1930's, Behrman attained to considerable prominence in his craft, as a playwright and as a producer-writer. In 1928, he sailed to England to oversee a production of *The Second Man* in London, with Noël Coward in the leading role. Indeed, over the years, the production of a Behrman play usually called for the talents of America's and England's most distinguished players: Alfred Lunt and Lynn Fontanne, Ina Claire, Catherine Cornell, and Laurence Olivier, among others. From 1929 to 1939, Behrman's work was produced on Broadway stages with general approval: *Serena Blandish*, *Meteor*, *Brief Moment*, *Biography*, *Rain from Heaven*, *End of Summer*, and *No Time for Comedy*. For Behrman, these years brought both regret (with the death by suicide of Daniel Asher in 1929) and personal fulfillment (including his marriage in 1936 to Elza Heifetz and the birth of their only child, David Arthur, in 1937).

In 1938, Behrman joined the Playwrights' Company, an independent guild of writer-producers that included Robert E. Sherwood, Maxwell Anderson, Elmer Rice, and Sidney Howard. Until 1945, when Behrman withdrew from the company, he produced *The Talley Method*, *The Pirate*, *Jacobowsky and the Colonel*, and *Dunnigan's Daughter*. During this time, he received a significant award, as well as academic recognition: In 1943, he was admitted to the Department of Arts and Literature of the National Institute of Arts and Letters, and in 1944, his *Jacobowsky and the Colonel*, based originally upon a sketch by Franz Werfel but almost completely reinterpreted by the playwright, won the New York Drama Critics Circle Award as the best foreign play of the season.

After 1945, Behrman divided his literary work—that is to say, writing not commissioned by Hollywood studios—between the stage and various kinds of prose. His later plays include *I Know My Love*, *Jane*, *Fanny*, *The Cold Wind and the Warm*, *Lord Pengo*, and his final production, *But for Whom Charlie*. Toward the end of his career, he turned with greater avidity to the expanded essay, which prose he called his "one hobby." In 1952, he published *Duveen*, a biography of Joseph Duveen, a notorious art dealer about whom Behrman had earlier written a profile entitled "The Days of Duveen" for *The New Yorker*. The autobiographical volume *The Worcester*

Account, as noted above, also had its genesis in *The New Yorker*. In 1960, he published *Portrait of Max*; in 1965, a sheaf of essays entitled *The Suspended Drawing Room*; in 1968 his only novel, *The Burning Glass*; and in 1972, a book of memoirs and appreciations, *People in a Diary*. Among the awards he received during the final decades of his life were an honorary degree from Clark University (1949) and the Brandeis University Creative Arts Award (1962); in the latter year, he was also appointed Trustee of Clark University. On September 9, 1973, Behrman died in New York of apparent heart failure.

Analysis

Although S. N. Behrman was not, except in *The Cold Wind and the Warm*, basically an autobiographical playwright, many of his themes can be traced to circumstances in his life. His economically deprived youth and his years of struggle as a journalist lay behind his frequent depiction of the clash between characters emerging from deprivation and those already privileged by birth or class. At the same time, his culturally enriched childhood, one that particularly emphasized traditional Jewish values of social justice and strict moral probity, sensitized him to the contrast between superficially upright but morally corrupt people and those of genuine integrity. Finally, in his early comedies—particularly those prior to 1936— Behrman transformed Horatio Alger stories that he had enjoyed as a youth into moral tales concerning the Midas touch that turns gold into dross.

Typically in Behrman's variations on these ambition myths, the major (sensible) character abandons his childish illusions, discovers his limitations, and accepts in a mature way his responsibilities or potentialities. Rarely, as in *Serena Blandish*, the character is a woman; on the whole, Behrman's female leads are more astute than their romantic counterparts. For men and women alike, the tests for Behrman's pattern of discovery/initiation are through friendship or through marriage. As a youth, Behrman was not physically robust or socially assertive; perhaps by way of compensation, he cherished throughout his lifetime generous friendships (an assumption supported by *People in a Diary*), and in his plays he established the values of supportive relationships. The greater test of maturity, however, was in the courtship clash that precedes marriage. Married late in life, at the age of forty-three, Behrman tended to view on the stage the "war of the sexes" from the vantage point of rationality, not idealistic romance. If couples in his plays achieve the promise of a satisfactory (rational) union, the credit always goes to the woman, whom Behrman—like Shaw—championed as the more sensible of the sexes. In all relationships—those of competition, of friendship, and of courtship—Behrman holds up the exemplary pattern of tolerance. Without tolerance, his characters could never come to self-knowledge, and their world of high comedy would fall apart.

In *The Second Man*, Mrs. Kendall Frayne, a wealthy widow whose chief asset is her common sense, and Monica Grey, a younger woman, are romantically interested in Clark Storey. Storey is a would-be poet and novelist, handsome but passionless. His counterpart is Austin Lowe, a chemist with meager social graces to match his rival's. Nevertheless, he wins the love of Monica; for her part, Mrs. Frayne is too worldly-wise to fall for the superficial Storey. By the end of the play, Storey escapes both romantic entanglements but discovers the unsettling truth that he possesses a "second man" in his nature, one that is "calm, critical, observant, unmoved, blasé, odious." Thus, Storey attains, at the very least, the reward of painful illumination.

For Behrman's original audience, the play offered both entertainment and a moral lesson that they were prepared to accept. By challenging the playgoers' intelligence, the writer allowed them to discern, without the heavy hand of editorial intrusion, that Mrs. Frayne's "sophistication" would prevent her from choosing a poor mate. In addition to flattering the audience's urbanity, Behrman taught them a sound moral lesson. For all of his protestations that he speaks honest truth, Clark Storey must—to protect his vanity—conceal his emotional shallowness and his greed to achieve status. Thus, the audience learns to reject an ambition that lacks the solid basis of integrity.

This lesson, presented with different variations upon the theme, appears in *Serena Blandish* and *End of Summer*. In both plays, fortune hunters attempt, without hiding their motives, to secure a marriage that will advance their ambitions. Subtitled *The Difficulty of Getting Married*, *Serena Blandish* showcases a charming, witty young woman who has emerged from an impoverished background. Serena catches the eye of Sigmund Traub, a wealthy, middle-aged, Jewish businessman. He takes her under his wing, provides her with social advantages and money (he even lends her a diamond ring), and generally acts like a Pygmalion to her Galatea. Her ambitions, however, are never realized. The money she displays to her rich suitors she does not really possess, and by the end of the play she remains unmarried. Similarly, in *End of Summer*, Dr. Kenneth Rice pursues but fails to snare two wealthy women. A "self-made man," as he likes to call himself, he courts Leonie Frothingham and her daughter Paula for the sake of their money, but Leonie, a sensible woman in the mold of Mrs. Frayne, rejects his advances, as does her idealistic daughter. At the "end of summer," he has neither wife nor money.

Dr. Rice, a Freudian psychoanalyst, resembles other power-obsessive character-types in Behrman's plays: Hobart Eldridge (*Rain from Heaven*), Allan Frobisher (*Jane*), Orrin Kinnicott (*Biography*), Raphael Lord (*Meteor*), Lord Pengo (*Lord Pengo*), and Dr. Axton Talley (*The Talley Method*). Although different in certain respects, all of these personalities are rigid, authoritarian, self-centered, and intolerant; most are politically conservative. They contrast with other male characters who, although less assertive, have more attractive personal qualities. Among these sensitive (but often unfocused and self-indulgent) types are a number of second-rate artists or aesthetes in the pattern of Clark Storey of *The Second Man*. They include Aaron (*The Cold Wind and the Warm*), Sasha Barashaev (*Rain from Heaven*), Daniel Chanler (*I Know My Love*), Roderick Dean (*Brief Moment*), Peter Crewe (*Jane*), Melchoir Feydak (*Biography*), Edgar Mallison (*Serena Blandish*), Derek Pengo (*Lord Pengo*), Willard Prosper (*But for Whom Charlie*), Miguel Riachi (*Dunnigan's Daughter*), and War-wick Wilson (*Biography*). Although these would-be artists range in appeal from the fragile Aaron to the radical Marxist painter Riachi, they share the qualities of self-indulgence, independence, and (to varying degrees) fecklessness.

In general, Behrman's male figures—whether petulantly dictatorial or dreamy—lack the balanced common sense of their female counterparts. Among his "strong" women in the pattern of Mrs. Frayne are Emily Chanler (*I Know My Love*), Fern Dunnigan (*Dunnigan's Daughter*), Linda Esterbrook (*No Time for Comedy*), Abbey Fane (*Brief Moment*), Marion Froude (*Biography*), Enid Fuller (*The Talley Method*), and Lael Wyngate (*Rain from Heaven*). To these may be added Leonie Frothingham (despite her naïveté) and Serena Blandish, whose good sense compensates, in large measure, for her deficiency in exaggerating the values of money and status.

Along with their common sense and emotional maturity, these women share a quality of tolerance. For Behrman, tolerance greatly humanizes his protagonists. To be sure, several leading males are wisely tolerant—chief among them Jacobowsky, but the "strong" women (as contrasted to frivo-lous types) best exemplify the virtue. In *The Second Man*, Clark Storey tells Mrs. Frayne that she possesses the two "great requirements" for mar-riage: money and tolerance. Running through many of Behrman's comedies is a conflict between the tolerant, blessed with habits of kindness and serenity, and the intolerant. In *Biography*, three characters hold narrowly rigid opinions: Orrin Kinnicott, Richard Kurt, and Bunny Nolan. Respond-ing to Marion Froude's open nature, Kurt upbraids her, for "what you call tolerance I call sloppy laziness." The audience, comparing the two per-sonalities—the woman cheerful and emancipated, the man egotistic, wrapped up in radical politics—can be expected to draw a different conclusion.

In *Rain from Heaven*, Behrman stigmatizes, in the words of Lael Wyngate, an "epidemic of hatred and intolerance that may engulf us all." Perhaps the playwright best expresses this theme in *Jacobowsky and the Colonel*. In the second act, the Nazi Colonel warns Marianne that he can-not tolerate being treated in any fashion that he believes is disrespectful.

The Nazi's counterpart in this moral tale of "strange bedfellows" is Jacobowsky, the "wandering Jew" who has learned to accept life's evils with a redeeming sense of good humor. Through his example, the Colonel undergoes an initiation in the rites of true manhood. By the end of the play, the Colonel is not entirely "mature," not wholly tolerant, but he has at least learned to make compromises.

Behrman's insights into the corrosive effects of intolerance derive, at least in part, from his life's education as a Jew. Curiously, most of his apprenticeship work and the plays of the late 1920's and early 1930's avoid all mention of Jews. To be sure, Sigmund Traub in *Serena Blandish* is a Jew, a Bond Street merchant, but Behrman reveals little about the man's psychological reasons for pampering a beautiful woman not linked to him by passion. Not until 1934 in *Rain from Heaven* did Behrman create a Jewish character who functions as spokesman for his own ideas: Hugo Willens, who, despite his Nordic appearance, had to flee Europe because his grandmother was a Jew.

Among the later plays, *The Cold Wind and the Warm* explores autobiographical themes already presented in Behrman's essays for *The New Yorker*; in this, his most touching play, Behrman comes to terms with his Jewishness, without evasion or apology. A drama of recollection, *The Cold Wind and the Warm* surprised some critics, who were accustomed to Behrman's usual "high comedy"; although reviews were mixed, the play lasted for 120 performances at the Morosco. The playwright's final stage offering, *But for Whom Charlie*—one of his least successful plays—included the minor character Seymour Rosenthal, a Jew who had once been excluded from a college fraternity because of his religion. Also in the play, however, was Brock Dunaway, a Jewish novelist seventy years old—a survivor, just as Behrman was to survive the hardships of his own past.

Fortunately for the decent characters in the author's drama, they do not stand alone in their struggle against prejudice. For Behrman, the links of friendship, perhaps more enduring than those of romantic passion, unite men and women of goodwill. By the final act of *Amphitryon 38*, Jupiter and Alkmena move toward a deeper appreciation of each other. Jupiter asks the rhetorical question: What is the object of friendship? Alkmena's answer is probably also Behrman's: "To bring together the most totally dissimilar people and make them equal." This judgment is crucial in accepting the friendship of men as dissimilar as the Colonel and Jacobowsky. The audience must grasp the idea that they not only tolerate each other but also become friends. If social antagonists can appreciate each other's values, then people of goodwill have an even greater obligation to join forces. In *Biography*, Marion Froude's friendship with Melchoir Feydak is based upon mutual respect and admiration. As decent, emphathetic persons, they stand out as the only fully tolerant characters in the play. Conversely, when

Behrman's characters lack a capacity for friendship, they become self-centered and obnoxious. Like Dr. Kenneth Rice (*End of Summer*), who cannot trust another person deeply enough to make him (or her) a friend, Raphael Lord (*Meteor*) and Dr. Axton Talley (*The Talley Method*) ultimately become monsters. Without meaningful attachments, Behrman believes, human beings lose their spiritual bearings and destroy themselves.

It is noteworthy that Behrman's defective characters invariably lack humor. For the dramatist, a sense of the comic, no less than a capacity for friendship, marks the true human being. In an interview with *The New York Times* in 1952, Behrman remarked: "The essence of the comic sense is awareness: awareness of the tragedy as well as the fun of life, of the pity, the futility, the lost hopes, the striving for immortality, for permanence, for security, for love."

Although Behrman's plays were crafted for theatrical performance, they are also admirably suitable for reading. Modeled after the scintillating comedies of Wilde and Shaw, Behrman's plays similarly are, by turn, clever, ironic, provocative. That is not to say, however, that Behrman was an original thinker on social issues, as Shaw was, or that his plays match Wilde's sense of whimsy. Indeed, Behrman's drama is uneven in quality. Plays such as *The Pirate* (adapted from Ludwig Fulda's play *Die Seerauber*) and *I Know My Love* (adapted from Marcel Achard) or the musical *Fanny* must be judged as entertainments, not against the highest standards of the dramatic art. Other plays are quite dated, products of their time. In particular, the comedies of the 1930's, for all of their surface brilliance, resemble certain clever mating comedies of the motion pictures of that decade. During the hard years of the Great Depression, many theatergoers appreciated escapist fantasies that would carry them in imagination away from their troubles. The drawing-room settings of Behrman's plays, with furnishings opulent and refined, provided an alternative world, one inhabited by mostly clever, attractive characters whose major problem in life was to find an appropriate mate. Behrman's characters—mostly upper-class, worldly, and well-educated—fit comfortably into this world, but for modern theatergoers, the Depression-era frame of reference has vanished.

Nevertheless, Behrman's plays still appeal to audiences interested in comedy of manners. He isolates universal human traits and observes them faithfully, without exaggeration. At his best, his comedies offer the viewer (or reader) moral choices that exercise the heart. Never vulgar, rarely sexually provocative, his comedies sparkle with ample appreciation for human potentialities: for the happiness of a true marriage; for friendship based upon trust; for common sense that cannot be swayed by political or social bias; for discovery of the authentic self; above all, for tolerance of others' foibles, together with the resolve never to injure innocent people through malice or ignorance.

Other major works

NOVEL: *The Burning Glass*, 1968.

NONFICTION: *Duveen*, 1952; *The Worcester Account*, 1954; *Portrait of Max: An Intimate Memoir of Sir Max Beerbohm*, 1960; *The Suspended Drawing Room*, 1965; *People in a Diary*, 1972 (reissued as *Tribulations and Laughter*, 1972).

SCREENPLAYS: *He Knew Women*, 1930 (adaptation of his *The Second Man*); *The Sea Wolf*, 1930 (adaptation of Jack London's novel); *Surrender*, 1931 (with Sonya Levien); *Rebecca of Sunnybrook Farm*, 1932 (with Levien; adaptation of Kau Douglas Wiggin's children's novel); *Brief Moment*, 1933 (adaptation of his play); *Anna Karenina*, 1935 (with Salka Viertel and Clemence Dane; adaptation of Leo Tolstoy's novel); *The Scarlet Pimpernel*, 1935 (with Lajos Biro, Robert E. Sherwood, and Arthur Wimperes); *Quo Vadis*, 1951 (with John Lee Makin and Levien; adaptation of Henryk Sienkiewicz's novel).

Bibliography

Asher, Donald. *The Eminent Yachtsman and the Whorehouse Piano Player*. New York: Coward, McCann & Geoghegan, 1973. In a 256-page memoir about Asher's late, suicidal father, Daniel Asher, upon whom is based a central character in Behrman's *The Cold Wind and the Warm*, the author includes a portrait of Behrman (his father's closest friend) and a vivid description of early twentieth century life in the tenement ghetto of Massachusetts' Worcester, where Behrman and Daniel Asher grew up.

Gassner, John. "S. N. Behrman: Comedy and Tolerance." In *The Theatre in Our Times*. New York: Crown, 1954. Gassner draws examples from Behrman's major plays to establish his distinction as an able writer of high comedy. He finds that the playwright's artistic and ideological vision encompasses comic detachment and a thematic advocacy of indulgence and tolerance in confronting a reality that is contradictory and commonly two-sided.

Gross, Robert F. *S. N. Behrman: A Research and Production Handbook*. Westport, Conn.: Greenwood Press, 1992. This sourcebook provides a detailed record of Behrman's work as a Broadway playwright and Hollywood screenwriter, from the 1920's to the mid-1960's, and encompasses published and unpublished primary materials (plays, film scripts, fiction, and essays) and the critical responses. Includes plot summaries and critical overviews for fifty-one plays, and an annotated bibliography, which is divided into chronological sections for reviews, books, articles, and the like. All materials are cross-referenced and indexed.

Klink, William R. *S. N. Behrman: The Major Plays*. Amsterdam, The Netherlands: Rodopi, 1978. Klink lucidly evaluates Behrman's major plays excluding those adapted or written in collaboration. The study includes an introduction briefly discussing published and unpublished material about Behrman, a summary conclusion, and a bibliography. Valuable as one of few books solely on Behrman.

Krutch, Joseph Wood. *The American Drama Since 1918: An Informal History.* New York: George Braziller, 1957. Krutch devotes twenty-five pages of a chapter on comedy to an admiring, relatively comprehensive discussion of Behrman's plays, concluding with *No Time for Comedy.* Identifies the thematic thrust of Behrman's comedies before 1940.

Reed, Kenneth T. *S. N. Behrman.* Boston: Twayne, 1975. Reed's biographical and critical study provides one of the most accessible, valuable, and comprehensive treatments of the playwright and his work. It contains a chronology, a detailed examination of Behrman's plays (including a chapter on the prose works) within the context of his life and career, an index, and a select bibliography that includes an annotated listing of major secondary sources. Reed encompasses chapters on the playwright's techniques and major themes. Contains a photograph of Behrman.

Sievers, W. David. *Freud on Broadway.* New York: Heritage House, 1955. Sievers investigates Freudian influence in American dramatists' work and identifies Behrman as one of the "post-Freudian playwrights of the thirties" who redirected psychoanalytical observations of the isolated individual to the socio-centered problems of Fascism, radicalism, racism, and greed. While overemphasizing Behrman's contribution to psychoanalytic drama, Siever's evaluation (fourteen pages) of the playwright's characters and themes is persuasively interesting. Contains an index.

Leslie B. Mittleman
(Updated by *Christian H. Moe*)

DAVID BELASCO

Born: San Francisco, California; July 25, 1853
Died: New York, New York; May 14, 1931

Principal drama

L'Assommoir, pr. 1879 (adaptation of Émile Zola's novel); *Within an Inch of His Life*, pr. 1879 (with James A. Herne); *Hearts of Oak*, pr. 1879 (with Herne; originally as *Chums*; adaptation of Henry Leslie's play *The Mariner's Compass*); *La Belle Russe*, pr. 1881, pb. 1882; *The Stranglers of Paris*, pr. 1881, pb. 1941 (adaptation of Adolphe Belot's novel *L'Estrangleur*); *May Blossom*, pb. 1883, pr. 1884; *Valerie*, pr. 1886 (adaptation of Victorien Sardou's *Fernande*); *Baron Rudolph*, pr. 1887, pb. 1941 (with Bronson Howard); *The Highest Bidder*, pr. 1887; *The Wife*, pr. 1887, pb. 1941 (with Henry C. De Mille); *Lord Chumley*, pr., pb. 1888 (with De Mille); *The Charity Ball*, pr. 1889, pb. 1941 (with De Mille); *Men and Women*, pr. 1890, pb. 1941 (with De Mille); *Miss Helvett*, pr. 1891; *The Girl I Left Behind Me*, pr. 1893, pb. 1941 (with Franklyn Fyles); *The Younger Son*, pr. 1893 (adaptation of O. Vischer's play *Schlimme Saat*); *The Heart of Maryland*, pr., pb. 1895; *Zaza*, pr. 1898 (adaptation of Pierre Berton and Charles Simon's French play); *Madame Butterfly*, pr. 1900, pb. 1935 (with John Luther Long; adaptation of Long's story); *Naughty Anthony*, pr. 1900, pb. 1941; *DuBarry*, pr. 1901, pb. 1928; *The Darling of the Gods*, pr. 1902, pb. 1928 (with Long); *Sweet Kitty Bellairs*, pr., pb. 1903 (adaptation of Agnes and Egeron Castle's *The Bath Comedy*); *Adrea*, pr. 1905, pb. 1928 (with Long); *The Girl of the Golden West*, pr. 1905, pb. 1928; *The Rose of the Rancho*, pr. 1906, pb. 1936 (with Richard W. Tully; adaptation of Tully's *Juanita*); *A Grand Army Man*, pr. 1907, pb. 1908 (with Pauline Phelps and Marion Short); *The Lily*, pr. 1909; *The Return of Peter Grimm*, pr. 1911, pb. 1928; *The Governor's Lady*, pr., pb. 1912 (with Alice Bradley); *The Secret*, pr. 1913; *The Son Daughter*, pr., pb. 1919 (with George Scarborough); *The Comedian*, pr. 1923; *Laugh, Clown, Laugh*, pr. 1923 (adaptation of Fausto Maria Martini's play *Ridi, pagliaccio*); *Fanny*, pr., pb. 1926 (with Willard Mack); *Mima*, pr. 1928 (adaptation of Ferenc Molnár's play *The Red Mill*); *Six Plays*, pb. 1928 (Montrose J. Moses, editor); *The Plays of Henry C. De Mille, Written in Collaboration with David Belasco*, pb. 1941 (Robert Hamilton Ball, editor).

Other literary forms

David Belasco published a number of human-interest essays and articles about stagecraft, including "How I Stage My Plays" and "Stage Realism of the Future." A serialized autobiography, "My Life's Story," was published in *Hearst's Magazine* from March, 1914, to December, 1915, followed four years later by a full-length memoir, *The Theatre Through Its Stage Door* (1919). With two of his most popular plays later turned into novels, Belasco was one of the first in the United States to capitalize on the success of dramatic works by revising them for a new reading audience.

Achievements

While contemporary critics frequently criticized Belasco's penchant for melodrama, his immense popular success was a product of his reliance upon heart-interest as well as a strict interpretation of the fourth-wall convention. Belasco paid meticulous attention to details, often rewriting extensively in rehearsal. Indeed, he is best remembered for his directing methods, his realism, and his technical effects.

Belasco was the directing genius behind many actors and actresses. David Warfield, for example, who began his career with the burlesque company Weber and Fields, under Belasco's tutelage moved from the farcical *The Auctioneer* to Belasco's own seriocomic *The Return of Peter Grimm* and later appeared in William Shakespeare's *The Merchant of Venice*. Perhaps "Mr. Dave's" greatest success was Leslie Carter, a society divorcée who undertook two years of acting lessons from Belasco. Best remembered for her electrifying performance in *The Heart of Maryland*, the fiery-haired actress exemplified the sensationalism that Belasco's audiences enjoyed. Such individual triumphs by no means detracted from Belasco's attention to his entire company. On the one hand, he encouraged every expression of individual talent, no matter how slender; on the other, he held long, painstaking rehearsals commencing at least six weeks before opening night.

Belasco believed that the purpose of the theater was to mimic nature, and he attempted to immerse his actors not merely in a realistic scene but in a mood as well. As Lise-Lone Marker points out, his goal seems similar to that of the proponents of the New Stagecraft, yet Belasco saw both light and color to be as essential to dialogue as music is to a song. He is noted for his ultrarealistic stage sets—sets that seem to answer August Strindberg's objection, in the preface to *Miss Julie*, to unstable canvas scenery. Belasco imported antique furniture and draperies for his sets; he offered his company his collection of authentic jewelry; he even introduced a flock of sheep on stage for his production of Salmi Morse's *The Passion Play*, and *The Governor's Lady* featured an exact replica of fashionable Child's restaurant. He followed the fourth-wall convention to its logical conclusion, forcing the famous tenor Enrico Caruso to sing his arias with his back to the audience in Giacomo Puccini's operatic version of *The Girl of the Golden West*.

Belasco's stage sets were complemented by his innovations in the use of movable spots, diffused lighting, and, above all, the baby spotlight (invented by Belasco's light man, Louis Hartmann), which eliminated the harshness of the ever-present footlight. His experiments with colored silks as filters and his discovery of the scrim, which was used in staging *The Darling of the Gods*, produced the spectacular effects that earned him the nickname "The Wizard."

Biography

David Belasco was born in San Francisco, California, on July 25, 1853. His father, Humphrey Abraham Belasco, was a London actor who, with his bride, Reina Martin Belasco, had succumbed to Gold Rush fever. Once in San Francisco, however, the couple settled into shopkeeping after David's birth. Five years later, news of a gold strike in British Columbia lured them north, where David's three brothers were born and where Humphrey Belasco maintained a tobacco shop while investing in real estate and digging for gold.

Belasco's published memories of British Columbia are highly imaginative accounts, containing references to a monastic education as well as to his appearance as "Davido, the Boy Wonder," with the Rio de Janeiro Circus. More sober accounts place him first at the Colonial School and then at the Anglican Collegiate School in 1862. Two years later, he made his first professional stage appearance, as the Duke of York in Charles Kean's *King Richard III*. Belasco's other theatrical efforts took place in San Francisco, to which his family returned when he was eleven. *The Roll of the Drum*, a childhood play strongly influenced by the penny dreadfuls, and a gold medal at Lincoln Grammar School for his impassioned rendition of Matthew Gregory Lewis' poem "The Maniac" were among Belasco's early achievements.

After graduation from Lincoln, Belasco entered a self-imposed, five-year apprenticeship during which he took a touring company up and down the West Coast, deriving much of the material by copying prompt books and pirating uncopyrighted Continental works. At twenty, he began a fifty-two-year marriage with Cecelia Loverich. His subsequent career in California was furthered by Tom Maguire, an unschooled Tammany barkeeper who opened a series of successful California theaters. As Maguire's prompter at the Baldwin, a magnificent hotel/theater, Belasco oversaw Salmi Morse's *The Passion Play*, which scandalized the citizens of San Francisco. During this period, he staged his Naturalistic version of Émile Zola's *L'Assommoir* and collaborated with James Herne in such works as *Chums*, which became known as *Hearts of Oak* after its New York success under that title. Before Maguire retired in 1882, Belasco had written and directed a number of works, among them *La Belle Russe* and *The Stranglers of Paris*, an adaptation of Adolphe Belot's earlier work.

Belasco's first New York assignment was as stage manager at the Madison Square Theatre, backed by Marshall and George Mallory, who sought wholesome productions by American playwrights. The interference and parsimony of the Mallory brothers caused Belasco to leave after only a few years, in 1885. After brief stints with Steele MacKaye and Lester Wallack, Belasco was hired by Daniel Frohman to direct the Lyceum Theatre. There, he collaborated with Henry C. DeMille to produce *The Wife, Lord Chumley, The Charity Ball*, and *Men and Women*. In 1889, Belasco undertook the training of a red-haired society divorcée, Leslie Carter, for the stage; finally, at forty, he had his first unqualified success with *The Heart of Maryland*, a Civil War drama written expressly for Carter, whose role called for her to swing on a bell clapper to keep the bell from ringing and to save her escaping Northern lover. After winning a lawsuit against N. K. Fairbank, Carter's financial backer, for withdrawing funding for another play, Belasco produced *Zaza*—inspired, in part, by Carter's determination to go upon the stage—and began training another star, Blanche Bates, who initially appeared in Belasco's *Naughty Anthony*. Ironically, the afterpiece with which Belasco bolstered his slender farce—an adaptation of John Luther Long's story "Madame Butterfly"—proved the more memorable production; in later years, it became one of Puccini's best-known operas.

In 1901, Belasco produced a dramatization of the life of Madame DuBarry, the mistress of King Louis XV. In staging *DuBarry*, another Carter vehicle, Belasco imported French antique draperies and furniture. The next year, he leased Oscar Hammerstein's theater, the Republic, which was remodeled and renamed the Belasco; his first new play, a collaboration with Long called *The Darling of the Gods*, featured the back-lit scrim. Although leasing the Republic gave him relative freedom from the Theatrical Syndicate which for sixteen years controlled bookings in New York and throughout the United States, Belasco entered a 1903-1904 lawsuit charging hidden partnerships and bribery against Marc Klaw and Abe Erlanger, a lawsuit often credited with breaking the syndicate's power. Immediately after the altercation, Belasco produced his very successful melodrama *The Girl of the Golden West*, which Puccini produced as *La fanciulla del West*.

In the same year, Carter deserted Belasco by remarrying; consequently, in 1907, it was Blanche Bates who helped inaugurate Belasco's new theater, the Stuyvesant, whose ornamental façade hid not only the finest lighting equipment then available but also Belasco's own private studio. Shortly thereafter, Belasco shocked his public by producing *The Easiest Way* (pb. 1908, pr. 1909), Eugene Walter's play about an unreformed prostitute. Belasco recouped with a production of his own *The Return of Peter Grimm*, a play known as much for its masterly lighting as for its afterlife theme— validated, according to the program notes, by psychologist William James himself.

From 1910 to 1920, Belasco produced thirty-two plays, mostly melodramas by other authors; his masterly 1920 production of *Deburau* (Harley Granville-Barker's adaptation of Sacha Guitry's play about pantomime) and his 1922 production of Shakespeare's *The Merchant of Venice*, with David Warfield, demonstrated that he was still a powerful figure in the theater. In November, 1930, Belasco fell ill with pneumonia during rehearsals of Frederic and Fanny Hatton's *Tonight or Never* and died the following year, on May 14, in New York.

Analysis

While David Belasco experimented with Naturalism, an overriding number of his plays are either melodramas or farces, whose strong emotion, light wit, and happy endings appealed to his audiences. Indeed, when Belasco was not writing adaptations of foreign novels and plays, he relied on a number of well-worn themes and used his magic realism to disguise the similarities. Many of his well-made plays feature the trials and tribulations of young lovers; his fascination with the lives of outcast women is equally evident.

A number of Belasco's melodramas have historical or ethnic backgrounds. *DuBarry*, set in the time of Louis XV, and *The Darling of the Gods*, set in Japan during the Samurai period, exhibit the same melodramatic characteristics as *The Girl of the Golden West*—slender character motivation, a romantic plot, strong appeal to the emotions, and a denouement characterized by poetic justice. Of the three heroines, DuBarry is the only one who fails to win a happy ending; the French milliner turned king's mistress, executed by the revolutionaries as an aristocrat, does nevertheless achieve a final reunion with Cossé, her former sweetheart. Yo-San, who dies for betraying the hide-out of her Samurai lover's band, meets Kara in the afterlife. Of the three, the Girl—Minnie—achieves the most enduring happiness, for although she leaves her beloved Sierra Nevada mountains, she does so in the company of Johnson, a reformed thief who has become her sweetheart. Perhaps the most sensational of Belasco's historical plays, *The Heart of Maryland* features a pair of Civil War lovers divided by opposing North/South sympathies and reunited after an act of heroism on the part of Maryland Calvert herself.

Belasco's farces were much less sumptuous in staging and considerably lighter in plot; like *Lord Chumley*, *Naughty Anthony* relies on complicated, improbable situations for its humor. Professor Anthony Depew, a teacher of moral behavior, when caught kissing one of his patients in a darkened park gazebo, gives his landlord's name instead of his own. An incompetent lawyer, another love triangle, and a vengeful wife are coupled with what was then a mildly shocking episode in which Cora, a hosiery saleswoman, strips off her stockings onstage. Handled differently, *Naughty Anthony* might have succeeded as a satire of moral hypocrisy; as it stands, however, the tangled skeins of the well-made play are too much in evidence.

Belasco attempted to deal with the outcast woman in historical plays such as *DuBarry* and in sheer melodrama such as *La Belle Russe*, in which a notorious prostitute tries to profit from the good fortune of her innocent twin. La Belle Russe herself is saved by the love for her illegitimate child; similarly, in *Zaza*, the heroine redeems herself by becoming a great actress. Other characters, not nearly as well received, face a more realistic end.

A lavish and sensational Civil War melodrama, *The Heart of Maryland* made Belasco independent. The play, backed by Max Blieman, a dealer in art, opened on October 9, 1895, in Washington, D.C., and moved to the Herald Square Theatre in New York two weeks later for a run of 229 performances.

The property and light cues for the play show that Belasco paid extraordinary attention to detail, even visiting Maryland so he could duplicate the atmosphere. The first scene opens on The Lilacs, a nostalgically reproduced mansion replete with fragrant lilac bushes and water lilies. In the near distance is a stream crossed by a rustic bridge; in the far appear the hills of Maryland. The plot interprets the conflict between North and South romantically: Maryland Calvert's Northern lover is Colonel Alan Kendrick, whose father commands the Southern forces; Nanny, a sharp-witted Yankee of sixteen, is wooed by Robert Telfair, a lieutenant in the Southern artillery unit encamped at The Lilacs. Further complications arise when Colonel Thorpe, a Southern officer in the employ of the Northern Secret Service, uses the information given to him by Lloyd Calvert—Maryland's brother, a Northern sympathizer—to further his own career rather than to warn General Hooker of General Kendrick's advance. When Alan is brought as a prisoner to The Lilacs, Maryland, despite her strong Dixie bias, passes the information to him.

In act 2, Lloyd is killed while he is carrying information, but not before he asks his sister to detain an anonymous "friend" of his—Alan. Captured while awaiting Maryland, Alan confronts his father, who keeps his military bearing with difficulty. Maryland becomes hysterical upon learning of her brother's death and impulsively accuses his "friend" of spying. As the scene closes, she understands that she has accused her lover in order to save her brother's name.

At the beginning of act 3, Alan is incarcerated in an old church that serves as a prison. Maryland, crossing the lines, brings a stay of execution, but Thorpe realizes that had the letter reached the now-dead Colonel Kendrick, he himself would have been indicted for spying. He brings Alan from the prison to torment him with the sight of Maryland; Alan, bound and helpless, watches as Maryland—like the operatic heroine Tosca—stabs her attacker and urges Alan to run. The climax of the scene occurs when she races up the stairs and leaps to grasp the clapper on the bell that is rung to alert the Southern artillery. As the act closes, Maryland swings back and forth on the bell, a tour de force supposedly reminiscent of Belasco's childhood fascination with Rosa Hartwicke Thorpe's poem "The Curfew Must Not Ring Tonight."

The resolution in the fourth act finds Nanny nursing the wounded Telfair while the Northern troops, led by Alan, cannonade The Lilacs, where Thorpe has imprisoned Maryland. Thorpe negotiates a retreat to Richmond but insists that Maryland accompany him to stand trial. Alan accepts but then, given safe conduct, delivers a letter from General Lee court-martialing Thorpe for double treachery and appointing Telfair commander. The curtain closes as Maryland and Alan are reunited.

Although Belasco, in a first-night curtain speech, had said, "Now I am encouraged to hope I have proved myself a dramatist," critical praise was not forthcoming; nevertheless, the play ran for nearly nine months and had a successful season in London. Although some British critics praised Leslie Carter's histrionics as Maryland and likened Belasco to the wildly popular French playwright Victorien Sardou, George Bernard Shaw (who also disliked Sardou) made sharp-tongued fun of American melodrama while conceding that the actors themselves were better trained than their British cousins and that Carter's intensity showed her to be an actress "of no mean powers."

One of the works that held the most personal meaning for Belasco, *The Return of Peter Grimm* is permeated not only by a sense of loss for departed family members but also by a belief in an afterlife. During the play's first performance at the Boston Hollis Street Theatre on January 2, 1911, Belasco's younger daughter Augusta, terminally ill with tuberculosis, impressed her father with her belief that dying is another form of living— or, in Peter Grimm's words, "knowing better." Other personal facts contributed to the production of the play about the old horticulturist who returns from the dead to right his mistakes, most notably Belasco's insistence in 1898 that his mother had appeared to him in a waking dream; the next morning, news was brought during the rehearsals for *Zaza* that she had died in San Francisco during the night.

Despite rumors to the contrary, Belasco reiterated publicly that Cecil B. DeMille was responsible only for the idea of the play and not for the actual script—a script which, Belasco noted, presented the serious problem of how to make Grimm's return believable. Three factors contributed to his success in solving this problem: naturalistic stage setting, acting, and lighting. First, the props were carefully selected to suggest not only a real room but also a wealth of memories that might be evoked by a cozy, homey house; likewise, the view shown from the onstage window conveys the close tie between Grimm's sense of well-being and his thriving business. Second, Belasco instructed his other actors to look *through* the Grimm "apparition" so as to highlight the reaction of the eight-year-old child medium. Third, the complex lighting system made use of the baby lens developed by Louis Hartmann. This lens concentrated spots of flesh-toned light on all of the characters but Grimm, who was bathed in a colder, bluer light; consequently, he seemed in contrast always to be shadowed. In addition, Belasco abolished the footlights and substituted bridge lights on beams above the set. The lighting schematic took almost a year to develop but was called "perhaps the most perfect example of stage lighting ever exhibited."

The melodramatic plot includes a love triangle, a villainous family member, and a child who dies young. In the long first act, the love that James Hartman, Grimm's secretary, has not only for Catherine Staats—Grimm's adopted daughter—but also for the plants themselves is juxtaposed to the money-hungry courtship of Grimm's nephew Frederick, whose dearest wish is to sell the house and nursery. Warned by his doctor that the condition of his heart may cause his death at any moment, Grimm forces an engagement between Catherine and Frederick so that he may be, he thinks, assured of the continuance of his business and of Catherine's happiness. William, the eight-year-old illegitimate son of a runaway servant, is also put under the protection of Frederick, who clearly dislikes him. At the end of the act, Peter dies.

An approaching storm, James's and Catherine's manifest unhappiness, an altercation among Grimm's old friends over their legacies—all produce a mood of suspense that builds toward the arrival of the ghost in act 2. When the ghostly Grimm does appear, however, it is very quietly; moreover, since he can make himself felt only indirectly, his efforts to save the business, to make Catherine break her engagement, and to reveal Frederick as William's father are all subtle (or else, indeed, the play would end abruptly). It is only to William, who is ill, that Grimm can speak directly; through Grimm's influence, William points out the incriminating letter from his mother, Annemarie. Frederick's perfidy revealed and the marriage broken off, the third act centers on William's death, a scene that escapes the bathetic partly by the circus motif that carries over from the first act and partly by Peter's insistence that he is taking William away "to know better." As the curtain falls, the two dance away to the clown's tune, "Uncle Rat Has Gone to Town." The play, which moved to the New York Stuyvesant Theatre on October 18, 1911, ran for 231 performances. Critical reception was warm, citing Belasco's triumph in making the impossible appear actual by his magic of lighting and directing.

A compound of memories of California (as well as of Bret Harte, as some contemporary critics charged), *The Girl of the Golden West* opened on October 3, 1905, at the Belasco Theatre in Pittsburgh and moved to New York on November 14. Puccini adapted the play, which Belasco believed his best, under the title *La fanciulla del West* (Puccini had brought about a similar musical transformation with Belasco's *Madame Butterfly* in 1904). As Belasco notes, teaching acting techniques to opera singers—Enrico Caruso among them—familiar only with vocal flourishes was a difficult task, considering that both he and Arturo Toscanini, the conductor, were autocratic in their methods. The December 10, 1910, premiere at the Metropolitan Opera House was, nevertheless, a success.

The melodramatic plot, which Belasco insisted was based on his father's stories, features the trusting, unlettered Minnie, owner of The Polka, a Western saloon. Most of her customers, including the gambler/sheriff Jack Rance, are in love with her. While the bartender, Nick, slyly keeps up business by encouraging her suitors, Minnie, who has fallen in love with a nameless stranger she has met on the road, cheerfully and faithfully serves as a "bank" for the prospectors' nuggets. In act 1, the stranger, Dick Johnson—in reality, Ramerrez, a bandit who has plotted to rob The Polka—appears. While Johnson is at The Polka, the Pony Express brings news that Ramerrez is in the area, and the Girl, who innocently admires Johnson, stoutly declares that she will protect the prospectors' hard-earned gold.

In act 2, Minnie welcomes Johnson to her cabin for dinner, where he becomes convinced that she is the one woman for whom he would reform. Trapped by a snowstorm, he hides when Rance and his men appear at the cabin to ascertain Minnie's safety. While there, they arouse Minnie's jealousy by mentioning Ramerrez's supposed lover, Nina Micheltorena. Minnie angrily sends Johnson out into the storm, but he is wounded by Rance and returns to take refuge in her loft. Rance is almost convinced that Ramerrez has escaped until a drop of blood from the loft falls on his handkerchief. As the act ends, Rance and the Girl play poker to win Ramerrez; during a diversion, Minnie uses the three aces she had hidden in her stocking to make a better hand, wins the right to let Ramerrez escape, and frees herself from Rance's power.

In act 3, Minnie opens the "Academy," a grammar school for prospectors, but is distracted by happiness at the thought of meeting Johnson and sadness at leaving The Polka. A crisis occurs when the Wells Fargo agent recaptures Johnson, much to the glee of Rance, who has kept his promise not to interfere but who can now take revenge. Rance proposes lynching Johnson, and the boys in The Polka are willing to follow his lead until they witness the reunion between Johnson and the Girl. Hearing her prayer, they become convinced that Providence protects Johnson. As the play concludes, Johnson and the Girl are leaving California for a new start in the "promised land" in the East.

Belasco introduced a number of special effects that enhanced the play's atmosphere. Before the first act, audiences saw a detailed panorama of the

Sierra Nevada, complete with the Girl's cabin on Cloudy Mountain. The panorama, a transparency painted in evocative colors and lit from behind, slowly unrolled to the bottom of the mountain, where The Polka appeared blazing with light. The sound effects were introduced at this point; Belasco discarded the usual orchestral accompaniment, using instead a small band of concertina and banjo, playing such favorites as "Camptown Races" and "Pop Goes the Weasel," partly, Belasco claimed, in memory of Jake Wallace, the famous banjo player of the mining camp. After the houselights were dimmed and the panorama removed, the act opened on the interior of The Polka, where all props were handled with meticulous detail, from the real pineboards in the walls to the riding paraphernalia piled carelessly on the floor. In addition, even the minor characters were costumed in distinctly individualistic ways to suggest a realistic and motley selection of prospectors. Perhaps the greatest tour de force of the play was the snowstorm that trapped Johnson in Minnie's cabin. Making use of the pathetic fallacy—the idea that natural events parallel emotional and moral situations—Belasco built the suspense of the scene. Blowers, fans, rock salt, snow bags, and air tanks to reproduce the sound of the storm were operated by a cadre of thirty-two stagehands, who formed, as William Winter notes, "a sort of mechanical orchestra."

On the whole, Belasco's plays are not classics and do not even lend themselves to serious criticism. In his own day, his appeal to the emotions did as much as his wizardry in the areas of lighting and directing to guarantee his plays full houses and long runs. Today's more sophisticated audiences would judge them overly sentimental, melodramatic, and simplistic. Yet Belasco did have an enduring impact on the theater, setting an example with his imaginative approach to extending what had become the usual boundaries of staging and his meticulous attention to the details of production.

Other major works

NOVELS: *The Girl of the Golden West*, 1911; *The Return of Peter Grimm*, 1912.

NONFICTION: *My Life's Story*, 1916 (2 volumes); *The Theatre Through Its Stage Door*, 1919.

Bibliography

Belasco, David. *The Theatre Through Its Stage Door.* Edited by Louis V. Defoe. New York: Harper & Brothers, 1919. This volume offers the playwright's own factual view of Broadway history. Supplemented by many rare illustrations.

De Mille, Henry Churchill. *The Plays of Henry C. De Mille, Written in Collaboration with David Belasco.* Edited by Robert Hamilton Ball. Princeton, N.J.: Princeton University Press, 1941. Contains a wide-ranging introductory essay by Robert Hamilton Ball and is part of America's lost-plays series.

Marker, Lise-Lone. *David Belasco: Naturalism in the American Theatre.* Princeton, N.J.: Princeton University Press, 1975. This volume is considered the standard and most scholarly biography of Broadway's most innovative producer, including his very successful collaboration with James A. Herne.

Timberlake, Craig. *The Bishop of Broadway: The Life and Work of David Belasco.* New York: Library Publishers, 1954. Although somewhat dated, Timberlake's book nevertheless presents a solid account of Belasco's popular plays and the many stars he created.

Winter, William. *The Life of David Belasco.* 1925. Reprint. Freeport, N.Y.: Books for Libraries Press, 1970. This reprint of the 1925 edition was completed by the author's son, William Jefferson Winter, after the author's death. It discusses the history of theater in the United States as well as the playwright's long career. Contains illustrations.

Patricia Marks
(Updated by *Peter C. Holloran*)

RUDOLF BESIER

Born: Java; July 2, 1878
Died: Elmhurst, England; June 13, 1942

Principal drama

The Virgin Goddess, pr. 1906, pb. 1907; *Olive Latimer's Husband*, pr. 1909; *Don*, pr., pb. 1909; *Apropos*, pr. 1910; *The Crisis*, pr. 1910 (adaptation of P. F. Berton's play *La Rencontre*); *Lady Patricia*, pr., pb. 1911; *Kipps*, pr. 1912 (with H. G. Wells; adaptation of Wells's novel); *Kings and Queens*, pr. 1915; *Kultur at Home*, pr. 1916 (with Sybil Spotiswoode); *A Run for His Money*, pr. 1916 (also as *Buxell*, pr. 1916); *Robin's Father*, pr. 1918 (with Hugh Walpole); *The Prude's Fall*, pr. 1920 (with May Edginton; originally as *The Awakening of Beatrice*); *The Ninth Earl*, pr. 1921 (with Edginton); *Secrets*, pr. 1922, pb. 1932 (with Edginton); *The Barretts of Wimpole Street*, pr., pb. 1930.

Other literary forms

Rudolf Besier is noted only for his dramatic works, although he was also engaged in journalism and translated from the French.

Achievements

Though he wrote a large number of plays, Besier's international reputation depends upon a single work, the historical drama *The Barretts of Wimpole Street*. This perennial favorite was produced for the first time at the Malvern Festival in England in 1930 by Sir Barry Jackson, following its rejection by two London producers. After twenty-seven American producers turned it down, Katharine Cornell accepted it and the play opened in Cleveland and, shortly thereafter, at the Empire Theatre in New York.

At the turn of the century, dramatic language on the English-speaking stage had increasingly tended to become dry and uninteresting, and, as a result, dialogue seemed stilted. Besier's first play, *The Virgin Goddess*, a classical tragedy written during a visit to the United States, clearly showed his eagerness to return colorful and lively dialogue to the stage. The play was greeted with mixed reviews. Three years later, Besier received considerable praise for his comedy *Don*, which centers on an eccentric and magnanimous poet. The play's formal language and heavy sentimentality have dated badly. *Lady Patricia*, a satire on English affectations, and *Kultur at Home*, which delighted audiences for the manner in which it depicted German domestic life at its worst, kept Besier before the critics and the public.

Besier first achieved genuine popular success with the dream play *Secrets*, in which he used the device of allowing the first act to take shape as a prologue, commencing the main action with the second act. In the opening episode, Lady Carlton, old and exhausted from constantly tending her dying husband, falls asleep in an armchair beside his bed. The drama itself consists of a series of flashbacks presented in the form of a dream. In these, the lives of the couple are presented as they marry, endure initial poverty, and gradually attain affluence. During this time, the husband has an affair with another woman; his wife forgives him, despite her bitter jealousy, because of her realization that he needs her. Like several of Besier's earlier plays, *Secrets* is highly sentimental, but it is distinguished by its acute perceptions into the psychology of the two main characters.

The success of *Secrets* did not prepare the public for Besier's masterpiece, which appeared some eight years later. Though many playgoers were surprised by the general popularity of *The Barretts of Wimpole Street*, one can see in retrospect the groundwork for this achievement. At the beginning of his career, Besier had demonstrated his ability to draw a portrait of a peculiar poet, and in *Secrets* he demonstrated his sharp and sensitive knowledge of human feelings. Further, several of his earlier plays revealed a flair for melodrama. Though *The Barretts of Wimpole Street* exhibits characteristics of the comedy (it was labeled by Besier as such), the psychological drama, and the historical drama, the play contains many of the traits of the melodrama. Above all, it is the intrinsic appeal of the story of Elizabeth Barrett and Robert Browning which has given the play its enduring appeal, yet Besier must be given full credit for realizing the dramatic potential in this well-known romance—particularly the role of Elizabeth Barrett's father, the quintessential Victorian tyrant.

Biography

Born in Java of Dutch extraction on July 2, 1878, Rudolf Besier was the son of Margaret (née Collinson) and Rudolf Besier. He was educated in England and Germany: at St. Elizabeth College, Guernsey, and at Heidelberg, respectively. For several years he was engaged in journalism, being for a time on the staff of C. Arthur Pearson, Ltd. In 1908, however, Besier left journalism, having decided to devote his efforts entirely to the theater. He married Charlotte Woodward, the daughter of the Reverend J. P. S. Woodward, of Plumpton, Sussex. He wrote a large number of plays; the most famous of these plays and the one that confirmed his dramatic reputation is *The Barretts of Wimpole Street*. Critics praised the play, but it was severely criticized by members of the Barrett family, who objected to the Freudian implications in the portrayal of Edward Moulton Barrett. Later, a film version of the play was made. An extremely tall, handsome man who shunned public exposure, Besier spent the last part of his life at his home in Elmhurst, Surrey, where he died suddenly of heart failure on June 13, 1942.

Analysis

Like any work that deals with actual personages, a play demands some understanding of the lives of its characters and the times in which they lived if it is to be thoroughly appreciated. Understanding the fullness of *The Barretts of Wimpole Street* necessarily entails historical knowledge not only of Elizabeth Barrett and Robert Browning but also of the general nature of Victorian customs, manners, and class distinctions. The oldest child in a wealthy, upper-middle-class family, Elizabeth Barrett was educated at home. As a result of a back injury at the age of fifteen, she became a chronic invalid. From her early teens until the end of her life, she read widely and concentrated on writing poetry. At the time of the play, Barrett for a number of years had been confined to her room in her father's London house on Wimpole Street. From there, she pursued her education, including the study of Greek, took frequent medication, and, with the exception of visits by her family and a few friends, remained by herself to write articles and the poetry which brought her recognition. Robert Browning, a poet then ignored by the public, one day came to pay his respects, and the celebrated literary romance began. The pair seemed ill-matched; she was six years older than he and her health was frail. Her father, moreover, had decided that none of his children should marry.

Despite such unpromising conditions, the two lovers secretly married and moved to Italy, where they lived for most of the fifteen years that remained of Elizabeth Barrett Browning's life. There, they wrote most of their now famous poems and had a son. Elizabeth Browning strongly devoted herself to the Italian struggle for independence against Austria. She wrote not only *The Cry of the Children* (1854), in which she passionately argued against child labor in England, but also *Sonnets from the Portuguese* (1850), her famous sonnet sequence celebrating her love for her husband. In 1861, she died and was buried in her beloved Italy.

The hero of Rudolf Besier's play, Robert Browning, was strong, spirited, and optimistic; like Barrett, he began writing when he was young. The criticism that attended his poetry early in his career failed to discourage him, for he continued to write prolifically. His whirlwind courtship overwhelmed Barrett's initial resistance, and their romance ended only with her death, after which he returned to England. His reputation today rests primarily on his dramatic monologues, in which the speakers' own words provide psychological insights into their characters. He died in Venice in 1889, but his body was returned to England and buried in Westminster Abbey, where many of England's great poets are buried.

Set against Browning in the play is the antagonist, Barrett's father, Edward Moulton Barrett, who at the age of nineteen left Cambridge University to marry a woman more than five years older than he. The union produced twelve children; one child, a girl, died in childhood, and two boys died as adults. After his wife died, he ruled his nine remaining children like a despot, refusing to explain any of his commands and forbidding any of the children to marry. Three eventually disobeyed him, and as a result, he disinherited them and refused to see them again.

The Barretts of Wimpole Street takes place during the early years of Queen Victoria's reign. Though the living and working conditions of the lower classes were slowly improving, the poor found it difficult to make gains through their employment. The exploitation of women and child laborers was common. Putting in long hours for pitifully low wages under oppressive and unhealthy conditions, workers were barely able to survive. Then, too, the class distinctions were rigidly structured and observed, with opportunities to rise to a higher class practically nonexistent. Though not of the aristocracy, Edward Moulton Barrett had inherited large sums of money and had land holdings on the British island of Jamaica. Consequently, he was able to attend Cambridge University. Supported by his own means and the wealth that came to him through his wife, he lived comfortably in a fashionable London district and reared his large family, though he was temporarily inconvenienced financially when all slaves were freed in the British Empire.

Both sons and daughters of the upper classes were dependent on their fathers for financial support. Robert Browning was himself supported by his parents until his poetry began to earn money for him. The various Barrett sons assisted their father in his office, taking orders while he attended to business in the financial quarter of London or while he was abroad supervising his land holdings. Daughters were never permitted to engage in business affairs, and, as a result, some, such as Bella, became social butterflies, while others, such as Arabel, worked in support of various social or religious causes. Certain others became little more than house decorations, awaiting the opportunity to marry. Elizabeth Barrett, therefore, stands out in contrast, for she had both a career of her own and a limited inheritance. She was fortunate also in being able to secure a respectable education. Women of the upper classes were generally encouraged to pursue only the refined graces of music, manners, and needlework. Barrett gained additional education through her own intense and varied reading and from her brothers' tutors.

Characterized by prudery, repression, and formality, the Victorian period was highlighted by a fear of outspokenness and by the evasion of facts. In *The Barretts of Wimpole Street*, for example, Arabel upbraids Bella for speaking of the birth of children and scolds Henrietta for describing their father with language she considers ugly. Houses of the wealthy were heavily and formally furnished. Women, moreover, dressed in voluminous layers of clothing, and men indulged in formal attire. When first calling on Elizabeth Barrett, Robert Browning faultlessly dressed in the manner of the times—a cape fastened around his neck, a high hat, lemon-colored gloves, and a cane. Edward Moulton Barrett, together with his sons, wore evening clothes for dinner with the family each night. The wealthy also were transported in fine carriages that were attended by coachmen and footmen wearing powdered wigs.

Besier's purpose necessitated many of the dramatic techniques he used in the play. His intention was not so much to present the love affair between Barrett and Browning as to portray a family dominated by a tyrannical, repressed father. The revolt of the most unlikely family member of the Barretts of Wimpole Street constitutes the romantic and dramatic climax, and, appropriately enough, the play is set entirely in Elizabeth Barrett's room. The use of only one setting focuses audience attention on the one room which every family member visited. By this means, Besier could portray the attitudes of the various sons and daughters toward their father and, in turn, his effect on them. The play's conclusion maintains and reinforces this dramatic focus: The audience does not view Elizabeth Barrett's marriage, nor is there any scene in Italy. The play closes with the father's frustrated endeavor to destroy her dog, Flush, a final indication of his unreasoning cruelty.

Terror affects each member of the Barrett family. Elizabeth continues to drink the porter that she so detests in order not to displease her father, while Henrietta, ever rebellious, accedes to Barrett's demands and swears upon the Bible that she will neither see nor communicate with her suitor, Captain Surtees Cook. Representing all the boys who through fear of their father are leading "a life which isn't a life at all," Octavius calls Barrett "His Majesty." The whole family is elated when informed that the father is undertaking a two-week business trip. Arabel, more placid than most of the other children, hopes that he will be detained. Elizabeth herself later declares that "our family life was one of unrelieved gloom." Besier relieves the tense, strained, family atmosphere with scenes of a lighter, even humorous, quality. The Browning story primarily supplies these brief interludes, but to a degree, the story of Henrietta and Captain Cook does so as well. Entertainment also is provided by the refreshingly frivolous Bella, whose ostentatiousness reveals an aspect of the father not brought out by any of the other characters.

Because his primary intention was not simply to dramatize the romance between two gifted poets, Besier was confronted by the problem of subordinating the literary activities and interests of his principal characters to the analysis of a family's spirit in the household of a tyrannical father. Besier's dramatic maturity is evident in the masterful manner in which he resolves the problem. He employs the play's various references to poetry either to delineate character or to move the plot forward. When Barrett, for example, is reflecting on what she perceives to be the obscure nature of

Browning's poetry ("No—it's quite beyond me! I give it up!"), the audience is prepared for the tender, more intimate scene in which the shared poetic sensibilities of the lovers establish their rapport and suggest their determination to overcome the obstacles that life sets before them.

The play is divided into the classical five acts, as opposed to the more modern three, and each act is given a title: "Porter in a Tankard," "Mr. Robert Browning," "Robert," "Henrietta," and "Papa." All five acts revolve around the commanding presence (or absence) of the father: act 1, his insistence that Barrett drink porter as medicine; act 2, the appearance of his as yet unknown opponent; act 3, Browning's deepening hold on Barrett's affections; act 4, the father's cruelty to Henrietta and Barrett's realization that she must agree with Browning's wedding plans; and act 5, Barrett's final interview with her father, in which she is so revolted by his words that she becomes distraught. Indeed, the father's influence, even when he is not actually onstage, is so extensive, so tangible, that in many ways he, and not Barrett or Browning, is the main character of the play.

Much of Besier's portrayal of the father accords with the known facts of his life and personality. Not only did he terrorize his children, but also he prohibited them to marry and actually disowned three who disobeyed his injunction. In other details, however, Besier used dramatic license. He collapsed the actual time of Barrett's romance with Browning from one year to approximately four months, and he inserted into the dialogue a remark that was not to achieve acclaim until some years later. When Browning finally achieved recognition, Browning societies were established all over England for the express purpose of discussing and analyzing his poetry. Browning, after receiving a letter from a member of one of these societies asking for an explanation of one particularly obscure poetic passage, replied: "When that passage was written, only God and Robert Browning understood it. Now only God understands it." Besier felt at liberty to include the remark in a conversation between Barrett and Browning, thereby reinforcing the warmth and the humanness of their relationship.

The reader can trace in *The Barretts of Wimpole Street* the change in Barrett's feelings for her father and, at the same time, her increasing health and desire for life as she comes increasingly under the influence of Robert Browning. When the first act begins, she is "so tired—tired—tired of it all," and later she admits that she "was often impatient for the end." To Browning, she declares that love can have no place in the life of a dying woman. Three months later, however, she is miraculously revitalized, full of energy and desirous of experiencing nature's passionate embrace, all of which she attributes not to the doctors or the porter but to Browning himself: "I wanted to live—eagerly, desperately, passionately—and only because life meant you—you—and the sight of your face, and the sound of your voice, and the touch of your hand." Carried along by Browning's inspiring vitality, she nevertheless continues to resist the idea of marriage simply because of the difference in their ages. When she views her father's brutal treatment of Henrietta, however, she becomes more sure about marriage, and following her final interview with her father, when she realizes that he is "not like other men," all of her doubts disappear. With a self-assurance and determination not earlier evident, she whispers to herself: "I must go at once—I must go—I must go. . . ."

Besier raised *The Barretts of Wimpole Street* from what could have been mere sentimentalism to the genuinely dramatic. The result was a play that has continued to please audiences on stage, television, and film.

Bibliography

Hochman, Stanley, ed. *McGraw-Hill Encyclopedia of World Drama.* 2d ed. Vol. 2. New York: McGraw-Hill, 1984. This biographical article covers the highlights of the playwright's career in the United States, including the production of *The Virgin Goddess* and *Lady Patricia.* The article features a photograph of Besier and Katharine Cornell in the first American production of *The Barretts of Wimpole Street.*

Hutchens, John. "The Actor's Month: Broadway in Review." *Theatre Arts Monthly* 15 (April, 1931): 273-277. Hutchens reviews the original American performance of Besier's most famous play, *The Barretts of Wimpole Street*, which featured Katharine Cornell as Elizabeth Barrett Browning. He reveals that Besier's script attributes incestuous impulses to Barrett's father as the root of his tyrannical behavior. At the time, this play was considered a shocking and psychologically advanced twist to a well-known romantic tale.

Isaacs, Edith J. R. "A Merry Feast of Play-Going." *Theatre Arts Monthly* 19 (April, 1935): 258. Isaacs critiques the revival of *The Barretts of Wimpole Street* that featured many of the original actors. She says that Besier's script "comes back enriched in character and story and presentation. It is distinctly a better play than it was," implying that Besier may have revised it for its second run. She says that this has helped "a play of medium worth grow to its present stature."

Skinner, Richard Dana. "The Barretts of Wimpole Street." *Commonweal* 13 (February 25, 1931): 469. *Commonweal* is a Catholic periodical and its theater critic is predictably conservative. Skinner applauds the romance of Besier's *The Barretts of Wimpole Street*, yet he condemns the psychosexual abnormality of the character of Edward Moulton Barrett as "gratuitous." He calls the abnormality "a discordant note in what is otherwise one of the most beguiling stage romances of recent years."

Van Doren, Mark. "Drama: Early Victorian Father." *The Nation* 132 (February 25, 1931): 224-225. Van Doren compliments *The Barretts of Wimpole Street* by saying that "Mr. Besier had the almost unique inspiration to make his famous hero and heroine behave as if they did not know they were famous. . . . This was delightful." He states that the play's weakness lies in Besier's characterization of the father as a perfect, predictable monster.

A. Gordon Van Ness III
(Updated by *Pamela Canal*)

ROBERT MONTGOMERY BIRD

Born: New Castle, Delaware; February 5, 1806
Died: Philadelphia, Pennsylvania; January 23, 1854

Principal drama

The Cowled Lover, wr. 1827, pb. 1941; *Caridorf: Or, The Avenger*, wr. 1827, pb. 1941; *'Twas All for the Best*, wr. 1827, pb. 1941; *The City Looking Glass: A Philadelphia Comedy*, wr. 1829, pr., pb. 1933; *Pelopidas: Or, The Fall of Polemarchs*, wr. 1830, pb. 1919; *The Gladiator*, pr. 1831, pb. 1919; *Oralloossa: Son of the Incas*, pr. 1832, pb. 1919; *The Broker of Bogotá*, pr. 1834, pb. 1917; *The Life and Dramatic Works*, pb. 1919 (includes *Pelopidas*, *The Gladiator*, *Oralloossa*); *News of the Night: Or, A Trip to Niagara*, pr. 1929, pb. 1941; *The Cowled Lover and Other Plays*, pb. 1941 (includes *Caridorf*, *'Twas All for the Best*, *News of the Night*).

Other literary forms

Robert Montgomery Bird is better known as a novelist than as a dramatist. In his dramas, Bird was clearly moving toward the subject matter that would form the basis for his two earliest novels, *Calavar: Or, The Knight of the Conquest* (1834) and *The Infidel: Or, The Fall of Mexico* (1835)—romances dealing with Mexican Indians. Yet Bird is better remembered for his novels that are set in indigenous North American settings—*The Hawks of Hawk-Hollow: A Tradition of Pennsylvania* (1835) and *Nick of the Woods: Or, The Jibbenainosay, a Tale of Kentucky* (1837)—than he is for his Mexican romances. In addition, Bird published a volume of short fiction, *Peter Pilgrim: Or, A Rambler's Recollections* (1838), and several works of nonfiction, including *Sketch of the Life, Public Services, and Character of Major Thomas Stockton of New-Castle, the Candidate for the Whig Party for the Office of Governor of Delaware* (1844) and *A Brief Review of the Career, Character, and Campaigns of Zachary Taylor* (1848).

Achievements

How one ranks the achievement of Bird depends on the backdrop against which one is viewing him. Compared with American dramatists since Eugene O'Neill, Bird must be viewed as a less than successful artist whose plays were somewhat contrived and stereotyped. Viewed against a different backdrop, that of the dramatists of the first half of the nineteenth century, Bird figures as one of the two or three most promising figures in the American drama of his time. It must be remembered that American theater audiences were unsophisticated and, at times, uncouth during this period. Bird himself called them "foolish and vulgar," and he was probably not much off the mark. Refined and cultivated Americans did not go to the theater. British audiences were not much better than those in the United States, and audiences in both countries preferred to attend performances of Shakespearean plays rather than performances of contemporary drama. Bird knew his audiences, and if he ever forgot their salient characteristics, Edwin Forrest, the great actor of the day, was always nearby to remind him, as Forrest's notations in surviving manuscripts of Bird's dramas attest.

Certainly, Bird's earliest plays are dramatically substandard. Some of them have never been performed and a few had their first performances only after Arthur Hobson Quinn drew scholarly attention to Bird, in his 1916 article in *The Nation*, "Dramatic Works of Robert Montgomery Bird," and in his compendious *A History of American Drama from the Beginning to the Civil War* (1923). It must be borne in mind, however, that Bird was only twenty-one or twenty-two years old when he wrote his earliest plays and that he was at the time a student in medical school, which surely distracted him substantially from his literary pursuits.

Bird began to come into his own as an American dramatist in 1830 with Forrest's acceptance as a prize play in the dramatic contest that the actor sponsored annually of *Pelopidas*, a work surging with the Romantic spirit that Bird brought to American drama. Although *Pelopidas* was never produced during Bird's lifetime, Forrest continued to hold ownership of the play. The next year, Forrest awarded the dramatic prize to Bird's *The Gladiator*, which turned out to be Bird's most popular play with audiences and which certainly vies with *The Broker of Bogotá* as his best drama. Forrest took *The Gladiator* to London in 1836, where it was received less enthusiastically than was Forrest himself as Spartacus. Nevertheless, it is significant that this was the first American drama to be transported to England. The play was performed at the Theatre Royal in Drury Lane in a run that began on October 17, and despite the less than warm reception it received, its author was elected to honorary membership in the English Dramatic Authors' Society within a fortnight of its opening.

Two more of Bird's plays were to win Forrest's drama prizes in the years immediately following the award given to *The Gladiator*. *Oralloossa*, one of Bird's Latin American plays, won the prize in 1832, and the following year *The Broker of Bogotá*, also set in Latin America, received the coveted award.

Bird had great literary ambitions. By the time he was twenty-two, he had a clearly laid plan for his career as a writer. He intended initially to establish himself as a dramatist and had already sketched the plans for fifty-five plays he hoped to write. Once established as a dramatist, he planned to write a series of romances, and finally he anticipated devoting the talents of his later years to the writing of history.

It is impossible to say whether Bird might have followed his plan had he not had a severe falling out with Edwin Forrest in 1837, confirming for him his earlier contention that one cannot fill one's purse with the proceeds that the writer receives from drama. Forrest was growing rich on Bird's plays, and Bird received little more than the prize money (one thousand dollars in each instance) awarded to the winning play. No copyright laws, as we know them today, existed in Bird's time to protect playwrights from the sort of exploitation that Bird was experiencing.

Bird turned his efforts to writing romances, the first two of which, *Calavar* and *The Infidel*, were set in Mexico and were well received. In 1835, Benjamin H. Brewster turned *The Infidel* into a play. Bird's novels *The Hawks of Hawk-Hollow* and *Nick of the Woods*, however, had the kind of indigenous North American setting for which Americans longed and for which many American intellectuals were calling in their writings—Washington Irving in his "English Writers on America" (1820), William Cullen Bryant in his *Lectures on Poetry* (1884), William Ellery Channing in his "On National Literature" (1830), Henry Wadsworth Longfellow in his "The Defence of Poetry" (1832), and, most notably, Ralph Waldo Emerson in his Phi Beta Kappa address, "The American Scholar" (1837). These two novels established Bird as an outstanding writer capable of dealing seriously and successfully with indigenous American themes. *The Hawks of Hawk-Hollow* told about the life of a Tory family in Pennsylvania a year after the Battle of Yorktown; *Nick of the Woods* told the tale of Nathan Slaughter, an Indian-hating Quaker living in Kentucky, who, because of his Quaker pacifism, refused to join his Kentucky neighbors in 1782 in taking up arms against the Indians. Given the temper of Bird's times, one would have to consider his ability to produce such writing as his outstanding literary achievement.

In the fifteen years between the publication of his last novel, *The Adventures of Robin Day* (1839), and his death, Bird, afflicted by recurrent ill health, wrote only two more significant works of any length: his sketch of Major Thomas Stockton in 1844 and *A Brief Review of the Career, Character, and Campaigns of Zachary Taylor* in 1848. He also revised his dramas, hoping that he might publish them; Edwin Forrest, however, would not relinquish his ownership of the works, so that Bird was unable to follow through on this idea.

Toward the end of his life, Bird joined forces with George H. Boker, renowned for his drama *Francesca da Rimini* (pr. 1855), to agitate for a copyright law that would protect writers. It was not until two years after Bird's death, however, that the Copyright Act of 1856 was finally passed. Certainly its passage must be numbered among Bird's notable achievements, because the passage of this act made careers in writing more attractive to Americans than they had previously been.

Biography

Robert Montgomery Bird's father died in 1810, when Robert was only four years old. Because the elder Bird was bankrupt at the time of his death, his young son went to live in the home of his kindly uncle, Nicholas Van Dyke, who had been a member of the Council for Safety in 1776, a framer of the constitution of the state of Delaware, and president of the state of Delaware from 1783 until 1786. Bird remained in his uncle's house for ten years. The young boy led a relatively happy life with his uncle and with his uncle's family, although he was not overly happy in school and was subjected to frequent beatings. When his uncle discovered this, he withdrew Robert from the New Castle Academy, which the boy had been attending. Bird had a passion for books and for reading, and he drew heavily upon the resources of the New Castle Library Company during these early years of his life. He became interested in music and in writing during this period, and by the time he moved to Philadelphia in 1820 to live with his mother and to attend a school run by Mr. Pardon Davis, he had written considerable verse. In Philadelphia, he became interested in drawing, an avocation that he continued to pursue in his later years.

Bird returned to New Castle in 1821 and enrolled in the same New Castle Academy from which his uncle had earlier withdrawn him. While there, he wrote some of his earliest descriptive pieces. He remained at New Castle Academy until 1823, when he entered Germantown Academy to pursue courses preparatory to his entering the University of Pennsylvania as a medical student. In the summer between leaving Germantown Academy and entering the university, Bird studied medicine, as was the custom in his day, with a practicing physician, Dr. Joseph Parrish.

Bird attended the University from 1824 until 1827, receiving the M.D. degree upon the completion of his studies. By that time, he had published a great deal of poetry in *Philadelphia Monthly Magazine* and had begun to write plays, although they all remained fragmentary at that point. He had also laid specific plans for his literary career and had begun reading widely in classical literature, in Shakespearean and Jacobean drama, and in Latin American history, archaeology, and literature as a means of implementing his literary plans.

Life as a physician did not appeal to Bird, although in 1827 he established himself as a doctor in Philadelphia and had a substantial number of patients. After a year in medical practice, during which time he completed a comedy, *'Twas All for the Best*, and two tragedies, *The Cowled Lover* and *Caridorf*, he left the medical profession to support himself by writing.

In 1828, Bird began work on three more plays, "King Philip," "The Three Dukes," and "Giannone." He also began work on his long poem, "The Cave," and on a novel, "The Volunteers." Although none of these works was ever produced or published, within a short time Bird had also finished *The City Looking Glass*, a comedy that would finally be staged in 1933, some hundred years after it was written.

Bird was working so unrelentingly that his health began to be adversely affected, and in 1829, he sought diversion in painting as a means of regaining his health. At the end of that summer, he began a long journey to what was then considered frontier territory, Pittsburgh and Cincinnati. He spent the winter in Cincinnati with John Grimes, an artist, and his circle. During that trip, Bird visited Kentucky and imbibed some of the local color that later was to appear in his most successful novel, *Nick of the Woods*.

Upon returning to Philadelphia in 1830, Bird learned that Edwin Forrest was again offering an annual prize, which he had instituted in 1828, for the best play written by an American author. The prize was one thousand dollars, and Forrest, who was to act in the prize play, was to own the property in return for awarding the prize. Bird entered the contest with *Pelopidas*, a classical tragedy set in Thebes, and this play won the prize quite handily. Forrest ultimately decided against producing the play, because it did not have the sort of clearly defined central character that he required in any play that was to be a vehicle for his talent. This being the case, Bird wrote for him another play, *The Gladiator*, which was declared a prize play but for which Forrest did not give the author another one thousand dollars in prize money, reasoning that this play was a substitute for *Pelopidas*.

The Gladiator provided Forrest with the perfect role, that of Spartacus, and the play opened to enormous acclaim in New York on September 26, 1831. It soon had played in both Boston and Philadelphia, and it always played to full houses and enthusiastic audiences. By the time Bird died in 1854, *The Gladiator* had been presented more than one thousand times, and its success was to continue until the turn of the century. Forrest grew rich from the proceeds, none of which he shared with the author.

Forrest and Bird were born in the same year, and they became not only close professional associates but also close friends. Bird was to win two more of Forrest's prizes, one for *Oralloossa* in 1832 and one for *The Broker of Bogotá* in 1834. In all, Forrest awarded nine prizes for American plays, and Bird took four of them, although he was paid for only three.

In 1833, Bird and Forrest traveled together for some months. They had planned to go to Mexico; they turned back at New Orleans, however, because of a cholera epidemic. Bird went on to Nashville, where he had a reunion with John Grimes, with whom he went to Mammoth Cave, which the two explored fully. As a result of this exploration, Bird returned to his work on the long poem "The Cave," which had occupied him earlier. He began work on *The Broker of Bogotá*, his last drama, which he completed the next year.

By that time, Bird had concluded that he could not support himself as a playwright, and he decided to devote his time to writing romances. His explanation was that "novels are much easier sorts of things and immortalize one's pocket much sooner. A tragedy takes, or should take, as much labor as two romances; and one comedy as much as six tragedies."

Drawing on the extensive reading he had done about Latin America, Bird wrote *Calavar* in 1834, following it the next year with *The Infidel: Or, The Fall of Mexico*. These novels were meticulously researched and found a ready audience, but Bird was to find his real métier in *The Hawks of Hawk-Hollow*, published in the same year as *The Infidel*, and in *Nick of the Woods*, published in 1837.

Bird set *The Hawks of Hawk-Hollow* in the area around the Delaware Water Gap on the Pennsylvania-New Jersey border, a region with which he had a particular affinity. A second edition of the novel was released in the first year of the book's publication, and that was followed by three English editions of the work by 1842. Because international copyright laws did not exist at that time, Bird did not profit financially from the English editions.

Nick of the Woods was published in 1837, the year of Bird's marriage to Mary Mayer, and was a resounding success. By 1839, the novel had been dramatized by J. T. Haines, and two other dramatizations of it were to follow, one in 1856 and another in 1940. *Nick of the Woods* was also translated into several foreign languages.

In 1837, largely at his wife's urging, Bird tried to convince Forrest to pay him some six thousand dollars that Bird believed was rightfully his. Forrest argued bitterly with Bird over this debt and stormed out of Bird's house, claiming to have complete ownership of Bird's major dramas—a claim that Forrest exercised through Bird's remaining years. Bird was never to write another play, although he revised his dramas in 1843, planning to publish them. That hope, however, was thwarted by Forrest's claim to exclusive rights to the plays.

Afflicted by a complete nervous collapse in 1840, Bird turned to farming on acreage he had bought two years earlier near Elkton, Maryland. He underwent substantial losses of his crops because of violent weather, but his health improved greatly during this interlude of intense physical activity as a farmer. In 1841, Bird was well enough to return to Philadelphia, where he had been appointed a professor at Pennsylvania Medical College, a post in which he served with high distinction until 1843, when the medical college disbanded.

Meanwhile, Bird had become active in politics. He attended the Whig Convention in Delaware as a delegate in 1842 and felt reasonably sure that he would be nominated as a representative to the United States Congress. This plan went awry when George Brydges Rodney, the incumbent, who had intended not to run for reelection, changed his mind, leaving no place for Bird on the Whig ticket. Nevertheless, Bird received a minor political appointment in 1846 when he was named to be a director of the New Castle Branch of the Farmers' National Bank. The following year, Bird was nominated for the positions of assistant director and librarian of the

Smithsonian Institution but was not appointed. Using thirty thousand dollars borrowed from his close friend Senator John M. Clayton, Bird bought a one-third interest in Philadelphia's *North American*, a newspaper that thrived under Bird's editorship, although the paper's success was marred by the mismanagement of his partners. Bird gave his full energies to his newspaper work and was considered an excellent literary editor.

During the presidential campaign of 1848, Bird was a vigorous supporter of Zachary Taylor, whose biography he wrote specifically to aid the candidate in his campaign. Bird hoped for some sort of government appointment, but, despite a meeting with President Taylor in 1849, Bird was not appointed to office. He spent his final years working hard on the *North American* to the detriment of his own health, as well as working with George H. Boker to help bring about copyright laws that would protect authors from the sort of exploitation that he, Bird, had suffered at the hands of Forrest and of English publishers who had pirated his work.

Bird was in ill health during the latter months of 1853. His condition worsened in the first days of 1854, and on January 23, he died of a cerebral hemorrhage at his country residence, Kittatiny House, in Delaware Water Gap. His wife and fifteen-year-old son, Frederick Mayer Bird, survived him.

Analysis

Robert Montgomery Bird's earliest plays were essentially derivative, at times suggestive of the closet dramas of the Elizabethan Revival, at times recalling Ben Jonson's plays or the Restoration drama of William Congreve, with whose work Bird was well acquainted. Most of the plays of this early period are set in such romantic locations as Spain ("The Three Dukes"), Italy ("Giannone"), or other foreign places. They depend heavily upon highly intricate plots in which the key characters are amply disguised; mistaken identity is central to the resolution of the plot, and coincidence is a *sine qua non* of the plays' rising action and denouement. Like many of the Restoration dramatists, Bird selected names that were either ironic—for example, "Nathan Slaughter" for a Quaker who refused to fight in *Nick of the Woods*—or descriptive—Sluggardly, the innkeeper; Ha'penny, the debtor; and Agony, the miserly uncle. These plays are no worse than much of the Restoration drama that sometimes served as Bird's model, but they can hardly be called good.

'Twas All for the Best is a complicated comedy of manners set in England. The language is stilted to the point of being painful to the modern reader. The plot revolves around Sir Noel Nozlebody, who steals his brother's daughter, rears her as his own child, and declares his own daughter to be a foundling. This play contains some scenes that are essentially tragic and that seem to have no place in a play that purports to be a comedy. In

'Twas All for the Best, Bird was not yet in control of his medium.

Similarly complicated in plot is another Bird farce of the same general period, *News of the Night*, which is set in Philadelphia but which follows a classical Roman story line with strong overtones of the comic spirit of Jonson. This play, with its stereotypical props of old chests, rope ladders, and women dressed as men, was first produced by the Columbia University Laboratory Players in New York on November 2, 1929.

The City Looking Glass, first published in an edition by Arthur Hobson Quinn in 1933, was subtitled *A Philadelphia Comedy*. It is ostensibly about the seamy side of life in Philadelphia, but there seems to be little that is American about it. Again, the plot is reminiscent of Jonson and involves two low-life creatures, Ravin and Ringfinger, who pursue two commonplace young ladies, only to discover that one of these girls, Emma, is really the daughter of a highly respected and wealthy Virginia gentleman. Act 4 provides small glimpses into Southern life and into the views of the times, but except for that act, the play has little relationship to anything authentically American. This drama was first performed by the Zelosophic Society of the University of Pennsylvania on January 20, 1933.

"The Fanatick," based on Charles Brockden Brown's Gothic novel *Wieland* (1798), was planned but was never completed. "The Three Dukes" and "Giannone" also exist only in fragments which are a part of the Robert Montgomery Bird Collection at the University of Pennsylvania; "Giannone" is the most promising of these fragmentary plays. It is interesting to note that in these works, members of the nobility speak in blank verse while the other characters speak in prose.

Bird all but completed two tragedies, *The Cowled Lover* and *Caridorf*. *The Cowled Lover* is modeled after William Shakespeare's *Romeo and Juliet*. The ardent Raymond disguises himself as a monk in order to be near his beloved, Rosalia. Ultimately, he and Rosalia are killed by the young woman's father. The play is highly Romantic and shows the strong Gothic influence of some of the authors Bird was reading at the time—Percy Bysshe Shelley and Lord Byron, for example.

Caridorf suffers from having a quite unconvincing hero, a man who refuses to come to the bedside of his dying father and who first seduces Genevra, then upbraids her for having lost her chastity. The audience is asked to overlook these inhumane acts and see through to Caridorf's essential goodness, a demand which strains credulity.

With *Pelopidas*, Bird showed signs of maturing into a significant playwright. Gone are the stereotypical plots of his earlier plays; gone are the heavy-handed props of a play such as *News of the Night*. *Pelopidas* has a typical Romantic setting, that of Thebes after the Spartans had conquered and grasped political power in the city. The tale of Pelopidas is told in Plutarch's *Parallel Lives*, which is the basic source for Bird's play. Bird, however, showing excellent critical judgment, distorted the Plutarchan version to suit his own artistic needs.

Pelopidas was a great hero of Thebes, and, with the conquest of the city by Sparta, he was forced into exile. His wife remained behind in the city, which was now controlled by four polemarchs. In Plutarch's account, these polemarchs were native Thebans who were appointed to their dictatorial positions by the conquerors. Bird, however, made two of the polemarchs, Philip and Archias, Spartan, thereby setting up an interesting contrast between them and the two Theban polemarchs, Leontidas and Philidas. Bird also established contrasts within the two pairs. Philip is the typical Spartan, businesslike, aggressive, suspicious; Archias is trusting, fun-loving, somewhat lazy. Of the two Thebans, Leontidas is a libertine whose actions really trigger the action of the plot; Philidas is a more complex character, a seeming traitor to his city who is in truth working with his fellow Thebans to unseat the Spartans.

Pelopidas leaves his exile and sneaks back into Thebes, drawn irresistibly to the city because word has reached him that Leontidas is trying to seduce his wife, Sibylla. Upon his return, it becomes known that Philidas, the seeming turncoat, is planning a feast with the Spartans and that he is plotting their destruction. During the very tense banquet scene, the Spartans come close to learning what is about to happen; Bird manages to keep the suspense high until Pelopidas arrives and sees that the Spartans are dispatched. Pelopidas returns to the prison-room of his house just in time to save his wife and son from being murdered by the evil Leontidas, whom he kills.

Pelopidas is well drawn. He is a brave, rash idealist. When he first returns to Thebes, he brashly tries to rescue his wife and is captured by the enemy, only to escape and, chastened, make his more calculated and successful attempt at the rescue.

Edwin Forrest appreciated the dramaticality of *Pelopidas*, but he never allowed the play to be performed, because the role of Philidas tended to overshadow the leading role, in which Forrest would have been cast. When William E. Burton, manager of Philadelphia's National Theater, wanted to produce *Pelopidas* in 1840, Bird demurred, despite the generosity of Burton's terms, because he did not wish to enter into a disagreeable fray with Forrest, who claimed ownership of the property.

Had the Copyright Act of 1856 been passed twenty-five years earlier, *The Gladiator* would have made Bird an exceptionally wealthy man. As it turned out, Forrest reaped the full benefit of this play's success, while Bird received nothing for it. The story of Spartacus was well-known in the early nineteenth century, and Bird adapted this popular tale to serve his purposes in *The Gladiator*. Spartacus is a Thracian, recently captured by the Romans. His fame as a fighter has preceded him to Rome, where

Phasarius, one of Rome's most renowned gladiators, is plotting with the other gladiators to overthrow the city while its generals and soldiers are away. Phasarius, however, delays the planned overthrow because he wants the challenge of fighting Spartacus. Spartacus agrees to the combat because by doing so he can win the freedom of his wife and child, who have been enslaved.

The combat is arranged, and the gladiators enter the ring, but upon seeing each other, they realize that they are brothers. They lay down their arms, reunite, and organize the gladiators into an army that is soon on the brink of conquering Rome. At this point, Phasarius wants to destroy Rome utterly, whereas Spartacus wishes only to take his family and return to Thrace. Phasarius, like Leontidas in *Pelopidas*, wants to seduce Julia, the daughter of a high Roman official and a captive of the gladiatorial forces. Spartacus intervenes and saves Julia. The gladiators are divided between loyalty to Phasarius and loyalty to Spartacus, and thus the Romans are able to defeat them. When Spartacus' wife and child are killed, largely through Phasarius' duplicity, Spartacus loses his will to live. Although offered a pardon from the Romans, who are grateful for his protection of Julia, Spartacus chooses to die with his sword in his hand.

Like *Pelopidas*, *The Gladiator* is concerned centrally with the human quest for liberty. Led by Spartacus as the strong, central hero, the gladiators are glorified for rebelling against their oppressors. Like many Americans of his day, Bird could appreciate the impulse toward freedom in the classical characters he idealized in this play, while at the same time supporting slavery in his own country and refusing to buy property in Philadelphia, opting instead for the eastern shore of Maryland, because he feared that Pennsylvania would soon enfranchise black people.

Plays about Indians were popular in America during the 1830's and 1840's. The idea of the noble savage was in the air, and Forrest had already been playing John Augustus Stone's *Metamora* (pr. 1829), which focused on these topics, for two years when he first met Bird. Indeed, in 1836, Forrest gave Bird *Metamora* to revise; although no copy of Bird's revision is extant, it is generally thought that he in essence wrote an entirely new play, the only copy of which he delivered to Forrest. *Oralloossa* was awarded another of Forrest's drama prizes and was a resounding success when it was first performed. Forrest did not perform the play often after its initial run, partly because it was an expensive play to stage and partly because he was more at home in the role of Spartacus in *The Gladiator*.

Oralloossa bears certain surface resemblances to *Pelopidas*. In it, the Peruvian Incas are pitted against Pizarro's invading forces. Pizarro and his young compatriot Almagro are roughly comparable to Philip and Archias in *Pelopidas*, while the two Incas, Oralloossa and Manco, are roughly comparable to Philidas and Leontidas. Oralloossa serves both Pizarro and

Almagro simultaneously, but he is planning the downfall of each. As in *Pelopidas*, the crucial scene is a banquet at which Pizarro's forces are to dispatch Almagro. Oralloossa, however, who has put Pizarro up to this, has also arranged that Almagro will first kill Pizarro. Only the latter event comes to pass, and Almagro, who loves Oralloossa's sister, Ooallie, survives.

Oralloossa and Ooallie are both imprisoned by the Spanish because Manco has betrayed them, but Oralloossa escapes. So infuriated is Oralloossa at his fellow Inca, Manco, that he forsakes his kinsmen and tells the new Spanish viceroy, De Castro, where Manco and Almagro are hiding. Meanwhile, Oralloossa's sister Ooallie is buried alive and dies, because the priest who is supposed to save her from this fate never arrives. Oralloossa kills Almagro and then dies himself, leaving the Christian Spanish firmly in charge of the pagan Incas.

The play presents some extremely intense moments, but the climax comes so early in the action that the last act seems unbearably anticlimactic. *Oralloossa* might better have been a three-act play, ending shortly after Pizarro's murder, but three-act plays were not in vogue at the time.

The Broker of Bogotá, Bird's last play, is better crafted than *Oralloossa*; many regard it as his finest play. It is set in Bogotá, in the Spanish territory of New Grenada, which comprised present-day Colombia, Ecuador, Panama, and Venezuela. The play's protagonist is Febro, a bourgeois moneylender who has two sons of opposite temperaments. Ramon is unbridled and unruly, although he shows regret at times when his demeanor causes his father pain. He is counterbalanced by a much more dutiful brother, Francisco, who is a comfort to his father. A daughter, Leonor, is in love with the viceroy's son, Fernando. In a plot that runs rather like that of an Italian opera, Ramon falls in love with Juana, but Juana's father will not permit Ramon, who has been disowned by his own father, to pay court to his daughter.

At this point, the villain enters in the person of the nobleman Cabarero; he convinces Ramon to steal from his father's safe, the key to which he has just found, a substantial sum of money that the viceroy has left with Febro for safekeeping. Coincidentally, right at this point, Febro is considering a reconciliation with his errant son, but Ramon is unaware of this. To complicate matters further, Febro is accused of the theft and is brought before the viceroy. Febro has no defense unless Ramon is willing to admit to his own guilt, and he does not have the strength of character to do this. Just at this point, the distraught Febro is told that his daughter has eloped with a suitor.

All might have ended happily because, through Juana, it is revealed that Ramon, not Febro, is the thief, and at the same time it is revealed that the lover with whom Leonor has eloped is the viceroy's son. In the tradition of

Elizabethan tragedy, however, Bird cannot allow this to happen: Ramon commits suicide, and Febro dies.

The Broker of Bogotá is contrived, as were most of the plays of its period. Nevertheless, the play has a great deal to recommend it. The trial scene has much of the dramatic tension of a modern television mystery; Febro's fatherly efforts to defend Ramon when his guilt becomes known are well presented. Here, Bird's characters are multidimensional, in contrast to the relatively stereotyped figures of his earlier works. Finally, the basic conflict between the father and son, out of which the central action of the play develops, is convincing and tenable.

Although he cannot be classified among the greatest authors the United States has produced, Bird was a highly gifted, ambitious literary figure who had a clear sense of what he hoped to accomplish artistically. His writings brought him considerable celebrity in his own time and have won for him an enduring place in America's literary history.

Other major works

NOVELS: *Calavar: Or, The Knight of the Conquest*, 1834; *The Infidel: Or, The Fall of Mexico*, 1835; *The Hawks of Hawk-Hollow: A Tradition of Pennsylvania*, 1835; *Sheppard Lee*, 1836; *Nick of the Woods: Or, The Jibbenainosay, a Tale of Kentucky*, 1837; *The Adventures of Robin Day*, 1839.

SHORT FICTION: *Peter Pilgrim: Or, A Rambler's Recollections*, 1838.

NONFICTION: *Sketch of the Life, Public Services, and Character of Major Thomas Stockton of New-Castle, the Candidate for the Whig Party for the Office of Governor of Delaware*, 1844; *A Brief Review of the Career, Character, and Campaigns of Zachary Taylor*, 1848.

Bibliography

Bird, Mary Mayer. *Life of Robert Montgomery Bird.* Edited by C. Seymour Thompson. Philadelphia: The University of Pennsylvania Library, 1945. The incomplete biography by Bird's wife, ending two years before his death. The various fragments of her manuscript have been pieced together and augmented by several letters and documents. A straightforward and modest accounting of his life.

Dahl, Curtis. *Robert Montgomery Bird.* New York: Twayne, 1963. Believing that earlier assessments of Bird's literary works have been too laudatory, Dahl examines Bird because of his historical significance, placing his work in the context of the literature of his time. Dahl concludes that although Bird was successful in writing for the theater, he never produced any drama of lasting literary value. Chronology, annotated bibliography, and index.

Foust, Clement E. *The Life and Dramatic Works of Robert Montgomery*

Bird. New York: The Knickerbocker Press, 1919. In this standard biography of Bird, Foust quickly recounts Bird's early life before discussing his major plays and subsequent association with Edwin Forrest. The majority of the book discusses Bird's life and works after the dispute with Forrest that drove him away from the theater. Genealogy, bibliography, and the complete texts of four major plays.

Quinn, Arthur Hobson. *A History of the American Drama from the Beginning to the Civil War.* 2d ed. New York: Appleton-Century-Crofts, 1951. Chronicles Bird, the rise of the Romantic play, and the treatment of nonclassical material in a realistic or idealistic manner. A brief biography describes Bird's dramatic development, including a consideration of his earliest plays, but focusing on the scripts written for Edwin Forrest. The commentary on the scripts is mixed with related biographical events, culminating in Bird's exit from playwriting in 1837 because of his dispute with Forrest over royalties.

Wilson, Garff B. *Three Hundred Years of American Drama.* Englewood Cliffs, N.J.: Prentice-Hall, 1973. Briefly recounts Bird's life and the association of his plays with actor Edwin Forrest. Describes Bird's five major plays, with primary consideration given to *The Broker of Bogotá.* Contains a photograph of Forrest portraying Febro.

R. Baird Shuman
(Updated by *Gerald S. Argetsinger*)

GEORGE H. BOKER

Born: Philadelphia, Pennsylvania; October 6, 1823
Died: Philadelphia, Pennsylvania; January 2, 1890

Principal drama

Calaynos, pb. 1848, pr. 1849; *Anne Boleyn*, pb. 1850; *The Betrothal*, pr. 1850, pb. 1856; *The World a Mask*, pr. 1851, pb. 1940; *Leonor de Guzman*, pr. 1853, pb. 1856; *Francesca da Rimini*, pr. 1855, pb. 1856 (revised); *The Bankrupt*, pr. 1855, pb. 1940; *The Widow's Marriage*, pb. 1856; *Königsmark*, pb. 1869; *Nydia*, wr. 1885, pb. 1929 (early version of *Glaucus*); *Glaucus*, wr. 1885-1886, pb. 1940; *Glaucus and Other Plays*, pb. 1940.

Other literary forms

Although George H. Boker is remembered primarily as a dramatist, he wanted to be remembered as a poet. To this end, he wrote hundreds of poems.

The Book of the Dead, written in 1859 and 1860 and published in 1882, is his vindication of his father's name. After his father, a banker, died, the Girard Bank tried unsuccessfully to sue his estate for more than a half million dollars. The emotion in these 107 poems is sincere and the events prompting the collection are interesting, but the poems are less well crafted than those in Boker's other volumes of poetry.

After Boker ceased to write about the problems of his father's estate, he wrote many poems about the Civil War. Nearly every poem of this type is precisely dated, offering a narrative of a particular battle. Published soon after they were written in periodicals and leaflets, these poems, sentimental yet sincere and richly detailed, inspired patriotism in Northern readers. In 1864, Boker collected his Civil War verse in *Poems of the War*.

Boker's third important collection of poetry, *Sonnets: A Sequence on Profane Love*, comprises poems written between 1857 and 1887, but the work was only published posthumously in 1929. Of the 313 sonnets in the sequence, the first 282 seem to be about one woman, the next thirteen about another, and the last eighteen about a third woman. Written in the Italian form, these sonnets are generally well constructed and evoke intense images. The classical allusions are forced, but the descriptions of nature are powerful. Writing in 1927, Edward Sculley Bradley, the eminent critic who served as Boker's biographer and as editor of the sequence, argued that Henry Wadsworth Longfellow was the only American to equal Boker as a sonneteer.

Achievements

Important American literary figures of the nineteenth century respected

Boker as both a dramatist and a poet. He received praise from William Cullen Bryant, Oliver Wendell Holmes, James Russell Lowell, and Henry Wadsworth Longfellow. He was also elected to the Authors' Club of New York and the American Philosophical Society. Boker failed, however, to achieve comparable recognition from the American public: *Francesca da Rimini* and *The Betrothal* were his only popular plays.

Although fame eluded him, Boker was a master of the romantic tragedy. Romantic tragedy, like classical tragedy, depicts a hero or heroine, usually an admirable aristocrat, who suffers defeat or death because of fate or a fatal character flaw. For example, Leonor, the noble mistress of a king in *Leonor de Guzman*, dies a victim of circumstance and her own determination to see her son crowned king. In *Francesca da Rimini*, Paolo and Francesca, both of royal birth, die because of their predestined love for each other and their inability to assert reason over emotion.

The conventions of romantic tragedy are less rigid than those governing classical tragedy; also, in contrast to classical tragedy, romantic tragedy emphasizes the emotions and personalities of the characters rather than the plot. In *Francesca da Rimini*, the personality of Lanciotto, Francesca's deformed and savage husband, is more interesting than the play's inevitable end. Similarly, Leonor's passionate and forceful personality is more interesting than the palace intrigue.

Other characteristics of romantic tragedy include blank verse and remote, exotic settings. Boker's two best tragedies, *Francesca da Rimini* and *Leonor de Guzman*, are both written in blank verse and take place during the fourteenth century, the former in Italy and the latter in Spain.

William Shakespeare was the finest playwright in the tradition of romantic tragedy. If Boker's works clearly do not belong in such company, he nevertheless wrote romantic tragedies superior to those of any of his contemporaries. The only other American to approach Boker's success with romantic drama was Robert Montgomery Bird, an earlier nineteenth century novelist and playwright. *Francesca da Rimini* marks the end of romantic tragedy as a viable form in America and stands as the best play written by an American before the twentieth century.

Biography

George Henry Boker, a lifelong citizen of Philadelphia, was born in 1823. He attended the College of New Jersey (now Princeton University), where he developed a keen admiration for Shakespeare and other Elizabethan dramatists. He was still at college when he published his first poems. When Boker was graduated in 1842, his father wanted him to be a businessman or diplomat. He tried to study law, but he could not commit himself to a business career and did not pursue law. In 1844, he married Julia Riggs, a woman he had courted for some years. They had three children, but only the first, George, survived into adulthood. This son married but did not have children.

Boker had a literary group of friends, all poets, including Charles Godfrey Leland, Bayard Taylor, Thomas Bailey Aldrich (also editor of the *Atlantic Monthly*), Edmund Clarence Stedman, and Richard H. Stoddard. Boker generously used his wealth and literary influence to help his friends become published writers.

From 1847 to 1853, Boker wrote the bulk of his work. *The Lesson of Life and Other Poems* (1848), containing several sonnets, anticipates his later sequence of sonnets. *Calaynos*, his first play, is a romantic tragedy about a man whose Moorish ancestry is not apparent. It was produced in London in 1849, apparently without the author's permission, and then produced with his permission in the United States in 1851. Angered by a playwright's lack of rights, Boker supported the Dramatic Authors' Bill, which Congress passed in 1856.

Anne Boleyn, Boker's second play, was never produced. His next two plays, which were produced, were *The Betrothal*, a comedy in blank verse, and *The World a Mask*, a social satire written largely in prose. In 1852, he published *The Podesta's Daughter*, a dramatic dialogue. That year he also wrote two more plays, *The Widow's Marriage*, a comedy which was never produced, and *Leonor de Guzman*, a romantic tragedy about two women trying to secure the Castilian throne for their sons. Boker began a sequel to this latter play but never finished it.

In nineteen intense days in March of 1853, Boker wrote his masterpiece, *Francesca da Rimini*, a reworking of Dante's account of Paolo and Francesca. It was first produced with moderate success in 1855. After writing his best play, he wrote one of his worst, *The Bankrupt*. Like *The World a Mask*, it is poorly written and shows Boker's inability to handle a contemporary setting well. Boker had it produced anonymously.

After *The Bankrupt*, Boker's dramatic production slowed down. He published *Plays and Poems* in 1856, a popular collection in two volumes which contained no new works. He labored longer than usual on *Königsmark*, a dramatic sketch never produced. Boker's dramatic career was impeded by a series of events—what appears to have been a long affair with a woman from Philadelphia, a lawsuit against his father's estate, his involvement in the Civil War, and, finally, his work as a diplomat.

From 1857 until 1871, Boker apparently carried on a love affair, and during this time he wrote almost three hundred sonnets in celebration of his love. These sonnets, along with two other short sequences probably inspired by subsequent affairs, were discovered in his daughter-in-law's house after his death and were published in 1929 with the help of his biographer, Edward Sculley Bradley. Boker was also preoccupied by a suit against his father's estate that lasted fifteen years. Soon after Boker's father died, representatives of the bank he had managed initiated a suit against his estate. Although Boker did not share his father's interest in business, he admired his father's business acumen and respected his integrity. Depressed and fearful of bankruptcy, Boker spent 1859 and 1860 writing vindictive poems against his father's enemies.

From 1861 to the end of the Civil War, Boker vigorously supported the Northern position. He wrote many poems in support of the war effort; they were published individually and were instantly successful. Boker had them published as a collection, *Poems of the War*, and they became his most widely read publication. He also helped to organize the Union League, a Philadelphia club in support of the Northern stance. Boker was its first secretary and served in that capacity until he began his diplomatic career. In 1871, Boker began an appointment in Turkey, and in 1875, he became a diplomat in Russia. He and his wife returned to the United States permanently in 1878.

Upon returning home, Boker finally achieved some of the recognition he had sought. He became president of the Union League and was elected to both the Authors' Club of New York and the American Philosophical Society. He also published previously written works—*The Book of the Dead*, comprising his poems in support of his father, and a reprint of *Plays and Poems*, in 1883. Most important, however, in 1883, Lawrence Barrett, a famous nineteenth century actor, successfully revived *Francesca da Rimini*.

Boker wrote only two more plays after his return to the United States, *Nydia*, a tragedy, and *Glaucus*, apparently a revision of *Nydia*. Neither version was produced. Ill for the last three years of his life, Boker died of a heart attack in 1890.

Analysis

Francesca da Rimini, in spite of its imitative blank verse, is the best dramatic rendering of the love story recorded both by Giovanni Boccaccio and by Dante. The first version of George H. Boker's masterpiece, written in 1853, was never published; the final version was published in 1856. There are important differences between these two versions. In the published version, the participants in the love triangle—Lanciotto, Francesca, and Paolo—are emphasized more or less equally. In the 1853 version, in contrast, Lanciotto was the central figure. Further, the love scenes involving Francesca and Paolo, including the one immediately preceding the consummation of their love, were largely absent in the 1853 version. These changes served not only to decrease Lanciotto's importance but also to increase the audience's sympathy for the two young lovers.

Because it is shorter, the 1853 version moves more briskly to the conclusion. For example, in the 1853 version, Boker immediately prepares the audience for the climax by having Francesca, the inadvertent cause of

Lanciotto and Paolo's strife, appear in the first scene. In the 1856 version, however, Francesca does not appear until act 2, and Boker uses the first act to reveal the personalities of the two brothers and their relationship to each other. On the other hand, the published play is generally superior to the earlier version because it allows for richer characterizations. Both versions, though, to Boker's credit, emphasize character rather than plot.

Paolo loves his brother, but, an idler, he has not the discipline necessary to ignore his feelings for his brother's wife. Francesca, while she has the audience's sympathy, is too much a victim to have their unreserved admiration. Forced to become engaged to a man she has never met, she is deceived about Lanciotto's hideous appearance by the three most important people in her life—her father, Guido; her servant and confidante, Ritta; and the man with whom she has just fallen in love, Paolo. She recognizes that Lanciotto has a more noble character than Paolo, but she is nevertheless repelled by his deformities. She displays free will in a single scene only, one not present in the 1853 version, where she, more than Paolo, seeks consummation of their love. Francesca becomes a victim again in the last scene when Lanciotto, in an effort to force Paolo to kill him, kills her.

Lanciotto, a more complex figure than the young lovers, both repels and attracts the audience. He first appears as a hideously deformed and vicious, almost barbaric, warrior. While his father pities the defeated citizens of Ravenna, Lanciotto wants to see the city burn and its women crying. An uncivilized man, he is also deeply superstitious. He believes a warning by his nurse that his blood will be mixed with Guido's, and later he fears doom when he thinks he sees blood on his sword. Paolo and Maletesta, the brothers' father, are more civilized than he and chide him for his superstitions, but he remains convinced that evil awaits him.

Juxtaposed to Lanciotto's savagery and superstition are his deeply felt emotions, which gain the audience's sympathy. The audience understands his desire to destroy Ravenna when he reveals the reason for such rage: His first memory is of the death of his nurse's husband at the hands of a citizen of Ravenna. Lanciotto ironically evokes the most sympathy from the audience when he discloses how much he hates his deformed body for creating fear and pity in others. He also wins the audience over when he says he will not force Francesca, who so obviously loathes his sight, to touch him.

The last act shows Lanciotto at war with himself, fighting both his savagery and his love for his brother. When Lanciotto learns that his brother and wife have betrayed him, he, the savage soldier, feels that he cannot live with such dishonor unavenged. He races to the lovers, only to find he cannot attack his beloved brother. He asks the lovers to lie about their adultery. When they refuse, he tries to goad Paolo into killing him, but Paolo, never a fighter, remains passive. Even when Lanciotto stabs Francesca, Paolo refuses to act. Finally, Lanciotto kills his brother, too. Momentarily, he is relieved to have avenged his honor, but as the play concludes, he falls upon Paolo, declaring that he "loved him more than honor—more than life." Paolo, paralyzed by his love for Lanciotto, cannot save himself or Francesca. Lanciotto, wrongly believing that his honor is more important than his love for Paolo, forces himself into violence. Thus, the play ends with two brothers—one passively, one actively—led into destruction.

Pepe, Maletesta's jester, is one reason that critics admire *Francesca da Rimini*. As Boker's own addition to the story of Francesca and Paolo, Pepe hastens the inevitable tragedy. Pepe frequently suggests to Lanciotto that Paolo and Francesca love each other, and he tells Lanciotto when their love is consummated. To assure that Lanciotto seeks vengeance, he also lies, telling Lanciotto that Paolo has hired him to kill his brother. As Pepe expects, in anger, Lanciotto kills him, but he dies glad that the two brothers will also be destroyed.

Pepe would be a completely malevolent figure except for the motivation behind his hatred for Paolo and Lanciotto. A proponent of democracy, he hates the brothers because they represent royalty. He tells Lanciotto that he would like to see marriage abolished so that everyone would be born equal. Later, in a scene not present in the 1853 version, Paolo reports that he overheard Pepe ranting about being treated as a toy. Both brothers indeed treat him like that; generally unconcerned about his desires, they expect him to do their bidding, and they fatally underestimate his anger. Pepe is a modern antihero, supporting the cause of democracy.

Critics agree that two other plays by Boker approach the excellence of *Francesca da Rimini*: *Leonor de Guzman*, another romantic tragedy, and *The Betrothal*, a romantic comedy.

In *Leonor de Guzman*, the King of Castile and Leon dies, leaving three rivals competing for power: his wife Maria, who wants the throne to remain with her son; his mistress Leonor, who wants her son to become king; and Alburquerque, the prime minister, who wants the power for himself. The play is effective particularly because of the struggle between Leonor, the spiritually pure mistress who unwaveringly manipulates events to ensure that her son will be king, and Maria, the betrayed wife whose bitterness leads her to murder Leonor. The play ends with Leonor dead and Maria's son ill and successfully manipulated by Alburquerque. It seems that the Prime Minister will be victorious, but Leonor, before her death, has prophesied her son's triumph and Alburquerque's downfall so convincingly that, even as he watches her die, the Prime Minister already feels the sting of defeat.

Centering as it does on three strong characters, each with his or her distinctive personality, the play sustains the audience's interest. Nevertheless, it is inferior to *Francesca da Rimini*. In *Leonor de Guzman*, too many humorous scenes inappropriately distract the audience from the ensuing tragedy, and too many characters participating in palace intrigue blur the development of the three principal characters.

The Betrothal is a comedy about Costanza, who unhappily agrees to marry the evil Marsio to save her aristocratic father from poverty and possibly from prison. When she falls in love with Count Juranio, the Count's kinsman Salvatore manipulates events so that Costanza may marry the man she loves without ruining her father. Like *Francesca da Rimini* and *Leonor de Guzman*, *The Betrothal* is written in blank verse and centers on characters of aristocratic birth, but in addition to the expected difference in tone, the differences in plot, character, and theme distinctly set this comedy apart from Boker's tragedies. Murder is plotted in *The Betrothal*, but, as is consistent with its comic tone, no death occurs. Furthermore, the romance between Costanza's cousin and Juranio's kinsman is developed into a subplot, something Boker avoids in the two tragedies.

The characters of *The Betrothal* are interesting figures, but, unlike the prominent characters in the two tragedies, they are merely types— Costanza and Juranio as the virtuous lovers, Filippia and Salvatore as the loyal confidants, and Marsio as the evil suitor. Little exists in their portrayal to make them other than hero, heroine, or villain.

All three plays have a major character who is not a proper aristocrat. Pepe is a mere jester in *Francesca da Rimini*; Leonor, by becoming a mistress, has relinquished the status with which she was born; Marsio represents the nouveau riche. An important theme of the two tragedies is that those set apart from elite society may defeat the aristocracy. Pepe dies victorious, knowing that he has made royalty suffer. Leonor also dies victorious, knowing that her son, a bastard, will be king. In *The Betrothal*, however, Marsio, who is despicable partly because he lacks aristocratic graces, suffers ignominious defeat so that two aristocrats may appropriately marry each other. Boker's admiration for democracy is not apparent in this comedy.

One reason Boker is little remembered today is that he excelled at romantic drama, a form which modern readers, with their love of realism, seldom appreciate. *Leonor de Guzman*, with its emphasis on palace intrigue, and *The Betrothal*, with its assumption that aristocrats are better than others, understandably have little appeal for the twentieth century American reader. *Francesca da Rimini*, however, deserves the attention of modern readers: The play's complex characterization and democratic theme can sustain interest even today.

Other major works

POETRY: *The Lesson of Life and Other Poems*, 1848; *The Podesta's*

Daughter and Other Miscellaneous Poems, 1852; *Poems of the War*, 1864; *The Book of the Dead*, 1882; *Sonnets: A Sequence on Profane Love*, 1929 (Edward Sculley Bradley, editor).

MISCELLANEOUS: *Plays and Poems*, 1856 (2 volumes).

Bibliography

Bradley, Edward Scully. *George Henry Boker: Poet and Patriot.* Philadelphia: University of Pennsylvania Press, 1927. The standard literary biography, examining Boker's works in conjunction with his life. Bradley concludes that Boker was the victim of nineteenth century provincials who were reluctant to praise anything American. He attempts to kindle interest in Boker now that there is a new generation that can evaluate his works on their own merit. Illustrations, bibliography of Boker's writings, general bibliography, and index.

—————————. Introduction to *"Glaucus" and Other Plays by George Henry Boker.* Princeton, N.J.: Princeton University Press, 1940. Bradley praises Boker highly, labeling three of his plays masterpieces. Here, however, Bradley introduces and critiques the three lesser works, published for the first time in this volume.

Mayorga, Margaret G. *A Short History of the American Drama.* New York: Dodd, Mead, 1932. Mayorga provides commentaries on plays written before 1920, including a description of Boker's works and an analysis of *Francesca da Rimini.* She concludes that even though popular, *Francesca da Rimini* generally sounded the death knell for the American romantic tragedy.

Moses, Montrose J. *The American Dramatist.* Boston: Little, Brown, 1925. A brief biography and critical introduction to the plays. Moses finds a sameness to the plays in theme and style. Boker took his plots and conflicts from foreign sources and thus did not create a uniquely American drama.

Quinn, Arthur Hobson. *A History of the American Drama, from the Beginning to the Civil War.* 2d ed. New York: Appleton-Century-Crofts, 1951. In this biography and critical introduction, Quinn concludes that Boker treated foreign material too exclusively. Even though Boker was overtly patriotic and critical of foreign shortcomings in his poetry, these qualities are not seen in his plays. Nevertheless, Boker wrote the finest tragedies of his day. Bibliography and index.

Margaret Ann Baker
(Updated by *Gerald S. Argetsinger*)

ROBERT BOLT

Born: Sale, England; August 15, 1924
Died: near Petersfield, England; February 20, 1995

Principal drama

A Man for All Seasons, pr. 1954 (radio play), pr. 1957 (televised), pr. 1960 (staged), pb. 1960; *The Last of the Wine*, pr. 1955 (radio play), pr. 1956 (staged); *The Critic and the Heart*, pr. 1957; *Flowering Cherry*, pr. 1957, pb. 1958; *The Tiger and the Horse*, pr. 1960, pb. 1961; *Gentle Jack*, pr. 1963, pb. 1965; *The Thwarting of Baron Bolligrew*, pr. 1965, pb. 1966 (children's play); *Brother and Sister*, pr. 1967, 1968 (revision of *The Critic and the Heart*); *Vivat! Vivat Regina!*, pr. 1970, pb. 1971; *State of Revolution*, pr., pb. 1977.

Other literary forms

Robert Bolt began his career in drama as a writer of radio plays for the British Broadcasting Company, starting in 1953 with *The Master*, a play about the wandering scholars of the Middle Ages. He wrote sixteen scripts for the British Broadcasting Corporation, including eight for children. The first version of *A Man for All Seasons* was broadcast as a radio drama in 1954, and his very first production on the legitimate stage, *The Last of the Wine*, originated as a radio script a year earlier.

Bolt's most noteworthy achievements outside the legitimate theater, however, have been as a screenwriter. He worked with the renowned British director David Lean on *Lawrence of Arabia*, creating a screenplay based on T. E. Lawrence's own writings. The film received the Academy Award for Best Picture of 1962, and Bolt's scenario received a special award from the British Film Academy. His adaptation of Boris Pasternak's novel *Doctor Zhivago*, another script written for David Lean, won an Oscar for the Best Screenplay of 1965, an honor repeated in 1966 when Bolt adapted his own play, *A Man for All Seasons* (directed by Fred Zinnemann). The movie version also earned for Bolt the British Film Academy Award and the New York Film Critics Circle Award in 1966. His next project was an original treatment of *Ryan's Daughter* for David Lean in 1970. In 1972, he wrote and directed *Lady Caroline Lamb*, based on the life of the mistress of Lord Byron, the famous English poet.

In the 1980's, Bolt concentrated on screenplays, teleplays, and adaptations, notably *The Mission* (1986; starring Robert DeNiro), *Nostromo* (an adaptation of the Joseph Conrad novel, with Christopher Hampton, which was not completed), and *Without Warning* (1991), based on the life of James Brady, the press secretary to President Ronald Reagan who was disabled by a would-be assassin's bullet in 1981.

Achievements

Bolt has earned the reputation of being a serious dramatist whose sense of stagecraft has made him popular with theater audiences. Critics have also recognized his talent for structure and his concern with language from the time of his appearance in the West End theaters of London with *Flowering Cherry* in 1957. This play, a popular and critical success during its 435 performances at the Haymarket Theatre, won for him the *Evening Standard* Drama Award for Most Promising Playwright of that year. Although Bolt launched his career in the heyday of the Angry Young Men, when playwrights as diverse as John Osborne, Harold Pinter, John Arden, and Arnold Wesker challenged the then reigning conventions of English theater, he has never been associated with the avant-garde. In fact, as John Fuegi has emphasized, Bolt has deliberately rejected many features of the new drama while responding to those influences that he could accommodate to his traditional aesthetic.

Bolt's own statements about his approach to his art reflect his conviction that conventional dramatic structure, with a clearly articulated plot and an organic unity, not only satisfies the legitimate expectations of the audience but also provides an effective vehicle "for conveying delicate but immediate insights." He compares highly conventional theater, "where both sides of the footlights understand thoroughly what's going on," to a taut drumskin that resounds at the lightest tap. "Take away these conventions and you find yourself with a slack drumskin; you've got to jump up and down on it before you get even the slightest tinkle." Bolt also maintains that the slice-of-life dramatists who let the audience supply the ending use the theater "as a therapeutic rather than dramatic medium."

Bolt's earliest dramas were traditional well-crafted plays, largely naturalistic in approach, with a fourth-wall style of dramaturgy. Even as early as *Flowering Cherry*, however, Bolt was striving to break out of the purely naturalistic mode while maintaining a clear, unified structure. *A Man for All Seasons* realizes these ambitions; the play that established Bolt as one of the most popular playwrights in the London theater, it ran more than nine months in London and enjoyed an even longer New York run of more than a year and a half, starting in November, 1961. Despite some demurrers such as the influential critic Kenneth Tynan, the drama won widespread critical acclaim. Robert Corrigan was among those who considered *A Man for All Seasons* "one of the finest achievements of the modern theatre." Jerry Tallman of *The Village Voice* could think of no play that surpassed it in almost forty years for dramatic tension, structure, meaning, and language. The stage version received two American drama awards in 1962: the Tony Award of the American Theatre Wing for the best play of that year and the New York Drama Critics Circle Award for the best foreign play.

Biography

Robert Oxton Bolt was born in 1924, the younger son of Ralph Bolt and Leah Binnion Bolt. His family lived in the small town of Sale in Lancashire, where his father owned a shop carrying mostly furniture, glass, and china. His mother was a schoolteacher. The playwright has spoken of his parents as loving, concerned, and not unduly strict, despite their high standards. Though Bolt has described his religious position as between agnosticism and atheism, he was reared a Methodist. He has stated, "I ought to be religious in the sense that I'm comfortable thinking in religious terms and altogether I seem naturally constituted to be religious."

Despite his good home background, Bolt distinguished himself as a youngster by constantly getting into trouble and remaining at the bottom of his class in the Manchester Grammar School until his graduation in 1940. Not really prepared to enter any career or qualified to go on to a university, he became an office boy for the Sun Life Assurance Company in Manchester in 1942—a position he thoroughly loathed. Determined to escape from this whole way of life, he leaped at the opportunity to study for a degree in commerce under special wartime arrangements for admission to a university program. Through intensive preparation for his Advanced Level examinations, he gained a place in an honors school at Manchester University rather than the school of commerce. There, he began work for a degree in history in 1943. During this period, he also became a Marxist; from 1942 to 1947, he was a member of the Communist Party, inspired by youthfully idealistic visions of the Party's ability to change the world. He has since described himself as a Marxist with so many reservations that he would be scorned by a true Marxist.

After a year at Manchester University, Bolt joined the Royal Air Force and later transferred to the army, serving as an officer with the Royal West African Frontier Force in Ghana. At the end of the war, he returned to the university, where he was awarded an honors degree in history in 1949. That same year, he married Celia Ann Roberts, a painter; the couple had three children—Sally, Benedict, and Joanna—prior to their divorce in 1967. Bolt has been remarried twice since then; his second wife was the actress Sara Miles, by whom he had one son and from whom he was divorced in 1976. In 1980, he married Ann Zane.

Following his graduation from Manchester, Bolt prepared for a career in education by studying for his teaching diploma, which he received from the University of Exeter in 1950. For the next eight years, he worked as an English teacher, first at a village in Bishopsteignton in Devon and then at Millfield School in Street, Devon. His desire to become a dramatist first developed in 1954 while he was searching for a nativity play to perform with the children at the village school. Finding none of the plays he had read satisfactory, he decided to compose his own. Bolt recalls vividly "the electric tension" that built up inside him after he had composed some of the dialogue, and he remembers telling his wife, "Listen, I think I've found what I want to do." At this point, he decided to combine teaching with writing and began composing his radio scripts.

An adaptation of his 1955 radio script, *The Last of the Wine*, was staged in London at Theatre in the Round in 1956. The success of Osborne's play *Look Back in Anger* that same year made Bolt feel that young playwrights might have a chance of breaking into the West End theaters, and Bolt sent his play *The Critic and the Heart* to the Royal Court Theatre, where the reader—Osborne himself—rejected it, claiming that it was a promising play but not the particular kind of drama that the theater was seeking. Although Bolt did not succeed in getting a West End showing, *The Critic and the Heart* was produced at the Oxford Playhouse in 1957 and was well received. This play represents Bolt at his most traditional. Bolt himself criticized the play for being too orthodox and completely naturalistic in form. He tells how, being inexperienced in the theater, he modeled the play on W. Somerset Maugham's *The Circle* (pr. 1921), doing a detailed structural analysis and following it closely in his own play, even down to the placement of climaxes and the lengths of acts. As Ronald Hayman emphasizes, however, the content and dialogue are distinctly Bolt's own; the playwright also demonstrates his capacity for closely interweaving characters and plot. Bolt later rewrote the play as *Brother and Sister*, which was produced at Brighton in 1967; another revised version appeared at Bristol in 1968.

With his next play, *Flowering Cherry*, Bolt caught the attention of director Frith Banbury, known for his promotion of promising young playwrights. Banbury arranged Bolt's first West End production in 1957 with a stellar cast, including Ralph Richardson and Celia Johnson in the leads. The highly successful London run was followed by a New York production in 1959, when critics received it far less enthusiastically. Bolt's next work, *The Tiger and the Horse*, about the effects a petition to ban the hydrogen bomb have on a middle-class university family, is another basically naturalistic domestic drama of the same type as *Flowering Cherry*. Like its predecessor, it was directed by Banbury, beginning a successful London run in August, 1960.

A Man for All Seasons began its run at the Globe Theater in July, 1960, with Paul Scofield as Sir Thomas More; *The Tiger and the Horse*, though written first, opened a month later. Thus, Bolt had the distinction of having two very different types of plays enjoying success at the West End theaters simultaneously. The 1960's also found Bolt branching out into screenwriting and winning distinction in that field as well. In 1961, he also went to jail briefly, along with other members of Bertrand Russell's Committee of One Hundred, for antinuclear protests that involved token breaches of the law. Bolt had been working on the screenplay for *Lawrence of Arabia* at the time, and progress on the film stopped while he was away from the scene. Finally, producer Sam Spiegel angrily pressured him into binding himself over and coming out of prison because people's jobs and thousands of dollars were at stake. Bolt speaks of this as a surrender, an action he has regretted, despite the good reasons for doing it.

Bolt's next drama for the legitimate stage was *Gentle Jack*, a highly experimental drama in which he sought to move even further away from naturalism. John R. Kaiser aptly described the play as "an adult fairy tale or an allegorical fantasy" dealing with the appearance of the god Pan in the modern world. Produced in 1963, with Dame Edith Evans and Kenneth Williams in the leading roles, *Gentle Jack* is perhaps the least successful of Bolt's major theatrical works, running for only seventy-five performances. Neither the critics nor the public received it favorably; many found it puzzling and obscure, a marked departure from Bolt's usual clarity and even from the types of drama that had made him one of the leading popular playwrights of his time.

For his next stage venture, Bolt turned to another fairy tale, but this time a highly successful one for children, *The Thwarting of Baron Bolligrew*, first performed in December, 1965, by the Royal Shakespeare Company at the Aldwich Theatre in London. It has been noted that Bolt's penchant for larger-than-life figures served him well in creating his fairy-tale characters, including the stout, elderly hero, Sir Oblong Fitz-Oblong, a knight with a strong sense of duty, and the villainous Baron Bolligrew. The knight is a humorous version of the uncommon man of principle who must fight against the evil and deception in the society around him. Ronald Hayman notes that, "like some children, he tries too hard to be good." Bolt also makes use of a Storyteller who, like the Common Man, provides a narrative link between episodes and occasionally takes part in the action, such as by making the moon rise when Sir Oblong asks for it.

Bolt has returned to historical subjects for the adult dramas that he has written since *Gentle Jack*. *Vivat! Vivat Regina!*—his treatment of the rival queens Mary Stuart and Elizabeth Tudor—had its premiere at the Chichester Festival in 1970; it then moved to the Piccadilly Theatre in London, where it proved a major hit of the season. The play also had a successful New York engagement in 1972. A play dealing with the Russian Revolution and Vladimir Ilich Lenin's central role in it, *State of Revolution*, was first produced in 1977 at the Birmingham Repertory Theatre and later at the National Theatre.

Bolt suffered a debilitating stroke in 1979, leaving him partially paralyzed but capable of walking with a cane. He felt an affinity to the experiences of Press Secretary James Brady, whose gunshot wound from an attempt on the life of then President Ronald Reagan left him similarly paralyzed.

Bolt's treatment of Brady's life in *Without Warning* is said to incorporate much of Bolt's own reactions to his illness. Interviewers in 1991 noted Bolt's speech difficulties but remarked on his total clarity of thought and expression. He died a few years later, on February 20, 1995.

Analysis

The full range of Robert Bolt's achievements can be illustrated most effectively through a more detailed consideration of four major plays. *The Tiger and the Horse* demonstrates the "uneasy straddling between naturalism and non-naturalism" that he found in his earlier plays; it also represents one of his attempts to give his contemporaries the larger-than-life significance he finds appropriate in theatrical characters. Marking a significant development in Bolt's dramaturgical skills, *A Man for All Seasons* shows how he turned to historical settings to escape the pitfalls of naturalism and to present individuals of significant dramatic dimension; the play remains his most penetrating examination of the individual in conflict with society. In *Vivat! Vivat Regina!*, he draws upon the artificiality of the theater in presenting the conflict between two striking historical figures. Finally, *State of Revolution* represents a serious attempt to explore some decisive events in contemporary history and the towering figure who gave them shape.

The Tiger and the Horse is a well-plotted domestic drama in which a petition to ban the bomb serves as a major catalyst in the action; its effects are skillfully interwoven with the crises of a seduction and growing insanity to provide some intensely pitched action.

The title alludes to an aphorism by the poet William Blake, from *The Marriage of Heaven and Hell*: "The tygers of wrath are wiser than the horses of instruction"; it suggests that the logic of the heart can express a higher wisdom than can the reasoning of the mind. In his review of the play, Richard Findlater aptly summarized the theme embedded in the drama "as the relative values of commitment in private and public life, and the balance of power between heart and head among members of the English thinking class." Through Bolt's craftmanship, public issues and private concerns are skillfully intertwined in the development of the plot.

Jack Dean, the Master of a university college who is in line for the vice chancellorship, is the horse of the play. Though a kindly, tolerant, and highly principled man, he has developed as his personal philosophy a detachment that is essentially a refusal to become involved, an emotional neutrality that he unwittingly carries over into personal relationships as well as into his approach to larger issues. Even his having abandoned astronomy to take up philosophy becomes significant in Bolt's careful delineation of his character. When his daughter Stella is looking through his telescope and taking comfort in the order she finds in nature, Dean launches into one of the "big speeches" found here and in *Flowering Cherry*; he speaks of the darkness, "ignorant of human necessities," that fills the spaces between the stars, and he adds that what appears to be a meaningful pattern in the universe is actually merely "Scribble." Thus, staid, imperturbable Dean reveals the terrifying vision of the existential void that led him to turn away from investigating the world around him and to take refuge in abstract philosophical speculation.

When Louis Flax, a research fellow from a working-class background, circulates a petition urging nuclear disarmament, Dean refuses to sign; one vote, he says, does not really matter, and he claims that he does not understand all the political and diplomatic considerations involved. The same lack of engagement is apparent in his personal life. When Stella tries to warn Dean that her mother is acting strangely and seems mentally unbalanced, he refuses to take her concern seriously. At first, too, he fends off Stella's confidences about Louis; only when she tells her father that she is pregnant and has no intention of marrying Louis because he does not really love her does she crack that mask of imperturbability. Dean responds with natural fatherly concern for Stella and indignation against Louis, yet while he offers his daughter his firm support and expresses distress on her behalf, he still insists, "I am not involved."

Dean's wife, Gwendoline, is the tiger of the play, a woman capable of passionate intensity, though she has obviously submerged her own feelings in her role as the Master's wife. A biologist before her marriage, she is profoundly moved by the issue of the bomb, aware of the mutation that radiation can cause in unborn children. She is ready to sign Louis' petition until Sir Hugo Slade, the present Vice Chancellor of the university, reminds her that such an action on her part could cost her husband the Vice Chancellor's post. She tries to find out what Dean wants her to do, but he refuses to coerce her in any way, even offering her the pen and urging her to sign the petition. She holds back out of concern for his position, even though she continues to brood over the petition—to the point of arousing Stella's concern.

Louis Flax, like Dean, is an intellectual who is out of touch with his emotions. The general concern for humanity that underlies his petition against the hydrogen bomb does not extend itself to a genuine love for the woman bearing his child. Even though he dutifully proposes marriage to Stella, he, too, must discover the place love should occupy in his life.

The climax comes when Dean discovers that Gwendoline has gone mad and has slashed the Holbein painting belonging to the college (one that depicts a deformed child); she has attached the petition to the damaged portrait. In the confrontation that follows, Dean realizes that he bears the responsibility for his wife's troubled state. His philosophy of dissociation, his unwitting failure to share anything with her, has led her to believe that he does not really love her and that he tolerated her only out of his "goodness." Her concern over the issues raised by Louis' petition finally pushed her over the edge. Though Sir Hugo Slade urges Dean publicly to dissociate himself from his wife's action, Dean accepts responsibility for what he has done to her. He expresses his love for her and refuses to dismiss her gesture as merely the aberration of an insane woman, even going so far as to add his own signature to the petition.

In many respects, *The Tiger and the Horse* is a conventional, well-made play, integrating a serious contemporary theme with the stuff of traditional domestic drama. The reservations that Hayman and others have expressed about the play are valid; in particular, the plot is so tightly developed that there is no room to develop the characters as effectively as Bolt might have done. For example, the progression of Gwendoline's madness is never really dramatized; her eccentricity and troubled behavior are only mentioned in the dialogue. Thus, her breakdown has a certain melodramatic edge. Similarly, Louis' changed attitude after his son is born—his discovery that he really does love Stella—is not dramatized; rather, it is tacked on to provide a conventional happy ending.

With *A Man for All Seasons*, Bolt shifted to a historical subject, but one that embodies themes relevant to contemporary life. He felt that the distancing effect of a play set in past centuries would provide a way of escaping from some of the constraints of naturalism, such as an overriding concern for the skillful use of realistic plot detail.

The play's protagonist, Sir Thomas More, exemplifies the man who has realized his full potential. The historical Thomas More was a charming, urbane man, extraordinarily successful in his public and private life—happy in his family and in his friendships, accomplished as a statesman, renowned for his intelligence and wit. Unlike Jack Dean, he was intensely involved in the life of his times, yet he retained enough detachment to keep his sense of values intact. As Bolt stresses in his preface to the play, he found More's most distinctive quality to be "an adamantine sense of his own self. He knew where he began and left off, what area of himself he could yield to the encroachments of his enemies, and what to the encroachments of these he loved." Though More loved life and did not court martyrdom, he was willing to die rather than betray his deepest principles. More could not falsely express approval of King Henry VIII's divorce and subsequent marriage to Anne Boleyn, particularly when this meant swearing an oath, pledging his integrity as a guarantor of the truth. Thus, Bolt describes More as "a hero of selfhood."

Tynan objected that Bolt does not show the audience what More's underlying convictions were or why he embraced them so uncompromisingly. He notes that the playwright is not concerned with whether these convictions are right or wrong but only that More clung to them and would not disclose them under questioning. More's speech before the death sentence is passed succinctly states his position that the Act of Parliament making King Henry Supreme Head of the Church is contrary to divine law, but Bolt's concern is not with exploring the soundness of More's view; rather, he dramatizes More's twofold struggle—to preserve his life, if possible, but above all to preserve his soul, or essential self.

Corrigan has described the main action of the play as a series of confrontations between More and those who seek to make him retreat from that last stronghold of the self and accede to the king's behest. Bolt effectively uses the Brechtian device of a series of semi-independent scenes to develop these confrontations. The scenes show More adroitly facing powerful opponents, as well as interacting with his family, which is deeply involved with his fate. Because of Bolt's emphasis on More's domestic life, Hayman has found *A Man for All Seasons* thin on social texture, a drama focusing on personal relationships rather than showing the individual pitted against society. Yet Bolt has correctly noted that More himself attached great importance to his family life. Moreover, the conflicts Bolt presents are skillfully orchestrated to show More facing questions, opposition, and misunderstandings in the small world of his home at the same time that he is battling them in the world at large.

Perhaps the two most important foils for More are Richard Rich and the Common Man. When Rich first appears, he is arguing with More, maintaining that "every man has his price," an opinion that his own subsequent career aptly illustrates. Not adequately defined by any strong sense of personal values, as More is, he is readily tempted to sell himself in order to procure advancement. Rich undergoes something of an interior struggle when he finds himself drifting toward betrayal of his king, but he soon sheds any semblance of self-respect to become a useful tool to Thomas Cromwell. Unlike More, who will not compromise himself by a false oath that is a mere formality, Rich boldly perjures himself in a capital case to help Cromwell secure More's conviction.

The Common Man, who assumes various roles within the play, starting as More's steward Matthew and ending as his executioner, provides another foil to the man of uncommon moral courage. Bolt indicates that he used "common" in the sense of "that which is common to us all"; he intended to have the audience identify to a degree with the character. In each role, the Common Man demonstrates his overriding concern with two basic human instincts, self-interest and self-preservation. Anselm Atkins has argued that, despite essential differences, the Common Man is made to resemble More sufficiently to have the audience recognize themselves in both characters. More represents what we could be, at our best; the Common Man indicates what we all too often are—concerned finally with slipping by comfortably in life, getting what we can without too many moral scruples.

Both characters are extremely rational and both seek with great care to keep themselves out of trouble. Like More, the Common Man draws a firm boundary between what he will and will not do, only in his case he draws a line where risks outweigh gains, as when Cromwell offers the jailer a dangerously large sum for information about his prisoner More. The Common Man, unlike More, is concerned with preserving his bodily life at all costs, not with the essential self, his soul.

Bolt's masterful handling of language, blending a Tudor flavor into modern dialogue and skillfully interpolating More's own words where appropriate, is a notable feature of the play. The dramatist has indicated that he sought to make thematic use of images, with dry land representing society and the sea and water representing "that larger context which we all inhabit, the terrifying cosmos." These references are so naturally interwoven into the rest of the play that they generally escape notice, yet the pattern is there; such remarks as King Henry's passing allusion to *his* river, where he is playing the role of pilot, and Matthew's reference to More's fear of drowning have additional resonance when seen in this context.

Bolt's preface to *Vivat! Vivat Regina!* makes evident his conviction that setting plays in the past is one method of giving characters the particularity they need to emerge as people rather than as archetypes while still enabling them to be "theatrical." By this the playwright means that the characters have "a continuously high pitch of speech and action" obviously different from the pace of real life but appropriate to the heightened intensity of drama and made convincing within the dramatic framework. Bolt feels that the audience accepts theatrical speech and action more readily in characters from the past "not because we seriously think they really did continuously speak and act like that but because we don't know how they spoke and only know the more dramatic of their actions."

Certainly Bolt selected a highly dramatic subject in the parallel careers of Elizabeth I of England and Mary, Queen of Scots, and the tragic rivalry between the two monarchs. Here the tension between the individual and society emerges as a study of the conflict between fulfillment in personal relationships and the exigencies of political power. Both women are strong-willed queens; as they steer their courses through troubled political waters, each recognizing a potential threat in the other, they must make crucial choices between love and political expediency. Elizabeth, who from her youth has had to be extremely self-controlled and politically calculating, can subordinate her needs as a woman to the requirements of her office, though at great psychological cost; she suppresses part of her personality, becoming hardened and neurotic even as she achieves greatness as a monarch. By contrast, Mary refuses to suppress the emotional side of her nature; she willfully chooses love, even though she risks political disaster.

Bolt's mastery of structure is evident in his handling of complex historical events unfolding over a number of years. He employs a series of parallel scenes, with the action shifting back and forth between Mary and Elizabeth in the same type of fluid staging that characterized *A Man for All Seasons*. He also uses patently theatrical devices to advance the action and to underscore the interconnections between the two monarchs' careers; in one such scene, Elizabeth is seated aloft on the throne as the baptism of Mary's son James, heir of the Tudor line, takes place in the foreground. The most stylized piece of action occurs at the Kirk o' Field incident, where Mary is shown acting in collusion with Bothwell, the murderer of her second husband, Darnley. She is seen dancing "puppet-like under Bothwell's compelling stare," then dancing alone and frightened. After an explosion rocks the stage and scatters the dancers, John Knox steps into the spotlight vacated by Mary and denounces her. When the lights come up, the other dancers are revealed to include Elizabeth and Lord Cecil, Philip of Spain, and the pope, who remonstrate with Mary over her involvement with Bothwell.

In discussing how he gave dramatic shape to the involved story of the two monarchs, Bolt notes that he sought "to present the confused eventfulness of Mary's life as a series of single theatrical happenings, and to present the torturous complexities of Elizabeth's policy as an immediate response." Bolt draws a sharply dramatic contrast between the two monarchs in terms of sexual politics. At the beginning of the play, Elizabeth, though deeply in love with Robert Dudley, reluctantly takes Lord Cecil's advice not to marry him because of his suspected involvement with his wife's death. The queen believes him innocent but realizes that such a marriage might cost her the throne. Her decision is partially affected by the knowledge that Mary, Queen of Scots, would welcome such a move. So much has she learned to subordinate her personal feelings to concerns of state that she later agrees to let Cecil propose Robert Dudley, now Earl of Leicester, as a "safe" suitor for Mary, Queen of Scots.

Instead, Mary makes a politically advantageous second marriage to Henry Stuart, Lord Darnley, which strengthens her claim to the English throne, yet even this marriage reflects Mary's determination to have a husband she can love. When Darnley proves weak and faithless, participating in the plot to kill the queen's favorite, David Rizzio, Mary falls deeply in love with Lord Bothwell. Unlike Elizabeth, she is portrayed as all too ready to risk her throne for love. Not only does she bring Darnley to Kirk o' Field under threat of otherwise losing Bothwell's love; she also refuses to repudiate Bothwell later, acting against Elizabeth's own admonition. Mary stubbornly maintains that he was tried and found innocent, despite the questionable nature of the verdict; she further reveals that she has married him. Even after she has surrendered herself to the Scottish nobility on condition that they let Bothwell go, she refuses to conciliate the lords by repudiating the marriage as a forced one and thus reclaiming her throne. Passionately, she declares, "I would follow him to the edge of the earth—in my shift!" When Bothwell is driven into exile and Mary is living as a royal prisoner in England, she still clings to the hope that he will keep his promise and return. Mary's pained acknowledgment that Bothwell will not return—she learns that he has taken service with the King of Denmark and has another woman in his house—leads her to renounce love to "study policy." This "policy," however, involves her in a conspiracy against Elizabeth and leads to her execution.

Because the two queens never met historically, Bolt does not invent any scene involving a direct confrontation between them as other dramatists, including Friedrich Schiller, have done. A key scene in the latter's *Mary Stuart* (pr. 1800) is a meeting between Elizabeth and Mary at Fotheringhay Castle, where Mary wins a moral victory over Elizabeth that ensures her death. In *Vivat! Vivat Regina!* the monarchs exchange words onstage twice in scenes that are obviously representational of exchanges that took place in letters. In addition, Bolt gains considerable dramatic impact by emphasizing the psychological effects of the rivalry. Elizabeth's reaction to the news of Mary's escape (following the murder of Rizzio) reveals her envy of Mary's more intense involvement in life; she particularly envies the passionate response the Queen of Scots can evoke in men such as Lord Bothwell, who "raises men, half-naked men . . . and drives her enemies from Edinburgh—and for what? Why, for herself." The English queen's envy is heightened by the awareness that the child Mary is carrying will be heir to the English throne, since Elizabeth is "barren stock." When Elizabeth is thought merciful for giving Mary refuge in England, even after hearing an impassioned letter from Mary to Bothwell that furnishes proof of Mary's involvement in the plot to kill Darnley, Lord Cecil astutely observes, "I do not think that this is altogether mercy. I think our Queen sees Mary in the mirror." On the other hand, Mary signs the letter giving her approval of the conspiracy against Elizabeth after she has learned that her son, James, has never received any of the letters and gifts she has sent and that Elizabeth "has played the mother's part." Her fury against the English queen impels Mary to an action that she knows might entrap her and lead to her death.

Bolt's psychobiographical approach presents both Mary and Elizabeth in human terms while fashioning an extremely effective structure for dramatizing the intertwined careers of the two monarchs. Hayman finds that the emphasis on personal relationships, which he sees as characteristic of Bolt's dramas, prevents Bolt from mining the complexity of his subject sufficiently. Similarly, Irving Wardle has called the play "an immensely skillful piece of cosmetic surgery: adding the common touch and the free-flowing action of epic theatre, while leaving the assumptions of heroic costume drama untouched." Other critics, however, such as Samuel Hirsch, have found *Vivat! Vivat Regina!* "exciting theater" that "illuminates history by putting it in the perspective of human personality."

When Bolt turned to twentieth century history and the Russian Revolution for the subject of his next play, *State of Revolution*, he focused on another uncommon man—this time a leader at odds not only with the capitalist society he sought to replace but also with his fellow revolutionaries. What fascinated the playwright was Vladimir Lenin's uncompromising dedication to the Marxist view of history and the Socialist Revolution as he saw it developing. Adopting the Marxist ethic that anything which promoted the establishment of the Socialist State was justified, Lenin often sanctioned extreme and brutal measures as necessary means to this great end. In an interview with Sally Emerson, Bolt stressed the paradox this man presented: "Viewed in one light, he was an indefensible monster, in another he was a great and good man. He did and said quite impermissible things but he was also selfless with no love of cruelty for its own sake."

Once again employing an episodic structure, Bolt moves from the pre-Revolutionary period in 1910, when the Bolshevik leaders were running a school to train Party activists at Maxim Gorky's villa in Capri, through the Revolution and its aftermath, ending with Vladimir Ilich Lenin's death and Joseph Stalin's rise to power in 1924. In order to provide a frame for the chronicle, the playwright uses as his narrator a historical figure, Anatole Lunacharsky, an associate of Lenin who became Commissioner for Education and Enlightenment in the Soviet State. Lunacharsky is portrayed as addressing a meeting of Young Communists around 1930, on the anniversary of Lenin's death. As critic David Zane Mairowitz has emphasized, Lunacharsky, a humane intellectual, reflects the original idealism within the revolutionary movement as well as the questioning and moral scruples that surfaced as its promise was betrayed. Mairowitz and others have also shown the basic problem with this particular framing device; the staged events purport to dramatize Lunacharsky's speech to his 1930 audience, yet such an account of the origins of Stalinism is inconceivable in that context: By 1930, the Stalinist rewriting of history was already well under way.

Nevertheless, Lunacharsky's account does present a compelling portrait of Lenin as a complex, driven man who acted with a terrible consistency in pursuing the goal of establishing a Socialist State. The play provides glimpses of the human warmth that Lenin too often suppressed in the name of revolutionary ideal, yet it also shows the cold detachment and ruthless determination he could exercise when personal feelings or human considerations seemed contrary to these greater goals. Despite his feeling of friendship for Lunacharsky, Lenin can brutally question why he is still in the Party with his baggage of humanistic notions. Lenin argues that "unconditional human love is nothing but a dirty dream" at a moment in history that requires "unconditional class hatred." He further indicates that he is willing to sacrifice cultural values, even the "moral amenities," to achieve the new society that will beget its own virtue—"its own new form of love and unimaginable music." Yet Lenin's words also suggest his own brand of revolutionary idealism and his intensity of purpose.

One of the deepest ironies underscored in the drama is the contradiction that Lenin's career offers to the Marxist view of history he embraced, which postulates that history finds the men it needs, contrary to the doctrine that great men shape events. At many crucial points, it is Lenin's "overwhelming, ruthless will" that determines the course of events, prevailing over the opposition of other Bolshevik leaders. Convinced that a Russian Revolution would lead to a worldwide Socialist revolution, he argues for an end to Russian participation in World War I and the immediate pursuit of a civil war. He is also determined to use the discontent of the peasants in promoting a Socialist revolution, even though the realistic Gorky emphasizes the disparity between the goals of the peasants and the aims of the Bolsheviks; the peasants desire individual ownership of the land, not the establishment of a collectivist society. Lenin also argues for the adoption of the Brest-Litovsk Treaty with Germany despite its harsh conditions, since his first priority is continuing the Revolution on any possible terms. After the Bolsheviks assume power, he continues to play the prime role in charting the development of the Socialist State. Following the Kronstadt uprising, he is the prime force shaping the New Economic Policy that permits a measure of capitalistic enterprise, because he deems this a necessary expedient. He also favors using the Cheka as a counterrevolutionary police force to root out the bourgeois elements in the Party.

The greatest irony, however, is the failure of Lenin's last supreme effort to exert his will and to influence the Party's choice of leader after his death. The Central Committee suppresses Lenin's "Testament" as the work of a sick man, even though its warning proves fatefully accurate. In this important document, Lenin expresses his preference for Leon Davidovich Trotsky as the next Party leader and warns that Stalin is too brutal. The irony is compounded by the fact that Stalin has been considered the ideal Party functionary for years, doing what needs to be done (like Thomas Cromwell in *A Man for All Seasons*). When he hears Lenin's warning that he will not use his power as Party Secretary with sufficient caution, Stalin can remind the Committee that he carried out all the jobs that Lenin asked him to do. He can also remind them that revolution is brutal—a statement Lenin himself often made. Lenin's collapse takes place onstage in the background during Stalin's delivery of his triumphant speech before the Thirteenth Congress—dramatically emphasizing Lenin's unsuccessful struggle to combat the menace he sees in Stalin. Bolt's drama portrays the development of Stalinism as a perverted outgrowth of Marxism-Leninism and makes clear the dangers of a philosophy that can dispense with the "moral amenities" in seeking to establish the dictatorship of the proletariat.

State of Revolution evoked mixed responses from the critics. Although the play confirms Bolt's talent for providing a clearly developed structure in treating the complex events of the Russian Revolution and its disastrous aftermath, Mairowitz has pointed out a number of oversimplifications in Bolt's treatment of the material, such as his failure to make clear that a civil war was in progress and his focusing upon the Bolshevik leaders with relatively little attention to the lower classes and their part in these historic events. Mairowitz and other critics have observed that the Bolshevik leaders tend to represent attitudes rather than fully articulated characters; Mairowitz adds that they sound like Englishmen in debate rather than impassioned Socialists. Despite such limitations, Bolt has managed to construct a compelling portrait of Lenin tragically caught up in the Marxist view of history, a drama culminating in a terrifying vision of the logical consequences of the Marxist ethic as Lenin himself formulated it.

Though Bolt has not matched the success of *A Man for All Seasons* in his subsequent dramas, he has effectively employed the open or epic style of that work to explore other historical subjects in *Vivat! Vivat Regina!* and *State of Revolution*. He has also continued to use the technical devices associated with a consciously theatrical style of dramaturgy for carefully planned effects. Bolt has never lost his concern for a realistic examination of human behavior or his ability to interweave close connections between plot and character. He continues to be one of the most skillful craftsmen in contemporary British theater, a popular playwright who has taken drama seriously and merits serious regard.

Other major works

NONFICTION: "English Theatre Today: The Importance of Shape," 1958 (in *International Theatre Annual*).

SCREENPLAYS: *Lawrence of Arabia*, 1962 (based on T. E. Lawrence's writings); *Doctor Zhivago*, 1965 (adaptation of Boris Pasternak's novel); *A Man for All Seasons*, 1966; *Ryan's Daughter*, 1970; *Lady Caroline Lamb*, 1972; *The Bounty*, 1984; *The Mission*, 1986.

TELEPLAY: *Without Warning: The James Brady Story*, 1991.

RADIO PLAYS: *The Master*, 1953; *Fifty Pigs*, 1953; *Ladies and Gentlemen*, 1954; *Mr. Sampson's Sundays*, 1955; *The Window*, 1958; *The Drunken Sailor*, 1958; *The Banana Tree*, 1961.

TRANSLATION: *The Sisterhood: A Play*, 1989 (of Molière's *Les Femmes savantes*).

Bibliography

Bolt, Robert. Introduction to *Vivat! Vivat Regina!* London: Heinemann, 1971. The introduction is a statement of principle regarding historical plays, the balance of historical factual accuracy, and the playwright's obligations. "I am Pro-Theatre," Bolt says. "I would claim . . . to be concerned for my own times. But I am not sure I relish them." Lists the cast of the first performance and contains designer notes.

Carpenter, Gerald. "Robert Bolt: Drama of the Threatened Self." *American Film: Magazine of the Film and Television Arts* 14 (September, 1989): 60-62. Reviews seven films available on video, written by Bolt under several directors (he directed *Lady Caroline Lamb* himself). Carpenter finds *The Mission*, with Robert DeNiro and directed by Roland Joffe, the most successful film.

Hayman, Ronald. *Robert Bolt.* London: Heinemann, 1969. The first book-length study of Bolt's work, devoting six chapters to single plays but adding two interviews, the first biographical and the second addressed directly to the present study. Bolt states that the volume is "certainly the most immediate and penetrating comment" on his work. Bibliography, a few illustrations, and a preface.

Kennedy, Harlan. "Nostromo." *American Film: Magazine of the Film and Television Arts* 15 (March, 1990): 28-31. A preproduction discussion of the filming of Joseph Conrad's novel, adapted by Bolt and Christopher Hampton, and directed by David Lean. Good biographical profiles and analysis of the novel's potential. Mentions two Bolt projects in preparation in 1990: *Buddha*, to be directed by Bernardo Bertolucci, and *Without Warning*, a teleplay on James Brady.

McCrindle, Joseph F., ed. *Behind the Scenes: Theater and Film Interviews from "The Transatlantic Review."* New York: Holt, Rinehart and Winston, 1971. Barry Pree interviewed Bolt in 1964 on the themes of his new play *Gentle Jack* and on his film work for director David Lean and producer Sam Spiegel—*Lawrence of Arabia* and *Doctor Zhivago.* "I love stars," Bolt says. "I like the grand manner and big personalities."

Marowitz, Charles, and Simon Trussler, eds. *Theatre at Work: Playwrights and Productions in the Modern British Theatre.* New York: Hill & Wang, 1967. An early interview with updates, covering Bolt's university upbringing and early experience, his concentration on radio plays before *Flowering Cherry*, and his admission that his plays do not reach working-class audiences.

Rusinko, Susan. *British Drama, 1950 to the Present: A Critical History.* Boston: Twayne, 1989. Rusinko places Bolt among the traditionalists, "a craftsman in the tradition of the well-constructed play middle-class audiences have come to expect." Contains a discussion of the controversy between critic Kenneth Tynan and Bolt regarding the Thomas More character in *A Man for All Seasons.*

Gertrude K. Hamilton
(Updated by *Thomas J. Taylor*)

EDWARD BOND

Born: Hollaway, North London, England; July 18, 1934

Principal drama

The Pope's Wedding, pr. 1962, pb. 1971; *Saved*, pr. 1965, pb. 1966; *Early Morning*, pr., pb. 1968; *Narrow Road to the Deep North*, pr., pb. 1968; *Black Mass*, pr. 1970, pb. 1971; *Lear*, pr. 1971, pb. 1972; *Passion*, pr., pb. 1971; *Bingo: Scenes of Money and Death*, pr. 1973, pb. 1974; *The Sea*, pr., pb. 1973; *The Fool*, pr. 1975, pb. 1976; *A-A-America!*, pr., pb. 1976; *Stone*, pr., pb. 1976; *We Come to the River*, pr., pb. 1976 (music by Hanz Werner Henze); *The Bundle: Or, New Narrow Road to the Deep North*, pr., pb. 1978; *The Woman*, pr. 1978, pb. 1979; *The Cat*, pr. 1980, pb. 1982; *Restoration*, pr., pb. 1981 (music by Nick Bicat); *Summer*, pr., pb. 1982; *Derek*, pb. 1983; *The English Cat*, pb. 1983 (opera libretto, music by Hans Werner Henze); *Red, Black, and Ignorant*, pb. 1985; *The War Plays*, pb. 1985; *Human Cannon*, pb. 1985; *Jackets*, pr. 1989, pb. 1990; *In the Company of Men*, pr. 1989, pb. 1990; *September*, pr., pb. 1990; *Two Post-Modern Plays*, pb. 1990.

Other literary forms

Edward Bond has adapted or translated classic plays, published several volumes of poetry and essays, and written a number of screenplays; he cowrote with Michelangelo Antonioni the screenplay for *Blow Up* (1967), also directed by Antonioni. Generally, Bond's essays deal with politics and the political responsibility of the artist.

Achievements

Bond's first major achievements occurred in the law court and in Parliament. His play *Saved* was the last British play prosecuted for obscenity; his *Early Morning*, the last banned entirely by the Lord Chancellor's office. The controversy stirred by these two plays focused attention on Britain's censorship laws and helped rally support to repeal them. Because of this notoriety and his association with London's Royal Court Theatre, long the home of experimental drama, Bond's detractors now dismiss him as an *enfant terrible* intent on shocking a complacent middle class. This view not only underestimates the excellence of Bond's early work but also denies the scope and richness of what has followed. A serious leftist, Bond has been concerned to show how social conditions generate moral ideas and how the past weighs on the present. Not surprisingly, then, Bond's later work has concentrated on mythic or historical subjects; he has written a play based on the Lear legend (*Lear*) and another about William Shakespeare in retirement (*Bingo*). *Early Morning* is set in Victoria's reign and *The Sea* in Edward's; *The Fool* is about the Romantic poet John Clare. In short, no other contemporary British playwright has explored the British past as thoroughly as has Bond in his search to find the sources of British ideas.

Bond disparages his film scripts because he believes that work in this medium cannot escape commercialism. Nevertheless, two of his screenplays, *Blow Up* (based on a story by Julio Cortázar) and *Walkabout* (1971) deserve mention. In *Blow Up*, a photographer discovers that he has accidentally taken a picture of what appears to be a murder. The film then explores the reactions of the photographer and his friends to this act of violence. This theme seems very close to those of Bond's major works. Similarly, *Walkabout*, the story of two children lost in the Australian Outback who are befriended by an aborigine, is informed by Bond's notion that innocence is available to primitives and children in a way that it is not available to civilized adults.

Biography

Born into a working-class family, Edward Bond, one of four children, was evacuated to Cornwall at the beginning of World War II, after which he returned to his grandparents' home near Ely. These country experiences were important to Bond and may be the source of his exceptional ability to capture a wide variety of speech mannerisms. After the war, he returned to London for grammar school and attended Crouch End Secondary Modern School; like many of his classmates, he left school at fifteen. He later attributed his interest in playwriting to two childhood experiences: first, his early exposure to the music hall, where one of his sisters was a magician's assistant, and second, his seeing, at age fourteen, the actor Daniel Wolfit in Shakespeare's *Macbeth*. Bond says of this experience, "It was the first thing that made sense of my life for me."

After leaving school, Bond worked in a factory until he was eighteen and then fulfilled his national service obligation (1953-1955). After basic training, he found himself stationed in Vienna, where he began seriously to try to write fiction. He returned to London in 1955 and again worked in factories. After submitting some plays to the Royal Court, he was asked in 1958 to join the writers' group there and to become a regular play reader for the theater. His first produced play, *The Pope's Wedding*, was directed by George Devine, who became Bond's favorite director and a champion of his work. Since 1966, Bond has lived by his writing, although his income has come more from the cinema than the theater. In 1971, Bond married Elisabeth Pablé. He has developed a coterie following in England and the United States and has been a popular playwright in Germany. His plays have won a number of awards, including the George Devine Award and the John Whiting Award in 1968, and in 1977 Yale University awarded him an honorary doctorate. Bond was writer-in-residence at the University of Essex from 1982 to 1983, and he subsequently served as a visiting professor at the University of Palermo in Italy.

Analysis

Edward Bond's early plays, *The Pope's Wedding* and *Saved*, realistically depict the English working class. His later plays move toward mythological and historical drama whose form seems to have been influenced by the works of both Bertolt Brecht and Shakespeare. In all of his work, Bond considers the connections of political power and violence in a society that reduces human beings to commodities.

Bond's second play, *Saved*, created a *succès de scandale*, and much of his subsequent fame depended on the notoriety of this first production at the Royal Court Theatre. The play tells the story of a young man, Len, who is picked up by a young woman, Pam, and taken home by her. The first scene depicts Pam's seduction of Len and his embarrassment at being interrupted by her father, Harry. Len rents a room in Pam's parents' flat, but the affair ends when Pam falls in love with another young man, Fred. All of these characters are clearly South London working class, but none is unemployed or desperate for money. The play instead examines emotional poverty and destructive relationships. Although Pam bears Fred's child, Len continues to live with her parents, who have arranged their lives so that they hardly see or speak to each other.

Fred abandons Pam, who continues to pursue him and enlists Len's aid in doing so. In scene 4, Len, Pam, Harry, and Mary, Pam's mother, studiously ignore the crying baby as the audience witnesses the emotional poverty of their lives. After a short domestic scene between Len and Pam, scene 6 provides the play's central action. It begins with Fred and Len talking to each other about Pam. Some of Fred's friends arrive and describe their rowdy activities. Pam enters, pushing the baby's carriage. She tells Fred that the baby will be quiet because she has doped it with aspirin, but eventually she argues with the men and exits. Len exits shortly afterward. More of Fred's friends arrive, and rough male joking begins. Soon, the youths notice the baby and begin pushing the carriage violently across the stage. As Fred watches passively, their actions escalate until they remove the baby's diaper and rub its own excrement on its face.

One of the men, Pete, then throws a stone to Fred, who lets it drop. There is a moment of silence, then some taunting. At last, Fred picks up the stone and throws it into the carriage. The other men then stone the child. The men run off and Pam enters and wheels the carriage away, cooing all the time to the baby, at whom she has not yet looked closely. In scene 7, the last in the first act, Pam and Len visit Fred in jail. Fred will be convicted of manslaughter, but, more important, the audience learns that Len witnessed the entire scene but did not come forward to the police. It is also apparent that Pam still loves Fred.

As Sir Laurence Olivier pointed out in his defense of the play, *Saved* is like Shakespeare's *Macbeth* and *Julius Caesar* in that a horrifying act of violence happens in the first part of the play, with the rest of the play devoted to examining the consequences of that action. The remaining six scenes of *Saved* portray Len's continuing efforts to establish human contact and to work out his feelings about the killing. Act 2 opens with Harry and Len talking about Harry's work. The audience is unclear about how much time has lapsed since Fred's trial. Pam enters and an argument erupts. Bond uses this scene to show how Pam has not been changed by the baby's death and how Len is still searching for a viable human relationship. In the next scene, Mary and Len are alone together; she tears her stocking, which Len repairs. As he kneels beside her to work on the stocking, the audience sees that despite their age difference there is a powerful sexual attraction between them. In a clear parallel to scene 1, Harry also interrupts this scene.

Scene 10 shows Fred's return to his friends after his prison sentence. Pam and Len both go to the pub in which this reunion occurs. Several times, Len tries to find out what Fred felt during the stoning of the baby. Fred has objectified the experience and refuses to talk to Len. Indeed, his comments are all about the awfulness of prison. At the end of this scene, he rejects Pam brutally and takes up with another girl. Pam blames Len for this rejection.

Scene 11 shows a violent fight between Mary and Harry, who has accused his wife of "goin' after [her] own daughter's leftovers." Pam and Len interrupt this scene but are unable to prevent Mary from breaking a teapot (significantly, a wedding present) over Harry's head. Pam, still distraught because of her rejection by Fred, blames Len for all of her troubles.

Scene 12 is a scene of reconciliation between Harry and Len, in which Harry, among other things, tells Len that he has missed his chance because there is no war. Harry remembers killing with fondness. This scene, in which Harry and Len acknowledge their similarities, is the closest to real human contact that any of the characters come. The final scene of the play presents the entire family onstage while Len attempts to fix a chair; they sit self-absorbed and silent as he works.

This plot summary, which suggests how Bond mixes the tedious and ordinary to reveal the deeper evils in human nature, cannot convey the real power of *Saved*. His control of speech rhythms enhances the believability of the characters, revealing the depth of feeling that lies beneath the mere content of their speeches. Their very inarticulateness motivates their violence; they can only lash out.

Most of the early critics of the play were so appalled by its violence that they overlooked its devastating and insightful comments on society as well as its literary merit. Bond himself chides these critics in his introduction to the play when he writes, "Clearly the stoning to death of a baby in a London park is a typical British understatement. Compared to the strategic bombing of German towns it is a negligible atrocity, compared to the cultural and emotional deprivation of most of our children its consequences are insignificant."

The play, in fact, has two intertwined stories—the death of the child and Len's growing attraction for Mary. This second plot Bond calls an "Oedipal comedy" which is resolved by Harry's and Len's reconciliation. The death of the baby, however, must be seen in context. Scene 4, in which the baby is ignored, the personal relations within Pam's family, and the personality of Fred and his friends all suggest the bleakness of the life that would await this child if it grew up; at best, it would become like its murderers. The stoning, then, is a metaphor for the life of such children and shows in one brief, horrid moment the damage that accumulates over a lifetime.

Len constantly seeks a way out of these destructive relationships. Instinctively, he knows the importance of human contact, and instinctively he seeks it. His world offers virtually no language and no social structure to facilitate these contacts. Actions, often small and discontinuous, are thus the characters' only real means of expression. The last scene, in which Len repairs the chair, is a fitting end to the play. Len's commitment to Harry, Mary, and Pam is affirmed by this action; the others' indifference to him is affirmed by the trivial tasks they perform. The only speech in the last scene is Len's request for a hammer—a request the others ignore. Bond calls *Saved* "almost irresponsibly optimistic" because Len retains his "natural goodness." To the extent that Len survives the horrors of the play, Bond may be right in his judgment.

In an early *Theatre Quarterly* interview, Bond suggested that *Saved* suffered from "too much realism." His next play, *Early Morning*, a political satire set vaguely in Victoria's court, suffers from no such disadvantage. The Prince of Wales is portrayed as Siamese twins; Victoria is having a lesbian relationship with Florence Nightingale; and Disraeli plans a coup. Many critics, notably Malcolm Hay, see *Early Morning* as the play which holds the clue to Bond's later work. Bond's next play, *Narrow Road to the Deep North*, however—also performed in 1968—uses similar themes and techniques, won wider critical acclaim, and is more accessible to the non-British audience.

Bond says that *Narrow Road to the Deep North* began from his reading of *The Narrow Road to the Deep North* (1933), by the seventeenth century Japanese poet Matsuo Bashō, who is a character in the play. In one section of this celebrated travel journal, "The Records of a Weather Beaten Skeleton," Bashō reports that he came across a child abandoned by a river and decided that it was fate or "the irresistible will of heaven" which had caused its abandonment. Bashō then concludes, "If it is so child, you must raise your voice to heaven, and I must pass on leaving you behind."

Bond was so shocked by this incident that he put the book down and refused to go on reading it. The memory of it festered, however, and Bond's play resulted. This genesis would suggest that Bond's play is about the social responsibility of the artist—a theme clear in two of Bond's later plays, *Bingo* and *The Fool*. Bond's Bashō, however, is a religious poet; he seeks enlightenment in his travels and therefore seeks the "Deep North." The play is thus about religion and society, and as Tony Coult observes, "Edward Bond is an atheist and a humanist. These facts are basic to what goes on in his plays. His work invariably embodies a tough critique of the unholy alliance between religion and politics."

There are numerous formal and stylistic differences between *Narrow Road to the Deep North* and *Saved*. First, *Narrow Road to the Deep North* makes no pretense at historical accuracy: The seventeenth century poet invites nineteenth century English missionaries into Japan. The audience is firmly in the world of fable. Second, Bond is willing to address the audience directly. In the introduction, as Bond calls his prologue, Bashō says, "I'm the seventeenth century poet Bashō." Scene 1 begins, "Thirty years since I was here!," and the next scene Bashō begins, "I've been back two years now." In short, Bond ignores the conventions of exposition and simply tells the audience directly what it needs to know and moves on. Third, Bond develops two techniques beyond their use in *Saved*. His ability to create the symbolic stage picture has increased, and he is more at home in an extended episodic structure which allows him to trace the development of a story through time. History is important to Bond, and he seeks forms that allow him to trace its consequence.

Narrow Road to the Deep North opens with a prologue in which Bashō leaves the abandoned child by the river. He returns thirty years later, having been "enlightened," to find the city ruled by the tyrant Shogo, who is discovered at the end of the play to be the child that Bashō left to die. Kiro, a young seeker after truth, wants to become Bashō's disciple, but Bashō rejects him. During this scene, prisoners are marched to the river to be drowned. Bashō is confronted face-to-face with Shogo's cruelty.

Two years later, Shogo summons Bashō to the palace to become the tutor of the Emperor's son, the legitimate ruler of the city. On the same day, Kiro, clowning about with two other monks, gets his head stuck in a sacred pot. Bashō brings him before Shogo and challenges him to resolve this dilemma. Shogo, having no respect for the sacredness of the pot, simply smashes it. Kiro is so entranced by the power of direct action that he becomes Shogo's follower despite reservations about his cruelty. Bashō, appalled by this sacrilege, persuades the British to invade and take over.

The British are represented by Georgina, a missionary, and the Commodore, her military brother. Bashō mistakenly assumes he can control the Commodore, only to discover that Georgina is the real power and that her morality is as destructive as Shogo's barbarity. Posing as priests, Kiro and Shogo escape to the deep north, where Shogo raises an army. He retakes the city and determines that the boy emperor shall not be used against him again. When Georgina, who has been left in charge of the children, cannot tell him who is the boy emperor, he kills them all. This act drives Georgina mad. The Commodore returns with reinforcements and retakes the city, capturing Shogo in the process.

The play's last scene shows Bond's growing strength and sophistication as a playwright. Shogo has been executed offstage. A procession of cheering townspeople enters carrying parts of Shogo's mutilated body on placards. After the crowd passes, Georgina and Kiro are left onstage. Kiro opens his robe, and Georgina comically and anxiously awaits rape. Instead, Kiro performs hara-kiri. Two British soldiers enter and lead the still expectant Georgina away. A shout is heard offstage, and a man, dripping wet, emerges from the river. Naked, except for a loincloth, he asks, "Didn't you hear me shout? I shouted 'help.' You must have heard and didn't come. . . . I could have drowned." He wrings out his loincloth and dries himself with a banner from the procession as Kiro's body pitches forward in its death spasm. Thus, Bond ends the play with a complex of rhythms and images that bring his humanist view center. The audience is left with the nude body of the bather drying himself, unaware of the corpse beside him. Men must help men. Magic pots, prayers, and ritual suicide are all useless. The play echoes Brecht's heroine Joan Dark, who learns "that only men help where men are."

Unquestionably Bond's greatest achievement is his play *Lear*, which is not an adaptation or rewrite of Shakespeare's *King Lear* but a new play based on the Lear story. In fact, because Cordelia survives and rules in Bond's play, he claims that his play more closely follows the sources. Many of his statements about his own work must be taken with a grain of salt; like George Bernard Shaw, Bond makes extreme statements to annoy his critics. Nevertheless, part of the power of Bond's play derives from the comparison with *King Lear*, and in many ways it forms an anti-*Lear*—that is, it acknowledges the very different social worlds that produced the two plays.

In their book on Bond's plays, Malcolm Hay and Philip Roberts describe how Bond worked and the changes he made in the manuscript during the year and a half it took him to write the play. In his notes, Bond says of *King Lear*, "As a society we use the play in the wrong way. And it's for that reason that I would like to rewrite it so that we now have to use the play for ourselves, for our society, for our time, for our problems."

Lear's plot is too complex to summarize in detail, but there are some essential similarities and differences between it and *King Lear*. Like Shakespeare's Lear, Bond's king moves from arbitrariness through insanity to understanding. Daughters rebel against their father, the kingdom is divided, and blindness and the imprisonment of father and daughter occur. Like *King Lear*, Bond's play presents its themes and characters through animal imagery.

The differences between the plays seem more important. Bond renames Regan and Goneril as Bodice and Fontanelle. Cordelia is not Lear's daughter but a guerrilla leader who overthrows Bodice and Fontanelle and finds herself condemned to repeat Lear's mistakes. The action does not start from Lear's laying down of his authority but from his arbitrary exercise of it. As Bond's play opens, Lear and his daughters are inspecting a wall that Lear is building around the entire kingdom to protect it from his enemies. Because the wall drains the local people of both land and money, they attempt to sabotage the wall. Lear executes a malingering worker without a trial; his daughters, appalled at this abuse of power, marry his enemies and lead a revolt.

All the positive characters (Edgar, Kent, Albany, Gloucester) disappear from Bond's play. Lear himself is blinded onstage. The Fool is transformed into the Ghost of the Gravedigger's Boy and functions opposite Shakespeare's fool. Instead of leading Lear to wisdom, the ghost offers Lear refuge in noninvolvement and self-pity; he is less responsible than the king.

The eighteenth century found *King Lear* too violent, and it was rewritten into a decorous tragedy. Bond seems not to have found it violent enough. Warick, Lear's counselor, is beaten onstage, and his eardrums are pierced by Bodice's knitting needle. The death of the Gravedigger's Boy is accompanied by the squeals of slaughtered pigs. A medical orderly blinds Lear with a suction device after trapping his head in a specially designed chair. Like a good doctor, he sprays an aerosol on the wound to "encourage scabbing." The play ends when Lear is shot trying to destroy the wall that Cordelia is in the process of rebuilding. Bond might not argue that human beings today are more cruel than they were in the seventeenth century, but he will not allow his audience to forget that the modern technology of cruelty far exceeds the devices of the past.

In his preface written after the first production, Bond defends himself against those critics who find his work too violent:

> I write about violence as naturally as Jane Austen wrote about manners. Violence shapes and obsesses our society and if we do not stop being violent, we have no future. People who do not want writers to write about violence want us to stop writing about us and our time. It would be immoral not to write about violence.

To see and to accept humankind's role in violence leads one to see clearly, to understand. In act 2, Fontanelle, imprisoned with Lear, is executed onstage, and the medical orderly performs an autopsy on her. Lear watches with intense interest, saying: "She sleeps inside like a lion and a lamb and a child. The things are so beautiful. I am astonished. I have never seen anything so beautiful. . . ." The human body is not as it is for King Lear, "a poor bare forked thing." Bodice, the other daughter, is brought in as a prisoner during the autopsy. In their ensuing argument, Lear "puts his hands into Fontanelle and brings them out with organs and viscera." He says to Bodice:

> Look! I killed her! Her blood is on my hands! Destroyer! Murderer! And now I must begin again. I must walk through my life, step after step, I must walk in weariness and bitterness. I must become a child, hungry and stripped and shivering in blood, I must open my eyes and see.

Lear's inability to shirk the violence that his world has created leads him to pity and sanity, but Bond will not stop here. At the end of this scene, Lear is blinded after witnessing the death of both of his daughters. In his blindness, he is led to insight. Bond's Lear finds no redemption; revolt, not order, is established at the end of the play. Cordelia's revolution leads to more violence because her "morality is a form of violence."

Restoration extended Bond's reworking of past genres to include Restoration drama. *Summer* concerns a group of survivors of Nazi occupation, and the trilogy *The War Plays* argues for societal responsibility in its depiction of a postnuclear world. It is perhaps *Lear* and *Narrow Road to the Deep North*, however, that suggest most of the concerns and techniques of Bond's theater. He stands to Shakespeare as the Greek tragedians stood to Homer. Like them, he rewrites old stories for a new time. Like Shakespeare, he makes myths out of English history—or rather, he deconstructs the myths of the past. In Bond's play *Bingo*, for example, Shakespeare is a character. Bond is not, however, concerned with the great playwright, but with the middle-class investor who allows himself to be bought off so that the big landlords can enclose the common fields. Bond's play *The Fool* centers on the Romantic poet John Clare. Instead of a private madness or the divine madness of the great poet, Bond shows a working-class writer driven mad by upper-class expectations and attitudes. In both of these plays, Bond attacks the romantic myth of the artist who is separated from and superior to society. By negative examples, he insists that the artist is shaped by his time and his responsibilities to it.

Major British playwrights have to move Shakespeare; he sits on their horizons like a threatening cloud. Shaw railed at him all the time; Bond has sought to demythologize him in *Lear* and in *Bingo.* Bond is a writer at the height of his powers; like Shaw and Shakespeare, Bond can tell a story about interesting people in compelling language. Above all, he creates a stage picture that burns into the memory.

Other major works

POETRY: *Theatre Poems and Songs*, 1978; *Poems, 1978-1985*, 1987.

SCREENPLAYS: *Blow Up*, 1967 (with Michelangelo Antonioni; adaptation of Julio Cortázar's short story "Las babas del diablo"); *Laughter in the Dark*, 1969 (adaptation of Vladimir Nabokov's novel); *Walkabout*, 1971.

Bibliography

Coult, Tony. *The Plays of Edward Bond.* London: Methuen, 1978. An early and important study of Bond's work. The book is designed as a companion critical reader to Bond's plays, with a valuable introductory essay. Coult takes a thematic approach, concentrating on *Narrow Road to the Deep North*, *Lear*, *Bingo*, and *The Sea.* Supplemented by a chronology.

Hay, Malcolm, and Philip Roberts. *Bond: A Study of His Plays.* London: Methuen, 1980. This definitive study single-handedly places Bond in a distinct scholarly category where he is compared with his contemporaries. The chapters are arranged by plays, with a chronological list of plays, a strong introductory essay, and two sections of production stills. Supplemented by notes, a bibliography, and an index.

McCrindle, Joseph F., ed. *Behind the Scenes: Theater and Film Interviews from "The Transatlantic Review."* New York: Holt, Rinehart and Winston, 1971. Giles Gordon interviews a reluctant, even recalcitrant, Bond, "the opposite of gregarious by inclination" (Gordon's question and Bond's affirmation), in this 1966 piece, but he manages to get him talking about Anton Chekhov, Henrik Ibsen, and the best of his contemporaries.

Mathers, Pete. "Edward Bond Directs *Summer* at the Cottesloe, 1982." *New Theatre Quarterly* 2, no. 6 (May, 1986): 136-152. A performance analysis of the production directed by Bond himself, this article outlines Bond's directorial and artistic themes and approaches, "examining every element through which its audiences experienced that production." Contains full illustrations, including posters.

Peacock, D. Keith. *Radical Stages: Alternative History in Modern British Drama.* New York: Greenwood Press, 1991. In a chapter on Bond's historical allegories, and in his introductory essay, Peacock finds Bond's "alternative and . . . iconoclastic interpretation of history" at the center of his art. Strong critical discussion of *Bingo* (on William Shakespeare) and *The Fool* (on the Romantic poet John Clare). Usable general bibliography.

Scharine, Richard. *The Plays of Edward Bond.* London: Associated University Presses, 1976. A strong study of Bond as a revolutionary, yelling

"Fire!" as others "sit and watch." The first chapter, an introduction to Bond, and the last, a summary of themes and techniques, bracket six chapters on specific plays and one on "incidental dramatic works." Index.

Stuart, Ian. "Answering to the Dead: Edward Bond's *Jackets*, 1989-1990." *New Theatre Quarterly* 7 (May, 1991): 171-183. Examines the theory and practice of "theatre events" and "theatre acting" and discusses a specific acting style necessary to realize Bond's plays, exploring the work in progress. The *New Theatre Quarterly* and its predecessor, *Theatre Quarterly*, began concentrating on the development of Bond's career in 1972.

Taylor, John Russell. *The Second Wave: British Drama for the Seventies.* New York: Hill & Wang, 1971. A good early analysis of Bond by one of his first supporters. Taylor provides overviews of *Saved, Early Morning,* and a few other early works. Sees *Narrow Road to the Deep North* as marking "a new stage in Bond's mastery of his material and his ability to display it to best advantage."

Sidney F. Parham
(Updated by *Thomas J. Taylor*)

GORDON BOTTOMLEY

Born: Keighley, England; February 20, 1874
Died: Oare, near Marlborough, England; August 25, 1948

Principal drama

The Crier by Night, pb. 1902, pr. 1916 (one act); *Midsummer Eve*, pb. 1905, pr. 1930 (one act); *Laodice and Danaë*, pb. 1909, pr. 1930 (one act); *The Riding to Lithend*, pb. 1909, pr. 1928 (one act); *King Lear's Wife*, pr. 1915, pb. 1916; *Britain's Daughter*, pb. 1921, pr. 1922; *Gruach*, pb. 1921, pr. 1923; *Scenes and Plays*, pb. 1929 (includes *Ardvorlich's Wife*); *The Acts of Saint Peter*, pr., pb. 1933; *Lyric Plays*, pb. 1932; *Choric Plays and a Comedy*, pb. 1939; *Fire at Calbart*, pb. 1939, pr. 1944; *Kate Kennedy*, pr. 1944, pb. 1945.

Other literary forms

Gordon Bottomley also wrote nondramatic poetry, much of it published privately, in anthologies and in the small literary magazines of his time. Bottomley also favored a form of minor dramatic poetry which appears in the form of monologues, "duologues" (his term), and preludes. He also wrote many one-act plays, a form fashionable in small theaters and theater festivals, religious and secular, in the early part of the twentieth century. Examples of such miniatures of dramatic experimentation include *Ardvorlich's Wife*, in *Scenes and Plays*, and the short plays with Celtic themes in *Lyric Plays* and *Choric Plays and a Comedy*.

In addition to his lyric poetry and poetic drama, Bottomley took an active interest in visual arts and the careers of colleagues in a wide range of the arts. Thus, he introduced works by Sir James Guthrie, the graphic artist, and poetry by William Morris and Isaac Rosenberg, prominent poets of his time. He left also a lengthy correspondence with the painter and illustrator Paul Nash. It was Bottomley's conviction that serious drama must embrace music and the visual arts.

Bottomley also practiced the art of the dedicatory poem or prologue. Nearly every one of his theatrical works is dedicated in verse to a prominent artistic friend or colleague, including those mentioned above. In this practice the playwright followed and enlivened a long-standing tradition. Often Bottomley's prologue poems contain not only the standard praise for their recipient but also a brief apologia for his work.

Achievements

Bottomley was the recipient of the Femina Vie Heureuse prize, given in Paris in 1923, and three honorary degrees, from the universities of Aberdeen, in Scotland, and Durham and Leeds, in England. Perhaps, however, the playwright's achievement should be measured less by official acknowledgment than by his influence on contemporaries and disciples. The intense artistic friendships which Bottomley maintained helped to give momentum and focus to the efforts of the Georgian poets and to aid the movement of poetic and dramatic theme, structure, and language toward a distinctly modern mode. Bottomley was a recognized leader of his contemporaries, reading other playwrights' work in progress, writing frequent letters in response, and providing opportunities for stimulating work to designers, producers, and actors.

One of Bottomley's principal contributions to the arts was his insistence upon proper vocal training and delivery of lines of verse on the stage. Seeking to reestablish verse as a proper medium for drama, Bottomley was active in the formulation of a verse-speaking society whose efforts were copied elsewhere in Britain, Ireland, and the United States. By working with this society—with John Masefield, the poet laureate, who maintained a small theater in Oxford, and with experimental groups at the theater at Dartington Hall in Devon—and by aiding in the production of his and others' works by smaller groups and amateur groups, such as the Festival Theatre in Cambridge and the Yale University Drama School, Bottomley revived emphasis on the words used by playwrights to convey their dramatic ideas. *A Stage for Poetry: My Purposes with My Plays*, published in the year of his death, encapsulates Bottomley's views on the necessity for an artistic theater, definitely not aimed at mass audiences and their tastes; appendices in this text delineate his views on the need for the spoken word, in formal verse lines, to predominate on the stage.

Biography

Gordon Bottomley was the son of Alfred and Ann Maria Bottomley (née Gordon). The senior Bottomley worked as a cashier in a Yorkshire worsted mill and sent his son to Keighley Grammar School. After he left school, Gordon worked as a bank clerk until illness caused him to go into near-seclusion. He married Emily Burton of Arnside in 1905 and lived quietly, settling permanently in 1914 in The Shieling, Silverdale, near Carnforth in Lancashire. The Bottomleys took lengthy holidays in North Wales and often stayed with literary friends. Although Gordon Bottomley shunned the literary life of London, he was always current with literary and artistic trends, enjoying frequent communication and correspondence with such scholars as Lascelles Abercrombie, a fellow Georgian poet-dramatist; John Drinkwater, who wrote poetic plays and produced one of Bottomley's; Paul Nash, the painter, who produced sketches and studies of scenes from those plays; and Sir Edmund William Gosse, who would eventually respond negatively to the work of Bottomley and the Georgians. Perhaps Bottomley's greatest literary friend and supporter, however, was Sir Edward Marsh, the editor of several volumes bearing the title *Georgian Poetry*

(1912-1922), in which Bottomley's work figured prominently.

For all of his Georgian traits, it should be noted that Bottomley was deeply influenced by the Celtic Twilight movement of the late nineteenth century, as well as by the closely related Pre-Raphaelite Brotherhood. These movements were both interdisciplinary; both celebrated an idyllic, nearly prelapsarian, era of innocence and a setting in the more remote Celtic regions of Britain. Much of Bottomley's work is set in Scotland and draws from its folklore and mythology. In this, he is seen often as imitating or paralleling the dramatic experiments of William Butler Yeats, who found his inspiration in specifically Irish material.

There is little of event to record of Bottomley's personal life, but the publication and performance of one of his plays brought him a certain notoriety. When *King Lear's Wife* was first published, it appeared as the first offering in one of Marsh's anthologies, *Georgian Poetry II, 1913-1915* (1916). The preceding volume had been published to nearly unanimous acclaim, and literary critics hailed the harder, cleaner images of the modern Georgian poets, who were self-proclaimed anti-Victorians. The young poets of the new century were successfully freeing themselves from the limitations of the past. When *Georgian Poetry II, 1913-1915* was issued, however, the general critical response was negative—in some cases outraged—by what was judged to be excessive realism. The works of Bottomley and Abercrombie in particular were singled out as being representative of a new form of ugliness which offered violent and negative images of nature and humankind. Following productions of *King Lear's Wife* in Birmingham in 1915 and in London the next year, this negative response continued, with its focus on a corpse-washing sequence and a song, based on a child's nursery rhyme, which was considered shocking. It should be noted, however, that later critics, such as Frank Lawrence Lucas and Priscilla Thouless, have not been offended by Bottomley's harshness, generally viewing his work as transitional: He was aware of and influenced by the past, but he looked to the modern age.

Although Bottomley was in poor health for most of his life, he lived to see literary fashion change a number of times and to witness a small rekindling of interest in his drama in the 1940's, shortly before his death.

Analysis

In his *A Stage for Poetry*, Gordon Bottomley, near the end of his life, gave a tidy history of his dramatic career, complete with photographs and sketches of sets and costumes. More important, he left his own record of his dramatic intentions and accomplishments. He divided his works into two parts: "A Theatre Outworn" and "A Theatre Unborn." The former includes all the major works of his early career, which are written in traditional blank verse and hold generally to the nineteenth century model of heroic drama in aristocratic settings. From this group came Bottomley's commercial, if limited, successes. The plays that constitute his "Theatre Unborn" are considerably starker, using black or white cloths as backdrops, avoiding the proscenium stage, reverting to classical choric groups in robes, and featuring not aristocrats but characters who are often only partially human—either supernatural or animalistic or both. These theatrical experiments never found a proper audience, but they were not totally alien from Bottomley's earlier works. The playwright maintained an interest in Celtic mythology which runs through his work until the very end of his career. Although he came too late to be considered a playwright of the Celtic Twilight, Bottomley's themes and their execution stay true to that late nineteenth century movement's ideals. Bottomley's plays, many of them set in Scotland, contain frequent references to humans' dealings with supernatural creatures who hold power over them. His heroes and heroines are also frequently dreamers, incapable of dealing with the rigors of the real world; such refined sensibility was the Romantic legacy to the Celtic Twilight.

The Riding to Lithend is, in many ways, a characteristic one-act play by Bottomley. It features a long dedicatory poem to a prominent contemporary, and it is based, however loosely, on saga and myth. It includes a small cast of characters, not all of which are entirely or identifiably human, and its female characters are atypically strong, if not ferocious.

The play, written in 1908 but not performed until 1928, opens with a poem to the poet Edward Thomas, who died in World War I. In the poem, Bottomley refers to a visit from Thomas in 1907 during which he encouraged Bottomley to breathe new life into the adventures of the Icelandic hero Gunnar. Bottomley also compares Thomas himself to this early type by emphasizing his Welsh heritage, likening him to one of the heroes of *The Mabinogion* (c. 1100-1200), the Welsh saga cycle.

The *dramatis personae* include Gunnar Hamundsson, the hero-warrior; his wife, Hallgerd Longcoat; his mother, Rannveig; three female servants, Oddny, Astrid, and Steinvor; and a female thrall (a slave, taken in war), Ormild. There are also three beggar-women—Biartey, Jofrid, and Gudfinn—and many Riders, or warrior-vigilantes. The play is set in an "eating hall" in Gunnar's manor in the year 990. The female servants are combing and spinning wool and stitching a royal garment. In many of Bottomley's plays, an elaborate garment, representing its owner and symbolic of wealth and power, is prominently displayed in the opening scene.

The servant women have a sense of foreboding because all the men of the manor have been sent by Gunnar, rather unwisely it is feared, to a late harvest on the islands nearby. The abnormality of the harvest season is emphasized, and the audience learns that the seemingly capricious decision is in keeping with Gunnar's irregular hours and habits. He is an outcast from local law, and it is believed that his house is haunted by ghostly victims of his past misdeeds. Despite the foreboding occasioned by the unseasonal harvest, it is noted that Gunnar's "singing bill" (or sword) is silent, so that imminent danger seems unlikely. (The convention of the enchanted singing sword is prominent in early Northern European sagas and tales, most notably in Excalibur of Arthurian legend.) Once the concept of magic or unnatural power is introduced, there is a reference to a minor clairvoyant character who has foretold Gunnar's death. So strong is the power of this prophecy that Gunnar's brother, previously his stalwart lieutenant, has left Iceland as a result, and also to fulfill an injunction imposed upon Gunnar to exile himself for three years to atone for political and other misdeeds. All of this is related by the four serving women, who conclude that Gunnar, to defy such a prophecy, must be "fey"—that is, in the power of supernatural forces.

Rannveig enters and, as mother to two sons, one in exile, wishes Gunnar would fulfill the "atonement" and thus avoid being murdered by enraged noblemen. Hallgerd, the source of the trouble, enters preoccupied and angry about her fading beauty. Gunnar and Hallgerd argue over their predicament, and as a defiant gesture she looses her hair from its covering—signifying widowhood. It is then revealed that she was a widow when Gunnar first met, wooed, and won her. Theirs has been a turbulent marriage, and in the past, when Hallgerd stole food so as not to shame her husband in time of famine and in the presence of guests, he publicly humiliated her by slapping her face. By law, he could have killed or maimed her for such an offense. In this and others of Bottomley's plays, thievery, in keeping with the era and the culture he is representing, is a crime of great import and beneath the dignity of gentlefolk. This instance of thievery was the beginning of the blood feud which has resulted in Gunnar's being under injunction of exile.

Three witchlike figures from Icelandic myth enter, posing as beggar-women. They admit to traveling by flying through the night sky in a westerly direction (which signifies death), but Gunnar nevertheless agrees to house them for the night. These crones tell of Gunnar's heroic reputation, which remains solid throughout the country, and explain that there is still one ship by which he can escape. Here it is related that he did try once to leave the country, but his horse threw him and he experienced a vision of his homeland which made him vow to stay.

The crones also engage in traditional witch behavior, taking over the spinning (which they destroy), speaking of curses, and reciting the aristocratic lineage of Hallgerd, who in many respects is a worthy wife for the heroic Gunnar. The witches incense Hallgerd, who eventually drives them out. Their true nature becomes apparent when entering characters cannot see them; they become invisible after they leave the manor.

The noblemen who have awaited Gunnar's compliance with the law arrive at his home, and a battle ensues. Gunnar fights single-handedly, while Rannveig urges prudence and Hallgerd thirsts for blood. Gunnar's bowstring is broken, and he asks Hallgerd for some of her hair to repair it. She refuses—choosing this moment to avenge the public humiliation of her that he inflicted years earlier. Gunnar dies in battle with Hallgerd laughing. Rannveig, the grieving mother, keeps Hallgerd from her son's corpse, pulling her by the hair she denied to her husband. Rannveig then tries to murder Hallgerd to avenge her son's death, and hers is the play's final soliloquy—including a lullaby which uses images of sleep and death to good effect. In a final tableau, she raises the singing bill aloft over the corpse of her son. It is still singing, signifying Gunnar's victory even in death.

The Riding to Lithend makes significant use of Irish references, indicating the playwright's knowledge of the early links of custom and commerce between Iceland and Ireland and thus allowing for the Celtic Twilight influence seen elsewhere in his work. Also prominent is bird imagery, especially sinister imagery of birds of prey. The witch figures resemble in appearance and powers the Morrigan, a bird-woman of Celtic mythology who is usually a figure of death or misfortune, and Gunnar is identified with a bird-god which appears on his family crest.

The play delivers a primitive message in a primitive setting, and its characters retain the necessary two-dimensional qualities of figures in saga literature, who are more important as types than as individuals. The law is irrevocable, and although Gunnar is viewed as the best of the warrior mold of his homeland, he is not above the law. Appropriately, he dies in battle.

The blank verse, in this and in nearly all of Bottomley's plays, is at times merely neo-Elizabethan, deriving from the Shakespearean model used so much in the nineteenth century theater, but it can rise to eloquence when the playwright molds an honored verse form to modern language and expression. Bottomley's servant characters often have lines of a cleaner, more precise language; unlike Shakespearean servants, they too speak in blank verse, like their masters and mistresses.

King Lear's Wife begins with a lengthy dedicatory poem to Thomas Sturge Moore, another multifaceted artist who wrote verse plays of Bottomley's type and who also achieved distinction as an illustrator and designer of books, costumes and stage sets. The poem, written in iambic quadrameter, is composed in three stanzas of irregular length, each of which opens and closes with a triplet, while the remainder is formed in couplets. Bottomley praises *The Dial*, a literary magazine of the day, in which he had first encountered Moore's poetry from his seclusion in Lancashire. He hails Moore as "prince of poets in our time" and reminisces about conversations they enjoyed at a meeting in Surrey. Bottomley closes by offering *King Lear's Wife* as a "token . . . of admiration and loyalty."

The *dramatis personae* include Lear, King of Britain; Hygd, his queen;

Goneril and Cordeil, his daughters; Gormflaith and Merryn, servants to the queen; a Physician and two Elderly Women. The setting is a primitive English castle, fitted with harsh fabrics which deny a hospitable atmosphere. Highlighted is an elaborate robe and crown which belong to the "emaciated" Queen Hygd, whose large four-poster bed dominates the stage. She is being attended by Merryn, a Cornish servant of many years' service, and it is very early in the morning—a bleak time for a bleak setting.

The immediate subject is death. Hygd wants to die, feeling unneeded in middle age, but lingers mournfully in her illness. Merryn, quite old, is characterized as superstitious and alien because of her Cornish heritage; she dreads the idea of her own death. Enter a very vital middle-aged Lear, not the old and crazed figure of Bottomley's Shakespearean model. He is accompanied by the court Physician, and he has arranged for Gormflaith, a young Scotswoman, to tend the queen.

The Physician, seeking a psychological explanation for the queen's failing health, asks what long-term bitterness nursed in secret is the cause. The king responds vituperatively, and then the Physician suggests a cure, of juniper berries, marrow of adder, and emerald dust. Only Lear has a valuable emerald, a gift from an Irish king whose daughter mothered many British kings. He refuses to destroy it to save his wife's life.

Hygd awakens alone and is joined by Goneril, who is on the edge of womanhood. Dressed in hunting garb, Goneril is described in terms associated with Diana, the Greek virgin goddess and hunter. Both Goneril and Gormflaith are representative of "life." It is Lear's belief that his wife will benefit from their presence, but Hygd is repelled by their vitality. Goneril describes a visionary encounter at a Druidic site (a holy place of the priest class which had earlier controlled Britain). In contrast, Hygd describes and dismisses the new Christian religion of Merryn. Hygd then asks about Regan (the third daughter of Lear, who appears as an important character in Shakespeare's play but not at all in Bottomley's).

Hygd warns Goneril to enjoy her freedom now because soon she will be obliged to marry. The aging queen offers a philosophy frequent in Bottomley's work—that the domestication of fine, brave young women in marriage yields bitter results. At best, claims Hygd, women can only be venerated in age, whereas men fare better and have wider choices later in life.

They are interrupted by the child Cordeil (Cordelia in Shakespeare), who is at the door seeking her father. She is called "my little curse" and "an evil child" by her mother, who denies her access to the sickroom. Hygd claims that she conceived Cordeil to keep Lear faithful, adding that Cordeil's birth has left her an invalid. After Goneril lulls her mother to sleep, Gormflaith enters, an attractive woman, too eager to please. She reads a letter arranging an assignation with Lear, who arrives and destroys the letter for the sake of security. He then softens the blow by allowing Gormflaith to wear his emerald.

The king intends to make Gormflaith his queen after Hygd's death, despite Gormflaith's cunning observations concerning the negative effect this will have in his court and within his family. In his desire for a male heir, Lear will not hear reason. Gormflaith, in a climactic moment, asks to wear Hygd's crown, and Lear chastises her: "You cannot have the nature of a queen/ If you believe that there are things above you." Lear softens again, however, and while Gormflaith is sitting on his knee, wearing Hygd's crown, the queen awakens and sees all. Hygd tries to follow the lovers to the garden, falls, has a dying vision of Lear's mother, and dies shouting to Goneril "Pay Gormflaith."

The play rapidly becomes less poetic as Merryn discusses the need to tend the dead queen before rigor mortis sets in. The irony and bitterness increase as Goneril mockingly pays homage when Gormflaith reenters, still wearing Hygd's crown. Since Gormflaith was meant to be tending the queen, the enraged Goneril demands of her father the penalty given for servants leaving their posts, knowing fully that Lear is the cause of Gormflaith's absence. Goneril snatches the crown and replaces it on the queen.

The momentum of the play, its imagery and tone, alter greatly with the entrance of two women to minister to the queen's body. Like the gravediggers in William Shakespeare's *Hamlet*, they are irreverent in the presence of death, haggling over Hygd's personal effects—traditional payment for such work. They sing a grisly work song to the tune of "Froggie's Gone a Courtin'," preparing the reader for the equally grisly entrance of Goneril with a bloody knife. In a somewhat surprising about-face, Lear, when confronted by his murderess-daughter, disowns the dead Gormflaith and calls Goneril his "true daughter." The play ends with Lear hoping to marry off and "break" Goneril, thus bearing out Hygd's earlier fear, and the corpse washers finish by enjoying the irony of Lear's having traded one predicament—a sick wife—for another—a fearless and cruel daughter.

King Lear's Wife observes the traditional dramatic unities scrupulously. It showcases Lear against a predominantly female cast to great effect, and it develops ideas seen often in Bottomley's corpus. Beauty is power, but it is transient; death and physical violence are always near. The play rings a gender change on the classic revenge drama, because here a daughter avenges the disgrace and death of her mother. Ultimately, it affirms the sense of hierarchy and order codified in the law: Evildoers receive their just deserts.

The language of *King Lear's Wife* is not as garrulous as it is in many of Bottomley's works, and the speeches of supporting characters, such as

Merryn and the two corpse washers, are effective in reinforcing the thematic message of the play. Animal imagery prevails and is well integrated. The corpse washers wear black, batlike or birdlike costumes, appropriate to their task, and the reader is prepared for Goneril's murderous role because as a huntress she has killed in cold blood and become exhilarated by the act.

Hygd, the title character, was first performed by Katherine Drinkwater, the producer's wife, and later by Lady Viola Tree, of the famous acting family. *King Lear's Wife* was the only play Bottomley wrote that provoked a significant critical response. Although that response was largely negative, it drew attention to Bottomley's work, and as a result, his plays were produced more readily in subsequent years.

Although Gordon Bottomley's work has evoked little interest among critics of his own or subsequent generations, it is an excellent example of the transitional nature of the Georgian movement. Like the work of his contemporary, Yeats, Bottomley's plays bridged the Victorian and modern eras. He employed ancient Celtic folklore and mythology as subject matter, the verse form of Elizabethan drama, and combined them with the realism and clarity of language characteristic of modern drama. The more realistic content and style already being employed by Henrik Ibsen and George Bernard Shaw, however, had moved Western drama into the twentieth century, while Bottomley's work remained part of an earlier era.

Other major works

POETRY: *Poems at White Nights*, 1899; *Chambers of Imagery*, 1907-1912 (2 volumes); *A Vision of Giorgione*, 1910; *Poems of Thirty Years*, 1925.

NONFICTION: *A Stage for Poetry: My Purpose with My Plays*, 1948; *Poet and Painter, Being the Correspondence Between Gordon Bottomley and Paul Nash, 1910-1946*, 1955, 1990.

MISCELLANEOUS: *Poems and Plays*, 1953.

Bibliography

Bottomley, Gordon. Author's Note to *Lyric Plays*. London: Constable, 1932. Bottomley offers hints for the successful performance of his plays, which are written in verse. He says that a nonrealistic approach is best. The verse must be performed by trained speakers, and their movement should be rhythmic and beautiful, like a dance. By 1932, Bottomley's work seemed hopelessly out of date. He blamed the public's lack of enthusiasm for his plays on a general decline in the theater.

_____. Author's Note to *Scenes and Plays*. New York: Macmillan, 1929. In this first volume of his collected plays, Bottomley compares his work to Japanese Nō drama. He encourages the use of a speaking chorus consisting of eight to twelve members to increase the dramatic effect of his poetry. Bottomley also insists on a minimum of scenery. He says that he wants the audience to experience his plays intimately, "a chamber-drama to set beside our most precious heritage of chamber-music."

Causey, Andrew. Introduction to *Poet and Painter: Letters by Gordon Bottomley*. 2d ed. Bristol, England: Redcliffe Press, 1990. Causey offers rare biographical details about Bottomley, who started his literary career before the beginning of the twentieth century and remained committed to the philosophy of the Pre-Raphaelites and the Arts and Crafts movement. Paul Nash, his friend, was born fifteen years later, and so was more easily able to adapt to changing artistic tastes.

Pollard, Arthur. "Gordon Bottomley." In *Webster's New World Companion to English and American Literature*. New York: World Publishing, 1973. Pollard gives a brief but fairly complete account of Bottomley's career, which he says came about when "ill health compelled him to cut short a career in banking." Pollard states that Bottomley's plays were once considered quite avant-garde and experimental.

Thornton, R. K. R. "The Georgians." In *Webster's New World Companion to English and American Literature*, edited by Arhtur Pollard. New York: World Publishing, 1973. Thornton's article explains Bottomley's poetical drama as part of a literary movement that began in about 1910. The poetry in this movement was easy to understand, traditional in form and meter, pastoral in subject matter, and popular—unlike the difficult, abstract poetry that was to follow it. The Georgian movement, as it was called, lasted until approximately 1925. Because it failed to react to the alienation and upheavals that came with World War I, it came to be seen as laughably out of touch and old-fashioned.

Christina Hunt Mahony
(Updated by *Pamela Canal*)

DION BOUCICAULT
Dionysius Lardner Boursiquot

Born: Dublin, Ireland; December 27, 1820(?)
Died: New York, New York; September 18, 1890

Principal drama

London Assurance, pr., pb. 1841 (as Lee Moreton); *Old Heads and Young Hearts*, pr. 1844, pb. 1845; *The Knight of Arva*, pr. 1848, pb. 1868; *The Corsican Brothers*, pr., pb. 1852 (adaptation of Eugène Grangé and Xavier de Montépin's *Les Frères Corses*); *Louis XI*, pr., pb. 1855 (adaptation from the French); *The Poor of New York*, pr. 1857 (also known as *The Poor of Liverpool*, pr. 1864, and as *The Streets of London*; adaptation of Édouard-Louis-Alexandre Brisbarre and Eugène Nus's *Les Pauvres de Paris*); *Jessie Brown: Or, The Relief of Lucknow*, pr., pb. 1858; *Dot*, pr. 1859, pb. 1940 (adaptation of Charles Dickens' *The Cricket on the Hearth*); *The Octoroon: Or, Life in Louisiana*, pr. 1859, pr. 1861 (revised), pb. 1953 (adaptation of Mayne Reid's novel *The Quadroon*); *The Colleen Bawn*, pr. 1860, pb. 1953 (adaptation of Gerald Griffin's novel *The Collegians*); *Arrah-na-Pogue: Or, The Wicklow Wedding*, pr. 1864, pb. 1865 (in Gaelic); *Rip Van Winkle*, pr. 1865, pb. 1944 (with Joseph Jefferson; adaptation of the story by Washington Irving); *The Flying Scud: Or, Four-Legged Fortune*, pr. 1866, pb. 1940; *After Dark: A Tale of London Life*, pr., pb. 1868; *Formosa: Or, The Railroad to Ruin*, pr., pb. 1869; *Babil and Bijou*, pr. 1872 (with James Robinson Planché); *The Shaughraun*, pr. 1874, pb. 1880; *Forbidden Fruit*, pr., pb. 1876; *The Jilt*, pr. 1885, pb. 1904 (adaptation of a story by Hawley Smart); *Forbidden Fruit and Other Plays*, pb. 1940, 1963; *Plays*, pb. 1984; *Selected Plays*, pb. 1987.

Dion Boucicault was responsible for well over one hundred plays during his lengthy career. Some have been anthologized, and the three Irish plays were published together as *The Dolmen Boucicault* (1964). The others are most accessible in the microprint series *English and American Drama of the Nineteenth Century*, edited by Allardyce Nicoll and George Freedley (1965-1971), which also includes promptbook reproductions for many of the plays.

Other literary forms

Dion Boucicault's only fictional work was a collaboration with Charles Reade, *Foul Play* (1868). A short, dramatized history, *The Story of Ireland* (1881), was also published in his lifetime; *The Art of Acting* (1926) and *The Art of Acting: A Discussion by Constant Coquelin, Henry Irving, and Dion Boucicault* (1926) were posthumous collections. Boucicault was a regular contributor to *North American Review* from 1887 to 1889 and had written two essays for that periodical: "The Decline of the Drama" (1877) and

"The Art of Dramatic Composition" (1878). Several of his articles appeared elsewhere.

Achievements

Boucicault was the mid-nineteenth century's complete man of the theater. For almost fifty years, on both sides of the Atlantic, he labored as playwright, dramaturge, actor, director, and manager. Many of his enduring contributions were in the realm of practical theater. He was, with playwright Thomas William Robertson, one of the early proponents of directed rehearsals and ensemble playing. This interest led later to his formation of touring casts to replace the traditional system in which traveling stars played virtually unrehearsed stock dramas with local companies. He improved theatrical conditions by shortening the lengthy triple bills frequently offered and by abolishing half-price admission for latecomers. As an author, he fought for changes in American copyright law and for the principle of the playwright receiving a percentage of the receipts from his play's performance. Late in his life, he invented a method of fireproofing scenery.

As a dramatist, Boucicault was both prolific and popular. Here it was his sense of what would work onstage that raised him above his contemporaries. While many of his productions were translations or adaptations of others' works, any piece was more stageworthy once he had left his mark on it. Notable examples of his talents in this area are *The Corsican Brothers*, which he adapted from a French adaptation of a story by Alexandre Dumas, *père*, and *Rip Van Winkle*, which Boucicault adapted for the actor Joseph Jefferson. The former Boucicault merely made more spectacular, but for the latter, he completely remodeled the title character. The early Rip became a young and thoughtless scamp, lovable but destructive of himself and his family. The contrast between the young and old Rip adds dramatic interest, as does the very real dilemma his early behavior creates for his wife.

Boucicault's earliest successes were original comedies of manners. With this form, he provides virtually the only link between the great comic dramatists of previous centuries and Oscar Wilde. Indeed, several of Boucicault's early plays have scenes and characters that are suggestive of *The Importance of Being Earnest* (pr. 1895). *London Assurance*, his first major comedy, has been revived successfully in the twentieth century.

Moving next to sentimental melodrama, the dominant form of his day, Boucicault quickly mastered the formulas that would please audiences. The plays themselves have been largely forgotten, but the spectacular scenes with which he enlivened all of them have had a more lasting effect. It was his *After Dark*, for example, that popularized the image of the hero rescued from railway tracks as a train thundered toward him. Here again,

Boucicault had taken his hint from another playwright, Augustin Daly, but had doubled the atmosphere of suspense and integrated the scene into a well-made plot. His presentation of sensational scenes has been seen to have parallels with later cinematographic techniques.

Boucicault's American career had a strong effect on the development of American theater, and playwright-producer David Belasco can certainly be considered his follower. In England, George Bernard Shaw included him on a brief list of dramatists worth reading. It is on the Irish dramas, however, that Boucicault has had his most lasting influence. The transformation of the stage Irishman that he effected in his three best Irish plays was a clear forerunner to John Millington Synge's and Sean O'Casey's greatest characters, and both acknowledged their debt to him. Aside from grand theatricality and memorable characters, these plays were full of a gentle patriotism that only once went too far for his English audience. It was Boucicault's new version of the old ballad "The Wearing of the Green," which is sung in *Arrah-na-Pogue*, that caused that song to be banned in Britain and hence popularized it in Dublin and New York.

Biography

Dion Boucicault was born Dionysius Lardner Boursiquot in Dublin, Ireland, apparently in 1820, although he claimed a date in 1822. His mother, née Anne Darley, was sister to George Darley the poet and editor, and to the Reverend Charles Darley, a minor playwright. She was married to Samuel Smith Boursiquot, a Dublin wine merchant from whom she separated in 1819. Nevertheless, his will acknowledged Boucicault as his legitimate son, and the latter always referred to Boursiquot as his father—although Dr. Dionysius Lardner, who lived with Boucicault's mother from the summer of 1820 and was the boy's guardian, was probably Boucicault's actual father. Lardner was the compiler of *Cabinet Cyclopedia* and the first professor of natural philosophy and astronomy at the University of London (from 1827). Although Lardner financed young Dion Boucicault's education in Dublin and in the London area, the affair with Boucicault's mother did not survive Lardner's relocation to England.

After a brief apprenticeship to Lardner as a civil engineer, Boucicault had embarked, by 1838, on a stage career under the name Lee Moreton. *London Assurance*, accepted for the 1841 season at Covent Garden, was a resounding success on whose proceeds Boucicault brought his mother to London. Living beyond his means, he soon exhausted the money his first few comedies and farces brought him. In 1845, he married a French widow, Anne Guiot, his elder by some twenty years. She died soon after their marriage, in the Swiss Alps, leaving Boucicault a large sum that kept him in Paris for several more years. There, he familiarized himself with the French plays that were becoming so popular in England and that were to bring him many later successes in his translated and adapted versions. Always the actor, he traveled as the Viscount de Bourcicault.

When Charles Kean took over the Princess Theatre in 1850, Boucicault, impecunious again, was hired as his literary adviser. The two learned from each other, for Kean always sought the spectacular in his productions, and Boucicault was soon presenting scenes such as the miraculous appearance of the ghost in *The Corsican Brothers*. After joining Kean, he met the young actress Agnes Robertson, the manager's ward, who was to be his companion and partner for thirty years. By September, 1853, the two were performing in New York. Boucicault was later to claim that they had never married, but all of their acquaintances believed that they were man and wife. They had six children.

Having written *The Colleen Bawn* in a white heat and opened it successfully in New York, Boucicault returned with it to London in 1860, where the play ran an unprecedented 360 consecutive nights at the Adelphi. The next year, the piece opened in Dublin to enthusiastic Irish audiences. Until 1872, Boucicault was prospering in England. Then, an expensive collaboration with James Robinson Planché, *Babil and Bijou*, sent him once again to the United States in temporary disgrace. For the next few years, he toured on both sides of the Atlantic, and *The Shaughraun*, another Irish play, scored heavily wherever it played.

By then, Boucicault was often on the road without Agnes, and in 1885, while the company was performing in Sydney, Australia, he married Louise Thorndyke, a young actress in his last great success, *The Jilt*. Agnes sued for a formal divorce, which was eventually granted in England. Time was running out for Boucicault, whom William Archer had already branded "a playwright of yesterday." In 1888, his last company disbanded for lack of funds. For the next two years, he worked for an acting school in New York, where he died after a heart attack, complicated by pneumonia, on September 18, 1890.

Analysis

Dion Boucicault never had literary pretensions, but he was, and knew himself to be, a superb theatrical craftsman. He prefaced his first publication, *London Assurance*, with an apology that answers for much of his later work as well: "It will not bear analysis as a literary production. In fact, my sole object was to throw together a few scenes of a dramatic nature, and therefore I studied the stage rather than the moral effect." He later rationalized this concentration on the individual dramatic scene by arguing the decline of an audience whose chief literary form had become the newspaper. It is also true that he had to make his living from his work, and, as he once said, "More money has been made out of guano than out of poetry."

Certainly, Boucicault did not concentrate on fine language. Indeed, when he wrote his Aristotelian essay "The Art of Dramatic Composition," he listed only action, character, and decoration as the components of a drama. Diction and thought were never an issue for him, except as they were directly applicable to the presentation of plot and character. Nevertheless, a very serviceable acting drama can be written by concentrating on plot, characters, and spectacle.

Boucicault's drama was always based on his impression, invariably correct, of what would work in the theater. At the outset of his career, this impression was founded on his reading of the masters of English comedy. Oliver Goldsmith, Richard Brinsley Sheridan, George Farquhar, Sir John Vanbrugh, and William Congreve were his sources, and he wrote well in the comic style that they had established. His best work was always in the comic vein, but as his theatrical experience grew, he perfected his skills in melodrama. His great Irish plays represent the successful synthesis of these two strains.

What Boucicault learned above all from the earlier comic dramatists was the presentation of character-types. "By character," Boucicault wrote, "we mean that individuality in a person made by the consistency of feelings, speech, and physiognomy." The intricacies of character development were not for him, but in the creation of consistent comic caricatures, he excelled. From the gentleman freeloader Dazzle and the befuddled pastor Rural, through the thoughtlessly alcoholic Rip Van Winkle, to the rogue heroes of the Irish plays, Boucicault forged a gallery of memorable acting parts. The essential ingredient in each is individuality. Every major role has a certain dimension of stereotype, but the successful ones are not mere stereotypes.

As in his creation of spectacle, Boucicault exploits local color to the full. Thus, the clever servant is given a distinctively Irish flavor; the soldiers defending the empire are also clannish Scots; and the inventory of national types in *The Octoroon* includes an American Indian, good and bad Yankees, Southern gentry, a heroine of mixed blood, and a cosmopolitan hero who cannot understand why he should not marry her. A character such as Lady Gay Spanker, a typical domineering wife, is given an extra dose of realism by being the complete English horsewoman.

Character is subordinated to plot in Boucicault's theoretical article, and plot shows the characters "suffering their fate." As in all melodrama, calamity dogs the sympathetic characters until poetic justice raises them to some form of final triumph. Financial ruin is the omnipresent threat, but there are also physical dangers to be faced by the innocent. A typical Boucicault play involves a number of threats and rescues, with a continuing major danger increasing in intensity until the final resolution. Some of his melodramas are historical, but most are set in the present. While none of them could be called serious social drama, many do deal with real social problems: the plight of the poor, the evils of gambling and drink, even race relations. Boucicault's position is never controversial, and he is careful to balance good and evil characters in every social or national class.

The final element in the construction of a drama is decoration, which Boucicault recognized as at once the least essential and the most impressive. The realistic portrayal of locality, whether it was London, Lucknow, Louisiana, or Wicklow, was the first aim in his set design. This interest in decoration began early, and *London Assurance*, Boucicault's first success, was also the first play in London to be staged with a box set simulating a real room. For this, he had Madame Vestris, manager of Covent Garden, to thank, but scenery was to remain of vital importance to him. He often sought out the exotic, but the representation had to be believable. His realism, however, was designed to impress rather than to probe social issues. Each play offers at least one truly sensational scene: a steamboat explosion, a near-drowning, a boat race, or a burning building. These thrilling moments of spectacle join with the dangers presented by the plot to involve the audience in a world of vicarious peril.

Boucicault's best drama discards none of the sensationalism of his more commercial melodrama. Rather, it adds a true sense of comedy and a skill in the creation of characters, particularly of Irish characters. He kept a rich brogue all of his life and frequently acted parts calling for a stage Irishman. By setting plays in Ireland, he was able to exploit some traditional attributes of this stereotype without condescension. The audience laughs more *with* Myles-na-Coppaleen, for example, than *at* him. The witty dialogue of Boucicault's early comedies returns in full force in these Irish plays in such a way as to make the sentimentality of their main actions palatable even to an age unused to melodrama.

London Assurance and *Old Heads and Young Hearts* are theatrical curiosities. Boucicault took London by storm with comedies of manners, a dramatic form at least fifty years out of date. The plays are set in a time that might be the Regency (1811-1820) but draw heavily on the comic situations and characters of eighteenth century drama. While the plots of both plays are intricate, it is their characters that make them memorable.

London Assurance offers two fine female roles: Grace Harkaway is a witty heroine in the tradition of Congreve's Millamant, while Lady Gay Spanker, "glee made a living thing," carries the last three acts with her enthusiasm. Dazzle, the man nobody knows, is essentially the clever comic servant in his manipulation of the action. He brazenly attaches himself to the company, and his discovery provides the comic conclusion to the play when he acknowledges that he himself has "not the remotest idea" who he is. The moral tag which succeeds this quip, with its tedious definition of a gentleman, is the only Victorian thing about the play.

The main action, the father-and-son opposition in a love triangle, is the stuff of traditional comedy. An interesting variation is the "disguise" adopted by the son—simply denying his identity to his own father. This barefaced lie is so improbable that it works both in the play and on the stage. In this matter, Boucicault shows a spark of the assurance that characterizes Dazzle and Charles Courtly.

Old Heads and Young Hearts was Boucicault's second well-deserved success. In this play, there are now two pairs of lovers and two fathers to be placated. The background of hunting has been replaced by that of politics, and the country retreat is run as a military post by Colonel Rocket. The family relationships of the Colonel and his daughter and of Lord and Lady Pompion are sensitively drawn. The plot is deliberately confusing, and the old heads cannot follow what is going on. Jesse Rural, a well-meaning old minister, compounds the confusion with his efforts to help the young hearts and remains baffled at the final curtain. The wit is defter than that of *London Assurance*, but *Old Heads and Young Hearts* was to be Boucicault's last effort at true comedy of manners. He would argue later that the public only thought it wanted comedy, while what it really demanded was a mixture of genres.

The majority of Boucicault's original plays may be classed under the general heading melodrama, of which *The Poor of New York* and *After Dark* may be considered representative. The former was suggested by the commercial panic of 1857 in New York, but with its local allusions changed, it reappeared as *The Poor of Liverpool* and as *The Streets of London*. The plot, shamelessly based on coincidence, sentiment, and sensation, was loosely borrowed from a French play. The villainous banker Bloodgood, who has cheated or ruined virtually all the other characters, is finally exposed when two men break into a burning tenement to secure evidence against him that is about to be destroyed.

The plot of *After Dark* is incredible to an extreme that approaches self-parody. Father and daughter, husband and wife, jailer and convict, and former fellow officers are reunited by a series of coincidences, schemes, and discoveries that is utterly fantastic. The action, which is set in the lurid atmosphere of a gambling den, exploits the possibilities of the newly opened underground railway as well as providing an attempted suicide under Blackfriars Bridge.

The Octoroon is an altogether better play, although it depends on the same sort of sentimentality and coincidence. Boucicault walked a fine line between pro- and antislavery elements, and somehow managed to offend no one. Salem Scudder, a crusty Yankee who has a soft heart, is one of Boucicault's finest sentimental characters. The discovery of the murderer's identity by a self-developing photograph exploited a topical scientific discovery in a sensational manner. The ending, however, is tragic, as it must be. Zoe, the octoroon forbidden by her own society from marrying the man who loves her, had to die if the play was not to support miscegenation and offend many in the audience of Boucicault's day. The comic dialogue that was to lighten the sentiment of the Irish plays is also absent.

It is probably no coincidence that Boucicault's best plays were those with the largest roles for himself. He was a comic actor of some versatility, limited mainly by his accent, yet it was not until 1860 that he wrote a really meaty part that took advantage of this handicap. *The Colleen Bawn*, *Arrah-na-Pogue*, and *The Shaughraun* were his greatest successes, and Boucicault saved his best writing for them. Several other Irish plays were baldly commercial and had poor receptions.

The Colleen Bawn drew its plot loosely from Gerald Griffin's novel *The Collegians*, but Boucicault created the characters. Drawing on his reading of Irish playwrights Samuel Lover and Charles Lever, as well as on his own skill at comic dialogue, he quickly sketched a romantic comedy with the framework of melodrama. For spectacle, he added a dramatic dive to save the drowning heroine and an elaborate series of sliding Irish backdrops. For himself, he penned the character of Myles-na-Coppaleen, the heroic vagabond, a type he would re-create as Shaun the Post and Conn the Shaughraun in succeeding plays. Yet much of the wittiest dialogue is given to Anne Chute, a strong heroine in the mold of Grace Harkaway. Danny Mann, the villain, is given unusual depth in that he sincerely believes himself to be the faithful servant of the hero, Hardress Cregan.

As in Boucicault's two other major Irish plays, the villains are home-grown and the only Englishman is a noble romantic. *Arrah-na-Pogue* and *The Shaughraun*, however, both present heroes pursued by the English simply for being patriots. The political overtones are softened in that pardons are granted in both cases, but the atmosphere of oppression has been created. In the Irish plays, the dispossessed nobility are shown as the victims of an English system administered by greedy Irish speculators. The union between Cregan and Eily O'Connor, who belongs to a lower social station, is romantically satisfying but ultimately unrealistic. In the real-life episode fictionalized by Griffin, the young gentleman did find it necessary to have his peasant mistress murdered.

Arrah-na-Pogue brings back many of the character-types and sentiments of the earlier play. The trial of Shaun the Post, who has confessed in order to shield others, is a masterful comic scene that may well have influenced Shaw in *The Devil's Disciple* (pr. 1897). O'Grady seems symbolic of the Irish way of doing things in these plays when he asks for acquittal on the grounds of the prisoner's eloquence. Shaun's spectacular escape up an ivy-covered wall, just in time to rescue his Arrah, provides an appropriately melodramatic climax.

The Shaughraun is certainly Boucicault's finest play. The dramatist coined the title word from the Irish *seachran*, a participle that means "wandering." Conn is at his irrepressible best when he sneaks drinks at his own wake, after a popular Irish motif. The banter between Molineux, whose English birth was not his fault, and the spirited Claire is unforgettable. These two, however, are united in their reaction to Conn's pretended death. On that occasion, Molineux asks permission to exclaim "You Irish!" and Claire readily grants it. The playwright's confident introduction of the farcical hogshead barrel sequence into the midst of his melodramatic climax shows his complete control of the medium.

The cast of Irish characters includes the spirited heroine; the romantic heroine and her Fenian lover; the genial priest Father Dolan (once acted by Sean O'Casey); his housekeeper Moya, in love with Conn; the villainous squireen and his informer accomplice; and Conn's old mother, as well as his dog Tatthers, whose presence seems inseparable from Conn's yet who never appears onstage. This collection comprises the major types from the earlier two plays, and all are handled with a surer touch. As in many comic masterpieces, only the romantic lovers seem faceless.

Boucicault did not write any great drama after *The Shaughraun*. Some would argue that he had not done so before. Nevertheless, in this fantastic blend of melodrama, genuine comic wit, and facetious Irish blarney, Boucicault concocted truly memorable theater.

Other major works

NOVEL: *Foul Play*, 1868 (with Charles Reade).

NONFICTION: *The Story of Ireland*, 1881; *The Art of Acting*, 1926.

MISCELLANEOUS: *The Art of Acting: A Discussion by Constant Coquelin, Henry Irving, and Dion Boucicault*, 1926.

Bibliography

Boucicault, Dion. *Dion Boucicault: Selected Plays*. Edited by Andrew Parkin. Washington, D.C.: Catholic University of America Press, 1987. This volume contains the texts of *London Assurance*, *The Corsican Brothers*, *The Octoroon*, *The Colleen Bawn*, *The Shaughraun*, and *Robert Emmet*.
_____. *Plays by Dion Boucicault*. Edited by Peter Thompson. Cambridge, England: Cambridge University Press, 1984. Contains the texts of some lesser-known Boucicault plays such as *Used Up*, *Old Hands and New Hearts* and *Jessie Brown*, as well as the better-known *The Octoroon* and *The Shaughraun*.
Fawkes, Richard. *Dion Boucicault: A Biography*. London: Quartet Books, 1979. A comprehensive life and times of Boucicault. The detailed narrative draws, in part, on a number of unpublished sources. The emphasis is on theatrical history and Boucicault's place in it, rather than on the playwright's character or the wider context of his work. Bibliography.

Hogan, Robert. *Dion Boucicault.* Boston: Twayne, 1969. A comprehensive overview of the playwright's life and times. Starting with a biography, this study goes on to examine three distinct phases of Boucicault's career, beginning with what are called his Regency comedies, such as *London Assurance*, after which his so-called commercial potboilers are discussed, and then his Irish plays. In conclusion, Hogan assesses Boucicault's influence. This work is especially valuable for its extensive bibliography.

Molin, Sven Eric, and Robin Goodfellow, eds. *Dion Boucicault: A Documentary Life.* 5 vols. Newark, Del.: Proscenium Press, 1979-1991. An ambitious attempt to characterize Boucicault's life and times in terms of the contemporary documentary record. Each part deals with a particular phase of Boucicault's prolific and protean career and has for its centerpiece a reprint of one or more of the playwright's texts. Supplemented by memoirs, theatrical histories, and similar documentary sources. An essential resource for students of theater history, melodrama, and Boucicault himself.

Philip Oxley
(Updated by *George O'Brien*)

HOWARD BRENTON

Born: Portsmouth, England; December 13, 1942

Principal drama

Ladder of Fools, pr. 1965; *A Sky-Blue Life*, pr. 1966, pb. 1989; *Gargantua*, pr. 1969 (adaptation of François Rabelais' novel); *Revenge*, pr. 1969, pb. 1970; *Heads*, pr. 1969, pb. 1970; *The Education of Skinny Spew*, pr. 1969, pb. 1970; *Christie in Love*, pr. 1969, pb. 1970; *Gum and Goo*, pr. 1969, pb. 1972; *Cheek*, pr. 1970; *Fruit*, pr. 1970; *Wesley*, pr. 1970, pb. 1972; *Scott of the Antarctic: What God Didn't See*, pr. 1971, pb. 1972; *Lay By*, pr. 1971, pb. 1972 (with Brian Clark, Trevor Griffiths, David Hare, Steven Poliakoff, Hugh Stoddart, and Snoo Wilson); *England's Ireland*, pr. 1972 (with David Elgar, Tony Bicât, Brian Clark, Francis Fuchs, Hare, and Wilson); *Hitler Dances*, pr. 1972, pb. 1982; *How Beautiful with Badges*, pr. 1972, pb. 1989; *Measure for Measure*, pr. 1972, pb. 1989 (adaptation of William Shakespeare's play); *A Fart for Europe*, pr. 1973 (with Elgar); *Mug*, pr. 1973; *Magnificence*, pr., pb. 1973; *Brassneck*, pr. 1973, pb. 1974 (with Hare); *The Churchill Play: As It Will Be Performed in the Winter of 1984 by the Internees of Churchill Camp Somewhere in England*, pr., pb. 1974; *The Saliva Milkshake*, pr. 1975 (staged and teleplay), pb. 1977 (adaptation of Joseph Conrad's novel *Under Western Eyes*); *Weapons of Happiness*, pr., pb. 1976; *Government Property*, pr. 1976; *Epsom Downs*, pr., pb. 1977; *Deeds*, pr. 1978 (with Griffiths, Ken Campbell, and Hare); *Sore Throats*, pr., pb. 1979; *Plays for the Poor Theatre*, pb. 1980; *The Romans in Britain*, pr., pb. 1980; *A Short Sharp Shock!*, pr. 1980, pb. 1981 (with Tony Howard); *Thirteenth Night*, pr., pb. 1981 (based on Shakespeare's play *Macbeth*); *The Genius*, pr., pb. 1983; *Sleeping Policemen*, pr. 1983, pb. 1984 (with Tunde Ikoli); *Bloody Poetry*, pr. 1984, pb. 1985; *Pravda: A Fleet Street Comedy*, pr., pb. 1985 (with Hare); *A Professional Exercise*, pr. 1985 (with Hare); *Plays, One*, pb. 1986; *Greenland*, pr., pb. 1988; *H. I. D.: Hess Is Dead*, pb. 1989; *Three Plays*, pb. 1989; *Iranian Nights*, pr., pb. 1989 (with Tariq Ali); *Moscow Gold*, pb. 1990 (with Ali); *Plays, Two*, pb. 1990; *Berlin Bertie*, pr. 1992.

Other literary forms

Although known primarily as a playwright, Howard Brenton has published the collections of poetry *Notes from a Psychotic Journal and Other Poems* (1969) and *Sore Throats and Sonnets of Love and Opposition* (1979). In 1989, he published *Diving for Pearls*, a novel.

Achievements

Brenton belongs to a small group of radical English playwrights known as the "wild bunch," which includes Snoo Wilson, Howard Barker, and David Hare. Brenton's achievements in drama have been principally in openly agitprop theater in the interest of revolutionary socialism. His plays depict matters of current public interest in Great Britain, though frequently he sets the drama in a specific, noncontemporary historical period, such as Roman Britain or nineteenth century Italy. Despite the directness of their Marxist propaganda, the plays hold their own in terms of dramatic plot and characterization. Like Edward Bond, Brenton employs graphic violence and pornographic images to convey his outrage against the social complacency he detects in his country. The plot forms resemble Samuel Beckett's Theater of the Absurd and Bertolt Brecht's epic drama, but Brenton dissociates himself from both playwrights: Beckett he has criticized for being a philosophical pessimist, Brecht for lacking awareness of the theater event. Brenton's play *Weapons of Happiness* won the *Evening Standard* Drama Award for Best Play of 1976, and he received commissions to write plays for the Royal Shakespeare Company and the National Theatre. Frequently, his plays are collaborations with other writers, notably his friend David Hare.

Biography

Howard Brenton was born in Portsmouth, England, on December 13, 1942, during the German blitzes of World War II. His parents were Donald Henry and Rose Lilian (née Lewis) Brenton. Donald Brenton retired in the early 1960's after twenty-five years as a law-enforcement officer and joined the Methodist Church, eventually becoming an ordained minister in that denomination. His avocations included the theater, in which he participated frequently as an amateur stage actor and director. Howard Brenton's interest in writing and the theater began quite early in life in imitation of his father. Traveling all over England and Wales with his family, Brenton was glum and rebellious even as a child, enjoying the nonauthoritarian environment of the stage and the privacy of writing. At age nine, he adapted a comic strip into a short play. The youthful Brenton also wrote poems and three novels, in addition to completing a biography of Adolf Hitler at age seventeen. Brenton attended grammar school and was graduated from Chichester High School in West Sussex. He initially wanted to be a visual artist specializing in abstract paintings, and with that end in mind, he enrolled at Corsham Court, an art college in Bath. Changing his mind at the last minute, he dropped art school and made plans to attend St. Catherine's College, Cambridge, to study writing. In later years, Brenton said that he hated his Cambridge years despite the fact that he was a promising student there. Majoring in English, he took courses with George Steiner, the distinguished literary critic; Brenton greatly admired Steiner for his social views and for his teaching. In 1965, Brenton saw the first production of one of his plays, *Ladder of Fools*, at Cambridge and received a B.A. degree with honors.

Upon leaving Cambridge, Brenton worked odd jobs, stage-managed, and acted part-time while continuing to write plays. In 1969, he performed as an actor with the Brighton Combination, for whom he also wrote the short experimental plays *Gargantua* and *Gum and Goo*. Later the same year, he worked with Chris Parr's theater group at Bradford University, which produced *Gum and Goo*, *Heads*, and *The Education of Skinny Spew* in conjunction with rock concerts given at the university. During this time, Brenton submitted a play script to the Royal Court Theatre and was invited for an interview. *Revenge*, his first full-length play, was produced at the Royal Court Theatre Upstairs, London, in September, 1969.

During the production of *Revenge*, Brenton met and befriended David Hare, a fellow playwright and director. Hare's company, the Portable Theatre, commissioned Brenton to write *Christie in Love*, which Hare directed in November, 1969, and for which Snoo Wilson (who, like Hare, was later to be professionally associated with Brenton) built the set and stage-managed. The play moved to the Royal Court Theatre Upstairs early the following year and received favorable reviews. As a result of *Christie in Love*, Brenton won the Arts Council's John Whiting Award in 1970 and received an Arts Council Drama Bursary for the next season. The play was the beginning of a long and prodigious professional relationship between Brenton and Hare. On January 31, 1970, between productions of *Christie in Love*, Brenton married Jane Margaret Fry.

As a playwright on the "Fringe" in the early 1970's, Brenton wrote a number of plays to be produced in unusual spaces. His play *Wesley* was performed at the Eastbrook Hall Methodist Church in Bradford, and *Scott of the Antarctic: What God Didn't See* was produced in an ice-skating rink. These works appeared as part of the Bradford Festival in 1970 and 1971. The playwright was also involved in several collaborative efforts during this time, notably *Lay By* and *England's Ireland*. In 1972, Brenton became a resident playwright at the Royal Court Theatre. It was at the Royal Court that Brenton began a succession of "anti-Brechtian" epic plays, which cemented his reputation: *Magnificence*, *Brassneck*, *The Churchill Play*, *Weapons of Happiness*, and *Epsom Downs*. *Weapons of Happiness*, which took its title from a phrase spray-painted on the set of *Magnificence*, was the first play to debut at the National Theatre's new Lyttelton Theatre. Brenton wrote *Epsom Downs* in 1977 for the Joint Stock Theatre Group. During the same period of time, Brenton wrote three plays for television: *Lushly* (1971), *The Saliva Milkshake*, and *The Paradise Run* (1976). *The Saliva Milkshake* was also adapted for the stage and eventually was performed in New York, marking Brenton's debut in the United States. In 1973, Brenton wrote a short screenplay for the British Film Institute, *Skin Flicker*, based on a novel by Tony Bicât, who worked with him at the Portable Theatre (founded by Bicât and Hare).

In its 1978-1979 season, the Royal Shakespeare Company staged a successful revival of *The Churchill Play* at the Warehouse Theatre in London. The next year, *Sore Throats*, also performed by the Royal Shakespeare Company at the Warehouse, departed from the theatrical epics which established Brenton as an important playwright in the 1970's. The play, which the writer calls "an intimate play in two acts," occurs in a Pinteresque *mise en scène* (an empty South London flat), with only three characters: two women and a man. Brenton followed *Sore Throats* with *A Short Sharp Shock!* in 1980, a collaboration with Tony Howard. The year 1980 was to become a landmark year for Brenton with the National Theatre production of *The Romans in Britain* at the new Olivier Theatre. The play, his second for the National Theatre, provoked a strong critical reaction that did not abate during its entire run. Indeed, not since Edward Bond depicted the brutal stoning of an infant in a perambulator in his 1965 play *Saved* had London theater critics raised such an outcry against a play and a playwright. Most of the outrage was directed at the production's liberal use of male nudity and the graphic representation onstage of a Roman soldier's attempted rape of a young Celtic priest. The director Michael Bogdanov was charged with obscene behavior under the Sexual Offenses Act of 1967, and there was an effort to stop the play and withdraw the Greater London Council's subsidy to the National Theatre. Despite, or perhaps because of, all the puritan indignation over the play's visual content, *The Romans in Britain* played to full houses during its six-month run in London. Also in 1980, the National Theatre presented Brenton's *The Life of Galileo* (1980; adaptation of Bertolt Brecht's play *Leben des Galilei*) which ran for more than a year.

The Royal Shakespeare Company's performance of *Thirteenth Night* in 1981 was a little less controversial than *The Romans in Britain*. The play, a political satire loosely adapted from William Shakespeare's tragedy *Macbeth*, drew criticism for its pointed, allegedly libelous references by name to prominent living British conservatives. A number of the play's offensive lines were subsequently deleted from performances. Brenton criticized academia and technology in *The Genius*, which the Royal Court Theatre produced in 1983. In the same year, the Foco Novo Theatre Company commissioned Brenton and Tunde Ikoli to write separate plays involving three black characters and three white characters. The two plays were then synthesized by the director Roland Rees into a single play, *Sleeping Policemen*. The next year, the same theater company commissioned Brenton to write *Bloody Poetry*, a play about Percy Bysshe Shelley, which the company produced at the Haymarket Theatre at Leicester. *Bloody Poetry* was subsequently moved to the Hampstead Theatre in London. In 1985, Howard Brenton and David Hare collaborated on a comedy called *Pravda*, a satire on the more commercial and sensationalistic aspects of English newspaper journalism. Presented under Hare's direction at the National Theatre, the play was both a popular and a critical success, with Anthony Hopkins' performance in the leading role being singled out for special praise.

A prolific playwright, Brenton has generated at least one play per year, always treating political and ethical themes in satirical ways. In 1989, his parody *H. I. D.: Hess Is Dead* appeared, as did *Iranian Nights*, his tongue-in-cheek treatment of the Salman Rushdie controversy, which one critic called a "juvenile, idiotic, and terribly expensive production," but which others praised for its defense of free speech; the play contrasts liberal and fundamentalist Muslims. *Berlin Bertie* was produced in 1992, continuing his fascination with the moral contradictions of German political history.

Analysis

Howard Brenton's plays aggressively and unapologetically exploit contemporary public issues to promote revolutionary socialism and antiestablishment social causes. Whether the dramatic setting is historical (*The Romans in Britain*, *Bloody Poetry*) or contemporary (*Magnificence*, *Sore Throats*) or futuristic (*The Churchill Play*, *The Genius*), the plays depict class struggle and the necessity of nonviolent change on a universal scale. Brenton's drama is, nevertheless, remarkably evenhanded in its treatment of the characters, sometimes critical of the radicals for their fuzzy thinking about politics and sometimes sympathetic toward the human foibles of the rich and powerful. It portrays even political conservatives, usually the villains of Brenton's stage conflicts, in the best possible light, notably in the touching dialogue between Alice and Babs in scene 4 of *Magnificence*, and in the sympathetic characterization of Captain Thompson, the physician at the English concentration camp in *The Churchill Play*. Brenton's plays frequently make the point that self-interest and misspent passion occur on all sides of a political issue, thus contributing to the general malaise in society. It is a point scored expertly in the 1969 play *Revenge*, in which opposing sides of the law are represented by a single actor.

Brenton's early one-act play, *Christie in Love*, demonstrates the writer's interest in the criminal mind and the banality of evil. Based on the case of the 1950's mass murderer John Reginald Halliday Christie, the play combines elements of psychological naturalism and self-conscious structuralist theater. The Constable and the Inspector, the only actors in the drama besides Christie, are intentionally flat characters, offsetting Christie himself, who is (after his initial entrance) dramatically believable and psychologically complex. In the first two scenes, the two law-enforcement officers exchange inane comments about their activity and sexist jokes which are painfully ill-timed and unfunny. When Christie appears, in scene 3, he arises slowly out of a grave of newspapers in the manner of a Count Dracula, wearing a large, disfiguring fright mask. In all the subsequent scenes, Christie is maskless, revealing a quite ordinary looking and surprisingly defenseless man. The contrasting imagery suggests that the concocted tabloid image of Christie (or, for that matter, any "villain") as a monster is a false one, and that the real person who was Christie performed his heinous crimes out of love, peculiarly defined and experienced by the individual. Moreover, in the context of the play, Christie is far more genuine in his passions than his interrogators, who delude themselves with ideas of normality and morality which they enforce through violence, willful ignorance, and deprecation of sex and love.

Certain elements of the play have appeared again in Brenton's later work. Christie's theatrical resurrection from the dead is very similar to Winston Churchill's escape from the catafalque in the play-within-a-play at the beginning of *The Churchill Play*. The startling synthesis of exclamations of true love and images of brutality appears again in *Sore Throats*, in which sudden dramatic reversals and extremely contradictory actions muddle the real nature of the characters' emotions. The bleak, Cold War background and the surrealistic middle-class setting of the play recur in numerous other Brenton works, including *The Churchill Play* and *The Genius*. At the same time, *Christie in Love* is unique among Brenton's plays in the comparative subtlety of its politics and theatrical violence. In the plays most characteristic of the playwright, revolutionary socialism is openly espoused, and terrorism and violence are gruesomely reified on the stage.

Critics and reviewers frequently complain that Brenton's theater is too violent, that it is in reality only sensationalistic. A certain amount of the outcry against his play *The Romans in Britain* was directed against its graphic portrayal of torture and murder, as well as its profuse male nudity. Brenton deliberately uses shock techniques, violence, profanity, nudity, and scatology to provoke his audiences. There is a prophetic intensity about his writing, particularly in the plays of the middle 1970's and early 1980's, which are public spectacles condemning oppression and collaboration with oppression through passivity. Brenton calls this element in drama "aggro," a British slang term which suggests a mix of aggression and aggravation. Its purpose is to draw the audience together into the play's (and playwright's) outrage. Brenton has commented that his agitprop theater frequently succeeds better at agitation than at propaganda, and the usual critical and public response to his plays seems to bear him out on this point.

Another aspect of Brenton's writing that draws criticism on occasion is the unevenness of his dramatic style. Scenes that are dark with pessimism and brooding alternate with slapstick comedy, and sensitive character drama intermixes with pornographic and Grand Guignol stage effects. For example, the ironically titled revenge play *Magnificence* begins with five young radicals occupying an abandoned flat in protest against the landowner's legal oppression of the poor tenants. The opening scenes center mainly on the two female members of the group: Mary, who is pregnant and whose approach to revolution is largely aesthetic, and Veronica, who formerly worked for the British

Broadcasting Corporation (BBC) and who is the most intellectual (and moderate) member of the group. A sort of climax is reached in the play at the end of scene 3, when Mr. Slaughter, the landlord, in the company of a constable, breaks into the room and bodily attacks the occupants. In the process, he kicks Mary in the stomach, accidentally causing a miscarriage. The setting of the play then changes to Cambridge College and two new characters are introduced: two men who are friends, Tory bureaucrats in government and academia, who go by the nicknames Alice and Babs. The scene, which is the center of the play, is peaceful, full of reminiscences and flirtations between the two old friends as they punt a flat-bottomed boat across the stage. In the course of the scene, Babs reveals to his friend that he is about to die, and at the scene's end, he expires quietly in Alice's arms. The final third of the play centers on Jed, a minor and mostly silent character in the opening scenes, who now seeks revenge for the death of Mary's child. The other members of the radical group have chosen a less active public course; in Jed's opinion, they have debased the principles for which they stood at the beginning. The play concludes with a riveting horror scene in which Jed attacks Alice and forces him to wear a bomb in the form of a mask upon his head. When, after agonizing dramatic suspense, the explosive fails to detonate, Jed and Alice attempt to strike some sort of bargain, and then unexpectedly the bomb explodes, killing them both.

In the end, *Magnificence* leaves the audience with a sense of having watched three individual plots, each with its own impetus and tone, and—except for the obvious continuation of characters from scene to scene—little coherence is evident between the three principal parts. Brenton treats each scene on its own terms without imposing unity of action. In respect to this professedly unconscious stylistic element, Brenton categorizes himself, along with Snoo Wilson and David Hare, as a "maximalist" playwright, in contrast to the dramatic minimalism of Samuel Beckett and Harold Pinter. Brenton's goal is to depict a situation realistically by incorporating into the play as many facets or aspects of the situation as possible. The result is a deliberate hodgepodge of styles, characters, and events.

Perhaps the quintessential Brenton protagonist is Josef Frank in *Weapons of Happiness*. Like Christie and Churchill, Frank is an actual historical figure whom Brenton "resurrects" in order to make a point about political activism. The real Josef Frank was one of the twelve prominent members of the Czechoslovakian Communist Party hanged by the Stalinists in Prague in 1952. Brenton's Frank survives to 1976 by emigrating to England, where he inadvertently becomes involved in a workers' strike at a potato chip factory. Frank, a sullen and silent old man plagued with painful memories of his interrogation in the 1950's and nightmare fantasies about Stalin, is alienated not only from the factory owner and managers but also from the youthful rebels who attempt a minor coup by taking over the factory. Unable to side with the capitalists and reactionary police who want him to betray the young radicals and also unable to side with the Communists for whom violent force and half-digested Marxist ideology are legitimate tools of revolution, Frank is forced once again into a solitary position. In the end, he is able to confide in Janice, one of the young English Communists, and warns her against the utopian and terrorist tendencies which have become a part of the radical movement. He dies alone in a drain leading out of the factory. The final scene shows Janice and her comrades establishing a Socialist commune in Wales, hopefully modeled on Frank's Trotskyism.

Aspects of Josef Frank's character are typical of Brenton's antiheroes— lapsed idealists who fall, at least temporarily, into inactivity because of disillusionment and embitterment about the status quo and the state of the revolution. In *The Genius*, the American physicist Leo Lehrer, perhaps modeled on Brecht's Galileo, invents a weapon capable of destroying the whole world at once. Distressed that the American military establishment has perverted his mathematical genius in the interest of power and oppression, he flees the United States for a small university in England, full of self-loathing and paranoid fears. There he meets Gilly Brown, another mathematical genius, who has accidentally completed the formula for the weapon also. In the closing scene, Gilly and Leo have left the university to camp outside the wire fences surrounding a military installation, which they, along with another student and the university bursar's wife, periodically invade in order to publicize the vulnerability of lethal military weapons to outside attack.

Another disillusioned radical is Percy Bysshe Shelley in *Bloody Poetry*. Like Frank and Lehrer, Shelley is a refugee. He has fled from England, where his female entourage (Mary Shelley and Claire Clairemont) and he are viewed with suspicion and moral repugnance, and sets up residence in Switzerland and Italy with George Gordon, Lord Byron, a fellow radical and anarchist whose moral dissipation is portrayed in his continual drunkenness and unawareness of the consequences of his sexual liaisons. Like Frank, Shelley is haunted by the ghosts of his past life, in this case the ghost of Harriet Westbrook, Shelley's first wife, who was unable to live the life of a revolutionary (or a revolutionary's wife) and so was abandoned, eventually to go mad and kill herself. Shelley's dilemma in the play is that his wild libertarian ideology contradicts his social conscience. The puritan indignation of his countrymen and the irresponsible self-destruction of Byron do not represent his own conscience and his own concept of personal liberty, which, moreover, he cannot quite reconcile within himself. The play concludes with Shelley jubilant and adrift at sea shortly before his death. He sings about the utopian future when the men of England will rid themselves of tyrants and become free. After a blackout, Byron is seen on stage with the sail-draped corpse of Shelley and the silent, brooding ghost of Harriet. Dismayed at the unexpected death of his friend, Byron shouts, "Burn him! Burn him! Burn him!

Burn us all!" thus crying down the old order in a renewed spirit of social revolution.

The Genius and *Bloody Poetry* also present examples of another class of Brenton character: the sideline observer who lacks the courage or will to act on his convictions. In *The Genius*, the university bursar, Graham Hay, is a liberal humanist who is initially sympathetic to Lehrer, even after, midway through act 1, Lehrer cuckolds the old man. Hay is a gentle man with somewhat rarefied academic tastes, but he is the lackey of the university vice-chancellor. In the end, Hay is interrogated by the English secret police and betrays Lehrer. Despite his right-thinking liberal humanist philosophy, Hay fails in the end for lack of moral passion. In *Bloody Poetry*, the sideline figure is Dr. William Polidori, whom Byron's publisher has sent to spy upon the circle of radical friends in Italy. Polidori lacks the involvement in the dramatic action which would make him a sympathetic character; his moralizing commentary on Shelley's and Byron's actions is invalidated by his own lack of commitment. In his final appearance, Polidori circulates solo in the theater with a glass of wine in one hand, lying to his listeners about his close ties with the Shelley circle and supplying grisly details about Shelley's "suicide."

Both Polidori and Hay are part of the "vast conspiracy of obedience" Morn describes in the last act of *The Churchill Play*. It is a bureaucratic conspiracy for which everyone is and is not responsible—one which leads ultimately, so Morn thinks, to military dictatorship. The most seductive aspect of the conspiracy is its anonymity. No one needs to feel individually accountable for the atrocities which one's government (or one's private organization) perpetrates. The conspiracy of obedience absolves the individual participant from personal guilt. Polidori accepts this absolution as a matter of fact. Hay, on the other hand, has to be "taught" through intimidation not to feel responsible. The character of Captain Thompson, the concentration camp physician in *The Churchill Play*, is perhaps the best developed of Brenton's sideline observers, and the play delineates a certain progress in the ethical development of Thompson.

Thompson is the chief supporter of the seditious entertainment the prisoners of the Churchill Camp are preparing for the visiting Members of Parliament. When first seen, Thompson is defending the play to Colonel Ball, the commanding officer of the prison. Shortly thereafter, Sergeant Baxter attempts to intimidate Thompson into withdrawing his support for the play. Thompson is so shaken by the threat that he becomes deaf to the story that the new prisoner Reese tries to tell him and walks officiously away. In act 3, Thompson takes an evening walk with his wife Caroline. Their conversation reveals that their position at the camp is repulsive to their liberal humanist ideals, but at the same time, Thompson feels powerless to take a stand. He is shocked at the unjust, murderous treatment of the prisoners, but since the injustice is apparently no one person's responsibility, he does not know where he can turn for justice. Thompson and Caroline's ideology, represented by their wish for seclusion and a quiet home, tends to be obscurantist; they are unable to face the harsh reality of the camp, much less to fight against it. At the end, Thompson offers to accompany the prisoners as they attempt to escape from the camp. To the prisoners, however, Thompson is a collaborator, and despite his professed goodwill toward them, he is not one of them. They turn from him in disgust, leaving him in the company of the right-wing Members of Parliament and the camp guards.

Brenton's focus on controversial themes has remained constant. *A Short Sharp Shock!* satirizes England's leading Tory politicians; *Pravda*, written in collaboration with David Hare, lambastes Fleet Street publishers; *Iranian Nights* parodies the Ayatollah Ruhollah Khomeini's call for novelist Salman Rushdie's death; and *Berlin Bertie* examines German political history.

Howard Brenton's plays represent an important contribution to radical and poststructuralist English drama. He belongs to the second wave of modernist English theater, the generation after Arnold Wesker, John Osborne, and Harold Pinter. Though sometimes attacked for the political content of the writing, Brenton's theater is vivid and powerful propaganda. As a playwright, he has never failed to excite critical and public comment and to stir controversy.

Other major works

NOVEL: *Diving for Pearls*, 1989.

POETRY: *Notes from a Psychotic Journal and Other Poems*, 1969; *Sore Throats and Sonnets of Love and Opposition*, 1979.

NONFICTION: "The Good Between Us," 1990.

SCREENPLAYS: *Skin Flicker*, 1973; *The Eleventh Crushing*, 1987.

TELEPLAYS: *Lushly*, 1971; *The Paradise Run*, 1976; *Dead Head*, 1986.

TRANSLATION: *The Life of Galileo*, 1980 (of Bertolt Brecht's play).

Bibliography

Boon, Richard. "Setting Up the Scaffolding: Howard Brenton's *Hitler Dances.*" *New Theatre Quarterly* 4 (November, 1988): 335-343. In this study, Boon provides a discussion of *Hitler Dances*, a transitional play that was developed in the Traverse Workshop, and reveals much about Brenton's working methods.

Brenton, Howard. "Petrol Bombs Through the Proscenium Arch: An Interview with Howard Brenton." Interview by Catherine Itzin and Simon Trussler. *Theatre Quarterly* 5 (March-May 1975): 4-20. An interview with production photographs of *Hitler Dances*, *Christie in Love*, and other plays. Brenton discusses whether "Fringe" theater has failed by 1975 and states his famous dictum "You don't write to convert. More . . . to stir things up."

_____. "The Red Theatre Under the Bed." *New Theatre Quarterly* 3 (August, 1987): 195-201. An interview on Brenton's later work and thinking. The playwright discusses his play *Pravda*, "the last of the dinosaurs"; his concerns with South Africa; his television work, specifically a series entitled *Dead Head*; the film *The Eleventh Crushing*; a play tentatively titled *Heaven Made*; and his "populist" leanings.

Bull, John. *New British Political Dramatists.* New York: Grove Press, 1983. Contains a major chapter on Brenton, entitled "Portable Theatre and the Fringe." Bull notes the playwright's preoccupation with children in his early work and sees his characters as inhabiting an urban England, "a pin-table map with the major cities flashing in multi-coloured lights." Strong list of plays by, and articles about, Brenton.

Mitchell, Tony. *File on Brenton.* London: Methuen, 1988. One of a series by Methuen designed for the information age. The volume is a valuable information source, organized by play title, with critical comments, review clippings, and similar short-stroke data, quickly retrieved. Strong chronology, bibliography, index.

Rusinko, Susan. *British Drama 1950 to the Present: A Critical History.* Boston: Twayne, 1989. Brenton's plays are here briefly outlined chronologically, quoting as a central theme his famous comment, "When it comes to agitprop, I like the agit, the prop I'm very bad at." Short bibliography on Brenton and other contemporary playwrights.

Theater 13 (Spring, 1981). A special edition on Brenton, featuring the text of his play *Sore Throats* (originally published in 1979) and three articles, one on his philosophy, one on *The Romans in Britain* controversy, and one (by fellow playwright Edward Bond) on the censorship furor of that play.

Joseph Marohl
(Updated by *Thomas J. Taylor*)

JAMES BRIDIE
Osborne Henry Mavor

Born: Glasgow, Scotland; January 3, 1888
Died: Edinburgh, Scotland; January 29, 1951

Principal drama

The Sunlight Sonata: Or, To Meet the Seven Deadly Sins, pr. 1928, pb. 1930; *The Switchback*, pr. 1929, pb. 1930; *What It Is to Be Young*, pr. 1929, pb. 1934; *The Anatomist*, pr. 1930, pb. 1931; *The Girl Who Did Not Want to Go to Kuala Lampur*, pr. 1930, pb. 1934; *Tobias and the Angel*, pr. 1930, pb. 1931; *The Amazed Evangelist*, pb. 1931, pr. 1932; *The Dancing Bear*, pr. 1931, pb. 1934; *Jonah and the Whale*, pr., pb. 1932; *The Proposal*, pr. 1932 (adaptation of Anton Chekhov's play *A Marriage Proposal*); *A Sleeping Clergyman*, pr., pb. 1933; *Colonel Wotherspoon*, pr., pb. 1934; *Colonel Wotherspoon and Other Plays*, pb. 1934; *Marriage Is No Joke*, pr., pb. 1934; *Mary Read*, pr. 1934, pb. 1935 (with Claud Gurney); *The Black Eye*, pr., pb. 1935; *Moral Plays*, pb. 1936; *Storm in a Teacup*, pr. 1936, pb. 1937 (adaptation of Bruno Frank's play); *Susannah and the Elders*, pr. 1937, pb. 1940; *Babes in the Wood*, pr., pb. 1938; *The King of Nowhere*, pr., pb. 1938; *The Last Trump*, pr., pb. 1938; *The Golden Legend of Shults*, pr. 1939, pb. 1940; *What Say They?*, pr., pb. 1939; *The Dragon and the Dove*, pr. 1942, pb. 1944; *Holy Isle*, pr. 1942, pb. 1944; *Jonah 3*, pr. 1942, pb. 1944 (based on his play *Jonah and the Whale*); *A Change for the Worse*, pr. 1943, pb. 1944; *Mr. Bolfry*, pr. 1943, pb. 1944; *It Depends What You Mean*, pr. 1944, pb. 1948; *Lancelot*, pb. 1944, pr. 1945; *Plays for Plain People*, pb. 1944; *The Forrigan Reel*, pr. 1945, pb. 1949; *Hedda Gabler*, pr. 1945 (adaptation of Henrik Ibsen's play); *The Wild Duck*, pr. 1946 (adaptation of Ibsen's play); *De Angelus*, pr. 1947, pb. 1949; *John Knox*, pr. 1947, pb. 1949; *Gog and Magog*, pr. 1948; *Daphne Laureola*, pr., pb. 1949 (with George Munro); *John Knox and Other Plays*, pb. 1949; *The Tintock Cup*, pr. 1949; *Mr. Gillie*, pr., pb. 1950; *The Queen's Comedy*, pr., pb. 1950; *Red Riding Hood*, pr. 1950 (with Duncan Macrae); *The Baikie Charivari: Or, The Seven Prophets*, pr. 1952, pb. 1953; *Meeting at Night*, pr. 1954, pb. 1956 (with Archibald Batty).

Other literary forms

Two autobiographical volumes constitute the major nondramatic writings of James Bridie. *Some Talk of Alexander*, derived from his experiences in the field ambulance unit of the British army during World War I in India, Mesopotamia, Persia, Transcaucasia, and Constantinople, was published in 1926. A second autobiography, *One Way of Living*, published in 1939, is a creative memoir written when Bridie had turned fifty. It is divided into ten chapters, each covering a five-year period of his life. There is an overlay of italicized portions in each chapter, in which an interior monologue of the author ranges freely over some imaginative, associative reflection, evoking the style of James Joyce in *A Portrait of the Artist as a Young Man* (1916). In addition to his two autobiographical works, Bridie wrote a collection of essays entitled *Mr. Bridie's Alphabet for Little Glasgow Highbrows* (1934); a collection of short plays, fragments, essays, poetry, and film and radio scripts entitled *Tedious and Brief* (1944); criticism in *The British Drama* (1945); and still another collection of essays entitled *A Small Stir: Letters on the English* (1949; with Moray McLaren). Finally, Bridie was a prolific writer of articles, described by Winifred Bannister, his biographer, as "witty, teasing admonitions usually aimed at drawing people into the theatre, and even that part of the Scottish public not interested in the theatre could hardly avoid being aware of Bridie as a personality, for almost everything he said and did in public was news."

Achievements

Bridie, like John Keats and Anton Chekhov, belongs to a long tradition of writers who were educated for a medical career but who eventually became major literary figures. The author of more than forty plays, he complemented that impressive achievement with a lifelong, active participation in the development of the Glasgow Citizens' Theatre, Glasgow's equivalent of London's National Theatre. His civic work on the Scottish Arts Council, the Edinburgh International Festival of music and drama, the film section of UNESCO, and the Scottish Community Drama Association was unflagging. He also developed into a more than proficient artist, for a time illustrating the *Scots Pictorial* as "O.H." His drawings and paintings have been exhibited at Glasgow art galleries.

Bridie's position in modern British drama is firmly established, and certainly in Scottish theater history he is a major dramatist. Gerald Weales in *Religion in Modern English Drama* (1961) links Bridie and George Bernard Shaw as modern religious dramatists who, at their deaths in 1951 (Bridie) and 1950 (Shaw), left religious drama "almost completely in the hands of the more orthodox practitioners," few of whom "approach Shaw and Bridie as playwrights." J. B. Priestley, a consummate crafter of the well-made play, while calling attention to some of Bridie's weaknesses, calls his best scenes "blazing triumphs." He also asserted that Bridie's "characters appear to exist more in their own right than Shaw's."

Indeed, for Priestley, Bridie is Scotland's major dramatist. In the preface to the posthumous publication of *Meeting at Night*, Priestley offers a measured evaluation of Bridie's work. He concludes his personal tribute to Bridie with the comment that since his death, "the Theatre has seemed only half the size, half the fun, it used to be."

Biography

James Bridie was born Osborne Henry Mavor on January 3, 1888, in Glasgow, Scotland, the son of Henry A. and Janet (Osborne) Mavor. Bridie said that in 1931, he started calling himself "James Bridie," after his grandfather James Mavor and his great-grandfather John Bridie, a sea captain. Gradually, the name Bridie—the dramatist half of Osborne Henry Mavor, the doctor—took over, so that by the time of his death, friends such as Priestley had thought of him strictly as Bridie, never as O. H. Mavor.

Near the beginning of his autobiography, *One Way of Living*, Bridie writes that on January 3, 1938, he takes pleasure, at the age of fifty, in having lived ten different lives in cycles of five years. He describes himself as a Lowland Scot who has no English or Highland blood, no Unconscious Mind, and who therefore is ill-qualified to write an autobiography. Yet he must write one, even though he makes of it a matter of mathematics rather than art, since a Lowland Scot is so ordered in his life, dividing it into three planes—intellectual, moral, and physical—that anyone out of step with it is considered disordered and abnormal. Indeed, Bridie's life was ordered, at first by a father whom he admired and who, unable to enter medicine because of financial difficulties, wished his son to become a doctor. Later, the order was of his own making.

At twenty-five, Bridie was still an undergraduate, having failed some of his medical courses, particularly anatomy. Eventually, however, he became a resident at the staff of the Royal Infirmary in Glasgow as house physician to W. R. Jack; he then moved to the eye, ear, and nose department. He served in the army field ambulance unit during World War I, returning from Soviet Russia in 1919. Joining the staff of the Victoria Infirmary in Glasgow, he led a pleasant life, and began writing, he contends, to subsidize his consulting practice. In 1923, he married Rona Locke Bremner, bought himself a car, and settled into what he describes as a happy bourgeois life; indeed, he remarks in his autobiography that a childhood admiration for a doctor who owned a car was his reason for wanting to become a doctor. His medical career was rewarded with a doctorate of law from Glasgow University in 1939, and a C.B.E. in 1946. Of the honors conferred on him, he enjoyed most the governorship of Victoria Infirmary in Glasgow, where he had earlier served as assistant physician and honorary consulting physician.

Amid the events of a physician's life, however, Bridie's writing and theatrical interests persisted. Undergraduate productions of his plays with titles such as *The Son Who Was Considerate of His Father's Prejudices*, *No Wedding Cake for Her*, *The Duke Who Could Sometimes Hardly Keep from Smiling*, *Ethics Among Thieves*, and *The Baron Who Would Not Be Convinced That His Way of Living Was Anything out of the Ordinary* were received with loud applause at school functions. He also wrote for the Glasgow University magazine under "unfamiliar names."

Because of his concern that playwriting, considered by some disreputable, could hurt his consulting practice, Bridie at first wrote under the pseudonym "Mary Henderson," who appears as a character in his first professionally produced play, *The Sunlight Sonata*. In addition, he feared that the hobby might become too absorbing. Another name, "Archibald Kellock" (a character in *Colonel Wotherspoon*), became the pseudonym under which he wrote other plays. In 1938, at the age of fifty, Dr. Osborne Henry Mavor and playwright James Bridie parted, and the latter devoted full time to his chosen career, one that included the development of the Glasgow Citizens' Theatre in particular and the Scottish theater in general.

Bridie died in 1951 of a vascular condition at the Edinburgh Royal Infirmary, one year after the death of George Bernard Shaw, whom Bridie knew and who attended some of Bridie's plays.

Analysis

At the heart of much of James Bridie's drama lies the conflict between science and religion. He explored this conflict in a variety of dramatic genres, including comedies, mystery and morality plays that have interesting resemblances to those of the medieval period, and problem dramas that suggest the influence of Henrik Ibsen. In all three general groupings, one can detect a stylistic hallmark: the use of medical language, characters who are members of the medical profession or who have something to do with a member of that profession, or situations in which science is involved in either a major or minor way. In Bridie's plays, however, as in his life, science takes second place to the moral problems of his characters, even when its virtues or vices are the basis for those problems. In a general sense, then, all of his dramas, including the most entertaining Shavian comedies, are morality plays.

Although Bridie's religious views were "so liberal minded, so humanitarian as to be unfixed," according to Bannister, they were, nevertheless, the driving force in his own life and in the characters of his plays. A moral fervor and rational humanism characterize his earliest performed play, *The Sunlight Sonata*, a comedy about seven characters affected by the traditional Seven Deadly Sins. Similarly, *The Baikie Charivari* is a Faustian confrontation between man and the Devil, containing seven potential evils in the form of visitors who would teach Bridie's "Faust." Indeed, Bridie's thesis resembles Johann Wolfgang von Goethe's: the necessity of never saying to the moment, "Stay, thou art fair."

Bridie's mystery plays, dramatizations of Bible stories, constitute an important part of his oeuvre. In the tradition of the medieval mystery play, in which Bible stories were dramatized for "plain people," Bridie modernizes the dilemmas in which biblical characters find themselves. In fact, he wrote three versions of the Jonah story: *Jonah and the Whale*, *The Sign of the Prophet Jonah* (1942), and *Jonah 3*. Bridie's stories were drawn not only from the Bible but also from the Apocrypha and from contemporary religious events and figures.

Some of Bridie's plays have evoked comparisons with Shaw and Ibsen. Clever turns of phrase, witty dialogue, puns, outrageous situations in which societal "outlaws" (such as the father and daughter in *Meeting at Night* who conduct a mail-order confidence racket) have earned for Bridie the label the "Scottish Shaw." Bannister records a comment that Shaw is supposed to have made to Bridie: "If there had been no me there would have been no you." The two dramatists are dissimilar, however, in a major way, for with the exception of *Daphne Laureola*, Bridie's characterizations of women lack the strength and conviction of Shaw's. Among influences on Bridie, perhaps that of Ibsen is the strongest. It can be seen in his adaptations of Ibsen's plays but more subtly in the satiric thrusts at status-quo science and religion in plays such as *A Sleeping Clergyman*, *The Switchback*, and *The Anatomist*.

In his autobiography, Bridie claimed that *A Sleeping Clergyman* "was the nearest thing to a masterpiece I shall probably ever write." Completed at the end of 1932, before he had decided to give up medicine in order to devote himself to the theater, the play was produced in London in 1933. He had worked on the play off and on for two years, with earlier productions in Birmingham and Malvern. He stated that the play was an attempt to combine two themes with which he had dealt earlier: the scientist as dictator in *The Anatomist* and as lost sheep in the wilderness in *The Switchback*, and the relation of human beings to God in *Tobias and the Angel* and *Jonah and the Whale*.

The play is in two acts, the first preceded by a prologue and the second by a "chorus." In these two introductory portions, the framework for the story is established. At a respectable men's club in Glasgow, Dr. Cooper, a specialist in diseases of women, and Dr. Coutts, a neurologist, are relaxing with a drink. Nearby, a "huge, whitebearded" clergyman sleeps. Coutts has just returned from the funeral service of ninety-seven-year-old Dr. William Marshall, a former visiting physician at the Royal Infirmary of Glasgow. Coutts, whose father had been a friend of Marshall, represented the faculty at the funeral. The conversation then turns to another funeral attendee, Sir Charles Cameron, a noted bacteriologist. Interest in Cameron, a relative of the deceased, is aroused as the matter of his illegitimate birth is mentioned by Coutts. With a brief reference to Cameron's grandfather, a dissipated medical student, the prologue ends, and the narration shifts to a dramatization of events in the lives of three generations of Camerons. In flashback style, the drama consists of two acts, with four scenes in each act. The action moves swiftly through more than sixty years, from 1867 to 1872, 1885, 1886, 1907, 1916, and finally to the 1930's, in a fascinating tale in which genius eventually conquers the predilection to dissipation which the latest Cameron had inherited from his grandfather.

In act 1, the first Cameron is a young medical reseacher, dying of tuberculosis but, above everything else, bent on finishing the medical research project in which he is currently engaged. The efforts of Dr. Will Marshall and his sister, Harriet, to convince Cameron to spend some time with them at their shore residence are futile. After visiting Cameron in his untidy room, Will leaves, having loaned Cameron three pounds. Later, Harriet arrives to inform Cameron that she is pregnant. He agrees to her proposal of marriage, but it is later revealed, in a conversation between two relatives on the day of a birthday party for little Wilhelmina (daughter of Harriet and Cameron), that the marriage had never taken place.

The story of the second generation of Camerons is dramatized in scene 3 of act 1. Wilhelmina, now a young woman, shows the effects of heredity as she asks her Uncle Will for a cigar she wishes to try. The incident evokes the scene in Ibsen's *Ghosts* in which Oswald, an artist returning from Paris to his hometown in Norway, smokes a pipe and then recalls being sick as a child after his father had given him a pipe to smoke. Ibsen's play is about an inherited syphilitic condition; Bridie's is about inherited genius and its accompanying Bohemian life-style.

Wilhelmina, reared by her Uncle Will, follows in the footsteps of her mother and father in her disregard of stifling, conventional conduct. During a lovers' quarrel over her decision to marry another man, a man of her own class—even though she is pregnant by her lover, a lower-class employee of her uncle—she poisons the latter. In covering up her act, her uncle asks Dr. Coutts (father of Coutts of the prologue) to carry out the investigation of the death. In the ensuing trial, Wilhelmina is found innocent, and then, in a reversal of her earlier intentions, refuses to marry Sutherland even though he proposed. Act 1 ends on this note. Without regard for the puritanical mores of Scottish respectability, the Camerons continue to exercise their individualism.

A "chorus" introducing the second act parallels the prologue to act 1. The clergyman still sleeps as Dr. Cooper listens to Dr. Coutts's tale of the Cameron generations. The audience learns of the trial of Wilhelmina and of the birth of her twins, Charles and Hope. The birth is followed by Wilhelmina's suicide one month later.

Act 2 continues with the third generation of Camerons, as Will Marshall once more assumes the duties of child-rearing. Charles Cameron follows in his grandfather's footsteps in the sowing of his wild oats and in his genius for medical research. Like the ghosts of the past in Ibsen's plays, the present repeats the past. When Cameron cites the pressure of exams as the reason for his disorderly conduct and consequent arrest, Uncle Will provides the three pounds for his release, an amount similar to that which he had loaned Cameron's grandfather long ago.

After service in World War I, this third-generation Cameron, through both hard work and genius, eventually becomes a noted bacteriologist. At the age of fifty, he heads a medical research organization, the Walker Institute, financed by a wealthy relative, Sir Douglas Todd Walker. In his consistently blunt manner, he proposes marriage to Lady Katharine, saying that, if he wants descendants, he will have to hurry. Katharine, a worker who supplies the Institute with flowers, accepts, returning his bluntness in her acceptance.

Cameron's sister, Hope, appears on the scene from Geneva with a message from the League of Nations asking Cameron to expedite research on his cure for influenza. Both sister and brother have experienced the triumph of virtue over evil, even though it required three generations to do so. Old Will Marshall, now in his nineties, lives to see the rewards of his efforts. Vindicated, he comments to Hope at the play's end that "Charlie Cameron the First had the spark in his poor diseased body. Now lettest thou thy servant depart in peace. I did my best to keep the spark alive, and now it's a great flame in Charlie and in you. Humanity will warm its hands at you."

Bridie's view of genius as the divine force working through man is reflected in Katharine's comment that perhaps Cameron is a law of biology himself. God, like the sleeping clergyman in the two prologues, is removed from the immediate goings-on. Old Dr. Will Marshall, having lived ninety-seven years and having encouraged the spark of genius through three generations of Camerons, is a variation of the God-principle. Like the sleeping clergyman, who is oblivious to his surroundings, Dr. Will has devoted nearly a lifetime to practicing status-quo medicine. Unlike the clergyman, however, he has nourished the genius in which he never loses faith.

In addition to the Ibsenite concern with heredity already mentioned, there is in Bridie's play the Shavian concern with a life force that works through genius, emerging in the medical breakthroughs by the Camerons in their contributions to civilization. Religious, not in the conventional doctrinaire sense but in his contribution to humankind, Cameron is the very essence of God. Bridie's God is a deistic entity that has provided human beings with laws and that has retired, like the sleeping clergyman, to a preprandial nap, to allow people to work out those laws. This working out of virtue is the personal and social morality of Bridie's plays. Weales claims that Bridie is one of the last two modern playwrights (Shaw is the other) to write religious plays based on a personal and unorthodox view of human beings' relationship to God.

The style of the play is as direct, unsentimental, and naturalistic as are the Camerons, whose disregard for the civilities of language and behavior provokes the censure of their conventional friends and relatives. Bridie's epic sweep of three generations has invited the criticism that the characters, particularly the supporting ones, are not fully developed.

Two of Bridie's last plays are companion pieces that deal yet again with human beings' relationship to their God or gods. The first of the two, *The Queen's Comedy*, is a reworking of books 14 and 15 of Homer's *Iliad.* Produced in 1950, a year before Bridie's death, the play is dedicated to its director, Tyrone Guthrie, famous in both England the United States. On the title page appears Gloucester's famous line from William Shakespeare's *King Lear.* "As flies to wanton boys are we to the gods: they kill us for their sport." The title of the play derives from the various goddesses' attitudes toward Jupiter, particularly toward his entanglement in the affairs of men. In a conversation with Minerva, Juno reflects on the absurdity of Jupiter changing himself into "swans and things," a reference to his love affair with Leda and, consequently, his peopling the whole world "with his little lapses—all demanding special consideration because of their remarkable parentage. . . ."

Reflecting the ravages of World War II, in which Bridie lost a son, the play modernizes Homer's view of the gods. Jupiter comments that it was "easier to make a Universe than to control it. It was full of mad, meaningless forces. I got most of them bound and fixed and working to rules and all of a sudden I felt lonely. I felt that I would rather my mother had given me a puppydog or a kitten. . . ." An extension of the sleeping clergyman as a symbol for God, Jupiter feels helpless and, more pointedly, is saddened by his inability to provide answers to the overriding questions of man's existence. It is this fact that humans discover when, slain on the battlefield of Troy, they reach Olympus. The gods in their personal habits and relationships are no better than humans. Bridie wrote this fiercely antiwar play at a time when his own deteriorating health intensified his awareness of the bleakness that pervaded postwar Great Britain.

If *The Queen's Comedy* is about the relationship between God and man, its companion piece, *The Baikie Charivari*, is an allegory about the relationship between man and the devils that besiege him during his life. The play can be seen as Bridie's final comment on his lifelong concern with good and evil forces at work in the life of man. Produced the year after his death, the drama bears an interesting resemblance to his first professionally produced play, *The Sunlight Sonata.* Like the Seven Deadly Sins of that earlier play, seven devils confront Sir James MacArthur Pounce-Pellott, the leading character, whose name is derived from that of Pontius Pilate and the comic character, Punch, of magazine fame. His wife's name is Judy, and they have a daughter whom they still call Baby, even though she is of marriageable age. Pounce-Pellott has returned to the town of Baikie on the

Clyde Estuary in Scotland to retire at the age of fifty. He has spent his life in the British Civil Service in Junglipore, India.

In the surrealistic prologue, the Devil appears as a mask in the moon and speaks to a beadle, the Reverend Marcus Beadle, and to a local policeman, Robert Copper. The names of the Baikie residents, like those of the characters in a medieval morality play, symbolize their professions or qualities. In the style of the Book of Job in the Old Testament, the Devil inquires of Beadle and Copper, "Have ye considered my servant Pounce-Pellott?" When the cock crows and the Devil vanishes, Pounce-Pellott appears, a good-looking man in his fifties, announcing himself as "Knight Commander of the Indian Empire, King of Ghosts and Shadows, sometimes District Commander of Junglipore and other places."

Like Faust in his quest for wisdom, Pounce-Pellott wishes to be educated in the knowledge of the West. To this end, various neighbors (and a woman from America) appear as his teachers: the Reverend James Beadle (religion), Robert Copper (law), Councillor John Ketch (sociology, labor and left-wing thinking), Joe Mascara (art), Dr. Jean Pothecary (psychiatry), Lady Maggie Revenant (the old aristocratic order, actually a ghost from the past), and Mrs. Jemima Lee Crowe (an American publisher who offers Pounce-Pellott money for his memoirs). These figures represent the current wisdom of the West.

In the end, Pounce-Pellott, like his predecessor Pilate, washes his hands of them all and, asking for his stick, kills them all, except Lady Maggie, whom he cannot kill because she is a ghost. The Devil reappears, announcing that only time will tell whether he has been defeated. He vanishes, and Pounce-Pellott reflects on his inability to answer the riddle of life. He does know, however, that he killed those who pretended to know. Like Cameron of *A Sleeping Clergyman*, he knows that he cannot know, but also that he cannot stop seeking to know.

The tone of the play shifts between the surrealism of scenes such as that in which the Devil appears to Pounce-Pellott, and the ironic comedy of a Punch-and-Judy world, in which the realistic antics of his wife, daughter, and the seven representatives of Western wisdom are observed by Pounce-Pellott. As the play progresses to its conclusion in the form of arguments presented by the seven teachers, the prosaic style subtly gives way to poetic and lyric passages.

As a final, highly poetic statement, *The Baikie Charivari* is a sophisticated extension of Bridie's lifelong moral earnestness and a paean to the necessary effort of the human spirit to extend virtue, not in any narrow dogmatic sense or through high-flown idealism, but in the dogged persistence with which a rational humanism can create some order out of chaos, even out of the remnants of civilization left in the wake of a Trojan War or a World War II.

Responding to the long-standing criticism that he had difficulty in concluding a play, Bridie, at the close of *One Way of Living*, writes: "Only God can write a third act, and He seldom does." Bridie expresses his anger at "doctrinaire duds" and insists that audiences should leave the theater with their heads "whirling with speculation" and "selecting infinite possibilities for the characters . . . seen on stage." These possibilities find focus from time to time in men of genius such as Charles Cameron of *A Sleeping Clergyman* and Pounce-Pellott of *The Baikie Charivari*, who can stand alone if necessary. The miracle, mystery, and morality plays of medieval times are given contemporary significance in Bridie's theater, in that it is the miracle of individuated man that gives meaning to the existence of a Maker. As reflected in the very structure of Bridie's plays, there is no concluding "third act" to man's Faustian effort to work miracles on earth.

Other major works

NONFICTION: *Some Talk of Alexander*, 1926; *Mr. Bridie's Alphabet for Little Glasgow Highbrows*, 1934; *One Way of Living*, 1939; *The British Drama*, 1945; *A Small Stir: Letters on the English*, 1949 (with Moray McLaren).

RADIO PLAY: *The Sign of the Prophet Jonah*, 1942 (based on his play *Jonah and the Whale*).

MISCELLANEOUS: *Tedious and Brief*, 1944.

Bibliography

Bannister, Winifred. *James Bridie and His Theatre.* London: Rockliff, 1955. Written by a personal acquaintance of Bridie, the book contains a biography and an analysis of the plays and their performances (almost one a year from 1928 to 1954). Depicts Bridie as a liberal, proud, even patriotic Scot, despite his satires on a hypocritical society. Includes a chronology, photographs, an index of characters, and a general index.

Bentley, Eric. *In Search of Theater.* New York: Alfred A. Knopf, 1953. In the context of many "well-made" playwrights of his time, Bentley sees Bridie, using the play *Gog and Magog* as an example, attempting new structures in each of his well-made plays.

Bridie, James. *One Way of Living.* London: Constable, 1939. A 299-page meanderingly intimate, humorous, autobiographical account of his life, in ten five-year segments, with emphasis on the productions of his plays. Bridie's opinions and views on a multitude of topics are a key to his more than forty plays and other writings.

Luyben, Helen L. *James Bridie: Clown and Philosopher.* Philadelphia: University of Pennsylvania Press, 1965. A thematic analysis of selected plays, showing Bridie's growth from idealism, through disillusion, and finally reconciliation, with focus on the demonic. Contains a chronology, a bibliography, and an index.

Tobin, Terence. *James Bridie.* Boston: Twayne, 1980. A chronological analysis of the complete multifaceted works of Bridie as a Renaissance man of the first half of the twentieth century. What William Butler Yeats and Lady Augusta Gregory were to the Abbey Theatre in Dublin, Bridie was to the Citizens' Theatre of Glasgow. All three wrote in religion-dominated cultures that frequently exercised hostility toward the theater. Includes a photograph, a chronology, a bibliography, and an index.

Weales, Gerald. *Religion in Modern English Drama.* Philadelphia: University of Pennsylvania Press, 1961. An incisive comparison (only part of a broad topic) of George Bernard Shaw and Bridie as two dramatists "exuberant in their confession of faith." Contains an appendix of commercial and church dramas and a bibliography.

Susan Rusinko

RICHARD BROME

Born: England; c. 1590
Died: England; c. 1652-1653

Principal drama

Christianetta, pr. 1623(?) (with George Chapman?; no longer extant); *A Fault in Friendship*, pr. 1623 (with "Young Johnson"; no longer extant); *The Love-sick Maid: Or, The Honor of Young Ladies*, pr. 1629 (no longer extant); *The Northern Lass*, pr. 1629, pb. 1632; *The City Wit: Or, The Woman Wears the Breeches*, pr. c. 1629, pb. 1653; *The Queen's Exchange*, pr. 1631-1632(?), pb. 1657; *The Novella*, pr. 1632, pb. 1653; *The Covent-Garden Weeded*, pr. 1632, pb. 1659; *The Love-sick Court: Or, The Ambitious Politique*, pr. 1633-1634(?), pb. 1659; *The Late Lancashire Witches*, pr., pb. 1634 (with Thomas Heywood); *The Life and Death of Sir Martin Skink*, pr. c. 1634 (with Heywood; no longer extant); *The Apprentice's Prize*, pr. c. 1634 (with Heywood?; no longer extant); *The Sparagus Garden*, pr. 1635, pb. 1640; *The New Academy: Or, The New Exchange*, pr. 1635(?), pb. 1659; *The Queen and the Concubine*, pr. 1635-1636(?), pb. 1659; *The Jewish Gentleman*, pr. 1636(?) (no longer extant); *The English Moor: Or, The Mock-Marriage*, pr. 1637, pb. 1659; *The Antipodes*, pr. 1638, pb. 1640; *The Damoiselle: Or, The New Ordinary*, pr. 1638(?), pb. 1653; *Wit in Madness*, pr. 1638-1639(?) (no longer extant); *A Mad Couple Well Matched*, pr. 1639, pb. 1653; *The Court Beggar*, pr. 1640, pb. 1653; *A Jovial Crew: Or, The Merry Beggars*, pr. 1641, pb. 1652.

Other literary forms

Besides plays, Richard Brome wrote only some brief commendatory poems attached to other writers' collections of poetry or plays. He also edited John Fletcher's play *Monsieur Thomas* (pb. 1639) and probably edited *Lachrymae Musarum: The Tears of the Muses* (1649), a collection of elegies, to which Brome contributed, on the death of Henry Hastings in 1645.

Achievements

The reputation of Caroline playwright Richard Brome has generally been haunted by some ambiguity or doubt. During his own time, Brome was extremely popular, but even then his success was marred by criticisms that he pandered to his audience's poor tastes. Such criticisms might have been motivated to some extent by irrelevant factors, such as envy of his success and scorn for his humble background as a servant. His popularity continued during the Restoration, when his work influenced the form of Restoration comedy, and lasted into the eighteenth century. During the Victorian period, Brome was roundly condemned as the most obscene of the Renaissance dramatists and frequently contrasted with Ben Jonson—Jonson and Brome respectively epitomizing a "good" versus a "bad" comic dramatist. Again, irrelevant factors appear to have clouded the critical estimates of Brome.

Brome's ambiguous reputation has continued into the modern period, when he has been known as the most outstanding minor Caroline dramatist, but his status has also been on the rise. Kathleen Lynch demonstrated that Brome is an important link between Renaissance and Restoration comedy in *The Social Mode of Restoration Comedy* (1926), and R. J. Kaufmann valued Brome's work as an accurate reflection of Brome's time, a pivotal period in English history, in *Richard Brome: Caroline Playwright* (1961). Brome, however, is not merely of historical interest: His plays, particularly his best works, are still entertaining, and the social conditions he depicts bear some close resemblances to conditions today. T. S. Eliot believed that Brome should be read more, and Catherine M. Shaw, Brome's latest chronicler, in her book *Richard Brome* (1980), states that his plays could be revived on stage.

A highly professional playwright, eclectic and practical, Brome had the ability to judge public taste and had the theatrical skills to satisfy it— through his use of both satiric and romantic elements, his plotting, his characters, and his language. Of these, his characters are perhaps most appealing today, offering an engaging cross section of Caroline England. Brome's diversity of characters resembles Jonson's, but, unlike Jonson, Brome seems to like his characters: His satire is tolerant rather than indignant or disgusted.

Also appealing is Brome's style. It is clear and direct, easy to follow, already anticipating the Restoration style, which T. S. Eliot called the first "modern" style. At the same time, it retains some of the old Renaissance figurative richness. Finally, Brome had an excellent ear for conversation, including cant, dialects, and speech mannerisms. The resulting blend is a particularly effective style for the theater. Brome's style is another indication that he was in tune with the theater and with his time.

Brome's success was consistent throughout his career, beginning with the early plays *The Love-sick Maid* (now lost) and *The Northern Lass*, but his art improved as he went along. To modern tastes, his best plays might include *The Covent-Garden Weeded* and *The Sparagus Garden*, written near the midpoint of his career, and *The Antipodes*, *A Mad Couple Well Matched*, and *A Jovial Crew*, written near the end. *A Jovial Crew* has generally been the favorite.

Biography

Little is known of Richard Brome's personal life, including date and place of birth and death. The conventionally accepted estimate of his birth date is 1590, but evidence for the date is scanty: In 1591, a Richard Brome was listed as the son of Henry Brome in the St. James Clerkenwell parish register, and depositions in 1639 and 1640 Chancery Court suits identified a Richard Brome "aged 50 years or thereabouts." Whether these records refer to Richard Brome the playwright is uncertain, since marriage and burial records of the period indicate several Richard Bromes in the London area alone. For the same reason, Brome's marriage and family relationships cannot be clearly identified, though he did apparently marry and rear a family: In 1640, he complained that the Salisbury Court Theatre's refusal to pay him caused him and his family to suffer hardship. His death can be pinned down only to the years 1652-1653.

Much more interesting information is available on Brome's career as a playwright. The most interesting fact is that, before becoming a playwright, Brome was the servant of Ben Jonson, a leading playwright and the main theorist of Renaissance English drama. The induction of Jonson's comedy *Bartholomew Fair* (pr. 1614) refers to "his man, Master Broome, behind the arras," and Jonson wrote a commendatory poem for Brome's *The Northern Lass* that includes the following lines:

> I had you for a servant, once, Dick Brome;
> And you performed a servant's faithful parts.
> Now, you are got into a nearer room,
> Of fellowship, professing my old arts.
> And you do do them well, with good applause,
> Which you have justly gained from the stage,
> By observation of those comic laws
> Which I, your master, first did teach the age.
> You learned it well, and for it served your time
> A prenticeship: which few do nowadays. . . .

Similarly, Brome gratefully acknowledged Jonson's influence and tutelage, proud to be one of the "Sons of Ben."

How well Brome learned from his mentor is indicated by an incident that occurred in 1629. That year, Jonson's *The New Inn* failed miserably at the Blackfriars Theatre; shortly afterward, the same company and theater presented Brome's *The Love-sick Maid*—to extraordinarily popular acclaim. Jonson was so upset that, in "Ben Jonson's Ode to Himself," he blasted popular taste in the theater, complaining that "Broom's sweepings do as well/ There as his master's meal." Other Sons of Ben seconded their master with puns on Brome's name and status and with allusions to the sweepings or dregs he was serving up. Apparently this incident ruffled Jonson and Brome's relationship only briefly, however, since Jonson left out the snide allusion to Brome when he published his ode in 1631, and in 1632, Jonson wrote his commendatory verses to Brome's *The Northern Lass*.

The coincidence of Jonson's failure and Brome's success in 1629 also indicates that Brome learned from other contemporary playwrights besides his mentor. Brome collaborated with Thomas Heywood and possibly with George Chapman, and a number of fellow dramatists, including James Shirley and John Ford, wrote commendatory verses for Brome's works. In addition, Brome's work shows the influence of still other playwrights, such as John Fletcher, Francis Beaumont, and Philip Massinger. These collaborations, commendations, and influences confirm that, if Jonson was Brome's mentor, Brome was also widely acquainted with other dramatists and their work.

Such a view of Brome is further supported by his associations with various companies and theaters. His early play with "Young Johnson," *A Fault in Friendship* (now lost), was produced by the Prince's Company, probably at the Red Bull Theatre. In 1628, Brome was listed with the Queen of Bohemia's Players, who apparently toured the provinces and sometimes acted at the Red Bull Theatre in London (whether Brome was an actor for the company is in dispute). From 1629 to 1634, Brome wrote for the King's Men, the leading troupe in London and also Jonson's company, who produced Brome's work at court and at the Globe and Blackfriars theaters. In 1635, Brome returned briefly to the Prince's Company at the Red Bull, then signed a three-year contract to write for the King's Revels (later Queen Henrietta's Men) at the Salisbury Court Theatre. Brome found this association unsatisfactory—there was a dispute about proper payment—and did not sign a new seven-year contract with Salisbury Court Theatre when it was offered to him in 1638. Instead, in 1639 he moved over to write for Beeston's Boys at the Cockpit Theatre—a happy association which continued until the end of Brome's career.

Brome's career ended abruptly, at its height, when the English Civil War started in 1642 and Parliament closed all the theaters. A creature of the theater, Brome lived on, sadly and in poverty, until 1652 or 1653. Appropriately, his last known literary effort involved a collection of elegies entitled *Lachrymae Musarum*.

Analysis

As R. J. Kaufmann observes, Richard Brome's work forms "an intelligible and complex commentary on a central phase of an historical evolutionary process." That historical process, though highly complex itself, with its many social, religious, and nationalistic side issues, can be briefly summarized as the growing challenge of the English middle class to the old aristocratic order. Although individuals did not line up neatly, the middle class as a group found its symbol of power in Parliament, while the king was the figurehead of the old order. The middle class also leaned toward the Puritan sects, while the aristocracy generally hewed to the established Anglican Church. These deep-rooted tensions and others came to a head during the ill-fated reign of Charles I, from 1625 to 1649, when Brome practiced his art, and culminated in the English Civil War and the beheading of King Charles in 1649.

As these bloody events show, Brome lived and wrote on the eve of destruction. While his tone is comic, Brome nevertheless sets forth the conditions which led to social paroxysm. As a playwright, he sets forth those conditions in human terms, in the terms of feeling individuals. Therefore, for students of seventeenth century English history, Brome has particular significance, but there are also some strong parallels between the social conditions in his plays and those of today. For people living in unstable times, possibly on the edge of cataclysm, Brome has a message.

Brome's message centers mostly on money, which dominates the life depicted in his plays, and money's erosion of all other values. Marriages and alliances are formed on the basis of money as much as on the basis of love or friendship. Degraded aristocrats, short on cash, join with the middle class or with crooks and coney-catchers in pursuit of lucre. Groups of beggars roam the countryside. Everywhere the middle class is rampant, feeling its oats and hoping to purchase the manners and pedigrees of the aristocracy it is replacing. The world itself seems turned upside down, former values inverted. For the general theme of Mammon-worship, Brome was probably indebted to his mentor, Jonson, but Brome elaborates the social details of his theme that were apparent in the society around him. Brome might also have been indebted to Jonson for his conservative, aristocratic sympathies; with the changing makeup of the Caroline audience, Brome had to tone down those sympathies and appeared to be a more evenhanded observer.

The Northern Lass is an example of Brome's early work. The play's immediate success, combined with that of *The Love-sick Maid*, which was produced the same year, firmly established Brome's popularity in his time. These two early hits proved Brome's ability to satisfy his audience's tastes, but *The Northern Lass* makes one question those tastes and wonder whether Jonson was not right, after all, to attack them. The play's overdone intrigue and disguising become tedious, and its main attraction is its sentimental portrait of Constance from England's North Country. Yet *The Northern Lass* does illustrate the typical Brome: It introduces the all-pervasive theme of money and Brome's use here, in one play, of both satiric and romantic elements.

Money's power is underlined by the play's opening scene: Sir Philip Luckless, a court gentleman, has contracted to marry Mistress Fitchow, a rich city widow. The marriage represents a common social expedient of the time, the uneasy alliance of aristocrats and members of the middle class as the aristocrats sought to replenish their funds while the middle class sought to obtain titles. Sir Philip learns how uneasy the alliance is when he meets his bride's relatives, "a race of fools," and discovers that the bride herself is a loud shrew. He regrets the marriage bargain even more when Constance, the sweet-voiced Northern lass who is in love with him, appears on the scene. Eventually, Sir Philip gets a divorce on a technicality (since he and Mistress Fitchow quarrel on their wedding day, their marriage is never consummated) and is able to marry Constance. Significantly, the conflicts between love and money, aristocracy and middle class, end in compromise: Half of Constance's rich uncle's estate comes with her hand, and Fitchow marries Sir Philip's cousin Tridewell, who rather unconvincingly falls in love with her. By Brome's time, dramatists had to give money and the middle class their due.

As the play's title suggests, it was the sentimental portrait of Constance—the romantic element—that charmed Brome's audience. Innocent and direct, Constance speaks in a fetching North Country dialect: "But for my life I could not but think, he war the likest man that I had seen with mine eyne, and could not devise the thing I had, might be unbeggen by him." Mistaking Sir Philip's courtly compliment for a marriage proposal, she pursues him all the way to London. Naïve and loving, Constance introduces another perspective into the scheming context of the play, particularly in contrast to Fitchow and the prostitute Constance Holdup. Yet even the prostitute, through confusion with Constance, takes on some of her halo, thus enabling the audience to sentimentalize both innocence and its loss. In short, Constance is a reminder that innocence exists out there somewhere—or so Brome's audience wanted to believe.

A much better play than *The Northern Lass* is *The Sparagus Garden*, written around the midpoint of Brome's career. A comedy in which the satiric element predominates, *The Sparagus Garden* might well win the appreciation of a modern audience. Brome warns in the prologue that the audience should not "expect high language or much cost," since "the subject is so low." In fact, the language is sharp, colorful, and varied (including courtly and Somersetshire accents and satire of gentlemen's cant), not to mention full of sexual innuendo. The "low subject" is the Sparagus Garden, a suburban garden-restaurant with beds upstairs—the best little rendezvous for lovers in London. Here they can also sate themselves with asparagus, which is described as full of wonderful properties in both its erect and limp states.

Aside from the sexual appetites of Londoners, much else is satirized in *The Sparagus Garden*. For example, neighborly feuding is satirized in the characters of Touchwood and Striker, two rich old justices whose enmity over the years has grown into a close and sustaining relationship: They love to hate each other, and the desire of each to strike the final blow keeps them alive. Marital strife is satirized through the relationship of Brittleware and Rebecca: Brittleware fears that Rebecca will make him a cuckold, and

Rebecca plays on her husband's anxiety by reciting her sexual yearnings and Brittleware's inability to satisfy them—"you John Bopeep." Anxiety about sexual promiscuity is also satirized through the figure of Sir Arnold Cautious, "a stale bachelor" and "a ridiculous lover of women" (a voyeur) who will marry no woman because he can find no virgin. Other objects of incidental satire in *The Sparagus Garden* are lawyers and poets.

The social change occurring in the Caroline period is strikingly dramatized in *The Sparagus Garden*. Not only is the Sparagus Garden a resort for gentlemen accompanying city wives, such as Mrs. Holyhock, the "precise" (that is, puritanical) draper's wife, but also its main agent (pimp/procurator/publicist) is Sir Hugh Moneylacks, a degraded knight who "lives by shifts." Having run through his own estate and that of his middle-class wife, whom he drove to an early grave, Sir Hugh is now Striker's disowned son-in-law.

A hardened hustler, Sir Hugh is not at all abashed by his father-in-law's rejection, nor is the Sparagus Garden his only money-making project. In addition, he and his confederates are instructing the Somersetshire bumpkin Tim Hoyden, who has four hundred pounds to invest in the project, on how to be a gentleman—a subject of further satire in *The Sparagus Garden*.

In contrast to *The Sparagus Garden*, *A Jovial Crew* is a Brome comedy in which the romantic element predominates. The last of Brome's plays, *A Jovial Crew* is generally considered his best. It was a favorite of the Restoration and of the eighteenth century, when it was turned into a comic opera at Covent Garden—a version no doubt suggested by the play's numerous songs and dances. Performed by a jolly crew of raffish beggars, the rousing songs and dances embody the beggars' carefree philosophy, which stands in stark contrast to the middle-class ethos. The bands of beggars roaming the countryside are both an indictment of and an alternative to the emerging middle-class order. Coming from all walks of life—soldiers, lawyers, courtiers, and poets as well as peasants—the beggars turn necessity into a virtue: They form a "beggars' Commonwealth" with its own language and values, values based on fellowship rather than money. In fact, they scorn money.

The middle-class characters view the beggars' commonwealth with fear and fascination. Oldrents, an old country esquire whose home epitomizes middle-class prosperity, stability, and dullness, is vexed by a fortune-teller's prediction that his two daughters will become beggars. His friend Hearty, "a decayed gentleman," urges him to laugh at the prediction (to look upon the carefree beggars and birds of the field and be as they) but to little avail. As it turns out, Oldrents has good reason to fear for his daughters— particularly since his rapacious grandfather wrested the family estate from a "thriftless heir," Wrought-on, whose own posterity became beggars. Oldrents fathered a son with one of Wrought-on's beggar-descendants; now the son, unknown to him, is his steward, Springlove, who has a yearning, each spring, to go wandering with the beggars.

Oldrents' daughters also feel the attraction of the wandering life, which promises an escape from Oldrents' dull household and worried disposition. The daughters, Rachel and Meriel, look on their begging venture as a lark, and they impose it upon Vincent and Hilliard, their boyfriends since childhood, as an ordeal, a test of loyalty more significant than such childish games as "tearing of books" or "piss and paddle in't." In fact, they are all failures at alternative life-styles, even though they have the services of Springlove, who equips and instructs them and gives them an introduction to the beggars. After experiencing the hardships of pricking their "bums" on a straw bed and waking without a mirror, they fly back to their middle-class nests.

Despite its fun and folly, its reminder of Shakespearean couples running through the forests of Arden and Athens, *A Jovial Crew* is a strong record of a deteriorating society on the verge of civil war. It was Brome's final statement. The record had been building, however, throughout his works—a record of growing middle-class dominance, of money's power, of declining loyalties and eroding values, of a vacuum at the heart of life. It is a record that today's world might do well to examine carefully.

Bibliography

Allen, Herbert F. *A Study of the Comedies of Richard Brome, Especially as Representative of Moral Decadence.* Ann Arbor: University of Michigan Press, 1912. Allen finds Brome's work decadent in the sense that it reveals a diseased falling off from an earlier, healthier comedy. It strains for originality, succumbs to subtle imitation, stresses art over matter, and portrays indecencies. Allen's grim anatomy leaves little to admire in Brome's comedies.

Andrews, Clarence Edward. *Richard Brome: A Study of His Life and Works.* New Haven, Conn.: Yale University Press, 1913. Reprint. Hamden, Conn.: Archon Books, 1972. This scholarly analysis proposes a chronology and a bibliography of Brome's work, devotes a long chapter to the qualities of Brome's plays, considers the influence on Brome of Ben Jonson, William Shakespeare, Thomas Dekker, and others, and sums up in two appendices the satire in, and the sources of, *The Antipodes.*

Davis, Joe Lee. "Richard Brome's Neglected Contribution to Comic Theory." *Studies in Philology* 40 (1943): 520-528. Davis argues that *The Antipodes*, first acted in 1638, "incorporates a theory of comic catharsis and what may be termed an *extra*-realistic conception of the relationship between comedy and actuality." *The Antipodes* was written under the influence of Thomas Randolph's *The Muse's Looking-Glasse* (1638).

_____. *The Sons of Ben: Jonsonian Comedy in Caroline England.* Detroit: Wayne State University Press, 1967. Brome is one of a group of minor dramatists called the Sons of Ben for their imitation of Ben Jonson. Caroline England was dominated by Puritanism and Platonism, and Davis traces the consequences of this domination for the comedy of the period, analyzing thirty-two plays by eleven dramatists.

Donaldson, Ian. *The World Upside-Down: Comedy from Jonson to Fielding.* London: Oxford University Press, 1970. Contains chapters on six comedies, including Brome's *The Antipodes.* Donaldson finds Brome's work "readable," his plays "brisk, well-made, seldom dull" but rarely showing "true comic originality," and his talent only "an engaging minor one." *The Antipodes* is "absurdist" but "basically comforting and conservative," and its moral premises are "strikingly simple and assured."

Kaufmann, R. J. *Richard Brome: Caroline Playwright.* New York: Columbia University Press, 1961. Kaufmann offers an informative and comprehensive overview of Brome's work, stressing Brome's conservative clinging to "Tudor culture." Appendix 1 provides "Undigested Records," and appendix 2 proposes a "Chronology of Brome's Plays."

Shaw, Catherine M. *Richard Brome.* Boston: G. K. Hall, 1980. An excellent introduction to Brome, with the standard chronology and bibliography of the Twayne volumes. Rather imaginative chapter topics include "The Ladies Take the Stage" and "The Gentlemen: Fathers, Fools, and Fops." This well-written study gives a good sense of the contents and qualities of Brome's work.

Harold Branam
(Updated by *Frank Day*)

ROBERT BROWNING

Born: Camberwell, England; May 7, 1812
Died: Venice, Italy; December 12, 1889

Principal drama

Strafford, pr., pb. 1837; *Pippa Passes*, pb. 1841; *King Victor and King Charles*, pb. 1842; *The Return of the Druses*, pb. 1843; *A Blot in the 'Scutcheon*, pr., pb. 1843; *Colombe's Birthday*, pb. 1844, pr. 1853; *Luria*, pb. 1846; *A Soul's Tragedy*, pb. 1846.

Other literary forms

Robert Browning is better known as a major Victorian poet and, in particular, as one who perfected the influential verse form called dramatic monologue. His achievement in poetry, for which he forsook the theater altogether in 1846, was unquestionably much greater than what he accomplished as a writer of stage plays, yet it is difficult and unwise to distinguish the subject matter and techniques of Browning's "failed" dramas from those of his successful poems. Although he was by nature and inclination a dramatic writer, it became apparent that his peculiar interests and talent in that line were more suited to the finer medium of poetry than to the practical exigencies of stagecraft. The verse confirms his acknowledged preoccupation with interior drama ("Action in character, not character in action"). Browning's verse masterpieces in this mode include "Porphyria's Lover," "My Last Duchess," "The Bishop Orders His Tomb at St. Praxed's Church," "Andrea del Sarto," "Love Among the Ruins," "The Last Ride Together," and *The Ring and the Book* (1868-1869). A dramatic monologue by Browning typically features an incandescent moment of crisis or of self-realization in the mental life of some unusual, often morally or psychologically flawed, character. Rather like a soliloquy except in being addressed to a present but silent listener, this type of poem enabled Browning to let his speakers' personalities, motives, obsessions, and delusions be revealed—inadvertently or otherwise—in speech and implied gesture. This preoccupation with inward, psychological drama—with the springs of action rather than with action itself—is the origin of Browning's greatness as a poet and of his limitations as a stageworthy playwright.

Achievements

In nineteenth and early twentieth century criticism, Browning was widely considered to be the best English writer of dramatic literature (though not of stageable plays) since the Renaissance. That judgment was probably accurate enough, if only because of the remarkable dearth of fine drama during the two hundred years in question. Even today, especially if Browning's splendid dramatic monologues are included in the estimate, there can be little doubt that his achievement was, under the circumstances, extraordinary. Nevertheless, any evaluation of his plays must begin by conceding that, despite his hopes, practical theatrical craft in the ordinary sense was never in Browning's vein of genius. He was a first-rate dramatic poet, not a good technical playwright. Indeed, the very themes and methods that mark the plays' literary value are the source of their unsuitability for successful performance. One historical explanation of this "failure" is the Romantic concept of acted and unacted drama, documented in Michael Mason's contribution to *Robert Browning* (1975). Mason associates Browning with a widespread and consciously antitheatrical attitude among authors that resulted in plays composed with indifference to performative—as opposed to literary or expressive—criteria. If Browning did believe on principle that actual staging is not necessary to serious drama, it is less surprising that his own plays are satisfactory chiefly as reading texts. On the other hand, we should remember that Browning did press persistently to see some of his work upon the boards. In any case, Browning's plays have never been popular and, with the exception of *Pippa Passes*, are not usually numbered among his most important contributions to the history of English dramatic writing. Their lasting excellence, then, is in their objective poetry and prose. As in the verse collections to which he gave titles such as *Dramatic Lyrics* (1842; in *Bells and Pomegranates*, 1841-1846), *Dramatis Personae* (1864), *Dramatic Idyls* (1879, 1880), and *Men and Women* (1855), Browning's mastery of inward action is demonstrated in the plays' delineation of moral and psychological crises and in their vivid intellectual and emotional energy. Understood as searching critiques of modern life, the psychological and moral bearings of some of these dramas—and their subversive frankness (about eroticism, for example, or respectability)— were original and significantly ahead of their time. Formal innovations in the reading plays (*Pippa Passes* and *A Soul's Tragedy*) and Browning's special gift for creating memorable female characters have also been praised.

Biography

As a young man, Robert Browning was tutored at his prosperous family's home near London. He spent much of a sheltered adolescence reading eagerly and eclectically in the fine library there, absorbing philosophical, artistic, and historical lore that would later emerge—sometimes rather obscurely—in his plays and poems. Devoted always to a literary career, Browning lived for many years dependent upon his indulgent parents. They exerted a deep personal influence: the father intellectually, the mother religiously. In literature, the works and example of Percy Bysshe Shelley were Browning's first and most enduring inspiration, though in drama itself the constant model would be, wisely and otherwise, William Shakespeare. The privately published verse and plays of Browning's early maturity were eccentric and poorly received. Most of the drama in particular was ill-suited to theatrical production, and in disappointment, he turned increasingly to a new type of poetry, the dramatic monologue, in order to fuse the variousness and objectivity of plays with the subtle effects of poems. Yet even after 1846, when elopement and marriage crowned his long, ardent courtship of Elizabeth Barrett, she was still the better-known writer of the two. The blithe years of his wedded life were spent mostly in Italy, where Browning's fascination with the rich and enigmatic sociocultural heritage of the Mediterranean bloomed and reflected itself in the great new poems collected in *Men and Women*. Mrs. Browning's sudden death in 1861 ended this golden era and was personally devastating for her husband. Thereafter, Browning resided in both England and Italy, continuing to write poetry— notably *The Ring and the Book*—and gradually winning a wide and appreciative audience for all of his work. This late adulation, including the international Browning Society's admiration of his religious and philosophical outlook, was in striking contrast with the humiliation he had felt during the early years. In 1888, he saw the publication of the first volumes of what would become a seventeen-volume collection of his dramatic and poetic canon.

Analysis

Robert Browning's best plays, whether for reading or performance, are the ones in which we are most aware of his genius for evoking "action in character": the drama of human personality in conscious or unconscious conflict with itself. Outward action and scenic spectacle are perhaps more incidental in Browning than in any other significant English playwright, though the extended implications for social morality are usually apparent. Instead, Browning concentrates on the self-articulation of minds that are devious or deviant or otherwise exceptional. One effect is to cast doubt upon the normative values and impulses contending in (or generated by) such mentalities, notably in politics or love. Indeed, love of one sort or another among socially prominent characters is usually the symbolic field in which Browning's flawed or obsessive personalities perform most ineffectually or tragically. Rationalizers of selfishness, greed, hypocrisy, or cruelty are frequently presented, as are characters who let themselves and others be destroyed by the paradoxes inherent in artificial codes or standards of conduct. In particular, egomania and other faults of willful pride (including excessive shame or guilt) would appear to be Browning's diagnosis of the moral neuroses and complacencies he detected in Victorian society at large. The characters are not so much evil as inveterately and anxiously deluded.

It is easy to misconstrue the sometimes grotesque, sentimental, or over-wrought behavior of Browning's characters as a lapse or compromise with popular taste on the playwright's part. In Browning, the trite or melodramatic overreaction is symptomatic—it is his subject, not his technique. The presence and perspective of intelligent, realistic, and sensible characters such as Guendolen in *A Blot in the 'Scutcheon* confirm Browning's deliberate exhibition of abnormality in others, such as the histrionic Mildred and Thorold Tresham. That contemporary readers and audiences (including Charles Dickens) could apparently value Browning's pathos for its own sake is a separate consideration. A more significant problem for Browning, and for modern readers, is the atheatricality of such refined psychological and metaphoric aims. The artistic intention may in fact be too subtle, the rendering too opaque, the intended medium too visual to elicit onstage anything like the appropriate effect. Nevertheless, as a reading text the typical Browning play yields the same kind of dramatic significance that is to be found in his poetry.

The verse tragedy *A Blot in the 'Scutcheon*, considered Browning's best play, indicates his special effort to create something both subtle and stageworthy. In fact, he described it to the celebrated actor-manager William Charles Macready as "a sort of compromise between my notion and yours. . . . There is *action* in it, drabbing, stabbing, et autres gentilesses." Nevertheless, the observable action and strong dialogue in this drama of eighteenth century aristocratic honor remain subordinated to Browning's real interest in portraying inward conflicts and destructive ideals. Moreover, the tragic situation derives entirely from the flawed psyches of proud, rash Lord Tresham and his guilt-tormented sister Mildred. The distraught girl and her illicit lover Lord Mertoun attempt through an elaborate charade of formal betrothal to bring their relationship within the bounds of social and class respectability. Here, then, is a combination of Browning's favorite dramatic themes: unusually heightened emotion, symbolic moments of intense individual crisis, thwarted or misdirected love and sexuality, and the inhibiting force of pride or conventionality upon free feeling and action. In all of these respects, *A Blot in the 'Scutcheon* shows divided loyalties and misguidedly good intentions causing tensions that explode in impulsive and fatal choices. Mildred Tresham is visibly going to pieces throughout much of the play, her virtual derangement the price she pays for being torn between her passionate love for Mertoun and her terror of offending her imperious brother. It is her panic that has necessitated the young lovers' gamble for respectability, and she thus initiates the sequence of disastrous dissimulations, exposures, and misunderstandings. Both men are doomed when, cracking under the strain, she blurts out half the truth; Tresham and Mertoun feel bound by honor to suppress the simple word that could avert the needless catastrophe. It is the kind of situation in which Browning excelled: dilemmas in which men and women are too hampered by mixed motives to act with candor, charity, courage, or imagination.

The proud folly of Thorold Tresham is likewise responsible for the tragic denouement in *A Blot in the 'Scutcheon*. He whips himself into a rage about Mildred's "dishonorableness" and the reputation of his ancestral house, despite having seen earlier the wisdom of embarrassed concealment. In his fury, he so aggravates her already excessive shame that she is unable to reveal that her secret paramour and her formal suitor are the same person. Again in the duel scene, Tresham's selfish, intemperate anger and taunting compel the unwilling Mertoun to fight and die. Thereafter, sorrowful but still obsessed with observing the niceties of maintaining the family name, Tresham kills himself in a gesture that would seem ludicrously melodramatic were it not so poignantly in keeping with the pernicious notions of heroism and dynastic obligation he has displayed all along. Guendolen's wry epitaph confirms that one is expected to pity Tresham but by no means to admire his "perfect spirit of honor" or to condone his pointless, self-righteous suicide. Here and elsewhere, Guendolen seems to reflect the author's bemusement by what she calls "the world's seemings and realities." If the Treshams are unstable and haunted, young Mertoun seems overly casual until it is too late, at which point he overreacts in dignified fatalism. His contribution to the tragedy, apart from maintaining, all too incautiously, the liaison with Mildred and misjudging her brother, is to defy Tresham unnecessarily before the duel and to perish more or less suicidally on the latter's sword. Murders, suicides, and (as in Mildred's case) expirings under stress are almost always associated in Browning's plays with willful or simplistic escapism, albeit in the name of some illusory notion of justice. The three deaths in *A Blot in the 'Scutcheon* are good examples of this tendency.

The thematic focus of this play is on the inhumanity of what is perversely done for the sake of personal, social, and dynastic honor. In scene after scene, Tresham, Mildred, and Mertoun are either driven or betrayed by such considerations, their relationships becoming increasingly complicated, frustrated, and dangerous. At the same time, Guendolen's frank and genial perspective reminds us (and ought to have convinced the other characters) that with a little more candor and a lot less preoccupation with "name" and "blots," the whole problem could have been resolved comedically rather than tragically. She notices almost prophetically, for example, how overready the others are to announce principles for which they are prepared to die. It is also Guendolen who gaily sees through Mertoun's pretense, Tresham's gullible complacency, and Mildred's guilty secret. Her insights are ignored or come too late, but her bright and ironic personality commands the stage at the end. It is significant that Tresham, Mildred, and Mertoun apparently die uncontrite: They regret the ghastly effects, but not the causes, of their actions. Tresham's dying utterances, which he imagines to embody heroic penance and self-sacrifice, are as banal, code-bound, and monomaniac as anything he has said before. Mildred likewise persists in considering her own death as a just retribution and relief from anguish. Mertoun, like the others, is none the wiser for bringing on his own end. Each demise is a wholly destructive martyrdom to some abstract, over-scrupulous notion of "duty" or "wrong." Moreover, these unexpected deaths are shocking; as in some of Browning's other plays (and in such dramatic monologues as "Porphyria's Lover" and "My Last Duchess"), the customary tragic effects of fear and pity are mingled with surprise and even revulsion. The conventions of drama do not easily embrace Browning's emphasis on extravagance and perversity in characters' motives and reactions. If pathology and tragedy do not mix, Browning is no tragedian. His work may nevertheless be a finer, more modern, and more disturbing criticism of life for having deviated from literary tradition.

Pippa Passes is Browning's most famous (though possibly least stageable) play and ranks among his best works. An early and experimental composition, the drama comprises four symbolic vignettes from Renaissance life in an Italian town. These independent scenes are structurally and thematically connected by the momentary overhearing, in each, of young Pippa's voice. The girl's innocent singing crucially affects the outcome of interviews that she unknowingly bypasses in her holiday journey. In every case, her song induces a hearer to make, at a point of personal crisis, a guilty choice in favor of just or noble action. *Pippa Passes* reveals Browning at his dramatically strongest and weakest. The situations, subtle effects, psychological focus, and tenuous framing story are quite unsuitable for theatrical performance. In reading, however, the play is successful and undoubtedly dramatic. The issues raised by the various personalities, conflicts, and resolutions of the four scenes are likewise typical of Browning at his best.

Perhaps the most memorable and evocative vignette in *Pippa Passes* is the scene that presents two adulterous lovers, Ottima and Sebald, who have just murdered Ottima's wealthy old husband. Even as the couple begin to talk, it becomes evident that their former "wild wicked" passion has become wearied and cloying. The crime designed to set them free has already started to gnaw the heart out of their love. Sebald in particular seems irritable, distracted, and resentful from the outset. He is also grimly obsessed with the man whose killing he now half regrets. Like Macbeth, he is weaker and more morbidly sensitive than his accomplice. Sebald surprises, and then alarms, Ottima by dwelling on his troubled conscience, self-disgust, and frank doubts about her value as his reward. The pace and drama intensify as Ottima grasps the seriousness of this threat to their relationship and fearfully sets out to argue and finally to seduce him back into her control. In lines of lush and powerfully sensual poetry, accompanied by indications of alluring gesture, she soon succeeds in diverting and arousing the febrile Sebald. As he excitedly begs forgiveness and names her his "queen . . . magnificent in sin," they embrace and ardently undress. At this instant, the passing song of Pippa is heard from outside the window—the famous little lyric ending, "God's in his heaven—/ All's right with the world." Grateful for being rescued by the intervention of this "miracle," a remorseful Sebald recoils at once from Ottima, bitterly repudiates her fascinations, and abruptly kills himself. It is typical of Browning that the impulsiveness and startling effect of the suicide, rather than its moral implications, are highlighted: The act's dramatic interest is in its psychology, its convincing exhibition of how that haunted mind might react, edifyingly or not, under such stress. Ottima's immediate responses—shock, envy, tender generosity, and self-recovery—are likewise rendered by Browning with skillful realism and irony. She is another of his brilliant portraits of women, and for all of her sins (a murder among them), the sanity of her final outlook underlines the strange extremism of Sebald's.

Each of the other sections of *Pippa Passes* similarly portrays two characters whose dilemma is interrupted and in some sense resolved by the passing voice of unworldly little Pippa, and, like the Ottima-Sebald scene, the others are Browningesque in their psychological verisimilitude, dramatic patterning, unusual feeling, and apparent moral opaqueness. Two parts employ a robust and naturalistic prose that confirms Browning's versatility and also indicates how emphatically his preference for "outmoded" verse drama was based on positive and theoretical considerations, not on any inability as a prose stylist. He never composed another play with the ingenuity and variety of *Pippa Passes*, but in the separate vignettes can be seen the germ of the great dramatic monologues to come, as well as the peculiarly psychological (or psychosocial) bearings of speeches and soliloquies in the later plays.

Briefer analyses of Browning's other dramas will suffice. Of these, *Strafford*, *King Victor and King Charles*, *The Return of the Druses*, and *Luria* are undistinguished. The first two are historical studies. *Luria* is a tragedy strongly reminiscent of (but much inferior to) Shakespeare's *Othello*. A convoluted romance, *The Return of the Druses* fails to integrate the politics with the love story. Features of two other plays do deserve attention. These are *Colombe's Birthday* (important as the happiest and most stageworthy Browning drama) and *A Soul's Tragedy* (very significantly the last).

Colombe's Birthday is a fairly conventional romantic comedy about the personal feelings and minor diplomatic stir associated with a young duchess' marriage. Graceful and gently satiric, the story interestingly follows good Duchess Colombe's birthday tribulations (both a threatened insurrection and the advent of a rival claimant to the throne, followed by two attractive marriage proposals) and the sound judgment (and luck) by which she satisfies both love and public duty. There are pleasing and eloquent characters, much fine verse, a genially searching critique of "courtier-ways," and a satisfying conclusion in which all receive as much or as little as their behavior warrants. Moreover, as a stage play *Colombe's Birthday* is workmanlike, accessible, and sedately agreeable. There is, however, a notable scarcity of Browning's customary dramatic concerns, tensions, and techniques. Indeed, to some extent this play indicates the literary limitations of work in which he most compromises with practicality and with popular taste. It may not be coincidental, then, that *Colombe's Birthday* was the last drama Browning designed expressly for theatrical presentation and that he soon abandoned playwriting altogether.

A Soul's Tragedy, Browning's most politically and philosophically serious play, has often been praised even though it is his last and his least stageable. Written in evident indifference to theatrical expectations, it dexterously traces the development and decline of a sixteenth century revolutionary's mind. The title itself seems to express the lifelong orientation of Browning's writing and the inevitability of his forsaking the theater. An entirely interior, possibly allegorical, process is being enacted in *A Soul's Tragedy*, called by its author a "wise metaphysical play." Only the inward action—defeat in the soul—is tragic, moreover; to all outward appearances the pattern and outcome are comedic. Well-articulated theories of statecraft, and much rhetoric about public responsibility, are simply vehicles for the playwright's exploration of moral psychology. The "tragedy" lies in the latter—in the conscious and unconscious mental life underlying an individual's outward behavior and rationalized principles. As critic Trevor Lloyd has shrewdly pointed out in connection with the political dramas, Browning handles well "the frame of mind of a man undertaking an imposture for the sake of something that he can convincingly regard as a good purpose." The mind that undergoes change in *A Soul's Tragedy* is that of Chiappino. During the first half of the play, he utters, in excellent verse, all the idealism (sincere and otherwise) of unselfish aspiration. Then, in the second part, he speaks—this time in lively prose—all the disillusionment (justifiable and otherwise) of realpolitik. That switch from "poetical" to "prosaic" thought and expression is not simply a political metaphor or an elegant gimmick on Browning's part. Both "voices" are rhetorical projections of what the self-preoccupied "soul" imagines or requires itself to believe at the moment. The touchstones against which Chiappino's development can be charted are two alter-ego characters: Luitolfo is the simple and genuine radical, while Onigben is the cynical legate whose droll Machiavellianism here is unsurpassed in English drama. As we might expect in Browning, Onigben gets the last word.

Browning published *A Soul's Tragedy* with *Luria* in 1846 as the eighth and last issue of the *Bells and Pomegranates* series. In more ways then one, this pamphlet marked the end of an era in his artistic life. The dedication to Walter Savage Landor announced the work as Browning's "last attempt for the present at dramatic poetry." He never wrote another play.

Other major works

POETRY: *Pauline*, 1833; *Paracelsus*, 1835; *Sordello*, 1840; *Dramatic Lyrics*, 1842 (in *Bells and Pomegranates*, 1841-1846); *Dramatic Romances and Lyrics*, 1845 (in *Bells and Pomegranates*); *Christmas Eve and Easter Day*, 1850; *Men and Women*, 1855 (2 volumes); *Dramatis Personae*, 1864; *The Ring and the Book*, 1868-1869 (4 volumes); *Balaustion's Adventure*, 1871; *Prince Hohenstiel-Schwangau: Savior of Society*, 1871; *Fifine at the Fair*, 1872; *Red Cotton Nightcap Country: Or, Turf and Towers*, 1873; *Aristophane's Apology*, 1875 (sequel to *Balaustion's Adventure*); *The Inn Album*, 1875; *Pacchiarotto and How He Worked in Distemper*, 1876; *La Saisiaz, and The Two Poets of Croisac*, 1878; *Dramatic Idyls (First Series)*, 1879; *Dramatic Idyls (Second Series)*, 1880; *Jocoseria*, 1883; *Ferishtah's Fancies*, 1884; *Parleyings with Certain People of Importance*, 1887; *The Poetical Works of Robert Browning*, 1888-1894 (17 volumes); *Asolando*, 1889; *Robert Browning: The Poems*, 1981 (2 volumes).

NONFICTION: *Browning's Essay on Chatterton*, 1948 (Donald A. Smalley, editor); *New Letters of Robert Browning*, 1950 (W. C. DeVane and Kenneth Knickerbocker, editors); *The Letters of Robert Browning and Elizabeth Barrett Barrett 1845-1846*, 1969 (Elvan Kintner, editor).

TRANSLATION: *The Agamemnon of Aeschylus*, 1877.

MISCELLANEOUS: *Bells and Pomegranates*, 1841-1846 (poetry and plays); *The Works of Robert Browning*, 1912 (10 volumes; F. C. Kenyon, editor); *The Complete Works of Robert Browning*, 1969-

Bibliography

Altick, Richard D., and James F. Loucks II. *Browning's Roman Murder Story: A Reading of "The Ring and the Book."* Chicago: University of Chicago Press, 1968. An important book devoted to an analysis of Browning's arguably greatest poem of dramatic monologues. Emphasizing the comedy and realism, the authors present in ten chapters the purpose, design, and meaning as a dramatic articulation of the poet's ideas of rhetoric, ethics, and language. Includes footnotes, an index, and a brief bibliographic note.

King, Roma A., Jr. *The Focusing Artifice: The Poetry of Robert Browning.* Athens: Ohio University Press, 1968. Reviewing Browning's total career, King analyzes individual poems and dramas as works of art focusing intellectual and cultural forces in Browning's modern tradition. This book is especially useful for its inclusion of a substantial chapter that focuses on the dramas as experiments in search of an adequate form for Browning's purposes. Contains notes, a bibliography, and an index.

Lawson, E. LeRoy. *Very Sure of God: Religious Language in the Poetry of Robert Browning.* Nashville: Vanderbilt University Press, 1974. Believing that Browning's religious views are compatible with those of such modern thinkers as Paul Tillich, Lawson presents the religious monologues sympathetically for modern readers. Reviewing references to God in poems and letters, the concluding chapter asserts that no word is adequate to express what is above human knowledge. Includes footnotes and a bibliography.

Ryals, Clyde de L. *Browning's Later Poetry, 1871-1889.* Ithaca, N.Y.: Cornell University Press, 1975. Looking at thematic structures, Ryals devotes a chapter each to major late poems, from *Balaustion's Adventure* to *Asolando.* Browning's governing idea is the Christian doctrine of the Incarnation as a continuing process of divine revelation in individual lives and poetry itself. Footnotes, bibliography, and index.

Shaw, W. David. *The Dialectical Temper: The Rhetorical Art of Robert Browning.* Ithaca, N.Y.: Cornell University Press, 1968. This major study borrows the ideas of the philosopher Søren Kierkegaard to analyze the drama and dramatic monologues as efforts to overcome opposing objective and subjective views. *The Ring and the Book* is presented as a masterful synthesis of multiple points of view in dialectical rhetoric, which resolves these views. Later works are generally ignored. Index.

Thomas, Donald. *Robert Browning: A Life Within Life.* New York: Viking Press, 1983. Relying more on Browning's poetry than on his correspondence, Thomas studies the problem of Browning's private, interior life as a brooding Romantic at the center of the robust Victorian savior of Elizabeth Barrett. Includes a sympathetic treatment of Browning's late writings, which are compared favorably with those of Alfred, Lord Tennyson. Helpful notes, select bibliography, and index.

Michael D. Moore
(Updated by *Richard D. McGhee*)

ED BULLINS

Born: Philadelphia, Pennsylvania; July 2, 1935

Principal drama

Dialect Determinism: Or, The Rally, pr. 1954, pb. 1973; *Clara's Ole Man*, pr. 1965, pb. 1969; *How Do You Do?*, pr. 1965, pb. 1968; *The Theme Is Blackness*, pr. 1966, pb. 1973; *A Son, Come Home*, pr. 1968, pb. 1969; *The Electronic Nigger*, pr. 1968, pb. 1969; *Goin' a Buffalo*, pr. 1968, pb. 1969; *In the Wine Time*, pr. 1968, pb. 1969; *The Gentleman Caller*, pb. 1968, pr. 1969; *Five Plays*, pb. 1969 (includes *Clara's Ole Man, A Son, Come Home, The Electronic Nigger, Goin' a Buffalo, In the Wine Time*); *We Righteous Bombers*, pr. 1969 (as Kingsley B. Bass, Jr.; adaption of Albert Camus' play *Les Justes*); *In New England Winter*, pb. 1969, pr. 1971; *A Ritual to Raise the Dead and Foretell the Future*, pr. 1970; *The Pig Pen*, pr. 1970, pb. 1971; *The Duplex*, pr. 1970, pb. 1971; *Street Sounds*, pr. 1970, pb. 1973; *The Devil Catchers*, pr. 1971; *The Fabulous Miss Marie*, pr. 1971, pb. 1974; *House Party*, pr. 1973 (lyrics; music by Pat Patrick); *The Theme Is Blackness*, pb. 1973 (collection); *The Taking of Miss Janie*, pr. 1974, pb. 1981; *Home Boy*, pr. 1976 (lyrics; music by Aaron Bell); *Jo Anne!*, pr. 1976; *Daddy*, pr. 1977; *Storyville*, pr. 1977, 1979 (revised; music by Mildred Kayden); *Sepia Star: Or, Chocolate Comes to the Cotton Club*, pr. 1977 (lyrics; music by Kayden); *Michael*, pr. 1978; *Leavings*, pr. 1980; *Steve and Velma*, pr. 1980; *A Teacup Full of Roses*, pr. 1989; *A Sunday Afternoon*, pr. 1989 (with Marshall Borden); *I Think It's Going to Turn Out Fine*, pr. 1990; *Salaam, Huey Newton, Salaam*, pr. 1991 (one act); *American Griot*, pr. 1991 (with Idris Ackamoor).

Other literary forms

Although known primarily as a playwright, Ed Bullins has also worked in forms ranging from fiction and the essay to the "revolutionary television commercial." His novel *The Reluctant Rapist* (1973) focuses on the early experience of Steve Benson, a semiautobiographical character who appears in several plays, including *In New England Winter*, *The Duplex*, and *The Fabulous Miss Marie*. *The Hungered Ones: Early Writings* (1971), a collection of Bullins' early stories and essays, some of which are loosely autobiographical, provides an overview of his early perspective. Active as an editor and a theorist throughout his career, Bullins has written introductions to anthologies such as *The New Lafayette Theater Presents* (1974) and *New Plays from the Black Theatre* (1969). Along with the introduction to his own collection *The Theme Is Blackness*, these introductions provide a powerful and influential theoretical statement on the aesthetics and politics of the African-American theater during the late 1960's and early 1970's. *The Theme Is Blackness* also contains scripts for "rituals" and mixed-media productions, including "Black Revolutionary Commercials," which reflect the concern with electronic media visible in many of his later plays.

Achievements

As much as any contemporary American playwright, Bullins has forged a powerful synthesis of avant-garde technique and revolutionary commitment challenging easy preconceptions concerning the relationship between politics and aesthetics. Like Latin American writers Carlos Fuentes and Gabriel García Márquez and African writers Ngugi wa Thiong'o and Wole Soyinka, Bullins sees no inherent contradiction between the use of experimental techniques and the drive to reach a mass audience alienated from the dominant social/economic/racial hierarchy. Separating himself from the cultural elite which has claimed possession of the modernist/postmodernist tradition, Bullins adapts the tradition to the frames of reference and to the immediate concerns of his audience, primarily but not exclusively within the African-American community. While he frequently comments on and revises the philosophical and aesthetic concerns of Euro-American modernism, he does so in order to clarify his audience's vision of an American culture riddled by psychological and political contradictions which intimate the need for a basic change.

Paralleling the political modernism advocated by Bertolt Brecht in his aesthetic/political debate with Georg Lukács, Bullins' synthesis takes on particular significance in the context of the Black Arts Movement of the late 1960's. As a leading figure in the movement for specifically black cultural institutions and modes of expression, Bullins refuted through example the casual stereotypes of black revolutionary artists as ideologically inflexible and aesthetically naïve. Although he supports the confrontational strategies of radical playwrights committed to what he calls the "dialectic of change," he works primarily within what he calls the "dialectic of experience," which entails a sophisticated confrontation with a "reality" he understands to be in large part shaped by individual perceptions. Drawing on Brecht, Jean Genet, Albert Camus, Amiri Baraka, Eugene O'Neill, John Cage, Anton Chekhov, and Langston Hughes with equal facility, Bullins is not primarily a literary dramatist or a political agitator. Rather, he is a playwright in the classic sense, concerned above all with bringing the experience of black Americans alive onstage in a manner which forces the audience to confront its metaphorically ambiguous but politically explosive implications. His most successful plays, such as *In New England Winter* and *The Taking of Miss Janie*, demonstrate conclusively that a revolutionary artist does not need to circumscribe his vision in order to defend a preestablished ideological position. Demonstrating his affinities with

Brechtian theory, as opposed to Brechtian practice, Bullins creates tensions between presentation style and content to alienate his audience, white or black, from its assumptions concerning race, class, sex, and ultimately the nature of perception.

Not surprisingly, this challenge frequently disturbs mainstream audiences and critics; typical is the response of Walter Kerr, who complained in a review of *The Taking of Miss Janie* that "no one likes having to finish—or trying to finish—an author's play for him; but that's the effort asked here." Ironically, Kerr's criticism accurately identifies the reason for Bullins' success in contexts ranging from the black community theaters of San Francisco and New York to the La Mama theater in New York's Soho district. Challenging the audience to confront the experience presented rather than to accept a mediated statement about that experience, Bullins rarely presents didactic statements without substantial ironic qualification. By refusing to advance simple solutions or to repress his awareness of oppression, Bullins attempts to force the audience to internalize and act on its responses. Effective as literature as well as theater, Bullins' plays have won numerous awards and grants from both African-American and Euro-American organizations. The best of them, especially the early sections of the Twentieth-Century Cycle, a projected twenty-play series, have led some critics to compare Bullins with O'Neill. While his ultimate stature depends in large part on the development of the cycle and his continuing ability to generate new forms in response to changing audiences and political contexts, Bullins' place in the history of American and African-American theater seems assured.

Biography

Intensely protective concerning the details of his private life, Ed Bullins has nevertheless been a highly visible force in the development of African-American theater since the mid-1960's. Reared primarily by his civil-servant mother in North Philadelphia, Bullins attended a predominantly white grade school before transferring to an inner-city junior high, where he became involved with the street gang called the Jet Cobras. Like his semiautobiographical character Steve Benson (*The Reluctant Rapist, In New England Winter, The Duplex*), Bullins suffered a near-fatal knife wound, in the area of his heart, in a street fight. After dropping out of high school, he served in the United States Navy from 1952 to 1955. In 1958, he moved to California, where he passed his high school graduation equivalency examination and attended Los Angeles City College from 1961 to 1963.

Bullins' 1963 move to San Francisco signaled the start of his emergence as an influential figure in African-American culture. The first national publication of his essays in 1963 initiated a period of tremendous creativity extending into the mid-1970's. Actively committed to black nationalist politics by 1965, he began working with community theater organizations such as Black Arts/West, the Black Student Union at San Francisco State College, and Black House of San Francisco, which he founded along with playwright Marvin X. The first major production of Bullins' drama, a program including *How Do You Do?*, *Dialect Determinism*, and *Clara's Ole Man*, premiered at the Firehouse Repertory Theater in San Francisco on August 5, 1965. At about the same time, Bullins assumed the position of Minister of Culture with the Black Panther Party, then emerging as a major force in national politics. Breaking with the Panthers in 1967, reportedly in disagreement with Eldridge Cleaver's decision to accept alliances with white radical groups, Bullins moved to Harlem at the urging of Robert MacBeth, director of the New Lafayette Theater.

Bullins' first New York production, *The Electronic Nigger*, ran for ninety-six performances following its February 21, 1968, debut at the American Place Theatre, where it was moved after the original New Lafayette burned down. Combined with his editorship of the controversial Summer, 1968, "Black Theatre" issue of *The Drama Review*, the success of *The Electronic Nigger* consolidated Bullins' position alongside Baraka as a major presence within and outside the African-American theatrical community. Between 1968 and 1976, Bullins' plays received an average of three major New York productions per year at theaters, including the New Lafayette (where Bullins was playwright-in-residence up to its 1973 closing), the American Place Theatre, the Brooklyn Academy of Music, Woodie King's New Federal Theatre at the Henry Street Settlement House, Lincoln Center, and the La Mama Experimental Theater.

A Teacup Full of Roses was staged at the Bay Area Playwrights' Festival in the summer of 1989. Bullins also wrote *A Sunday Afternoon* with Marshall Borden and "a pseudo-satiric monster horror play, a take-off on B-movies," called *Dr. Geechie and the Blood Junkies*, which he read at the Henry Street Settlement House in New York in the summer of 1989. The La Mama theater staged *I Think It's Going to Turn Out Fine*, based on the Tina Turner legend, in 1990, and *American Griot* (coauthored with Idris Ackamoor, who also acted in the play) in 1991. *Salaam, Huey Newton, Salaam*, a one-act play on the aftermath of the Black Revolution, premiered at the Ensemble Studio Theater in 1991.

Bullins won the 1968 Vernon Rice Award for *The Electronic Nigger*, the 1971 Obie Award for *In New England Winter* and *The Fabulous Miss Marie*, and in 1975 both the Obie and the New York Drama Critics Circle Award for *The Taking of Miss Janie*. In addition to teaching at Fordham, Columbia, the University of Massachusetts (Boston), Bronx Community College, Manhattan Community College, and Amherst College, Bullins has received grants from the Guggenheim Foundation (1971, 1976), the Rockefeller Foundation (1968, 1970, 1973), the Creative Artists Program Service (1973), the Black Arts Alliance (1971), and the National Endowment for the Arts (1974). As public interest in African-American theater diminished in the 1980's, Bullins continued supporting community theater in California, working on the Twentieth-Century Cycle and occasionally acting in New York productions, including the revival of *Clara's Ole Man* and Wallace Shawn's *The Hotel Play* (pr. 1981). Despite his critical success, however, no Bullins play has been produced on Broadway and no collection of his work remained in print.

Bullins has also taught American humanities, black theater, and play making at Contra Costa College, in San Pablo, California. He settled in Emeryville, near Oakland, and started a theater there called the BMT Theatre (Bullins Memorial Theatre, named after his son, who died in an automobile accident).

Analysis

A radical playwright in both the simple and the complex senses of the term, Ed Bullins consistently challenges the members of his audience to test their political and aesthetic beliefs against the multifaceted reality of daily life in the United States. Committed to a revolutionary black nationalist consciousness, he attacks both liberal and conservative politics as aspects of an oppressive context dominated by a white elite. Equally committed to the development of a radical alternative to Euro-American modernist aesthetics, he incorporates a wide range of cultural materials into specifically black performances. The clearest evidence of Bullins' radical sensibility, however, is his unwavering refusal to accept any dogma, white or black, traditional or revolutionary, without testing it against a multitude of perspectives and experiences. Throughout a career that has earned for him serious consideration alongside Eugene O'Neill and Tennessee Williams as the United States' greatest dramatist, Bullins has subjected the hypocrisies and corruptions of Euro- and African-American culture to rigorous examination and reevaluation. Refusing to accept any distinctions between aesthetics and politics or between the concerns of the artist and those of the mass community, Bullins demands that his audience synthesize abstract perception and concrete experience. Providing a set of terms useful to understanding the development of these concerns in his own work, Bullins defines a constituting dialectic in the black theatrical movement which emerged in the mid-1960's:

> This new thrust has two main branches—the *dialectic of change* and the *dialectic of experience*. The writers are attempting to answer questions concerning Black survival and future, one group through confronting the Black/white reality of America, the other, by heightening the dreadful white reality of being a modern Black captive and victim.

Essentially, the dialectic of change focuses attention on political problems demanding a specific form of action. The dialectic of experience focuses on a more "realistic" (though Bullins redefines the term to encompass aspects of reality frequently dismissed by programmatic realists) picture of black life in the context in which the problems continue to condition all experience. Reflecting his awareness that by definition each dialectic is in constant tension with the other, Bullins directs his work in the dialectic of change to altering the audience's actual experience. Similarly, his work in the dialectic of experience, while rarely explicitly didactic, leads inexorably to recognition of the need for change.

Bullins' work in both dialectics repudiates the tradition of the Western theater, which, he says, "shies away from social, political, psychological or any disturbing (revolutionary) reforms." Asserting the central importance of non-Western references, Bullins catalogs the "elements that make up the alphabet of the secret language used in Black theater," among them the blues, dance, African religion and mysticism, "familial nationalism," myth-science, vodun ritual-ceremony, and "nigger street styles." Despite the commitment to an African-American continuum evident in the construction and content of his plays, Bullins by no means repudiates all elements of the Euro-American tradition. Even as he criticizes Brechtian epic theater, Bullins employs aspects of Brecht's dramatic rhetoric, designed to alienate the audience from received modes of perceiving theatrical, and by extension political, events. It is less important to catalog Bullins' allusions to William Shakespeare, O'Neill, Camus, or Genet than to recognize his use of their devices alongside those of Baraka, Soyinka, and Derek A. Walcott in the service of "Black artistic, political, and cultural consciousness."

Most of Bullins' work in the dialectic of change, which he calls "protest writing" when addressed to a Euro-American audience and "Black revolutionary writing" when addressed to an African-American audience, takes the form of short satiric or agitprop plays. Frequently intended for street performance, these plays aim to attract a crowd and communicate an incisive message as rapidly as possibly. Influential in the ritual theater of Baraka and in Bullins' own "Black Revolutionary Commercials," this strategy developed out of association with the black nationalist movement in cities such as New York, Detroit, Chicago, San Francisco, and Newark. Reflecting the need to avoid unplanned confrontations with police, the performances described in Bullins' influential "Short Statement on Street Theater" concentrate on establishing contact with groups unlikely to enter a theater, especially black working people and individuals living on the margins of society—gang members, junkies, prostitutes, street people. Recognizing the impact of the media on American consciousness, Bullins frequently parodies media techniques, satirizing political advertising in "The American Flag Ritual" and "selling" positive black revolutionary images in

"A Street Play." Somewhat longer though equally direct, "Death List," which can be performed by a troupe moving through the neighborhood streets, alerts the community to "enemies of the Black People," from Vernon Jordan to Whitney Young. Considered out of their performance context, many of these pieces seem simplistic or didactic, but their real intent is to realize Bullins' desire that "each individual in the crowd should have his sense of reality confronted, his consciousness assaulted." Because the "accidental" street audience comes into contact with the play while in its "normal" frame of mind, Bullins creates deliberately hyperbolic images to dislocate that mind-set in a very short period of time.

When writing revolutionary plays for performance in traditional theaters, Bullins tempers his rhetoric considerably. To be sure, *Dialect Determinism*, a warning against trivializing the revolutionary impulse of Malcolm X, and *The Gentleman Caller*, a satiric attack on master-slave mentality of black-white economic interaction, both resemble the street plays in their insistence on revolutionary change. *Dialect Determinism* climaxes with the killing of a black "enemy," while *The Gentleman Caller* ends with a formulaic call for the rise of the foretold "Black nation that will survive, conquer and rule." The difference between these plays and the street theater lies not in message but in Bullins' way of involving the audience. Recognizing the different needs of an audience willing to seek out his work in the theater but frequently educated by the dominant culture, Bullins involves it in the analytic process leading to what seem, from a black nationalist perspective, relatively unambiguous political perceptions. Rather than asserting the messages at the start of the plays, therefore, he developed a satiric setting before stripping away the masks and distortions imposed by the audience's normal frame of reference on its recognition of his revolutionary message.

Along with Baraka, Marvin X, Adrienne Kennedy, and others, Bullins helped make the dialectic of change an important cultural force at the height of the black nationalist movement, but his most substantial achievements involve the dialectic of experience. Ranging from his impressionistic gallery plays and politically resonant problem plays to the intricately interconnected Twentieth-Century Cycle, Bullins' work in this dialectic reveals a profound skepticism regarding revolutionary ideals which have not been tested against the actual contradictions of African-American experience. *Street Sounds*, parts of which were later incorporated into *House Party*, represents Bullins' adaptation of the gallery approach pioneered by poets such as Robert Browning, Edgar Lee Masters (*Spoon River Anthology*, 1915), Melvin B. Tolson (*Harlem Gallery*, 1969), Gwendolyn Brooks (*A Street in Bronzeville*, 1945) and Langston Hughes (*Montage of a Dream Deferred*, 1951). By montaging a series of thirty- to ninety-second monologues, Bullins suggests the tensions common to the experience of seemingly disparate elements of the African-American community. Superficially, the characters can be divided into categories such as politicians (Harlem Politician, Black Student), hustlers (Dope Seller, The Thief), artists (Black Revolutionary Artist, Black Writer), street people (Fried Brains, Corner Brother), working people (Errand Boy, Workin' Man), and women (The Loved One, The Virgin, Harlem Mother). None of the categories, however, survives careful examination; individual women could be placed in every other category; the Black Revolutionary Artist combines politics and art; the Harlem Politician, politics and crime. To a large extent, all types ultimately amount to variations on several social and psychological themes which render the surface distinctions far less important than they initially appear.

Although their particular responses vary considerably, each character in *Street Sounds* confronts the decaying community described by The Old-timer: "They changin' things, you know? Freeways comin' through tearin' up the old neighborhood. Buildings goin' down, and not bein' put up again. Abandoned houses that are boarded up, the homes of winos, junkies and rats, catchin' fire and never bein' fixed up." As a result, many share the Workin' Man's feeling of being "trapped inside of ourselves, inside our experience." Throughout the play, Bullins portrays a deep-seated feeling of racial inferiority which results in male obsession with white women (Slightly Confused Negro, The Explainer) and a casual willingness to exploit or attack other blacks (The Thief, The Doubter, Young West Indian Revolutionary Poet). Attempting to salvage some sense of freedom or self-worth, or simply to find momentary release from the struggle, individuals turn to art, sex, politics, or drugs, but the weight of their context pressures each toward the psychological collapse of Fried Brains, the hypocritical delusions of the Non-Ideological Nigger, or the unfounded self-glorification of The Genius. Even when individuals embrace political causes, Bullins remains skeptical. The Theorist, The Rapper, and The Liar, who ironically echoes Bullins' aesthetic when he declares, "Even when I lie, I lie truthfully. . . . I'm no stranger to experience," express ideological positions similar to those Bullins advocates in the dialectic of change. None, however, seems even marginally aware that his grand pronouncements have no impact on the experience of the black community. The Rapper's revolutionary call—"We are slaves now, this moment in time, brothers, but let this moment end with this breath and let us unite as fearless revolutionaries in the pursuit of world liberation!"—comes between the entirely apolitical monologues of Waiting and Bewildered. Similarly, the Black Revolutionary Artist's endorsement of "a cosmic revolution that will liberate the highest potential of nationhood in the universe" is followed by the Black Dee Jay's claim that "BLACK MEANS BUY!" The sales pitch seems to have a great deal more power than the nationalist vision in the lives of the Soul Sister and the Corner Brother, whose monologues frame the Black Revolutionary

Artist-Black Dee Jay sequence.

One of Bullins' characteristic "signatures" is the attribution of his own ideas to characters unwilling or unable to act or inspire others to act on them. Reflecting his belief that without action ideals have little value, Bullins structures *Street Sounds* to insist on the need for connection. The opening monologue, delivered by a white "Pig," establishes a political context similar to the one that Bullins uses in the dialectic of change, within which the dialectic of experience proceeds. Reducing all blacks to a single type, the nigger, Pig wishes only to "beat his nigger ass good." Although Bullins clearly perceives the police as a basic oppressive force in the ghetto, he does not concentrate on highlighting the audience's awareness of that point. Rather, by the end of the play he has made it clear that the African-American community in actuality beats its own ass. The absence of any other white character in the play reflects Bullins' focus on the nature of victimization as experienced within and perpetuated by the black community. The Harlem Mother monologue which closes the play concentrates almost entirely on details of experience. Although she presents no hyperbolic portraits of white oppressors, her memories of the impact on her family of economic exploitation, hunger, and government indifference carry more politically dramatic power than does any abstraction. This by no means indicates Bullins' distaste for political analysis or a repudiation of the opening monologues; rather, it reflects his awareness that abstract principles signify little unless they are embedded in the experience first of the audience and, ultimately, of the community as a whole.

While Bullins consistently directs his work toward the African-American community, his work in the dialectic of experience inevitably involves the interaction of blacks and whites. *The Taking of Miss Janie*, perhaps his single most powerful play, focuses on a group of California college students, several of whom first appeared in *The Pig Pen*. In part a meditation on the heritage of the 1960's Civil Rights movement, *The Taking of Miss Janie* revolves around the sexual and political tensions between and within racial groups. Although most of the characters are readily identifiable types—the stage directions identify Rick as a cultural nationalist, Janie as a California beach girl, Flossy as a "soul sister"—Bullins explores individual characters in depth, concentrating on their tendency to revert to behavior patterns, especially when they assume rigid ideological or social roles. The central incident of the play—the "rape" of the white Janie by Monty, a black friend of long standing—provides a severely alienating image of this tendency to both black and white audiences. After committing a murder, which may or may not be real, when the half-mythic Jewish beatnik Mort Silberstein taunts him for his inability to separate his consciousness from Euro-American influences, Monty undresses Janie, who does not resist or cooperate, in a rape scene devoid of violence, love, anger, or physical desire. Unable to resist the pressures which make their traditional Western claim to individuality seem naïve, both Janie and Monty seem resigned to living out a "fate" which in fact depends on their acquiescence. Monty accepts the role of the "black beast" who rapes and murders white people, while Janie plays the role of plantation mistress. While these intellectually articulate characters do not genuinely believe in the reality of their roles, their ironic attitude ultimately makes no difference, for the roles govern their actions.

While the rape incident provides the frame for *The Taking of Miss Janie*, Monty and Janie exist in a gallery of characters whose collective inability to maintain individual integrity testifies to the larger dimensions of the problem. Rick and Len enact the classic argument between nationalism and eclecticism in the black political/intellectual world; Peggy tires of confronting the neuroses of black men and turns to lesbianism; "hip" white boy Lonnie moves from fad to fad, turning his contact with black culture to financial advantage in the music business; several couples drift aimlessly into interracial marriages. Alternating scenes in which characters interact with monologues in which an individual reflects on his future development, Bullins reveals his characters' inability to create an alternative to the "fate" within which they feel themselves trapped. While none demonstrates a fully developed ability to integrate ideals and experiences, several seem substantially less alienated than others. In many ways the least deluded, Peggy accepts both her lesbianism and her responsibility for her past actions. Her comment on the 1960's articulates a basic aspect of Bullins' vision: "We all failed. Failed ourselves in that serious time known as the sixties. And by failing ourselves we also failed in the test of the times." Her honesty and insight also have a positive impact on the black nationalist Rick, who during a conversation with Peggy abandons his grandiose rhetoric on the "devil's tricknology" (a phrase adopted from the Nation of Islam)—rhetoric which masks a deep hostility toward other blacks. Although he has previously attacked her as a lesbian "freak," Rick's final lines to Peggy suggest another aspect of Bullins' perspective: "Ya know, it be about what you make it anyway." Any adequate response to *The Taking of Miss Janie* must take into account not only Peggy's survival strategy and Rick's nationalistic idealism but also Janie's willed naïveté and the accuracy of Mort's claim that, despite his invocation of Mao, Malcolm X, and Franz Fanon, Monty is still on some levels "FREAKY FOR JESUS!" Bullins presents no simple answers nor does he simply contemplate the wasteland. Rather, as in almost all of his work in both the dialectic of change and the dialectic of experience, he challenges his audience to make something out of the fragments and failures he portrays.

The Twentieth-Century Cycle, Bullins' most far-reaching confrontation with the American experience, brings together most of his theatrical and thematic concerns and seems destined to stand as his major work. Several of the projected twenty plays of the cycle have been performed, including *In the Wine Time, In New England Winter, The Duplex, The Fabulous Miss Marie, Home Boy*, and *Daddy*. Although the underlying structure of the cycle remains a matter of speculation, it clearly focuses on the experience of a group of black people traversing various areas of America's cultural and physical geography during the 1950's, 1960's, and 1970's. Recurring characters, including Cliff Dawson, his nephew Ray Crawford, Michael Brown (who first appeared in a play not part of the cycle, *A Son, Come Home*), and Steve Benson, a black intellectual whose life story resembles Bullins' own, serve to unify the cycle's imaginative landscape. In addition, a core of thematic concerns, viewed from various perspectives, unites the plays.

In the Wine Time, the initial play of the cycle, establishes a basic set of thematic concerns, including the incompatibility of Ray's romantic idealism with the brutality and potential violence of his northern urban environment. Stylistically, the play typifies the cycle in its juxtaposition of introverted lyricism, naturalistic dialogue, technological staging, and African-American music and dance. Individual plays combine these elements in different ways. *In New England Winter*, set in California, draws much of its power from a poetic image of the snow which takes on racial, geographical, and metaphysical meanings in Steve Benson's consciousness. Each act of *The Duplex* opens with a jazz, blues, or rhythm-and-blues song which sets a framework for the ensuing action. *The Fabulous Miss Marie* uses televised images of the Civil Rights movement both to highlight its characters' personal desperation and to emphasize the role of technology in creating and aggravating their problems of perception. Drawing directly on the reflexive rhetoric of Euro-American modernism, *In New England Winter* revolves around Steve Benson's construction of a "play," involving a planned robbery, which he plans to enact in reality but which he also uses as a means of working out his psychological desires.

Ultimately, Bullins' *Salaam, Huey Newton, Salaam* extends Bullins' vision into an imaginary future to depict the former Black Panther leader down and out in the wake of a black revolution. Bullins suggests that each of these approaches reflects a perspective on experience actually present in contemporary American society and that any vision failing to take all of them into account will inevitably fall victim to the dissociation of ideals and experience which plunges many of Bullins' characters into despair or violence. While some of his characters, most notably Steve Benson, seem intermittently aware of the source of their alienation and are potentially capable of imaginative responses with political impact, Bullins leaves the resolution of the cycle plays to the members of the audience. Portraying the futility of socially prescribed roles and of any consciousness not directly engaged with its total context, Bullins continues to challenge his audience to attain a perspective from which the dialectic of experience and the dialectic of change can be realized as one and the same.

Other major works

NOVEL: *The Reluctant Rapist*, 1973.

POETRY: *To Raise the Dead and Foretell the Future*, 1971.

SCREENPLAYS: *Night of the Beast*, 1971; *The Ritual Masters*, 1972.

ANTHOLOGIES: *New Plays from the Black Theatre*, 1969 (with introduction); *The New Lafayette Theater Presents: Plays with Aesthetic Comments by Six Black Playwrights*, 1974 (with introduction).

MISCELLANEOUS: *The Hungered Ones: Early Writings*, 1971 (stories and essays).

Bibliography

Bigsby, C. W. E. *The Second Black Renaissance: Essays in Black Literature.* Westport, Conn.: Greenwood Press, 1980. A strong chapter, "Black Drama: The Public Voice," includes a protracted discussion of Bullins' work as "a moving spirit behind the founding of another black theatre institution, the New Lafayette Theatre." Index.

DeGaetani, John L. *A Search for a Postmodern Theater: Interviews with Contemporary Playwrights.* New York: Greenwood Press, 1991. After writing more than fifty plays, Bullins still admires Samuel Beckett and still deals with the theme of "the breakdown of communications among loved ones, and misunderstanding among good intentions." Contains an excellent update of his activities and a strong discussion of the themes of rape in his work.

Fabre, Genevieve. *Drumbeats, Masks, and Metaphor: Contemporary Afro-American Theatre.* Translated by Melvin Dixon. Cambridge, Mass.: Harvard University Press, 1983. This study, translated by Dixon, treats Bullins in a full chapter, "The Language of the Blues," an essay on themes and objectives as well as a critical overview of his major works. Contains an index and notes, including a comment on Bullins' West Coast organizing of theaters.

Gayle, Addison, Jr., ed. *Black Expression: Essays by and About Black Americans in the Creative Arts.* New York: Weybright and Talley, 1969. A brief description of four Bullins plays, followed by an essay by Bullins entitled "The So-Called Western Avant-garde Drama." Describes Bullins as the minister of culture of the Black Panther Party and resident playwright of the New Lafayette Theater.

Hay, Samuel A. "Structural Elements in Ed Bullins' Plays." In *The Theater of Black Americans.* Vol. 1, edited by Errol Hill. Englewood Cliffs, N.J.: Prentice-Hall, 1980. Examines structural consistencies in *The Du-*

plex but adds valuable comments on earlier works. Begins with Walter Kerr's review, comparing his remarks with Bullins' structural elements, such as "desultory conversation," "unplanned and casual action," and "frequently disconnected dialogue." Compares Bullins' work with Anton Chekhov's *Tri Sestry* (pr., pb. 1901; *Three Sisters*, 1920).

Herman, William. *Understanding Contemporary American Drama.* Columbia: University of South Carolina Press, 1987. A long chapter on Bullins, "The People in This Play Are Black," details his major plays to 1984. Good biographical sketch of Bullins' New Lafayette connections, including his editorship of *Black Theatre*, the theater company's journal.

Williams, Mance. *Black Theatre in the 1960's and 1970's: A Historical-Critical Analysis of the Movement.* Westport, Conn.: Greenwood Press, 1985. By concentrating on theater movements rather than on the playwright, this study underlines Bullins' strong administrative and inspirational contributions to the African-American theater experience. Includes discussion of his literary style, use of music, views on street theater, and his relationship with the New Lafayette Theater. Index and bibliography.

Craig Werner
(Updated by *Thomas J. Taylor*)

EDWARD BULWER-LYTTON

Born: London, England; May 25, 1803
Died: Torquay, England; January 18, 1873

Principal drama

The Duchess de la Vallière, pb. 1836, pr. 1837; *The Lady of Lyons: Or, Love and Pride*, pr., pb. 1838; *Richelieu: Or, The Conspiracy*, pr., pb. 1839; *The Sea-Captain: Or, The Birthright*, pb. 1839; *Money*, pr., pb. 1840; *Dramatic Works*, pb. 1841; *Not So Bad as We Seem: Or, Many Sides to a Character*, pb. 1851.

Other literary forms

Edward Bulwer-Lytton was one of the most versatile and prolific writers of a far-from-laconic age. Though he held the stage during the late 1830's as the foremost contemporary English playwright, Bulwer-Lytton was more generally known in his own day for his novels, which gained an international readership. Today, what reputation remains to this once celebrated Victorian writer rests on a handful of his twenty-odd novels. Bulwer-Lytton the fiction writer was deft in many veins. Among his works are witty and elegant society novels, the best being *Pelham: Or, The Adventures of a Gentleman* (1828); the so-called Newgate novels, dealing with the dark impulses of the criminal mind, such as *Eugene Aram* (1832); historical romances, such as the famous *The Last Days of Pompeii* (1834); metaphysical works in the *Bildungsroman* tradition of Johann Wolfgang von Goethe, including *Ernest Maltravers* (1837) and its sequel *Alice: Or, The Mysteries* (1838); and even, at the end of his life, a precursor of utopian science fiction, *The Coming Race* (1871). Bulwer-Lytton, who despite his aristocratic background was obliged to support himself through his literary labors, also wrote short stories, his best piece being "The Haunted and the Haunters" (1857), and poetry, including *The New Timon* (1846), now chiefly remembered for having provoked Alfred, Lord Tennyson, and *King Arthur* (1848-1849, 1870). His *England and the English* (1833), a multifaceted study of pre-Reform Bill England, remains one of the most insightful social histories of early nineteenth century British culture, politics, education, and manners.

Achievements

Bulwer-Lytton is an author whose breadth leads the public, rightly or wrongly, to undervalue the depth of his achievements. When he aimed for high seriousness in the philosophical novels devoted to such abstractions as the Ideal and the Beautiful, he proved himself superficial, but when he set his sights lower, he excelled. He produced in *Pelham* one of the earliest and finest examples of the "silver fork" novel, a genre that proved its intrinsic worth in its culminating work, William Makepeace Thackeray's *Vanity Fair* (1847-1848), and demonstrated its endurance by continuing to flourish, if only in a debased form, down to the present day. He wrote historical novels exemplary in their learning and accuracy, books that remain models for that genre, whatever one chooses to make of its worth. Finally, Bulwer-Lytton's utopian novel *The Coming Race*, though less than a finished literary achievement, prefigures in its title, theme, and format the sort of "scientific romances" produced by H. G. Wells at the beginning of the twentieth century.

Bulwer-Lytton's achievements as a dramatist are less substantial. Solidly researched, structurally sound, but inexcusably melodramatic by modern standards, his historical dramas served at best to keep playwriting alive in an age when few good British writers were making the effort to do so. In *Money*, Bulwer-Lytton offered for the Victorian world what *Pelham* had given the Regency: an incisive and detailed study of the forms folly, pretension, hypocrisy, and honor take in a particular milieu at a particular time.

Biography

Edward George Earle Lytton Bulwer (later, on inheriting his mother's estate, to be called E.G.E.L. Bulwer-Lytton, and later still, E.G.E.L. B.L., first Baron Lytton) was the third and last son of General William Bulwer and his wife Elizabeth Barbara Lytton, the heiress of Knebworth. Both of his parents were descendants of ancient families. Bulwer's early education was erratic but intensive. He read widely and deeply in the notable library of his maternal grandfather, Richard Warburton Lytton, and instead of attending a public school, he was placed with a tutor at Ealing. In 1822, Bulwer went up to Cambridge. He earned a bachelor of arts degree in 1826 and a master of arts in 1835. His university awarded him an honorary doctor of laws in 1864.

Having finished his education, Bulwer led the life of traveler and man of fashion. He toured the Lake District and Scotland and frequented the most exclusive circles of society in London and Paris. Handsome, elegantly dressed, proficient at all the fashionable sports and pursuits, he was one of the great dandies of England's "age of cards and candlelight." Like many another literary gentleman of his day, Bulwer had been dazzled by the glamour and notoriety of the late Lord Byron, and he made the mistake of embarking upon a curious romance with one of Byron's former mistresses, the mentally unbalanced Lady Caroline Lamb. This liaison led him to a yet worse error: In 1827, he married Lady Caroline's protégée Rosina Doyle Wheeler, a lovely but volatile Irishwoman, against the wishes of his mother, upon whose inclinations all of his financial prospects rested.

As short of income as they were lavish in their tastes, the young couple had to rely upon Bulwer-Lytton's pen to pay their bills. It proved dependable. Throughout the 1820's and 1830's, Bulwer-Lytton worked rapidly and industriously to churn out a succession of novels that gained for him a wide public and a sufficient income. This taxing labor impaired his temper and ultimately contributed to the breakdown of his marriage, however, for Rosina was suited by neither temperament nor training to suffer neglect and ill-use with composure. After traveling abroad to Naples in 1833, the Bulwer-Lyttons reached the point at which they could no longer live together. They agreed to a legal separation in 1836, but Rosina's financial dependence and monomaniacal hatred made her a recurring torment to her husband throughout the rest of his life.

Besides working hard as an author and as editor of the *New Monthly Magazine*, Bulwer-Lytton had in 1831 been elected to Parliament as member for St. Ives. A Radical Reformer, he was acquainted with the younger members of the utilitarian school. He supported liberal causes throughout his first parliamentary period, which ended when he lost his seat in 1841. The late 1830's and 1840's found him continuing his career as novelist, launching himself as a successful dramatist, and traveling, often for his health. On returning from one such trip abroad in 1849, he joined his friend Charles Dickens in forming a Guild of Literature and Art for the relief of impoverished authors. To benefit this guild, he wrote *Not So Bad as We Seem*, which an amateur troupe managed by Dickens staged in 1851. The philanthropic venture did not prosper, but the friendship of the two men of letters did. Dickens was to name one of his own sons after Bulwer-Lytton; at his fellow author's urging, Dickens rewrote the ending of *Great Expectations* (1860-1861), so that the Victorian reading public could have the affirmative sort of conclusion it tended to prefer.

In 1852, after having published his political *Letters to John Bull, Esquire* in 1851, Bulwer-Lytton was returned to Parliament as member for Hertfordshire, a position he was to hold until his elevation to the peerage in 1866. On rejoining the ranks of the Commons, he stationed himself among the conservatives, though his positions were more philosophical than were those of the usual Tory gentleman. In 1858, Lord Derby made him secretary for the Colonies. He was to raise Bulwer-Lytton to the peerage as first Baron Lytton of Knebworth in 1866.

On receiving his barony, Bulwer-Lytton retired from political life but continued his literary efforts until his death at Torquay early in 1873. His son Edward Robert Bulwer-Lytton (later the first Earl of Lytton and himself a man of letters) was with him in his last days.

Analysis

A combination of versatile talent and personal glamour made Edward Bulwer-Lytton a literary star of the first magnitude in his own day. His apparent brilliance has waned considerably since his death, and readers no longer see him as the literary peer of such novelists as Dickens or Thackeray—or Anthony Trollope, for that matter. Instead, he is remembered for writing a handful of works quite different from one another: an urbanely witty "silver fork" novel, an abstruse metaphysical romance, an impressively learned historical novel or two. Even though Bulwer-Lytton was more widely read and diversely educated than were many better-remembered literary figures of his day and despite the fact that his literary craftsmanship is sound, there are several reasons for his descent, if not into obscurity at least into a sort of twilight.

First, the passage of time has made the personal notoriety that surrounded Bulwer-Lytton's literary image—his violently unhappy marriage, his friendship with the "most gorgeous" Lady Blessington and the still more decorative Alfred, Count d'Orsay, his political adventures and editorial skirmishes—matters of historical curiosity rather than compelling contemporary interest. Second, the "high moral tone" so agreeable and edifying to Victorian readers sounds bombastic or bathetic to twentieth century ears; thus, the grandiose rhetoric to which Bulwer-Lytton, no less than most of his fellow writers, regularly resorted often blights what might otherwise be engaging books. Finally, and most important, Bulwer-Lytton's very ambition works against him for a modern audience. He was a writer who, as Sir Leslie Stephen acutely remarked, had talent enough to believe himself a genius; perpetually straining to be more of a philosopher or poet than he had power to be, Bulwer-Lytton conveyed the impression of being more superficial and insincere than he actually was. Thus, even Bulwer-Lytton's soundest literary achievements today have a smaller audience than they deserve. His plays, which are very far from being masterpieces, would no doubt have been completely forgotten had they not been written in what may be the Dark Age of British drama, that mediocre century between Richard Brinsley Sheridan and Oscar Wilde.

Bulwer-Lytton's literary detractors have accused him, both in his own day and subsequently, of being an opportunist who shrewdly gauged the reading public's desires and accommodated them. This charge is not entirely accurate—one of Bulwer-Lytton's ruling characteristics was that temperamental mobility that makes its possessor innately responsive to shifts in the climate of his milieu—but a clear sense of the marketplace does dominate his career as a dramatist. His interest in the public theater of the day predated his writing for it. He worked in Parliament to correct or simplify certain legal abuses or complexities that handicapped the contemporary theater, and his sociocultural study *England and the English* (1833) contains a chapter assessing the state of the British stage. By the early 1830's, he had even written two dramatic pieces: a stage version of his novel *Eugene Aram* (the play, in fact, preceded the novel) and a historical drama centering on Cromwell. Bulwer-Lytton's serious theatrical career, however, dates from February, 1836, when he invited the popular actor-manager William Charles Macready, renowned for his championing of "true" Shakespearean texts and his partisanship of contemporary British ventures in legitimate theater, to meet him at the Albany. With this visit began a fruitful professional relationship that is chronicled in the two men's letters to each other. Macready's advice on dramatic affairs enabled Bulwer-Lytton to discard one embryonic play ("Cromwell") and to strengthen another (*The Duchess de la Vallière*) until it became stageable—though despite Macready's presence in a leading role, this maiden venture failed when presented in January, 1837. Bulwer-Lytton was to write a number of other mediocre and unsuccessful plays in his career, but between 1837 and 1840, he created for Macready, at this time managing a theatrical company, three plays that attained a measure of distinction and considerable popular success: *The Lady of Lyons*, *Richelieu*, and *Money*.

Three of Bulwer-Lytton's plays—*The Duchess de la Vallière*, *The Lady of Lyons*, and *Richelieu*—take French incidents for their subject matter and contemporary French drama for their inspiration: Bulwer-Lytton, a political liberal and a writer who believed in giving his politics literary embodiment, admired the early promise of France's republican revolution of 1830 and her political playwrights, particularly Victor Hugo and Alexandre Dumas, *père*. Bulwer-Lytton's own French plays, as he observes in the introductory remarks to his *Dramatic Works*, offer a trilogy that follows the passage of France's reins of power from the one (in *Richelieu*) to the many (in *The Lady of Lyons*).

As theater, the first of these plays fails. Dealing with the career of Louise de la Vallière, one of Louis XIV's mistresses, *The Duchess de la Vallière* offers an always melodramatic and sometimes downright hysterical moral battle waged within and on behalf of the heroine. A virtuous provincial maiden, Louise goes to court, where she both falls (morally) and rises (socially) when the Sun King makes her his mistress and a duchess. Too good a woman to be continually interesting, too sincere a lover of Louis the man to be a stimulating and appreciative companion for Louis the King or the sort of intermediary courtiers find useful, Louise is soon supplanted by a more worldly mistress. After many a scene of debate, escape, pursuit, and lament, the duchess takes her leave of the king and the world and enters a nunnery.

The Lady of Lyons: Or, Love and Pride, based on a slight tale called "The Bellows Mender," proved more successful than had its predecessor, for a number of reasons. As the critic Charles Shattuck observes, Bulwer-Lytton the Radical selected just the sort of story—"that of the noble commoner winning out against the entrenched social prejudices of decadent aristocracy"—to please the public in an age of reform. In addition, the play is not high drama but romantic comedy: The temptations to grandiose posturing, moralizing, and philosophizing are less frequent. The lady of the play's title is Pauline Deschappelles, the beautiful daughter of a rich merchant. She inspires the love and possesses the pride that combine in the subtitle.

As the play opens, Pauline, with the encouragement of her mother, a woman as stupid and matrimonially obsessed as is Mrs. Bennet in Jane Austen's novel *Pride and Prejudice* (1813), has refused the proposal of Beauseant, *ci-devant* marquis, who bitterly states the absurdity of the lovely girl's goals in life: "Now as we have no noblemen left in France,—as we are all citizens and equals, she can only hope that, in spite of the war, some English Milord or German Count will risk his life, by coming to Lyons, that this *fille du Roturier* may condescend to accept him."

To revenge himself on the proud beauty and her family, Beauseant enlists the aid of one of "Nature's noblemen"—Claude Melnotte, the handsome and self-educated son of a gardener. Melnotte, known ironically, because of his efforts at self-improvement, as "Prince Claude," is himself a man who loves and has been brutally scorned by Pauline. Disguised as the Prince of Como and financed by Beauseant, Claude is to woo, win, and thereby disgrace the ambitious girl. Because he has been insulted by her, the gardener's son agrees, but because he truly loves her, he repents of his deception as soon as Pauline agrees to marry him, for in so doing, she reveals herself partly charmed by his title but also partly alive to his real excellence. No sooner has he wed the girl than Claude nobly offers her an annulment, which Pauline, by now seriously attached to him, is not disposed to accept. Having thus won her love, Claude goes off as a soldier to acquire a name and fortune worthy of the lady he has gained.

Two and a half years pass, and Claude, now known as the mysterious and heroic Colonel Morier, returns to Lyons to claim Pauline's hand. He is crushed to learn that the woman who vowed to wait for him is on the verge of marrying Beauseant—but relieved to discover that her apparent fickleness is only filial concern to save her now-bankrupt father's good name by giving him a rich son-in-law. Having arrived at the eleventh hour, the gardener's son, now risen to eminence in the Grande Armée, can stoop to save the little bourgeoise who once scorned him. Thus, the play's outcome is shrewdly calculated to please both republicans and romantics.

Whereas *The Lady of Lyons* offered a timely political message in a palatable comic form, Bulwer-Lytton's next play for Macready, *Richelieu*, proved more ambitious. Initially conceived as a romance set in the days of Louis XIII, and only incidentally dealing with the cardinal, the play gradually changed, as Bulwer-Lytton's fascination with the complex man who was one of the great architects of the prerevolutionary French state drew Richelieu to center stage.

Accordingly, the romantic comedy was elevated to a blank-verse drama. The love conflict—a triangular relationship whose three parties are the cardinal's ward Julie de Mortemar; her honorable admirer the Chevalier de Mauprat, at first the cardinal's foe, then his stout ally; and Louis XIII, who wants Julie for his mistress—was subordinated to a political problem: a conspiracy against the cardinal's strategies and life by a cabal allied with the Spanish powers. Bulwer-Lytton, well-read in French history, condensed a number of events occurring between 1630 and 1642 for his *Richelieu*. In one grand chain of events, the shrewd, brave, ruthless, but jovial cardinal successfully deals with the Duc de Bouillon's conspiracy, the "Day of Dupes," the apostasy of Baradas, and the treason of Cinq Mars. Not surprisingly, then, the play is full of melodramatic action. It contains an abundance of the intrigues and counterintrigues, betrayals, escapes, and pursuits admired by nineteenth century audiences. Bulwer-Lytton's chief interest, though, is in doing justice to the cardinal's character: His preface and occasional footnotes guarantee that the reader's attention remains on the cardinal's character as revealed through events, rather than on the events themselves. As statesman and private person, the Richelieu whom Bulwer-Lytton presents is a plausible mixture of vices and virtues. For a reading audience, the playwright comes close to his professed goal of "not disguising his foibles or his vices, but not [being] unjust to the grander qualities (especially the love of country), by which they were often dignified, and, at times, redeemed."

Bulwer-Lytton's third play for Macready, the piece first called "Norman," then "The Inquisition," next "The Birthright," and finally *The Sea-Captain*, failed disastrously in 1839; and Bulwer-Lytton was not immediately eager to resume his playwriting. In May, 1840, however, Macready's company was having a slow season at the Haymarket, so Bulwer-Lytton, willing to oblige a friend in need, embarked upon the composition of a social comedy. He began and then abandoned "Appearances," a play conceived as "a satire on the way appearances of all kinds impose on the public." The play he then proceeded to write, *Money*, is a refinement on this theme.

In *Money*, which is the most enduring of his plays, Bulwer-Lytton deals rather as Molière might have done with the manner in which the hypocritical world's regard for a man changes as his financial position improves or deteriorates. The play's hero is Alfred Evelyn, a high-minded but impoverished gentleman serving as private secretary to his worldly cousin Sir John Vesey, a man who lives luxuriously on the reputation of wealth, as do more than a few suave deceivers in Bulwer-Lytton's society novels. Evelyn loves and proposes to his equally poor and equally admirable cousin Clara, who, like him, is an exploited retainer of the Vesey family. Clara returns his love but knows from her parents' experience that affection without money is not enough to make a man happy. With Evelyn's best interests at heart, she refuses him. Directly thereafter, Evelyn inherits a great fortune, and Clara proves too scrupulous to confess the love she had not permitted herself to avow when he was poor. He therefore engages himself to the mercenary Sir John's charming, calculating daughter Georgina, but, suspicious of her avowed attachment, pretends to ruin himself through extravagant spending, particularly gambling. As a result of this test, Georgina's insincerity and Clara's generous love become evident. The play ends with the virtuous man whom money alone cannot please gaining true wealth: As Evelyn tells his fiancée, Clara, "You have reconciled me to the world and to mankind."

As a comedy of manners, *Money* falls short of such masterpieces as William Congreve's *The Way of the World* (pr. 1700) or Wilde's *The Importance of Being Earnest* (pr. 1895), but it is of all Bulwer-Lytton's plays the one that proves most rewarding to twentieth century readers. *Money* demonstrates how a chronic moral disease, the avarice of the fashionable world, afflicts the denizens of a particular place and time. The Victorian symptoms of this malaise, the coldhearted courtships, the mutual deceptions of extravagant worldlings and greedy tradesmen, the compelling drama of the gaming table, are interesting historical curiosities for a modern audience. Thus, ironically, the one play that Bulwer-Lytton chose to set in the present is the one in which posterity finds the most telling observations of a vanished age.

Other major works

NOVELS: *Falkland*, 1827; *The Disowned*, 1828; *Pelham: Or, The Adventures of a Gentleman*, 1828; *Devereux: A Tale*, 1829; *Paul Clifford*, 1830; *Eugene Aram*, 1832; *Godolphin*, 1833; *The Last Days of Pompeii*, 1834; *Rienzi, the Last of the Roman Tribunes*, 1835; *Ernest Maltravers*, 1837; *Alice: Or, The Mysteries*, 1838; *Zanoni*, 1842; *The Last of the Barons*, 1843; *Harold, the Last of the Saxons*, 1848; *The Caxtons: A Family Picture*, 1849; *My Novel*, 1852; *What Will He Do with It?*, 1859; *A Strange Story*, 1861; *The Coming Race*, 1871; *Kenelm Chillingly: His Adventures and Opinions*, 1873; *The Parisians*, 1873.

SHORT FICTION: "The Haunted and the Haunters," 1857.

POETRY: *The New Timon*, 1846; *King Arthur: An Epic Poem*, 1848-1849, 1870.

NONFICTION: *England and the English*, 1833; *Letters to John Bull, Esquire*, 1851.

Bibliography

Bulwer-Lytton, Edward. *Bulwer and Macready: A Chronicle of the Early Victorian Theatre.* Urbana: University of Illinois Press, 1958. This edition of letters related to Bulwer-Lytton's theatrical ventures principally contains letters from Bulwer-Lytton himself, from the actor and producer of plays William Charles Macready, and from the literary man John Forster. A concise introduction, supplemented by period illustrations, provides useful background for the correspondence and for Bulwer-Lytton's involvement with theater.

Campbell, James L., Sr. *Edward Bulwer-Lytton.* Boston: Twayne, 1986. This accessible critical and biographical overview of Bulwer-Lytton's life and literary career emphasizes his fiction and pays comparatively little attention to his dramas.

Christensen, Allan. *Edward Bulwer-Lytton: The Fiction of New Regions.* Athens: University of Georgia Press, 1976. This critical study focuses chiefly on Bulwer-Lytton's novels. Aimed at presenting him as a dedicated artist rather than a facile opportunist, it traces the literary development of his aesthetic ideas and philosophical ideals.

Escott, T. H. *Edward Bulwer: First Baron Lytton of Knebworth.* Port Washington, N.Y.: Kennikat Press, 1970. This reprint of a 1910 monograph considers personal, social, and political aspects of Bulwer-Lytton's many-sided career, especially his involvement with Victorian Tory government.

Lytton, Victor A. *The Life of Edward Bulwer, First Lord Lytton.* 2 vols. London: Macmillan, 1913. Written by a family member, this detailed biography quotes extensively from Bulwer-Lytton's letters and journals as well as from other primary sources. Many plates appear in the handsomely produced two volumes.

Sadleir, Michael. *Bulwer: A Panorama.* Boston: Little, Brown, 1931. In this first and only volume of a projected but unfinished longer study, Sadleir covers Bulwer-Lytton's life and writings to 1836. Effective analysis of early works blends with an insightful biography solidly grounded in the contexts of Regency and early Victorian society.

Peter W. Graham

ALEXANDER BUZO

Born: Sydney, Australia; July 23, 1944

Principal drama

Norm and Ahmed, pr. 1968, pb. 1969; *The Front Room Boys,* pr. 1969, pb. 1970; *Rooted,* pr. 1969, pb. 1973; *The Roy Murphy Show,* pr. 1970, pb. 1973; *Macquarie,* pb. 1971, pr. 1972; *Tom,* pr. 1972, pb. 1975; *Batman's Beachhead,* pb. 1973; *Coralie Lansdowne Says No,* pr., pb. 1974; *Martello Towers,* pr., pb. 1976; *Makassar Reef,* pr. 1978, pb. 1979; *Big River,* pr. 1980, pb. 1981; *The Marginal Farm,* pr. 1983, pb. 1985.

Other literary forms

Alexander Buzo has written for both film and television, coauthoring the script for the television production of *Ned Kelly* (1970) and writing the screenplay for the short film *Rod* (1972). He has also contributed articles to journals such as *The Australian Financial Review, National Times,* and *POL Magazine.*

Achievements

Buzo was playwright-in-residence for the Melbourne Theatre Company in 1972-1973. During that period, his historical play *Macquarie* and a satire on big business, *Tom,* were produced. He was awarded the Australian Literature Society Gold Medal for those two plays in 1972. Buzo also received a fellowship from the Commonwealth Literary Fund in 1970 and a grant from the Literature Board of the Australia Council in 1973 and 1979.

One of Buzo's greatest achievements has been to alter the image of the Australian theater. He belongs to the "New Wave" of Australian playwrights who began to come to prominence in the 1960's and whose spiritual mentor was Ray Lawler, whose *Summer of the Seventeenth Doll* (pr. 1955) was the first Australian play to win international attention.

Buzo's first important play, the one-act *Norm and Ahmed,* won for him as much notoriety as fame. It was the subject of a number of prosecutions for indecency, provided by the play's obscene closing line. *Norm and Ahmed* was introduced to the public in 1968, at the Old Tote Theatre in Sydney, as part of an experimental Australian play season; it was accompanied by another one-act play, *The Fire on the Snow* (pr. 1941), by Douglas Stewart, which had been first produced as a radio play. In the original production, the closing line was delivered onstage in a Bowdlerized form, but in the play's production in Brisbane, in April and May of 1969, the final speech was delivered as written in Buzo's script. The actor playing Norm, who speaks the offending line, was arrested after about two weeks of production, having ignored warnings by the police. He was tried, convicted, and fined, but he took the case to the State Supreme Court of Queensland, where the conviction was overturned. The state authorities appealed to the High Court of Australia, which upheld the State Supreme Court's decision.

The play was produced in Melbourne, the capital of the state of Victoria, in July of 1969, and the producer and the actor playing Norm were prosecuted for indecency in that state as well. After a number of adjournments, during one of which the magistrate, counsel, and witnesses saw a special performance, the producer and actor were each fined ten dollars. They appealed, but the appeal was dismissed, and the judge decided that the line in question violated contemporary standards of decency.

Norm and Ahmed was first published as a supplement to *Komos*, the journal of drama and theater arts of Monash University in Victoria, Australia. The publishers mentioned that they had had extreme difficulty obtaining a firm to set the type because of the obscenity charge which was then before the courts.

The controversy over *Norm and Ahmed* received a considerable amount of publicity. The net effect was to liberate Australian drama from censorship, and many playwrights have followed Buzo's lead, using strong language wherever they feel it to be appropriate.

Biography

Alexander Buzo was born in Sydney, the capital of the state of New South Wales, on July 23, 1944, the son of an Albanian-born, American-educated civil-engineer father and an Australian mother. Buzo spent his childhood in Armidale, an inland town in New South Wales, near the border between New South Wales and Queensland, an area devoted primarily to the raising of sheep.

Buzo attended primary school in Armidale and high school at the International School in Geneva, Switzerland. After completing high school, he returned to Australia. He was graduated from the University of New South Wales in Sydney.

Buzo has firmly committed himself to earning a living as a writer and has succeeded in doing so—no mean feat in Australia. Producing plays almost annually since the age of twenty-five, he has achieved world renown as a dramatist. His plays reflect many of his personal beliefs; he detests bullies and cowards and satirizes them mercilessly, as demonstrated by his portrayal of the central character of Norm in *Norm and Ahmed*; he is sympathetic to women's attempts to achieve equality and to make a mark in the traditionally male-chauvinist society of Australia; and, finally, he deplores the insularity of Australia and Australians, and his writings reflect his attempts to change his people's view of themselves.

Analysis

All Alexander Buzo's plays may be classified as socially pertinent and controversial. He writes to shock, or at least to make his audience uncomfortable, even when they are laughing uproariously. In his earlier plays, his tone is satiric, bordering sometimes on the morbid, while in his later work it tends to be ironic. If his plays seem to lack a definite structure much of the time, this failing is balanced by his superlative dialogue.

There is a universality of character and setting that more than makes up for the Australian idioms that Buzo employs, particularly in his early plays—idioms that will frequently baffle the non-Australian playgoer (or reader). Indeed, as Buzo has matured, his characterizations have become increasingly rich and complex. His early characters, although representing recognizable types, border on caricature. Norm, in *Norm and Ahmed*, for example, is drawn in bold strokes but with little detail. In contrast, Coralie Lansdowne, of *Coralie Lansdowne Says No*, is a fine character portrait of a troubled woman, uneasy with herself, and Weeks Brown, the protagonist of *Makassar Reef*, has a depth of character seldom met in modern drama, Australian or European, American or English.

As noted above, Buzo's recurring theme as a playwright is Australia's national identity. While he has many other concerns as well, it is this theme that links plays as diverse as *Norm and Ahmed*, *Macquarie*, and *Makassar Reef*. *Norm and Ahmed*, which has been called "probably the best Australian one-act play staged for many years," is primarily a study of an uncertain Australian, one who cannot come to terms with the "invasion" of his country by immigrants who have different values and different mores. Indeed, Norm is portrayed as the archetypal Australian; the attitudes he expresses are those ascribed to the conservative middle-class, median-educated "Aussie." Ahmed personifies everything that this class of Australian has come to dislike: the immigrant who is not only disturbingly "different" but also ambitious, hardworking, and self-possessed. Confronted by a "boong" such as Ahmed, the typical Aussie feels a need to reestablish his uneasy sense of superiority.

The historical background to the play, which needs no explanation for an Australian audience, will be less familiar to non-Australians. Traditionally, immigrants to Australia, of whom there were more than two million after World War II, were drawn from Great Britain and continental Europe, and for many years there was in effect a "White Australia" policy. This policy has changed, however, as the Australian government has come to realize that the country is situated in Southeast Asia, with many nonwhite neighbors. While nonwhites have been permitted to immigrate to Australia, attitudes toward them have changed slowly, and many white Australians have retained racist tendencies.

Both Norm and Ahmed are types rather than fully developed characters.

Norm, who mentions that his father was Irish, fits the stereotype of the Irish-Australian: antigovernment but politically conservative, boozing, rebellious, suspicious of foreigners. Ahmed is a leftist, unhappy with the government both in Australia and in Pakistan. He is formal, polite, and reserved.

Buzo's gift for dialogue is evident in this early play. Indeed, the play depends entirely on dialogue to hold the audience's attention. There is no plot and, with the exception of the kick to Ahmed's stomach that provides the conclusion, no action. Norm is a natural storyteller, and he keeps Ahmed engaged with tales of himself and his exploits during the war, at the same time freely expressing his attitudes toward various facets of Australian life. Norm is not only a fine raconteur but also a born actor, and he acts out many of his tales for Ahmed. His speech is glib, and he cleverly conceals his true self from Ahmed throughout the play, until the culmination. The play made a deep impression in Australia, and much has been written about why Norm kicks Ahmed. Why indeed?

Norm has received only politeness from Ahmed, but Ahmed's reserve implies a feeling of superiority, which Norm cannot tolerate. As Katherine Brisbane observes in her introduction to *Three Plays by Alexander Buzo* (1973): "His powers of reasoning may have betrayed him in the past but his prejudice he can rely on."

Buzo's first historical play, *Macquarie*, is about one of Australia's early colonial governors, Lachlan Macquarie. The play is important in that it marks Buzo's first foray into the roots of Australia's national identity. One must remember that the first settlement in Australia took place in 1788. Buzo uses the historical genre to draw parallels between the past and the present. He makes his audience realize that no matter how much things have changed, there are certain human characteristics that are constant. Greed, avarice, honesty, and high-mindedness are still as significant in maintaining societal values as they were in the nineteenth century.

The play retains a twentieth century flavor by a series of rapid changes on a permanent set—using lighting to focus on particular parts of the set, leaving other parts darkened, and employing a commentator to narrate the action. These devices, given currency by the epic theater of Bertolt Brecht, reminds the audience that they are in contemporary times. Stage presentations of *Macquarie* rely heavily on technical effects of this nature, and the sparse setting that Buzo calls for compels the playgoer or reader to use his imagination to fill in the blanks. The play is not naturalistic; it does not try to present the history of the era as much as it delves into the motivations of an honorable man who is opposed by a number of self-interested factions. It stresses moral struggles which are universal.

Governor Macquarie is opposed by the ultraconservative, anticonvict faction of "established" Australians, among whom are his lieutenant governor and a prominent Methodist minister, Samuel Marsden, one of the wealthiest landowners of the time. The latter group wishes to maintain the status quo and violently opposes Macquarie's reform efforts.

The action opens in Sydney, in the colony of New South Wales, which, at the time, constituted all of settled Australia, except for Tasmania, then known as Van Diemen's Land. The colony extended along the entire east coast of Australia, much of which had not yet been explored. There are rapid shifts in time and place (between Sydney and London) and a lot of action. So many changes in locale occur at such a rapid pace that the audience will wonder, now and then, exactly where the action is taking place.

Considerable social commentary is included in the play, amounting almost to allegory. The clergyman Marsden represents the evil forces in the colony, whereas Macquarie represents the forces of good, overcome by deceit, greed, and politicizing. The play dramatizes the visions of fairness and right as exemplified in a just, farsighted governor, who, although he makes errors in judgment, is basically a sincere and compassionate man. While he made mistakes because of his own character faults, nevertheless he was a heroic figure in early Australia.

Macquarie provides audiences with an insight into the beginnings of Australia and, implicitly, a standard by which to judge the present. That judgment is made more explicit in *Makassar Reef*, a play which differs in style from *Macquarie* as much as *Macquarie* differs from *Norm and Ahmed* yet which continues Buzo's investigation of the Australian experience.

The setting for *Makassar Reef* is the Celebes Islands of Indonesia. The plot concerns a no-longer-young Australian couple: Weeks Brown, a government economist in his thirties, and his fiancée, Beth Fleetwood. Other characters are Wendy Ostrow and her daughter, recently back from Geneva and now on their way to Australia, where Wendy was born but which her daughter has never seen; Perry Glasson, an Australian yachtsman-drifter, who will do almost anything to make a little money; Silver, a thief who passes as a Dutch hippie but who was really born in Australia; and two Indonesians: Karim, a corrupt government official, and Abidin, a disillusioned but still politically active journalist who earns his living as an English teacher and guide. There is also an offstage character, Madame Yu, who owns the hotel and restaurant in which much of the action takes place, and who also has a hand in prostitution, drugs, and, presumably, many other illegal affairs.

There are many parallels between this play and William J. Lederer's novel *The Ugly American* (1958). As travel has become cheaper and Australians more mobile, they have usurped the place of the American, especially in locations closer to Australia, displaying all the characteristics despised for so many years in American tourists: smug superiority, conspicuous display of wealth, and disregard for local customs.

Disillusionment pervades *Makassar Reef*. Weeks either is on vacation, has resigned, or has been fired from his post as a government economic adviser in Australia; it appears that one of the policies he advised his superiors to put into effect has had disastrous results. Almost penniless in Makassar, reduced to selling his personal possessions, Weeks is drunk through much of the play.

In this demoralized state, Weeks looks for solace in an affair with Wendy, and thus the plot is set in motion. Beth is aware of the affair but will not relinquish Weeks. Wendy's daughter, Camilla, thinks that Weeks and Beth are married; indeed, they have lived together for nine years and it would appear there is nothing left for them to do but marry. Camilla is shattered by the revelation of Weeks's affair with her mother.

Beth retaliates by having an affair with the yachtsman, Perry, who is subsequently falsely arrested in a conspiracy between the Indonesian official, Karim, and the thief, Silver. Silver, however, learns that Madame Yu, determined to rid her territory of all competition, intends to eliminate him. Needing passage from the island, he strikes a bargain with Weeks to liberate Perry, who, in return, is supposed to take Silver with him to Singapore, far from Madame Yu's influence. Upon liberation, however, Perry leaves the island by himself, abandoning Silver to his well-deserved fate.

At the close of the play, the audience learns that Weeks has obtained work with the World Bank in Washington, and Beth, who earlier claimed that she was pregnant by him but who casually mentions that she is now menstruating, is to go with him. Wendy and Camilla are booked on the next plane to Australia, much to Camilla's distress: She wants to return to her friends and school in Geneva, the only life she has ever known.

Makassar Reef is a dark play enlivened with occasional sparks of humor. The dialogue, as is typical of Buzo, is fast-paced, and the action shifts rapidly from point to point on the set. As noted above, there is a feeling of senselessness about life, an utter disillusionment pervading this play, a pressing-in of the world that is forcefully communicated to the audience. The mood of the play reminds one of post-World War I European theater and film; it is redolent with a feeling of defeat.

The play is noteworthy for its superb characterizations, its trenchant examination of the difficulties people experience in establishing and maintaining intimacy. The stereotyped characters and broad satire of Buzo's early plays have given way to fully rounded characters and subtle irony. At the same time, Buzo has developed the theme of Australia's isolation introduced in *Norm and Ahmed*. In *Makassar Reef*, he stresses Australia's position, geographically and economically, as a Southeast Asian nation. Thus, both stylistically and thematically, *Makassar Reef* gives evidence of Buzo's continuing growth as a dramatist.

Other major works

NOVEL: *The Search for Harry Allway*, 1985.
NONFICTION: *Tautology*, 1981; *Meet the New Class*, 1981.
SCREENPLAY: *Rod*, 1972.
TELEPLAY: *Ned Kelly*, 1970.

Bibliography

Fitzpatrick, Peter. "Alexander Buzo." In *After "The Doll": Australian Drama Since 1955*. Sydney: Edward Arnold, 1979. In this six-page essay, Fitzpatrick examines the qualities shared by Buzo and David Williamson: the fact that "they were the first to be granted the token of legitimacy," that "their developing 'professionalism' was marked by their writing for film," and that they "share a preoccupation with the values and lifestyles of their own generation." Analyzes the language in Buzo's plays.

McCallum, John. "Coping with Hydrophobia: Alexander Buzo's Moral World." *Meanjin* 39, no. 1 (April, 1980): 60-69. Analyzes the characters in Buzo's early plays (up to *Tom*), portrayed mostly as victims of an "amoral and dehumanising society." Also examines the shift in style from these early "angry" plays, as Buzo called them, to a new style of romantic comedy and witty characters. Discusses several plays, among them *Big River*, *Makassar Reef*, and *Martello Towers*.

New Theatre Quarterly 2 (February, 1986). Half the issue is devoted to Australian theater, with six articles addressing the drama since 1975. Discusses Buzo throughout but especially in Peter Fitzpatrick's article "After the Wave," in which he observes that "Buzo's more recent plays have moved away from specific local settings." Chronology from 1977 to 1983.

Rees, Leslie. *The Making of Australian Drama: A Historical and Critical Survey from the 1830's to the 1970's*. Sydney: Angus and Robertson, 1973. Discusses Buzo's work in chapters on university theater, on *The Front Room Boys*, on drama experimentation, and in an appendix on the courtroom furor over *Norm and Ahmed*. Good bibliography and index.

Sturm, T. L. "Alexander Buzo: An Imagist with a Personal Style of Surrealism." In *Contemporary Australian Drama: Perspectives Since 1955*, edited by Peter Holloway. Sydney: Currency Press, 1981. Sturm's five-page essay begins by linking Buzo's drama to the "sociological pattern" of Australian "national self-consciousness," but then focuses on Buzo's rejection of such reception of his plays: "Some people regard my plays as documentaries on the Australian way of life and that disturbs me. . . . My plays are meant as works of fiction." Includes discussions of *Macquarie* and *Coralie Lansdowne Says No*, among others.

Peter Goslett
(Updated by *Thomas J. Taylor*)

GEORGE GORDON, LORD BYRON

Born: London, England; January 22, 1788
Died: Missolonghi, Greece; April 19, 1824

Principal drama

Manfred, pb. 1817, pr. 1834; *Marino Faliero, Doge of Venice*, pr., pb. 1821; *Sardanapalus: A Tragedy*, pb. 1821, pr. 1834; *The Two Foscari: A Tragedy*, pb. 1821, pr. 1837; *Sardanapalus: A Tragedy, The Two Foscari: A Tragedy, Cain: A Mystery*, pb. 1821; *Heaven and Earth*, pb. 1822 (fragment); *Werner: Or, The Inheritance*, pb. 1823, pr. 1830; *The Deformed Transformed*, pb. 1824 (fragment).

Other literary forms

George Gordon, Lord Byron, is considerably better known as a poet than as a dramatist, and the relative importance of the poetry is quickly evident in any review of Byron's literary career. His first book, *Fugitive Pieces,* was printed at his own expense in November of 1806, and though it consisted primarily of sentimental and mildly erotic verse, it also contained hints of the satiric wit that would be so important to Byron's later reputation. The volume is also notable for having inspired the first accusations that Byron lacked poetic chastity; at the urging of some of his friends, he withdrew the book from private circulation and replaced it with the more morally upright *Poems on Various Occasions*, printed in Newark in January of 1807 by John Ridge, who had also printed *Fugitive Pieces*.

In his first attempt at public recognition as a man of letters, Byron published *Hours of Idleness* in June of 1807. The volume shows the obvious influence of a number of Augustan and Romantic poets, but despite its largely derivative nature, it received several favorable early reviews. Fortunately for Byron's development as a poet, however, the praise was not universal, and subsequent critical attacks, notably by Henry Brougham of *The Edinburgh Review*, helped inspire the writing of Byron's first poetic triumph, *English Bards and Scotch Reviewers* (1809). In the tradition of Alexander Pope's *The Dunciad* (1728-1743) but written under the more direct influence of *Baviad* (1794) and *Maeviad* (1795), by William Gifford, *English Bards and Scotch Reviewers* is the earliest significant example of Byron's satiric genius. Three more satiric poems soon followed, but none of these—*Hints from Horace* (1811), *The Curse of Minerva* (1812), and *Waltz: An Apostrophic Hymn* (1813)—attracted as much admiring attention as *English Bards and Scotch Reviewers*.

During this same period, Byron was composing the poem with which he would be most closely associated during his lifetime and which would make him the most lionized literary figure of his day, *Childe Harold's Pilgrimage*,

Cantos I-IV (1812-1818, 1819). The first two cantos of the poem, an imaginative meditation loosely based on two years of travel on the Continent, were published on March 10, 1812, and produced an immediate sensation. In his own words, Byron "awoke one morning and found myself famous." Cantos III and IV were greeted with equal excitement and confirmed the identification of Byron in the popular mind with his poem's gloomy protagonist.

In the meantime, Byron published a series of poetic tales that further exploited the knowledge derived from his Eastern travels and that continued the development of the Byronic hero, the brooding, titanic figure whose prototype within Byron's canon is Childe Harold. These tales include *The Giaour* (1813), *The Bride of Abydos* (1813), *The Corsair* (1814), *Lara* (1814), *Parisina* (1816), and *The Siege of Corinth* (1816). Illustrative of the diversity of Byron's poetic output is the publication, during this same period, of *Hebrew Melodies Ancient and Modern* (1815), short lyrics based largely on passages from the Bible and accompanied by the music of Isaac Nathan. Although Byron lacked the lyric mastery of a number of his extraordinary contemporaries, he produced well-crafted lyrics throughout his literary career, none of which is more admired or more often quoted than the first poem of *Hebrew Melodies Ancient and Modern*, "She Walks in Beauty."

Also published in 1816 was "The Prisoner of Chillon," a dramatic monologue on the theme of human freedom, which Byron was inspired to write after a visit to the castle where François de Bonivard had been imprisoned during the sixteenth century. *The Lament of Tasso* (1817), written during the following year, is a less successful variation on the same theme and, more important, an early manifestation of Byron's fascination with the literature and history of Italy. This fascination is also seen in *The Prophecy of Dante* (1821), "Francesca of Rimini" (inspired by Canto V of Dante's *Inferno*), and the translation of Canto I of Luigi Pulci's *Morgante Maggiore* (1483), which were produced in the years 1819 and 1820.

The importance of Pulci to Byron's poetic career is immeasurable. Through *Whistlecraft* (1817-1818), by John Hookham Frere, Byron became indirectly acquainted with the casual, facetious manner of the *Morgante Maggiore* and adapted the Pulci/Frere style to his own purposes in his immensely successful tale of Venetian dalliance, *Beppo: A Venetian Story*. Written in 1817 and published in 1818, *Beppo* is the direct stylistic precursor of *Don Juan*, Cantos I-XVI (1819-1824, 1826), the seriocomic masterpiece whose composition occupied Byron at irregular intervals throughout the last six years of his life.

Although the final years of Byron's literary career are important primarily for the writing of *Don Juan*, several other of Byron's works deserve passing or prominent mention. *Mazeppa* (1819) is a verse tale in Byron's earlier manner which treats heavy-handedly a theme which the first cantos of *Don Juan* address with an adroit lightness: the disastrous consequences of an illicit love. *The Island* (1823) is a romantic tale inspired by William Bligh's account of the *Bounty* mutiny, a tale that possesses some affinities with the Haidée episode of *Don Juan.* The years from 1821 to 1823 produced three topical satires, *The Blues: A Literary Ecologue* (written in 1821 but first published in *The Liberal* in 1823), *The Vision of Judgment* (1822), and *The Age of Bronze* (1823), the second of which, a devastating response to Robert Southey's obsequious *A Vision of Judgment,* is one of Byron's undoubted masterworks.

Finally, no account of Byron's nondramatic writings would be complete without making reference to his correspondence, among the finest in the English language, which has been given its definitive form in Leslie A. Marchand's multivolume edition, *Byron's Letters and Journals* (1973-1982).

Achievements

In his *The Dramas of Lord Byron: A Critical Study* (1915), Samuel C. Chew, Jr., makes it abundantly clear that Byron was simultaneously fascinated with the theater and contemptuous of the accomplishments of contemporary dramatists. He was frequently to be found in the playhouses, especially during his days as a student and during the period immediately following his Eastern travels, and on at least two occasions, he acted, with considerable success, in amateur theatrical productions. His comments on the stage suggest, however, that he was appalled by the reliance of early nineteenth century playwrights on melodramatic sensationalism and visual spectacle. His letters mention the scarcity of fine plays, and his poetry castigates modern dramatists for their tastelessness. *English Bards and Scotch Reviewers,* for example, calls contemporary drama a "motley sight" and deplores the "degradation of our vaunted stage." It cries out to George Colman and Richard Cumberland to "awake!" and implores Richard Brinsley Sheridan, who had achieved a recent success with *Pizarro: A Tragedy in Five Acts* (pr. 1799), an adaptation of a play by August von Kotzebue, to "Abjure the mummery of the German schools" and instead to "reform the stage." It asks, in indignant mockery, "Shall sapient managers new scenes produce/ From Cherry, Skeffington, and Mother Goose?" and makes sneering reference to the extravagances of Matthew Gregory "Monk" Lewis' *The Castle Spectre* (pr. 1797). It suggests, on the whole, that the once glorious English theater is in woeful decline.

Despite Byron's sense of the theater's decay, or perhaps because of it, evidence exists, in epistolary references to destroyed manuscripts and in a surviving fragment or two of attempted drama, that, as early as 1813-1814, he had ambitions of becoming a playwright, but he had completed nothing for the stage when, in 1815, he was appointed a member of the Drury

Lane Committee of Management. Although he found his committee work "really good fun," it did nothing to improve his opinion of the taste of contemporary dramatists and their audiences, and when he finally finished a dramatic work, it was not intended for popular presentation.

Like the rest of his completed drama, *Manfred* was written during Byron's final, self-imposed exile from England. Begun in Switzerland and finished in Venice, the play is psychosymbolic rather than realistic and may have been inspired, as any number of commentators have pointed out, by Byron's acquaintance with Johann Wolfgang von Goethe's *Faust* (pb. 1808, 1833). Byron appears to have known of Goethe's masterpiece through translated passages in Madame de Staël's *De l'Allemagne* (1810) and through an extensive oral translation by Monk Lewis during a visit to the poet in August of 1816. Considerable controversy has occurred, however, over the extent of *Faust*'s influence on *Manfred*, the consensus now being that *Faust* is simply one of many sources of the play's intricate materials, albeit an important one. Chew makes mention of Chateaubriand's *René* (1802), Goethe's *The Sorrows of Young Werther* (1774), Horace Walpole's *The Castle of Otranto* (1764) and *The Mysterious Mother* (1768), Samuel Taylor Coleridge's *Remorse* (1813), John Robert Maturin's *Bertram: Or, The Castle of St. Aldobrand* (1816), William Beckford's *Vathek* (1782), and Lewis' *The Monk* (1796) as other works with which *Manfred* has affinities and from which borrowings may have occurred. More important, however, *Manfred* is a cathartic projection of Byron's own troubled psyche, an attempt, which some critics have called Promethean rather than Faustian, to cope with the seemingly unconquerable presence of evil in the world, to deal with his frustrated aspirations toward an unattainable ideal, and, on a more mundane level, to come to terms with his confused feelings toward his half sister Augusta. With respect to *Manfred*'s place in theatrical history, Malcolm Kelsall, in *The Byron Journal* (1978), has made an excellent case for grouping Byron's play both with *Faust* and with Henrik Ibsen's *Peer Gynt* (pb. 1867). Kelsall states that "the new kind of stage envisaged" in these plays "is unfettered by any kind of limitation of place, and that assault, which is as much upon the conceived possibilities of stage allusion as upon unity of place, demands of the imagination that it supply constantly shifting visual correlatives for the inner turmoil of the hero's mind."

Byron's next play, *Marino Faliero, Doge of Venice*, is of an entirely different sort and ushers in a period in which Byron attempted to return to classical dramatic principles to produce plays whose themes are essentially political. He sought to counteract the undisciplined bombast and sprawling display of the drama with which he had become familiar in England by making use, without becoming anyone's slavish disciple, of theatrical techniques exploited by the ancient Greeks and Romans, the neoclassical French, and the contemporary Italians, notably Conte Vittorio Alfieri.

Because he did this during a time when his involvement in Italian political intrigue was beginning to develop, Byron's decision to center his play on Marino Faliero, the fourteenth century Doge of Venice who was executed for conspiring to overthrow the oppressive aristocratic class to which he himself belonged, is hardly surprising. He wrote the play as a closet drama—to be read rather than staged—considering its classical regularity an impossible barrier to its popular success, and he was furious when he learned of Drury Lane's intention of producing it. As he summarized the matter in a journal entry of January 12, 1821, how could anything please contemporary English theatergoers which contained "nothing melodramatic—no surprises, no starts, nor trap-doors, nor opportunities 'for tossing of their heads and kicking their heels'—and no *love*—the grand ingredient of a modern play"?

In *Sardanapalus*, Byron extended his experimentation with classical regularity and continued his exploration of political themes while at the same time appealing in two particular ways to popular taste. The play's setting, ancient Nineveh, accorded well with popular interest in Eastern exoticism, an interest that Byron's own Eastern tales had intensified, and the devotion of the slave Myrrha to Nineveh's troubled ruler satisfied the public's desire to witness pure, selfless love.

The Two Foscari, the third of the classically constructed political plays, again makes use of Venice for its setting. Although generally considered to be less successful than the earlier of the Venetian dramas, *The Two Foscari* contains autobiographical elements, embodied in Jacopo Foscari, that give a certain fascination to the play. Jacopo, after a youth of aristocratic gaiety, has been unjustly exiled from his native land. He had been the boon companion of the city's most promising young men, had been admired for his athletic vigor, particularly in swimming, and had drawn the attention of the city's most beautiful young women. Then the powerful had intrigued against him, and his banishment had begun. Byron's contemporaries could hardly have missed the personal significance of this situation or have overlooked the note of defiant anguish in such an exchange as the following:

> GUARD: And can you so much love the soil which hates you?
> JAC. FOS: The soil!—Oh no, it is the seed of the soil
> Which persecutes me; but my native earth
> Will take me as a mother to her arms.

Jacopo's persecution is carried out as an act of vengeance by an enemy of the Foscari family, an act which corrupts its perpetrator, but unlike Percy Bysshe Shelley's *The Cenci* (pb. 1819), whose theme is much the same, *The Two Foscari* is not effective theater.

Cain was published as part of a volume that also contained *Sardanapalus* and *The Two Foscari*, but it ought instead to be grouped with *Heaven and*

Earth, which was written at about the same time but whose publication was delayed because of the controversy inspired by *Cain*. In *Cain* and *Heaven and Earth*, Byron returned to the style of *Manfred*, but he derived his materials from biblical lore and from previous literary treatments of these same stories. He called the plays "mysteries," a reference both to the medieval mystery plays and to the mystified response Byron was expecting from the general public. *Cain* is a reinterpretation of the tale of the primal murder, a reinterpretation in which Cain is clearly the superior of his brother Abel and kills his brother, as Chew observes, in an "instinctive assertion of freedom against the limitations of fate." *Heaven and Earth* is based on the passage in Genesis which states that "the sons of God saw the daughters of men that they were fair; and they took them wives of all which they chose." Its plot culminates in the nearly total destruction of the flood, a destruction so general and arbitrary that the play becomes, in Chew's summary, "a subtle attack on the justice of the Most High." The heretical themes of the two works suggest why Murray, during a period of reactionary conservatism, was involved in litigation over the publication of *Cain* and was reluctant to associate himself with *Heaven and Earth*.

Werner was much more in keeping with the literary tastes of the time than Byron's other plays, a fact that can be at least partially explained by its having been begun in 1815, during the period of Byron's closest association with Drury Lane. A surprisingly faithful rendering of "The German's Tale" from Sophia and Harriet Lee's *The Canterbury Tales* (1797-1805), *Werner* centers on the title character and his perfidious son, Ulric, an ambitious villain of the deepest dye. Making no pretense of adhering to the classical unities, the play moves with Gothic ponderousness toward its dark conclusion, in which Ulric is revealed to be the cold-blooded murderer of his own fiancée's father, Stralenheim, the one man who stood between Ulric's family and their return to hereditary wealth and power.

The Deformed Transformed is one of Byron's two dramatic fragments (the other being *Heaven and Earth*). As its prefatory "Advertisement" states, Byron based it on Joshua Pickersgill's novel *The Three Brothers* (1803) and on Goethe's *Faust*. Chew points out the autobiographical significance of Byron's adding lameness to the other deformities from which his central character, Arnold, escapes by dealing with the Devil, but the play's incompleteness and incoherence make it difficult to comment further on Byron's dramatic intention. The fragment was composed in 1822 and published in February of 1824 by John Hunt.

The history of Byron's plays in theatrical production appears largely to be a tale of creative misinterpretation in the twentieth century and commercial adaptation and exploitation in the nineteenth. Margaret Howell's 1974 account in *The Byron Journal* of Charles Kean's June 13, 1853, production of *Sardanapalus* is particularly instructive. Reduced from its full length of 2,835 lines to 1,563, the play was presented almost solely as spectacle and required the approval of the local fire inspectors, because of one of its more impressive effects, before it could be performed. The production seems to have embodied everything that most disgusted Byron about London theater.

Biography

Born in London, England, on January 22, 1788, George Gordon, Lord Byron, who, since birth, suffered from a deformed foot, was the son of Captain John Byron, nicknamed "Mad Jack" because of his wild ways, and the former Catherine Gordon. On his mother's side, the poet claimed descent from James I of Scotland and on his father's, with less certainty, from Ernegis and Radulfus de Burun, estate owners in the days of William the Conqueror. Newstead Abbey, which the poet would inherit at age ten as the sixth Lord Byron, had been granted to Sir John Byron by King Henry VIII, though the title of lord was first held by General John Byron, follower of Charles I and Charles II, the latter of whom is said to have seduced the general's wife. The poet received the title upon the death, in 1798, of his great-uncle, William Byron, nicknamed "the Wicked Lord."

Because the poet's grandfather, Admiral John Byron, himself something of a rake, had disinherited Mad Jack for his even greater irresponsibility and because his father, before his death at age thirty-six, had squandered nearly all the wealth of both of the heiresses he had married, the poet's earliest years were spent in genteel poverty in his mother's native Aberdeen, Scotland, where he attended Aberdeen Grammar School. During these years, he developed his lifelong interests in both athletics and reading and was imbued, under the influence of his nurse, Agnes Gray, and his Presbyterian instructors, with the sense of predestined evil that marked so much of his later life.

After coming into his inheritance in 1798, Byron and his mother moved to Nottinghamshire, the location of Newstead Abbey, in which the young lord proudly took up residence despite the warning of John Hanson, the family attorney, that the abbey was in such disrepair that it ought not to be lived in. During 1799, Byron's clubfoot was incompetently treated by a local quack physician, Dr. Lavender, and Byron was physically and sexually abused by his new nurse, May Gray, events that left the poet with permanent emotional scars. Later in the same year, Byron was taken to London to be treated by a more reputable physician. He was also placed in the Dulwich boarding school of Dr. Glennie, who was to prepare young Byron for admission to Harrow.

Byron entered Harrow in April of 1801, and despite an occasional period of haughty aloofness, he soon became a favorite of his schoolmates. Some of his most intense friendships dated from his Harrow days, friendships the intensity of which was probably an expression, as his biographers have pointed out, of his fundamentally bisexual nature. Nevertheless, the instances of Byron's overt amatory passion, especially early in his life, more often involved women than men. He had become infatuated with a cousin, Mary Duff, perhaps as early as age seven; had written his first love poetry for another cousin, Margaret Parker, at age twelve; and had fallen so deeply in love with Mary Chaworth during a hiatus in Nottinghamshire in 1803 that he at first refused to return to Harrow. Nevertheless, he did return, and after completing his course of studies, he enrolled in Trinity College, Cambridge, during the fall of 1805.

During his Cambridge days, Byron formed romantic attachments with two male friends, won acceptance by the university's liberal intellectual elite, kept a bear in his living quarters, and became thoroughly acquainted with the distractions of London, including the theater. He also assembled his first books of poetry, most notably *Hours of Idleness*, and, almost incidentally, earned a Cambridge master's degree, which was granted in July of 1808. After a short retirement to Newstead Abbey, during which he worked on *English Bards and Scotch Reviewers*, Byron left for London, where he became a member of the House of Lords on March 13, 1809, and where *English Bards and Scotch Reviewers* was anonymously published several days thereafter. The authorship of the scathing satire was soon discovered, and Byron had the satisfaction of being lauded for his poem by Gifford and others before his departure on July 2, 1809, for his Continental tour.

Traveling with John Cam Hobhouse and several retainers, Byron disembarked in Lisbon and made the journey to Seville and later to Cadiz by horseback. The frigate *Hyperion* then took them to Gibraltar, after which they sailed for Malta, where he managed a romantic interlude with the fascinating Mrs. Constance Spencer Smith. The brig *Spider* next delivered them to Patras and Prevesa in Greece, then ruled by the Turks, whence they set out for Janina, capital of the kingdom of the barbarous Ali Pasha, sovereign of western Greece and Albania and prototype of *Don Juan's* piratical Lambro. Ali Pasha's court was located seventy-five miles away, in Tepelene, where Byron arrived on October 19, 1809, and where the colorful ruler flattered the young poet with an audience. The Tepelene adventure was one of the most memorable of Byron's memorable life, and when he returned to Janina, he began *Childe Harold's Pilgrimage* in an attempt to capture the poetic essence of his travels.

Following his perilous return to Patras by way of Missolonghi, where he was to die fifteen years later, Byron journeyed on to Athens, stopping first at Mount Parnassus and writing several stanzas to commemorate the event. In Athens itself, he and Hobhouse lived with the Macri family, whose twelve-year-old Theresa was immortalized by Byron as "the Maid of Athens." The two travelers explored the city and its historic surroundings from Christmas Day, 1809, through March 5, 1810. The sloop *Pylades* then carried them to Smyrna, where they took a side trip to Ephesus, after which they embarked for Constantinople aboard the frigate *Salsette*. On May 3, 1810, during a pause in the voyage, Byron swam the Hellespont from Sestos to Abydos, an accomplishment about which he would never tire of boasting.

Byron's stay in Constantinople brought him further invaluable knowledge of the decadent splendors of the East and also involved him in several petty disputes over matters of protocol, disputes in which Byron's aristocratic arrogance, one of his least attractive traits, came repulsively to the fore. Such matters appear to have been smoothed over, however, by the time Byron left Constantinople on July 14, 1810.

Hobhouse returned directly to England, but Byron spent the next several months in Greece, where he added to his sexual conquests, contracted a venereal disease, saved a young woman from threatened execution, and continued his exploration of a country for whose freedom he was eventually to offer up his life. On April 22, 1811, he sailed from Greece for Malta, where he temporarily renewed his affair with Mrs. Smith, and then returned home to England, stepping ashore on July 14, 1811.

Within a month of his landing, Byron's mother died, an event which caused him considerable distress despite the uneasy relationship that had long existed between them. The year also brought news of the deaths of three of Byron's closest friends. The poet dealt with his grief as best he could and continued preparations for the publication of *Childe Harold's Pilgrimage*, Cantos I and II. He also resumed his place in the House of Lords, delivering his maiden speech on February 27, 1812, an effective denunciation of a bill requiring the execution of frame breakers (workers who violently resisted the mechanization of the weaving trade). Byron delivered two more parliamentary speeches, on April 21, 1812, and June 1, 1813, but the sudden fame that *Childe Harold's Pilgrimage* brought him after its appearance on March 10, 1812, drew his attention away from politics and changed his life forever.

The immediate effect of Byron's renown was that he became the most sought-after guest in London society and the most avidly pursued of handsome bachelors. In particular, Lady Caroline Lamb, despite being already married, descended upon him with extraordinary enthusiasm. She found him "mad—bad—and dangerous to know," a description which might, with equal or greater justice, have been applied to Lady Caroline herself. Their tempestuous liaison occupied much of Byron's attention during the spring and summer of 1812 and involved indiscreet meetings, plans of elopement, threats of suicide, and a great deal of public scandal. Although they parted in September, to Byron's infinite relief, occasional further storms broke out in the months thereafter.

During the years 1812 and 1813, Byron began the series of Oriental tales that would solidify his literary fame and involved himself in affairs with various other women, most peculiarly and most deeply with his half sister, Mrs. Augusta Leigh. He spent much of the summer of 1813 with Augusta, and Elizabeth Medora Leigh, born on April 15, 1814, has always been assumed to be the poet's daughter. Though Byron never publicly acknowledged her, various passages in his letters, especially those to his close confidante, Lady Melbourne, suggest his paternity.

Lady Melbourne's brilliant niece, Annabella Milbanke, also figured prominently in Byron's life during this period. Although he despised "bluestockings" (intellectual women), Byron was unaccountably drawn to Annabella, whose intelligence and wide reading distinguished her so completely from the impulsively romantic Lady Caroline and the passively maternal Augusta. Perhaps as a means of escaping the chaos of his unstable love life, Byron proposed to Milbanke on two occasions, in September of 1812 and again in September of 1813. Unfortunately for both of them, Byron's second proposal was accepted. After various delays, apparently involving visits to Augusta, Byron and Annabella Milbanke were married on January 2, 1815.

The several months of Byron's marriage were marked by continuing literary activity (especially work on the later Oriental tales and on *Hebrew Melodies Ancient and Modern*), by visits to and from Augusta, by Byron's association with the Drury Lane Committee of Management, and by fits of temper, related to the poet's marital and financial problems, which terrified both his wife and his half sister. The birth of the poet's only legitimate child, Augusta Ada Byron, in December of 1815, did nothing to improve the situation, and when mother and daughter left on January 5, 1816, for what was purportedly a temporary visit to Annabella's parents, the marriage was effectively at an end. By March of 1816, a separation had been agreed upon, and Byron affixed his signature to the necessary legal documents on April 21, 1816. A week earlier, he had spoken for the last time to his beloved Augusta, and on April 25, still experiencing financial difficulties and being roundly denounced by the press for his marital problems, Byron left England forever.

Once more on the Continent, Byron visited the Waterloo battlefield, journeyed up the Rhine Valley, crossed into Switzerland, and began looking for accommodations near Lake Geneva. Along the lakeshore, he and his traveling companion, Dr. John Polidori, were approached by Claire Clairmont, who, as a result of an affair earlier in the spring, was pregnant with Byron's child. Clairmont was accompanied by her stepsister, Mary Godwin (later to become Mary Shelley), and Percy Bysshe Shelley. The poets were soon fast friends and by early June had established households very near each other and within two miles of Geneva. Their animated conversations deeply influenced the lives of both poets, with the inspiration of their contact communicating itself, on one particular evening, to two other members of the group. During a gathering at the Villa Diodati, where Byron had taken up residence, a challenge to compose ghost stories resulted in the eventual publication of Dr. Polidori's *The Vampyre* (1819), the first English vampire tale, and Mary Shelley's classic Gothic novel, *Frankenstein* (1818). During the several weeks of his almost daily talks with Shelley, Byron himself wrote "The Prisoner of Chillon" and worked diligently on *Childe Harold's Pilgrimage*, Canto III.

Although Claire had at first kept her relationship with Byron a secret from Mary and Percy, they inevitably became aware of Claire's pregnancy, after which Percy and Claire approached Byron in an attempt to resolve matters. Because Byron did not feel the same affection for Claire that she felt for him, it was decided that they should not live together. It was further decided that the child should be cared for by Byron, with Claire being addressed as its aunt. The child, Allegra Byron, was born in Bath, England, on January 12, 1817, and died in Ravenna, Italy, on April 20, 1822.

John Cam Hobhouse arrived at the Villa Diodati with another of Byron's friends, Scrope Davies, on August 26, 1816, and following the departure for England of the Shelley household on August 29, the two toured the Alps with Byron and Polidori. Another tour, with Hobhouse only, began on September 17. Byron's combined impressions of the Alps helped inspire *Manfred*, whose composition was well advanced when the poet gave up the Villa Diodati on October 5 and journeyed with Hobhouse to Milan.

After a sojourn of less than a month in Milan, during which he met the Italian poet Vincenzo Monti and the French novelist Stendhal, rescued Polidori from an encounter with the local authorities, and came under the surveillance of the Austrian secret police, Byron left with Hobhouse for Venice, where they arrived on or about November 10. Hobhouse soon departed to see other areas of Italy, but Byron, having fallen in love with Venice and with Marianna Segati, his landlord's wife, settled in for an extended stay. In the several months of this first Venetian interlude, he completed *Manfred* and overindulged during the Carnival period.

On April 17, 1817, Byron set out, by way of Arqua, Ferrara, and Florence, for Rome, where Hobhouse showed him the local antiquities. He returned on May 28 with the completed *The Lament of Tasso* and with vivid impressions that would be incorporated in *Childe Harold's Pilgrimage*, Canto IV. Soon thereafter, he and Marianna established themselves at the Villa Foscarini in La Mira, outside Venice. There, Byron formed another liaison, this time with the beautiful Margarita Cogni; worked at what was to become the final canto of *Childe Harold's Pilgrimage*; and began the precursor of *Don Juan*, the charming *Beppo*. Late in 1817, he returned to

Venice with the visiting Hobhouse and, on January 7, 1818, said goodbye to his friend after a last ride together. Byron entrusted Hobhouse with the manuscript of *Childe Harold's Pilgrimage*, Canto IV, whose publication in April brought the poet further literary fame during a time when his personal life had rendered him infamous.

In 1818, Byron's Venetian dissipations reached a level of obsessive frequency that threatened his health. Nevertheless, he continued to write, producing *Mazeppa* and Canto I of *Don Juan* and beginning Canto II. He was showing signs of physical exhaustion by April of 1819, when he became reacquainted with a woman whom he had casually encountered during the previous year. With this woman, the nineteen-year-old Countess Teresa Guiccioli, he was soon involved in one of the most long-lasting and passionate relationships of his life. In June, he followed her to Ravenna, in August to Bologna, and in September back to Venice, where they spent some of their time at Byron's quarters in the Palazzo Mocenigo and longer periods at the Villa Foscarini in La Mira. At the end of the year, when Teresa's husband cajoled her to return to Ravenna, Byron followed again.

The continuation of *Don Juan* had been one of Byron's primary literary projects in 1819, and further material was written in 1820. The year was significant for other reasons, too, including the writing of *Marino Faliero, Doge of Venice*, Byron's increasing entanglement in the revolutionary Carbonari movement, and Teresa's formal separation from Count Guiccioli. When the Carbonari movement collapsed in 1821 and Teresa's family was exiled from Ravenna, Byron accepted Shelley's invitation to move himself, his lover, and her banished relatives to Pisa, where Shelley had taken up residence. Despite this political and personal upheaval, Byron completed three plays during 1821 (*Sardanapalus*, *The Two Foscari*, and *Cain*) and wrote the magnificent *The Vision of Judgment*.

Byron became part of the Pisan Circle in November of 1821, and he remained a resident of the general Pisa area until September of 1822. These months witnessed the writing of much of *Don Juan*, which Byron had previously ceased composing upon the request of Teresa and which he now resumed with her permission. The period also saw the beginnings of Byron's acquaintance with the colorful Edward John Trelawny and the less satisfactory relationship between Byron and the improvident Hunt family. Most sadly, however, these were the months in which Byron's daughter, Allegra, died in a convent at Ravenna and in which Shelley, with Edward Williams, was drowned off the Italian coast. What ultimately drove Byron from Tuscany, however, was the latest banishment of Teresa's family, this time to Genoa, where Byron joined them in late September.

In Genoa, Byron wrote his last Augustan satire, *The Age of Bronze*, and a romantic verse narrative, *The Island*, while continuing *Don Juan*. He also began making serious plans to leave for Greece, where a war of independence had recently broken out. After a traumatic parting with Teresa, he set sail from Italy aboard the *Hercules* in July of 1823, accompanied by Trelawny and Teresa's brother, Pietro Gamba. In early August, they reached Cephalonia, and in late December, they left for Missolonghi, where Byron arrived on January 4, 1824, to be greeted the next day by Prince Alexandros Mavrocordatos, the Greek military leader.

During the previous August, Byron had been taken ill after an excursion to Ithaca. At Missolonghi, on February 15, he became ill once again. His recovery was slow and was hampered by terrible weather, the disunity of the Greek leadership, and their constant demands that he supply them with money. After riding through a rainstorm on April 9, he experienced a relapse. His condition worsened during the following days, and after being bled by his physicians until his strength was gone, he died on April 19, 1824. His remains were returned to England, where they were denied burial in Westminster Abbey. Instead, he was interred on July 16, 1824, in Hucknall Torkard Church, near his ancestral home of Newstead Abbey.

Analysis

Although a number of George Gordon, Lord Byron's, plays are more easily approached as dramatic poetry than as theatrical drama, the political tragedies are readily accessible to dramatic analysis. The following discussion will center on three such works, the classically constructed *Marino Faliero, Doge of Venice* and *Sardanapalus*, and the Gothic, melodramatic *Werner*.

Because it more closely resembles the popular theater of Byron's day, *Werner* will be considered first. Despite being the last play which Byron completed, *Werner* is the earliest of the plays in terms of initial composition, having been begun during the year preceding Byron's final exile from England. Byron's fascination with the story upon which the play is based dates from an even earlier period. As he explains in the play's preface, he had read "The German's Tale" from the Lees' *The Canterbury Tales* at about age fourteen, and it had "made a deep impression upon" him. It "may, indeed, be said to contain the germ of much that" he wrote thereafter, an admission that suggests the importance of the play within the Byron canon, despite the play's obvious literary deficiencies.

The play's title character embodies many of the traits of the Byronic hero and has much in common, too, with Byron's father, "Mad Jack" Byron. As the play begins, Werner is a poverty-stricken wanderer, who, like Mad Jack, has been driven out by his father because of various youthful excesses resulting from the indulgence of his overly passionate nature. Although a marriage that his father considered improvident was the immediate cause of this estrangement, Werner was guilty of other, unstated transgressions before this, transgressions that prepared the way for the final severing of the parental tie. Since then, Werner has been a proud exile, burdened by a sense of personal guilt and too familiar with the weaknesses of human nature to rely on his fellowman for consolation. His love for Josephine, herself an exile, partially sustains him, but his realization that her sufferings are a product of his own foolish actions exacerbates his gloom.

The one embodiment of hope for Werner and Josephine is their son, Ulric, who has been reared by Werner's father, Count Siegendorf, after Werner's banishment. Ulric, however, possesses his father's passions without possessing the sense of honor that would prevent those passions from expressing themselves in hideous crimes. As the play begins, Ulric is missing from his grandfather's court, disturbing rumors are circulating concerning his possible whereabouts, and the nobleman Stralenheim, a distant relation, is poised to usurp the family inheritance in the event of Werner's father's death.

The play's elements of Gothic melodrama are obvious from the opening of the first scene. The play begins at night during a violent thunderstorm, and act 1 is set in "The Hall of a decayed Palace" in a remote section of Silesia. The palace is honeycombed with secret passages, which receive considerable use during the course of the play's action. The Thirty Years' War has just ended, rendering the profession of soldier superfluous and lending glamour to professional thievery, that favorite occupation of many a *Sturm und Drang* hero-villain. Ulric, as we eventually discover, is himself the leader of a band of soldiers turned marauders.

Ulric, another avatar of Byronic heroism, is something of a superman, possessing traits that render him capable of great good and great evil. One of the play's characters, the poor but honorable Gabor, describes him as a man

> Of wonderful endowments:—birth and fortune,
> Youth, strength and beauty, almost superhuman,
> And courage as unrivall'd, were proclaim'd
> His by the public rumour; and his sway,
> Not only over his associates, but
> His judges, was attributed to witchcraft,
> Such was his influence. . . .

Ulric's dual nature expresses itself most clearly in his treatment of the potential usurper, Stralenheim. When Ulric is unaware of Stralenheim's identity, he courageously rescues him from the floodwaters of the River Oder, but later, when he learns that Stralenheim is a threat to his family's wealth and power, he cold-bloodedly murders him. He then conceals his responsibility for the crime and hypocritically questions his father about his possible role in Stralenheim's death. Werner has compromised his honor by stealing gold coins from Stralenheim's room, a crime that suggests the family's moral weakness, but he is incapable of murder. Freed of restraint by one additional generation of moral decay, Ulric, by contrast, is capable of almost anything.

Because of Stralenheim's murder and the nearly simultaneous death of Werner's aged father, Werner becomes Count Siegendorf and Ulric his heir apparent. All goes well for a year, although Werner, troubled by his possession of the tainted gold and by the mysterious circumstances of his rise to power, is plagued by a guilty conscience. There are manifestations of guilt in Ulric's behavior, too, but that strength of will which allowed him to rescue Stralenheim from the flood and later to cut his throat sustains him through subsequent unsavory deeds. He continues his clandestine command of the marauders who threaten the fragile peace and accepts betrothal to the loving and innocent Ida, daughter of the murdered Stralenheim. The ultimate proof of Ulric's reprobate nature occurs when Gabor, who had witnessed the hideous crime and had been unjustly branded as its likely perpetrator, comes forward to accuse Ulric. In an attempt to silence this threat to everything he has striven to accomplish, Ulric sends his minions in pursuit of the innocent man, at the same time uttering a defiant confession of his guilt before the startled Ida, who immediately falls dead in shocked disbelief.

Werner deviates from classical restraint in both content and form. In addition to relying on melodramatic plot devices, *Werner* violates the unities of place and time, a major shift in location and period occurring between acts 3 and 4. *Marino Faliero, Doge of Venice* and *Sardanapalus*, on the other hand, are much more regular, with only slight changes in setting and time taking place from one scene to the next. Like *Werner*, however, both plays center on the consequences of having men of powerful but uncertain character in positions of responsibility.

The tenuous thread on which the plot of *Marino Faliero, Doge of Venice* hangs is the apparent historical fact that the title character, while he was Doge of Venice, conspired against the tyrannous Venetian oligarchy partly because he found their rule unjust and, more important, because they failed to punish one of their number severely enough for a scrawled insult to the Doge's wife. When Faliero discovers that Michel Steno is to receive one month of imprisonment instead of death for an unsavory comment inscribed on the ducal throne, he becomes furious, although his wife, Angiolina, counsels restraint. His rage is motivated by his disgust that the oligarchy, with its facelessly diffused and inflexibly selfish power, refuses, on the one hand, to recognize the rights of the common people and neglects, on the other, to show the deference due superior spirits. His rebelliousness (like Byron's own) is simultaneously an assertion of individual, proud will and a genuine concern for democratic principles. He detests the oppressive rule of the privileged few and joins a conspiracy against them, but he maintains an aristocratic haughtiness among the "common ruffians leagued to ruin states" with whom he throws in his lot.

Ultimately, his joining the conspirators is an expression of that irrepressible, restless pride which he shares with Byron's other heroes. He exhibits not simply the temporal pride of a Coriolanus but also the everlasting, self-assertive pride of a Lucifer. Indeed, his is

> . . . the same sin that overthrew the angels,
> And of all sins most easily besets
> Mortals the nearest to the angelic nature:
> The vile are only vain: the great are proud.

In addition to treating, with considerable complexity, the frequently self-contradictory motivations of the rebel, *Marino Faliero, Doge of Venice* explores the moral ambiguities of instigating violent actions to achieve just ends. Like the French revolutionaries, the Venetian conspirators are about to sweep away the old order in a bath of blood, but one of their number, Bertram, refuses to abandon his humanity and warns an aristocratic friend that his life is in danger. The ironic result of this humane gesture is that the rebellion is discovered and the conspirators themselves, including the proud Doge, are put to death. Victory belongs to those whose ruthlessness wins out over their compassion, and he who would be kind becomes a Judas.

In *Sardanapalus*, this conflict between humanity and harsh political reality is again examined. Sardanapalus is a lover of life whose mercy and whose desire for peace, love, and pleasure bring down a dynasty. As a descendant of Nimrod and the fierce Semiramis, he is expected to conduct the affairs of state by means of bloodshed and unrelenting conquest. Instead, he allies himself with the forces of vitality against those of death and thereby earns a reputation for weakness. He knows the harem and the banquet hall better than the battlefield and is judged effeminate because he prefers the paradisiacal celebration of life to the ruthless bloodletting of war and political persecution. Even when he knows that two of his most powerful subjects, the Chaldean Beleses and the Mede Arbaces, have plotted against him, he refuses to have them killed and thereby opens the way to successful rebellion. After merely banishing the two from Nineveh, he finds himself, during a symbolically appropriate banquet, beset by a usurping army.

Despite his seeming weakness, Sardanapalus, like Byron's other heroes, possesses unquenchable pride and courage. Assuming the weapons of the warrior but refusing to wear full armor, so that his soldiers will recognize and rally to him, he enters battle and temporarily staves off defeat. His lover, Myrrha, a character added to the play, significantly enough, at the suggestion of Teresa Guiccioli, shows an equally fierce courage, as do Sardanapalus' loyal troops, and for a time, victory seems possible. Still, the kingly worshiper of life is troubled in his dreams by the image of the worshiper of death, Semiramis, and there are dark forebodings of approaching catastrophe.

When it finally becomes clear that defeat is inevitable, Sardanapalus expresses regret that the fallen world in which he found himself was unwilling to accept the temporary renewal which he attempted to offer:

> I thought to have made mine inoffensive rule
> An era of sweet peace 'midst bloody annals,
> A green spot amidst desert centuries,
> On which the future would turn back and smile,
> And cultivate, or sigh, when it could not
> Recall Sardanapalus' golden reign.
> I thought to have made my realm a paradise,
> And every moon an epoch of new pleasures.

When the world refuses his great gift, he turns to the only paradisiacal sanctuary available in a universe of spiritual disorder. He unites himself with the one individual who most loves him. He has his last loyal subjects build a funeral pyre, symbolic of his and Myrrha's passion, and the lovers die amid its flames.

Byron's political tragedies are literary explorations of the relationship, in an unregenerate world, of the extraordinary individual to the state. They examine the place of the almost superhumanly proud and passionate man within corporate humanity. They express the fascination with the link between earthly power and individual freedom and fulfillment that manifested itself in Byron's first speech before Parliament and that would lead him, finally, to his death at Missolonghi.

Other major works

POETRY: *Fugitive Pieces*, 1806; *Poems on Various Occasions*, 1807; *Hours of Idleness*, 1807; *Poems Original and Translated*, 1808; *English Bards and Scotch Reviewers*, 1809; *Hints from Horace*, 1811; *Childe Harold's Pilgrimage*, Cantos I-IV, 1812-1818, 1819 (4 cantos published together); *The Curse of Minerva*, 1812; *Waltz: An Apostrophic Hymn*, 1813; *The Giaour*, 1813; *The Bride of Abydos*, 1813; *The Corsair*, 1814; *Ode to Napoleon Buonaparte*, 1814; *Lara*, 1814; *Hebrew Melodies Ancient and Modern*, 1815; *Monody on the Death of the Right Honourable R. B. Sheridan*, 1816; *Parisina*, 1816; *Poems*, 1816; *The Prisoner of Chillon, and Other Poems*, 1816; *The Siege of Corinth*, 1816; *The Lament of Tasso*, 1817; *Beppo: A Venetian Story*, 1818; *Mazeppa*, 1819; *Don Juan*, Cantos I-XVI, 1819-1824, 1826 (16 cantos published together); *The Prophecy of Dante*, 1821; *The Vision of Judgment*, 1822; *The Age of Bronze*, 1823; *The Blues: A Literary Eclogue*, 1823; *The Island*, 1823; *The Complete Poetical Works of Byron*, 1980-1986 (5 volumes).

NONFICTION: *Letter to [John Murray] on the Rev. W. L. Bowles' Strictures on the Life and Writings of Pope*, 1821; "A Letter to the Editor of *My Grandmother's Review*," 1822; *The Parliamentary Speeches of Lord Byron*, 1824; *Byron's Letters and Journals*, 1973-1982 (12 volumes; Leslie A. Marchand, editor).

Bibliography

Brisman, Leslie. "Troubled Stream from a Pure Source." In *George Gordon, Lord Byron*, edited by Harold Bloom. New York: Chelsea House, 1986. Brisman's essay is a readable and pithy examination of the Romantic origins of Byron's major drama that places Cain within the context of the Romantic task of returning fallen man to his original state of innocence. The volume contains a brief chronology of Byron's life as well as a useful select bibliography.

Chew, Samuel C., Jr. *The Dramas of Lord Byron: A Critical Study*. 1915. Reprint. New York: Russell & Russell, 1964. The first sustained analysis of Byron's plays, Chew's book remains the best single introductory examination of Byron's dramatic works and his career as a dramatist. Although methodologically dated, Chew offers a sensible investigation of Byron's development of dramatic structure in the light of the larger context of Romantic drama, in addition to some solid insights into the connections between Byron's poems and plays. The volume includes appendices that examine Byron's use of the dramatic unities and compares Byron's *Manfred* with Johann Wolfgang von Goethe's *Faust* (pb. 1808, 1833).

Elledge, W. Paul. *Byron and the Dynamics of Metaphor*. Nashville, Tenn.: Vanderbilt University Press, 1968. This monograph analyzes the dualistic split often evident in Byron's work, concluding that the antithetical pulls of human thought and conduct provide the central tension for Byron's plays. The book contains superb discussions of *Cain*, *Manfred*, and *Sardanapalus*.

Foot, Michael. *The Politics of Paradise: A Vindication of Byron*. New York: Harper & Row, 1988. Foot's inclusive analysis of Byron's poetics as it relates to his dynamic life, which Foot divides into formative periods linked to Byron's place of residence, includes incisive analyses of *Cain*, *Manfred*, and *Sardanapalus*. The book also includes a pithy select bibliography that would serve as a good starting point for in-depth research on Byron. Also included are two appendices, one containing Byron's maiden speech to the House of Lords, the other a comparison of Byron and Alexander Pope.

Martin, Philip. *Byron: A Poet Before His Public*. Cambridge, England: Cambridge University Press, 1982. This fine biographical-historical analysis of Byron's plays, with chapters on *Manfred*, *Cain*, and *Sardanapalus*, places Byron's work within the context of his contemporaries of the second generation of Romantic poets. The analyses of the plays include an excellent discussion of the placement of Byron's plays within the dramaturgical context of the time, particularly the mannered expressionism of Edmund Kean, Sarah Siddons, and Charles Kemble. Contains a number of illustrations and a complete bibliography.

Robert H. O'Connor
(Updated by *Gregory W. Lanier*)

MRS. SUSANNAH CENTLIVRE

Born: Whaplode(?), England; c. 1667
Died: London, England; December 1, 1723

Principal drama

The Perjur'd Husband: Or, The Adventures of Venice, pr., pb. 1700; *The Beau's Duel: Or, A Soldier for the Ladies*, pr., pb. 1702; *The Stolen Heiress: Or, The Salamanca Doctor Outplotted*, pr. 1702, pb. 1703; *Love's Contrivance: Or, Le Medecin Malgré Lui*, pr., pb. 1703; *The Gamester*, pr., pb. 1705; *The Basset-Table*, pr. 1705, pb. 1706; *Love at a Venture*, pr. 1706(?), pb. 1706; *The Platonick Lady*, pr. 1706, pb. 1707; *The Busie Body*, pr., pb. 1709; *The Man's Bewitch'd: Or, The Devil to Do About Her*, pr., pb. 1709; *A Bickerstaff's Burying: Or, Work for the Upholders*, pr., pb. 1710; *Mar-Plot: Or, The Second Part of the Busie Body*, pr. 1710, pb. 1711; *The Perplex'd Lovers*, pr., pb. 1712; *The Wonder: A Woman Keeps a Secret*, pr., pb. 1714; *The Gotham Election*, pb. 1715; *A Wife Well Manag'd*, pb. 1715, pr. 1724; *The Cruel Gift: Or, The Royal Resentment*, pr. 1716, pb. 1717; *A Bold Stroke for a Wife*, pr., pb. 1718; *The Artifice*, pr., pb. 1722; *The Dramatic Works of the Celebrated Mrs. Centlivre*, pb. 1872 (3 volumes); *The Plays of Susanna Centlivre*, pb. 1982 (3 volumes).

Other literary forms

In addition to her plays, Mrs. Susannah Centlivre published literary letters and some verse celebrating state occasions.

Achievements

From 1700 until her death in 1723, Mrs. Centlivre was probably the most prolific and popular playwright in England. In her first ten years as a professional, she turned out a dozen plays for the stage; in the second half of her career, another seven.

Some of her plays closed after one or two nights, but others became exceptionally popular. *The Busie Body*, *The Wonder*, and *A Bold Stroke for a Wife* were major successes for Mrs. Centlivre, although these pieces had their longest runs after 1750. *The Busie Body*, her most popular play, was mounted at least 475 times between its premiere and 1800. David Garrick, the greatest actor of the century, gained at least part of his fame by his frequent portrayal of Marplot, the good-natured bungler in *The Busie Body*. For the last role of his career, Garrick chose Don Felix, a jealous lover in *The Wonder*. *The Busie Body* and *The Wonder* even survived the doldrums of Victorian theater, becoming repertory pieces on the modern British stage and the American stage.

Mrs. Centlivre never became rich writing plays, but she did achieve some celebrity in literary circles. As a woman playwright, she was something of a novelty; other women published plays, but very few. In her lifetime, Mrs. Centlivre had only two serious female rivals, Mary Manley and Mary Pix. Neither woman wrote so much or so well. Mrs. Centlivre competed with male writers also, becoming a friendly rival to such accomplished dramatists as George Farquhar, Nicholas Rowe, and Sir Richard Steele.

Modern critics generally view Mrs. Centlivre as a competent professional whose plays make great theater, if not great literature.

Biography
The life of "celebrated Mrs. Centlivre," as she is commonly known to stage history, is poorly documented. A Susannah Freeman, born in Lincolnshire, probably to William and Ann Freeman of Whaplode, who had her baptized on November 20, 1669, is thought to have become Mrs. Susannah Centlivre. She was educated at home, but she left in her teens, evidently to escape a stern stepmother. Legend has it that she had some "gay adventures" during her early wanderings. One contemporary of Mrs. Centlivre related that when she left home, she stopped by the side of the road one day to rest, where she was spotted by a passing student from Cambridge University, Anthony Hammond, who—as the story goes—took pity on the fatigued and tearful girl and brought her to his quarters at the university. Disguised as Hammond's cousin Jack, Mrs. Centlivre is said to have studied at the university for two months, after which she left with Hammond's letter of recommendation. The story is probably apocryphal, but it exemplifies the kind of mythology that contemporaries used to explain Mrs. Centlivre's mysterious early years.

Mrs. Centlivre joined a company of strolling players around 1684. By most accounts she was always attractive to men, including, some sources say, a Mr. Fox, who either married her or simply shared the same quarters with her for a while. Fox apparently died, and she seems to have married a Mr. Carroll, an army officer, in 1685. Carroll died within a year and a half from wounds sustained in a duel.

By 1700, Mrs. Centlivre had settled in London, where she began life as a professional playwright. Her early plays were not well received; not until *The Gamester* was produced in 1705 did she have a genuine success.

After three more failures, Mrs. Centlivre enjoyed another success with *The Busie Body*, which, premiering in 1709, became her most popular play ever. Still, the kind of success that she enjoyed with *The Gamester* and *The Busie Body* did not provide an adequate living. For her income, Mrs. Centlivre, like most playwrights, depended on three sources: gifts from patrons of the arts, sales of play copies, and author benefit nights at the theater, in which she would receive all the ticket receipts, less the house's operating expenses. None of these sources was reliable, and there is evidence that between 1700 and 1707 Mrs. Centlivre spent some time as a strolling actor in the provinces, presumably supplementing the income she made from playwriting.

The burden of supporting herself was relieved considerably when, in 1707, she married the man with whom she would live for the rest of her life, Joseph Centlivre. As a cook for the Crown, Joseph could expect to make at least fifty-five pounds per annum, not a negligible income at the time.

After *The Busie Body*, Mrs. Centlivre was never to see another true success. She tried to take advantage of the play's popularity by writing the sequel, *Mar-Plot*, but, like most sequels, it had a short run, lasting only six days during the 1710-1711 season. *The Wonder* in 1714 and *A Bold Stroke for a Wife* in 1718 had respectable runs, but they did not achieve real popularity until after 1750.

Mrs. Centlivre died on December 1, 1723, in her house in London's Buckingham Court, where she had lived the last ten years of her life. She was buried in St. Paul's, Covent Garden.

Analysis

If Mrs. Susannah Centlivre became the most popular playwright of her time, there was good reason for it. As a professional playwright, she wrote to eat, and thus to please. She gave the audience what they wanted, and she gave them plenty of it.

Writing to please the audiences of the early eighteenth century was no easy task. In the preface to *Love's Contrivance*, Mrs. Centlivre complains that "Writing is a kind of Lottery in this fickle Age, and Dependence on the Stage as precarious as the Cast of a Die; the Chance may turn up, and a Man may write to please the Town, but 'tis uncertain, since we see our best Authors sometimes fail." If audiences were notoriously fickle, playwrights were careful also not to anger the moral reformers, who needed only the scantest traces of profanity or bawdy language to brand a play licentious.

Mrs. Centlivre's solution was to write entertaining plays that would offend very few theatergoers and, with any luck, please most of them. Thus, she avoided tough satiric material. Her plays may poke fun, but they rarely abuse; they mock, but rarely malign. In English drama written between 1660 and 1685, so-called Restoration drama, comedy was often savagely satiric—and there was a good stock of comic butts: merchants, Puritans, fops, pedants, coquettes, and old lechers. Mrs. Centlivre adopted many of the comic types of the Restoration stage but treated them with a tolerance uncharacteristic of her models.

Indeed, the stock character is a major component of Mrs. Centlivre's drama and is usually found in formulaic plots, often variations on the boy-gets-girl theme. Mrs. Centlivre created characters not for the ages but for the Friday-afternoon show. She expected that her audience would recognize the character types and take delight in the predictable action, as the greedy merchant loses his money or the resourceful maid wins her beau. Indeed, in a play by Mrs. Centlivre, plot is often preeminent, featuring disguises, chance meetings, lovers' assignations, schemes and counterschemes—all the elements that we would expect from a busy play of intrigue. Centlivre's characters never stop to ponder aloud the ethics of their actions; rather, they pursue their aims until they are either fulfilled or frustrated. Much of Mrs. Centlivre's art, then, depended on giving new life to old characters and old plots, and in this she was very successful.

In *The Gamester*, she wrote a didactic play showing the reformation of a compulsive gambler. The main action concerns Valere, who is in love with Angelica. Angelica returns his love but will not marry him unless he gives up gambling. Valere has another reason to forsake the dice when his father, Sir Thomas Valere, announces that he is tired of paying his son's debts and that he must marry Angelica or lose his inheritance. Thus, Valere asks Angelica's forgiveness one more time, which she bestows, giving him a diamond-studded portrait of herself to seal the bargain.

Predictably, Valere cannot resist the gaming tables even now, and he loses all of his money to a pert young gentleman who turns out to be Angelica disguised in breeches; she has come to verify a rumor that Valere has broken his promise. Having won all of his cash, Angelica convinces him to stake the precious portrait, which she also wins, and she dashes out before he has a chance to win it back.

When Valere goes to Angelica to claim her hand, she demands the portrait as proof of his faith. When he cannot produce it, she reveals it herself, making Valere believe that their relationship is over. Indeed, the situation looks desperate: When Sir Thomas enters the scene and learns what has happened, he disinherits his son. Sir Thomas' severity seems to shock Angelica, though, and she takes Valere back, recognizing, perhaps, her own hand in his downfall. Convinced that the couple will marry, Sir Thomas restores his son's fortune.

In writing *The Gamester*, Mrs. Centlivre was trying to capitalize on the vogue for didactic comedy that developed in the first decade of the eighteenth century. Didactic comedy, in which a character is reformed from vicious ways, never dominated the stage, but professionals such as Colley Cibber, Sir Richard Steele, and Sir John Vanbrugh all wrote plays of this type, with various degrees of success. Steele's *The Lying Lover* (pr. 1703) was a failure, but, as noted above, *The Gamester* enjoyed a successful run. Steele had written a ponderous, preachy play; Mrs. Centlivre wrote something quite different.

Unlike *The Lying Lover*, *The Gamester* does not take itself too seriously. In his play, Steele works in a sermon on the evils of dueling, but Mrs. Centlivre never rails against gambling. Her prime interest is in the gamester, not in gaming itself. By reclaiming a gambler, she gives her play a moral pretext and a handy plot formula. Shocking people into giving up gambling was not her purpose; in fact, as a compulsive gambler, Valere does not have a bad life. He must occasionally avoid his creditors, and his dealings with Angelica and Sir Thomas are sometimes a bit awkward, but, ultimately, his vice causes him relatively little hardship or distress. At the end of the play, he is a bit richer, and he has the girl.

In one sense, Valere's gaming works as Angelica's rival for his attentions. Since Mrs. Centlivre does not portray the life of a gamester as a difficult one, Valere's prime motive in giving up the dice is to win Angelica (and his inheritance). Mrs. Centlivre is, in effect, giving us another version of the boy-gets-girl plot. As in many dramatic versions of this old story, the couple must overcome some difficult elders, represented by Sir Thomas, who threatens disinheritance, and his brother Dorante, a minor character with amorous designs on Angelica.

In keeping with the spirit of the play, Mrs. Centlivre makes neither her characters nor any of their fates very nasty. Perhaps she was worried that her play could be considered immoral if she portrayed vice too graphically. Valere is not Vice incarnate, nor is he even vicious—he simply has a vice, gaming. His habit is like a disease, and the audience is free to hate the disease while sympathizing with Valere himself. The audience forgives him and celebrates his happy end.

In *The Busie Body*, a different kind of play, Mrs. Centlivre produced what some critics have called a romantic intrigue. Sir George Airy, a rich young gentleman, is in love with Miranda, who lives with her amorous old guardian, Sir Francis Gripe. Miranda wants no part of her guardian's romancing, but she is also rather coy with Sir George, whom she does fancy. The situation has a parallel in the plight of Isabinda, who is sequestered by her father, Sir Jealous Traffic. Traffic wants to save his daughter for a Spanish merchant, but Charles, the poor son of Sir Francis, provides some competition. The young lovers do eventually marry, but not before having many of their best-laid plans dashed by ill luck and by the good-natured but witless bungling of Marplot, the "busie body" of the title.

After viewing *The Gamester*, Mrs. Centlivre's audience could conceivably debate whether Valere deserved such good fortune at the end of the play. He does very little to earn it. *The Busie Body* does not pose the same kind of question. The play exhibits plot with a vengeance, and the characters are all familiar types, preventing the audience from taking any of them seriously. Sir Francis and Sir Jealous, for example, are typically stubborn, overbearing fathers who hinder true love by proposing and championing unsuitable matches for their children. In the rebellious lovers of *The Busie Body*, the audience recognizes more stock characters. Miranda is the familiar resourceful woman who seems to control much of the play's action and wins her man as much as he wins her. Miranda does not immediately express her love for Sir George: She keeps him dangling for a while. (The type is coy as well as cunning.) For all of her schemes, though, the resourceful woman is generally a sympathetic character. So, too, is the sequestered maiden, the damsel in distress, of which Isabinda is a prime example. Locking up fair maidens for inevitable rescue was a staple of Spanish romance, but playwrights such as William Wycherley and Mrs. Centlivre put the device to good use on the English stage.

Mrs. Centlivre's rescuers, Sir George and Charles, would also have been familiar to the audience of 1709. As in many comedies with two pairs of lovers, the gentlemen are good friends. Both characters resemble the male half of Restoration comedy's "gay couple." Typically, the gay couple, while trying to outmaneuver scheming elders, engage in battles of wit, man and woman guardedly measuring the depth of each other's affection. Contests of wit were not Mrs. Centlivre's strong point, but there is a sparring match of sorts in the first meeting between Miranda and Sir George.

In Marplot, Mrs. Centlivre presented to her audience a character-type less familiar than the others but still not entirely original. As the well-meaning bungler, Marplot has forebears in John Dryden's Sir Martin in *Sir Martin Mar-All: Or, The Feign'd Innocence* (pr. 1667), for example. Of all the characters in *The Busie Body*, Marplot may be the most attractive. Although his mere presence is ruinous to the plans of the couples, his good heart and feeble wit keep one from really blaming him. In trying to delay Sir Jealous, Marplot succeeds only in confirming the father's suspicions that Charles is in his daughter's bedroom. At one point in the play, Sir George, to escape the eyes of Sir Francis, hides behind the chimney board. The fastidious Sir Francis wants to throw an orange peel in the chimney, so Miranda tells him that she is keeping a monkey there, a monkey that should be released only when the trainer is present. Sir Francis accepts this story and walks off, but Marplot cannot contain his curiosity and reveals George behind the board. Marplot yells out, and Sir George must bolt out of the room to remain undetected by the returning Sir Francis. Perhaps the audience never really becomes emotionally attached to Marplot—after all, he remains a type—but he is fresher than the other characters, charming and amusing.

No character, however, overshadows the action of *The Busie Body*. The play offers virtually a smorgasbord of comic plot devices. Secret meetings between lovers are interrupted by the unseasonable return of parents. Charles dispatches a letter to Isabinda, but the woman servant, Patch, accidentally drops it for Sir Jealous to find. Miranda gets rid of Sir Francis by telling him that he must attend the funeral of Squeezum the Usurer, but her guardian meets Squeezum on the street, hastening his return. There is little suspense—the audience knows that young love will conquer parental tyranny—but great pleasure in seeing the complex plot brought to a satisfactory conclusion.

Mrs. Centlivre's last great success, *A Bold Stroke for a Wife*, is a comedy with some scenes that border on pure farce. The business of the play is to get Colonel Fainwell, a soldier, married to his lover, Ann Lovely, whose dead father has left her the ward of four eccentric guardians: Sir Philip Modelove, an aging fop; Periwinkle, an antiquarian; Tradelove, a stockbroker; and Obadiah Prim, a Quaker. Ann cannot claim her fortune unless she marries a man agreed upon by all four of her guardians—a requirement which, given their radically different dispositions, appears to be impossible to satisfy. The couple could not live on a soldier's wages; thus, Fainwell must find a way to trick all four into accepting him as Ann's match. This he accomplishes through disguise and deception.

Unlike *The Busie Body*, *A Bold Stroke for a Wife* does not give the audience an endless series of comic devices. Fainwell uses one basic tactic throughout the play: impersonation. He appears as a fop to Sir Philip, as a collector of odd facts and curios to Periwinkle, as a Dutch trader to Tradelove, and as a Quaker to Prim. After winning the confidence of each guardian, he uses transparent tricks to gain their consent. For the most part, his ploys run smoothly, although there are some predictable complications. In general, the plot of *A Bold Stroke for a Wife* is not very compelling. We enjoy seeing the guardians duped, but our pleasure comes from the justice, not the methods.

The play works, in part, because some comic butts get their richly deserved rewards. Fops, stockbrokers, antiquarians, and puritans had long been targets of satire when Mrs. Centlivre wrote her play. Rarely, however, had so many types of butts appeared in one play. If tricking one kind of butt was funny, tricking four kinds would be even funnier—the more, the merrier.

The audience laughs because each of the butts, in his own way, is prideful and narrow-minded. Sir Philip affects French dress and the French language and disdains anything associated with his native England. Periwinkle is obsessed with the unauthentic artifacts of ancient history. The prime mover of Tradelove's existence is money, while Prim cares only for parading his piety and condemning the wicked ways of others.

In Restoration comedy, such figures would be abused and ridiculed. In contrast, Mrs. Centlivre does not treat her butts ruthlessly. Refusing to heap scorn upon them, she laughs good-naturedly at their follies and invites us to do the same. She may have realized that there is a bit of Prim and Periwinkle in everyone.

Other major works

POETRY: *The Masquerade*, 1713; *A Poem Humbly Presented to His Most Sacred Majesty George* . . . , 1714; *An Epistle to the King of Sweden from a Lady of Great Britain*, 1715.

Bibliography

Bowyer, John Wilson. *The Celebrated Mrs. Centlivre.* Durham, N.C.: Duke University Press, 1952. The standard biography and literary analysis. Provides a thorough survey of Mrs. Centlivre's life and writings. Portrait, bibliography of Mrs. Centlivre's writings, and index.

Hume, Robert D. *The Development of English Drama in the Late Seventeenth Century.* Oxford, England: Clarendon Press, 1976. Primarily, Hume analyzes *The Busie Body* and concludes that Mrs. Centlivre breathes life into standard devices and knows how to develop comic suspense and laughter. Complemented by an index.

Lock, F. P. *Susannah Centlivre.* Boston: Twayne, 1979. Lock's focus on Mrs. Centlivre's plays is literary and critical as opposed to biographical and historical. He analyzes the plays in their historical context and concludes that her work fluctuates broadly. When at her best, she wrote amusing, light comedy of distinction. Chronology, bibliography, and index.

Nettleton, George Henry. *English Drama of the Restoration and Eighteenth Century, 1642-1780.* New York: Macmillan, 1923. Nettleton briefly describes Mrs. Centlivre's major works and acknowledges her success with dramatic structure and dialogue, but he is ultimately unimpressed with her contribution to the "moral reawakening" of the English theater.

Scouten, A. H. "Comic Dramatists of the Augustan Age." In *The Revels History of Drama in English, 1660-1750.* Vol. 5. London: Methuen, 1976. Scouten labels Mrs. Centlivre a professional hack. Her best work is intrigue comedy, primarily derived from Spanish sources.

Sutherland, James R. "The Progress of Error: Mrs. Centlivre and the Biographers." *The Review of English Studies: A Quarterly Journal of English Literature and the English Language* 17 (April, 1942): 167-182. Sutherland demonstrates how many of the "facts" of Mrs. Centlivre's life are not substantiated and in some cases have even been invented. He tracks down the sources of these errors and warns that all biographers must be diligent in avoiding such pitfalls.

Ward, Adolphus William. *A History of English Dramatic Literature to the Death of Queen Anne.* Vol. 2. London: Macmillan, 1875. Ward describes Mrs. Centlivre as unique among her contemporaries in constructing light comedy, universal comic characters, and the elements of farce.

Douglas R. Butler
(Updated by *Gerald S. Argetsinger*)

GEORGE CHAPMAN

Born: Near Hitchin, England; c. 1559
Died: London, England; May 12, 1634

Principal drama

The Blind Beggar of Alexandria, pr. 1596, pb. 1598 (fragment); *An Humourous Day's Mirth*, pr. 1597, pb. 1599; *All Fools*, wr. 1599, pr. 1604, pb. 1605 (also known as *The World Runs on Wheels*); *Sir Giles Goosecap*, pr. c. 1601 or 1603, pb. 1606; *The Gentleman Usher*, pr. c. 1602, pb. 1606; *Bussy d'Ambois*, pr. 1604, pb. 1607; *Monsieur d'Olive*, pr. 1604, pb. 1606; *Eastward Ho!*, pr., pb. 1605 (with John Marston and Ben Jonson); *The Widow's Tears*, pr. c. 1605, pb. 1612; *The Conspiracy and Tragedy of Charles, Duke of Byron*, pr., pb. 1608; *May Day*, pr. c. 1609, pb. 1611; *The Revenge of Bussy d'Ambois*, pr. c. 1610, pb. 1613; *The Masque of the Middle Temple and Lincoln's Inn*, pr. 1613 (masque); *The Wars of Caesar and Pompey*, pr. c. 1613, pb. 1631; *The Ball*, pr. 1632, pb. 1639 (with James Shirley); *Chabot, Admiral of France*, pr. 1635, pb. 1639 (with Shirley).

Other literary forms

George Chapman was a poet and scholar as well as a playwright. His literary career began with the publication of the poem *The Shadow of Night* in 1594 and included the completion of a poem begun by Christopher Marlowe, *Hero and Leander* (1598). Chapman seemed to have been proudest of his achievements as a self-taught scholar. He translated Homer's *Iliad* (part of book 18 appeared in 1598, and the entire work was published in 1611) and *Odyssey* (1614). He also translated the lesser works of Homer (*The Crown of All Homer's Works*, 1624) and Hesiod's *Georgics* (1618). Although a few of Chapman's plays enjoyed popularity into the eighteenth century, he was best known for his translations. His versions of Homer's works were read well into the nineteenth century and influenced John Keats, among others. Chapman regarded his work on Homer as his life's mission and believed that Homer's spirit had visited him and urged him on in his labors; his translation ends with the assertion, "The work that I was born to do, is done."

Achievements

With the exception of *Chabot, Admiral of France*, Chapman's plays were written and first produced over a seventeen-year span, from 1596 to 1613. Chapman regarded himself as a scholar; he wrote plays simply to earn a living. In his own day, his plays enjoyed varying degrees of success, with his comedies and *Bussy d'Ambois* meeting with the greatest public favor. Today, Chapman's plays are seldom performed. They are generally well-written, usually reflect his scholarly interests, and have dialogue that is sometimes difficult to speak. In his own day and in subsequent eras, Chapman's dialogue has been cited as the principal weakness of his plays. The syntax is sometimes so convoluted that actors would have difficulty speaking their lines. On the other hand, the good-natured wit of his best comedies, such as *All Fools*, makes them appealing even to modern audiences. Chapman lived when both William Shakespeare and Ben Jonson were writing some of the best plays written in any language. His plays suffer in comparison with theirs and thus are not performed as often as they might be. Nevertheless, his comedies have their own special qualities that make them interesting apart from the writings of his great contemporaries.

Chapman's dark and brutal tragedies lack the universal appeal of the comedies. They are interesting studies of character and moral issues and make for good reading. They are so seldom performed that one has difficulty ascertaining how they might be received by a modern audience.

Scholars place Chapman among the historically important English playwrights. He is credited with several innovations—such as the comedy of humors—that were later used by Ben Jonson and the Restoration dramatists. In overall achievement, he must rank behind Shakespeare and Jonson, but he might be fairly rated as ahead of his other contemporaries, although many of them, such as John Marston, Francis Beaumont, and John Fletcher, might be his superior in some aspects of drama. Having written in an era of great playwrights and great dramas, Chapman has the distinction of having been an innovator and of having created a style uniquely his own.

Biography

Little is known of George Chapman's life before the publication of *The Shadow of Night*. He was born near Hitchin, a town in rural Herfordshire, England, in about 1559. His parents were Thomas and Joan Chapman; Thomas was wealthy, and Joan was the daughter of George Nodes, who had served Henry VIII. Chapman's older brother, Thomas, inherited nearly all the family estate, and Chapman was in financial straits for most of his adult life.

In about 1574, George Chapman may have attended a university, possibly Oxford. If he did so, he did not attend for long. He eventually joined Sir Ralph Sabler's household and was there until 1583 or 1585. From 1591 to 1592, he served in the battles against Spain in the Low Countries. After returning to England, Chapman fell under the influence of a group of prominent young men that included Christopher Marlowe and was nominally led by Sir Walter Raleigh. Their theories about philosophy and the occult provide much of the substance of Chapman's first poem, *The Shadow of Night*. With the publication of this poem and *Ovid's Banquet of*

Sense (1595), Chapman became a prominent poet, but he remained poor.

Much of Chapman's adult life was marred by periodic imprisonment and battles with creditors. He had bad luck with his patrons, and his plays, even when successful, did not pay him enough to achieve permanent security. In 1600, he was jailed on fraudulent charges of failing to pay his debts. After certain passages of *Eastward Ho!* were perceived as insulting to the king, he was jailed in 1605 along with one of his coauthors, Ben Jonson. Chapman adamantly protested his innocence of intent to mock the king; he and Jonson were eventually released. He was almost imprisoned again in 1608 for some offending scenes in *The Conspiracy and Tragedy of Charles, Duke of Byron*. This play angered the ambassador of France, whose protests resulted in heavy cutting of scenes by censors. In 1612, one of Chapman's few patrons, Prince Henry, died; King James did not fulfill Henry's pledge to support Chapman, and the playwright was again imprisoned for debt. Good fortune seemed his at last when the Earl of Somerset became his patron and he gained favor in the royal court, but the earl was arrested for murder in 1615. Chapman remained loyal to Somerset, who was eventually pardoned (although he was not guilty) and released in 1622. During the intervening years, Chapman had to fight the old legal charges of debt until he was acquitted in 1621.

Chapman's public life was filled with difficulties, but what his private life was like is unclear. Certainly, his financial and legal problems must have clouded his personal relationships, but whether he was married or had a family is unknown. What little is known of his friendships indicates that he was loyal and formed long-lasting bonds. He seems to have been faithful to the memory of Christopher Marlowe; he was loyal to the Earl of Somerset during the nobleman's most difficult moments; and he had a close friendship with Inigo Jones, the Jacobean court's chief architect and designer of sets for masques. His long friendship with Ben Jonson was stormy, particularly because of Jonson's bitter enmity with Jones.

Throughout debts, his imprisonment, and other setbacks, Chapman remained dedicated to an ideal. His life and achievements are colored by his determination to render in English the works of Homer. The classical structures of some of his plays reflect his researches; his studies of the nature of power are informed by his classical readings; his style is influenced by the classics of antiquity. He endured hardship, in part, because of his belief that he had a special purpose in life and because of his belief in the importance of literature.

Analysis

George Chapman's plays are diverse in structure, topic, and style, yet they are united by his interests in learning and learned people, his dismay at the unfairness of human society, and his moral beliefs. Beginning with boisterous and exuberant comedy, moving through satire and tragicomedy, then through violently dynamic tragedies, and ending with philosophical tragedies, Chapman's plays reveal a remarkably coherent ethos and a mastery of poetry and prose that allows for wonderful diversity in the dramas.

The first extant play by Chapman, *The Blind Beggar of Alexandria*, exists only in a truncated version. It was very popular and was often performed, but only its subplot was printed in 1598. Its main plot can be interpolated only from fragments found in the subplot's story of Iris, the blind beggar. It shares with the play that followed it, *An Humourous Day's Mirth*, the distinction of being a comedy of humours—a play in which each of the characters represents an aspect of human nature, such as greed or sloth. Although Ben Jonson's *Every Man in His Humour* (pr. 1598) is sometimes credited with being the first comedy of humors, both of Chapman's plays predate it. Thus, Chapman's first two plays have historical importance as the earliest extant examples of an important late Renaissance form of comedy, although the question of who actually invented the form is problematic. It is a form that remained important for Jonson throughout his career, but one that was abandoned by Chapman after 1602.

Neither *The Blind Beggar of Alexandria* nor *An Humourous Day's Mirth* is important for its artistry. Both are funny, and both have intricate plots typical of much of Chapman's comedy. The first shows his use of classical sources for inspiration, also typical of much of his dramatic writing. *The Blind Beggar of Alexandria* is peopled by Greek characters—King Ptolemy, Aegiale, Cleanthes, Prince Doricles, and others. The elements of Greek comedy, such as magic, are combined with Renaissance themes, such as comedy inspired by social manners. In his later plays, Chapman combines classical and contemporary forms to refresh stock ideas. *An Humourous Day's Mirth* is a weak play overcrowded with superfluous characters and is awkwardly constructed. Its significance for Chapman's later achievements is found in its scholarly heroine Florilla, whose true learning is contrasted with the pretenses of those around her. The assuming by characters of false humors, such as melancholy, in order to appear learned or sensitive, and the gulling of fools are reminiscent of the comedies of Jonson, but the concern for genuine learning, as personified by Florilla, distinguishes Chapman's work. Other playwrights of Chapman's day, including Jonson, mocked false learning and admired true scholarship, but none examines them as consistently as Chapman.

An Humourous Day's Mirth was followed by a minor masterpiece of comedy, *All Fools*. The play is about Rinaldo, a schemer roughly related to the Vice of medieval morality plays and to the intriguing servant of classical drama; Valerio, Rinaldo's friend and favored son of Gostanzo; and Fortunio, Rinaldo's virtuous brother. Around these three young men revolve their fathers, a jealous husband, and the women—Gratiana and

Bellanora—whom Valerio and Fortunio love. The intricate plot of the play is representative of comedies of its day. Rinaldo schemes to dupe various characters, and according to the weaknesses in their personalities, various characters are duped; some, such as Gostanzo, think that they are gulling others even as they are gulled.

The plot of Chapman's *All Fools* comes mainly from Terence's comedy *Heautontimorumenos* (163 B.C.; *The Self-Tormentor*), although Chapman reworks it into a play that is more Elizabethan than classical in character and colors it with a strong moral point of view not found in Terence's play. Gostanzo is deluded about himself and his son Valerio; he believes himself to be wise and his son to be virtuous when, in fact, he is foolish and his son is a profligate gambler who is heavily in debt. Valerio marries Gratiana but keeps the marriage secret from Gostanzo because she is not wealthy enough for Gostanzo's approval and because he is supposed to be innocent of worldly matters such as male-female relationships. Gostanzo also has a daughter, Bellanora, who loves Fortunio, a modest and virtuous young man who is also not wealthy enough to satisfy Gostanzo. Once, when Valerio, Gratiana, Fortunio, and Rinaldo are together, they see Gostanzo approaching them, and all save Rinaldo flee. Rinaldo tells Gostanzo that Gratiana and Fortunio are secretly married and wish to keep the marriage secret from Fortunio's father, Marc Antonio. Gostanzo believes Rinaldo's story and tells it to Marc Antonio at the first opportunity, even though he had promised to keep the story secret. Under Rinaldo's influence, Gostanzo convinces Marc Antonio that Fortunio is in danger of becoming a dissolute young man and that Valerio might prove to be a good influence on him if Fortunio and Gratiana lived in Gostanzo's home. Thus, without his knowing it, Gostanzo arranges for Valerio and Gratiana to live together and leaves Fortunio free to court Bellanora.

All Fools might remain a funny but unexceptional comedy, but Chapman is enough of an artist to allow his characters to learn, grow, and change. The plot becomes increasingly complex as Gostanzo suspects that Valerio is having a love affair with Fortunio's wife (who is really Valerio's wife), and under Rinaldo's influence, he pretends to Marc Antonio that Gratiana is really Valerio's wife (which she is, but Gostanzo does not know it) and persuades Marc Antonio to take Gratiana into his house and to allow Valerio to visit her. Gostanzo, proud of his wisdom, believes he has gulled Marc Antonio. The plot expands to include Cornelio, a jealous husband, and Gazetta, his wife. Rinaldo tricks Cornelio into believing that Gazetta has a lover, and Cornelio attacks the supposed lover and arranges to divorce his wife. In the meantime, Gostanzo is tricked into giving his blessing to the marriage of Valerio and Gratiana, believing that he is tricking Marc Antonio because he thinks Fortunio is married to Gratiana. Cornelio learns of Rinaldo's deceit and decides to trick Rinaldo and Valerio. He tells Rinaldo that Valerio has finally been arrested for his debts and is held at the Half Moon Tavern. Rinaldo and Gostanzo rush to the tavern and find Valerio gaming and drinking. Gostanzo, learning of his son's profligacy and recognizing the trick that has been played on him, is at first enraged. He discovers that Fortunio and Bellanora have also married and that he is not as clever and wise as he thought. He has acquired enough wisdom to recognize his own limitations, however, and he accepts what has happened. With Cornelio's reconciliation with Gazetta, all parties are reconciled, and *All Fools* ends with its characters happy.

Although the play's ending seems a bit contrived, Gostanzo's growth is believable. His pride was immoral; it helped to drive Valerio and Rinaldo to their deceitful behavior. Rinaldo is also proud; he takes pride in his ability to manipulate Gostanzo, Marc Antonio, and Cornelio. The comeuppance delivered by Cornelio is a necessary lesson for Rinaldo; he, too, can be tricked. Happiness is possible at the end of the play because the characters learn to accept themselves and others as they are; pride and trickery had prevented such acceptance.

All Fools has much charm and much good comedy; its mad plot can still entertain a modern audience. *May Day* also retains the ability to entertain, although it is not as strong a play as *All Fools*. In *May Day*, the schemer is Lodovico; other figures based on classical conventions appear in the play, including Quintiliano, a representative of the *miles gloriosus* (braggart soldier) commonly found in classical comedies. As in *All Fools*, conventions, classical or otherwise, serve as foundations for Chapman's development of complex characterizations and his sophisticated comedy. Like *All Fools*, *May Day* is a comedy of humors; Chapman wrote one more such play, *Sir Giles Goosecap*. Although still amusing, it lacks the spirited activity of its predecessors. By 1602, Chapman was working on a new kind of comedy.

A tragicomedy is a play that has a plot like that of a tragedy but ends like a comedy. It is a genre that allows for much variety in plot and character, and one that can incorporate elements of other genres, such as romantic comedy. Shakespeare's *Measure for Measure* (pr. 1604), for example, could be classified as a tragicomedy because its plot focuses on the possible execution of an innocent man and the potential debauchment of a chaste woman. The potential tragic ending is averted only when the Duke of Vienna reappears as himself. Of Chapman's tragicomedies, *The Gentleman Usher* is notable for its excellent characterizations and variety of action; it does not match Shakespeare's plays for depth of feeling or suspenseful plotting, but it compares well with any Elizabethan comedy in its richness of ideas and events. On the other hand, *Monsieur d'Olive* is a good play but not as well designed as its predecessor. It is notable more for its subplot than for its romantic central plot.

As in *All Fools*, notions of what constitutes virtuous conduct are called into question by *The Gentleman Usher* in the conflict between a father and his son. This time, the father and son both love the same woman. The son, Prince Vincentio, must, like Valerio, hide his intentions and behavior from his father, Duke Alphonso. Like Gostanzo, Alphonso is deluded about his own nature and that of his son. The rivalry of father and son is played out in a plot of treachery and danger. In *All Fools*, the scheming Rinaldo was mostly playful; he did some harm but was not inherently malicious. His counterpart in *The Gentleman Usher* is Medice, who is vengeful, ambitious, and willing to murder to get what he wants.

The malice of Medice is balanced by the pompous foolishness of Bassiolo, usher to Count Lasso, the father of Margaret, who is loved by Alphonso and Vincentio. Bassiolo fancies himself to be a schemer and agrees to be the go-between for Margaret and Vincentio after Vincentio flatters him. The bumbling Bassiolo provides much of the play's laughter, but even in his character, there is an element of menace. While Vincentio has been privately making fun of Bassiolo, he and his friend, Count Strozza, have also mocked Medice. Favorite of Alphonso, and ambitious, the proud Medice is angered by the two men. He graphically shows how the seemingly innocent conniving of Vincentio can be turned into tragedy. Alphonso has arranged for a boar hunt near the home of Count Lasso and Margaret; Strozza joins him in the hunt. Medice arranges for Strozza to be shot by an arrow and Strozza barely lives. This near-tragedy is a prelude to a seemingly complete tragedy. The foolish Bassiolo comes to know that he has been tricked; forced by Vincentio to continue as go-between, he overplays his role, and Alphonso and Medice discover that Vincentio has secretly courted Margaret. Vincentio flees, and Margaret, who has promised herself to Vincentio, covers her face with an ointment that disfigures it horribly; she hopes to repel Alphonso with her hideous looks. Only a doctor, acting as a *deus ex machina*, saves a comic ending by curing her disfigurement after Vincentio has shown that he loves her regardless of her looks. Medice is exiled and the other characters are reconciled.

The characters of *The Gentleman Usher* are well drawn, with the villain Medice comparing well even with the villains of Shakespeare's comedies. The play is full of activity, merriment, and suspense. Its main plot and subplot are well interwoven, and no event is without importance to the play as a whole. *The Gentleman Usher* ranks with *All Fools* as the best of Chapman's comedies and is representative of the best in English comedic traditions.

On the other hand, *Monsieur d'Olive* is more satiric, with its subplot portraying the silliness of courtly ambassadorships. Its comic variety has been admired by such critics as Algernon Charles Swinburne. It, too, might be well received by a modern audience. Chapman would write only one more comedy, *The Widow's Tears*.

Chapman's first tragedies, *Bussy d'Ambois* and *The Conspiracy and Tragedy of Charles, Duke of Byron* (consisting of two mated plays, *The Conspiracy* and *The Tragedy*), feature angry and robust protagonists whose courage is offset by ignorance of human nature and misguided ambition. Both Bussy d'Ambois and the Duke of Byron are betrayed and murdered. Although both plays are good and make for interesting reading, *Bussy d'Ambois* is superior in thematic construction and dramatic structure.

Bussy gains access to the court of Henry III, King of France, through Monsieur, the king's brother. A proud man, Bussy rapidly alienates the venal courtiers surrounding the king. He excites the jealousy of the Duke of Guise by making pleasant conversation with Guise's wife, Eleanor, and he persists even after Guise asks him to stop. Bussy also angers the courtiers Barrisor, l'Anou, and Pyrhot; they duel Bussy and two of Bussy's friends. All are killed save Bussy. Even though his blunt manner of speaking and proud demeanor have resulted in the deaths of five men and jeopardized his own life, Bussy learns little from his experiences. He receives a pardon for the killings from King Henry, who grants the pardon at Monsieur's behest, and he then begins a love affair with Tamyra, the wife of the Count of Montsurry; she is also coveted by Monsieur. The play gains momentum and moves toward a seemingly inevitable conclusion. Bussy becomes the favorite of the king, and Monsieur grows jealous of his status in the court.

A friar acts as go-between for Bussy and Tamyra and in a secret chamber invokes spirits to show them the future. They warn Bussy of the conspiracy of Monsieur, Guise, and Montsurry to murder him. Later, Montsurry stabs and then tortures Tamyra on the rack in order to force her to confess to her affair with Bussy. The friar is exposed as the go-between and is killed. His ghost warns Bussy of danger. Proud, headstrong, and not given to thoughtfulness, Bussy ignores all warnings and is tricked by Montsurry into walking into an ambush. He struggles mightily but is mortally wounded; in a gesture of defiance, he dies while leaning on his sword and speaking forgiveness of those who had betrayed him.

Bussy d'Ambois is one of the most popular of Chapman's plays. Its bloody scenes rival the most awful scenes of the revenge tragedies of the period, and its atmosphere is rank with the corruption and perversity characteristic of the Jacobean theater, but it is superior to most plays of its time in its intellectual themes and fully drawn characters. All of Chapman's tragedies are concerned at least in part with knowledge and the lack of it, especially self-knowledge. None of the characters in *Bussy d'Ambois* truly understands his or her nature, even after that nature is exposed; thus, these characters are unable to control events fully. King Henry cannot save his favorite; Monsieur cannot use Bussy to advantage; the friar cannot save himself; Tamyra cannot save her lover; Montsurry is driven to murder; and Bussy walks into his own death trap. Bussy, like Byron in *The Conspiracy and Tragedy of Charles, Duke of Byron*, is a man of action and forthright in speech and behavior, but he lacks tact and thoughtfulness. Without intellectual substance, he is all bluster and blunder—a killing machine who cannot adequately battle lies, conspiracies, and corruption.

Bussy d'Ambois can be interpreted as an elaborate satire on the Renaissance individualist. Bussy's blunderings are unheroic and even silly. His loud manner of speaking is more offensive and egotistical than it is honest. The notion that he can reshape society is shown to be foolish by his susceptibility to the trickeries of those who are his moral inferiors. The horrible sufferings of his lover and the deaths of his friends are made to seem pointless by his empty gesture of standing and mouthing clichéd forgiveness as he succumbs to treachery he could easily have avoided if he had taken only a moment to think about what he was doing.

Chapman's *The Revenge of Bussy d'Ambois*, *The Wars of Caesar and Pompey*, and *Chabot, Admiral of France* complete his study of character and knowledge and give his dramatic canon a well-rounded wholeness. These tragedies lack the dynamism of Chapman's other plays; they are static and devoted more to contemplation than to action. They make good reading and are moving in their portraits of good, thoughtful men trapped in insane events and corrupt societies.

The Wars of Caesar and Pompey suffers from a corrupt text. It depicts Cato's efforts to save Rome from war and Pompey's downfall: The man of action, Pompey, and the thoughtful man, Cato, both die nobly, with Pompey having learned some wisdom and Cato having learned to act. Their deaths seem futile in terms of Rome's survival, but they both grow into better, more complete men than they were at the play's start.

Clermont d'Ambois of *The Revenge of Bussy d'Ambois* is a thoughtful man like Cato, and he is typical of Chapman's introspective heroes. Scholarly, contemplative, and courageous, Clermont displays the potential weakness of the thoughtful person—he tends to hesitate and to accept evils he might change through well-considered action. A capable fighter, he nevertheless lacks the boldness of his recently murdered brother, Bussy. He does not believe that revenge is a worthy act, but the ghost of his brother exacts from him a promise to avenge his murder. Charlotte, the sister of Clermont and Bussy, shares Bussy's active and thoughtless nature. She exacts from her husband, Baligny, his promise to avenge Bussy's murder, and her foolish and poorly considered actions contrast with Clermont's caution.

Through Baligny, Clermont tries to challenge Montsurry to a duel, but Montsurry is frightened of him and avoids the challenge. Baligny is a malicious man who contrives to make trouble for those around him. He talks his way into King Henry III's confidence by arguing that crimes committed on behalf of a king are justified. The Duke of Guise, who has atoned for his role in Bussy's death, has become Clermont's friend and a powerful member of the king's court. While behaving in a friendly manner toward Guise, Baligny encourages King Henry to fear and distrust the duke and the duke's friend Clermont. The flatteries and lies of Baligny do not sway Clermont one way or another because of his secure self-knowledge, but Clermont's insistence on not thinking ill of his brother-in-law makes him susceptible to trickery. When warned that Baligny has arranged his ambush, Clermont repeats his brother's error and ignores the warning. When ambushed, Clermont fights with great strength, drives away his attackers, and flees on foot until exhaustion forces him to stop. Once captured, he is surprisingly calm and accepting of his fate.

The Duke of Guise persuades King Henry, who often vacillates under the influence of others, to release Clermont from prison, and Clermont goes to Guise's house. There, the ghost of Bussy again urges revenge. King Henry, angered by Guise's defense of Clermont, orders the duke's death. The king's men murder him as he comes to visit Henry.

Tamyra, wife of Montsurry and once Bussy's lover, helps Clermont enter Montsurry's house. Inside, his sister Charlotte has been stopped by Bussy's ghost in her own scheme to kill Montsurry. In a duel, Montsurry fights well but is slain by Clermont. A short time later, Clermont learns of the death of his close friend Guise, and in grief, he kills himself.

Clermont is a fine figure. The play is an exploration of his character and the nature of worldly knowledge and self-knowledge. The focus on Clermont's character, however, detracts from the action of the play. Some scenes are set pieces for expositions, and the action scenes come as bursts in the middle of a contemplative play. Clermont is like Shakespeare's Hamlet in his tendency to think rather than act, and like Hamlet, he is urged into revenge by a ghost. Unlike Hamlet, he exacts revenge not in an outburst forced by events but in a planned duel. In addition, Clermont is a man who does not worry about fate; although introspective, he does not waffle in indecision. He does not act because he does not want to act.

Chapman devoted much of his life to the scholarly ideal. His characters Clermont and Cato reflect the learning and self-understanding that enable people to know themselves well enough to endure most of life's vicissitudes with calm and to be impervious to flattery and the dangerous lure of personal ambition. His plays are united by characters such as Florilla, the knowledgeable heroine of *An Humourous Day's Mirth*, by his themes of knowledge and ignorance and wisdom and foolishness, by his mastery of dramatic forms and techniques, and by his humane point of view. The range of human emotions is covered by his plays, from joy to sorrow and from laughter to pathos. The plays reflect Chapman's high-minded seriousness about his art and his compassion for humanity. That Chapman is a good playwright, not a great one, speaks well for the great ones. His plays will reward those who read them, stage them, or attend them.

Other major works

POETRY: *The Shadow of Night*, 1594; *Ovid's Banquet of Sense*, 1595; *Hero and Leander*, 1598 (a completion of the poem begun by Christopher Marlowe); *The Tears of Peace*, 1609; *Andromeda Liberata*, 1614.

TRANSLATIONS: *Iliad*, 1598, 1609, 1611 (of Homer's *Iliad*); *Odyssey*, 1614 (of Homer's *Odyssey*); *Georgics*, 1618 (of Hesiod's *Georgics*); *The Crown of All Homer's Works*, 1624 (of Homer's lesser-known works).

Bibliography

Bradbrook, Muriel C. *George Chapman*. Edited by Ian Scott-Kilvert. London: Longman, 1977. This brief general overview of Chapman's life and work contains sections on the lyric poetry, including *Hero and Leander* and the translations of Homer and Hesiod. The individual chapters on the comedies and tragedies conclude that Chapman's modern reputation will have to be based on only the best of the lyrics plus two tragedies, *Bussy d'Ambois* and the two parts of the Byron play.

MacLure, Millar. *George Chapman: A Critical Study*. Toronto: Toronto University Press, 1966. A general study of the author and his writings, with detailed analyses of the poems and translations as well as the plays. Emphasizes the highly varied nature of Chapman's thought and works and offers a good discussion on Chapman's classicism. The book's writing style is sometimes difficult.

Rees, Ennis. *The Tragedies of George Chapman: Renaissance Ethics in Action*. Cambridge, Mass.: Harvard University Press, 1954. Rees sees Chapman as a Christian Humanist primarily involved with doctrine and ethical significance, indicating a concern for the individual and his place in the "body politic." The author considers Chapman to be a successful tragedian.

Solve, Norma Dobie. *Stuart Politics in Chapman's Tragedy of Chabot*. Ann Arbor: University of Michigan Press, 1928. Solve argues that Chapman's service to two different patrons led to the particular nature of *Chabot, Admiral of France*: From Prince Henry, Chapman developed his interest in French history; from the arrest and trial of Robert Carr and the attendant rise to favor of George Villiers came Chapman's disgust with court intrigue, which is shown as the cause of the downfall of the great Chabot in France.

Spivack, Charlotte. *George Chapman*. New York: Twayne, 1967. Spivack provides valuable insights into Chapman's friendships and stresses his classicism in a section on nondramatic verse, much of which is analyzed as "metaphysical." Considers the comedies of two types (early comedies of humors and later plays of satire and romance) and the tragedies also of two types (early ones with Herculean heroes and later ones with stoical heroes).

Waith, Eugene M. *The Herculean Hero in Marlowe, Chapman, Shakespeare, and Dryden.* New York: Columbia University Press, 1962. Discusses Bussy D'Ambois as a type of hero who once belonged to epic: the great warrior type who lives above the laws of his time and shows striking disregard for his society's conventional morality. Emphasizes Bussy's failings as well as his efforts to live by a code of heroic action. Illustration.

Wieler, John William. *George Chapman: The Effect of Stoicism upon His Tragedies.* New York: King's Crown Press, 1949. Wieler believes that Chapman's involvement with Stoic doctrine is a key to his entire development as a tragedian and a main cause for the failure of his tragedies. The analysis of Stoic ethics influences the conclusion that *The Wars of Caesar and Pompey* rather than *Chabot, Admiral of France* might have been Chapman's final dramatic work.

Kirk H. Beetz
(Updated by *Howard L. Ford*)

FRANK CHIN

Born: Berkeley, California; February 25, 1940

Principal drama

The Chickencoop Chinaman, pr. 1972, pb. 1981; *The Year of the Dragon*, pr. 1974, pb. 1981.

Other literary forms

In addition to his plays, Frank Chin has published a collection of short stories, the novel *Donald Duk* (1991), and numerous essays and articles on Chinese American literature and culture. He has also coedited a breakthrough anthology of Asian American writing entitled *Aiiieeeee!* (1974), revised in 1991 as *The Big Aiiieeeee!*

Achievements

Chin is the first Chinese American playwright to have had serious drama produced on the New York stage (at the American Place Theater) and on national television (by the Public Broadcasting Service). Having come into prominence in the 1960's and 1970's, he represents the consciousness of Americans of Chinese descent—those born and reared in the United States, who thus have only tenuous ties to the language and culture of China. Chin has sometimes been considered the John Osborne, the angry young man, of his generation of Chinese Americans. His plays turn on themes of identity— anguished and indignant probings into ethnic identity, gender identity, and self-identity. In them, Chin mirrors the issues and realities of Chinese American life and history as lived in Chinatown ghettos; they seek to expose and explode generally held stereotypes of Chinese Americans as an emasculated model minority with a quaintly exotic culture. Painful truths told with exuberant verbal pyrotechnics are trademarks of Chin's theater, and the characteristic gamut of his language ranges from black ghetto dialect to hipster talk to authentic Chinatown Cantonese (not Hollywood's "Charlie Chan–ese").

In addition to his achievement as a playwright, Chin is important as an editor of Asian American literature, a fiction writer, and an essayist. Chin's work has been recognized by many awards, among them prizes and grants from the Rockefeller Foundation, the American Place Theater (New York), and the National Endowment for the Arts.

Biography

Frank Chew Chin, Jr., was born a fifth-generation Californian of Chinese American parentage on February 25, 1940, in Berkeley, California, near Oakland, where his parents lived and worked. During his infancy, his family sent him to the sierra, where he was cared for by a retired vaudeville acrobat and a silent-film bit player. After World War II, he rejoined his family and grew up in the Chinatowns of Oakland and San Francisco, attending Chinese as well as English schools. During these years, he identified closely with his father, who was prominent in Chinatown governance and who became the president of the Six Companies (roughly the Chinatown equivalent of being elected mayor). Chin was graduated from the University of California at Berkeley, where he won several prizes for fiction writing; during his student years, he undertook the adventure of traveling to Fidel Castro's Cuba. In 1961, he was awarded a fellowship at the Writers' Workshop at the University of Iowa.

After leaving Iowa, Chin spent some time with the Southern Pacific Railroad, becoming the first Chinese American to work as a brakeman on the rails laid by his forefathers. Chin left the railroad company to become a writer-producer for KING-TV in Seattle, and several of his shows were aired by the Public Broadcasting Service (PBS) and on *Sesame Street.*

Chin left Seattle to teach Asian American studies at San Francisco State University and the University of California, Davis. With a group of scholars, he organized the Combined Asian American Resources Project (CARP), which collected literary, documentary, and oral history materials now kept in the Bancroft Library of the University of California, Berkeley. CARP has since been responsible for the publication of key Asian American texts by the University of Washington Press. In 1972, Chin founded the Asian American Theater Workshop in San Francisco with the support of the American Conservatory Theater (where he has been a writer-in-residence). During the 1980's and early 1990's, Chin maintained his residence in Southern California (living with his third wife and third child), where he channeled his energies toward the writing of fiction and children's literature rather than drama. Meanwhile, his continuing research in Asian American folklore and history has been supported by several grants (including a Rockefeller Fellowship at the University of California, Los Angeles) and has borne fruit in several important exhibitions.

Analysis

Frank Chin's plays center on a protagonist's confrontation with the problematics of identity. *The Chickencoop Chinaman* is the more experimental in technique, with an almost cinematic use of montage, flashbacks, symbolic stage sets, and surrealistic, dreamlike sequences. *The Year of the Dragon* is more conventional, a drama of family and psychological conflict set in a San Francisco Chinatown apartment.

The Chickencoop Chinaman is a play that treats the theme of identity through dispelling stereotypes and myths. The play is divided into two acts. Each act has a scene in Limbo (a surreal transitional time-space located between realistic time-spaces), a sequence recollecting a past obsession with a mythic figure (for example, the miracle-working Helen Keller in act 1, the popular-culture hero the Lone Ranger in act 2), and scenes set in the realistic location of 1960's Pittsburgh, where the problem of the protagonist's identity is worked out.

The play's action centers on Tam Lum, a Chinese American filmmaker who is making a documentary about a black boxing champion named Ovaltine Jack Dancer, a boyhood idol with whom he once shared a moment of mystic brotherhood urinating in unison in a roadside bush. Tam comes to Pittsburgh from San Francisco in search of Dancer's father, Charley Popcorn, who was a quintessential formative figure for Dancer and who now runs a Pittsburgh theater. Allegorically, Tam's making a film about Dancer is an effort to express an identity for himself, and his search for Charley is his search for a father figure.

Before arriving in Pittsburgh, Tam is introduced in a Limbo scene on his airliner from San Francisco. The air hostess is transformed into a Hong Kong Dream Girl clad in a drill team uniform and twirling a baton (hence an American dream girl, too). Indeed, the woman represents the American stereotype of Asian women—attractive, compliant, trained to give pleasure. Although Tam scoffs at the Hong Kong Dream Girl's stereotypical identity, it becomes apparent that his own identity is problematic. For example, when asked what his mother tongue is, Tam can speak no Chinese, but instead begins speaking in tongues, using a startling array of American dialects. Tam also points out that Chinese American identity is not one ordained by nature; Chinese Americans are not born to an identity but must synthesize one out of the diverse experiences of living in crowded Chinatown tenements, metaphorical chickencoops. This opening sequence, then, poses the play's central theme: the problem of stereotyping and identity.

In Pittsburgh, Tam stays with a boyhood friend, a Japanese American dentist named "Blackjap" Kenji. Kenji's apartment in Pittsburgh's black ghetto, Oakland, ironically underlines the circularity of Tam's search (since San Francisco has its Oakland too), and its location within earshot of a railroad yard is a symbolic reminder of the Chinese American contribution to American history. Tam and Kenji, who grew up in the black ghetto of Oakland, California, talk in exuberant black dialect and express themselves by slapping skin; they have, to a great degree, adopted the style and expressiveness of a black identity.

Kenji's ménage includes Lee, a part-Chinese woman who is passing for white. She has a young son, Robbie, by a previous liaison or marriage. Lee has a love-hate relationship with men of color, men whom she collects and then uses her whiteness and sexuality to dominate and intimidate. Thus, Lee lives platonically and parasitically with Kenji, in fact reducing him to a sexless host.

During their reunion scene in act 1, Tam and Kenji reenact a past obsession that they had with the figure of Helen Keller, imitating and parodying her. This may seem pointlessly cruel until one realizes that, in Chin's play, Keller symbolizes the myth of the disadvantaged person who overcomes all handicaps and pulls herself up by her own bootstraps. In other words, she epitomizes what American society fondly thinks that every disadvantaged minority group can do for itself. When Tam and Kenji mock and demythologize the figure of Helen Keller, they are, in particular, rejecting the popular American myth that Asian Americans are a model minority capable of miracles of self-help.

Act 2 opens with another scene in which Tam and Kenji again recollect a mythic figure, this time the Lone Ranger. As a boy, Tam had fantasized that, behind his mask, the Lone Ranger was a Chinese, and Tam had therefore identified with him as a heroic role model who represented the possibility that a Chinese American could become an idol of the American public. As Tam reenacts his past fantasy in his adulthood, however, he realizes that the Lone Ranger is a racist, as is clear in his treatment of Tonto, and that he is not by any means a Chinese. In fact, the Lone Ranger is an obese white man who sadistically shoots Tam in the hand (symbolically handicapping him physically), then lays on him the curse of being an honorary white (handicapping him psychologically with this false identity). This episode, then, demythologizes the private fantasies of any Chinese American who might believe that he can easily achieve heroic status in the American imagination; it also shows the wounding consequences of the Chinese American fantasy that they can be accepted as honorary whites.

Tam and Kenji then track down Charley Popcorn. They are crushed, however, when Charley reveals that he is not, in fact, Dancer's father—that Dancer had constructed a myth around his memories of their association. Thus Tam's search for a surrogate and idolized father figure in a black man ends in disillusionment.

Returning to the apartment, Tam and Kenji undergo another identity crisis, this time precipitated by Lee's former husband, Tom. His name suggests the stereotype of the subservient minority, "Uncle Tom," and he is the very model of the minority that has attained middle-class success. Tom has heard of Kenji's decent but sexless relationship with Lee and wants to take Lee and Robbie back. Yet now Kenji authoritatively stands his ground, sends Robbie to bed, and asserts that he wants Lee to stay and that he will father children with her.

Tam, too, appears to recover from his shattering disillusionment with Charley. In the surrealistic penultimate scene, he is shown being borne to Kenji's apartment on Charley's back, and in this position, Tam recalls the unmanning events when his wife left him on his birthday. In the play's last scene, however, Tam makes a great effort and stumbles into Kenji's apartment carrying Charley on his back. This reversal of position symbolically denotes Tam's freedom from his past reliance on an identity borrowed from the blacks and a new determination to find the wherewithal for a future identity from sources within himself. He is thus able to keep his integrity despite the needling of Lee and the blandishments of Tom's imitation whiteness. Just as Kenji and Lee are united in a new relationship, so Tam is shown coming to terms with an identity grounded on his own ethnicity. Before the curtain falls, Tam is shown in the kitchen unashamedly practicing the craft of his ethnic group *par excellence*. As he prepares the food, he reminisces about the Chinese American legend of the Iron Moonhunter, a mythic train which the Chinese railroaders supposedly created out of parts stolen from the railroad companies, and which wanders the West searching out the souls of dead Chinese to bear them home to their families. Chin seems to understand that people need myths, and in the end, his protagonist, disillusioned with the black myth that is unavailable to him and rejecting a white myth that he finds contemptible, shapes his own myth of identity in the heroism and craft of Chinese America.

Chin's second play, *The Year of the Dragon*, is more conventionally structured than its predecessor and was accorded a national audience in a television production on "PBS Theatre in America" in 1975. This play also treats the theme of identity, but it focuses more sharply and poignantly upon the question of self-worth: the worth of an individual self to loved ones (family) and the worth of a minority ethnic group to the majority society (white-dominated America). Again, stereotypes form the chief factor that obscures individual worth and identity—stereotypes about family relationships, stereotypes about ethnicity. These thematic strands are worked out in the exposition of the many psychological conflicts and confrontations in the well-established Eng family of San Francisco's Chinatown.

The exposition, and exposé, of ethnic stereotypes is presented chiefly through two elements of the play: the family business of providing tours of Chinatown and the new Anglo son-in-law whom their daughter has brought from Boston. The family owns Eng's Chinatown Tour and Travel agency, and the eldest son, forty-year-old Fred, conducts tours of San Francisco's Chinatown. For the sake of business, however, Fred cannot show Chinatown as it really is; rather, he must pander to the stereotypes of Chinatown held by the American public—that it is an exotic place of delicious foods, mysterious (but safe) goings on, and incomprehensible (but happy) inhabitants composed of attractively available women, complaisant men, and harmonious families with above-average children. Fred knows that he is being false to himself and his people when he gives his happy tour-guide's spiel, and he mutters curses at his customers under his breath beneath his patter. In reality, Fred would like to tell the truths of Chinatown, which he sets down in short stories, but no one will publish his work. Through Fred's situation, then, Chin portrays the stifling effects of ethnic stereotypes.

The other element in the play that deals with ethnic stereotypes is presented through the character Ross, the Eng family's Boston-bred son-in-law on a honeymoon visit from the East. He is portrayed as a well-meaning but oafish Sinophile who has studied Chinese (although in a dialect different from the Eng family's), admires Chinese culture and customs, and thinks of Chinese Americans as the only minority group that does not dislike white dominance. Such stereotypes prevent him from seeing the Chinese American realities which trip him up constantly. His type of cultural voyeurism is subtly captured in the play's final scene, in which he is appointed photographer to take posed pictures of the Eng family. In this technically effective scene, Chin uses spatial form as adroitly as did Gustave Flaubert in the "agricultural fair" scene of *Madame Bovary* (1857). Through a kind of auditory montage, Chin creates an ironic counterpoint commenting on Ross's photography by interspersing the scene with the sounds and spiel of a tour guide describing a Chinese New Year's parade offstage. Just as the tourists are gawking at the Chinatown parade, so is Ross ogling his new Chinese American family.

In probing the stereotypes of familial relationships, Chin makes a painful but necessary criticism of stereotypes held by his own ethnic group. He also dispels the Charlie Chan–esque stereotype held by many Americans, that Chinese families are uniformly harmonious and hierarchical.

Much of the conflict in the family swirls around its patriarch, Pa Eng, who came to the United States in 1935 accompanied only by his infant son Fred, for he was forced to leave his wife in China because United States immigration laws excluded Chinese women from entering America. Pa Eng soon married a fifteen-year-old American-born Chinese girl (Ma Eng), who risked losing her American citizenship by marrying the man she loved (her citizenship was at risk not because she married a bigamist but because another American anti-Chinese law forbade American-born women to marry Chinese men on pain of forfeiting their citizenship). Ma Eng bore and reared two children, meanwhile pampering Pa Eng in his stereotypical Chinese view of the patriarch as a kind of semidivinity.

When the play opens, Pa Eng has prospered, to the point that he has been elected mayor of Chinatown. Yet he is now old and ill, and he believes that his days are numbered. He wants to die in the bosom of his family, so he has sent for his first wife (China Mama). This he has done without communicating his intent to his family. (In fact, throughout the play, the family members can hardly be said to communicate; they never bother to listen to what others have to say.) China Mama's arrival, as can be expected, precipitates several crises during which Pa Eng appears an inconsiderate, uncomprehending, ego-bound patriarch. He commands Ma Eng, who is unnerved by this presence in her household, either to relinquish her home or to be subservient to China Mama and begin teaching her English. It is in his relationship with Fred, however, that Pa Eng's authoritarian role becomes most apparent.

Pa Eng's patriarchal dominance and his Chinese values have acted as long-standing denials of Fred's identity and self-worth. Fred had aspired to be a writer, but his father scoffed at this: According to stereotypes he holds, if one is not a doctor or a lawyer, one is nothing at all. Pa Eng gives his mayoral speech to Ross to edit, not to Fred, who majored in English. Nevertheless, Fred is a dutiful son, nursing his father when he spits blood and even going through a daily ritual of accompanying him to the toilet and wiping him after a defecation, a viscerally affecting scene to stage. Fred has also sacrificed his own college career to work and provide for his sister's college expenses, but his father does not appreciate that, probably because his stereotypical values do not accord much importance to daughters. Fred also is aware that his younger brother, Johnny, is deteriorating into a gun-wielding Chinatown mobster and wants him to leave his environment and go to college in the East. This Johnny resists. Fred knows that Johnny will comply if Pa Eng orders him to go, but Pa Eng refuses. Instead, Pa Eng wants Fred to accompany him as he delivers his mayoral speech. In this speech, he plans to acknowledge Fred as his heir, but he will do it in such a way that Fred will always be fitted with the stereotypical identity of a Number One Son, a person who has no self-worth beyond that which derives from his father. This is unacceptable to Fred, who refuses to go with his father as long as he refuses to order Johnny to leave Chinatown. In attempting to impose his will on his son, Pa Eng resorts to violence and slaps him repeatedly. Yet the physical exertion is too much for the sick old man, and he dies in this pitiable moment of futile tyranny. Tragically, Pa Eng's death does not free Fred. The closing tableau of the play shows Fred being submerged by his milieu as he slips into the spiel of the Chinatown tour guide, and as the spotlight singles him out, Fred is shown dressed glaringly in white, the Chinese symbol of death.

In sum, it may be said that Frank Chin has pioneered in the field of Asian American literature. His daring and verbally exuberant theater has asserted the presence of the richly unique and deeply human complexities of Chinese American life, and his work has brought this presence to the attention of the American public. He has criticized the false myths and the deadening stereotypes of self and ethnicity held by Asians and whites alike. At a time when it was ripe and necessary to do so, Chin proclaimed and proved that there is such an entity as Asian American literature. American literary history must henceforth reckon with that claim if it is to be true to itself.

Other major works

NOVEL: *Donald Duk*, 1991.

SHORT FICTION: *The Chinaman Pacific and Frisco R.R. Co.*, 1988.

TELEPLAYS: *S.R.T., Act Two*, 1966; *The Bel Canto Carols*, 1966; *A Man and His Music*, 1967; *Ed Sierer's New Zealand*, 1967; *Searfair Preview*, 1967; *The Year of the Ram*, 1967; *And Still Champion . . . .* 1967; *The Report*,

1967; *Mary*, 1969; *Rainlight Rainvision*, 1969; *Chinaman's Chance*, 1971.
ANTHOLOGIES: *Aiiieeeee!*, 1974 (Asian American writing); *The Big Aiiieeeee!*, 1991.

Bibliography

Barnes, Clive. "Theater: Culture Study." *The New York Times*, June 3, 1974, p. 39. A balanced review of *The Year of the Dragon* in performance at The American Place Theater in New York City. Barnes notes that the play has "gaps" and "lacks energy at times" but is still "interesting." He praises the "absolutely fascinating . . . insights" that Chin provides while dispelling stereotypes about Chinese Americans, investigating Chinese American identity, and exploring generational differences.

Kim, Elaine H. *Asian American Literature: An Introduction to the Writings and Their Social Context.* Philadelphia: Temple University Press, 1982. In chapter 6 of this essential and pioneering study of Asian American literature, Kim discusses Chin together with other writers of his generation. Kim's focus is on Chin's short fiction and *The Chickencoop Chinaman.* She analyzes the play as a forum for Chin's ideas on Chinese American culture, identity, and manhood, ideas that are darkened by a pervading sense of futility, decadence, and alienation. Kim also faults Chin for the use of "unbalanced" dialogues (that is, monologic lectures) and stereotyped women characters.

_____. "Frank Chin: The Chinatown Cowboy and His Backtalk." *Midwest Quarterly* 20 (Autumn, 1978): 78-91. This essay by the doyenne of Asian American literary critics is an earlier version of the previous bibliographic entry. The essay, however, is more acerbic than the book chapter; it finds that *The Chickencoop Chinaman* conveys "contempt for the Asian-American identity" and portrays the "pathetic futility of the male protagonist."

Kroll, Jack. "Primary Color." *Newsweek*, June 19, 1972, 55. Extolls *The Chickencoop Chinaman* as "the most interesting play of the American Place Theater" that year. Compares Chin with John Osborne and Chin's protagonist to Lenny Bruce, sees Chin's thematic concerns as his generation's search for identity, and characterizes Chin's language as "rogue poetry of deracination" enlivened by the "beat and brass, the runs and rim-shots of jazz."

McDonald, Dorothy Ritsuko. Introduction to *The Chickencoop Chinaman and the Year of the Dragon: Two Plays by Frank Chin.* Seattle: University of Washington Press, 1981. This extensive introduction provides information on Chin's background and his views on Chinese American history. Makes an intelligent thematic commentary on Chin's plays. Sees Chin's intent as attempting to dispel stereotypes about Chinese Americans and to recover mythic archetypes (such as Kwan Kung, patron deity of war and letters) to validate the Chinese American male. A valuable essay marred by some errors of detail.

Oliver, Edith. "Off Broadway." *The New Yorker* 48 (June 24, 1972): 46. An enthusiastic response to *The Chickencoop Chinaman* that hails its historical importance for bringing "the first news (theatrically speaking) of the Chinese Americans in our midst." Characterizes the play as "moving, funny, pain-filled, sarcastic, bitter, ironic . . . in a furious and dazzling eruption of verbal legerdemain." Notices a "few paltry things that are wrong" with it but finds that these "hardly matter," given the play's theatrical inventiveness.

C. L. Chua